W9-BZA-300

Successes and New Directions in Data Mining

Florent Masseglia
Project AxIS–INRIA, France

Pascal Poncelet
Ecole des Mines d'Ales, France

Maguelonne Teisseire
Universite Montpellier, France

INFORMATION SCIENCE REFERENCE

Hershey · New York

Acquisitions Editor:	Kristin Klinger
Development Editor:	Kristin Roth
Editorial Assistants:	Jessica Thompson and Ross Miller
Senior Managing Editor:	Jennifer Neidig
Managing Editor:	Sara Reed
Copy Editor:	April Schmidt
Typesetter:	Jamie Snavely
Cover Design:	Lisa Tosheff
Printed at:	Yurchak Printing Inc.

Published in the United States of America by
Information Science Reference (an imprint of IGI Global)
701 E. Chocolate Avenue, Suite 200
Hershey PA 17033
Tel: 717-533-8845
Fax: 717-533-8661
E-mail: cust@igi-global.com
Web site: http://www.igi-global.com/reference

and in the United Kingdom by
Information Science Reference (an imprint of IGI Global)
3 Henrietta Street
Covent Garden
London WC2E 8LU
Tel: 44 20 7240 0856
Fax: 44 20 7379 0609
Web site: http://www.eurospanonline.com

Library of Congress Cataloging-in-Publication Data

Successes and new directions in data mining / Florent Messeglia, Pascal Poncelet & Maguelonne Teisseire, editors.

    p. cm.

 Summary: "This book addresses existing solutions for data mining, with particular emphasis on potential real-world applications. It captures defining research on topics such as fuzzy set theory, clustering algorithms, semi-supervised clustering, modeling and managing data mining patterns, and sequence motif mining"--Provided by publisher.

 Includes bibliographical references and index.

 ISBN 978-1-59904-645-7 (hardcover) -- ISBN 978-1-59904-647-1 (ebook)

 1. Data mining. I. Masseglia, Florent. II. Poncelet, Pascal. III. Teisseire, Maguelonne.

 QA76.9.D343S6853 2007

 005'74--dc22

                                2007023451

British Cataloguing in Publication Data
A Cataloguing in Publication record for this book is available from the British Library.

All work contributed to this book set is new, previously-unpublished material. The views expressed in this book are those of the authors, but not necessarily of the publisher.

Table of Contents

Detailed Table of Contents

In recent years, several extensions of data mining and knowledge discovery methods have been developed on the basis of fuzzy set theory. Corresponding fuzzy data mining methods exhibit some potential advantages over standard methods, notably the following: Since many patterns of interest are inherently vague, fuzzy approaches allow for modeling them in a more adequate way and thus enable the discovery of patterns that would otherwise remain hidden. Related to this, fuzzy methods are often more robust toward a certain amount of variability or noise in the data, a point of critical importance in many practical application fields. This chapter highlights the aforementioned advantages of fuzzy approaches in the context of exemplary data mining methods, but also points out some additional complications that can be caused by fuzzy extensions.

With the growth in the number of Web users and the necessity for making information available on the Web, the problem of Web personalization has become very critical and popular. Developers are trying to customize a Web site to the needs of specific users with the help of knowledge acquired from user navigational behavior. Since user page visits are intrinsically sequential in nature, efficient clustering algorithms for sequential data are needed. In this chapter, we introduce a similarity preserving function called sequence and set similarity measure S3M that captures both the order of occurrence of page visits as well as the content of pages. We conducted pilot experiments comparing the results of PAM, a standard clustering algorithm, with two similarity measures: Cosine and S3M. The goodness of the clusters resulting from both the measures was computed using a cluster validation technique based on average levensthein distance. Results on the pilot dataset established the effectiveness of S3M for sequential data. Based on these results, we proposed a new clustering algorithm, SeqPAM, for clustering sequential data. We tested the new algorithm on two datasets, namely cti and msnbc datasets. We provided recommendations for Web personalization based on the clusters obtained from SeqPAM for the msnbc dataset.

XML is a rather verbose representation of semistructured data, which may require huge amounts of storage space. Several summarized representations of XML data have been proposed, which can both provide succinct information and be directly queried. In this chapter, we focus on compact representations based on the extraction of association rules from XML datasets. In particular, we show how patterns can be exploited to (possibly partially) answer queries, either when fast (and approximate) answers are required, or when the actual dataset is not available; for example, it is currently unreachable. We focus on (a) schema patterns, representing exact or approximate dataset constraints, (b) instance patterns, which represent actual data summaries, and their use for answering queries.

In this chapter, we consider the problem of constrained clustering of documents. We focus on documents that present some form of structural information, in which prior knowledge is provided. Such structured data can guide the algorithm to a better clustering model. We consider the existence of a particular form of information to be clustered: textual documents that present a logical structure represented in XML format. Based on this consideration, we present algorithms that take advantage of XML metadata (structural information), thus improving the quality of the generated clustering models. This chapter also addresses the problem of inconsistent constraints and defines algorithms that eliminate inconsistencies, also based on the existence of structural information associated to the XML document collection.

Patterns can be defined as concise, but rich in semantics, representations of data. Due to pattern characteristics, ad-hoc systems are required for pattern management, in order to deal with them in an efficient and effective way. Several approaches have been proposed, both by scientific and industrial communities, to cope with pattern management problems. Unfortunately, most of them deal with few types of patterns and mainly concern extraction issues. Little effort has been posed in defining an overall framework dedicated to the management of different types of patterns, possibly user-defined, in a homogeneous way. In this chapter, we present PSYCHO (pattern based system architecture prototype), a system prototype providing an integrated environment for generating, representing, and manipulating heterogeneous patterns, possibly user-defined. After presenting the PSYCHO logical model and architecture, we will focus on several examples of its usage concerning common market basket analysis patterns, that is, association rules and clusters.

Chapter VI
Deterministic Motif Mining in Protein Databases /
Pedro Gabriel Ferreira and Paulo Jorge Azevedo 116

Protein sequence motifs describe, through means of enhanced regular expression syntax, regions of amino acids that have been conserved across several functionally related proteins. These regions may have an implication at the structural and functional level of the proteins. Sequence motif analysis can bring significant improvements towards a better understanding of the protein sequence-structure-function relation. In this chapter, we review the subject of mining deterministic motifs from protein sequence databases. We start by giving a formal definition of the different types of motifs and the respective specificities. Then, we explore the methods available to evaluate the quality and interest of such patterns. Examples of applications and motif repositories are described. We discuss the algorithmic aspects and different methodologies for motif extraction. A brief description on how sequence motifs can be used to extract structural level information patterns is also provided.

Chapter VII
Data Mining and Knowledge Discovery in Metabolomics /
Christian Baumgartner and Armin Graber 141

This chapter provides an overview of the knowledge discovery process in metabolomics, a young discipline in the life sciences arena. It introduces two emerging bioanalytical concepts for generating biomolecular information, followed by various data mining and information retrieval procedures such as feature selection, classification, clustering, and biochemical interpretation of mined data, illustrated by real examples from preclinical and clinical studies. The authors trust that this chapter will provide an acceptable balance between bioanalytics background information, essential to understanding the complexity of data generation, and information on data mining principals, specific methods and processes, and biomedical applications. Thus, this chapter is anticipated to appeal to those with a metabolomics background as well as to basic researchers within the data mining community who are interested in novel life science applications.

Chapter VIII
Handling Local Patterns in Collaborative Structuring /
Ingo Mierswa, Katharina Morik, and Michael Wurst 167

Media collections on the Internet have become a commercial success, and the structuring of large media collections has thus become an issue. Personal media collections are locally structured in very different ways by different users. The level of detail, the chosen categories, and the extensions can differ completely from user to user. Can machine learning be of help also for structuring personal collections? Since users do not want to have their hand-made structures overwritten, one could deny the benefit of automatic structuring. We argue that what seems to exclude machine learning, actually poses a new learning task. We propose a notation which allows us to describe machine learning tasks in a uniform manner. Keeping the demands of structuring private collections in mind, we define the new learning task of localized alternative cluster ensembles. An algorithm solving the new task is presented together with its application to distributed media management.

Chapter IX

Analysing and mining image data to derive potentially useful information is a very challenging task. Image mining concerns the extraction of implicit knowledge, image data relationships, associations between image data and other data or patterns not explicitly stored in the images. Another crucial task is to organise the large image volumes to extract relevant information. In fact, decision support systems are evolving to store and analyse these complex data. This chapter presents a survey of the relevant research related to image data processing. We present data warehouse advances that organise large volumes of data linked with images, and then we focus on two techniques largely used in image mining. We present clustering methods applied to image analysis, and we introduce the new research direction concerning pattern mining from large collections of images. While considerable advances have been made in image clustering, there is little research dealing with image frequent pattern mining. We will try to understand why.

Environmental research and knowledge discovery both require extensive use of data stored in various sources and created in different ways for diverse purposes. We describe a new metadata approach to elicit semantic information from environmental data and implement semantics-based techniques to assist users in integrating, navigating, and mining multiple environmental data sources. Our system contains specifications of various environmental data sources and the relationships that are formed among them. User requests are augmented with semantically related data sources and automatically presented as a visual semantic network. In addition, we present a methodology for data navigation and pattern discovery using multiresolution browsing and data mining. The data semantics are captured and utilized in terms of their patterns and trends at multiple levels of resolution. We present the efficacy of our methodology through experimental results.

This chapter gives a survey of some existing methods for visualizing multidimensional data, that is, data with more than three dimensions. To keep the size of the chapter reasonably small, we have limited the methods presented by restricting ourselves to numerical data. We start with a brief history of the field and a study of several taxonomies; then we propose our own taxonomy and use it to structure the rest of the chapter. Throughout the chapter, the iris data set is used to illustrate most of the methods since this is a data set with which many readers will be familiar. We end with a list of freely available software and a table that gives a quick reference for the bibliography of the methods presented.

Intense work in the area of data mining technology and in its applications to several domains has resulted in the development of a large variety of techniques and tools able to automatically and intelligently transform large amounts of data in knowledge relevant to users. However, as with other kinds of useful technologies, the knowledge discovery process can be misused. It can be used, for example, by malicious subjects in order to reconstruct sensitive information for which they do not have an explicit access authorization. This type of "attack" cannot easily be detected, because, usually, the data used to guess the protected information, is freely accessible. For this reason, many research efforts have been recently devoted to addressing the problem of privacy preserving in data mining. The mission of this chapter is therefore to introduce the reader to this new research field and to provide the proper instruments (in term of concepts, techniques, and examples) in order to allow a critical comprehension of the advantages, the limitations, and the open issues of the privacy preserving data mining techniques.

Data analysis or data mining have been applied to data produced by many kinds of systems. Some systems produce data continuously and often at high rates, for example, road traffic monitoring. Analyzing such data creates new issues, because it is neither appropriate, nor perhaps possible, to accumulate it and process it using standard data-mining techniques. The information implicit in each data record must be extracted in a limited amount of time and, usually, without the possibility of going back to consider it again. Existing algorithms must be modified to apply in this new setting. This chapter outlines and analyzes the most recent research work in the area of data-stream mining. It gives some sample research ideas or algorithms in this field and concludes with a comparison that shows the main advantages and disadvantages of the algorithms. It also includes a discussion and possible future work in the area.

Preface

Since its definition, a decade ago, the problem of mining patterns is becoming a very active research area and efficient techniques have been widely applied to problems either in industry, government, or science. From the initial definition and motivated by real-applications, the problem of mining patterns not only addresses the finding of itemsets but also more and more complex patterns. For instance, new approaches need to be defined for mining graphs or trees in applications dealing with complex data such as XML documents, correlated alarms, or biological networks. As the number of digital data is always growing, the problem of the efficiency of mining such patterns becomes more and more attractive.

One of the first areas dealing with a large collection of digital data is probably text mining. It aims at analyzing large collections of unstructured documents with the purpose of extracting interesting, relevant, and nontrivial knowledge. However, patterns become more and more complex and lead to open problems. For instance, in the biological networks context, we have to deal with common patterns of cellular interactions, organization of functional modules, relationships and interaction between sequences, and patterns of genes regulation. In the same way, multidimensional pattern mining has also been defined and a lot of open questions remain according to the size of the search space or to effectiveness consideration. If we consider social networks on the Internet, we would like to better understand and measure relationships and flows between people, groups, and organizations. Many real-world applications data are no more appropriately handled by traditional static databases since data arrives sequentially in the form of continuous rapid streams. Since data-streams are contiguous, high speed, and unbounded, it is impossible to mine patterns by using traditional algorithms requiring multiple scans, and new approaches have to be proposed.

In order to efficiently aid decision making and for effectiveness consideration, constraints become more and more essential in many applications. Indeed, an unconstrained mining can produce such a large number of patterns that it may be intractable in some domains. Furthermore, the growing consensus that the end user is no longer interested by a set of all patterns verifying selection criteria led to demand for novel strategies for extracting useful, even approximate knowledge.

The goal of this book is to provide theoretical frameworks and present challenges and their possible solutions concerning knowledge extraction. It aims at providing an overall view of the recent existing solutions for data mining with a particular emphasis on the potential real-world applications. It is composed of XIII chapters.

The first chapter, by Eyke Hüllermeier, explains "Why Fuzzy Set Theory is Useful in Data Mining". It is important to see how much fuzzy theory may solve problems related to data mining when dealing with real applications, real data, and real needs to understand the extracted knowledge. Actually, data mining applications have well-known drawbacks, such as the high number of results, the "similar but hidden" knowledge or a certain amount of variability or noise in the data (a point of critical importance in many practical application fields). In this chapter, Hüllermeier gives an overview of fuzzy sets and then demonstrates the advantages and robustness of fuzzy data mining. This chapter highlights these advantages in the context of exemplary data mining methods, but also points out some additional complications that can be caused by fuzzy extensions.

Web and XML data are two major fields of applications for data mining algorithms today. Web mining is usually a first step towards Web personalization, and XML mining will become a standard since XML data is gaining more and more interest. Both domains share the huge amount of data to analyze and the lack of structure of their sources. The following three chapters provide interesting solutions and cutting edge algorithms in that context.

In "SeqPAM: A Sequence Clustering Algorithm for Web Personalization", Pradeep Kumar, Raju S. Bapi, and P. Radha Krishna propose SeqPAM, an efficient clustering algorithm for sequential data and its application to Web personalization. Their proposal is based on pilot experiments comparing the results of PAM, a standard clustering algorithm, with two similarity measures: Cosine and S3M. The goodness of the clusters resulting from both the measures was computed using a cluster validation technique based on average levensthein distance.

XML is a rather verbose representation of semistructured data, which may require huge amounts of storage space. Several summarized representations of XML data have been proposed, which can both provide succinct information and be directly queried. In "Using Mined Patterns for XML Query Answering", Elena Baralis, Paolo Garza, Elisa Quintarelli, and Letizia Tanca focus on compact representations based on the extraction of association rules from XML datasets. In particular, they show how patterns can be exploited to (possibly partially) answer queries, either when fast (and approximate) answers are required, or when the actual dataset is not available (e.g., it is currently unreachable).

The problem of semisupervised clustering (SSC) has been attracting a lot of attention in the research community. "On the Usage of Structural Information in Constrained Semi-Supervised Clustering of XML Documents" by Eduardo Bezerra, Geraldo Xexéo, and Marta Mattoso, is a chapter considering the problem of constrained clustering of documents. The authors consider the existence of a particular form of information to be clustered: textual documents that present a logical structure represented in XML format. Based on this consideration, we present algorithms that take advantage of XML metadata (structural information), thus improving the quality of the generated clustering models. The authors take as a starting point existing algorithms for semisupervised clustering documents and then present a constrained semisupervised clustering approach for XML documents, and deal with the following main concern: how can a user take advantage of structural information related to a collection of XML documents in order to define constraints to be used in the clustering of these documents?

The next chapter deals with pattern management problems related to data mining. Clusters, frequent itemsets, and association rules are some examples of common data mining patterns. The trajectory of a moving object in a localizer control system or the keyword frequency in a text document represent other examples of patterns. Patterns' structure can be highly heterogeneous; they can be extracted from raw data but also known by the users and used for example to check how well some data source is represented by them and it is important to determine whether existing patterns, after a certain time, still represent the data source they are associated with. Finally, independently from their type, all patterns should be manipulated and queried through ad hoc languages. In "Modeling and Managing Heterogeneous Patterns: The PSYCHO Experience", Anna Maddalena and Barbara Catania present a system prototype providing an integrated environment for generating, representing, and manipulating heterogeneous patterns, possibly user-defined. After presenting the logical model and architecture, the authors focus on several examples of its usage concerning common market basket analysis patterns, that is, association rules and clusters.

Biology is one of the most promising domains. In fact, it has been widely addressed by researchers in data mining these past few years and still has many open problems to offer (and to be defined). The next two chapters deal with sequence motif mining over protein base such as Swiss Prot and with the biochemical information resulting from metabolite analysis.

Proteins are biological macromolecules involved in all biochemical functions in the life of the cell and they are composed of basic units called amino acids. Twenty different types of amino acids exist, all with well differentiated structural and chemical properties. Protein sequence motifs describe regions of amino acids that have been conserved across several functionally related proteins. These regions may have an implication at the structural and functional level of the proteins. Sequence motif mining can bring significant improvements towards a better understanding of the protein sequence-structure-function relation. In "Deterministic Motif Mining in Protein Databases", Pedro Gabriel Ferreira and Paulo Jorge Azavedo go deeper in the problem by first characterizing two types of extracted patterns and focus on deterministic patterns. They show that three measures of interest are suitable for such patterns and they illustrate through real applications that better understanding of the sequences under analysis have a wide range of applications. Finally, they described the well known existing motif databases over the world.

Christian Baumgartner and Armin Graber, in "Data Mining and Knowledge Discovery in Metabolomics", address chemical fingerprints reflecting metabolic changes related to disease onset and progression (i.e., metabolomic mining or profiling). The biochemical information resulting from metabolite analysis reveals functional endpoints associated with physiological and pathophysiological processes, influenced by both genetic predisposition and environmental factors such as nutrition, exercise, or medication. In recent years, advanced data mining and bioinformatics techniques have been applied to increasingly comprehensive and complex metabolic datasets, with the objective to identify and verify robust and generalizable markers that are biochemically interpretable and biologically relevant in the context of the disease. In this chapter, the authors provide the essentials to understanding the complexity of data generation and information on data mining principals, specific methods and processes, and biomedical applications.

The exponential growth of multimedia data in consumer as well as scientific applications poses many interesting and task critical challenges. There are several inter-related issues in the management of such data, including feature extraction, multimedia data relationships, or other patterns not explicitly stored in multimedia databases, similarity based search, scalability to large datasets, and personalizing search and retrieval. The two following chapters address multimedia data.

In "Handling Local Patterns in Collaborative Structuring", Ingo Mierswa, Katharina Morik, and Michael Wurst address the problem of structuring personal media collection of data by using collaborative and data mining (machine learning) approaches. Usually personal media collections are locally structured in very different ways by different users. The main problem in this case is to know if data mining techniques could be useful for automatically structuring personal collections by considering local structures. They propose a uniform description of learning tasks which starts with a most general, generic learning task and is then specialized to the known learning tasks and then address how to solve the new learning task. The proposed approach uses in a distributed setting are exemplified by the application to collaborative media organization in a peer-to-peer network.

Marinette Bouet, Pierre Gançarski, Marie-Aude Aufaure, and Omar Boussaïd in "Pattern Mining and Clustering on Image Databases" focus on image data. In an image context, databases are very large since they contain strongly heterogeneous data, often not structured and possibly coming from different sources within different theoretical or applicative domains (pixel values, image descriptors, annotations, trainings, expert or interpreted knowledge, etc.). Besides, when objects are described by a large set of features, many of them are correlated, while others are noisy or irrelevant. Furthermore, analyzing and mining these multimedia data to derive potentially useful information is not easy. The authors propose a survey of the relevant research related to image data processing and present data warehouse advances that organize large volumes of data linked with images. The rest of the chapter deals with two techniques largely used in data mining: clustering and pattern mining. They show how clustering approaches could be applied to image analysis and they highlight that there is little research dealing with image frequent pattern mining. They thus introduce the new research direction concerning pattern mining from large collections of images.

In the previous chapter, we have seen that in an image context, we have to deal with very large databases since they contain strongly heterogeneous data. In "Semantic Integration and Knowledge Discovery for Environmental Research", proposed by Zhiyuan Chen, Aryya Gangopadhyay, George Karabatis, Michael McGuire, and Claire Welty, we also address very large databases but in a different context. The urban environment is formed by complex interactions between natural and human systems. Studying the urban environment requires the collection and analysis of very large datasets, having semantic (including spatial and temporal) differences and interdependencies, being collected and managed by multiple organizations, and being stored in varying formats. In this chapter, the authors introduce a new approach to integrate urban environmental data and provide scientists with semantic techniques to navigate and discover patterns in very large environmental datasets.

In the chapter "Visualizing Multi Dimensional Data", César García-Osorio and Colin Fyfe focus on the visualization of multidimensional data. This chapter is based on the following assertion: finding information within the data is often an extremely complex task and even if the computer is very good at handling large volumes of data and manipulating such data in an automatic manner, humans are much better at pattern identification than computers. They thus focus on visualization techniques when the number of attributes to represent is higher than three. They start with a short description of some taxonomies of visualization methods, and then present their vision of the field. After they explain in detail each class in their classification emphasizing some of the more significant visualization methods belonging to that class, they give a list of some of the software tools for data visualization freely available on the Internet.

Intense work in the area of data mining technology and in its applications to several domains has resulted in the development of a large variety of techniques and tools able to automatically and intelligently transform large amounts of data in knowledge relevant to users. However, as with other kinds of useful technologies, the knowledge discovery process can be misused. In "Privacy Preserving Data Mining, Concepts, Techniques, and Evaluation Methodologies", Igor Nai Fovino addresses a new challenging problem: how to preserve privacy when applying data mining methods. He proposes to the study privacy preserving problem under the data mining perspective as well as a taxonomy criteria allowing giving a constructive high level presentation of the main privacy preserving data mining approaches. He also focuses on a unified evaluation framework.

Many recent real-world applications, such as network traffic monitoring, intrusion detection systems, sensor network data analysis, click stream mining, and dynamic tracing of financial transactions, call for studying a new kind of data. Called stream data, this model is, in fact, a continuous, potentially infinite flow of information as opposed to finite, statically stored datasets extensively studied by researchers of the data mining community. Hanady Abdulsalam, David B. Skillicorn, and Pat Martin, in the chapter "Mining Data-Streams", focus on three online mining techniques of data streams, namely summarization, prediction, and clustering techniques, and show the research work in the area. In each section, they conclude with a comparative analysis of the major work in the area.

Acknowledgment

The editors would like to acknowledge the help of all involved in the collation and review process of the book, without whose support the project could not have been satisfactorily completed.

Special thanks go to all the staff at IGI Global, whose contributions throughout the whole process from inception of the initial idea to final publication have been invaluable.

We received a considerable amount of chapter submissions for this book and the first idea for reviewing the proposals was to have the authors reviewing each other's chapters. However, in order to improve the scientific quality of this book, we finally decided to gather a high level reviewing committee. Our referees have done an invaluable work in providing constructive and comprehensive reviews. The reviewing committee of this book is the following:

Larisa Archer	Gabriel Fung
Mohamed Gaber	Fosca Giannotti
S.K. Gupta	Ruoming Jin
Eamonn Keogh	Marzena Kryszkiewicz
Mark Last	Paul Leng
Georges Loizou	Shinichi Morishita
Mirco Nanni	David Pearson
Raffaele Perego	Christophe Rigotti
Claudio Sartori	Gerik Scheuermann
Aik-Choon Tan	Franco Turini
Ada Wai-Chee Fu	Haixun Wang
Jeffrey Xu Yu	Jun Zhang
Benyu Zhang	Wei Zhao
Ying Zhao	Xingquan Zhu

Warm thanks go to all those referees for their work. We know that reviewing chapters for our book was a considerable undertaking and we have appreciated their commitment.

In closing, we wish to thank all of the authors for their insights and excellent contributions to this book.

Florent Masseglia, Pascal Poncelet, & Maguelonne Teisseire

Chapter I
Why Fuzzy Set Theory is Useful in Data Mining

Eyke Hüllermeier
Philipps-Universität Marburg, Germany

ABSTRACT

In recent years, several extensions of data mining and knowledge discovery methods have been developed on the basis of fuzzy set theory. Corresponding fuzzy data mining methods exhibit some potential advantages over standard methods, notably the following: Since many patterns of interest are inherently vague, fuzzy approaches allow for modeling them in a more adequate way and thus enable the discovery of patterns that would otherwise remain hidden. Related to this, fuzzy methods are often more robust toward a certain amount of variability or noise in the data, a point of critical importance in many practical application fields. This chapter highlights the aforementioned advantages of fuzzy approaches in the context of exemplary data mining methods, but also points out some additional complications that can be caused by fuzzy extensions.

INTRODUCTION

Tools and techniques that have been developed during the last 40 years in the field of fuzzy set theory (FST) have been applied quite successfully in a variety of application areas. Still the most prominent example of the practical usefulness of corresponding techniques is perhaps *fuzzy control*, where the idea is to express the input-output behavior of a controller in terms of fuzzy rules.

Yet, fuzzy tools and fuzzy extensions of existing methods have also been used and developed in many other fields, ranging from research areas like approximate reasoning over optimization and decision support to concrete applications like image processing, robotics, and bioinformatics, just to name a few.

While aspects of knowledge representation and reasoning have dominated research in FST for a long time, problems of *automated learn-*

ing and *knowledge acquisition* have more and more come to the fore in recent years. There are several reasons for this development, notably the following: First, there has been an internal shift within fuzzy systems research from "modeling" to "learning", which can be attributed to the awareness that the well-known "knowledge acquisition bottleneck" seems to remain one of the key problems in the design of intelligent and knowledge-based systems. Second, this trend has been further amplified by the great interest that the fields of *knowledge discovery in databases* (KDD) and its core methodological component, *data mining*, have attracted in recent years (Fayyad, Piatetsky-Shapiro, & Smyth, 1996).

It is hence hardly surprising that data mining has received a great deal of attention in the FST community in recent years (Hüllermeier, 2005a, b). The aim of this chapter is to convince the reader that data mining is indeed another promising application area of FST or, stated differently, that FST is useful for data mining. To this end, we shall first give a brief overview of potential advantages of fuzzy approaches. One of these advantages, which is in our opinion of special importance, will then be discussed and exemplified in more detail: the increased expressive power and, related to this, a certain kind of robustness of fuzzy approaches for expressing and discovering patterns of interest in data. Apart from these advantages, however, we shall also point out some additional complications that can be caused by fuzzy extensions.

The style of presentation in this chapter is purely nontechnical and mainly aims at conveying some basic ideas and insights, often by using relatively simple examples; for technical details, we will give pointers to the literature. Before proceeding, let us also make a note on the methodological focus of this chapter, in which data mining will be understood as the application of computational methods and algorithms for extracting useful patterns from potentially very large data sets. In particular, we would like to distinguish between *pattern discovery* and *model*

induction. While we consider the former to be the core problem of data mining that we shall focus on, the latter is more in the realm of machine learning, where predictive accuracy is often the most important evaluation measure. According to our view, data mining is of a more explanatory nature, and patterns discovered in a data set are usually of a *local* and *descriptive* rather than of a *global* and *predictive* nature. Needles to say, however, this is only a very rough distinction and simplified view; on a more detailed level, the transition between machine learning and data mining is of course rather blurred.[1]

As we do not assume all readers to be familiar with fuzzy sets, we briefly recall some basic ideas and concepts from FST in the next section. Potential features and advantages of fuzzy data mining are then discussed in the third and fourth sections. The chapter will be completed with a brief discussion of possible complications that might be produced by fuzzy extensions and some concluding remarks in the fifth and sixth sections, respectively.

BACKGROUND ON FUZZY SETS

In this section, we recall the basic definition of a fuzzy set, the main semantic interpretations of membership degrees, and the most important mathematical (logical resp. set-theoretical) operators.

A fuzzy subset of a reference set $\mathbf{D}$ is identified by a so-called membership function (often denoted $\mu(\cdot)$), which is a generalization of the characteristic function $I_A(\cdot)$ of an ordinary set $A \subseteq \mathbf{D}$ (Zadeh, 1965). For each element $x \in \mathbf{D}$, this function specifies the *degree of membership* of x in the fuzzy set. Usually, membership degrees are taken from the unit interval [0,1]; that is, a membership function is a $\mathbf{D} \rightarrow [0,1]$ mapping, even though more general membership scales L (like ordinal scales or complete lattices) are conceivable. Throughout the chapter, we shall use the same notation for ordinary sets and fuzzy sets. Moreover, we shall not distinguish between a fuzzy set and its membership function; that is, $A(x)$ (instead of $\mu_A(x)$) denotes the degree of membership of the element x in the fuzzy set A.

Fuzzy sets formalize the idea of *graded membership*, that is, the idea that an element can belong "more or less" to a set. Consequently, a fuzzy set can have "nonsharp" boundaries. Many sets or concepts associated with natural language terms have boundaries that are nonsharp in the sense of FST. Consider the concept of "forest" as an example. For many collections of trees and plants, it will be quite difficult to decide in an unequivocal way as to whether or not one should call them a forest. Even simpler, consider the set of "tall men". Is it reasonable to say that *185 cm* is tall and *184.5 cm* is not tall? In fact, since the set of tall men is a vague (linguistic) concept, any sharp boundary of this set will appear rather arbitrary. Modeling the concept "tall men" as a fuzzy set A of the set $\mathbf{D}=(0,250)$ of potential sizes (which of course presupposes that the tallness of a men only depends on this attribute), it becomes possible to express, for example, that a size of *190 cm* is completely in accordance with this concept ($A(190=1)$), *180 cm* is "more or less" tall ($A(180)=1/2$, say), and *170 cm* is definitely not tall ($A(170)=0$).[2]

The above example suggests that fuzzy sets provide a convenient alternative to an interval-based discretization of numerical attributes, which is a common preprocessing step in data mining applications (Dougherty, Kohavi, & Sahami, 1995). For example, in gene expression analysis, one typically distinguishes between *normally expressed* genes, *underexpressed* genes, and *overexpressed* genes. This classification is made on the basis of the expression level of the gene (a normalized numerical value), as measured by so-called DNA-chips, by using corresponding thresholds. For example, a gene is often called overexpressed if its expression level is at least twofold increased. Needless to say, corresponding thresholds (such as 2) are more or less arbitrary. Figure 1 shows a *fuzzy partition* of the expression level with a "smooth" transition between under, normal, and overexpression. (The fuzzy sets $\{F_i\}_{i=1}^{m}$ that form a partition are usually assumed to satisfy $F_1 + ... + F_m \equiv 1$ (Ruspini, 1969), though this constraint is not compulsory.) For instance, according to this formalization, a gene with an expression level of at least 3 is definitely considered overexpressed, below 1 it is definitely not overexpressed, but in-between, it is considered overexpressed to a certain degree.

Fuzzy sets or, more specifically, membership degrees can have different semantical interpretations. Particularly, a fuzzy set can express three types of cognitive concepts which are of major importance in artificial intelligence, namely *uncertainty*, *similarity*, and *preference*

Figure 1. Fuzzy partition of the gene expression level with a "smooth" transition (grey regions) between underexpression, normal expression, and overexpression

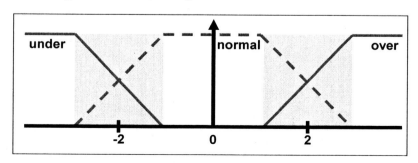

(Dubois & Prade, 1997). To exemplify, consider the fuzzy set *A* of mannequins with "ideal size", which might be formalized by the mapping $A : x \to \max(1 - |x - 175|/10, 0)$, where *x* is the size in centimeters.

- **Uncertainty:** Given (imprecise/uncertain) information in the form of a linguistic statement *L*, saying that a certain mannequin has ideal size, $A(x)$ is considered as the *possibility* that the real size of the mannequin is *x*. Formally, the fuzzy set *A* induces a so-called possibility distribution $\pi(\cdot)$. Possibility distributions are basic elements of *possibility theory* (Dubois & Prade, 1988; Zadeh, 1978), an uncertainty calculus that provides an alternative to other calculi such as probability theory.

- **Similarity:** A membership degree $A(x)$ can also be considered as the *similarity* to the prototype of a mannequin with ideal size (or, more generally, as the similarity to a set of prototypes) (Cross & Sudkamp, 2002; Ruspini, 1991). In our example, the prototypical "ideal-sized" mannequin is of size *175 cm*. Another mannequin of, say, *170 cm* is similar to this prototype to the degree $A(170) = 1/2$.

- **Preference:** In connection with *preference* modeling, a fuzzy set is considered as a *flexible constraint* (Dubois & Prade, 1996, 1997). In our example, $A(x)$ specifies the degree of satisfaction achieved by a mannequin of size *x*: A size of *x*=175 is fully satisfactory ($A(x)$=1), whereas a size of *x*=170 is more or less acceptable, namely to the degree 1/2.

To operate with fuzzy sets in a formal way, fuzzy set theory offers generalized set-theoretical resp. logical connectives and operators (as in the classical case, there is a close correspondence between set theory and logic). In the following, we recall some basic operators that will reappear in later parts of the chapter.

- A so-called t-norm $\otimes$ is a generalized logical *conjunction*, that is, a $[0,1] \times [0,1] \to [0,1]$ mapping which is associative, commutative, monotone increasing (in both arguments), and which satisfies the boundary conditions $\alpha \otimes 0 = 0$ and $\alpha \otimes 1 = \alpha$ for all $0 \leq \alpha \leq 1$ (Klement, Mesiar, & Pap, 2002; Schweizer & Sklar, 1983). Well-known examples of t-norms include the minimum $(\alpha, \beta) \mapsto \min(\alpha, \beta)$, the product $(\alpha, \beta) \mapsto \alpha\beta$, and the Lukasiewicz t-norm $(\alpha, \beta) \mapsto \max(\alpha + \beta - 1, 0)$. A t-norm is used for defining the *intersection* of fuzzy sets $F, G : X \to [0,1]$ as follows: $(F \cap G)(x) \overset{df}{=} F(x) \otimes G(x)$ for all $x \in X$. In a quite similar way, the *Cartesian product* of fuzzy sets $F : X \to [0,1]$ and $G : Y \to [0,1]$ is defined: $(F \cap G)(x, y) \overset{df}{=} F(x) \otimes G(y)$ for all $(x, y) \in X \times Y$.

- The logical *disjunction* is generalized by a so-called t-conorm $\oplus$, a $[0,1] \times [0,1] \to [0,1]$ mapping which is associative, commutative, monotone increasing (in both places), and such that $\alpha \otimes 0 = \alpha$ and $\alpha \oplus 1 = 1$ for all $0 \leq \alpha \leq 1$. Well-known examples of t-conorms include the maximum $(\alpha, \beta) \mapsto \alpha + \beta - \alpha\beta$, the algebraic sum $(\alpha, \beta) \mapsto \max(\alpha, \beta)$, and the Lukasiewicz t-conorm $(\alpha, \beta) \mapsto \min(\alpha + \beta, 1)$. A t-conorm can be used for defining the union of fuzzy sets: $(F \cup G)(x) \overset{df}{=} F(x) \oplus G(x)$ for all *x*.

- A generalized *implication* $\rightsquigarrow$ is a $[0,1] \times [0,1] \to [0,1]$ mapping that is monotone decreasing in the first and monotone increasing in the second argument and that satisfies the boundary conditions $\alpha \rightsquigarrow 1 = 1$, $0 \rightsquigarrow \beta = 1$, $1 \rightsquigarrow \beta = \beta$. (Apart from that, additional properties are sometimes required.) Implication operators of that kind, such as the Lukasiewicz implication $(\alpha, \beta) \mapsto \min(1 - \alpha + \beta, 1)$, are especially important in connection with the modeling of fuzzy rules, as will be seen in the fourth section.

ADVANTAGES OF FUZZY DATA MINING

This section gives a brief overview of merits and advantages of fuzzy data mining and highlights some potential contributions that FST can make to data mining. A more detailed discussion with a special focus will follow in the subsequent section.

Graduality

The ability to represent gradual concepts and fuzzy properties in a thorough way is one of the key features of fuzzy sets. This aspect is also of primary importance in the context of data mining. In fact, patterns that are of interest in data mining are often inherently vague and do have boundaries that are nonsharp in the sense of FST. To illustrate, consider the concept of a "peak": It is usually not possible to decide in an unequivocal way whether a timely ordered sequence of measurements has a "peak" (a particular kind of pattern) or not. Rather, there is a gradual transition between having a peak and not having a peak; see the fourth section for a similar example. Likewise, the spatial extension of patterns like a "cluster of points" or a "region of high density" in a data space will usually have soft rather than sharp boundaries.

Taking graduality into account is also important if one must decide whether a certain property is frequent among a set of objects, for example, whether a pattern occurs frequently in a data set. In fact, if the pattern is specified in an overly restrictive manner, it might easily happen that none of the objects matches the specification, even though many of them can be seen as approximate matches. In such cases, the pattern might still be considered as "well-supported" by the data; again,

we shall encounter an example of that kind in the fourth section. Besides, we also discuss a potential problem of frequency-based evaluation measures in the fuzzy case in the fifth section.

Linguistic Representation and Interpretability

A primary motivation for the development of fuzzy sets was to provide an interface between a numerical scale and a symbolic scale which is usually composed of linguistic terms. Thus, fuzzy sets have the capability to interface quantitative patterns with qualitative knowledge structures expressed in terms of natural language. This makes the application of fuzzy technology very appealing from a knowledge representational point of view. For example, it allows association rules (to be introduced in the fourth section) discovered in a database to be presented in a linguistic and hence comprehensible way.

Despite the fact that the user-friendly representation of models and patterns is often emphasized as one of the key features of fuzzy methods, it appears to us that this potential advantage should be considered with caution in the context of data mining. A main problem in this regard concerns the high subjectivity and context-dependency of fuzzy patterns: A rule such as "multilinguality usually implies high income", that might have been discovered in an employee database, may have different meanings to different users of a data mining system, depending on the concrete interpretation of the fuzzy concepts involved (multilinguality, high income). It is true that the imprecision of natural language is not necessarily harmful and can even be advantageous.[3] A fuzzy controller, for example, can be quite insensitive to the concrete mathematical translation of a linguistic model. One should realize, however, that in fuzzy control the information flows in a reverse direction: The linguistic model is not the end product, as in data mining; it rather stands at the beginning.

It is of course possible to disambiguate a model by complementing it with the semantics of the fuzzy concepts it involves (including the specification of membership functions). Then, however, the complete model, consisting of a qualitative (linguistic) and a quantitative part, becomes cumbersome and will not be easily understandable. This can be contrasted with interval-based models, the most obvious alternative for dealing with numerical attributes: Even though such models do certainly have their shortcomings, they are at least objective and not prone to context-dependency. Another possibility to guarantee transparency of a fuzzy model is to let the user of a data mining system specify all fuzzy concepts by hand, including the fuzzy partitions for the variables involved in the study under consideration. This is rarely done, however, mainly since the job is tedious and cumbersome if the number of variables is large.

To summarize on this score, we completely agree that the close connection between a numerical and a linguistic level for representing patterns, as established by fuzzy sets, *can* help a lot to improve interpretability of patterns, though linguistic representations also involve some complications and should therefore not be considered as preferable *per se*.

Robustness

It is often claimed that fuzzy methods are more robust than nonfuzzy methods. In a data mining context, the term "robustness" can of course refer to many things. In connection with fuzzy methods, the most relevant type of robustness concerns sensitivity toward variations of the data. Generally, a data mining method is considered robust if a small variation of the observed data does hardly alter the induced model or the evaluation of a pattern. Another desirable form of robustness of a data mining method is robustness toward variations

of its parametrization: Changing the parameters of a method slightly should not have a dramatic effect on the output of the method.

In the fourth section, an example supporting the claim that fuzzy methods are in a sense more robust than nonfuzzy methods will be given. One should note, however, that this is only an illustration and by no means a formal proof. In fact, proving that, under certain assumptions, one method is more robust than another one at least requires a formal definition of the meaning of robustness. Unfortunately, and despite the high potential, the treatment of this point is not as mature in the fuzzy set literature as in other fields such as *robust statistics* (Huber, 1981).

Representation of Uncertainty

Data mining is inseparably connected with uncertainty. For example, the data to be analyzed are imprecise, incomplete, or noisy most of the time, a problem that can badly deteriorate a mining algorithm and lead to unwarranted or questionable results. But even if observations are perfect, the alleged "discoveries" made in that data are of course afflicted with uncertainty. In fact, this point is especially relevant for data mining, where the systematic search for interesting patterns comes along with the (statistical) problem of multiple hypothesis testing, and therefore with a high danger of making false discoveries.

Fuzzy sets and possibility theory have made important contributions to the representation and processing of uncertainty. In data mining, like in other fields, related uncertainty formalisms can complement probability theory in a reasonable way, because not all types of uncertainty relevant to data mining are of a probabilistic nature, and because other formalisms are in some situations more expressive than probability. For example, probability is not very suitable for representing ignorance, which might be useful for modeling incomplete or missing data.

Generalized Operators

Many data mining methods make use of logical and arithmetical operators for representing relationships between attributes in models and patterns. Since a large repertoire of generalized logical (e.g., t-norms and t-conorms) and arithmetical (e.g., Choquet- and Sugeno-integral) operators have been developed in FST and related fields, a straightforward way to extend standard mining methods consists of replacing standard operators by their generalized versions.

The main effect of such generalizations is to make the representation of models and patterns more flexible. Besides, in some cases, generalized operators can help to represent patterns in a more distinctive way, for example, to express different types of dependencies among attributes that cannot be distinguished by nonfuzzy methods; we shall discuss an example of that type in more detail in the fourth section.

INCREASED EXPRESSIVENESS FOR FEATURE REPRESENTATION AND DEPENDENCY ANALYSIS

Many data mining methods proceed from a representation of the entities under consideration in terms of *feature vectors*, that is, a fixed number of features or attributes, each of which represents a certain property of an entity. For example, if these entities are employees, possible features might be gender, age, and income. A common goal of feature-based methods, then, is to analyze relationships and dependencies between the attributes. In this section, it will be argued that the increased expressiveness of fuzzy methods, which is mainly due to the ability to represent *graded* properties in an adequate way, is useful for both feature extraction and dependency analysis.

Fuzzy Feature Extraction and Pattern Representation

Many features of interest, and therefore the patterns expressed in terms of these features, are inherently fuzzy. As an example, consider the so-called "candlestick patterns" which refer to certain characteristics of financial time series. These patterns are believed to reflect the psychology of the market and are used to support investment decisions. Needless to say, a candlestick pattern is fuzzy in the sense that the transition between the presence and absence of the pattern is gradual rather than abrupt; see Lee, Liu, and Chen (2006) for an interesting fuzzy approach to modeling and discovering such patterns.

To give an even simpler example, consider again a time series of the form:

$$x = (x(1), x(2)....x(n)).$$

To bring again one of the topical application areas of fuzzy data mining into play, one may think of x as the expression profile of a gene in a microarray experiment, that is, a timely ordered sequence of expression levels. For such profiles, the property (feature) "decreasing at the beginning" might be of interest, for example, in order to express patterns like[4]

P: "A series which is decreasing at the beginning is typically increasing at the end."

(1)

Again, the aforementioned pattern is inherently fuzzy, in the sense that a time series can be more or less decreasing at the beginning. In particular, it is unclear which time points belong to the "beginning" of a time series, and defining it in a nonfuzzy (crisp) way by a subset $B=\{1,2,...,k\}$, for a fixed $k \in \{1...n\}$, comes along with a certain arbitrariness and does not appear fully convincing.

Besides, the human perception of "decreasing" will usually be tolerant toward small violations of the standard mathematical definition, which requires:

$$\forall t \in B : x(t) \geq x(t+1), \qquad (2)$$

especially if such violations may be caused by noise in the data.

Figure 2 shows three exemplary profiles. While the first one at the bottom is undoubtedly decreasing at the beginning, the second one in the middle is clearly not decreasing in the sense of (2). According to human perception, however, this series is still approximately or, say, almost decreasing at the beginning. In other words, it does have the corresponding (fuzzy) feature to some extent.

By modeling features like "decreasing at the beginning" in a nonfuzzy way, that is, as a Boolean predicate which is either true or false, it will usually become impossible to discover patterns such as (1), even if these patterns are to some degree present in a data set.

To illustrate this point, consider a simple experiment in which 1,000 copies of an (ideal) profile defined by $x(t) = |t - 11|$, $t = 1...21$ that are corrupted with a certain level of noise. This is done by adding an error term to each value of every profile; these error terms are independent and normally distributed with mean 0 and standard deviation σ. Then, the relative support of the pattern (1) is determined, that is, the fraction of profiles that still satisfy this pattern in a strict mathematical sense:

$$(\forall t \in \{1 \ ... \ k\} : x(t) \geq x(t+1))$$

$$\wedge (\forall t \in \{n - k \ ... \ n\} : x(t-1) \geq x(t))$$

Figure 3 (left) shows the relative support as a function of the level of noise (σ) and various values of k. As can be seen, the support drops off quite quickly. Consequently, the pattern will be discovered only in the more or less noise-free scenario but quickly disappears for noisy data.

Fuzzy set-based modeling techniques offer a large repertoire for generalizing the formal

Figure 2. Three exemplary time series that are more or less "decreasing at the beginning"

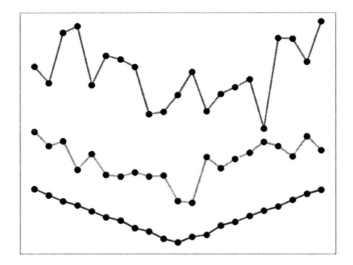

Figure 3. Left: Relative support of pattern (1) as a function of the level of noise σ and various values of k; Right: Comparison with the relative support for the fuzzy case

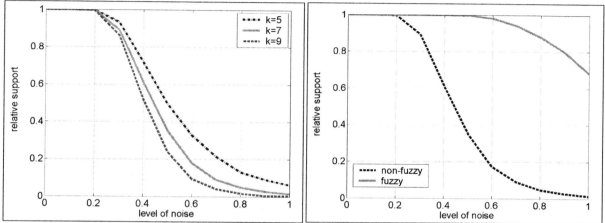

(logical) description of a property, including generalized logical connectives such as t-norms and t-conorms, fuzzy relations such as MUCH-SMALLER-THAN, and fuzzy quantifiers such as FOR-MOST. Making use of these tools, it becomes possible to formalize descriptions like "for all points t at the beginning, $x(t)$ is not much smaller than $x(t+1)$, and for most points it is even strictly greater" in an adequate way:

$$F_1(x) = (\tilde{\forall} t \in B : x(t+1) > x(t))$$

$$\otimes (\forall t \in B : \neg MS(x(t+1), x(t)))$$

where B is now a *fuzzy* set characterizing the beginning of the time series, $\tilde{\forall}$ is an exception-tolerant relaxation of the universal quantifier, $\otimes$ is a t-norm, and MS a fuzzy MUCH-SMALLER-THAN relation; we refrain from a more detailed description of these concepts at a technical level.

In any case, (3) is an example for a fuzzy definition of the feature "decreasing at the beginning" (we by no means claim that it is the best characterization) and offers an alternative to the nonfuzzy definition (2). According to (3), every time series can have the feature to some extent.

Analogously, the fuzzy feature "increasing at the end" (F_2) can be defined. Figure 3 (right) shows the relative support:

$$\text{supp}(P) = \frac{1}{1000} \sum_{x_i} \text{supp}_{x_i}(P) = \frac{1}{1000} \sum_{x_i} F_1(x_i) \otimes F_2(x_i)$$

$$(4)$$

of the pattern P for the fuzzy case, again as a function of the noise level. As can be seen, the relative support also drops off after a while, which is an expected and even desirable property (for a high enough noise level, the pattern will indeed disappear). The support function decreases much slower, however, so the pattern will be discovered in a much more robust way.

The above example shows that a fuzzy set-based modeling can be very useful for extracting certain types of features. Besides, it gives an example of increased robustness in a relatively specific sense, namely robustness of pattern discovery toward noise in the data. In this connection, let us mention that we do not claim that the fuzzy approach is the only way to make feature extraction more adequate and pattern discovery more robust. For example, in the particular setting considered in our example, one may think of a probabilistic alternative, in which the individual support $\text{supp}_{x_2}(P)$ in (4) is replaced by the probability that the underlying noise-free profile does satisfy the pattern P in the sense of (2). Apart from pointing to the increased computational complexity of this alternative, however, we like to repeat our argument that patterns like (1) are inherently fuzzy in our opinion: Even in a completely noise-free scenario, where information is exact and nothing is random, human perception may consider a given profile as somewhat decreasing at the beginning, even if it does not have this property in a strict mathematical sense.

Mining Gradual Dependencies

Association Analysis

Association analysis (Agrawal & Srikant, 1994; Savasere, Omiecinski, & Navathe, 1995) is a widely applied data mining technique that has been studied intensively in recent years. The goal in association analysis is to find "interesting" associations in a data set, that is, dependencies between so-called itemsets **A** and **B** expressed in terms of rules of the form $\mathbf{A} \to \mathbf{B}$. To illustrate, consider the well-known example where items are products and a data record (transaction) **I** is a shopping basket such as {butter, milk, bread}. The intended meaning of an association $\mathbf{A} \to \mathbf{B}$ is that, if **A** is present in a transaction, then **B** is likely to be present as well. A standard problem in association analysis is to find all rules $\mathbf{A} \to \mathbf{B}$ the *support* (relative frequency of transactions **I** with $\mathbf{A} \cup \mathbf{B} \subseteq \mathbf{I}$) and *confidence* (relative frequency of transactions **I** with $\mathbf{B} \subseteq \mathbf{I}$ among those with $\mathbf{A} \subseteq \mathbf{I}$) that reach user-defined thresholds *minsupp* and *minconf*, respectively.

In the above setting, a single item can be represented in terms of a binary (0/1-valued) attribute reflecting the presence or absence of the item. To make association analysis applicable to data sets involving numerical attributes, such attributes are typically discretized into intervals, and each interval is considered as a new binary attribute. For example, the attribute *temperature* might be replaced by two binary attributes *cold* and *warm*, where *cold* =1 (*warm* =0) if the temperature is below 10 degrees and *warm* =1 (*cold* =0) otherwise.

A further extension is to use fuzzy sets (fuzzy partitions) instead of intervals (interval partitions), and corresponding approaches to fuzzy association analysis have been proposed by several authors (see, e.g., Chen, Wei, Kerre, & Wets, 2003; Delgado, Marin, Sanchez, & Vila, 2003 for recent overviews). In the fuzzy case, the presence of a feature subset $\mathbf{A} = \{A_1 \dots A_m\}$, that is, a *compound feature* considered as a conjunction of primitive features $A_1 \dots A_m$, is specified as:

$$\mathbf{A}(x) = A_1(x) \otimes A_2(x) \otimes \dots \otimes A_m(x)$$

where $A_i(x) \in [0,1]$ is the degree to which x has feature A_i, and $\otimes$ is a t-norm serving as a generalized conjunction.

There are different motivations for a fuzzy approach to association rule mining. For example, again pointing to the aspect of *robustness*, several authors have emphasized that, by allowing for "soft" rather than crisp boundaries of intervals, fuzzy sets can avoid certain undesirable threshold or "boundary effects" (see, e.g., Sudkamp, 2005). The latter refers to the problem that a slight variation of an interval boundary may already cause a considerable change of the evaluation of an association rule, and therefore strongly influence the data mining result.

In the following, we shall emphasize another potential advantage of fuzzy association analysis, namely the fact that association rules can be represented in a more *distinctive* way. In particular, working with fuzzy instead of binary features allows for discovering *gradual* dependencies between variables.

Gradual Dependencies Between Fuzzy Features

On a logical level, the meaning of a standard (association) rule $A \rightarrow B$ is captured by the material conditional; that is, the rule applies unless the consequent B is true and the antecedent A is false. On a natural language level, a rule of that kind is typically understood as an IF-THEN construct: If the antecedent A holds true, so does the consequent B.

In the fuzzy case, the Boolean predicates A and B are replaced by corresponding fuzzy predicates which assume truth values in the unit interval $[0,1]$. Consequently, the material implication operator has to be replaced by a generalized connective, that is, a suitable $[0,1] \times [0,1] \rightarrow [0,1]$ mapping. In this regard, two things are worth mentioning. First, the choice of this connective is not unique; instead there are various options. Second, depending on the type of operator employed, fuzzy rules can have quite different semantical interpretations (Dubois & Prade, 1996).

A special type of fuzzy rule, referred to as *gradual rules*, combines the antecedent A and the consequent B by means of a *residuated* implication operator $\rightsquigarrow$. The latter is a special type of implication operator which is derived from a t-norm $\otimes$ through residuation:

$$\alpha \overset{df}{\rightsquigarrow} \beta = \sup\{\gamma \mid \alpha \otimes \gamma \leq \beta\} \qquad (5)$$

As a particular case, so-called *pure* gradual rules are obtained when using the following implication operator:[5]

$$\alpha \rightsquigarrow \beta = \begin{cases} 1 & if \ \alpha \leq \beta \\ 0 & if \ \alpha > \beta \end{cases} \qquad (6)$$

The above approach to modeling a fuzzy rule is in agreement with the following interpretation of a gradual rule: "THE MORE the antecedent A is true, THE MORE the consequent B is true" (Dubois & Prade, 1992; Prade, 1988); for example "The larger an object, the heavier it is". More specifically, in order to satisfy the rule, the consequent must be *at least* as true as the antecedent according to (6), and the same principle applies for other residuated implications, albeit in a somewhat relaxed form.

The above type of *implication-based* fuzzy rule can be contrasted with so-called *conjunction-based* rules, where the antecedent and consequent are combined in terms of a t-norm such as minimum or product. Thus, in order to satisfy a conjunction-based rule, both the antecedent and the consequent must be true (to some degree). As an important difference, note that the antecedent and the consequent play a symmetric role in the case of conjunction-based rules but are handled in an asymmetric way by implication-based rules.

The distinction between different semantics of a fuzzy rule as outlined above can of course also be made for association rules. Formally, this leads to using different types of support and confidence measures for evaluating the quality (interestingness) of an association (Dubois, Hüllermeier, & Prade, 2006; Hüllermeier, 2001). Consequently, it may happen that a data set supports a fuzzy association $A \rightarrow B$ quite well in one sense, that is, according to a particular semantics, but not according to another one.

The important point to notice is that these distinctions cannot be made for nonfuzzy (association) rules. Formally, the reason is that fuzzy extensions of logical operators all coincide on the extreme truth values 0 and 1. Or, stated the other way round, a differentiation can only be made on intermediary truth degrees. In particular, the consideration of gradual dependencies does not make any sense if the only truth degrees are 0 and 1.

In fact, in the nonfuzzy case, the point of departure for analyzing and evaluating a relationship between features or feature subsets A and B is a contingency table (see Table 1).

In this table, n_{00} denotes the number of examples x for which $A(x) = 0$ and $B(x) = 0$, and the remaining entries are defined analogously. All common evaluation measures for association rules, such as support (n_1/n) and confidence ($n_{11}/n_{1\bullet}$) can be expressed in terms of these numbers.

In the fuzzy case, a contingency table can be replaced by a *contingency diagram,* an idea that has been presented in Hüllermeier (2002). A contingency diagram is a two-dimensional diagram in which every example x defines a point $(\alpha,\beta) = (\mathbf{A}(x),\mathbf{B}(x)) \in [0,1] \times [0,1]$. A diagram of that type is able to convey much more information about the dependency between two (compound) features $\mathbf{A}$ and $\mathbf{B}$ than a contingency table. Consider, for example, the two diagrams depicted in Figure 4. Obviously, the dependency between $\mathbf{A}$ and $\mathbf{B}$ as suggested by the left diagram is quite different from the one shown on the right. Now, consider the nonfuzzy case in which the fuzzy sets $\mathbf{A}$ and $\mathbf{B}$ are replaced by crisp sets $\mathbf{A}_{bin}$ and $\mathbf{B}_{bin}$, respectively, for example, by using a

$[0,1] \rightarrow \{0,1\}$ mapping like $\alpha \mapsto (\alpha > 0.5)$. Then, identical contingency tables are obtained for the left and the right scenario (in the left diagram, the four quadrants contain the same number of points as the corresponding quadrants in the right diagram). In other words, the two scenarios cannot be distinguished in the nonfuzzy case.

In Hüllermeier (2002), it was furthermore suggested to analyze contingency diagrams by means of techniques from statistical regression analysis. Among other things, this offers an alternative approach to discovering gradual dependencies. For example, the fact that a linear regression line with a significantly positive slope (and high quality indexes like a coefficient of determination, R^2, close to 1) can be fit to the data suggests that indeed a higher $\mathbf{A}(x)$ tends to result in a higher $\mathbf{B}(x)$; that is, the more x has feature $\mathbf{A}$, the more it has feature $\mathbf{B}$. This is the case, for example, in the left diagram in Figure 4. In fact, the data

Table 1.

	$\mathbf{B}(y) = 0$	$\mathbf{B}(y) = 1$	
$\mathbf{A}(x) = 0$	n_{00}	n_{01}	$n_{0\bullet}$
$\mathbf{A}(x) = 1$	n_{10}	n_{11}	$n_{1\bullet}$
	$n_{\bullet 0}$	$n_{\bullet 1}$	n

Figure 4. Two contingency diagrams reflecting different types of dependencies between features $\mathbf{A}$ and $\mathbf{B}$.

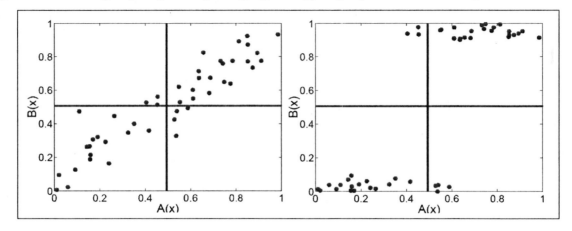

in this diagram support an association $\mathbf{A} \rightarrow \mathbf{B}$ quite well in the sense of the THE MORE-THE MORE semantics, whereas it does not support the nonfuzzy rule $\mathbf{A}_{bin} \rightarrow \mathbf{B}_{bin}$.

Note that a contingency diagram can be derived not only for simple but also for compound features, that is, feature subsets representing conjunctions of simple features. The problem, then, is to derive regression-related quality indexes for all potential association rules in a systematic way, and to extract those gradual dependencies which are well-supported by the data in terms of these indexes. For corresponding mining methods, including algorithmic aspects and complexity issues, we refer to Hüllermeier (2002).

Before concluding this section, let us note that the two approaches for modeling gradual dependencies that we have presented, the one based on fuzzy gradual rules and the other one using statistical regression analysis, share similarities but also show differences. In particular, the logical modeling of gradual dependencies via suitable implication operators does not assume a relationship between $\mathbf{A}(x)$ and $\mathbf{B}(x)$ which is, say, indeed "strictly increasing". For example, if $\mathbf{B}(x) \equiv 1$, then the rule $\mathbf{A} \rightarrow \mathbf{B}$ will be perfectly satisfied, even though $\mathbf{B}(x)$ is constant and does not increase with $\mathbf{A}(x)$. In fact, more specifically, the semantical interpretation of a gradual rule should be expressed in terms of a *bound* on the degree $\mathbf{B}(x)$ rather than the degree itself: The more x is in $\mathbf{A}$, the higher is the guaranteed *lower bound* of the membership of x in $\mathbf{B}$. Seen from this point of view, the statistical approach is perhaps even more in line with the intuitive understanding of a THE MORE-THE MORE relationship.

COMPUTATIONAL AND CONCEPTUAL COMPLICATIONS

In the previous sections, we have outlined several potential advantages of fuzzy data mining, with a special focus on the increased expressiveness of fuzzy patterns. Needless to say, these advantages of fuzzy extensions do not always come for free but may also produce some complications, either at a computational or at a conceptual level. This section is meant to comment on this point, albeit in a very brief way. In fact, since the concrete problems that may arise are rather application-specific, a detailed discussion is beyond the scope of this chapter.

Regarding computational aspects, scalability is an issue of utmost importance in data mining. Therefore, the usefulness of fuzzy extensions presupposes that fuzzy patterns can be mined without sacrificing computational efficiency. Fortunately, efficient algorithmic solutions can be assured in many cases, mainly because fuzzy extensions can usually resort to the same algorithmic principles as nonfuzzy methods. To illustrate, consider again the case of association rule mining, the first step of which typically consists of finding the frequent itemsets, that is, the itemsets $\mathbf{A} = \{A_1 \dots A_m\}$ satisfying the support condition *supp* $(\mathbf{A}) \geq minsupp$. Several efficient algorithms have been developed for this purpose (Agrawal & Srikant, 1994). For example, in order to prune the search space, the well-known Apriori principle exploits the property that every superset of an infrequent itemset is necessarily infrequent by itself or, vice versa, that every subset of a frequent itemset is also frequent (downward closure property). In the fuzzy case, where an itemset is a set $\mathbf{A} = \{A_1 \dots A_m\}$ of fuzzy features (items), the support is usually defined by:

$$\sum_x A(\mathbf{x}) = \sum_x \mathbf{A}_1(\mathbf{x}) \otimes \mathbf{A}_2(\mathbf{x}) \otimes \dots \otimes \mathbf{A}_m(\mathbf{x})$$

where $A_i(x) \in [0,1]$ is the degree to which the entity x has feature A_i. So, the key difference to the nonfuzzy case is that the support is no longer an integer but a real-valued measure. Apart from that, however, it has the same properties as the nonfuzzy support, in particular the aforementioned closure property, which means that the basic algorithmic principles can be applied in exactly the same way.

Of course, not all adaptations are so simple. For example, in the case of implication-based association rules (Hüllermeier, 2002), the generation of candidate rules on the basis of the support measure becomes more intricate due to the fact that the measure is now asymmetric in the antecedent and the consequent part; that is, the support of a rule $\mathbf{A} \to \mathbf{B}$ is no longer the support of the itemset $\mathbf{A} \cup \mathbf{B}$.

Apart from computational issues, fuzzy extensions may of course also produce complications at a conceptual level which are of a more principled nature. As an example, we already mentioned a problem of ambiguity which is caused by using linguistic terms for representing patterns: as long as the precise meaning of such terms is not made explicit for the user (e.g., by revealing the associated membership function), patterns of that type remain ambiguous to some extent. We conclude this section by indicating another complication which concerns the scoring of patterns in terms of frequency-based evaluation measures. An example of this type of measure, which is quite commonly used in data mining, is the aforementioned support measure in association analysis: A pattern P is considered "interesting" only if it is supported by a large enough number of examples; this is the well-known support condition *supp* $(P) \geq minsupp$.

As already mentioned, in the fuzzy case, the individual support $supp_{x_i}(P)$ given to a pattern P by an example x_i is not restricted to 0 or 1. Instead, every example x_i can support a pattern to a certain degree $s_i \in [0,1]$. Moreover, resorting to the commonly employed sigma-count for computing the cardinality of a fuzzy set (Zadeh, 1983), the overall support of the pattern is given by the sum of the individual degrees of support. The problem is that this sum does not provide any information about the *distribution* of the s_i. In particular, since several small s_i can compensate for a single large one, it may happen that the overall support appears to be quite high, even though none of the s_i is close to 1. In this case, one may wonder whether the pattern is really well-supported. Instead, it seems reasonable to require that a well-supported pattern should at least have a few examples that can be considered as true prototypes. For instance, imagine a database with 1,000 time series, each of which is "decreasing at the beginning" to the degree 0.5. The overall support of this pattern (500) is as high for this database as it is for a database with 500 time series that are perfectly decreasing at the beginning and 500 that are not decreasing at all. A possible solution to this problem is to replace the simple support condition by a "level-wise" support threshold, demanding that, for each among a certain set of membership degrees $0 < \alpha_1 < \alpha_2 \leq ... \leq \alpha_m \leq 1$, the number of examples providing individual support $\geq \alpha_i$ is at least *min-supp$_i$* (Dubois, Prade, & Sudkamp, 2005).

The purpose of the above examples is to show that fuzzy extensions of data mining methods have to be applied with some caution. On the other hand, the examples also suggest that additional complications caused by fuzzy extensions, either at a computational or conceptual level, can usually be solved in a satisfactory way. In other words, such complications do usually not prevent from using fuzzy methods, at least in the vast majority of cases, and by no means annul the advantages thereof.

CONCLUSION

The aim of this chapter is to provide convincing evidence for the assertion that fuzzy set theory can contribute to data mining in a substantial way. To this end, we have mainly focused on the increased expressiveness of fuzzy approaches that allows one to represent features and patterns in a more adequate and distinctive way. More specifically, we argued that many features and patterns of interest are inherently fuzzy, and modeling them in a nonfuzzy way will inevitably lead to unsatisfactory results. As a simple example, we discussed features of time series, such as "decreasing at the beginning", in the fourth section, but one may of course also think of many other useful applications of fuzzy feature extraction, especially in fields that involve structured objects, such as graph mining, Web mining, or image mining. Apart from extracting features, we also argued that fuzzy methods are useful for representing dependencies between features. In particular, such methods allow for representing *gradual* dependencies, which is not possible in the case of binary features.

Several other merits of fuzzy data mining, including a possibly increased interpretability and robustness as well as adequate means for dealing with (nonstochastic) uncertainty and incomplete information, have been outlined in the third section. Albeit presented in a quite concise way, these merits should give an idea of the high potential of fuzzy methods in data mining.

REFERENCES

Agrawal, R., & Srikant, R. (1994). Fast algorithms for mining association rules. In *Proceedings of the 20th Conference on VLDB,* Santiago, Chile (pp. 487-499).

Chen, G., Wei, Q., Kerre, E., & Wets, G. (2003, September). Overview of fuzzy associations mining. In *Proceedings of the 4th International Symposium on Advanced Intelligent Systems,* Jeju, Korea.

Cross, V., & Sudkamp, T. (2002). *Similarity and computability in fuzzy set theory: Assessments and applications* (Vol. 93 of Studies in Fuzziness and Soft Computing). Physica-Verlag.

Delgado, M., Marin, D., Sanchez, D., & Vila, M.A. (2003). Fuzzy association rules: General model and applications. *IEEE Transactions on Fuzzy Systems, 11*(2), 214-225.

Dougherty, J., Kohavi, R., & Sahami, M. (1995). Supervised and unsupervised discretization of continuous features. In A. Prieditis & S. Russell (Ed.), *Machine learning: Proceedings of the 12th International Conference* (pp. 194-202). Morgan Kaufmann.

Dubois, D., Fargier, H., & Prade, H. (1996a). Possibility theory in constraint satisfaction problems: Handling priority, preference and uncertainty. *Applied Intelligence, 6,* 287-309.

Dubois, D., Fargier, H., & Prade, H. (1996b). Refinements of the maximin approach to decision making in fuzzy environment. *Fuzzy Sets and Systems, 81,* 103-122.

Dubois, D., Hüllermeier, E., & Prade, H. (2006). A systematic approach to the assessment of fuzzy association rules. *Data Mining and Knowledge Discovery, 13*(2), 167.

Dubois, D., & Prade, H. (1988). *Possibility theory.* Plenum Press.

Dubois, D., & Prade, H. (1992). Gradual inference rules in approximate reasoning. *Information Sciences, 61*(1-2), 103-122.

Dubois, D., & Prade, H. (1996). What are fuzzy rules and how to use them. *84,* 169-185.

Dubois, D., & Prade, H. (1997). The three semantics of fuzzy sets. *90*(2), 141-150.

Dubois, D., Prade, H., & Sudkamp, T. (2005). On the representation, measurement, and discovery of fuzzy associations. *IEEE Transactions on Fuzzy Systems, 13*(2), 250-262.

Fayyad, U.M., Piatetsky-Shapiro, G., & Smyth, P. (1996). From data mining to knowledge discovery: An overview. In *Advances in Knowledge Discovery and Data Mining.* MIT Press.

Huber, P.J. (1981). *Robust statistics.* Wiley.

Hüllermeier, E. (2001). Implication-based fuzzy association rules. In *Proceedings of the 5th Eu-*

ropean Conference on Principles and Practice of Knowledge Discovery in Databases, Freiburg, Germany (pp. 241-252).

Hüllermeier, E. (2002). Association rules for expressing gradual dependencies. In *Proceedings of the 6ᵗʰ European Conference on Principles and Practice of Knowledge Discovery in Databases*, Helsinki, Finland (pp. 200-211).

Hüllermeier, E. (Ed.). (2005a). Fuzzy sets in knowledge discovery [Special Issue]. *Fuzzy Sets and Systems, 149*(1).

Hüllermeier, E. (2005b). Fuzzy sets in machine learning and data mining: Status and prospects. *Fuzzy Sets and Systems, 156*(3), 387-406.

Klement, E.P., Mesiar, R., & Pap, E. (2002). *Triangular norms*. Kluwer Academic Publishers.

Lee, C.H.L., Liu, A., & Chen, W.S. (2006). Pattern discovery of fuzzy time series for financial prediction. *IEEE Transactions on Knowledge and Data Engineering, 18*(5), 613-625.

Prade, H. (1988). Raisonner avec des règles d'inférence graduelle: Une approche basée sur les ensembles flous. *Revue d'Intelligence Artificielle, 2*(2), 29-44.

Ruspini, E.H. (1969). A new approach to clustering. *Information Control, 15*, 22-32.

Ruspini, E.H. (1991). On the semantics of fuzzy logic. *International Journal of Approximate Reasoning, 5*, 45-88.

Savasere, A., Omiecinski, E., & Navathe, S. (1995, September). An efficient algorithm for mining association rules in large databases. In *Proceedings of the 21ˢᵗ International Conference on Very Large Data Bases*, Zurich, Switzerland (pp. 11-15).

Schweizer, B., & Sklar, A. (1983). *Probabilistic metric spaces*. New York: North-Holland.

Sudkamp, T. (2005). Examples, counterexamples, and measuring fuzzy associations. *Fuzzy Sets and Systems, 149*(1).

Zadeh, L.A. (1965). Fuzzy sets. *Information and Control, 8*, 338-353.

Zadeh, L.A. (1973). New approach to the analysis of complex systems. *IEEE Transactions on Systems, Man, and Cybernetics, 3*(1).

Zadeh, L.A. (1978). Fuzzy sets as a basis for a theory of possibility. *1*(1).

Zadeh, L.A. (1983). A computational approach to fuzzy quantifiers in natural languages. *Comput. Math. Appl., 9*, 149-184.

ENDNOTES

[1]   Our distinction between machine learning and data mining can roughly be seen as a "modern" or extended distinction between descriptive and inductive statistics. We note, however, that this view is not an *opinio communis*; for example, some people prefer having an even more general view of data mining that includes machine learning as a special case.

[2]   This example shows that a fuzzy set is generally context-dependent. For example, the Chinese conception of tall men will differ from the Swedish one.

[3]   See Zadeh's (1973) principle of incompatibility between precision and meaning.

[4]   Patterns of that kind may have an important biological meaning.

[5]   This operator is the core of all residuated implications (5).

Chapter II
SeqPAM:
A Sequence Clustering Algorithm for Web Personalization

Pradeep Kumar
University of Hyderabad, India

Raju S. Bapi
University of Hyderabad, India

P. Radha Krishna
Institute for Development & Research in Banking Technology, India

ABSTRACT

With the growth in the number of Web users and necessity for making information available on the Web, the problem of Web personalization has become very critical and popular. Developers are trying to customize a Web site to the needs of specific users with the help of knowledge acquired from user navigational behavior. Since user page visits are intrinsically sequential in nature, efficient clustering algorithms for sequential data are needed. In this chapter, we introduce a similarity preserving function called sequence and set similarity measure S3M that captures both the order of occurrence of page visits as well as the content of pages. We conducted pilot experiments comparing the results of PAM, a standard clustering algorithm, with two similarity measures: Cosine and S3M. The goodness of the clusters resulting from both the measures was computed using a cluster validation technique based on average levensthein distance. Results on pilot dataset established the effectiveness of S3M for sequential data. Based on these results, we proposed a new clustering algorithm, SeqPAM for clustering sequential data. We tested the new algorithm on two datasets namely, cti and msnbc datasets. We provided recommendations for Web personalization based on the clusters obtained from SeqPAM for msnbc dataset.

INTRODUCTION

The wide spread evolution of global information infrastructure, especially based on Internet and the immense popularity of Web technology among people, have added to the number of consumers as well as disseminators of information. Until date, plenty of search engines are being developed, however, researchers are trying to build more efficient search engines. Web site developers and Web mining researchers are trying to address the problem of average users in quickly finding what they are looking for from the vast and ever-increasing global information network.

One solution to meet the user requirements is to develop a system that personalizes the Web space. Personalizing the Web space means developing a strategy, which implicitly or explicitly captures the visitor's information on a particular Web site. With the help of this knowledge, the system should decide what information should be presented to the visitor and in what fashion.

Web personalization is an important task from the point of view of the user as well as from the application point of view. Web personalization helps organizations in developing customer-centric Web sites. For example, Web sites that display products and take orders are becoming common for many types of business. Organizations can thus present customized Web pages created in real time, on the fly, for a variety of users such as suppliers, retailers, and employees. The log data obtained from various sources such as proxy server and Web server helps in personalizing Web according to the interest and tastes of the user community. Personalized content enables organizations to form lasting and loyal relationships with customers by providing individualized information, offerings, and services. For example, if an end user visits the site, she would see pricing and information that is appropriate to her, while a re-seller would see a totally different set of price and shipping instructions. This kind of personalization can be effectively achieved by using Web mining approaches. Many existing commercial systems achieve personalization by capturing minimal declarative information provided by the user. In general, this information includes user interests and personal information about the user. Clustering of user page visits may help Web miners and Web developers in personalizing the Web sites better.

The Web personalization process can be divided into two phases: off-line and online (Mobasher, Dai, & Luo, 2002). The off-line phase consists of the data preparation tasks resulting in a user transaction file. The off-line phase of usage-based Web personalization can be further divided into two separate stages. The first stage is preprocessing of data and it includes data cleaning, filtering, and transaction identification. The second stage comprises application of mining techniques to discover usage patterns via methods such as association-rule mining and clustering. Once the mining tasks are accomplished in the off-line phase, the URL clusters and the frequent Web pages can be used by the online component of the architecture to provide dynamic recommendation to users.

This chapter addresses the following three main issues related to sequential access log data for Web personalization. Firstly, for Web personalization we adopt a new similarity metric S^3M proposed earlier (Kumar, Rao, Krishna, Bapi & Laha, 2005). Secondly, we compare the results of clusters obtained using the standard clustering algorithm, *Partition Around Medoid (PAM),* with two measures: *Cosine* and S^3M similarity measures. Based on the comparative results, we design a new partition-clustering algorithm called

Table 1. Table of notations

Symbol	Description
D	Dataset
N	Total number of item sets in D
k	Number of clusters
$\grave{t}_j$	Medoid of jth cluster
t_{j_s}	s^{th} member of jth cluster
$|C_j|$	Total number of items in the jth cluster
τ	Tolerance on total benefit

SeqPAM. Finally, in order to validate clusters of sequential item sets, *average Levensthein distance* was used to compute the intra-cluster distance and *Levensthein distance* for inter-cluster distance.

The rest of the chapter is organized as follows. In the next section, we review related work in the area of Web personalization. Subsequently, we discuss background knowledge on similarity, sequence similarity, as well as cluster analysis techniques. Following this is a brief description of our proposed similarity metric, S^3M. Description and preprocessing of *cti* and *msnbc* datasets are provided in the next section. Then we present clustering of Web usage data using *PAM* with *cosine* as well as S^3M similarity measures over the pilot dataset. After that, we propose a new partitional clustering algorithm, *SeqPAM*. Finally, we conclude with the analysis of results on pilot, *cti,* and *msnbc* datasets. Also, a recommendation for Web personalization on *msnbc* dataset is presented. Table 1 provides the symbols used in this chapter and their description.

RELATED WORK

Web mining techniques are generally used to extract knowledge from Web data repository related to the content, linkage and usage information by utilizing data mining techniques. Mining Web usage data enables capturing users' navigational patterns and identifying users' intentions. Once the user navigational behaviors are effectively characterized, it provides benefits for further Web applications such as facilitation and improvement of Web service quality for both Web-based organizations and for end-users. As a result, Web usage mining recently has become active topic for the researcher from database management, artificial intelligence, and information systems, etc (Buchner & Mulvenna, 1998; Cohen, Krishnamurthy, & Rexford, 1998; Lieberman, 1995; Mobasher, Cooley, & Srivastava, 1999; Ngu & Sitehelper, 1997; Perkowitz & Etzioni, 1998; Stormer, 2005;

Zhou, Hui, & Fong, 2005). Meanwhile, with the benefits of great progress in data mining research, many data mining techniques such as clustering (Han,, Karypis, Kumar & Mobasher, 1998; Mobasher et al., 2002; Perkowitz & Etzioni, 1998), association rule mining (Agarwal & Srikant, 1994; Agarwal, Aggarwal, & Prasad, 1999), and sequential pattern mining (Agarwal & Srikant, 1995) are adopted widely to improve the usability and scalability of Web mining techniques.

In general, there are two types of clustering methods performed on the usage data-user transaction clustering and Web page clustering (Mobasher, 2000). One of the earliest applications of Web page clustering was adaptive Web sites where initially non-existing Web pages are synthesized based on partitioning Web pages into various groups (Perkowitz & Etzioni, 1998, 2000). Another way is to cluster user-rating results. This technique has been adopted in collaborative filtering application as a data preprocessing step to improve the scalability of recommendation using k-Nearest- Neighbor (kNN) algorithm (O'Conner & Herlocker, 1999). Mobasher et al. (2002) utilized user transaction and page view clustering techniques, with traditional *k-means* clustering algorithm, to characterize user access patterns for Web personalization based on mining Web usage data. Safar (2005) used kNN classification algorithm for finding Web navigational path. Wang, Xindong, and Zhang (2005) used support vector machines for clustering data. Tan, Taniar, and Smith (2005) focus on clustering using the estimated distributed model.

Most of the studies in the area of Web usage mining are very new and the topic of clustering Web sessions has recently become popular. Mobahser et al. (2000) presented automatic personalization of a Web site based on Web usage mining. They clustered Web logs using cosine similarity measure. Many techniques have been developed to predict HTTP requests using path profiles of users. Extraction of usage patterns from Web logs has been reported using data mining techniques (Buchner et al., 1998; Cooley, Mobasher, & Srivastava, 1999; Spiliopoulou & Faulstich, 1999).

Shahabi, Zarkesh, Adibi, and Shah (1997) introduced the idea of Path Feature Space to represent all the navigation paths. Similarity between a pair of paths in the Path Feature Space is measured by the definition of Path Angle, which is actually based on the Cosine similarity between two vectors. They used k-means clustering to group user navigation patterns. Fu, Sandhu, and Shih (1999) grouped users based on clustering of Web sessions. Their work employed attribute oriented induction to transfer the Web session data into a space of generalized sessions and then they applied the *BIRCH* (Balanced Iterative Reducing and Clustering using Hierarchies) clustering algorithm (Zhang, Ramakrishnan, & Livny, 1996) to this generalized session space. Their method scaled well over large datasets also. Banerjee and Ghosh (2001) introduced a new method for measuring similarity between Web sessions. They found the longest common sub-sequences between two sessions through dynamic programming. Then the similarity between two sessions is defined as a function of the frequency of occurrence of the longest common sub-sequences. Applying this similarity definition, the authors built an abstract similarity graph and then applied the graph partition method for clustering. Wang, Wang, Yang, and Yu (2002) had considered each Web session as a sequence and borrowed the idea of sequence alignment from the field of bio-informatics to measure similarity between sequences of page access. Pitkow and Pirolli (1999) explored predictive modeling techniques by introducing a statistic called Longest Repeating Sub-sequence model, which can be used for modeling and predicting user surfing paths. Spiliopoulou et al. (1999) built a mining system, *WUM* (Web Utilization Miner), for discovering of interesting navigation patterns. In their system, interestingness criteria for navigation patterns are dynamically specified by the human expert using WUM's mining language

MINT. Mannila and Meek (2000) presented a method for finding partial orders that describe the ordering relationship between the events in a collection of sequences. Their method can be applied to the discovery of partial orders in the data set of session sequences. The sequential nature of Web logs makes it necessary to devise an appropriate similarity metric for clustering. The main problem in calculating similarity between sequences is finding an algorithm that computes a common subsequence of two given sequences as efficiently as possible (Simon, 1987). In this work, we use S^3M similarity measure, which combines information of both the elements as well as their order of occurrences in the sequences being compared.

This chapter aims at designing a semi-automatic system that will tailor the Web site based on user's interests and motivations. From the perspective of data mining, Web mining for Web personalization consists of basically two tasks. The first task is clustering, that is, finding natural groupings of user page visits. The second task is to provide recommendations based on finding association rules among the page visits for a user. Our initial efforts have been to mine user Web access logs based on application of clustering algorithms.

BACKGROUND: SIMILARITY, SEQUENCE SIMILARITY, AND CLUSTER ANALYSIS

In this section, we present the background knowledge related to similarity, sequence similarity, and cluster analysis.

Similarity

In many data mining applications, we are given with unlabelled data and we have to group them based on the similarity measure. These data may arise from diverse application domains. They may be music files, system calls, transaction records, Web logs, genomic data, and so on. In these data, there are hidden relations that should be explored to find interesting information. For example, from Web logs, one can extract the information regarding the most frequent access path; from genomic data, one can extract letter or block frequencies; from music files, one can extract various numerical features related to pitch, rhythm, harmony, etc. One can extract features from sequential data to quantify parameters expressing similarity. The resulting vectors corresponding to the various files are then clustered using existing clustering techniques. The central problem in similarity based clustering is to come up with an appropriate similarity metric for sequential data.

Formally, similarity is a function S with nonnegative real values defined on the Cartesian product $X \times X$ of a set X. It is called a metric on X if for every $x, y, z \in X$, the following properties are satisfied by S.

1. **Non-negativity:** $S(x, y) \geq 0$.
2. **Symmetry:** $S(x, y) = S(y, x)$.
3. **Normalization:** $S(x, y) \leq 1$.

A set X along with a metric is called a metric space.

Sequence Similarity

Sequence comparison finds its application in various interrelated disciplines such as computer science, molecular biology, speech and pattern recognition, mathematics, etc. Sankoff and Kruskal (1983) present the application of sequence comparison and various methodology adopted. Similarity metric has been studied in various other domains like information theory (Bennett, Gacs, Li, Vitanyi, & Zurek, 1988; Li, Chen, Li, Ma, & Paul, 2004; Li & Vitanyi, 1997), linguistics setting, (Ball, 2002; Benedetto, Caglioti, & Loreto, 2002), bioinformatics (Chen, Kwong, &

Li, 1999), and elsewhere (Li & Vitanyi, 2001; Li et al., 2001).

In computer science, sequence comparison finds its application in various respect, such as string matching, text, and Web classification and clustering. Sequence mining algorithms make use of either distance functions (Duda, Hart, & Stork, 2001) or similarity functions (Bergroth, Hakonen, & Raita, 2000) for comparing pairs of sequences. In this section, we investigate measures for computing sequence similarity. Feature distance is a simple and effective distance measure (Kohonen, 1985). A feature is a short sub-sequence, usually referred to as N-gram, where N being the length of the sub-sequence. Feature distance is defined as the number of sub-sequences by which two sequences differ. This measure cannot qualify as a distance metric as two distinct sequences can have zero distance. For example, consider the sequences $PQPQPP$ and $PPQPQP$. These sequences contain the same bi-grams (PQ, QP and PP) and hence the feature distance will be zero with $N = 2$.

Another common distance measure for sequences is the Levenshtein distance (LD) (Levenshtein, 1966). It is good for sequences of different lengths. LD measures the minimum cost associated with transforming one sequence into another using basic edit operations, namely, replacement, insertion, and deletion of a sub-sequence. Each of these operations has a cost assigned to it. Consider two sequences $s_1 =$ *"test"* and $s_2 =$ *"test."* As no transformation operation is required to convert s_1 into s_2, the LD between s_1 and s_2, is denoted as LD $(s_1, s_2) = 0$. If $s_3 =$ *"test"* and $s_4 =$ *"tent,"* then LD $(s_3, s_4) = 1$, as one edit operation is required to convert sequence s_3 into sequence s_4. The greater the LD, the more dissimilar the sequences are. Although LD can be computed directly for any two sequences, in cases where there are already devised scoring schemes as in computational molecular biology (Mount, 2004), it is desirable to compute a distance that is consistent with the similarity score of the sequences. Agrafiotis (1997) proposed a method for computing distance from similarity scores for protein analysis, classification, and structure and function prediction. Based on Sammon's non-linear mapping algorithm, Agrafiotis introduced a new method for analyzing protein sequences.

When applied to a family of homologous sequences, the method is able to capture the essential features of the similarity matrix, and provides a faithful representation of chemical or evolutionary distance in a simple and intuitive way. In this method, similarity score is computed for every pair of sequences. This score is scaled to the range [0,1] and distance d is defined as: $d = 1-ss$, where ss is the scaled similarity score. Besides practical drawbacks, such as high storage requirements and non-applicability in online algorithms, the main problem with this measure is that it does not qualify as a metric in biology applications. The self-similarity scores assigned to amino acids are not identical. Thus scoring matrices such as *PAM* (point accepted mutation) or *BLOSUM* (BLOck SUbstitution Matrix) used in biological sequence analysis have dissimilar values along the diagonal (Mount, 2004). Thereby, scaling leads to values different from 1 and consequently to distances different from 0 for identical amino acid sequences, thus violating one of the requirements of a metric.

Setubal and Meidanis (1987) proposed a more mathematically founded method for computing distance from similarity score and vice versa. This method is applicable only if the similarity score of each symbol with itself is the same for all symbols. Unfortunately, this condition is not satisfied for scoring matrices used in computational molecular biology.

Many of the metrics for sequences, including the ones previously discussed, do not fully qualify as being metrics due to one or more reasons. In the next section, we provide a brief introduction to the similarity function, S^3M, which satisfies all the requirements of being a metric. This function considers both the set as well as sequence similarity across two sequences.

Cluster Analysis

The objective of sequential pattern mining is to find interesting patterns in ordered lists of sets. These ordered lists are called item sets. This usually involves finding recurring patterns in a collection of item sets. In clustering sequence datasets, a major problem is to place similar item sets in one group while preserving the intrinsic sequential property.

Clustering is of prime importance in data analysis. It is defined as the process of grouping N item sets into distinct clusters based on similarity or distance function. A good clustering technique would yield clusters that have high inter-cluster and low intra-cluster distance.

Over the years, clustering has been studied by across many disciplines including machine learning and pattern recognition (Duda et al., 2001; Jain & Dubes, 1988), social sciences (Hartigan, 1975), multimedia databases (Yang & Hurson, 2005), text mining (Bao, Shen, Liu, & Liu, 2005), etc. Serious efforts for performing efficient and effective clustering started in the mid 90's with the emergence of data mining field (Nong, 2003). Clustering has also been used to cluster data cubes (Fu, 2005).

Clustering algorithms have been classified using different taxonomies based on various important issues such as algorithmic structure, nature of clusters formed, use of feature sets, etc (Jain et al., 1988; Kaufman & Rousseeuw, 1990). Broadly speaking, clustering algorithms can be divided into two types—partitional and hierarchical. In partitional clustering, the patterns are partitioned around the desired number of cluster centers. Algorithms of this category rely on optimizing a cost function. A commonly used partitional clustering algorithm is k-Means clustering algorithm. On the other hand, hierarchical clustering algorithms produce hierarchy of clusters. These types of clusters are very useful in the field of social sciences, biology and computer science. Hierarchical algorithms can be further subdivided into two types, namely, divisive and agglomerative. In divisive hierarchical clustering algorithm, we start with a single cluster comprising all the item sets and keep on dividing the clusters based on some criterion function. In agglomerative hierarchical clustering, all item sets are initially assumed to be in distinct clusters. These distinct clusters are merged based on some merging criterion until a single cluster is formed. Clustering process in both divisive and agglomerative clustering algorithms can be visualized in the form of a dendrogram. The division or agglomeration process can be stopped at any desired level to achieve the user specified clustering objective. Commonly used hierarchical clustering algorithm is single linkage based clustering algorithm.

There are two main issues in clustering techniques. Firstly, finding the optimal number of clusters in a given dataset and secondly, given two sets of clusters, computing a relative measure of goodness between them. For both these purposes, a criterion function or a validation function is usually applied. The simplest and most widely used cluster optimization function is the sum of squared error (Duda et al., 2001). Studies on the sum of squared error clustering were focused on the well-known k-Means algorithm (Forgey, 1965; Jancey, 1966; McQueen, 1967) and its variants (Jain, Murty, & Flynn, 1999). The sum of squared error (SSE) is given by the following formula,

$$SSE = \sum_{j=1}^{k} \sum_{s=1}^{|C_j|} |t_j - \hat{t}_{j_s}| \qquad (1)$$

where is the cluster center of jth cluster, t_{js} is the sth member of jth cluster, $|C_j|$ is the size of jth cluster and k is the total number of clusters (refer to Table 1 for notations used in the chapter).

In the clustering algorithms previously described, the data predominantly are non-sequential in nature. Since pairwise similarity among sequences cannot be captured directly, direct

application of traditional clustering algorithms without any loss of information over sequences is not possible. As computation of centroid of sequences is not easy, it is difficult to perform k-Means clustering on sequential data.

S^3M: SIMILARITY MEASURE FOR SEQUENCES

In this section, we describe a new similarity measure S^3M that satisfies all the requirements of being a metric. This function considers both the set as well as sequence similarity across two sequences. This measure is defined as a weighted linear combination of the length of longest common subsequence as well as the Jaccard measure.

A sequence is made up of a set of items that happen in time or happen one after another, that is, in position but not necessarily in relation with time. We can say that a sequence is an ordered set of items. A sequence is denoted as follows: $S = <a_1, a_2, ... a_n>$, where $a_1, a_2, ..., a_n$ are the ordered item sets in sequence S. Sequence length is defined as the number of item sets present in the sequence, denoted as $|S|$. In order to find patterns in sequences, it is necessary to not only look at the items contained in sequences but also the order of their occurrence. A new measure, called sequence and set similarity measure (S^3M), was introduced for network security domain (Kumar et al., 2005). The S^3M measure consists of two parts: one that quantifies the composition of the sequence (set similarity) and the other that quantifies the sequential nature (sequence similarity). Sequence similarity quantifies the amount of similarity in the order of occurrence of item sets within two sequences. Length of longest common subsequence (LLCS) with respect to the length of the longest sequence determines the sequence similarity aspect across two sequences. For two sequences A and B, sequence similarity is given by,

$$SeqSim(A,B) = \frac{LLCS(A,B)}{\max(|A|,|B|)} \qquad (2)$$

Set similarity (Jaccard Similarity measure) is defined as the ratio to the number of common item sets and the number of unique item sets in two sequences. Thus, for two sequences A and B, set similarity is given by:

$$SetSim(A, B) = \frac{|A \cap B|}{|A \cup B|} \qquad (3)$$

Let us consider two sequences A and B, where $A = <a, b, c, d>$ and $B = <d, c, b, a>$. Now, the set similarity measure for these two sequences is 1, indicating that their composition is alike. But we can see that they are not at all similar when considering the order of occurrence of item sets. This aspect is quantified by the sequence similarity component. For example, sequence similarity component is 0.25 for these sequences. LLCS keeps track of the position of occurrence of item sets in the sequence. For two sequences, $C=<a, b, c, d>$ and $D=<b, a, k, c, t, p, d>$, LLCS(C, D) works out to be 3 and after normalization, the sequence similarity component turns out to be 0.43. The set similarity for these two sequences is 0.57. The above two examples illustrate the need for combining set similarity and sequence similarity components into one function in order to take care of both the content as well as position based similarity aspects. Thus, S^3M measure for two sequences A and B is given by:

$$S^3M(A, B) = p * \frac{LLCS(A,B)}{\max(|A|,|B|)} + q * \frac{|A \cap B|}{|A \cup B|}$$

$$(4)$$

Here, $p + q = 1$ and $p, q \geq 0$. p and q determine the relative weights to be given for order of occurrence (sequence similarity) and to content (set similarity), respectively. In practical applications, user could specify these parameters. The LLCS between two sequences can be found by the dynamic programming approach (Bergroth et al., 2000).

Characteristics of S³M Similarity Measure

Let S be a set of finite sequences generated from a given set of symbols, A. Let $\mathfrak{R}$ denote the set of real numbers then $sim(s_i, s_j) : S \times S \rightarrow \mathfrak{R}$ is called an index of similarity between sequences $s_i, s_j \in S$ if it satisfies the following properties (Dunham, 2003):

1. **Non-negativity:** $Sim(s_i, s_j) \geq 0$.
2. **Symmetry:** $Sim(s_i, s_j) = Sim(s_j, s_i)$.
3. **Normalization:** $Sim(s_i, s_j) \leq 1$.

Proposed similarity function has six parameters namely *p, q, LLCS (A, B), max (|A|, |B|), |A∩B| and |A∪B|*. By the two conditions $p+q = 1$ and $p, q \geq 0$, we can infer that p and q can never be negative. Rest of the four parameters, being absolute values, cannot attain negative values. Hence, the parameters cannot be negative. Finally, the sum and division operations on non-negative values will always result in positive values. Thus, it is straightforward to see that the first condition of similarity holds true. Since all the operations used in computing the similarity score are symmetric, it is easy to see that the proposed similarity function also obeys the symmetry property. Here, since the proposed measure is a convex combination with two parameters p and q lying between 0 and 1, the third property of normalization also holds true.

Theoretical Justification for Choice of "P" Parameter

When the length of longest common subsequence is used as a measure of similarity between pair of sequences then it becomes important to have an idea of expected length of longest common subsequence between them. Equation (5) gives the expected length of a longest common subsequence over an alphabet of size k over all the pair of sequences of length n (Paterson & Dancik, 1994).

$$EL_n^{(k)} = \frac{1}{k^{2n}} \sum_{|u|=|v|=n} LLCS(u,v) \qquad (5)$$

A bound γ_k on the expected length of the Longest Common Subsequence has been derived by Paterson et al. (1994). For every $k \geq 2$ there is some γ_k such that,

$$\gamma_k = \lim_{n \to \infty} \frac{EL_n^{(k)}}{n} \qquad (6)$$

Exact values of γ_k are not known. Upper bound on γ_k for $k = 1, 2, \ldots, 15$ as calculated by Paterson et al. (1994) is 0.47620 for alphabet size 14 and 0.46462 for alphabet size of 15. The upper bound of γ_k can be used to specify the value of p and q for S^3M similarity measure. In this work, since the alphabet size is 17 for the *msnbc* dataset a p value of 0.5 is chosen for experimentations. The alphabet size for *cti* dataset is 16 hence p = 0:45 is chosen. However, in general since p value is domain dependent, this should be chosen based on user's experience.

WEB USAGE DATA

In this section, we describe the necessary pre-processing steps on the dataset. We also outline here the description of the Web usage data that we have taken for experimental purposes.

Data Preprocessing

A prerequisite step in all of the techniques for providing users with recommendations is the identification of a set of user sessions from the raw usage data provided by the Web server. Ide-ally, each user session gives an exact account of who accessed the Web site, what pages were requested and in what order, and for how long each page was viewed.

In addition, to identify user sessions, the raw log must also be cleaned or transformed into a list of page views. Cleaning the server log involves removing all of the file accesses that are redundant, leaving only one entry per page view. This includes handling page views that have multiple frames and dynamic pages that have the same template name for multiple page views. It may also be necessary to filter the log files by mapping the references to the site topology induced by physical links between pages. This is particularly important for usage-based personalization, since the recommendation engine should not provide dynamic links to "out-of-date" or non-existent pages.

Each user session can be thought of in two ways: either as a single transaction of many page references or as a set of many transactions each consisting of a single page reference. The goal of transaction identification is to dynamically create meaningful clusters of references for each user. Based on an underlying model of the user's browsing behavior, each page reference can be categorized as a content reference, auxiliary (or navigational) reference, or hybrid. In this way, different types of transactions can be obtained from the user session file, including content-only transactions involving references to content pages and navigation-content transactions involving a mix of page types. The details of methods for transaction identification are discussed in Cadez, Heckerman, Meek, Smyth, and White (2000). For the purpose of this chapter, we assume that each user session is viewed as a single transaction containing reference to multiple pages in a session. Finally, the session file may be filtered to remove very small transactions.

Description of the Dataset

In this section, we describe two datasets taken for experimentation. First, we describe the *msnbc* dataset and then followed by *cti* dataset.

Description of the *msnbc* Dataset

We collected data from the UCI dataset repository (http://kdd.ics.uci.edu/) that consists of Internet Information Server (IIS) logs for *msnbc.com* and news-related portions of *msn.com* for the entire day of September 28, 1999 (Pacific Standard Time). Each sequence in the dataset corresponds to page views of a user during that twenty-four hour period. Each event in the sequence corresponds to a user's request for a page. Requests are not recorded at the finest level of detail but they are recorded at the level of page categories as determined by the site administrator.

There are 17 page categories, namely, "frontpage," "news," "tech," "local," "opinion," "on-air," "misc," "weather," "health," "living," "business," "sports," "summary," "bbs" (bulletin board service), "travel," "msn-news," and "msn-sports." Table 2 shows the characteristics of the dataset.

Each page category is represented by an integer labels. For example, "frontpage" is coded as 1, "news" as 2, "tech" as 3, etc. Each row describes the hits of a single user. For example, the fourth user hits "frontpage" twice, and the second user hits "news" once and so on as shown in Figure 1.

In the total dataset, the length of user sessions ranges from 1 to 500 and the average length of session is 5.7.

Description of the *cti* Dataset

The second data set, *cti*, is from a university Web site log and was made available by the authors of Mobasher (2004) and Zhang et al. (2005). The data is based on a random collection of users visiting university site for a 2-week period during the month of April 2002. After data preprocessing, the filtered data contains 13745 sessions and 683 pages. We further preprocessed *cti* dataset where the root pages were considered in the page view of a session. This preprocessing step resulted in total of 16 categories namely, search, programs, news, admissions, advising, courses, people, research, resources, authenticate, cti, pdf, calendar, shared, forums, and hyperlink. These page views were given numeric labels as 1 for search, 2 for programs and so on. Table 3 shows the complete list of numeric coded Web pages.

Figure 2 shows the sample cti Web navigation data. Each row describes the hits of a single user. For example, the seventh user hits "research" twice then "course" followed by "news" twice. The session length in the dataset ranges from 2 to 68. Since comparing very long sessions with small sessions would not be meaningful, hence we considered only sessions of length between 3 and 7. Finally, we took 5915 user sessions for our experimentation.

Figure 1. Example msnbc web navigation data

```
T1: on-air misc misc misc on-air misc
T2: news sorts tech local sports sports
T3: bbs bbs bbs bbs bbs bbs
T4: frontpage frontpage sports news news local
T5: on-air weather weather weather sports
T6: on-air on-air on-air on-air tech bbs
T7: frontpage bbs bbs frontpage frontpage news
T8: frontpage frontpage frontpage frontpage frontpage bbs
T9: news news travel opinion opinion m sn-news
T10: frontpage business frontpage news news bbs
```

Table 2. Description of the msnbc dataset

Total Dataset	
Number of users	989,818
Minimum session length	1
Maximum session length	500
Average number of visits per user	5.7

Figure 2. Example cti web navigation data

```
news people
programs programs admissions programs courses
resources forums
courses courses courses courses
courses people
hyperlink news
reasearch research courses news news
authenticate cti programs cti cti
authenticate cti news
people admissions cti cti admissions admissions people people
```

Table 3. Number coding of Web pages for cti dataset

Web Page Name	Number Coding	Web Page Name	Number Coding
Search	1	Resources	9
Programs	2	Authenticate	10
News	3	cti	11
Admissions	4	Pdf	12
Advising	5	Calendar	13
Courses	6	Shared	14
People	7	Forums	15
Research	8	Hyperlink	16

CLUSTERING OF WEB USAGE DATA

Web personalization techniques are often based on matching the current user's profile against clusters of similar profiles obtained by the system over time from other users. Clustering user transactions based on mined information from access logs does not require explicit ratings or interaction with users.

In this chapter, we used *PAM*, a standard clustering algorithm that represents data in a vectorial form and partitions the space into groups of items that are close to each other based on cosine similarity measure. *PAM* is also used here with

S^3M, our proposed similarity measure with a representation scheme that preserves sequence information within a session.

In the case of Web transactions, each cluster represents a group of transactions that are similar, based on co-occurrence patterns of page categories. Let $\Sigma = \{p_1, p_2, p_3, ..., p_m\}$ be the set of page categories, t be a user session and $t \in \Sigma^*$, where Σ^* represents the set of all sessions made up of sequences of page categories.

Let D be the training dataset consisting of N user sessions, i.e., $D = \{t_1, t_2, t_3, ..., t_N\}$. Each user session can be represented in two ways. In the vectorial representation, $t_i = < f(p_1), f(p_2), f(p_3), ..., f(p_m) >$, where each $f(p_j)$ can be formulated in three different ways. $f(p_j) \in \{0,1\}$ indicating the presence or absence of jth page category in the ith user session, t_i. Boolean representation has been used in the literature (Shahabi et al., 1997; Yan et al., 1996). If $f(p_j)$ could represent the duration of time user spends in the jth page category in the ith user session, then user session can be vectorially formulated with respect to the time spent. It has been commented that time spent is not a good indicator of interest (Konstan et al., 1997). $f(p_j)$ can be used to represent the frequencies of page categories for a user session. In this chapter, for experiments with *PAM* using cosine measure, we used the third approach.

In the sequence representation scheme, the user session consisting of page categories, i.e., $t \in \Sigma^*$ is considered directly. We have used this formulation in all the experiments where S^3M similarity measure was considered.

Cosine similarity is a common vector based similarity measure. This metric calculates the angle of difference in the direction of two vectors, irrespective of their lengths. Cosine similarity between two vectors, V_1 and V_2 is given by,

$$S(V_1, V_2) = \frac{V_1 \bullet V_2}{|V_1||V_2|} \qquad (7)$$

Table 4. Sum of squared error for PAM with cosine similarity measure

	C1	C2	C3	C4
C1	0	0.85	0.155	0.889
C2	0.85	0	0.749	0.25
C3	0.155	0.749	0	0.906
C4	0.889	0.25	0.906	0

Table 5. Sum of squared error for PAM with S^3M similarity measure

	C1	C2	C3	C4
C1	0	0.723	0.162	0.123
C2	0.723	0	0.749	0.79
C3	0.162	0.749	0	0.044
C4	0.123	0.79	0.044	0

Table 6. Comparison of clusters formed with the two similarity measures

	LD with *cosine* measure	LD with S^3M measure
C1	4.514	4.448
C2	4.938	4.62
C3	5.593	3.7
C4	4.92	3.908
ALD	4.9905	4.169

Table 7. LD between cluster representatives obtained using cosine measure

	C1	C2	C3	C4
C1	0	5	3	6
C2	5	0	5	2
C3	3	5	0	6
C4	6	2	6	0

Pilot Experiments with PAM

We took 200 arbitrarily chosen Web transactions from the msnbc dataset and performed the pilot experiments. The sum of squared error is used to find the optimal number of clusters in the *PAM* clustering technique. Tables 4 and 5 show the inter-cluster distance between clusters obtained with *cosine* and S^3M similarity measures, respectively. It is evident from the Tables that the inter-cluster distance among clusters with *PAM*, the cosine metric is better than the clusters obtained using S^3M metric.

As these clusters are composed of sessions that are sequential in nature, the cost associated with converting the sequences within a cluster to the cluster representative must be minimum. At the same time, the cost of converting the sequences from two different clusters must be high. We computed a well known measure of the conversion cost of sequences, namely, the levensthein distance for each cluster. The average levensthein distance reflects the goodness of the clusters. Average Levenshtein distance (ALD) is expressed as,

$$ALD = \frac{1}{k} \sum_{j=1}^{k} \frac{\sum_{j_s}^{|C_j|} LD(\hat{t}_j, t_{j_s})}{|C_j|} \qquad (8)$$

where, k is the total number of clusters, $|C_j|$ is the number of item sets in j^{th} cluster and LD(is the levensthein distance between s^{th} element of jth cluster to its corresponding cluster representative.

As can be seen from Table 6, the ALD for the clusters formed with the S^3M measure is less than that computed for clusters formed with the cosine measure. So, the user sessions within the clusters formed based on S^3M have retained more sequential information than those obtained by the cosine measure.

Table 8. LD between cluster representatives obtained using S³M measure

	C1	C2	C3	C4
C1	0	6	5	6
C2	6	0	5	5
C3	5	5	0	5
C4	6	5	5	0

Table 9. comparative results of PAM and SeqPAM on pilot dataset

	LD using *PAM*		LD using *SeqPAM*
	Cosine	S³M	
C1	4.514	4.448	3.427
C2	4.938	4.62	3.493
C3	5.593	3.7	4.04
C4	4.92	3.908	3.78
ALD	4.9905	4.169	3.685

Table 10. LD between cluster representatives obtained from SeqPAM

	C1	C2	C3	C4
C1	0	6	5	5
C2	6	0	5	6
C3	5	5	0	5
C4	5	6	5	0

Table 11. LD using SeqPAM and PAM on cti dataset

	LD using SeqPAM	LD using PAM
C1	3.412	3.972
C2	3.125	3.784
C3	4.014	4.235
C4	3.762	3.984
C5	3.521	4.024
C6	3.834	4.173
ALD	4.361	4.028

So far, we have looked at the intra-cluster LD measure where S^3M seems to perform better. The quality of a cluster is also measured by how well various clusters differ from each other and it is usually denoted as inter-cluster distance.

Tables 7 and 8 show the LD measure across cluster representatives formed using the two similarity measures. Since we considered only user sessions of length 6, the theoretical maximum and minimum inter-cluster LD would be 6 and 0, respectively. In Table 7, we find that a minimum cost of 2 is required to convert a cluster representative to another cluster representative (shown in bold face in Table 7). Whereas, the minimum cost needed for conversion across clusters is 5 with the S^3M measure (see Table 8).

These results clearly point out the advantage of using a measure such as S^3M that preserves order information for the pilot dataset.

SeqPAM: PARTITION AROUND MEDOID FOR SEQUENTIAL DATA

From the pilot results presented in the previous section, it has been observed that the *PAM* partitioning algorithm performed better for Web usage data when sequential information was considered. With this inspiration, we modified the standard *PAM* algorithm and named it *SeqPAM*, partition around medoid algorithm for sequential data.

Description of *SeqPAM* Algorithm

Consider a dataset D with N item sets, $D = \{t_1, t_2, ..., t_N\}$ where each $t_i = <p_1, p_2, ..., p_m>$ where p_2 follows p_1, p_3 follows p_2, and so on. Our objective is to cluster these item sets into k distinct clusters. The sequence clustering problem is to identify the underlying clusters based on a given sample of sequences. Because of the variability of the lengths of sequences and lack of good distance metrics for comparing sequences, the sequence clustering problem is non-trivial.

SeqPAM differs from *PAM* in two aspects. The first difference is in the medoid selection process and the second aspect is in the formulation of objective function. The optimization function used in *SeqPAM* accounts for sequence information. The algorithm constructs similarity matrix using *S³M* function.

The initial medoid selection process starts by randomly selecting the first medoid. The first medoid guides the process of selecting the remaining *k-1* medoids. The remaining medoids are selected such that the similarity value between any two adjacent medoids is approximately equal to *1/(k−1)*. The process of selection from guidance of the first medoid ensures that the difference between the similarity values of the first and the kth medoid is maximal (close to one). These *k* medoids form the

initial representatives of *k* clusters. Each item set from the dataset *D* is now assigned to the cluster around its nearest medoid. Thus, the entire dataset is partitioned around *k medoids*.

The objective of *SeqPAM* is to find clusters such that they have maximal intra-cluster similarity and minimal inter-cluster similarity. To ensure this property, an optimization function called total benefit (*TB*) is devised. Since the aim of *SeqPAM* is to cluster sequential data, total benefit is formulated using our *S³M* similarity metric. Total benefit reflects the average intra-cluster similarity with respect to the *k medoids*. Total benefit is given by,

$$TB = \frac{1}{k}\sum_{j=1}^{k}\frac{1}{|C_j|}\sum_{s=1}^{|C_j|}S^3M(\hat{t}_{j_l},t_{j_s}) \qquad (9)$$

A new set of cluster medoids is selected based on the process of maximizing pairwise similarity within the respective clusters. For each cluster, pairwise similarity values among the members of the cluster are computed and a new cluster representative, $\hat{t}_j$, is chosen that has the maximal average pairwise similarity as shown next.

$$\hat{t}_j' = \underset{t_{j_l}}{\arg\max}\left\{\frac{1}{|C_j|}\sum_{s=1}^{|C_j|}S^3M(\hat{t}_{j_l},t_{j_s})\right\} \qquad (10)$$

where, $j_l = 1, 2, ..., |C_j|$.

All the item sets in the dataset D are re-partitioned around the new set of medoids. The total benefit with respect to new set of medoids is computed. The process of selection of new medoids and re-partitioning is continued till the di®erence in the successive total benefit values is within the user specified tolerance value, τ. An outline of *SeqPAM* algorithm is given in Algorithm 1.

Pilot Experiments with *SeqPAM*

Experiments with *SeqPAM* were conducted on the pilot dataset consisting of 200 Web transactions and the results are shown in Tables 9 and

Algorithm 1. Algorithm for SeqPAM

```
Input:
   D = Dataset of N item sets
   k = number of desired clusters
   τ = Tolerance on total benefit
   (stopping criterion)
Output:
   Set of k clusters
Begin
   Construct the similarity matrix
      for the dataset D using S³M.
   Select initial medoids.
repeat
   Partition the dataset D
      around k medoids.
   Compute the total benefit.
   for all Clusters
      do
         Compute the new cluster
      resentatives.
   end for
until the change in total benefit
   is within τ
End
```

10. For the sake of comparison, results of *PAM* with cosine and S^3M measures are replicated in Table 9 from Table 6. ALD values are also shown for all the experiments in Table 9. The ALD obtained with *SeqPAM* (3.685) is better compared to that obtained with cosine (4.9905) and S^3M (4.169) measures used with the *PAM* clustering algorithm.

Minimum value for LD based inter-cluster similarity using *SeqPAM* is 5 (see Table 10) whereas, for *PAM* with cosine measure is 2. Hence, a better inter-cluster as well as intra-cluster similarity is achieved using *SeqPAM* over *PAM* with cosine measure. Also, *SeqPAM* results in better intra-cluster similarity than *PAM* with S^3M measure.

Thus, from the pilot experiments we can conclude that the new sequence clustering algorithm *SeqPAM* is more suitable for sequential data such as Web usage data. In the next subsection, we report results on the larger *msnbc* dataset as well as the *cti* dataset.

Experimental Results with SeqPAM and PAM on cti Dataset

Experiments were conducted on the final pre-processed *cti* dataset with *SeqPAM* and *PAM* clustering algorithm. For the experimentation purpose *k* was fixed to 6. Table 11 shows the ALD (intra-cluster distance) using *SeqPAM* and *PAM* clustering algorithms. Table shows the superiority of *SeqPAM* over *PAM*. It can be observed that the ALD value (intra-cluster distance) for *SeqPAM* was lower than that of *PAM*. That is, the cost associated in converting the sequence taken from *SeqPAM* cluster to its corresponding representative is less compared to that in *PAM* clusters. The results point out that in *SeqPAM* the sequences more similar with respect to the editing operation are grouped together whereas in *PAM* this might not have been possible.

Table 12. Inter-cluster LD with SeqPAM on cti dataset

	C1	C2	C3	C4	C5	C6
C1	0	4	3	6	4	5
C2	4	0	5	6	5	6
C3	3	5	0	4	4	5
C4	6	6	4	0	4	6
C5	4	5	4	4	0	5
C6	5	6	5	6	5	0

Table 13. Inter-cluster LD with PAM on cti dataset

	C1	C2	C3	C4	C5	C6
C1	0	2	3	6	5	3
C2	2	0	4	2	6	3
C3	3	4	0	5	2	4
C4	6	2	5	0	6	5
C5	5	6	2	6	0	6
C6	3	3	4	5	6	0

Table 14. LD using SeqPAM and PAM on msnbc dataset

	LD using SeqPAM	LD using PAM
C1	3.265	3.291
C2	3.532	3.919
C3	4.952	4.672
C4	3.905	4.012
C5	3.997	4.619
C6	4.238	4.735
C7	4.713	4.962
C8	4.538	4.829
C9	4.681	4.124
C10	5.293	4.892
C11	3.991	4.726
C12	4.117	4.721
ALD	4.2685	4.4585

LD measure across each cluster reflects the inter-cluster distance. Tables 12 and 13 show the LD (inter-cluster distance) measure with *SeqPAM* and *PAM* clustering algorithms on *cti* dataset. The values in these Tables establish that sequences which require more edit distance are placed in different groups in the case of *SeqPAM*. In other words, if we choose two sequences randomly from two distinct clusters, the cost of converting one to the other is very high in *SeqPAM* compared to that in *PAM*. Randomly if two sequences are picked from *SeqPAM* and *PAM* clusters there is high chance that the cost associated in editing one sequence to another is high for *SeqPAM* cluster.

Experimental Results on msnbc Dataset using *SeqPAM* and *PAM* Clustering Algorithms

All the experiments (pilot, cti, and msnbc dataset) were carried out on a 2.4 GHz, 256 MB RAM, Pentium-IV machine running on Microsoft Windows XP 2002 and the code was developed in Java 1.4. Preprocessed msnbc dataset with 44,062 user sessions was given as input to *SeqPAM*. The results are summarized in Tables 14 and 15. For this larger datset, k was fixed at 12.

The *ALD* obtained on the larger msnbc dataset using *SeqPAM* clustering algorithm is 4.2685 as shown in Table 14 and the inter-cluster levensthein distances among the 12 clusters ranged from 4 to 6 (see Table 15). Both the values indicate that the preprocessed as well as pilot dataset groupings have preserved sequential information embedded in the *msnbc* dataset.

As can be seen from the Table 14, the ALD obtained with *SeqPAM* is less than *PAM* (4.2685 < 4.4585) thus indicating that the intracluster distance for *SeqPAM* is minimum. We also recorded the LD for each cluster and observed that for *SeqPAM* the LD value was less than that for *PAM* (except for the 3 clusters out of the 12 clusters). This figure indicates that in the *SeqPAM* clustering algorithm the cost of converting a sequence to its cluster representative is less as compared to *PAM*. Tables 15 and 16 show the LD (inter-cluster distance) using *SeqPAM* and *PAM*, respectively for *msnbc* dataset. These values are indicators of

Table 15. Inter-cluster LD with SeqPAM

	C1	C2	C3	C4	C5	C6	C7	C8	C9	C10	C11	C12
C1	0	5	5	4	6	4	4	5	6	5	5	6
C2	5	0	6	6	4	4	4	5	6	6	4	5
C3	5	6	0	5	6	6	6	4	5	5	6	6
C4	4	6	5	0	5	4	6	4	4	5	6	6
C5	6	4	6	5	0	4	4	5	6	6	5	5
C6	4	4	6	4	4	0	5	5	6	6	6	5
C7	4	4	6	6	4	5	0	5	4	4	5	6
C8	5	5	4	4	5	5	5	0	6	5	5	6
C8	5	5	4	4	5	5	5	0	6	5	5	6
C9	6	6	5	4	6	6	4	6	0	6	6	5
C10	5	6	5	5	6	6	4	5	6	0	5	6
C11	5	4	6	6	5	6	5	5	6	5	0	4
C12	6	5	6	6	5	5	6	6	5	6	4	0

Table 16. Inter-cluster LD with PAM

	C1	C2	C3	C4	C5	C6	C7	C8	C9	C10	C11	C12
C1	0	4	2	3	4	5	2	6	4	3	5	2
C2	4	0	6	5	5	5	2	4	5	4	5	5
C3	2	6	0	4	5	3	4	6	4	2	5	5
C4	3	5	4	0	4	5	2	3	5	2	4	6
C5	4	5	5	4	0	3	6	5	2	4	5	3
C6	5	5	3	5	3	0	4	6	5	2	3	6
C7	2	2	4	2	6	4	0	4	5	3	5	3
C8	6	4	6	3	5	6	4	0	4	4	5	3
C9	4	5	4	5	2	5	5	4	0	4	6	3
C10	3	4	2	2	4	2	3	4	4	0	4	5
C11	5	5	5	4	5	3	5	5	6	4	0	6
C12	2	5	5	6	3	6	3	3	3	5	6	0

Table 17. Recommendation set

	C1	C2	C3	C4	C5	C6	C7	C8	C9	C10	C11	C12
frontpage	√				√			√		√		
news	√	√				√			√	√	√	
tech			√		√			√				
local							√	√				
opinion			√									√
on-air				√		√			√			√
misc				√			√			√		
weather					√					√		
health	√				√							
living		√										
business	√						√					
sports		√										√
summary				√				√		√		
bbs		√	√			√				√		√
travel				√						√		
msn-news	√								√		√	
msn-sports					√		√		√			

distance between cluster representatives. The high values obtained for LD indicate better clustering result as compared to *PAM*.

Since the length of sequences being considered for experimentation from *msnbc* dataset is 6, the maximum value for inter-cluster distance

(LD) can be 6. It can be clearly observed from Tables 15 and 16 that for *SeqPAM* we obtained the value of 6 for 26 pairs of clusters whereas for *PAM* it was observed only among 9 pairs. Thus, these results indicate that the cost of converting a sequence taken from two different clusters formed in *SeqPAM* is higher than those from the clusters of PAM.

The previous results show that the clusters formed in *SeqPAM* have high inter-cluster distance and low intra-cluster distance than those formed in *PAM*.

The aim of this chapter is to suggest ways of improving personalization using clustering technique. To this end, we have come up with a recommendation scheme wherein four most frequent page categories within each cluster are identified as shown in Table 17. From the Table, it can be seen that if a new session falls within the first cluster, then the following page categories are recommended for personalizing the user page: "frontpage," "news," "health," and "business." Table 17 shows the recommendation sets for all the clusters formed using *SeqPAM* algorithm for *msnbc* dataset.

CONCLUSION

Clustering is an important task in Web personalization. User sessions comprising Web pages exhibit intrinsic sequential nature. We introduced a similarity measure for sequential data called S^3M. We compared the performance of the standard clustering algorithm PAM with *cosine* as well as S^3M measures over a *pilot* dataset consisting of 200 Web transactions. Results of the pilot experiments established that using sequence sensitive similarity measure such as S^3M results in better clusters. Cluster quality is measured using a cluster validation index called, average Levensthein distance (ALD). Based on the pilot experiments, we devised *SeqPAM*, a modified *PAM* algorithm for clustering sequential data.

SeqPAM differs from *PAM* in medoid selection process and optimization criterion. Results on *cti* and *msnbc* dataset were demonstrated to establish the validity of *SeqPAM* clustering algorithm. A simple personalization scheme based on clusters obtained from *SeqPAM* for *msnbc* dataset has been formulated.

Although the number of clusters (k) has been fixed in this work, optimal number of clusters can be automatically determined based on the cluster validity index proposed in the chapter. The Web transaction data considered for all our experiments had a fixed session length of 6 and so results need to be replicated for various fixed session lengths. In future, *SeqPAM* algorithm needs to be generalized for clustering sequences of variable lengths. Recommendation schemes for Web personalization can be formulated by mining rules from the sequence clusters determined by *SeqPAM* and this needs to be investigated in future.

ACKNOWLEDGMENT

We are thankful to Dr. Guandong Xu, Victoria University, for providing us the *cti* dataset to establish our arguments more strongly. The authors are also thankful to the anonymous referees for valuable comments which resulted in an improved presentation of the chapter.

REFERENCES

Agarwal, R., & Srikant, R. (1994). Fast algorithms for mining association rules. In *Proceedings of the 20th International Conference on Very Large Data Bases* (pp. 487-499). Morgan Kaufmann.

Agarwal, R., & Srikant, R. (1995). Mining sequential patterns. In *Proceedings of the International Conference on Data Engineering* (pp. 3-14), Taipei, Taiwan: IEEE Computer Society Press

Agarwal, R., Aggarwal, C., & Prasad, V. (1999). A tree projection algorithm for generation of frequent item sets. *Journal of Parallel and Distributed Computing, 61*(3), 350-371.

Agrafiotis, D. K. (1997). A new method for analyzing protein sequence relationships based on Sammon maps. *Protein Science, 6*(2), 287-293.

Ball, P. (2002). Algorithm makes tongue tree. *Nature, 22,* January.

Banerjee, A., & Ghosh, J. (2001). Clickstream clustering using weighted longest common subsequences. In *Proceedings of Workshop on Web Mining in the 1st International SIAM Conference on Data Mining* (pp. 33-40).

Bao, J., Shen, J., Liu, X., & Liu, H. (2005). The heavy frequency vector-based text clustering. *International Journal of Business Intelligence and Data Mining, 1*(1), 42-53

Benedetto, D., Caglioti, E., & Loreto, V. (2002). Language trees and zipping. *Physics Review Letters, 88*(4), 1-4.

Bennett, C. H., Gacs, P., Li, M., Vitanyi, P. M. B., & Zurek, W. (1998). Information distance. *IEEE Transactions on Information Theory, 44*(4), 1407-1423.

Bergroth, L., Hakonen, H., & Raita, T. (2000). A survey of longest common subsequence algorithm. The *7th International Symposium on String Processing and Information Retrieval* (pp. 39-48).

Buchner, A., & Mulvenna, M. D. (1998). Discovering internet marketing intelligence through online analytical Web usage mining. *SIGMOD Record, 27*(4), 54-61.

Cadez, I. V., Heckerman, D., Meek, C., Smyth, P., & White, S. (2000). Visualization of navigation patterns on a Web site using model-based clustering. In *Proceedings of the Sixth International Conference on Knowledge Discovery and Data Mining,* (pp. 280-284). Boston:

ACM Press

Chen, X., Kwong, S., & Li, M. (1999). A compression algorithm for DNA sequences and its applications in genome comparison. In K. Asai, S. Myano, & T. Takagi (Eds.), *Genome informatics* (pp. 51-61). *Proceedings of the 10th Workshop on Genome Informatics, Universal Academy Press, Tokyo,* (Also in RECOMB 2000).

Cohen, E., Krishnamurthy, B., & Rexford, J. (1998). Improving end-to-end performance of the Web using server volumes and proxy liters. *Proceedings of the ACM SIGCOMM,* Vancouver, British Columbia, Canada: ACM Press.

Cooley, R., Mobasher, B., & Srivastava, J. (1999). Data preparation for mining world wide Web browsing patterns. *Knowledge and Information Systems, 1*(1), 5-32.

Duda, R. O., Hart, P. E., & Stork, D. G. (2001). *Pattern classification* (2nd ed.). New York: John Wiley & Sons.

Dunham, M. H. (2003). *Data mining: Introductory and advanced topics.* NJ: Prentice Hall.

Forgey, E. W. (1965). Cluster analysis of multivariate data efficiency vs. interpretability of classifications. *Biometrics, 21*(3), 768-769.

Fu, L. (2005). Novel efficient classifiers based on data cube. *International Journal of Data Warehousing and Mining, 1*(3), 15-27.

Fu, Y., Sandhu, K., & Shih, M. (1999). Clustering of Web users based on access patterns. *Workshop on Web Usage Analysis and User Profiling.*

Han, E. H., Karypis, G., Kumar, V., & Mobasher, B. (1998). Hypergraph based clustering in high-dimensional data sets: A summary of results. *Bulletin of the Technical Committee on Data Engineering, 21*(1), 15-22.

Hartigan, J. A. (1975). *Clustering algorithms.* New York: John Wiley & Sons.

Jain, A. K., & Dubes, R. C. (1988). *Algorithms for clustering data.* NJ: Prentice Hall.

Jain, A. K., Murty, M. N., & Flynn, P. J. (1999). Data clustering: A review. *ACM Computing Surveys, 31*(3), 264-323.

Jancey, R. C. (1966). Multidimensional group analysis. *Australian Journal on Botany, 14*(1), 127-130.

Joachims, T., Freitag, D., & Mitchell, T. (1997). Webwatcher: A tour guide for the world wide Web. The 15th *International Joint Conference on Artificial Intelligence* (pp. 770-777). Nagoya, Japan.

Kaufman, L., & Rousseeuw, P. J. (1990). *Finding groups in data: An introduction to cluster analysis.* New York: John Wiley & Sons.

Kohonen, T. (1985). Median strings. *Pattern Recognition Letters, 3*(1), 309-313.

Konstan, J. A., Miller, B. N., Maltz, D., Herlocker, J. L., Gordon, L. R., & Riedl, J. (1997). GroupLens: Applying collaborative filtering to Usenet news. *Communications of the ACM, 40*(3), 77-87.

Kumar, P., Rao, M. V., Krishna, P. R., Bapi, R. S., & Laha, A. (2005). Intrusion detection system using sequence and set preserving metric. *Proceedings of IEEE International Conference on Intelligence and Security Informatics* (pp. 498-504). Atlanta: LNCS Springer Verlag

Levenshtein, L. I. (1966). Binary codes capable of correcting deletions, insertions, and reversals. *Soviet Physics-Doklady, 10*(7), 707-710.

Li, M., & Vitanyi, P. M. B. (1997). *An introduction to Kolmogorov complexity and its applications* (2nd ed.). New York: Springer-Verlag.

Li, M., & Vitanyi, P. M. B. (2001). Algorithmic complexity. In N. J. Smelser, & P. B. Baltes (Eds.), *International Encyclopedia of the Social & Behavioral Sciences* (pp. 376-382). Oxford: Pergamon.

Li, M., Badger, J. H., Chen, X., Kwong, S., Kearney, P., & Zhang, H. (2001). An information-based sequence distance and its application to whole mitochondrial genome phylogeny. *Bioinformatics, 17*(2), 149-154.

Li, M., Chen, X., Li, X., Ma, B., & P. M. B. Vitányi (2004). The similarity metric. *IEEE Transactions on Information Theory, 50,* 3250-3264.

Lieberman, H. L. (1995). Letizia: An agent that assists Web browsing. *Proceedings of the International Joint Conference on Artificial Intelligence* (pp. 924-929). Montreal, Canada: Morgan Kaufmann.

Mannila, H., & Meek, C. (2000). Global partial orders from sequential data. *Proceedings of the 6th International Conference on Knowledge Discovery and Data Mining* (pp. 161-168).

McQueen, J. (1967). Some methods for classification and analysis of multivariate observations. *Proceedings Fifth Berkeley Symposium on Math. Statistics and Probability.*

Mobasher, B. (2004). Web usage mining and personalization. In M. P. Singh (Ed.), *Practical handbook of Internet computing.* CRC Press.

Mobasher, B., Cooley, R., & Srivastava, J. (1999). Creating adaptive Web sites through usage based clustering of URLs. *Proceedings of the 1999 Workshop on Knowledge and Data Engineering Exchange.*

Mobasher, B., Colley, R., & Srivastava, J. (2000). Automatic personalization based on Web usage mining. *Communications of the ACM, 43*(8), 142-151.

Mobasher, B., Dai, H., & Luo, M. N. T. (2002). Discovery and evaluation of aggregate usage profiles for Web personalization. *Data Mining and Knowledge Discovery, 6,* 61-82.

Mount, D. W. (2004). *Bioinformatics: Sequence and genome analysis* (2ⁿᵈ ed.). Cold Spring Harbor, NY: Cold Spring Harbor Laboratory Press.

Ngu, D. S. W., & Wu, X. (1997). SiteHelper: A localized agent that helps incremental exploration of the world wide Web. *Proceedings of the 6ᵗʰ International World Wide Web Conference* (pp. 691-700). Santa Clara, CA: ACM Press.

Nong, Y. (2003). *The handbook of data mining.* NJ: Lawrence Erlbaum Associates.

O'Conner, M., & Herlocker, J. (1999). Clustering items for collaborative filtering. *Proceedings of the ACM SIGIR Workshop on Recommender Systems.* Berkeley, CA: ACM Press.

Paterson, M., & Danc'ik, V. (1994). Longest common subsequences. *Proceedings of the 19ᵗʰ International Symposium Mathematical Foundations of Computer Science* (pp. 127-142).

Perkowitz, M., & Etzioni, O. (1998). Adaptive Web sites: Automatically synthesizing Web pages. *Proceedings of the 15ᵗʰ National Conference on Artificial Intelligence* (pp. 727-732). Madison, WI: AAAI.

Perkowitz, M., & Etzioni, O. (2000). Adaptive Web sites. *Communications of the ACM, 43*(8), 152-158.

Pitkow, J., & Pirolli, P. (1999). Mining longest repeating subsequences to predict world wide Web surfing. *Proceedings of 2ⁿᵈ USENIX Symposium on Internet Technologies and Systems.*

Safar, M. (2005). K nearest neighbor search in navigation systems. *Mobile Information Systems, 1*(3), 207-224

Sankoff, D., & Kruskal, J. B. (1983). *Time warps, string edits, and macromolecules: The theory and practice of sequence comparison.* Reading, MA: Addison-Wesley Publishing Company.

Setubal, J. C., & Meidanis, J. (1987). *Introduction to computational molecular biology.* Boston: PWS Publishing Company.

Shahabi, C., Zarkesh, A. M., Adibi, J. & Shah, V. (1997). Knowledge discovery from users Web-page navigation. *Proceedings of the 7ᵗʰ International Workshop on Research Issues in Data Engineering High Performance Database Management for Large-Scale Applications* (p. 20). Washington, DC: IEEE Computer Society

Simon, I. (1987). Sequence comparison: Some theory and some practice. In M. Gross, & D. Perrin (Eds.), *Electronic dictionaries and automata in computational linguistics* (pp. 79-92). Berlin: Springer-Verlag, Saint Pierre d'Oeron, France.

Spiliopoulou, M., & Faulstich, L. C. (1999). WUM A tool for Web utilization analysis. In Extended version of *Proceedings of EDBT Workshop* (pp. 184-203). Springer Verlag.

Stormer, H. (2005). Personalized Web sites for mobile devices using dynamic cascading style sheets. *International Journal of Web Information Systems, 1*(2), 83-88.

Tan, L., Taniar, D., & Smith, K. A. (2005). A clustering algorithm based on an estimated distribution model. *International Journal of Business Intelligence and Data Mining, 1*(2), 229-245

Wang, H., Wang, W., Yang, J., & Yu, P. S. (2002). lustering by pattern similarity in large data sets, *SIGMOD Conference* (pp. 394-398).

Wang, J., Xindong Wu, X., & Zhang, C., (2005). Support vector machines based on K-means clustering for real-time business intelligence systems. *International Journal of Business Intelligence and Data Mining, 1*(1), 54-64

Yan, T. W., Jacobsen, M., Garcia-Molina, H., & Dayal, U. (1996). From user access patterns to dynamic hypertext linking. *Proceedings of the*

5th International World Wide Web Conference on Computer Networks and ISDN Systems (pp. 1007-1014). The Netherlands, Elsevier Science Publishers B. V. Amsterdam.

Yang, B., & Hurson, A. R., (2005). Similarity-based clustering strategy for mobile ad hoc multimedia databases. *Mobile Information Systems,* *1*(4), 253-273.

Zhang, T., Ramakrishnan, R., & Livny, M. (1996). BIRCH: An efficient data clustering method for very large databases. In *ACM SIGKDD Interna-*

tional Conference on Management of Data (pp. 103-114).

Zhang, Y., Xu, G., & Zhou, X. (2005). A latent usage approach for clustering Web transaction and building user profile. *ADMA* (pp. 31-42).

Zhou, B., Hui, S. C., & Fong, A. C. M. (2005). A Web usage lattice based mining approach for intelligent Web personalization. *International Journal of Web Information Systems,* *1*(3) 137-145.

This work was previously published in International Journal of Data Warehousing and Mining, Vol. 3, Issue 1, edited by D. Taniar, pp. 29-53, copyright 2007 by IGI Publishing, formerly known as Idea Group Publishing (an imprint of IGI Global).

Chapter III
Using Mined Patterns for XML Query Answering

Elena Baralis
Dip. di Automatica e Informatica, Politecnico di Torino, Italy

Paolo Garza
Dip. di Automatica e Informatica, Politecnico di Torino, Italy

Elisa Quintarelli
Dip. di Electronic e Informazione, Politecnico di Milano, Italy

Letizia Tanca
Dip. di Electronic e Informazione, Politecnico di Milano, Italy

ABSTRACT

XML is a rather verbose representation of semistructured data, which may require huge amounts of storage space. Several summarized representations of XML data have been proposed, which can both provide succinct information and be directly queried. In this chapter, we focus on compact representations based on the extraction of association rules from XML datasets. In particular, we show how patterns can be exploited to (possibly partially) answer queries, either when fast (and approximate) answers are required, or when the actual dataset is not available; for example, it is currently unreachable. We focus on (a) schema patterns, representing exact or approximate dataset constraints, (b) instance patterns, which represent actual data summaries, and their use for answering queries.

INTRODUCTION

The extensible markup language (XML) (World Wide Web Consortium, 1998) was initially pro- posed as a standard way to represent, exchange, and publish information on the Web, but its usage has recently spread to many other application fields. To name but a few, XML is currently used for publishing legacy data, for storing data that cannot be represented with traditional data models, and for ensuring interoperability among software systems.

However, XML is a rather verbose representation of data, which may require huge amounts of storage space. We propose several summarized representations of XML data, which can both provide succinct information and be directly queried. In particular, we propose *patterns* as abstract representations of the (exact or approximate) constraints that hold the data, and their use for (possibly partially) answering queries, either when fast, though approximate, answers are required, or when the actual dataset is not available; for example, it is currently unreachable. In this last case, the service of a "semantic" proxy, which caches patterns instead of actual data pages, can be provided.

In this chapter, we focus on (a) *schema patterns*, representing exactly or approximately the dataset constraints, and (b) *instance patterns*, which represent, again exactly or approximately, actual data summaries. Our summarized representations are based on the extraction of association rules from XML datasets, and queried by means of the GSL graphical query language (Damiani, Oliboni, Quintarelli, & Tanca, 2003).

Patterns can be exploited to provide intensional query answering. An intensional answer to a query substitutes the actual data answering the query (the extensional answer) with a set of properties characterizing them (Motro, 1989). Thus, our intensional answers are in general more synthetic than the extensional ones, but usually approximate. Applications of intensional query answering become more and more useful as the technology offers improved means for information handling; query optimization in large datasets, decision support, and context based data summarization are only the most important.

Approximate intensional answers may replace the extensional ones whenever a short response time is required, even to the cost of a controlled lack of precision. Furthermore, decision support may take advantage of the inherently synthetic nature of intensional answers. Consider, for example, the query: *What are the papers written by John Doe?* While an extensional answer, listing all the papers, is in order in case further transactional processing is required, an answer like *80% of John Doe's papers are about Data Mining* may be more interesting if a subsequent decision has to be taken, as, for instance, the choice of John Doe as a conference PC member.

Another interesting application domain is the storage and query of patterns instead of data in context-based data personalization for mobile users. Here, data summarization and tailoring are needed because of two main reasons: (a) the need to keep information manageable, in order for the user not to be confused by too much noise, and (b) the frequent case that the mobile device be a small one, like a palm computer or a cellular phone, in which condition only a summary of the information may be kept on board. In this case, patterns are kept on the mobile device instead of the actual data, and context-awareness can be enforced by keeping on board only the patterns which are relevant to the current situation. Finally, extracted patterns may also be used to provide an integrated representation of information mined from different XML documents, in order to answer queries by using all the available information gathered from different (heterogeneous) data sources.

The chapter is organized as follows. In the next section, the background is discussed. The Mined Patterns: A New Approach to XML Intensional Query Answering section introduces the type of patterns we propose and describes how we represent them in our graph-based language. In the Using Patterns to Answer Queries subsection, we propose an approach to provide intensional answers to user queries. The Representing and Querying Instance Patterns section discusses how patterns are physically represented and queries actually performed in this representation. The

Experimental Results section shows some experimental results on schema patterns and instance patterns, while A Prototype Tool section discusses a prototype tool we have implemented. Finally, conclusions and possible lines for future work are presented.

BACKGROUND

In the recent years, the database research community has devoted significant efforts to the design of XML query languages, which are both expressive and intuitive. LOREL (Abiteboul, Quass, McHugh, Widom, & Wiener, 1997) is the first proposal of a query language to support XML data querying. LOREL has a SQL-like syntax and was originally developed for general semistructured databases. It includes a mechanism for type coercion and introduces the notion of path expressions in the query composition process. After this first attempt, the World Wide Consortium (W3C) promoted the discussion on a standard XML language that had in XML-QL (Deutch, Fernandez, Florescu, Levy, & Suciu, 1998) the first initiative. However, XML-QL is a quite verbose language because it is based on an XML-like hierarchical organization of tags.

XPATH (World Wide Web Consortium, 1999) is a non-XML language developed for specifying only path expressions, that is, the description of the paths that the desired portions have to satisfy. XPATH has been extended by introducing XQuery (World Wide Web Consortium, 2002), a standard functional query language to process XML data which mainly use *FLWOR expressions*, nested to arbitrary depth to build queries. The syntax of FLWOR expressions is similar to select statements of SQL: *For* expressions are used for iteration; the *Let* clause allows one to bind variables; in the *Where* part, the conditions on the documents to be retrieved are specified; and the *Return* expression is used to generate the result. Logical expressions and built-in functions can be part of XQuery expressions.

At the same time, graphical, visual interfaces were proposed, with the main aim to be intuitive for naive users: XML-GL (Ceri, Comai, Damiani, Fraternali, Paraboschi, & Tanca, 1999) is the first proposal of visual interface for XQuery, which has been revised and extended by XQBE (Braga, Campi, & Ceri, 2005), a more intuitive interface inspired by the query by example (QBE) (Elmasri & Navathe, 1994) language. It is based on the use of annotated trees for composing queries; such trees are automatically mapped into XQuery expressions and processed by an XQuery engine. XQBE includes most of the expressive power of XPath expressions and operators but is more limited than XQuery, which is Turing-complete.

In this work, we represent both queries and mined patterns by means of the common formalisms of GSL (Damiani et al., 2003), which is an intuitive, graph-based query paradigm for semistructured data. GSL generalizes many features of several languages proposed in the literature, in which queries are graphical or based on patterns. Furthermore, it has the expressive power to represent the set of simple and more complex queries we can effectively manage with our approach.

Many query engines have been proposed in previous work; some are listed on the W3C website (World Wide Web Consortium, 1998). Some approaches are based on ad-hoc XML native databases, for example, Berkeley DB XML (Sleepycat Software, 2006); others store and encode XML documents in relational databases, for example, the Monet DB (Boncz, Flokstra, Grust, van Keulen, Manegold, Mullender, et al., 2006), while other engines directly query the XML documents without storing them on disk, for example, Saxon-B8.4 (Kay, 2006). XML native databases allow achieving high performance by means of ad-hoc indices and structures for XML data. However, XML indices are not efficient as relational indices yet. Hence, currently the best performance is provided by engines based on relational databases, for example, the Monet DB (Boncz et al., 2006), because they can exploit the mature relational data management infrastructure. Many XML engines directly store entire XML documents in memory, for example, Saxon-B8.4 (Kay, 2006). This approach is more system independent, and can directly query the XML documents without permanently storing them on disk. However, it is usually less efficient, because it accesses the original XML documents, which are often larger (more verbose) than the internal database representation of the same information.

The problem of providing intensional answers by means of integrity constraints has been initially addressed in Motro (1989) in the relational databases context. In this work we extend the approach to graph-based probabilistic patterns and XML documents.

In particular, the summarized representations we propose are based on the extraction of association rules from XML datasets. Association rules describe the co-occurrence of data items in a large amount of collected data (Agrawal & Srikant, 1994). Rules are usually represented as implications in the form $X \Rightarrow Y$, where X and Y are two arbitrary sets of data items, such that $X \cap Y = \emptyset$. In our framework, a data item is a pair (data-element,value), for example, (Author,Smith).

The quality of an association rule is usually measured by means of *support* and *confidence*. Support corresponds to the frequency of the set $X \cup Y$ in the dataset, while confidence corresponds to the conditional probability of finding Y, having found X, and is given by $\dfrac{\sup(X \cup Y)}{\sup(Y)}$. Association rule mining is a well-known problem, extensively dealt with (see, e.g., Agrawal et al., 1994), and we do not address it in this chapter.

Several works (Buneman, Davidson, Fan, Hara, & Tan, 2001a; Buneman, Fan, Siméon, & Weinstein, 2001b) address the problem of defin-

ing constraints for XML data. In Buneman et al. (2001b), it is argued that, analogously to traditional databases, XML data need a formal definition of constraints, and an effort to define the most important categories of constraints for XML data is performed. In particular, path constraints, keys, and foreign keys are considered. Buneman et al. (2001a) proposes a deeper analysis of the definition of absolute and relative keys and describes a new key constraint language for XML, which can handle keys with a complex structure.

In Grahne and Zhu (2002), adopting the key definition proposed in Buneman et al. (2001b), a technique is proposed for obtaining a compact set of keys from an XML document. In particular, only a minimal set of keys is mined as representative keys. To identify representative keys, two interest measures similar to support and confidence are associated to a key, and precise (confidence = 100%) and valid (confidence ≥ 95%) keys are mined.

The discovery of functional dependencies in XML documents is still an open problem. Arenas and Libkin (2004) have devoted some efforts to the definition of XML functional dependencies, but, to the best of our knowledge, automatic extraction of XML functional dependencies from an XML corpus has not been addressed. On the other hand, discovery of functional dependencies from relational databases has been extensively explored (e.g., Huhtala, Karkkainen, Porkka, & Toivonen, 1999), but these techniques cannot be straightforwardly applied to XML documents.

Besides constraint extraction, our work also addresses the exploitation of the extracted knowledge to provide approximate answers to XML queries. Several structural and value indexing techniques to improve XML query execution time have been proposed (Boncz et al., 2006; Chung, Min, & Shim, 2002; He & Yang, 2004; Kay, 2006; Qun, Lim, & Ong, 2003). Our approach is different, since we achieve efficiency by querying instance patterns, which provide a summarized representation of XML documents in the style of materialized views for data warehouses (Harinarayan, Rajaraman, & Ullman, 1996), rather than traditional indexing techniques. Hence, summarized representation yields a general-purpose, portable, and condensed representation of XML documents than can be easily exploited by any XML query engine. Differently from materialized views, our summarized representation may leave out some (less frequent) information.

A Graphical Language to Present and Query XML Documents

Once rule extraction has been performed by using data mining algorithms, an intuitive and effective language is needed both to represent and query the extracted knowledge.

We propose the graph-based XML query language GSL (Damiani et al., 2003) with the twofold aim to seamlessly represent both summarized information (i.e., patterns) and queries over it. Graphical query expressions in GSL, which should allow non-expert users to approach our method more easily, can be easily translated into XQuery expressions, in a similar way as in Augurusa, Braga, Campi, and Ceri (2003) and Braga et al. (2005).

In this way, XML documents, queries, and patterns admit a uniform representation. Indeed, most of the well known graph based models proposed in the past lend themselves well to represent XML

data by graphs where nodes denote either objects (i.e., abstract entities) or values (i.e., primitive values), and edges represent relationships between them. See, for example, OEM (Papakonstantinou, Garcia-Molina, & Widom, 1995), UnQL (Bunemann, Davidson, Hillebrand, & Suciu, 1996), GraphLog (Consens & Mendelzon, 1990), and G-Log (Paredaens, Peelman, & Tanca, 1995). Accordingly, we represent an XML document by a labeled tree[1] (Damiani et al., 2003), where the nodes have a tag, a type label, which indicates whether the node is the root, an element, text, or attribute, and a content label, which can assume as value a PCDATA or an undefined value ($\perp$) for nonterminals.

Edges represent the "containment" relationship between different items of a XML document, thus edges do not have names. Moreover, since in this work we are interested in finding relationships among elementary values of XML documents, and such values may occur either as textual content of leaf elements or as attribute values, we do not distinguish between the two kinds of nodes and do not include edge labels in the figures.

The tree-based representation (with the considered labels for nodes and edges) of (a portion of) a well-formed XML document, which will be used as a running example in the rest of the chapter, is pictorially represented in Figure 1. The document reports information about Conference Proceedings, based on a slight variation of the

Figure 1. A simplified labeled tree of a portion of the XML Sigmod Record document

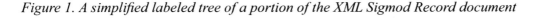

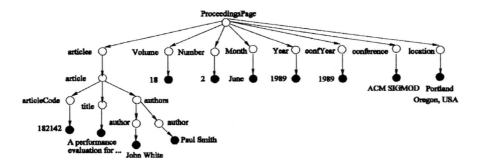

SIGMOD Record XML document (Merialdo, 2003) (e.g., information about abstracts has been added). Attributes and elements are characterized by empty circles, whereas the textual content of elements and the value of attributes is reported as a black-filled circle (denoted as content node in the following). The generality of this model accommodates the representation of XML documents as well as information originally represented by means of a different data model.

In general, a GSL query is represented by a *graph*, which is used to identify the subgraphs (i.e., the portions of a semistructured document) where the query is to be applied. Queries are represented as graphs with colored nodes and edges. A query is characterized by two colors: *thin* (t) specifies positive conditions, while *thick* (T) indicates a desired situation in the resulting instance. We represent the t color by thin lines and the T color by thick lines. A GSL query can also express the aggregate function COUNT, grouping criterions, and the possibility to extract the best k answers with respect to a countervalue.

Informally, an instance (i.e., the tree based representation of an XML document) satisfies a query if, whenever the thin part of the query matches (i.e., it is similar to) a part of the instance, the whole query matches it too. Note that, at the node level, matching corresponds to the well-known concept of *unification* (Staples & Robinson, 1986). At the graph level, the notion of similarity used in matching is formally defined later.

Query semantics is given as a set of pairs of instances (I,I'), where I' is the result of applying the query to I. In other words, a GSL query is applied to an instance that normally does not satisfy it, and query application consists in a change to that instance, so that the query is satisfied by the resulting instance.

For example, the query in Figure 2(a) requires finding *the articles with "XML" among the index terms*. We point out that the T part of the graph (thick lines) is used to add to the original XML document an element with tag result (for example,

a sub-element of the root node) that contains a copy[2] of the subtrees similar to the t part (thin line) of the pattern. The query in Figure 2(b) contains an aggregate function and requires *counting the articles written by the author Paul Smith.*

In order to apply queries to XML trees, we need to define a notion of similarity between graphs, to compare trees (or more in general graphs) representing queries to trees representing document instances. We formalize the concept of similarity between graphs through *bisimulation*, a relation between graphs that was initially introduced in Park (1980) and Milner (1980) for studying concurrent languages semantics.

We say that two labeled graphs G_0 and G_1 are *functionally bisimilar* ($G_0 \overset{b}{\longrightarrow} G_1$) or that there is an *embedding* of G_0 into G_1 if: (1) b is a total binary relation on $G_0 \times G_1$; (2) two nodes belonging to relation b have exactly the same type and the same label; (3) if two nodes n_0, n_1 are in relation b, then every edge having n_0 as an endpoint should find as a counterpart a corresponding edge with n_1 as an endpoint; (4) the relation b is a function.

Figure 2. Two GLS queries: (a) to find the articles with "XML" among the index terms and (b) to count the articles written by Paul Smith

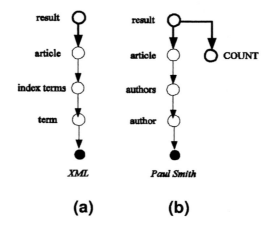

(a)   **(b)**

MINED PATTERNS: A NEW APPROACH TO XML INTENSIONAL QUERY ANSWERING

The notion of pattern introduced in this chapter yields a general-purpose and summarized representation of XML documents that can be easily exploited to provide answers to XML queries. In this section, we first classify the set of possible patterns and introduce a graph-based representation of the pattern concept. Then, we describe the classes of queries we can manage with our approach. Finally, we explain how to provide intensional answers to user queries.

Pattern Based Representation of XML Datasets

Patterns are classified in two orthogonal ways. The first type of classification refers to the accuracy with which the pattern represents the dataset.

1. An **exact pattern** expresses a property which holds on *any* instance of the dataset. Thus exact patterns represent *constraints*. For instance, in this chapter, we show how to represent functional dependencies between schema elements by means of schema patterns. An example of exact pattern is *A conference name and edition determines the conference location.*

2. A **probabilistic pattern** holds only on a given (large) fraction of the instances in the dataset. It is a weak constraint on the dataset, characterized by a quality index describing its reliability. An example of a probabilistic pattern is *With a confidence 0.5 the author John Doe is likely to have the word XML as one of the index terms of his articles.*

The second classification dimension corresponds to the different levels of detail (i.e., summarization level) of the represented information.

In particular:

- **Schema patterns** are expressed on the structure of the dataset. They are used to describe general properties of the schema, which apply to all instances. A schema pattern may be derived as an abstraction of a set of association rules.
- **Domain patterns** express constraints on the values of the instances of a dataset. Examples are domain constraints, which restrict the admissible values of a given element.
- **Instance patterns** are expressed on the instances of the dataset. In particular, in this chapter, they are used to summarize the content of a dataset by means of the most relevant (frequent) association rules holding on the dataset. We use them to derive an approximate answer to a query, without requiring actually access of the dataset to compute the answer. The answer may contain a subset or a superset of the required information, depending on the form of the query and of the considered instance pattern.

In this chapter, we focus on data summaries represented by means of probabilistic schema and instance patterns. We apply the graphical model for XML documents introduced in Damiani et al. (2003) to describe summarized XML information.

Representing Patterns

In this section, we represent instance and schema patterns by means of GSL colored trees.

Instance Patterns

Definition 1. A (probabilistic) instance pattern is a pair $<G,<c,s>>$, such that:

- *G* is a rooted GSL tree.
- The thin (t) and thick (T) parts of *G* are not empty and the root *r* is thin.
- Each leaf of *G* is a content node with a defined content label (i.e., a value).
- $<c,s>$ are the confidence and the support of the instance pattern; $0<c\leq1$ and $0<s\leq1$. Note that when $c = 1$ the instance pattern is exact and *c* may be omitted.

For example, the instance pattern in Figure 3 represents an association rule. In the graphical representation, we place confidence and support

Figure 3. An instance pattern: with confidence 0.5 and support 0.9, the author Paul Smith is likely to have the XML term among the index terms.

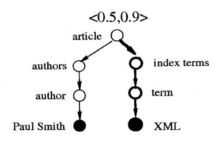

Figure 4. A more complex instance pattern: with a confidence 0.2 and a support 0.85, the author Paul Smith is likely to have a publication at the VLDB 2000 Conference.

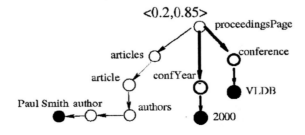

of the instance pattern near the graph root. A more complex instance pattern expressing an association rule with more than one path in the T part of the graph is depicted in Figure 4. Note that here the confidence is associated to the conjunction of the two conditions in the T part (i.e., the consequent) of the instance pattern.

It is also interesting to combine instance patterns and represent them in a compact way (i.e., by a unique GSL tree). For example, in Figure 5(a), we show a representation of the instance pattern which summarizes two patterns relating an author to conferences where he/she published a paper. The new instance pattern contains two paths in the T part (consequent), graphically linked by an arc, with each confidence reported on the leaf (note the difference with Figure 4, reporting instead a conjunctive condition in the T part).

When considering instance patterns whose T part is composed by a unique path, we call *index* a colored tree summarizing a set of instance patterns which differ only in the content node of the T path. In Figure 5(b), we extend the pattern in Figure 5(a) and represent an index summarizing the *relationships between the author Paul Smith and the conferences* where he published a paper.

In general, instance patterns can have more than one path both in the t and in the T part. This means that multiple elements or attributes are considered simultaneously when extracting association rules; we recall that multiple paths in the same part of the graphical association rule are read as a conjunction of conditions.

Schema Patterns

As introduced earlier, schema patterns are a special case of constraints and, in particular, lend themselves to represent the notion of functional dependency as it is used in the relational databases context. A schema pattern represents a type of implication that differs from a functional dependency for two main reasons: (1) it is inferred

Figure 5. (a) A disjunctive instance pattern; (b) an index that summarizes some similar instance patterns

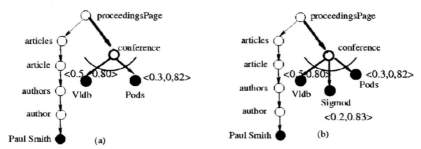

(a)   (b)

from a dataset (and not given at the schema level) and (2) it can be probabilistic. We now discuss how to represent probabilistic schema patterns by means of GSL rules.

A *Bisimilar Rule Base (BRB) R* is a set of instance patterns $\{<A_1,<c_1,s_1>>,...,<A_n,<c_n,s_n>>\}$ such that $\forall i, j \in \{1,...,n\}$ the instance patterns A_i and A_j representing association rules, deprived of their content nodes, are functional bisimilar.

A *probabilistic schema pattern P* can be derived from a BRB $\{A_1,<c_1,s_1>>,...,<A_n,<c_n,s_n>>\}$ (we say that the BRB constructs *P*) and is represented by a GSL graph. For example, if the BRB is composed by instance patterns with the form reported in Figure 6, then the corresponding

schema pattern – *"for each element Item A if an element B exists, then it must be unique"* – is represented as in Figure 7.

The weight *p* near the transaction root *r* is the *probabilistic schema pattern weight* which is a quality index that describes the reliability of the probabilistic schema pattern. It is computed as a function of the supports and confidences of the instance patterns which contribute to P as follows.

Let $\{<A_1,<c_1,s_1>>,...,<A_n,<c_n,s_n>>\}$ be a BRB. The weight *p* is given by $p = \sum_{i \in \{1,...,n\}} c_i \times s_i$, where c_i and s_i are confidence and support of association rule A_i.

Figure 6. An instance pattern

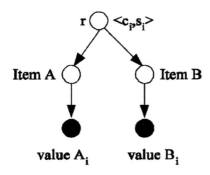

Figure 7. A probabilistic schema pattern

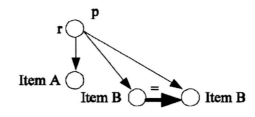

Note that when $p = 1$, the schema pattern is exact and p may be omitted. The graphical form of a schema pattern represents the "implication" whose antecedent is the path rooted in the node r without any outgoing T edge (in Figure 7, condition *for each element Item A child of r*), and whose consequent is composed by two identical paths connected by a "=" labeled edge. The consequent is used to represent the functional dependency property (in Figure 6, *if two paths with a node Item B child of r exist, they must be the same path*). For example, the probabilistic schema pattern of Figure 8 is extracted from the BRB relating author names to index terms. Note that in probabilistic schema patterns, the content label of leaf nodes is undefined (i.e., no black filled nodes are represented).

When all leaf elements of a probabilistic schema pattern, both in the t and T part, are *single-valued* elements, then $0 < p <= 1$. This general property is proved by Theorem 2 below. In the special case in which all the instance patterns in the BRB have confidence $c_i = 1$ and the sum of all association rule supports is 1, then $p = 1$ and the schema pattern *becomes exact*, as asserted by Theorem 1. In particular, it represents a functional dependency between the corresponding elements. The proofs of both theorems are provided in Baralis, Garza, Quintarelli, and Tanca (2006).

Figure 8. A probabilistic schema pattern

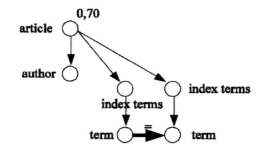

Theorem 1
Let $e_1,...,e_k$ be the k different single-valued leaf elements of a probabilistic schema pattern P ($G_{\{t\}}$ includes the first l leaf elements and $G_{\{T\}}$ the last k-l leaf elements), and $R = \{<A_1,<c_1,s_1>>,...,<A_n,<c_n,s_n>>\}$ the rule base determining P. Then, for all $<A_i,<c_i,s_i>> \in R$, $c_i = 1$ if and only if $p = 1$.

Theorem 2
Let $e_1,...,e_k$ be the k different single-valued leaf elements of a probabilistic schema pattern P ($G_{\{t\}}$ includes the first l leaf elements and $G_{\{T\}}$ the last k-l leaf elements), and $R = \{<A_1,<c_1,s_1>>,...,<A_n,<c_n,s_n>>\}$ the rule base associated to P. Then, $0 < p <= 1$.

Classification of Very Simple Queries

In this section, we classify the general forms of the query types we can effectively manage with our approach, which are called very simple queries (VSQ).

More complex queries can be dealt with by means of query decomposition. In this case, the query answering process consists of several steps: a complex query is first decomposed, possibly partially, into very simple queries; then, intermediate, but fast, results yielded by the very simple queries on patterns are collected; finally, these partial results are appropriately integrated to provide the final answer to the original complex query. Hence, our summarized representation, similar to a traditional database management system (DBMS) index, may be exploited to compute (a portion of) a query result. This technique is rather effective, for instance, with counting subqueries, over which our method is particularly efficient. Note that if some portions of a complex query cannot be translated into very simple queries, we may directly query the real datasets for those portions while retaining the fast answering method for the rest of the query.

Select Queries

Queries in this class select information satisfying simple or complex conditions on the value of content nodes. The class can be further specialized as follows:

- Queries imposing a restriction on the value of the content nodes (see Figure 2(a) for an example of this kind of query).
- Queries with AND conditions on the content nodes (see the lefthand side graph of Figure 9).
- Queries with OR conditions on the content nodes (see the righthand side graph of Figure 9).

Counting Queries

An example of a GSL counting query is in Figure 2(b), where the articles written by Paul Smith are counted. To answer this query, we use an instance pattern whose thin part matches the thin part of the query, and obtain as an answer *sup/conf* (where *sup* and *conf* are support and confidence of the instance pattern used to answer the query). More specifically, to count the items satisfying a condition on a content node, we use the equal-

ity $conf(A \Rightarrow B) = sup(A \Rightarrow B)/sup(A)$, where $A \Rightarrow B$ is an association rule. For example, in the SIGMOD Record XML document, we can count the different root instances (e.g., articles) having XML as an index term. We can use an association rule $A \Rightarrow B$ having the pair <Term, XML> in the body, thus the number of articles is given by $sup(A) = sup(A \Rightarrow B)/conf(A \Rightarrow B)$.

Counting and Grouping Queries

They are used for expressing some grouping criteria and then for counting the number of items satisfying a property in each group. A general GSL representation of a counting and grouping query is position in Figure 10(a), where we want to count the number of Item1 for each Item2.

Top k Queries

This kind of query selects the best *k* answers satisfying a counting condition. Queries in this class can be seen as GSL counting and grouping queries with a *TOP K* thick node. See Figure 10(b) for the general GSL form. In this case, the answer contains the *k* groups with the highest support value.

Figure 9. The GSL representation of select queries with AND and OR conditions

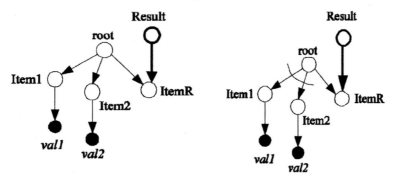

Figure 10. The GSL representation of (a) a counting and grouping query and (b) a top k query

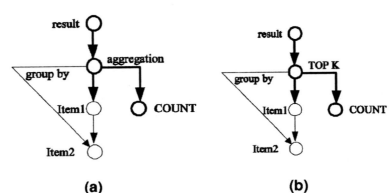

(a) **(b)**

Using Patterns to Answer Queries

We now show the rationale behind our proposal of using patterns for intensional answers. Consider the instance pattern in Figure 5(a) specifying that with a confidence of *0.5*, the author Paul Smith published a paper in the VLDB Conference Proceedings and with a confidence *0.3* he published in the PODS Conference Proceedings. If we consider the query in Figure 11(a), asking for all proceedings pages of Paul Smith, we can use the instance pattern of Figure 5(a) to answer that, with a confidence of 0.5 (i.e., *50%* of Paul Smith's publications), Paul Smith published in the VLDB Conference (the query matches with

each path in the thin part of the instance pattern in Figure 5(a)), and with a confidence 0.3, he published in the PODS Conference Proceedings. If we consider the index in Figure 5(b) (reporting the conferences where Paul Smith published), we can still provide a partial but more complete answer to the query in Figure 11(a), by saying that with a confidence of *0.5*, Paul Smith published in the VLDB Conference, with a confidence of *0.2* in the SIGMOD Conference, and so forth. The answer may be partial because instance patterns are extracted, enforcing support and confidence thresholds.

Consider now the query in Figure 11(b), asking for information about articles with the keyword

Figure 11. Two GSL queries: (a) to find information on the author Paul Smith; (b) to find information about the article with XML in the index terms

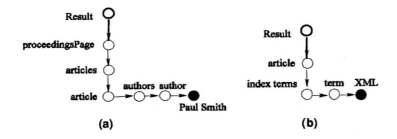

(a) **(b)**

XML among the index terms. If we use the instance pattern of Figure 3, a (partial) answer is that the author Paul Smith published on the XML topic (note that here the query matches the thick part of the instance pattern in Figure 3).

In the first case, where the query matches the thin part of the instance pattern, we obtain an answer that has the meaning of an implication. In the second case, where the query matches the thick part of the instance pattern, the answer is a set of items, each with its own reliability value.

Consider now a more complex query (Figure 12), asking for conferences where articles written by Paul Smith on the XML or the XQuery topic have been published; here a disjoint condition,

which is graphically represented by an arc, is required between the two terms. The query answering process first decomposes the query into the simple GSL queries in Figure 13, each one representing an AND condition; the result of the global query is the union of the answers to the two simple queries in Figure 13. To provide an intensional answer to these queries, we have to consider three-item instance patterns similar to them, that is, patterns with two items about the author Paul Smith and the XML (or XQuery) term in the antecedent and one item in the consequent of the related association rules.

If no three-item patterns have been mined, it is possible to introduce a further approximation in the result, by using two-item instance patterns (e.g., instance patterns with the antecedent describing either articles written by Paul Smith or articles containing XML as term and a conference name as consequent) and estimating the answer of the query as the intersection of the two-item patterns similar to a part of the query.

Mined schema patterns can be used to enlarge the set of instance patterns that can be used to answer a given user's query. Consider for example the query in Figure 14(a) asking for articles published on the LNCS series and suppose the schema pattern in Figure 14(b), stating that the conference name univocally determines the series where the articles will be published, has been ex-

Figure 12. A GSL complex query with AND and OR conditions

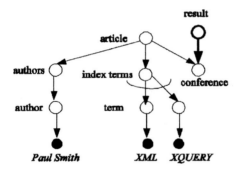

Figure 13. Two GSL queries with an AND condition

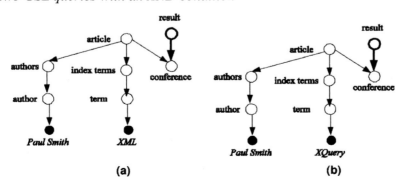

tracted from the dataset. Note that the thick part (consequent) of the schema pattern is similar to the thin part of the GSL query. Then, if it is know that the proceedings of a conference (e.g., ICDT) are published on the LNCS series, then the index relating that conference with other information can be used to provide an approximate answer. Figure 15 shows an example of such an index. Since schema patterns are extracted from datasets, conferences with LNCS proceedings are known. Furthermore, the BRB to determine a schema pattern has been mined. Hence, instance patterns relating conferences to series can be queried.

In the sequel, we give the formal definition of the semantics of queries when applied to patterns. Intuitively, applying selection queries to instance patterns has the effect of producing other patterns (see Definition 2) which correspond to (a fraction of) the actual data instances, thus representing a summarized description of the documents resulting from the query.

Definition 2. Given a class 1 query $Q = <<N,E,r>,Col>$ ($N_{Aggr} = \emptyset^3$) and a set of instance patterns $G = \{<G_1,<c_1,s_1>>,..., <G_n,<c_n,s_n>>\}$ the semantics of the application of Q to G (named S_Q) is as follows:

$$S_Q(G) = \begin{cases} \{\langle G_{i\{t\}},\langle c_i, s_i \rangle\rangle\} & if \ Q_{\{t\}} \xrightarrow{b} G_{i\{T\}} \cup \{r_i\} \\ \bigcup \{\langle G_{i\{T\}},\langle c_i, s_i \rangle\rangle\} & if \ Q_{\{t\}} \xrightarrow{b} G_{i\{t\}} \end{cases}$$

Figure 15. A GSL index

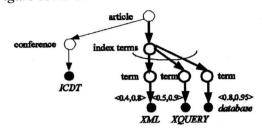

Applying a class 2 query to a set of instance patterns has the effect of producing the numeric value (see Definition 3) *support/confidence* of an instance pattern whose thin part matches the thin part of the query:

Definition 3. Given a class 2 query $Q = <<N,E,r>,Col>$ ($N_{Aggr} \neq \emptyset$, $N_{Gr} = \emptyset^4$) and a set of instance patterns $G = \{<G_1,<c_1,s_1>>,..., <G_n,<c_n,s_n>>\}$, the semantics of the application of Q to G (named S_Q) is as follows:

$$S_Q(G) = \frac{s_i}{c_i} \text{ such that } \exists i \in \{1,...,n\} \text{ such that } Q\{t\} \xrightarrow{b} G_i\{t\}$$

Applying a class 3 query to a set of instance patterns has the effect of producing a set of pairs (see Definition 4), where each pair is composed by the numeric value *support/confidence* of an

Figure 14. (a) A GSL query; (b) a schema pattern

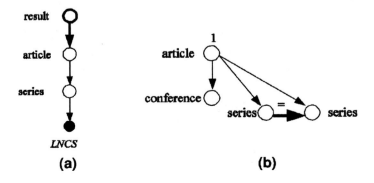

instance pattern whose thin part matches the thin part of the query, and the nodes of such a pattern matching the grouping nodes of the query.

Definition 4. Given a class 3 query $Q = <<N,E,r>,Col>$ ($N_{Aggr} \neq \emptyset$,

N_{Gr} $\{\langle aggregation, sub-element\_of, \perp \rangle\}$) and a set of instance patterns $G = \{<G_1,<c_1,s_1>>,...,$ $<G_n,<c_n,s_n>>\}$, the semantics of the application of Q to G (named S_Q) is as follows:

$$S_Q(G) = \left\{ \left\langle \frac{s_1}{c_1}, X_1 \right\rangle, ..., \left\langle \frac{s_l}{c_l}, X_l \right\rangle \right\}$$

if $Q\{_t\} \setminus E_{Gr} \xrightarrow{b} G_j\{_t\}$ and $j \in \{1,...,n\}$

Where the set $X_j \subseteq G_j$ is such that $X_j \xrightarrow{b} Y$, with $Y \subseteq Q$ such that $\forall y \in Y$ there exists an edge $\langle t, group\_by, y \rangle$.

A class 4 query is a counting and grouping query with an extra condition imposing an upper bound on the cardinality of the answer set. Therefore, the semantic is as follows:

Definition 5. Given a class 4 query $Q = <<N,E,r>,Col>$ ($N_{Aggr} \neq \emptyset$, $N_{Gr} = \{\langle top\_k, sub-element\_of, \perp \rangle\}$) and a set of instance patterns $G = \{<G_1,<c_1,s_1>>,...,$ $<G_n,<c_n,s_n>>\}$, the semantics of the application of Q to G (named S_Q) is as follows:

Let $S_Q(\underline{G}) = \left\{ \left\langle \frac{s_1}{c_1}, X_1 \right\rangle, ..., \left\langle \frac{s_l}{c_l}, X_l \right\rangle \right\}$ be the semantics of the corresponding counting and grouping query $\underline{G}$. We order in descending order the set $S_Q(\underline{G})$ w.r.t. the numeric value $\frac{s_i}{c_i}$ and obtain a set $\left\{ \left\langle \frac{s'_1}{c'_1}, X'_1 \right\rangle, ..., \left\langle \frac{s'_l}{c'_l}, X'_l \right\rangle \right\}$ and then we sort the set w.r.t. the $\frac{s'_i}{c'_i}$, descending, and give as a result the first k pairs $\left\{ \left\langle \frac{s'_1}{c'_1}, X'_1 \right\rangle, ..., \left\langle \frac{s'_k}{c'_k}, X'_k \right\rangle \right\}$ (with $k < l$).

The result of the application of queries to patterns instead of documents is correct by construction. It follows from the fact that each $<A_i,<c_i,s_i>>$ has been extracted from G, and the confidence c_i means that the number of subtrees of G matching A_i, given the number of subtrees matching $A_{i\{t\}}$, is c_i. Moreover, for queries with the count aggregation function, the semantics has been based on the fact that given an association rule $X \Rightarrow Y$ then $\sup(X) = \dfrac{\sup(X \Rightarrow Y)}{conf(X \Rightarrow Y)}$.

REPRESENTING AND QUERYING INSTANCE PATTERNS

In this section, we describe how queries, specified by means of our graphical representation, are actually applied to XML documents and instance patterns. We first discuss how instance patterns are generated. Next, we discuss the physical representation of the generated patterns. Finally, we discuss how queries are implemented on the actual physical data representations.

Generating Instance Patterns

The known algorithms for mining association rules (e.g., Agrawal et al., 1994) consider a collection of transactions, each containing a set of items. In the XML context, a transaction is a collection of pairs *(data-element, value)*. To define the concept of transaction, we select a *transaction root*, which is the lowest common ancestor of all the nodes involved in the considered transaction, within the labeled graph representing the structure of the considered XML document. Each subtree of the transaction root defines a transaction. *Data-element* is the label of an element with a content, rooted in the transaction root and specified as a complete path from the transaction root to the element. *Value* is the content of the considered element. For example, in our experiments on the DBLP XML document (Ley, 2005), each transaction is associated to an article (transaction root), and includes all the elements that characterize it (authors, title, year, conference name, etc.).

The *(data-element,value)* representation for data items yields a single item when the XML element contains a single data value. Instead, when the XML element has a textual content, in principle, each word of the text, coupled with the element label, may yield a data item. In practice, before transformation into data items, textual elements are subject to stopword elimination (i.e., elimination of very frequent and "noisy" words such as articles) and stemming (i.e., reduction of words to their semantic stem) (Porter, 1980). Both operations are commonly performed in textual data management.

Physical Representation of Instance Patterns

Two different physical representations may be used for instance patterns:

- **Rule-based physical representation**. Each instance pattern corresponds to one association rule; that is, there is a one-to-one mapping between instance patterns and association rules.
- **Itemset-based physical representation**. The set of instance patterns is stored as a set of itemsets, which are sets of items. Itemsets are the building blocks from which

association rules are generated (Agrawal et al., 1994). In particular, an arbitrary association rule $r:A \rightarrow B$, is generated by means of itemsets A and $A \cup B$, where $support(r)$ = $support(A \cup B)$, and $confidence(r)$ = $support(A \cup B)/support(A)$.

Since each itemset may contribute to the generation of several rules, the cardinality of the itemset set is always smaller than the cardinality of the corresponding association rule set. Hence, the itemset-based physical representation provides a more compact representation of the instance patterns.

Both representations may be stored either in a XML document (DTDs in Figure 16 and Figure 18, for rules and itemsets respectively), or in a relational database (schemata in Figure 17 and Figure 19). Any XQuery engine can directly be used on the XML document representation of patterns. Hence, both the original document and its pattern representation can be queried by using the same engine and the same query language (e.g., XQuery). Furthermore, when needed, both XML documents can be used in the same query (e.g., the pattern set representation is used to solve a subquery and the original XML document is used in the outer part of the query). On the other hand, the relational representation is stored in a relational database and queried by means of SQL. In this case, the pattern representation and the original XML document cannot be used in

Figure 16. DTD associated to the XML document for the rule-based physical representation

```
<?xml version="1.0" encoding="UTF-8"?>
<!ELEMENT RuleSet (AssociationRule+)>
<!ELEMENT AssociationRule (RuleBody, RuleHead*)>
<!ATTLIST   AssociationRule NumberItemHead CDATA #REQUIRED
                NumberItemBody CDATA #REQUIRED
                support CDATA #REQUIRED
                confidence CDATA #REQUIRED>
<!ELEMENT RuleBody (item+)>
<!ELEMENT RuleHead (item+)>
<!ELEMENT Item (#PCDATA)>
<!ATTLIST   Item DataElement CDATA #REQUIRED>
```

the same query (they are stored by means of two different approaches).

To efficiently query instance patterns, independently of the selected representation, the indexing techniques provided by the query engine of choice may be exploited.

Physical Representation of Queries on Instance Patterns

Queries over XML documents expressed in GSL find a straightforward implementation in XQuery (Braga et al., 2005). Figure 20(a) shows the XQuery corresponding to select GSL queries. The implementation of the same GSL query on a set of instance patterns is less immediate. Such implementation must take into account on the one hand, the physical representation of patterns (itemset-based or rule-based), and, on the other hand, the support system, that is, XML or relational.

To describe how query implementation takes place, we consider select queries as a represen-tative class of very simple queries. Consider the general form of select queries *"select value of element Item1 where element Item = 'val'"*. Figure 20 shows the XQuery and SQL expressions needed to provide the answer to this query on instance patterns.

In particular, Figure 20(b) and Figure 20(c) show the XQuery and SQL expressions on the itemset-based physical representations of the instance patterns. The general transformation process is independent of the instance pattern physical representation. Hence, the XQuery and SQL expressions on the rule-based representation are similar.

The transformation process for select queries produces a query that selects instance patterns which:

1. Correlate *Item* and *Item1*.
2. Satisfy the selection predicate *Item = "val"*. This predicate is transformed into a predicate selecting the items satisfying the condition *Item[@DataElement="Item1"]="val"*.

Figure 17. Schema of the relational tables for the rule-based physical representation

```
Rules(IDRule, Support, Confidence, Number Item Head, Number Item Body)
ItemRules(IDRule, DataElement, Value, Head_Body)
```

Figure 18. DTD associated to the XML document for the itemset-based physical representation

```
<?xml version="1.0" encoding="UTF-8"?>
<!ELEMENT ItemsetSet(Itemset+)>
<!ELEMENT Itemset (Item+)>
<!ATTLIST   Itemset NumberItem CDATA #REQUIRED
                    support CDATA #REQUIRED>
<!ELEMENT Item (#PCDATA)>
<!ATTLIST   Item DataElement CDATA #REQUIRED>
```

Figure 19. Schema of the relational tables for the itemset-based physical representation

```
Itemsets(IDItemset, Support, Number Item)
ItemItemsets(IDItemset, DataElement, Value)
```

3.   Yield as result set the values of items where ***DataElement="Item1"***.

All the very simple queries described earlier can be implemented by applying similar transformations.

Long Patterns Support Estimation

The proposed physical representations are general and allow representing patterns with an arbitrary number of items. However, if all patterns are extracted without enforcing any threshold on the maximum length, the number of patterns rapidly grows and the size of the pattern representation becomes similar to that of the original XML document. Hence, access may become inefficient. In this work, we propose to mine only patterns with at most two items to reduce the size of the instance pattern set. These patterns may also be exploited to give approximate answers to queries requiring longer patterns (e.g., queries in the Using Patterns to Answer Queries subsection).

Pavlov, Mannila, and Smyth (2001) proposed an approach to estimate the support of an arbitrary itemset X (i.e., a query Q in their context)

by using a probabilistic model generated on the complete set of T-frequent itemsets (i.e., itemsets with support higher than T without enforcing any maximum length constraint). Differently from Pavlov et al. (2001), we need to estimate the support of an arbitrary itemset X (i.e., pattern) by using only T-frequent itemsets with at most two items. We propose a simple approach based on the downward closure property of itemsets (Agrawal et al., 1994).

From the downward closure property of itemsets, the support sup(X) of a generic itemset X is lower than or equal to the support sup(Y) of all the itemsets $Y \subset X$. Hence:

$$\text{sup}(X) \leq \min_{(I,J)|I \in X, J \in X, I \neq J} \text{sup}(I \cup J)$$

where I and J are items included in X, $I \cup J$ is the itemset obtained by joining I and J, and sup$(I \cup J)$ is its support. The support of a pattern X with more than two items may be estimated as:

$$EstimatedSup(X) = \min_{(I,J)|I \in X, J \in X, I \neq J} \text{sup}(I \cup J)$$

EstimatedSup is an upper bound for the value of X's support. Experimental evaluation of this approximation (see the Experimental Results section) shows that it provides a fairly accurate estimation of the actual support of X.

Figure 20. Select query on content node and its rewritings

```
for $res in distinct-values(for $r in doc("document.xml")//root
                    where $r/Item="val"
                    return $r/Item1)
return $res
(a) Query on the original XML dataset


for $res in distinct-values(for $r in doc("itemsetSet.xml")/ItemsetSet/Itemset
                    where $r/Item[@DataElement="Item"]="val"
                    return $r/Item[@DataElement="Item1"])
return $res
(b) Query on the itemset-based physical representation (XML)


SELECT DISTINCT II2.Value FROM ItemItemsets II1, ItemItemsets II2
WHERE II1.IDItemset=II2.IDItemset
AND II1.DataElement='Item' AND II1.Value='val'
AND II2.DataElement='Item1';
(c) Query on the itemset-based physical representation (SQL)
```

We also considered a different approach, based on the independence assumption of items. Given the support of all items (i.e., patterns of length one), the support of a generic pattern X can be estimated by computing the joint probability of all items composing it (i.e., as the product of the supports of all the items in X). Experimental results show that this approach is less accurate than the former.

EXPERIMENTAL RESULTS

A set of experiments on real and synthetic XML datasets were performed to evaluate efficiency and effectiveness of schema and instance patterns. We performed our experiments on schema and instance patterns including at most two items. In particular, the itemset-based physical representation includes itemsets with one or two items, while the rule-based physical representation includes both one-element rules (i.e., with an empty head) and two-element rules (one in the body and one in the head). The experiments show that patterns composed by at most two items yield quite accurate answers for the classes of very simple queries introduced in this chapter.

Table 1 describes the XML datasets considered in our experiments. DBLP is a real-life dataset, downloaded from Ley (2005), where instance patterns have been extracted by defining the article element as transaction root. TPC-H is a suite of synthetic datasets generated from the TPC-H relational tables saved in XML format (TPC-H,

2005). In this case, the record element has been defined as transaction root.

The experiments have been performed on a 3.2GHz Pentium IV system with 2GB RAM, running Debian Linux 3.1. To validate execution time on instance patterns, queries have been performed by means of three well-known XQuery engines: the Monet DB (Boncz et al., 2006), Saxon-B8.4 (Kay, 2006), and Berkeley DB XML (Sleepycat Software, 2006). For itemset and association rule extraction, we use a publicly available version of Apriori (Agrawal et al., 1994) downloaded from Goethals and Zaki (2004).

Schema Patterns

In this section, we analyze the characteristics of the probabilistic schemata that have been extracted from the TPC-H datasets (Table 1) and discuss appropriate values of the p quality index. In this case, where the main issue consists in identifying all schema patterns, instance patterns have been extracted without enforcing any support threshold.

On all the considered XML datasets (part, orders, lineitem), exact schema patterns ($p = 1$) have been found. The exact schema patterns highlight the already known functional dependencies between primary keys and all the other elements, and between candidate keys and all the other elements. However, also previously unknown functional dependencies have been found.

Some of the previously unknown exact schema patterns are the following:

Table 1. Datasets characteristics

Dataset	Number of Transactions	File size (MB)	Description
Part-250	50000	15MB	Part table in XML (0.25 scale factor)
Orders-250	375000	129MB	Order table in XML (0.25 scale factor)
Lineitem-250	1499579	773MB	Lineitem table in XML (0.25 scale factor)
DBLP	618145	259MB	DBLP XML records (year 2005)

brand → manufacturer
order-clerk → ship-priority
order-customer → ship-priority
order-priority → ship-priority
lineitem-ship-date → linestatus

All these patterns highlight functional dependencies in the data, which may be exploited to optimize query computation. Also probabilistic schema patterns with a high value of p ($p > 0.95$) have been obtained:

Probabilistic schema pattern	p
lineitem-receipt-date → linestatus	0.996
lineitem-returnflag → linestatus	0.987
orderkey → linestatus	0.987
lineitem-commit-date → linestatus	0.981
Order-date → order-status	0.978

These probabilistic schema patterns highlight "quasifunctional" dependencies, that is, dependencies which hold with very few exceptions. Experimental results highlight that "useful" schema patterns are characterized by a very high value of the p quality index ($p > 0.9$).

Instance Patterns

In this section, we analyze the effectiveness of instance patterns as a summarized representation of an XML dataset. In particular, we considered (1) the compression factor of the instance pattern representation, (2) the query execution time and accuracy of the returned result set, and (3) the scalability of the approach.

Compression Factor

To analyze the compression provided by the XML instance pattern representation, we compared the size of the original XML dataset with the size of the XML pattern set when varying the minimum support threshold. We considered both XML rule-based and XML itemset-based physical representations. Since XML is a rather verbose information representation format, the size of the relational tables for instance patterns (not reported here) is obviously significantly smaller than that of the corresponding XML pattern representation. To analyze the compression provided by the instance pattern representation, we define the compression factor as:

(size(original dataset) - size(instance pattern set)) / size(original dataset)

Figure 21(a) compares the size (in MB) of the rule and itemset-based XML physical representations to the size of the original order TPC-H dataset when varying the (absolute) minimum support threshold. It also reports the corresponding compression factor. Figure 21(b) plots the number of extracted rules and itemsets for the same support configurations. The y-axis of both diagrams is in log scale.

The instance pattern representation is more compact than the original dataset for most minimum support thresholds. Since the number of rules grows more rapidly than the number of itemsets, for very low support values (e.g., below 5 in the orders TPC-H dataset), only the itemset-based physical representation provides a compact representation of the original dataset (positive compression factor value). Similar results (not reported here) have been obtained for all the considered datasets.

Query Execution Time

We compared query execution on instance patterns and on the original dataset by considering execution time, as well as recall and precision of the obtained result. Recall measures the fraction of data in the complete query result which is actually returned by querying instance patterns:

$Recall = |S_{ip} \cap S_d| / |S_d|$

Figure 21. TPC-H order dataset: effect of the minimum support threshold on the size of the instance pattern set

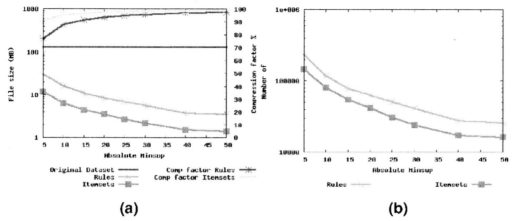

(a)　　　　　　　　　　　　　　**(b)**

Table 2. Benchmarking queries

Query	Class	Dataset	Query
Q1	select query	orders-250	select the values of the order status element where customer key is equal 370.
Q2	count query	orders-250	count the number of orders for customer 370.
Q3	select, group, and count query	DBLP	For each conference count how many of the accepted papers have been written by "NameX SurnameX".

where S_d is the dataset returned by querying the original dataset, while S_{ip} is the dataset obtained by querying instance patterns. Precision measures the fraction of the returned data which correctly matches the query:

$$Precision = |S_{ip} \cap S_d| / |S_{ip}|$$

Both measures take values in the range [0%,100%]. Instance patterns are characterized by 100% precision for very simple queries, while recall depends on the support threshold the instance patterns have been generated with.

Our experiments cover some significant kinds of very simple queries (select and count queries). The considered queries are reported in Table 2. We

have performed the queries on the XML datasets (original XML document and XML pattern representation) by means of three XQuery engines: Saxon-B8.4 (Kay, 2006), the Monet DB (Boncz et al., 2006), and Berkeley DB XML (Sleepycat Software, 2006). However, since the Monet DB query engine has achieved the best overall performance, in this section, we only report its results. Comparable results have been obtained for the other engines. Queries on the relational pattern representation have been performed by means of the Oracle 9i relational database. Figure 22 through Figure 24 show execution time and recall for the queries reported in Table 2. The values of execution time have been represented in log scale. All queries have been performed without defining indices on the corresponding datasets.

The recall value for instance patterns strongly depends on the frequency of the searched data. Only frequent events (i.e., events with frequency above the minimum support threshold in the original dataset) are represented into the instance pattern set. Hence, infrequent pairs *(element,value)* cannot be retrieved. In particular, if an element domain is small, high recall may be achieved when instance patterns are extracted with adequate support thresholds (e.g., query Q1 in Figure 22). Differently, when the element domain is large, recall is on average low. Consider, for example, query Q3 (Figure 24). By querying instance patterns, the system can only retrieve conferences frequently associated with *(author,"NameX SurnameX")*. Hence, the conferences where less than minimum support articles written by *"NameX SurnameX"* have been published cannot be retrieved.

Execution time depends both on query type and exploited indices. Current experiments have been performed without indexing XML documents and patterns. The effect of indexing on the execution time is discussed in the Scalability subsection. We first consider a select query (Q1) where the predicate selectivity is around 0.16%. Results are reported in Figure 22. Since no indices are defined, one full scan of the dataset is needed. The XQuery engine scans the original dataset and selects data satisfying the constraints. Similarly, when instance patterns are used, one full scan of the pattern set is needed. Hence, file size has a significant impact on query execution time, while predicate selectivity only slightly affects it. In Figure 22, the performance of the query on the relational representation of instance patterns is also reported. Since this relational representation still provides a significant performance improvement with respect to state of the art XQuery engines, this query may outperform the same query on the corresponding XML representation by an order of magnitude. Similar results have been obtained for all considered queries.

To answer select and count queries (Q2) on the original dataset, the XQuery engine scans all data and counts the instances satisfying the selection predicate. When the instance pattern set is considered, each instance provides, by means of its support value, the precomputation of the query result. Hence, it is possible to answer the query by retrieving the first instance pattern satisfying the selection predicate. In the worst case, when the first useful pattern is near the end of the instance pattern set, the XQuery engine may need a full scan of the set (see Figure 23).

Group and count query (Q3) performance is reported in Figure 24. Queries on the original dataset require a full scan, followed by grouping and counting on each group. When instance patterns are used, the XQuery engine selects one instance pattern for each group by performing a full scan of the instance pattern set and exploits the support value to answer the query. Since no grouping operation is needed (each instance pattern already represents a group with its cardinality), the contribution of the full scan operation dominates the execution time.

Scalability

To evaluate the scalability of the proposed approach with respect to the size of the original dataset, we exploited the TPC-H orders XML file. In particular, a set of order XML files has been generated by varying the scale factor parameter of the dbgen code (TPC-H, 2005). The order XML file size ranges from 5MB (scale factor 0.01) to 5GB (scale factor 10). Rules and itemsets have been extracted with minimum support threshold 5.

Scalability experiments have been performed on (a) non-indexed XML documents and (b) indexed XML documents. We report performance results for the Monet DB (the most efficient and scalable) and for Berkeley DB XML (the only one implementing indices).

Figure 25 reports the execution time for the Monet DB and Berkeley DB XML. We considered query Q2 (see Table 2) as a representative example.

Figure 22. Q1: Select query

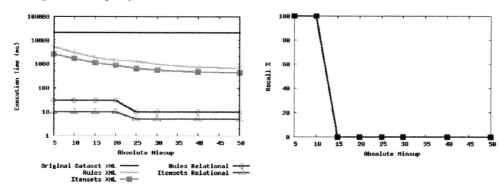

Figure 23. Q2: Select and count query

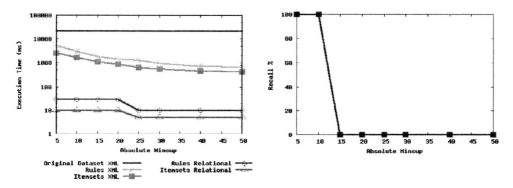

Figure 24. Q3: Group by query

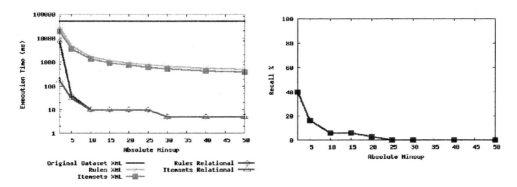

With the Monet DB, the advantage of our summarized representation becomes evident when the size of the original XML document exceeds 1GB (scale factor 2). In this case, our summarized representation allows us to perform queries that could not be completed on the original (not summarized) XML document. Hence, by accepting a slight approximation in the completeness of the query answer, our approach allows us to extend the query power of XML query engines. Furthermore, on average the XML itemset-based physical representation yields an 85% reduction in query execution time.

Since Berkeley DB XML requires more memory than the Monet DB, it was not possible to perform the same query on original XML documents larger than 500MB (scale factor 1) on our workstation. However, by appropriately trimming the support threshold, the size of the summarized XML file may always be kept lower than 400MB, even when the original XML document is 5GB. In this case, also Berkeley DB XML may be exploited to query summarized data.

We have analyzed the effect of indices on query execution time by using Berkeley DB XML (BDBXML). Performance is reported in Figure 25(b). Appropriate indices improve query performance on both the original XML document and its instance pattern representations. The comparison of query performance on the *indexed* original XML document and on its *non-indexed* summarized representation shows that our representation is always more effective than indices in reducing execution time.

Long Patterns Support Estimation

We performed experiments to evaluate the accuracy of the support estimation formula for patterns with more than two items (*EstimatedSup*) proposed earlier in the Long Patterns Support Estimation subsection. In particular, we evaluated on the TPC-H dataset the number of patterns of length N for which the support estimated by *EstimatedSup* corresponds to the real support of the pattern. We used the following formula to estimate the number of errors:

$$error = \frac{\#\ of\ wrong\ estimations}{\#\ of\ frequent\ patterns\ of\ length\ N}$$

We exploited the set of two-item frequent patterns to estimate the support of all frequent patterns of length three. Figure 26 shows the error behavior when varying the minimum support threshold.

Globally, the average number of incorrect estimations is about 19%. Hence, by using only patterns with two items, accurate answers can be obtained also for counting queries including more than two elements. We also measured the average difference between actual and estimated supports when the estimate is not correct (i.e.,

Figure 25. Execution time on the TPC-H order dataset when varying the scale factor

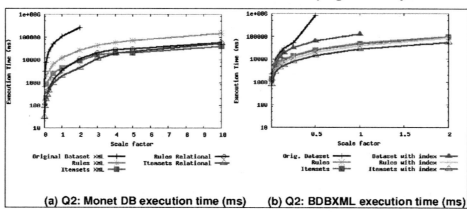

actual support≠*EstimatedSup*). In this case, on average, the estimated support is about twice the actual support.

A PROTOTYPE TOOL

We have built a first prototype environment implemented in Java to demonstrate the effectiveness of our approach. It is basically formed by two components, used to extract instance patterns from XML documents, and by a graphical interface which allows the user to pose very simple queries and to obtain an approximate answer. The first component visualizes the DTD of an XML document in a graph-based representation. The user chooses the elements (the transaction root and all the other elements) to be included in the extraction process of instance patterns by indicating also where stemming, stopwords, and discretization procedures are to be applied. The native XML document is then prepared for processing by the Apriori algorithm, and instance and schema patterns are mined. The second component stores the output of the miner into an Oracle database or in an XML document by using the physical representations discussed earlier.

The graphical interface supports the user in querying the extracted knowledge by writing very simple queries. The system automatically composes the corresponding SQL queries to be applied to the MySQL database of patterns, or the XML queries to be applied to the XML pattern physical representation.

CONCLUSION AND FUTURE WORK

In this chapter, we have proposed a graph-based formalism for specifying patterns on XML documents, and discussed how to exploit patterns to provide intensional answers to user queries. Experimental results show both the effectiveness of schema patterns in highlighting the schema properties of XML documents, and the efficiency of instance patterns in answering queries. Instance patterns provide a summarized representation of XML documents which allowed us to overcome current limitations of current XML query engines on the size of queried XML documents.

As an on-going work, we are considering extensions of our language to deal with more complex queries and patterns (e.g., containing negative information and multiple paths both in the thin and thick part). We are also formalizing query rewriting rules to seamlessly perform queries on the different instance pattern representations.

Figure 26. Number of estimation errors when varying the minimum support threshold

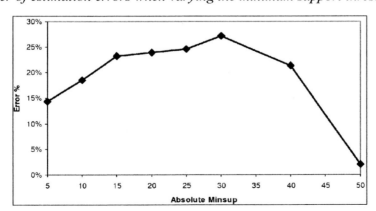

REFERENCES

Abiteboul, S., Quass, D., McHugh, J., Widom, J., & Wiener, J. (1997). The Lorel query language for semistructured data. *International Journal on Digital Libraries, 1*(1).

Agrawal, R., & Srikant, R. (1994). Fast algorithms for mining association rules in large data-bases. In J. B. Bocca, M. Jarke, & C. Zaniolo (Eds.), *International Conference on Very Large Data Bases* (pp. 487-499). Morgan Kaufmann.

Arenas, M., & Libkin, L. (2004). A normal form for XML documents. *ACM Transactions on Database Systems, 29*(1), 195-232.

Augurusa, E., Braga, D., Campi, A., & Ceri, S. (2003). Design and implementation of a graphical interface to XQuery. In *Proceedings of the ACM Symposium on Applied Computing* (pp. 1163-1167). ACM Press.

Baralis, E., Garza, P., Quintarelli, E., & Tanca, L. (2006). *Answering XML queries by means of data summaries* (Tech. Rep. No. 2006.43). Milano, Italy: Politecnico di Milano, Dipartimento di Elettronica e Informazione.

Boncz, P., Flokstra, J., Grust, T., van Keulen, M., Manegold, S., Mullender, S., Nes, N., Rittinger, J., Teubner, J., & Zhang, Y. (2006). *MonetDB/XQuery*. Retrieved June 13, 2007, from http://monetdb.cwi.nl/XQuery/

Boncz, P. A., Grust, T., Manegold, S., Rittinger, J., & Teubner, J. (2005). *Pathfinder: Relational XQuery over multi-gigabyte XML inputs in interactive time* (Tech. Rep. No. INS-E0503). Amsterdam: CWI.

Braga, D., Campi, A., & Ceri, S. (2005). XQBE (XQuery by example): A visual interface to the standard XML query language. *ACM Transaction on Database Systems, 30*(2), 398-443.

Buneman, P., Davidson, S., Fan, W., Hara, C., & Tan, W. (2001a). Reasoning about keys for XML. In G. Ghelli & G. Grahne (Eds.), *8ᵗʰ International Workshop on Database Programming Languages* (pp. 133-148). Springer-Verlag. Lecture Notes in Computer Science 2397.

Buneman, P., Davidson, S. B., Hillebrand, G. G., & Suciu, D. (1996). A query language and optimization techniques for unstructured data. In H. V. Jagadish & I. S. Mumick (Eds.), *ACM SIGMOD International Conference on Management of Data* (pp. 505-516). ACM Press.

Buneman, P., Fan, W., Siméon, J., & Weinstein, S. (2001b). Constraints for semistructured data and XML. *ACM SIGMOD Record, 30*(1), 47-54.

Ceri, S., Comai, S., Damiani, E., Fraternali, P., Paraboschi, S., & Tanca, L. (1999). XML-GL: A graphical languaguage for querying and restructuring XML documents. *Computer Networks, 31*(1-2), 1171-1188.

Chung, C.-W., Min, J.-K., & Shim, K. (2002). Apex: An adaptive path index for xml data. In M. J. Franklin, B. Moon, & A. Ailamaki (Eds.), *ACM SIGMOD International Conference on Management of Data* (pp. 121-132). ACM Press.

Consens, M. P., & Mendelzon, A. O. (1990). Graphlog: A visual formalism for real life recursion. In *Proceedings of the ACM SIGACT-SIGMOD-SIGART Symposium on Principles of Database Systems* (pp. 404-416). ACM Press.

Damiani, E., Oliboni, B., Quintarelli, E., & Tanca, L. (2003). *Modeling semistructured data by using graph-based constraints* (Tech. Rep. No. 27/03). Milano, Italy: Politecnico di Milano, Dipartimento di Elettronica e Informazione.

Deutch, A., Fernandez, M., Florescu, D., Levy, A., & Suciu, D. (1998). *XML-QL: A query language for XML*. Paper presented at QL'98–W3C Workshop on Query Languages.

Elmasari, R., & Navathe, S. B. (1994). *Fundamentals of database systems* (2nd ed.). Benjamin/ Cummings.

Goethals, B., & Zaki, M. J. (2004). *Advances in frequent itemset mining implementation: Report on FIMI'03. SIGKDD Explorations Newsletter,* 6(1), 109-117.

Grahne, G., & Zhu, J. (2002). Discovering approximate keys in XML data. In *Proceedings of the 11th International Conference on Information and Knowledge Management* (pp. 453-460). ACM Press.

Harinarayan, V., Rajaraman, A., & Ullman, J. D. (1996). Implementing data cubes efficiently. In H. V. Jagadish & I. S. Mumick (Eds.), *1996 ACM SIGMOD International Conference on Management of Data* (pp. 205-216). ACM Press.

He, H., & Yang, J. (2004). Multiresolution indexing of XML for frequent queries. In *Proceedings of the 20th International Conference on Data Engineering* (pp. 683-694). IEEE Computer Society.

Huhtala, Y., Karkkainen, J., Porkka, P., & Toivonen, H. (1999). TANE: An efficient algorithm for discovering functional and approximate dependencies. *The Computer Journal, 42*(2), 100-111.

Kay, M. (2006). *Saxon: The XSLT and XQuery processor.* Retrieved June 13, 2007, from http:// saxon.sourceforge.net/

Ley, M. (2005). *DBLP bibliography server.* Retrieved June 13, 2007, from http://dblp.uni-trier. de/xml

Merialdo, P. (2003). *SIGMOD RECORD in XML.* Retrieved June 13, 2007, from http://www.acm. org/sigmod/record/xml

Milner, R. (1980). A calculus of communicating system. *Lecture Notes in Computer Science, 92.* Berlin: Springer-Verlag.

Motro, A. (1989). Using integrity constraints to provide intensional answers to relational queries. In P. M. G. Apers & G. Wiederhold (Eds.), *Fifteenth International Conference on Very Large Data Bases* (pp. 237-245). Morgan Kaufmann.

Papakonstantinou, Y., Garcia-Molina, H., & Widom, J. (1995). Object exchange across heterogeneous information sources. In P. S. Yu & A. L. P. Chen (Eds.), *Eleventh International Conference on Data Engineering* (pp. 251-260). IEEE Computer Society.

Paredaens, J., Peelman, P., & Tanca, L. (1995). G-Log: A declarative graphical query language. *IEEE Transactions on Knowledge and Data Engineering, 7*(3), 436-453.

Park, D. (1980). Concurrency and automata on infinite sequences. *Lecture Notes in Computer Science, 104,* 167-183. Berlin: Springer-Verlag.

Pavlov, D., Mannila, H., & Smyth, P. (2001). *Beyond independence: Probabilistic models for query approximation on binary transaction data* (Tech. Rep. No. 09/01). University of California Irvine, Information and Computer Science.

Porter, M. F. (1980). An algorithm for suffix stripping. *Readings in Information Retrieval, 14*(3), 130-137. Morgan Kaufmann.

Qun, C., Lim, A., & Ong, K. W. (2003). D(k)-index: An adaptive structural summary for graph-structured data. In *Proceedings of the 2003 ACM SIGMOD International Conference on Management of Data* (pp. 134-144). ACM Press.

Sleepycat Software. (2006). *Berkeley DB XML.* Retrieved June 13, 2007, from http://www.sleepy-cat.com/products/bdbxml.html/

Staples, J., & Robinson, P. J. (1986). Unification of quantified terms. In R. M. K. J. H. Fasel (Ed.), Graph reduction. *Lecture Notes in Computer Science, 279,* 426-450. Springer-Verlag.

TPC-H. (2005). *The TPC benchmark H. Transaction Processing Performance Council*. Retrieved June 13, 2007, from http://www.tpc.org/tpch/default.asp

World Wide Web Consortium. (1998). *Extensible markup language (XML) 1.0*. Retrieved June 13, 2007, from http://www.w3C.org/TR/REC-xml/

World Wide Web Consortium. (1999). *XML Path Language XPath Version 1.0*. Retrieved June 13, 2007, from http://www.w3C.org/TR/xpath.html

World Wide Web Consortium. (2002). *XQuery: An XML Query Language*. Retrieved June 13, 2007, from http://www.w3C.org/TR/REC-xml/

ENDNOTES

[1] Note that XML documents are here tree-like structures (and not generic graphs) because, following the so-called "literal semantics", we do not interpret referencing attributes as pointers.

[2] We recall that we use references formalisms in this chapter. Thus, since arcs can only represent containment, the result tag contains a copy of the required information.

[3] N_{Aggr} represents aggregate nodes.

[4] N_{Gr} represents grouping nodes.

Chapter IV
On the Usage of Structural Information in Constrained Semi-Supervised Clustering of XML Documents

Eduardo Bezerra
CEFET/RJ, Federal Center of Technological Education CSF, Brazil

Geraldo Xexéo
Programa de Sistemas, COPPE, UFRJ, Institute of Mathematics, UFRJ, Brazil

Marta Mattoso
Programa de Sistemas, COPPE/UFRJ, Brazil

ABSTRACT

In this chapter, we consider the problem of constrained clustering of documents. We focus on documents that present some form of structural information, in which prior knowledge is provided. Such structured data can guide the algorithm to a better clustering model. We consider the existence of a particular form of information to be clustered: textual documents that present a logical structure represented in XML format. Based on this consideration, we present algorithms that take advantage of XML metadata (structural information), thus improving the quality of the generated clustering models. This chapter also addresses the problem of inconsistent constraints and defines algorithms that eliminate inconsistencies, also based on the existence of structural information associated to the XML document collection.

INTRODUCTION

The problem of semisupervised clustering (SSC) has been attracting a lot of attention in the research community. This problem can be stated as follows: given a set of objects X and some prior knowledge about these objects, the clustering algorithm must produce a partition of X guided by this prior knowledge. According to Grira, Crucianu, and Boujemaa (2004), there are two approaches for semisupervised clustering: *distance-based* and *constraint-based*. In distance-based semisupervised clustering, the prior knowledge about the data is used to modify the distance metric or the objective function in order to make distant objects farther and to make close objects closer (Chang & Yeung, 2004; Xing, Ng, Jordan, & Russell, 2002). In constraint-based semisupervised clustering, the prior knowledge is used to guide the clustering algorithm to a solution that reflects the user needs; this prior knowledge is usually in the form of *must-link constraints* and *cannot-link constraints* defined on the objects to be clustered (Basu, Banerjee, & Mooney, 2002, 2004; Wagstaff & Cardie, 2000). A must-link constraint $ML(o_i, o_j)$ states that objects o_i and o_j must be in the same cluster, whereas a cannot-link constraint $CL(o_i, o_j)$ states that o_i and o_j must be put in separate clusters. There are also hybrid approaches, which try both to learn a metric and to force the algorithm to obey the user-provided constraints (Basu, Bilenko, & Mooney, 2004; Bilenko, Basu, & Mooney, 2004).

Most semisupervised clustering algorithms are extensions of the well-known K-Means partitional clustering algorithm (MacQueen, 1967), although there are also approaches for hierarchical algorithms (Davidson & Ravi, 2005b). Experimental results show that the quality of the clustering models produced by these algorithms increases with the amount of provided prior knowledge. Nevertheless, despite the huge success of the semisupervised approach for clustering in recent years, there are still some open problems, especially when it comes to clustering of semistructured documents. Below, we summarize some of these problems.

- Associated to the characteristic of using external information, there is a first problem with current semisupervised clustering algorithms: they assume that the user is supposed to provide a significant amount of prior knowledge to allow the algorithm to produce a clustering model of a reasonable quality. However, in complex application domains (like textual document clustering), the user has to provide an amount of constraints that reaches the hundreds. Certainly, this is not a practical scenario. Usually, the user does not want (or is not able) to provide such a large amount of prior knowledge, particularly in an online system. Therefore, a first open problem in semisupervised clustering is to define approaches to reduce the amount of necessary constraints to be provided by the user.

- Another issue that we identified in current semisupervised clustering algorithms is that they are not prepared to take advantage of metadata. Thus, they require the provided constraints to be in the form $ML(o_i, o_j)$ or $CL(o_i, o_j)$, where o_i and o_j are two objects in the collection to be clustered. However, assuming that there is structural information associated with the collection of objects, the constraints could also be defined at such a level of abstraction. In other words, it should be possible for the user to define constraints in which the component objects are extracted from the metadata associated with the collection.

In addition, the amount of document collections associated to some form of structural information, particularly in XML (Bray, Paoli, & Sperberg-McQueen, 2000), is growing at a fast rate. The idea of the *Semantic Web*, for example, in which the Internet can be automatically navigated by software agents, assumes that data in this environment are in XML format. Another domain where textual documents are increasingly growing is in bioinformatics. Huge databases of textual information about proteins and amino acids, along with repositories of technical articles, have annotations or metadata information represented in XML. Frequently, these databases also present metadata in the form of ontologies and taxonomies (e.g., the *Gene Ontology* and the *Medical Subjects Headings*). Furthermore, several existing document collections are being converted to XML format (Chu, 2000). Considering that the semisupervised clustering task is going to be used to organize these XML document repositories, the possibility of using structural information to guide or restrict the clustering process cannot be ignored. Hence, the problem of how to incorporate structural information (coming from metadata) in the clustering process is highly relevant.

We take as a starting point existing algorithms for semisupervised clustering documents. We present a *constrained semisupervised clustering approach for XML documents*, and we deal with the following main concern: how can a user take advantage of structural information related to a collection of XML documents in order to define constraints to be used in the clustering of these documents? The mission of this chapter is to discuss in detail the following aspects:

- To show how to extend the possibilities of the user to define constraints over the objects to be clustered by defining a representation of XML documents that enables this user to specify constraints over the *structural information* of the documents. The representation we adopt is relevant to several domains of applications that work with semistructured textual documents in general, and text-centric XML documents in particular.
- To define ways of using the same structural XML information to expand the set of constraints defined by the user; this minimizes the overload on the user side with respect to the amount of prior knowledge that he/she must provide to the system in order to obtain a clustering model of reasonable quality.
- Another goal we have in this chapter it to describe ways of dealing with an *inconsis-*

tent set of constraints, in which there are the constraints $ML(o_i, o_j)$ and $CL(o_j, o_j)$, for some pair of objects o_j and o_j. We show that this problem is of practical interest and propose some solutions for it.

This chapter is organized as follows. We first describe some preliminary information, give some definitions, and describe related work. In the second section, we detail our approach for semisupervised clustering of XML documents. In the following section, we describe some issues we think are possible avenues of future research on the application of semisupervised clustering to structural information. Finally, in the last section, we give some concluding remarks.

BACKGROUND

In this section, we describe related work. We divide this description according to several aspects that we explore in this chapter. In Section 2.1, we provide some definitions about the terminology we use throughout the chapter. In Section 2.2, we describe some constraint-based algorithms for SSC in the literature. We also discuss some problems raised when the set of constraints provided to a semisupervised clustering algorithm is inconsistent. In Section 2.3, we finally. In Section 2.4, we describe attempts in the literature to assign a weight to each user-provided constraint.

Terminology

We use the letters r, s, t, and so forth to denote constraints. We use d_i and d_j to denote documents in a collection. Finally, we use v_a, v_b, v_c, v_d, and so on to refer to the values of a multivalued attribute att_k.

We define the *centroid* of a cluster of documents as the vector representative of such cluster. Given a cluster C, its centroid, denoted by $\mu(C)$, is the sum of all the vectors corresponding to the documents within C.

We use $ML(o_i, o_j)$ to denote a must-link constraint between objects o_i, o_j. Analogously, we use $CL(o_i, o_j)$ to denote a must-link constraint between objects o_i, o_j.

We say that a constraint r *refers* to a pair of documents d_i and d_j whenever they are used in the definition of the unordered pair corresponding to r. In other words, the constraint r refers to documents d_i and d_j if either $r = ML(o_i, o_j)$ or $r = CL(o_i, o_j)$. Analogously, we say that constraint r is referred by both d_i and d_j.

Constraint Based Algorithms for SSC

An inconsistent set of constraints is characterized by the (implicit or explicit) existence of one or more constraints (r1, r2), where we have $r1 = ML(d_i, d_j)$ and $r2 = CL(d_i, d_j)$. In Section 2.2.1, we present two SSC algorithms in the literature and describe how the existence of inconsistency can prevent them from finding a good clustering model. After that, in Section 2.2.2, we discuss the problems that these algorithms address when the set of constraints is inconsistent.

It is important to note that the SSC algorithms we describe in this section are extensions of classical K-Means (MacQueen, 1967). In K-Means, the main goal is to define K centroids (one for each cluster) by locally optimizing an objective function.

COP-KMeans and PC-KMeans

A representative algorithm in the constraint based approach to SSC is COP-KMeans (Wagstaff, Cardie, Rogers, & Schröedl, 2001). This algorithm is a variant of classical K-Means. It incorporates previous knowledge (in the form of constraints) to the clustering process. In its initialization step, COP-KMeans selects seeds (initial centroids)

randomly. However, as each seed is selected, the constraints referring to this seed are respected (not violated) by the algorithm. In other words, given a seed o_s, all the objects o_i, such that there exists a constraint in the form $ML(o_s, o_i)$, are allocated to the same cluster as o_s. In addition, these objects o_i cannot be assigned as the centroids of new clusters. After the initialization phase, COP-KMeans iteratively runs the two following steps:

- Assignment of each object o_j to the cluster C, such that μ_C is the closer centroid to o_j and no constraint (be it a must-link or a cannot-link) is violated.
- Updating of the centroid of each cluster C_i:
$$\mu_i = \sum_{x \in C_i} x.$$

It is relevant to note the inability of COP-KMeans to deal with inconsistent information. When the set of constraints provided is inconsistent, this algorithm simply stops running and reports that it was unable to produce a clustering model.

In Basu et al. (2004), the PC-KMeans algorithm is presented. This algorithm is another extension of K-Means that considers must-link and cannot-link constraints. Like Kim and Lee (2002) and Xing et al. (2002), the authors of PC-KMeans also use pair-wise constraints to train the distance metric. In PC-KMeans, the seed initialization occurs in two phases. First, the set R of user provided constraints is augmented to produce the set Closure(R). This is done by applying the following steps:

1. Add all the must-link constraints in R to Closure(R).
2. If constraints $ML(d_i, d_j)$ and $ML(d_j, d_k)$ are in R, then add the constraint $ML(d_i, d_k)$ to Closure(R).
3. If constraints $ML(d_i, d_j)$ and $CL(d_j, d_k)$ are in R, then add the constraint $CL(d_i, d_k)$ to Closure(R).

4. Repeat Steps 2 and 3 until there are no more constraints to be added to the set Closure(R).

From the steps above, we can see that PC-KMeans computes the *transitive closure* of the set of user-provided constraints. After augmenting the set R of user-provided constraints, PC-KMeans proceeds to the second phase in the initialization. In this phase, the algorithm forms several partitions by applying the following rule: objects that participate in a must-link constraint are put in the same partition. These partitions are then used to compute the initial centroids. The centroids are computed by interpreting the objects as vectors and by computing the average vector of the objects in each partition. Hence, instead of selecting the seeds in a random way (as the COP-KMeans algorithm does), PC-KMeans uses the user-provided constraints to select good seeds for the initialization.

The advantage of applying this procedure of transitive closure is that the amount of constraints that are passed as input to the SSC algorithm is greater than the amount provided by the user. This is a good thing, since quality of the clustering results of a SSC algorithm improve as the amount of constraints provided to it also increases. Indeed, in Basu et al. (2004), the authors of PC-KMeans show through empirical experiments that PC-KMeans generates clustering models that are much better than COP-KMeans. One of their conclusions is that this improvement is due to the initialization procedure adopted by PC-KMeans, which augments the user-provided set of constraints by applying the transitive closure. This conclusion is in conformity with the fact that partitional clustering algorithms (like K-Means and its variants) are very dependent on the initial seeds.

Inconsistent Sets of Constraints

From the above discussion, we can see that both SCOP-KMeans and PC-KMeans assume the user-provided constraints are consistent. However, in practical situations and for several reasons, the constraints provided by the user can be inconsistent. In the particular case of PC-KMeans, the application of the transitive closure procedure is only effective when the input set of constraints is consistent. Consequently, the initialization procedure of PC-KMeans only works if the user-provided constraints are consistent. If these constraints are not consistent, the use of the transitive closure operation in the initialization process will generate a new set of constraints even more inconsistent, and the improvement in clustering quality would certainly not be achieved. This drawback of PC-KMeans naturally raises the following question: can inconsistent constraints be used in a SSC task, in such a way that the results are better when compared to the situation in which no constraints are used? This is one of the main topics in this chapter, and in the third section, we describe our approach to solve this problem.

Another aspect that we consider in this chapter is how to use weights assigned to the constraints to resolve possible inconsistencies. In Bezerra, Xexéo, and Mattoso (2006), we propose a semisupervised clustering algorithm that work on XML documents, MAC-KMeans. Like COP-KMeans and PC-KMeans, our algorithm also assumes that user-provided constraints are consistent. In fact, this is a general assumption in the field of SSC. In Section 3.3, we move in the direction of removing such assumption by proposing some algorithms to remove inconsistency in the set of user-provided constraints before passing it to our SSC algorithm.

Defining Constraints Beyond Document-Level

Most works on semisupervised constrained document clustering consider only one type of constraint, the document-level constraints. A document-level constraint is defined over two documents and states that they must be put in the same or in different clusters. The algorithms COP-KMeans and SP-KMeans (see Section 2.2) are examples of algorithms that process document-level constraints.

However, it has been recognized by some authors that it is desirable to allow the user to define constraints in more expressive forms, not only at the document-level. This certainly gives the user more flexibility to state its clustering needs. One of the works that follow this direction is Davidson and Ravi (2005a), in which two new types of constraints are defined, the ε-constraint and the δ-constraint. The ε-constraint enforces that each instance x in a cluster must have another instance y in the same cluster such that the distance between x and y is at most ε. The δ-constraint enforces that every instance in a cluster must be at a distance of at least δ from every instance in every other cluster. Both constraints specify background information on the minimum distance between the clusters/objects.

In Klein, Kamvar, and Manning (2002), the authors present a method for clustering in the presence of supervisory information, given as pairwise instance constraints. Their approach is to allow instance-level constraints to have space-level inductive implications. They are able to successfully incorporate constraints for a wide range of datasets. They also show that their method improves on COP-KMeans. Although this work does not define a new type of constraint, they use a technique to infer space-level constraints from the user-provided constraints. We also use inference of constraints in our work, but using information in the structure (metadata) of the collection of XML documents to be clustered.

In Section 3.1, we describe our approach to enable the user to define constraints at the metadata level; that is, the user can define constraints using information found in the schema of the collection of XML documents. What we do is to define a representation for XML documents that enables the user to define must-link and cannot-link constraints both in the document level (as is already possible in some works) and in the *metadata level*. We also devise a method to automatically infer document-level constraints from user-provided metadata-level constraints.

Defining Weights for Constraints

Most works on SSC assume that the user-provided constraints have equal importance, or that the user can also provide weights for each constraint she/he defines. Constraints that are considered to be equally important are called *hard constraints*. On the other hand, there are also other works that consider *soft constraints*, that is, constraints assigned to a weight. This weight corresponds to the degree of reliability in this constraint. Therefore, while a hard constraint has the form (d_i, d_j), a soft constraint has the form (d_i, d_j, w_{ij}), where w_{ij} is the weight associated with the pair (d_i, d_j).

One work that uses soft constraints is Davidson and Ravi (2005a). In their formulation of a soft constraint model, Kleinberg and Tardos (1999) allow the definition of constraints in the object level. Furthermore, they assume that each constraint states that its components have the same label (which means that they must be put in the same cluster). Consequently, the constraint model proposed in Davidson and Ravi (2005a) only considers must-link constraints. They incorporate the constraints in the objective function of the clustering algorithm by computing a penalty that is proportional to the weights of the violated constraints. The approach used in this work for adding constraints to the clustering process uses a linear programming technique, which makes it computationally expensive.

In Wagstaff and Cardie (2000), the author of COP-KMeans proposes an extension to it, named SCOP-KMeans (Soft COP-KMeans). The SCOP-KMeans algorithm considers soft constraints, whose weights vary between -1 and +1 for both must-link and cannot-link constraints. Another extension of COP-KMeans is PC-KMeans (Basu et al., 2004). This algorithm also uses must-link and cannot-link soft constraints and its definition permits the definition of variable weights for constraint. However, this information must be provided to the algorithm along with the constraints.

USING XML METADATA IN SEMISUPERVISED CLUSTERING

In this section, we cover several aspects concerning the use of structural information on SSC of XML documents. In Section 3.1, we present our representation of XML documents that allows us to take advantage of their structure (i.e., their metadata). Section 3.2 describes our approach to use structural information automatically generate document-level constraints from constraints that the user defines on the metadata level. Finally, in Section 3.3, we describe some algorithms to deal with the existence of inconsistency in the set of user provided constraints.

Considering Both Structure and Content of XML Documents

There are several SSC algorithms that work only on the textual contents of XML documents to be clustered. However, clustering using only the textual content ignores any metadata information associated to the XML documents. However, the adequate cluster for a XML document may be highly correlated to the structural information (i.e., metadata) available inside the document. This fact motivated us to use the *dual representation for XML documents* that we describe in this

section. This representation is important because in our approach we need to query both structure (metadata) and textual content of the XML documents in the collection to be clustered. A typical XML document that we consider in our work is presented in Figure 1.

In XML literature, XML documents are categorized in two types: data-centric and document-centric. Data-centric XML documents are documents with a regular structure and typically represent relational data. Document-centric documents have a less regular structure, with portions of mixed content for XML elements. In this chapter, we consider a somewhat hybrid type of XML document that we call *text-centric*. This is for two reasons. First, the XML documents we consider have some of their elements with textual content (e.g., Title and Abstract) (text that can be indexed from the information retrieval point of view). On the other hand, a text-centric XML document also has descriptive elements (e.g., AuthorList and MeshHeadingList). According to our view, this descriptive information makes part of the metadata associated to the documents.

The conventional approach to preprocessing textual documents (removing stop words, stemming, and dimensionality reduction) ignores any existing structural information. Since our goal is to use structural information of XML documents to improve clustering results, we adopt a different approach: we preprocessed the text-centric XML documents in a collection according to two perspectives. Consider a collection of text-centric XML documents. Let E be the set of all XML subtrees in the schema of this collection. Also, consider two subsets of E, which we denote by E_{vsm} and E_{desc} described below:

- E_{vsm}, the set of subtrees whose content is used to represent the documents as a bag of words. This first perspective represents an XML document as $d_i = (w_{i1}, w_{i2}, ..., w_{im})$, where w_{ij} is the degree of importance of the j-th term in relation to d_i. There are several

Figure 1. A text-centric XML document

```
<MedlineCitation >
  <PMID>8651511</PMID>
  <ArticleTitle>
    The morphology of valves and valve-like
    structures in the canine and feline thoracic duct.
  </ArticleTitle>
  <Abstract>
    <AbstractText>
      The microanatomy and ultrastructure of ... (t r u n c a t e d)
    </AbstractText>
  </Abstract>
  <AuthorList>
    <Author>Bannykh S. S.</Author>
    <Author>Mironov A. A.</Author>
    <Author>Bannykh G. G.</Author>
    <Author>Mironov A. A. Jr.</Author>
  </AuthorList>
  <MeshHeadingList>
    <MeshHeading>Animals</MeshHeading>
    <MeshHeading>Cats</MeshHeading>
    <MeshHeading>Dogs</MeshHeading>
    <MeshHeading>Endothelium</MeshHeading>
    <MeshHeading>Thoracic Duct</MeshHeading>
    (t r u n c a t ed)
  </MeshHeadingList>
  <PublicationTypeList>
    <PublicationType>Journal</PublicationType>
  </PublicationTypeList>
</MedlineCitation>
```

ways of computing w_{ij}. In this work, we use the well-known TF/IDF measure (Salton & Buckley, 1988). The representation obtained by preprocessing the elements of the set E_{vsm} corresponds to a *bag of words*, in which d_i is a vector in a m-dimensional space. This *geometric interpretation* of d_i is usually adopted in classical document clustering algorithms.

- E_{desc}, the set of XML subtrees whose content is used to represent the documents as a bag of characteristics corresponding to categorical attributes. This second perspective views an XML document as a set of multivalued categorical attributes. When we interpret XML documents this way, a measure of similarity for categorical attributes can be applied to two documents d_i and d_j, and their similarity (or complementarily, their dissimilarity) is a function of the intersection of the sets of values of the elements in the set E_{desc}.

Figure 2 illustrates the sets E_{vsm} and E_{desc} described above. There are four subtrees extracted from the structure of the XML document shown in Figure 1. From the first subtree, we can extract a bag of words to represent the documents in the collection according to the geometrical perspective. On the other hand, the subtrees presented to the right in Figure 2 (with dotted rectangles) represent multivalued descriptive attributes. For example, the subtree whose root is *AuthorList*, is equivalent to a multivalued categorical attribute, and the domain of this attribute is the set of all authors.

Figure 2. Dual interpretation of an XML document

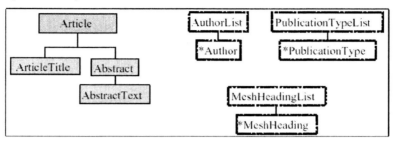

Let us now formalize the interpretation of an XML document as a set of multivalued categorical attributes. Initially, consider an operator ψ that when applied to E_{desc} results in a *sequence* of subtrees of E_{desc}, and labels each subtree in this sequence with a positive sequential integer number. Now, given a collection of XML documents, we represent the attributes of each document d_i by the tuple $T_{di} = (att_1, att_2, ..., att_{|Edesc|})$. Each att_k is a pair $[f_1(k), f_2(di, k)]$, where the function $f_1(\cdot)$ returns the label of the *k*-th element in the sequence generated by $\psi(E_{desc})$, and function $f_2(\cdot, \cdot)$ returns the set V_k of values corresponding to the k-th element of $\psi(E_{desc})$ that appear in document d_i (note that $Vk \subset Dom(att_k)$). In order to exemplify the construction of a tuple T_{di} for a document d_i, consider that the subtrees whose roots *AuthorList*,

PublicationType-List, and *MeshHeadingList* are elements of E_{desc} (see Figure 1). Figure 3 presents the tuple T_{di} corresponding to the document of Figure 1.

In order to exemplify the construction of a tuple T_{di} for a document d_i, consider again the document in Figure 1. Also, consider that the subtrees whose roots AuthorList, PublicationTypeList, and MeshHeadingList are elements of E_{desc}. Figure 3 presents the tuple T_{di} corresponding to the document of Figure 1.

Now consider the definition of document-level ML and CL constraints given in Section 0. When documents in a collection are represented only through the geometric perspective, the user can only define must-link and cannot-link constraints in the document level; that is, the user has only the option of defining constraints in the form $ML(d_i, d_j)$ or $CL(d_i, d_j)$, where d_i and d_j are document identifiers. We call these the *document-level* constraints. On the other hand, if we adopt a dual representation for XML documents as explained in this Section, new possibilities arise for the user to define constraints. In the following, we enumerate these possible scenarios.

1. **Document-level constraints:** The possibility of specifying must-link and cannot-link constraints between a pair of documents remains in our dual representation. For example, the user can define that two documents whose identifiers are d_3 and d_{14} must be put in different clusters: $CL(d_3, d_{14})$.

Figure 3. Tuple of multivalued categorical attributes extracted from an XML document

```
T_di = (att_1, att_2, att_3)

att_1 = (AuthorList, {"Bannykh S.",
                      "Mironov. A. Jr.",
                      "Bannykh G.",
                      "Mironov A"})

att_2 = (PublicationTypeList, {"Journal Article"})

att_3 = (MeshHeadingList, {"Animals",
                           "Cats",
                           "Dogs",
                           "Microscopy. Electron",
                           "Endothelium",
                           "Thoracic Duct"})
```

2. **Hybrid set of constraints:** Now the user can define constraints at the metadata level and combine them with constraints at the document level. For example, given two authors identified by a_1 and a_{10}, and the documents identified by d_2 and d_8, the user can define that $ML(d_2, d_8) \wedge ML(a_1, a_{10})$.

3. **Metadata-level constraints:** The user can also define constraints only by using metadata (descriptive) attributes. For example, consider an attribute att_k, where v_a and v_b are values of att_k. The user could define that documents annotated with value v_a and documents annotated with value v_b must remain in the same cluster, that is, $ML(v_a, v_b)$.

Another relevant aspect is that there is a mapping between each multivalued categorical attribute att_k and the set $\{d_i\}$ of documents that are annotated with values of att_k. We denote by $Docs(v, k)$ the set of documents associated to the value v of the attribute att_k. Inversely, we can also obtain the list of values of attribute att_k that are used to annotate a document d_i. We denote by V_{ik} the set of values of att_k that are used to annotate document d_i. This two-way mapping is going to be explored in the Section 3.2.

Definition 1. Docs(v, k). *Given a multivalued attribute att_k and a value $v \in Dom(att_k)$, we define $Docs(v, k)$ as the set of the documents annotated with value v.*

Definition 2. V_{ik}. *Given a document d_i and a multivalued attribute att_k, we define V_{ik} as the set of values of att_k that are used to annotate d_i.*

Expansion of User-Defined Constraints

As we stated in Section 0, a difficulty in the constrained clustering task is that, in complex domains of application, the user must provide a relatively large amount of semisupervision for the algorithm to reach a good clustering quality. In Basu et al. (2004) and in Bilenko et al. (2004), learning curves are presented that show quality results for 500 and 1,000 constraints. Although these quality results are much better when compared to an unsupervised version of the algorithm, it is not reasonable to think that the user is willing to provide such a large amount of constraints. The situation gets worse when we think of an online search engine that uses semisupervised clustering to group the relevant documents to a user-given query before presentation.

In this section, we intend to describe an algorithm that takes as input user-provided metadata-level constraints. Given m metadata-level constraints, this algorithm can infer n document-level constraints. The important fact here is that, depending on the metadata attribute chosen by the user to define metadata-level constraints, the value of m can be much greater than the value of n. The consequence of applying this algorithm is that the burden on the user is reduced, since he/she can specify fewer constraints and have the system infer an equivalent set of constraints of greater cardinality.

To explain our algorithm for inference of document-level constraints, consider U_{ML} and U_{CL} to be the sets of user-provided (metadata-level) must-link and cannot-link constraints, respectively. Taking the set $U_{ML} \cup U_{CL}$ as input, the system can infer two new sets, S_{ML} and S_{CL}, of document-level must-link and cannot-link constraints by applying algorithm InferDocDoc-Constraints, shown in Figure 1. This algorithm uses the set $Docs(v, k)$ (see Definition 1) in the following way: for each metadata-level constraint referring to values v_a and v_b, the algorithm uses the sets $Docs(v_a, k)$ and $Docs(v_b, k)$ to infer a set of document-level constraints. Therefore, the output of this algorithm is a set of document-level constraints, $S = S_{ML} \cup S_{CL}$.

It is important to note that our approach used to infer document-level constraints from the user-provided metadata-level constraints can be easily

Figure 4. Algorithm InferDocDocConstraints

```
Algorithm: InferDocDocConstraints

Input: set 𝒰 = 𝒰_{ML} ∪ 𝒰_{CL} of user-provided metadata-level constraints

Output: set 𝒮 = 𝒮_{ML} ∪ 𝒮_{CL} of inferred document-level constraints

Steps:
1. 𝒮 ← ∅

2. For each constraint r(v_a, v_b) ∈ 𝒰, do
   If r.linkType = MUSTLINK, then
      a. 𝒮 ← 𝒮 ∪ {ML(d_i, d_j) | d_i, d_j ∈ Docs(v_a), i ≠ j}
      b. 𝒮 ← 𝒮 ∪ {ML(d_i, d_j) | d_i, d_j ∈ Docs(v_b), i ≠ j}
      c. 𝒮 ← 𝒮 ∪ {ML(d_i, d_j) | d_i ∈ Docs(v_a), d_j ∈ Docs(v_b)}
   Else If r.linkType = CANNOTLINK, then
      a. V_1 ← Docs(v_a) − Docs(v_b)
      b. V_2 ← Docs(v_b) − Docs(v_a)
      c. 𝒮 ← 𝒮 ∪ {CL(d_i, d_j) | d_i ∈ V_1, d_j ∈ V_2, i ≠ j}
```

coupled with systems that have SSC algorithms that only work on document-level constraints. This is because the final output of InferDocDoc-Constraints is a set of document-level constraints. In this situation, InferDocDocConstraints can be used in a preprocessing phase, taking constraints at the metadata level and creating equivalent constraints at the document level.

Dealing with Inconsistent Constraints

In this section, we analyze a premise that is commonly assumed in the SSC task: that the set of user-provided constraints is consistent, and that consequently the *transitive closure* of this set can be generated. We also intend to show that this assumption is not acceptable in many situations, and that it can lead to an even more inconsistent set of constraints. We will finally describe algorithms to deal with such inconsistency.

An important aspect about the InferDocDoc-Constraints algorithm is that it infers document-level constraints from metadata-level constraints without considering the fact that the resulting constraint set S can be inconsistent. Therefore,

we need some method to process S (the output of InferDocDocConstraints) to extract a set S' (S' ⊂ S) of constraints that is consistent. Let us first formalize the concept of inconsistent set of constraints. To do that, we now describe a property of the document-level constraints: given a metadata-level constraint $ML(v_a, v_b)$, the algorithm InferDocDocConstraints generates must-link document-level constraints in the form $ML(d_i, d_j)$, where $(d_i, d_j) \in Docs(v_a, k) \times Docs(v_b, k)$ and $d_i \neq d_j$. Based on this property, we now define the *positive neighborhood* generated by a metadata-level constraint.

Definition 3. Positive neighborhood generate from a metadata-level constraints. *Let $r = ML(v_a, v_b)$ be a metadata level constraint. Let $R_{ML}(v_a, v_b)$ be the set of must-link constraints inferred from r. The positive neighborhood of r is the set of documents that participate in at least one constraint in the set $R_{ML}(v_a, v_b)$. We denote this set by V(r).*

According to Definition 3, we have an amount of neighborhoods that is equal to the quantity of metadata-level constraints provided by the user.

We can now define the concept of *inconsistent set of constraints.*

Definition 4. Inconsistent set of constraints. *Consider the sets of constraints U and S, where $S = S_{ML} \cup S_{CL}$ is obtained by applying InferDocDocConstraints taking U as input. The set S is inconsistent if exists at least one pair of documents d_i and d_j such that $d_i, d_j \in V(r)$, for some constraints $r \in U$, and $CL(d_i, d_j) \in S_{CL}$.*

Note that Definition 4 does not consider trivial constraints of the form $CL(d_i, d_i)$, for some document d_i, since algorithm InferDocDocConstraints, by construction, does not infer constraints of this kind.

The fact that a set of document-level constraints S is inconsistent can be viewed graphically if we interpret this set as an undirected graph. In such a graph, the vertices are the documents referenced by at most one constraint in S. In addition, there exists an edge between documents d_i and d_j if and only if there is a document-level (must-link or cannot-link) constraint involving the pair (d_i, d_j) and contained in S. In such interpretation, the set of document-level constraints inferred from a metadata-level constraint $r = ML(v_a, v_b)$ cor-

responds to a complete graph, where the vertices are documents in V(r), and each edge corresponds to a must-link constraint inferred from r by InferDocDocConstraints. To give an example, Figure 5 presents an undirected graph that represents the constraints inferred from the set U = {ML(v_a, v_b), CL(v_b, v_c)} of metadata-level constraints. The sets Docs(v_a, k), Docs(v_b, k), and Docs(v_c, k) are also presented. We represent must-link constraints by solid edges and cannot-link constraints by dotted edges. The set S inferred from U is represented by the graph. Note, for example, that this graph contains an edge corresponding to a cannot-link constraint that involves the pair of documents (d_1, d_3) and that both of them are contained in V(r_1), the positive neighborhood of constraint r_1. The same holds for pair (d_1, d_4). Therefore, according to Definition 4, the set of constraints represented by the graph presented in Figure 5 is inconsistent. It is important to note that, in this example, the document d_5 is not involved in any inconsistency.

Now, consider the subset $S_{ML} \in S$, composed of the must-link constraints inferred by algorithm InferDocDocConstraints. Here, we would like to point out an important aspect of our approach: we do not apply a procedure to generate the transitive

Figure 5. Example of inconsistency in a set of constraints represented as a undirected graph

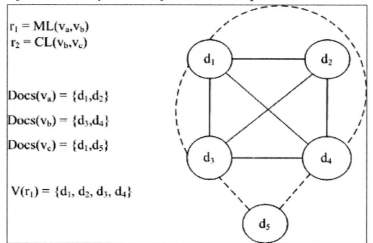

closure of the user-provided set of constraints. The reasons for such a decision are given below.

A first reason is that there can be inconsistencies in the set of user-provided metadata-level constraints. In addition, the algorithm InferDoc-DocConstraints also infers inconsistent constraints inherently (see Figure 5). Therefore, if the user-provided set of constraints is inconsistent, the application of the transitive closure procedure would introduce even more inconsistency.

Another reason for not applying the transitive closure is related to the document-level must-link constraints inferred by algorithm InferDocDoc-Constraints. Without loss in generality, consider that $ML(v_a, v_b)$ and $ML(v_c, v_d)$ are two metadata-level constraints provided by the user. We already know that the values v_a, v_b, v_c, and v_d are associated to the set $Docs(v_a, k)$, $Docs(v_b, k)$, $Docs(v_c, k)$, and $Docs(v_d, k)$, respectively (see Definition 1). Also, consider that $R_{ML}(a,b)$ and $R_{ML}(c,d)$ are the sets of must-link constraints inferred from $ML(v_a, v_b)$ and $ML(v_c, v_d)$, respectively. Now, consider Figure 6, which illustrates the situation we want to describe. According to Figure 6, a document d_j participates in a must-link constraint along with some document referenced by the set $R_{ML}(a,b)$. Also, in Figure 6, the "clouds" represent the sets of documents referenced by $R_{ML}(a,b)$ and $R_{ML}(c,d)$. As we can see from Figure 6, if $R_{ML}(a,b)$ and $R_{ML}(c,d)$ have at least one document in common, the application of the transitive closure procedure

(see Section 2.2.1) would collapse these two sets in a unique set. Further, this collapsed set would be joined to any other set with at least one element in common. In an extreme situation, all the inferred must-link constraints would end up joined in a unique big set. In addition, consider that two constraints exist, one must-link and a cannot-link. Consider also that these constraints reference document d_j that is not referenced in the sets $R_{ML}(a,b)$ and $R_{ML}(c,d)$. Then, the transitive closure on the $R_{ML}(a,b)$ and $R_{ML}(c,d)$ would result in the creation of additional inconsistencies related to d_j. To see this, note that new must-link constraints would be created between d_j and the documents referenced by $R_{ML}(a,b)$, if the transitive closure were applied.

Therefore, our decision to not use the transitive closure avoids the appearance of additional inconsistencies. However, as we stated before, the creation of inconsistencies is inherent to the behavior of InferDocDocConstraints, because this algorithm processes each constraint in its input separately. On the other hand, as the inconsistencies in the input increase, the improvement in clustering quality due to using this set decreases. In fact, our experiments show that an inconsistent set of constraints results in poorer quality when compared to the complete unsupervised case. Therefore, we need some way to remove inconsistencies from S (the input set). We describe some procedures to accomplish this goal in the next section.

Figure 6. Situation in which new inconsistencies are generated, if the transitive closure is applied on two sets of must-link constraints

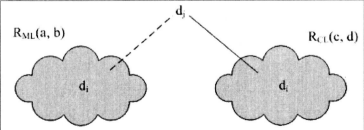

Removing Inconsistent Constraints

A first solution that we propose for dealing with an inconsistent set is to define an algorithm to remove constraints from this set until it becomes consistent. The following proposition serves as a starting point for the definition of such an algorithm.

Proposition (necessary condition for the existence of inconsistency in a set of constraints). *Let $S = S_{ML} \cap S_{CL}$ be the set of must-link and cannot-link document-level constraints. Let D_{ML} and D_{CL} be the sets of documents referenced in S_{ML} and S_{CL}, respectively. If S is inconsistent, then at least one of its constraints references some document in the set $D_{MLCL} = D_{ML} \cap D_{CL}$.*

The above proposition declares that, in a given set S of document-level constraints, constraints that are involved in inconsistencies always refer to documents pertaining to D_{MLCL}, the set of documents referenced by must-link and cannot-link constraints. (However, note that this proposition does not imply that all the documents within D_{MLCL} are involved in inconsistencies.) Therefore,

a possible algorithm to remove inconsistencies from S consists of scanning the elements in D_{MLCL} and, for each one of them, assess if it is involved in some inconsistency. If this is the case, the algorithm removes the corresponding constraints. We call this algorithm EI1, and its pseudocode is presented in Figure 7.

Steps 1, 2, and 3 of EI1 are self-descriptive. Steps 4 and 5 deserve some further explanation. Step 4 considers that there exists a function that we call MustLinkNeighborhoods. Given the set S_{ML} of must-link metadata-level constraints, let $m = |S_{ML}|$. This function generates m sets (not necessarily disjoints) of documents. Each one of these sets generated by MustLinkNeighborhoods corresponds to the documents within the set $\text{Docs}(v_a, k) \cup \text{Docs}(v_b, k)$, where v_a and v_b are such that $ML(v_a, v_b) \in S_{ML}$. Step 5 corresponds to a loop to iterate over each constraint $r(d_i, d_j)$ that refers to at least one document in the set D_{MLCL}. If r is a cannot-link constraint, and if both d_i and d_j are found in some set generated by MustLinkNeighborhoods, then r is removed from the constraint set.

EI1's main characteristic is to remove cannot-link constraints in favor of must-link con-

Figure 7. Algorithm EI1

```
Algorithm: EI1

Input: set of document-level constraints S = S_ML ∪ S_CL
       set of metadata-level must-link U_ML
Output: set of constraints S_c, such that S_c ⊆ S e S_c has no
        inconsistencies.

Steps:
1. S_c ← S
2. D_MLCL ← set of documents {d_i}, in which each d_i is referred to
            at least one must-link constraint r_1 and at least one
            cannot-link constraint r_2, where r_1, r_2 ∈ S
3. R_MLCL ← set of constraints that refer to at least one
            document in D_MLCL
4. {V_k}_{k=1..|U_ML|} ← PositiveNeighborhoods(U_ML)
5. For each constraint r(d_i, d_j) ∈ R_MLCL, do
       If r.linkType = CANNOTLINK and ∃V_k such that {d_i, d_j} ⊂ V_k, then
           S_c ← S_c − {r}
6. Return S_c
```

straints. To see this, note that once EI1 detects an inconsistency in some positive neighborhood, it always removes the cannot-link constraint that participates in this inconsistency. The disadvantage of this is that the algorithm can remove a cannot-link constraint that reflects the user need in relation to the resulting clustering model, and consequently the undesirable must-link constraint remains in the set. Therefore, EI1 can take the set of constraints to a consistent state, but by doing this, the algorithm potentially removes some useful constraints.

The EI2 algorithm, which we present in Figure 8, is similar to EI1. The difference is that, when EI2 detects a pair of documents d_i and d_j in a positive neighborhood, and the constraints $r1 = ML(d_i, d_j)$ and $r2 = CL(d_i, d_j)$ exist, both $r1$ and $r2$ are removed. This way, differently from EI1, EI2 does not favor one type of constraint over the other.

Algorithms EI1 and EI2 are based only on the information about the *structure* that is the source of inconsistencies. In the specific case of EI2, it considers the pair of constraints equivalently and removes both constraints. However, if an algorithm for removing inconsistencies could have access to the degree of relevance (or weight) for each constraint, then it could rely on this information to decide which constraint(s) to remove. This algorithm could follow a simple heuristics: for each pair of constraints that conflict with each other, the constraint with greater weight remains, and the other (weaker) constraint is removed. Therefore, we now describe a third algorithm, named EI3, for elimination of inconsistencies.

To start with the definition of EI3, let us first describe our approach to generate weights for the constraints. First, note that for each constraint the user provides, she/he does it with some degree of confidence, even though he/she does not state this explicitly. A solution to have weights associated to the user-provided constraints is to have the user provide these values. This is the solution adopted in Wagstaff and Cardie (2000),

Figure 8. Algorithm EI2

Algorithm: *EI2*

Input: set of document-level constraints $\mathcal{S} = \mathcal{S}_{ML} \cup \mathcal{S}_{CL}$
      set of metadata-level must-link constraints $\mathcal{U}_{ML}$
Output: set of contraints $\mathcal{S}_c$, such that $\mathcal{S}_c \subseteq \mathcal{S}$ and $\mathcal{S}_c$ has no
      inconsistencies.

Steps:
1. $\mathcal{S}_c \leftarrow \mathcal{S}$
2. $\mathcal{D}_{MLCL} \leftarrow$ set of documents $\{d_i\}$, where each d_i is referenced
      by at least one must-link constraint r_1 and at least one
      cannot-link constraint r_2, where $r_1, r_2 \in \mathcal{S}$
3. $\mathcal{R}_{MLCL} \leftarrow$ set of constraints that refer to at least one
      document in $\mathcal{D}_{MLCL}$
4. $\{\mathcal{V}_k\}_{k=1..|\mathcal{U}_{ML}|} \leftarrow$ PositiveNeighborhoods($\mathcal{U}_{ML}$)
5. **For each** constraint $r1(d_i, d_j) \in \mathcal{R}_{MLCL}$, **do**
    If $r1$.linkType = CANNOTLINK **and** $\exists \mathcal{V}_k$ such that $\{d_i, d_j\} \subset \mathcal{V}_k$, **then**
      5.1. $\mathcal{S}_c \leftarrow \mathcal{S}_c - \{r1\}$
      5.2. For each $r2$ such that $r2$.linkType = MUSTLINK and $d_i, d_j \in \mathcal{V}_k$, **do**
        $\mathcal{S}_c \leftarrow \mathcal{S}_c - \{r2\}$
6. **Return** $\mathcal{S}_c$

---

although the authors use the weights in a context different from the elimination of inconsistencies. However, this solution decreases the autonomy of the system. Instead, we want to describe an algorithm to automatically generate weights for the constraints. For this, we assume that the user defines the constraints at the metadata-level. Our strategy is to automatically assign weights to the constraints inferred by the InferDocDoc-Constraints algorithm. To automatically assign weights for the inferred constraints, we rely on the structural information associated to the collection of XML documents to be clustered. We now describe our strategy do derive weights.

After applying the InferDocDocConstraints algorithm, the system has two sets of document-level constraints, S_{ML} and S_{CL} (see Section 3.2). Without loss in generality, assume that one of these sets refers to the documents d_i and d_j. According to our dual representation of XML documents (see Section 3.1), there is a mapping between d_i and the values of attribute $att_k \in T_{di}$, $\forall k$ (the same holds form d_j). Therefore, the system can easily compute the two sets of values of att_k that are used to label d_i and d_j, respectively. Let us call these sets V_{ik} and V_{jk} (V_{ik}, $V_{jk} \in Dom(att_k)$).

We adopt the following hypothesis: given two sets of values V_{ik} and V_{jk} (V_{ik}, $V_{jk} \in Dom(att_k)$), the similarity (or dissimilarity) between these sets is correlated to the strength of the constraint define on (d_i, d_j), whether this constraint is a must-link or a cannot-link. As an example, consider the MEDLINE collection, from which we extracted the document presented in Figure 1. In this collection, if two documents are referred in a must-link constraint and have similar lists of authors, we assume this fact as clue that the user is looking for a clustering model that cluster the documents by authors. Besides, the facts that (1) two documents have similar lists of descriptors and (2) participate in a positive constraint intuitively accounts for a stronger constraint. An analogous argument can be constructed in relation to the dissimilarity between

two documents. Therefore, given a constraint r = (d_i, d_j), the similarity (dissimilarity) between d_i and d_j can be interpreted as the weight of r. To compute the similarity (dissimilarity) between two documents, we use the tuples of multivalued attributes associated with each document in the collection (see Section 3.1).

If we consider all the unordered pairs in the sets S_{ML} and S_{CL}, two symmetric matrices WML and WCL can be formed. The ij-th element of matrix WML is the weight of must-link constraint between documents d_i and d_j. Elements of matrix WCL are defined analogously. We use the elements of these matrices as the similarities (dissimilarities) between the sets V_{ik} and V_{jk}. Since these are sets of values of multivalued categorical attribute, several existing measures of similarity for categorical attributes can be applied to obtain the costs corresponding to the elements of these two matrices.

Now, we finally describe EI3, our third algorithm to remove inconsistencies. Consider Figure 9, in which we again interpret a set of constraints as an undirected graph. Figure 9(a) schematically illustrates a situation in which there is inconsistency, because documents d_i and d_j simultaneously satisfy the two following conditions: (1) they participate in a cannot-link constraint and (2) they are contained in a positive neighborhood. Note that there are cycles (in the graph) involving the edge corresponding to the cannot-link constraint r = CL(d_i, d_j). On the other hand, Figure 9(b) provides an instance of such a situation for a neighborhood of four documents, d_1, d_2, d_3, and d_4.

There are three possible ways to remove the inconsistency described in Figure 9: (1) remove the cannot-link constraint between d_i and d_j; (2) remove the must-link constraints in which document d_i participates; and (3) remove the must-link constraints in which d_j participates. The main question is what alternative is better. To give an answer to this question, we define the problem

Figure 9. (a) Situation in which documents d_i and d_j participate in a inconsistent set; (b) specific example for a neighborhood of four documents

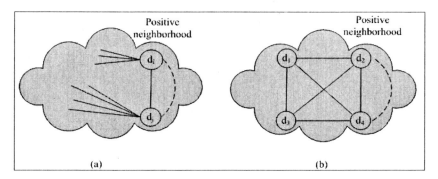

of removing constraints as an integer linear programming (ILP) problem. In the definition of this problem, consider the following variables:

- x_{cl} is equal to 1 if the cannot-link constraint should remain; or else 0.
- xi_{ml} is equal to 1 if the must-link constraints in which d_i participates should remain; or else 0.
- xj_{ml} is equal to 1 if the cannot-link constraints in which d_j participates should remain; or else 0;

Note that the three variables above have an integer domain. We can now define the two components of the ILP problem: the objective function (to be maximized) and the constraints over the variables x_{cl}, xi_{ml}, and xj_{ml}. This ILP problem is defined in Figure 10. In this problem, we have three coefficients, c_1, c_2, and c_3. The coefficient c_1 is equal to the value w_{ij} obtained from the matrix of cannot-link weights, and corresponds to the weight of the cannot-link constraint $r = CL(d_i, d_j)$. We define the coefficients c_2 and c_3 as the average values of the weights associated to the must-link constraints in which d_i and d_j participate, respectively. The values of coefficients c_2 and c_3 are obtained from the weight matrices.

Note that these values are fixed, given two documents d_i and d_j.

The values for the variables x_{cl}, xi_{ml}, and xj_{ml} are obtained by solving the PLI problem. These values can then be used to determine what constraints must be removed. If we solve this PLI problem for each pair of documents involved in a constraint that pertain to a positive neighborhood, the inconsistencies in the set of constraints are completely removed. We summarize all this process in the algorithm EI3, presented in Figure 10.

Figure 10. ILP problem associated with the EI3 algorithm

$$\text{maximize } Z = c_1 x_{cl} + c_2 xi_{ml} + c_3 xj_{ml}$$

subject to
$$p = x_{cl} + xi_{ml} + xj_{ml}$$

and to the following bound variables
$$2 \le p \le 2$$
$$x_{cl} \in \{0, 1\}$$
$$xi_{ml} \in \{0, 1\}$$
$$xj_{ml} \in \{0, 1\}$$

Figure 11. Algorithm EI3

Algorithm: *EI3*

Input: set of document-level constraints $S = S_{ML} \cup S_{CL}$.

Output: set of constraints S_c, such that $S_c \subseteq S$ e S_c has no
      inconsistencies.

Steps:
1. $S_c \leftarrow S$
2. $\mathcal{D}_{MLCL} \leftarrow$ set of documents $\{d_i\}$, in which each d_i is referred
      by at least ont must-link constraint r_1 and at least one
      cannot-link constraint r_2, where $r_1, r_2 \in S$
3. $\mathcal{R}_{MLCL} \leftarrow$ set of constraints that refer to at least one
      document in $\mathcal{D}_{MLCL}$
4. $\{\mathcal{V}_k\}_{k=1..|\mathcal{U}_{ML}|} \leftarrow$ PositiveNeighborhoods($\mathcal{U}_{ML}$)
5. **For each** constraint $r(d_i, d_j) \in \mathcal{R}_{MLCL}$, **do**
   If r.linkType = CANNOTLINK **and** $\exists \mathcal{V}_k \in \mathcal{V}$ such that $\{d_i, d_j\} \subset \mathcal{V}_k$, **then**
     5.1. Get the values x_{cl}, xi_{ml} and xj_{ml} that solve the ILP in Figure 10
     5.2. **If** $x_{cl} = 0$, **then**
        $S_c \leftarrow S_c - \{r\}$
     Else If $xi_{ml} = 0$, **then**
        $S_c \leftarrow S_c - \{$Constraints in V_k that refer to $d_i\}$
     Else If $xj_{ml} = 0$, **then**
        $S_c \leftarrow S_c - \{$Constraints inV_k that refer to $d_j\}$
6. Return S_c

FUTURE TRENDS

It is natural to conjecture that researchers in the field of semisupervised clustering will start to look for new kinds of data in which methods can be applied. In fact, this has already started, as we can see in some works (Ceccarelli & Maratea, 2005; Grira, Crucianu, & Boujemaa, 2005), where semisupervised clustering methods are applied to biological data and to image data.

Another avenue for future work is to investigate how structural information (i.e., XML metadata) can be used in the fuzzy clustering case. An open problem here is how to define the concepts of must-link and cannot-link constraints when a document can be put in more than one cluster. In addition, in our present work, we used MeSH, a hierarchy of concepts (descriptors) used to annotate documents in MEDLINE. However, we did not consider the relationships between descriptors.

Therefore, we also intend to investigate how a hierarchical taxonomy of concepts associated to the collection of documents can be used to both improve and explain clustering results.

Another issue that could be further explored is on defining more expressive ways for the user to define constraints. In this chapter, we introduced the concept of metadata-level constraints, which are more expression than document-level constraints. But we think there is much more space for investigation here. For example, in a fully expressive language for defining constraint, the user could define that her/his clustering need is related to grouping the documents that have the same authors or the same descriptors. We think such a language could be defined as a subset of first order logics.

Finally, an experimental evaluation of the algorithms we proposed for elimination of inconsistency is highly relevant. We are planning to provide such results in future work.

CONCLUSION

In this chapter, we have presented a new approach to take advantage of structural information associated with textual documents in semisupervised clustering. We first defined our dual view of an XML document, in which it can be viewed both as a bag of words and as a bag of multivalued categorical attributes. This view unleashed the possibility of defining constraints at the metadata level. In addition, we used this dual view to derive a procedure to expand the user-provided metadata level constraints into document-level constraints. This approach alleviates the burden on the user, since he/she now is required to provide much less constraints to the semisupervised clustering algorithm, without loss in the clustering quality.

Our dual representation for XML documents also opens up new possibilities in the definition of constraints: now, the user can define *metadata-level constraints*. Such dual representation also makes structural information available to guide execution of the SSC algorithm itself, as we have done in Bezerra et al. (2006). By using such representation, instead of only working on the textual content of text-centric XML documents, a SSC algorithm can also query structural information associated with the collection. We want to stress that the representation for XML documents we adopt is relevant to several domains of applications that work with semistructured textual documents in general and text-centric XML documents in particular. For example, in digital libraries, it is common to add some descriptive information to articles. Authors, keywords in a predefined set, and concepts of a taxonomy are examples of information frequently found in such repositories.

REFERENCES

Basu, S., Banerjee, A., & Mooney, R. J. (2002). Semisupervised clustering by seeding. In *Proceedings of the 19th International Conference on Machine Learning (ICML-2002)*, Sydney, Australia (pp. 19-26).

Basu, S., Banerjee, A., & Mooney, R. J. (2004). Active semisupervision for pairwise constrained clustering. In *Proceedings of the SIAM International Conference on Data Mining (SDM-2004)*, Lake Buena Vista, Florida (pp. 333-344).

Basu, S., Bilenko, M., & Mooney, R. J. (2004). A probabilistic framework for semisupervised clustering. In *Proceedings of KDD-2004*, Seattle, Washington (pp. 59-68).

Bezerra, E., Xexéo, G. B., & Mattoso, M. L. Q. (2006, April). *Semisupervised clustering of XML documents: Getting the most from structural information*. Paper presented at the 3rd International Workshop on XML Schema and Data Management (XSDM'06), Atlanta, Georgia.

Bilenko, M., Basu, S., & Mooney, R. J. (2004). Integrating constraints and metric learning in semisupervised clustering. In *Proceedings of the 21st International Conference on Machine Learning (ICML-2004)*, Banff, Canada (pp. 81-88).

Bray, T., Paoli, J., & Sperberg-McQueen, C. M. (2000). Extensible markup language (XML) 1.0 (2nd ed., W3C Recommendation).

Ceccarelli, M., & Maratea, A. (2005). Semisupervised fuzzy c-means clustering of biological data. Paper presented at WILF 2005 (pp. 259-266).

Chang, H., & Yeung, D.-Y. (2004). Locally linear metric adaptation for semisupervised clustering. In *Proceedings of the Twenty-first International Conference on Machine Learning*, New York, New York (p. 20). ACM Press.

Chu, W. W. (2000). Medical digital library to support scenario specific information retrieval. In *Proceedings of the Kyoto International Conference on Digital Libraries* (p. 388).

Davidson, I., & Ravi, S. (2005a). Clustering under constraints: Feasibility issues and the k-means algorithm. In *Proceedings of the 5th SIAM Data Mining Conference.*

Davidson, I., & Ravi, S. (2005b). *Hierarchical clustering with constraints: Theory and practice.* Paper presented at the Ninth European Conference on Principles and Practice of Knowledge Discovery in Databases (PAKDD-2005), Porto, Portugal.

Grira, N., Crucianu, M., & Boujemaa, N. (2004). Unsupervised and semisupervised clustering: A brief survey. In *A review of machine learning techniques for processing multimedia content: Report of the MUSCLE European Network of Excellence (FP6)* (p. 11).

Grira, N., Crucianu, M., & Boujemaa, N. (2005, November 6-12). Active semisupervised fuzzy clustering for image database categorization. In *Proceedings of the 6th ACM SIGMM International Workshop on Multimedia Information Retrieval,* Singapore.

Kim, H. J., & Lee, S. G. (2002). User-feedback driven document clustering technique for information organization. *IEICE Transactions on Information and Systems, E85-D*(6), 1043-1048.

Klein, D., Kamvar, S. D., & Manning, C. D. (2002). From instance level constraints to space-level constraints: Making the most of prior knowledge in data clustering. In *Proceedings of the ICML-2002* (pp. 307-314).

Kleinberg, J., & Tardos, E. (1999). Approximation algorithms for classification problems with pairwise relationships: Metric labeling and Markov random fields. In *Proceedings of the FOCS '99 40th Annual Symposium on Foundations of Computer Science,* Washington, DC (p. 14). IEEE Computer Society.

MacQueen, J. B. (1967). Some methods for classification and analysis of multivariate observations. In L. M. LeCam & N. Neyman (Eds.), *Proceedings of the Fifth Berkeley Symposium on Mathematical Statistics and Probability* (vol. 1, pp. 281-297).

Salton, G., & Buckley, C. (1988). Term-weighting approaches in automatic text retrieval. *Information Processing and Management, 24*(5), 513-523.

Wagstaff, K., & Cardie, C. (2000). Clustering with instance-level constraints. In *Proceedings of the Seventeenth International Conference on Machine Learning,* (pp. 1103-1110) San Francisco: Morgan Kaufmann Publishers.

Wagstaff, K., Cardie, C., Rogers, S., & Schröedl, S. (2001). Constrained kmeans clustering with background knowledge. In *Proceedings of the Eighteenth International Conference on Machine Learning (ICML-2001)* (pp. 577-584). San Francisco: Morgan Kaufmann Publishers.

Xing, E. P., Ng, A. Y., Jordan, M. I., & Russell, S. (2002). Distance metric learning with application to clustering with side-information. In S. T. S. Becker & K. Obermayer (Eds.), *Advances in neural information processing systems* (vol. 15, pp. 505-512). Cambridge, MA: MIT Press.

Chapter V
Modeling and Managing Heterogeneous Patterns:
The PSYCHO Experience

Anna Maddalena
University of Genoa, Italy

Barbara Catania
University of Genoa, Italy

ABSTRACT

Patterns can be defined as concise, but rich in semantics, representations of data. Due to pattern charac-teristics, ad-hoc systems are required for pattern management, in order to deal with them in an efficient and effective way. Several approaches have been proposed, both by scientific and industrial communities, to cope with pattern management problems. Unfortunately, most of them deal with few types of patterns and mainly concern extraction issues. Little effort has been posed in defining an overall framework dedicated to the management of different types of patterns, possibly user-defined, in a homogeneous way. In this chapter, we present PSYCHO (Pattern based SYstem arCHitecture prOtotype), a system prototype providing an integrated environment for generating, representing, and manipulating hetero-geneous patterns, possibly user-defined. After presenting the PSYCHO logical model and architecture, we will focus on several examples of its usage concerning common market basket analysis patterns, that is, association rules and clusters.

INTRODUCTION

The large volume of heterogeneous raw data collected from various sources in real-world ap-plication environments usually does not constitute knowledge by itself for the end users. Indeed, little information can be deduced by simply observing such a huge quantity of data, and advanced knowledge management techniques are required to extract from them concise and relevant information that can help human users to drive and specialize business decision processes. Of course, since raw data may be very heterogeneous, different kinds of knowledge artifacts, representing knowledge hidden into raw data, can be extracted.

We use the generic term *patterns* to denote in a concise and general way such compact but rich in semantics knowledge artifacts. Patterns reduce the number and size of data, to make them manageable from humans while preserving as much as possible their hidden information or discovering new interesting correlations.

Pattern management is an important issue in many different contexts and domains. However, without doubt, the most relevant context in which pattern management is required is data mining. Clusters, frequent itemsets, and association rules are some examples of common data mining patterns. The trajectory of a moving object in a localizer control system or the keyword frequency in a text document represent other examples of patterns.

Since patterns can be generated from different application contexts, their structure can be highly heterogeneous. Moreover, patterns can be extracted from raw data by applying some data mining tools (*a-posteriori patterns*) but also known by the users and used, for example, to check how well some data source is represented by them (*a-priori patterns*). In addition, it is important to determine whether existing patterns, after a certain time, still represent the data source they are associated with, possibly being able to change pattern information when the quality of the representation changes. Finally, independently from their type, all patterns should be manipulated (e.g., extracted, synchronized, deleted) and queried through ad hoc languages. Those specific characteristics make traditional database management systems (DBMSs) unsuitable for pattern representation and management. Therefore, the need arises for the design of ad hoc *pattern management systems (PBMSs)*, that is, systems for handling (storing/processing/retrieving) patterns defined over raw data (PANDA, 2001).

Many efforts have been devoted towards this issue. Scientific community efforts are mainly devoted to develop frameworks providing a full support for heterogeneous pattern management. The 3W Model (Johnson, Lakshmanan, & Ng, 2000) and the PANDA framework (PANDA, 2001) are examples of such approaches, in which raw data are stored and managed in a traditional way by using, for example, a DBMS whereas patterns are stored and managed by a dedicated PBMS. On the other hand, under the inductive databases approach, mainly investigated in the context of the CINQ project (CINQ, 2001), raw data and patterns are stored by using the same data model and managed in the same way by the same system. Industrial proposals mainly deal with standard representation purposes for patterns resulting from data mining, in order to support their exchange between different platforms. Examples of such approaches are the predictive model markup language (PMML, 2003), an XML-based language for common data mining representation, and the Java data mining aPI (JDM, 2003), a Java API for pattern management. In both cases, no user-defined patterns can be specified, and manipulation functionalities are quite limited. Finally, in the commercial world, the most important DBMSs address the pattern management problem by offering features for representing and managing typical data mining patterns.

In general, existing proposals do not provide a unified framework dealing with heterogeneous patterns in a homogeneous way. Indeed, usually they cope with some predefined pattern types, and they do not provide advanced capabilities for pattern extraction, querying, and management.

Starting from the limitations of existing proposals and taking into account the results presented in the context of the PANDA project (Bertino, Catania, & Maddalena, 2004; Catania, Maddalena, Mazza, Bertino, & Rizzi, 2004; Rizzi,

Bertino, Catania, Golfarelli, Halkidi, Terrovitis, et al., 2003), we have designed and implemented a PBMS coping with most of the features previously introduced.

The system, called *PSYCHO*, from *Pattern based management SYstem arCHitecture prOtotype*, allows the manipulation of heterogeneous patterns and the definition of user-defined patterns, not necessarily coming from a data mining context. It provides a pattern manipulation language (PSY-PML) for the management of both a-posteriori and a-priori patterns, which also supports synchronization between patterns and raw data, in order to reflect changes occurred in source data to the pattern extent, and a pattern query language (PSY-PQL), offering query capabilities for selecting and combining patterns, possibly of different types, and for combining patterns and data, in order to get a deeper knowledge of their correlations (*cross-over queries*).

The aim of this chapter is to present the main features of PSYCHO. To this end, we present an application experience in the context of market basket analysis. In particular, we describe how PSYCHO can be effectively used to model and manage common types of data mining patterns, that is, association rules, 2D point clusters, and clusters of association rules (Han & Kamber, 2001). The choice to focus PSYCHO presentation over these simple pattern types is basically motivated by the fact that these are well known patterns that, at the same time, raise interesting issues concerning modeling management. They are therefore a good choice in order to explain the basic peculiarities of PSYCHO, giving to the reader the basic intuition of its flexibility.

The remainder of this chapter is organized as follows. We first discuss the application needs requiring the management of different types of patterns. Then, we survey existing proposals coming from scientific and industrial communities for pattern management. After that, we present PSYCHO, describing the underlying pattern model and architecture. Then, before concluding

the chapter, we present some examples of PSYCHO usage focused over market basket analysis patterns. Such examples are primarily aimed at demonstrating the following two PSYCHO features: (1) management of data mining patterns and (2) management of user-defined patterns based on pattern hierarchies.

HETEROGENEOUS PATTERN: BACKGROUND

Patterns resulting from data mining tasks can be quite different. As an example, in the context of the market basket analysis, association rules over sale transactions are often generated. Moreover, in order to perform a market segmentation, the user may also be interested in identifying clusters of customers, based on their buying preferences, or clusters of products, based on customer buying habits.

According to that previously stated, patterns can be generated from different application contexts resulting in very heterogeneous structures. Besides that, the process by which they are generated can be different. Indeed, as already said, patterns can be a-posteriori patterns (i.e., resulting from a mining process) but also a-priori patterns (i.e., known by the users).

Nevertheless, heterogeneous patterns often have to be managed together. For instance, in a Web market basket analysis context, in order to understand well the e-commerce buying habits of Web users, the following patterns can be combined: (1) navigational patterns (identified by clickstream analysis) describing their surfing and browsing behavior; (2) demographic and geographical clusters, obtained with market segmentation analysis based on personal data and geographical features; and (3) association rules, describing correlations between sold items. By leveraging from their heterogeneity, all kinds of patterns should be manipulated (e.g., extracted, synchronized, deleted) and queried through dedicated languages.

All the previous reasons motivate the need for the design of ad hoc (PBMSs), that is, systems for handling (storing/processing/retrieving) patterns defined over raw data in order to efficiently support pattern matching and to exploit pattern-related operations generating intensional information. The set of patterns managed by a PBMS is called *pattern base* (Rizzi et al., 2003).

We remark that a PBMS is not a simple knowledge repository; it is an engine supporting pattern storage (according to a chosen logical model) and processing (involving also complex activities requiring computational efforts). Thus, the design of a PBMS relies on solutions developed in several disciplines such as data mining and knowledge discovery, for a-posteriori pattern extraction; database management systems, for pattern storage and retrieval; data warehousing, for providing raw data sets; artificial intelligence and machine learning, for pattern extraction and reasoning; and metadata management, for data exchange and interoperability.

In the following, we point out which requirements must be supported by a PBMS in order to cope with heterogeneous patterns in an effective and efficient way. In particular, we first discuss pattern model characteristics, making the PBMS able to represent heterogeneous patterns in a unified way; then we introduce query language features, for retrieving heterogeneous patterns in a homogeneous way, possibly combining patterns of different types inside the same query process; and, finally, we focus on manipulation language features, for manipulating patterns according to their specific characteristics.

In presenting those requirements, we give particular attention to the market analysis context, where two well-known data mining pattern types arise, that is, association rules and clusters.

An association rule expresses a correlation between sold itemsets. In more detail, given a domain D of values and a set of sale transac-

tions T, each corresponding to a subset of D, an association rule has the form A→B, where A ⊆ D, B ⊆ D, A ∩ B ≠∅ formalizes that "often, when the set of items A is sold, the set of items B is sold as well". Usually, A is called the "body" of the rule, whereas B is the "head" of the rule. In order to quantify the meaning of the word "often", statistical measures are associated with each rule. The most common measures are *support* and *confidence*, expressing, respectively, how many sale transactions contain items in A with respect to the total number of transactions and, among them, how many contain also items in B. On the other hand, a cluster is a group of elements sharing some similar characteristics or behaviors. Therefore, due to their diffusion, in presenting PBMS requirements, we use association rules and clusters as reference examples in order to point out and clarify the basic aspects we cope with.

Pattern Model Characteristics

The logical model adopted for representing patterns is a formalism by which patterns are described and manipulated inside the PBMS. We claim that, in order to be able to deal with heterogeneous patterns, the logical model should take into account at least the following issues:

- **Multi pattern types support:** The ability to model heterogeneous patterns is very important to make the PBMS flexible and usable in different contexts.
- **User-defined pattern types support:** The ability to support user-defined pattern types, generated in any possible application context, is fundamental for a PBMS guaranteeing full support for pattern heterogeneity and extensibility.
- **Relation between raw data and patterns:** By definition, each pattern represents a possibly huge set of source data. There exists, therefore, a relationship between each

pattern and the data source it represents. Thus, in order to enhance pattern semantics and provide additional significant information for pattern retrieval, it may be useful to store some information concerning such relation. In case of patterns generated by applying a mining technique, the data source corresponds to the data set from which the patterns have been mined. Besides the source data set, it may be useful to exactly know the subset of the source data set represented by the pattern. For examples, the rule bread → milk represents only transactions containing "bread" and "milk" in the overall set of transactions in the source data set. This subset can be represented in a precise way, by listing its components (i.e., all transactions containing "bread" and "milk"), or in an approximate way, by providing a formula satisfied by the transactions of the source data set from which the pattern has been generated.

- **Quality measures support:** It is important to be able to quantify how well a pattern represents a raw data set, by associating each pattern with some quantitative measures. For example, each association rule mined from transactional data is usually associated with confidence and support values. However, we may want to associate with a certain pattern type quality measures different from the usual ones. For instance, considering association rules, confidence and support are the most widely used, but there exist other quality measures such as coverage, leverage, and lift (Han & Kamber, 2001), which could be used. The capability of considering different quality measures could be useful in order to support heterogeneous patterns, even if it is supported by only a few existing systems.

- **Pattern validity support:** As already discussed, data change with a frequency rate higher than the pattern change rate. There-

fore, it is important to establish whether existing patterns, after a certain time, still represent the data source from which they have been generated or, more in general, which they represent. To this end, some notion of pattern validity should be exploited. In particular, we devise two different notions of validity that could be associated with a pattern: a semantic validity and a temporal validity. We say that a pattern p, inserted in the system at time t and representing a certain raw dataset D, is *semantically valid* at an instant of time $t' > t$ with respect to D if at t' p still represents raw data in D with measure values over a given threshold. In practice, it may also be useful to assign to each pattern a validity period, representing the interval of time in which it can be considered reliable with respect to its data source. We say that a pattern p is *temporally valid* at an instant of time t if t falls inside the pattern validity interval.

- **Pattern type hierarchy support:** Another important feature a model for heterogeneous pattern representation should provide is the capability to define some kind of hierarchy over the existing pattern types, in order to increase expressivity, reusability, and modularity. For instance, a shop vendor dealing with association rules can be interested in more complex patterns corresponding to groups or clusters of association rules. In this case, the considered patterns—that is, association rules and clusters of association rules—share two distinct hierarchical relationships: a first one expressing the fact that clusters have been generated from a source data set of association rules and a second one specifying that a cluster structure is indeed defined based on association rules (e.g., the cluster representative could be an association rules). We call the first hierarchical relationship "refinement hierarchy" and the second one "composition hierarchy".

Querying Features

The following querying features are considered fundamental for any PBMS in order to support pattern retrieval and analysis:

- **Queries against patterns:** The PBMS has to provide a query language supporting pattern retrieval according to some specified conditions. For example, all association rules having "bread" in their body may need to be retrieved. To support the pattern query processing in a DBMS-like manner, pattern collections have to be supported by PBMs in order to be used as input for queries.
- **Pattern combination:** Operations for combining patterns together should be provided as an advanced form of reasoning over heterogeneous patterns. Combination can be seen as a sort of "join" between patterns. For example, transitivity between association rules can be seen as a kind of pattern join.
- **Queries involving patterns and raw data:** A system managing heterogeneous patterns should provide operations not only for querying patterns in isolation, but also data by applying a cross-over processing between them. Cross-over queries are fundamental in order to get a deeper knowledge concerning the relationship between a pattern and data it represents.

Manipulation Features

Besides querying capabilities, a PBMS has to provide manipulation capabilities in order to support at least pattern generation, modification, and deletion. To this extent, we claim that any PBMS should support, as minimum requirements, the following manipulation features:

- **Automatic extraction:** In order to support a-posteriori patterns management, a PBMS has to provide the capability to generate patterns starting from raw data. This pattern generation process corresponds to the application of an extraction algorithm over raw data, and it constitutes a special case of insertion operation.
- **Direct insertion of patterns:** Besides a-posteriori patterns, the user may know a-priori some patterns and may wish to verify whether they represent a certain data source. Such patterns are not extracted from raw data, but directly inserted from scratch in the system. Ad hoc manipulation primitives are therefore needed to perform this operation.
- **Modification and deletion:** Patterns can be modified or deleted. For example, users may be interested in updating information associated with patterns (such as their validity in time or their quality measure values) or in dropping patterns having (or not having) certain characteristics. Moreover, when considering hierarchical patterns, the system has to provide support for cascade modifying or deleting patterns involved in a hierarchy.
- **Synchronization over source data:** An important issue to be taken into account is the ability to address unexpected, unforecasted changes in raw data, which may require changing the patterns representing them. Indeed, since source data change with high frequency, it becomes fundamental to determine whether existing patterns, after a certain time, still represent the data source from which they have been generated (i.e., whether they are still semantically valid), possibly being able to change pattern information when the quality of the representation changes (i.e., synchronizing raw data

and patterns). This issue constitutes a key feature for any pattern management system, and it is an interesting topic for researches in the areas of machine learning and data mining. It is often referred in literature as the *virtual concept drift* problem (Tsymbal, 2004). In the presence of concept drifts, it could be useful to be able to synchronize patterns with the modified source data set. This realignment may update the measure values associated with the patterns. Synchronization can be performed against the source data set the pattern is associated with or with respect to a different data set. In this second case, we call this operation *recomputation*. For example, suppose a shop vendor knows that association rules AR1 and AR2 hold over a data set D concerning sales in the month of January 2005 in her shop. Assuming that during February new sales are recorded into D, if the shop vendor is interested in determining whether association rules AR1 and AR2 still hold for the updated data set D, she has to apply a synchronization operation. On the other hand, suppose she receives a new data set D', concerning sales in the months of January and February 2005 in another shop. In order to check whether association rules AR1 and AR2 are reasonable patterns also for D', she has to apply a recomputation of the association rules AR1 and AR2 over D'.

- **Mining function:** As we have already said, patterns can be extracted from raw data by applying some kind of mining function. For example, the APriori (Agrawal & Srikant, 1994) or the FP-growth (Han, Pei, & Yin, 2000) algorithms can be used to generate association rules; on the other hand, the Single-Link, Complete-link, or K-means (Han & Kamber, 2001) are possible algorithms to be used for generating clusters.

The presence of a library of mining functions and the possibility to define new functions, if required, makes pattern manipulation much more flexible.

HETEROGENEOUS PATTERNS: THE CURRENT APPROACHES

As we have already stressed, the need for a framework supporting heterogeneous pattern management in a homogeneous way is widespread and it impacts over many different contexts and domains. For this reason, many efforts have been put in this direction from the academic and the industrial communities. In the remainder of this section, we briefly present existing proposals starting from theoretical solutions and moving towards industrial and commercial ones.

Theoretical Proposals

Within the scientific world, many efforts have been put in the formalization of the overall principles under which a PBMS can be realized, providing the theoretical foundations for the development of pattern-based technologies. The most important research efforts are the following:

- Inductive databases approach (De Raedt, 2002; Imielinsky & Mannila, 1996) particularly investigated in the context of the CINQ Project (CINQ, 2001);
- 3-worlds model (Johnson et al., 2000);
- PANDA Project (Bertino et al., 2004; Catania et al., 2004; PANDA, 2001; Rizzi et al., 2001).

Inductive databases. The research area of inductive databases is very active, and many research efforts have been devoted in laying the foundations of an inductive framework where both data and patterns are stored in the same layer. Under this integrated perspective, the knowledge repository is assumed to contain both data and patterns. Thus, the same data model is used for both data and pattern representation, and the knowledge discovery process is interpreted as an extended querying process (De Raedt, Jaeger, Lee, & Mannila, 2002; Meo, 2004). Therefore, a language for an inductive database is an extension of a database language that allows one to (1) select, manipulate, and query data as in standard queries; (2) select, manipulate, and query patterns; and (3) execute cross-over queries over patterns. Queries can also be stored in the repository as views; in this way, data sets and pattern sets are intensionally described. From a practical point of view, several languages extending SQL with data mining algorithm have been provided (Han, Fu, Wang, Koperski, & Zaiane, 1996; Imielinski & Virmani, 1999; Meo, Psaila, & Ceri, 1998). However, in general, they rely on specific types of patterns, mainly association rules or clusters.

3-worlds model. The 3-worlds model (3W model) is a unified framework for pattern management based on the definition of three distinct worlds: an intensional world (I-World), containing intensional descriptions of patterns; an extensional world (E-World), containing an explicit representation of patterns; and a world representing raw data (D-World). The type of patterns that can be represented in the I-World is a region in the collection of points representing the data space, described by means of linear constraints. For example, a cluster of customers based on their age can be described by the following constraint: "18<=age <=35". More complex regions, called *dimensions*, can be defined, composed of a set of constraints. In the E-World, each region is extensionally represented by listing all members of the source space satisfying the constraint characterizing the region. Finally, the D-World corresponds to the source data set, in the form of relations, from which regions and dimensions can be created as a result of a mining process. Note that regions

in the I-World are not predefined, thus user-defined patterns are allowed. Each region can be associated with a number of attributes, including measures, which do not have a special treatment. No pattern temporal management is provided. From the manipulation side, the framework does not support a-priori patterns. Indeed, operations to directly insert patterns in the system are not provided. Query languages for all the worlds have been proposed. In particular, for the D-World and the E-World, traditional relational languages can be used (with some minor extensions for the E-World). On the other hand, a specific algebra has been defined over regions in the I-World, providing support for basic queries over regions and for cross-over queries involving patterns, their extensions, and data.

PANDA model. Within the PANDA Project, a unified framework for the representation of heterogeneous patterns has been proposed. The PANDA solution relies on an ad hoc, dedicated logical model for representing heterogeneous pattern types, possibly user-defined. It also provides support for both a-priori and a-posteriori patterns, and it allows the user to define ad-hoc mining functions for generating a-posteriori patterns. Moreover, pattern quality measures and pattern validity notions are modeled, as well as relationships between patterns and raw data that can be stored in an explicit or approximated way. For instance, a cluster of customers can be explicitly (or extensionally) described by listing all customers belonging to it, or it can be approximately (or intensionally) described through a formula expressing the characteristics raw data should have in order to belong to the cluster. For example, an age-based cluster can be described by a constraint formula of the form "$m<=age<=n$" saying that only customers whose age is between m and n belong to the cluster. Furthermore, complex pattern types based on composition and refinement hierarchies can be defined by using the PANDA model.

Considering pattern manipulation and querying, the PANDA approach proposes specific languages for patterns (Bertino et al., 2004; Catania et al., 2004) taking into account temporal characteristics of pattern validity. In particular, the pattern manipulation language supports pattern manipulation operations involving both a-posteriori and a-priori patterns, such as pattern insertion, modification (e.g., update, synchronization, and recomputation), and deletion. On the other hand, by using the proposed pattern query language, patterns can be retrieved and queried by specifying filtering conditions involving all pattern characteristics supported by the model. Additionally, different patterns can be combined and correlated with raw data (i.e., cross-over operations are supported).

By concluding, for what concerns pattern representation, the more general model seems the one proposed in the context of the PANDA Project, where there is no limitation on the pattern types that can be represented. PANDA is also the only approach taking into account temporal aspects, hierarchies, and providing both a precise and an approximated relationship between patterns and source data. In particular, it can be shown that the approximated representation in PANDA is quite similar to the region representation in 3W.

Concerning the manipulation language, the 3W Model and inductive database approaches do not explicitly support direct insertion of patterns as well as deletion and update operations. On the other hand, all the proposals take into account synchronization (recomputation) issues, either by providing explicit recomputation operations or by exploiting the logical integration of patterns with raw data in the case of the inductive database approach. Concerning the query language, all the approaches propose one (or more) calculus-based or algebraic languages. As a final consideration, we observe that when dealing with applications managing different types of patterns (this is the case of advanced knowledge discovery applica-

tions), the 3W Model and PANDA theoretical frameworks are the best solutions since they provide support for heterogeneous patterns in a unified way. On the other side, the inductive databases approach provides better solutions for specific data mining context, such as association rules management, with a low impact on existing SQL-based applications.

Standards

The industrial community proposed some standards to support pattern representation and management in order to achieve interoperability and knowledge sharing between different environments. Thus, they provide the right front-end for pattern management applications.

In general, they do not support generic patterns and, similarly to the inductive database approach, specific representations are provided for specific types of patterns and usually low support for interpattern manipulation is provided. In the following, the most important standard proposals are briefly reviewed.

- **Predictive model markup language:** The predictive model markup language (PMML, 2003) is an XML-based standard aimed at describing data mining models (i.e., data mining results, algorithms, procedures, and parameters). It is mainly devoted to representing data mining information in order to facilitate their exchange between different application environments providing import/export support for PMML data.
- **SQL/MM – DM:** The ISO efforts rely on SQL technology and it is called SQL/MM – DM (ISO SQL/MM Part 6, 2001). By exploiting SQL potentialities, it provides support not only for data representation, but also for pattern representation. Therefore, data and pattern manipulation and querying can be performed in an SQL-based environment.

- **Java data mining API:** With a similar aim, in order to provide data mining support in the context of the Java programming language, the Java data mining API specification has been proposed (JDM, 2003). It can be considered a pattern management solution supporting the integration of data mining applications with other Java-based applications. Similarly to the case of SQL/MM, using JDM, manipulation and querying are possible by using typical languages used for accessing data.
- **Common warehouse metamodel:** The common warehouse metamodel (CWM, 2001) approach is another standardization effort of the Object Management Group aimed at representing metadata for exchanging patterns of knowledge between warehouse platforms.

Among the presented standards, PMML and CWM-DM simply address the problem of pattern representation and they mainly deal with data mining and data warehousing patterns. On the other hand, SQL/MM and JDM cope with both pattern representation and management. All standards provide a support for the representation of common data mining patterns. However, the set of pattern types is not extensible; thus, no user-defined patterns can be modeled.

All standards allow the user to specify the mining algorithms to apply. However, in the case of PMML, this is just a string used only for user information purposes. Furthermore, all considered approaches support measure computation and description of the source data set, which is used in SQL/MM and JDM for pattern extraction. None of the standards supports advanced modeling features concerning patterns such as temporal information management and pattern hierarchy definition.

Concerning pattern management, no dedicated languages for pattern manipulation are supported. Moreover, a-priori patterns cannot be handled by

using the proposed standards; actually, a limited support for them is provided by JDM, which allows pattern import.

Finally, we remark that SQL/MM and JDM can be used for developing specific data mining applications on top of existing technologies. In particular, SQL/MM can be put on top of an ORDBMS environment, whereas JDM works in a Java-based environment. Differently, PMML and CWM-DM are mainly used for pattern exchange between different environments.

Pattern Support in Commercial DBMSs

Since the ability to support business intelligence solutions enhances the market competitiveness of a DBMS product, all the most important DBMS producers supply their products with solutions for business intelligence supporting data mining and pattern management processes. In the remainder of this section, we briefly discuss data mining solutions proposed by three leading companies in database technology—Oracle, Microsoft, and IBM—with respect to the previously identified PBMS requirements.

- **Oracle data mining:** Oracle Data Mining (ODM, 2005) is a tool tightly integrated with Oracle DBMS supporting several data mining activities (such as classification, prediction, clustering, and association rule discovery) generating different kinds of patterns (such as Naïve Bayes network or support vector machine classifiers, clusters, and association rules) from source data stored in the underlying Oracle database. We outline that mining algorithms and machine learning methods are built-in in ODM, but the user may change some settings and/or define new parameters for the mining model through the ODM Java API. Statistical measures can be associated with classifiers and association rules.

- **Microsoft SQL Server:** The approach for business intelligence proposed by Microsoft SQL Server 2005 exploits OLAP, data mining, and data warehousing tools (MS SQL, 2005). SQL server 2005 allows the user to build different types of mining models dealing with traditional patterns (such as decision trees, clusters, Naïve Bayes classifiers, time series, association rules, and neural networks) and to test, compare, and manage them in order to drive business decision processes. The entire knowledge management process is performed through a mining model editor, that allows the user to define, view, compare, and apply models. Besides this editor, additional tools are provided to exploit other mining phases (for example, data preparation). Within SQL server 2005, through OLE DB for data mining (OLEDB, 2005), it is possible to integrate data-mining capabilities in other database applications. Indeed, it provides SQL-like storage and manipulation features for mined patterns, which are stored in a relational database. To create a mining model, a CREATE statement, similar to the SQL CREATE TABLE statement, can be used; to insert new patterns in a mining model, the INSERT INTO statement can be used; finally, patterns can be retrieved and predictions made by using the usual SQL SELECT statement. For the sake of interoperability and compatibility with standards, OLE DB for data mining specification incorporates PMML.

- **DB2 Intelligent Miner:** The DB2 database management environment provides support for knowledge management by means of a suite of tools, called DB2 Intelligent Miner (DB2, 2005), dedicated to the basic activities involved in the whole data mining process. In particular, the latest version of DB2 Intelligent Miner supports fraud detection, market segmentation, customer profiling, and market basket analysis. Thus, users

may use data mining functionalities as any other traditional relational function provided by the DBMS. The interaction among DB2 Intelligent Miner's tools takes place through PMML, SQL, and Java. In particular, the DB2 Extender for data mining tool allows the construction of PMML mining models within DB2/SQL applications and their update with respect to changes occurring in the underlying data. The generated PMML mining models are stored as Binary Large Objects (BLOBs). The other DB2 tools supporting training, scoring (or prediction), and visualization of a model works on PMML models, thus they can manage, without additional overhead, third-party PMML models. Finally, since the mining results are stored as BLOB, the user may interact with the system through an SQL API, and through ODBC/JDBC or OLE DB, data mining results can be integrated within business applications developed using a general-purpose programming language such as Java.

From the previous discussion, it follows that commercial DBMSs do not provide a dedicated logical model for pattern representation and querying, since these aspects are demanded to the applications using the mined results. An exception is represented by SQL Server 2005 where, through OLE DB, pattern storage, manipulation, and querying is made through OLE DB for Data Mining.

Moreover, we outline that in all commercial systems only a set of predefined pattern types can be used and mining functions are built-in in the system even if the user can modify some settings in order to specialize the algorithm to the case he/she is interested in. Finally, none of the considered DBMSs takes into account advanced modeling aspects involving patterns, such as temporal information management and the existence of hierarchical relationships between patterns. Actually, only DB2 considers pattern-data synchronization issues, through a scoring mechanism that can be started up by some triggers monitoring raw data changes.

PSYCHO: AN INTRODUCTION

From the discussion presented in the previous section, it follows that a unified framework dealing with heterogeneous patterns in a homogeneous way, addressing all the identified requirements, is still missing. In order to determine what the impact is of the identified characteristics over advanced data-intensive applications, we have developed PSYCHO (Pattern based SYstem arCHitecture prOtotype), a PBMS system prototype for heterogeneous pattern management. In the remainder of this section, we introduce PSYCHO in terms of its underlying data model and architecture, and we discuss how it addresses the previously discussed requirements.

PSYCHO: THE MODEL

The PSYCHO data model relies on the PANDA logical model first introduced in Rizzi et al. (2003) and then extended with temporal features in Catania et al. (2004). According to those proposals, the PSYCHO logical model is based on three basic concepts: *pattern types*, providing a formal description of the structure of a specific type of patterns; *patterns*, instances of a given pattern type; and *classes*, sets of semantically related patterns used for querying purposes. All such logical entities along with their relationships are graphically shown in Figure 1.

A pattern type acts as a template for patterns, since it defines the schema of a group of patterns. It is characterized by six components: (1) the pattern name; (2) the structure schema, describing the structure of the patterns instances of the pattern type being defined; (3) the source schema, describing the data set from which patterns, instances of the pattern type being defined, are constructed; (4)

Figure 1. The PSYCHO logical model

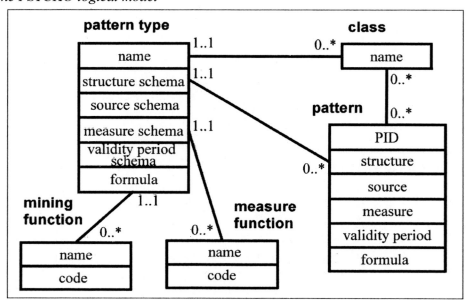

the measure schema, which is a tuple describing the measures expressing the quality of the source data representation achieved by the pattern; (5) the validity period schema, defining the schema of the temporal validity interval associated with each instance of the pattern type; and (6) the formula, describing, possibly in an approximate way, the relation between data represented by the pattern and the pattern structure. Within the current PSYCHO implementation, the formula is a conjunction of linear disequalities, whose free variables range over pattern structure schema elements and pattern source schema elements. The formula component then represents a constraint that is true for all the items of the data source which are represented by the pattern.

Patterns are instances of a specific pattern type, containing the proper instantiation of the corresponding schema components in the pattern type. In particular, the formula component of a pattern is obtained from the one in the corresponding pattern type by instantiating each

Table 1. PSYCHO support for the identified PBMS requirements

	Requirement	PSYCHO support	PSYCHO module
Pattern modeling	Multipattern type support	No predefined pattern type set	Pattern Base
	User-defined pattern types support	PSY-PDL primitives for defining new pattern types	PDL Interpreter + Pattern Base
	Relationship between raw data and patterns	Source data information represented inside the logical model in two different ways	Pattern Base + PQL Interpreter + Formula Handler
	Quality measure support	Pattern quality measures represented inside the logical model	Pattern Base + PQL Interpreter
	Pattern validity support	Pattern validity information represented inside the logical model	Pattern Base + PQL Interpreter
	Pattern type hierarchy support	PSY-PDL primitives for defining complex hierarchical pattern types	PDL Interpreter + Pattern Base
Pattern querying	Queries against patterns	PSY-PQL primitives for performing different types of queries	Query Processor + Formula Handler + Pattern Base
	Pattern combination	PSY-PQL primitives to perform pattern joins	Query Processor + Pattern Base
	Queries involving patterns and raw data	PSY-PQL primitives supporting cross-over queries	Query Processor + Pattern Base + Datasource
Pattern manipulation	Automatic extraction	PSY-PML primitive for generating a-posteriori patterns	PML Interpreter + Datasource + Pattern Base
	Direct insertion	PSY-PML primitive for a-priori pattern insertion	PML Interpreter + Pattern Base
	Modification and deletion	PSY-PML primitives for updating and dropping existing pattern types, patterns, and classes	PML Interpreter + Pattern Base
	Synchronization over source data	PSY-PML primitives for synchronizing and/or recomputing patterns	Query Processor + Pattern Base + Datasource
	Mining function	PSY-PML primitive for defining new mining functions	PDL Interpreter + Pattern Base

attribute appearing in the structure schema with the corresponding value and letting the attributes appearing in the source schema ranging over source space elements.

A class is a collection of semantically related patterns and constitutes the key concept in defining a pattern query language (see below). A class is defined for a given pattern type and contains patterns instances of that type. A pattern may belong to any number of classes defined for its patterns type. If a pattern does not belong to any class, it cannot be queried.

Concerning pattern extraction, several different mining functions can be defined to extract patterns of a certain pattern type. A mining function, defined for a certain pattern type, takes in input a raw data set and some threshold values for pattern measures and produces as output a set of instances of the proper pattern type, whose measure values are equal to or better than the specified thresholds. Generally, a set of built-in mining functions for standard patterns can be assumed to be available in the system. However, the user can define new mining functions in order to tailor pattern extraction with respect to specific needs. Similarly to the case of mining functions, several different measure functions can be defined to evaluate the measure values associated with a pattern of a certain type over a certain input data set.

In the context of the PANDA Project (Catania et al., 2004; Rizzi et al., 2003), some interesting relationships supporting hierarchical pattern definition have also been proposed. Among them, we recall the composition relationship—between a pattern and those used to define its structure—and the refinement relationship—between a pattern and those belonging to its data source. PSYCHO, which implements the logical model for patterns proposed in the context of the PANDA Project, supports both hierarchies.

According to the logical model used for pattern representation, PSYCHO supports two types of validity: *temporal validity* and *semantic validity*. A pattern is temporally valid with respect to a certain date (or a date interval) if its validity period contains the specified date (or the date interval). A pattern is semantically valid with respect to a certain data set and a set of thresholds if the pattern measure values computed over the input data set are better than the threshold values provided as input. The pattern validation process, which is primarily aimed at determining whether a pattern is still a good representation of a certain data set, essentially relies on the pattern semantic validity notion. Indeed, it often happens that a pattern, representing a data source at a certain instant of time, does not represent the same data source after several modifications occur in it (see below the first scenario for more details). As far as we know, no system supports this kind of analysis.

Based on the considered pattern model, PSYCHO provides three languages for pattern management:

- The *pattern definition language (PSY-PDL)*, used for defining new pattern types, classes, mining, and measure functions;
- The *pattern manipulation language (PSY-PML)*, used to perform operations such as insertions, extraction, deletions, updates, synchronization, and recomputation of the patterns in the system with respect to source data. Moreover, it allows the user to insert or remove a pattern into or from a class;
- The *pattern query language (PSY-PQL)*, used to query the PBMS in order to retrieve patterns and correlate them with data they represent (cross-over queries).

For all the three languages, an SQL-like syntax has been provided to simplify the request specification.

Table 1, for each cited requirement, summarizes how PSYCHO supports it (third column) and which are the involved PSYCHO software components (last column). We refer the reader to the next section for more details about the PSYCHO software architecture.

PSYCHO: THE ARCHITECTURE

In designing the PSYCHO architecture, we rely on object-relational technology: raw data are stored as tables of complex values in an object-relational DBMS and patterns corresponds to complex objects, which can be easily implemented within an object-relational DBMS. More precisely, the PSYCHO architecture relies on Oracle and Java technologies and can exploit Oracle Data Mining (ODM) server functionalities when dealing with standard data mining patterns. The architecture is composed of three distinct layers (Catania, Maddalena, & Mazza, 2005):

- **Physical layer:** It contains the *Pattern Base* and the *Data Source*. The Pattern Base stores

pattern types, patterns, and classes and it provides the implementation of the basic operations dealing with patterns. Concerning the pattern formula, we consider two distinct representations: an operational one, by which the formula is indeed a predicate over data source elements implemented as an Oracle PL/SQL stored function, and a declarative one, by which the formula is a linear constraint formula, managed by the Formula Handler component (see below). The Data Source stores all raw data from which patterns have been extracted. For the sake of simplicity, in the current PSYCHO version, we assume source data is stored in an Oracle DBMS.

- **Middle layer:** It contains the *PBMS Engine*, which corresponds to the kernel of the system. It supports all functionalities for pattern manipulation and retrieval interacting with both the Pattern Base and the Data Source components in the physical layer. The PSYCHO Engine takes a request from the

Figure 2. The PSYCHO architecture

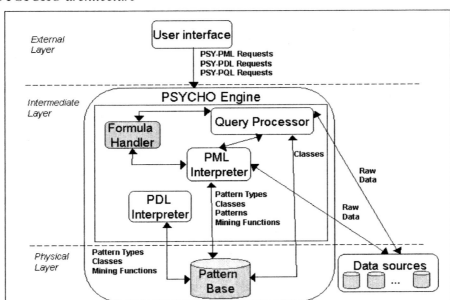

external layer – specified by using a specific SQL-like PSYCHO command—and calls the right functions/procedures at the physical layer. It is entirely written in Java, and it contains four different software modules: the *PDL Interpreter* and the *PML Interpreter*, which deal with the execution of PSY-PDL and PSY-PML commands, respectively; the *Query Processor*, which is dedicated to execute queries expressed using PSY-PQL; and the *Formula Handler*, which provides support for the management of intensional aspects related to pattern formulas through the usage of a Prolog constraint solver engine (Sicstus, 2004), which can be accessed by the Java application through the Jasper package (Jasper, 2005).

- **External layer:** It corresponds to a user interface from which the user can send requests to the engine by using the primitives of the provided languages (i.e., PSY-PDL, PSY-PML, and PSY-PQL).

The whole PSYCHO architecture is shown in Figure 2, where the software components populating the three layers of the architecture are depicted along with their interactions.

An important aspect concerning the PSYCHO architecture is how the different components communicate between them. We start our description bottom-up, from the lowest layer to the highest. The Pattern Base, as stated before, is integrated within the DBMS. The PSYCHO Engine is placed immediately above the Pattern Base. It creates and manages the connection with the DBMS and, therefore, with the Pattern Base. The communication is, therefore, the classical communication between a Java application and a DBMS, through a JDBC driver.

On the other hand, the communication between the PSYCHO Engine and the external layer is established using sockets. In this way, the system is more flexible, and a completely distributed architecture can be realized. In details,

the PSYCHO Engine opens a socket on a fixed port and waits for connections from the outside. When the external module needs to communicate with the server, it makes a connection, creates a serializable object that encapsulates the request, and sends it to the PSYCHO Engine. In this way, using serialization, sockets and JDBC driver, the different components corresponding to patterns and data sources, the engine, and external modules can be placed on different hosts.

PSYCHO USAGE

When using PSYCHO, we may identify several basic phases that occur in almost every pattern management session, independently from the handled pattern types and the considered reference domain. Such phases are: (1) set-up of the PBMS environment; (2) population of the pattern base; (3) analysis of the pattern base contents; and (4) pattern maintenance and updating phase. In general, we may assume that several standard data mining pattern types (such as association rules), along with their mining and measure functions, are built-in in the system.

In case the required pattern types are missing in the PBMS, phase 1 allows the user to set up the PSYCHO environment by creating all schema objects required for representing and managing the instances of the new pattern type. More precisely, phase 1 allows the definition of the following elements: (1) the pattern type we are interested in (if it does not already exist in the system); (2) at least one mining function implementing an extraction algorithm generating instances of the pattern type of interest; and (3) one (or more) measure functions computing measure values to be associated with pattern instances of the new pattern type. The syntax of the PSY-PDL commands to be used for the goals listed above is shown in Figure 3.

In the remainder of this section, we present various scenarios describing different PSYCHO

Figure 3. PSY-PDL syntax for creating pattern types, mining functions, and measure functions

```
1: CREATE PATTERN TYPE <Pattern_Type_Name> (
2:    STRUCTURE <Field_Declaration> [DEFINE EQUALS ON <Pattern_Variable> USING <Field_Declaration>
3:                    CODE <Code> RETURN <Name>],
4:    MEASURE <Field_Declaration> [DEFINE THETA ON <Pattern_Variable> USING <Field_Declaration>
5:                    CODE <Code> RETURN <Name>],
6:    FORMULA EXTENSIONAL ON <Data_Source_Name> USING <Field_Declaration>
7:         CODE <Code> RETURN <Name>
8:    FORMULA INTENSIONAL <Name>);
9:
10: CREATE MINING FUNCTION <Name> FOR <Pattern_Type_Name>
11: USING <Data_Source_Name>
12: WITH  <Field_Declaration> AS <Field_Declaration>
13: BEGIN
14:    <Mining_Code>
15: END;
16:
17: CREATE MEASURE FUNCTION <Name> FOR <Pattern_Type_Name>
18: USING <Data_Source_Name> AS <Field_Declaration>
19: BEGIN
20:    <Code>
21:    RETURN Measure(<List_of_Values>);
22: END;
```

applications. For each scenario, we point out the main goal and several operations, written in PSYCHO languages, aimed at showing the potentialities of the system.

SCENARIO 1: DATA MINING PATTERNS

The aim of the first scenario is to illustrate representation, generation, manipulation, and querying activities for patterns of the same type in PSYCHO. To this purpose, as already said, we consider association rules and clusters of 2-dimensional points. We remark that such data mining pattern types are managed by any commercial system dealing with data mining. However, PSYCHO allows one to perform several operations that are not directly supported by other existing tools.

Association Rules

Set-up. We assume source data are stored in a table with schema (DSid, Item_1,...,Item_n), where each tuple represents a sales transaction identified by

DSid, Item_i is either 1 or 0, and Item_i = 1 means that the corresponding transaction identified by DSid contains Item_i. Furthermore, we assume a basic Oracle type, named *CharArray*, for modeling arrays of chars is available and provides a method for checking equality between pairs of *CharArray* instances, named *Chararray_Equal*.

As already said, in this phase, we define the pattern type, the mining function required to extract association rules from source data, and the measure function, required to recompute measures upon a given data source. For association rules, we may assume such objects already exist in the system, since the association rule type is a standard data mining pattern.

The code required to set up the pattern type *AssociationRule* is shown in Figure 4. We notice that:

- As default, an extensional formula (lines 16-18) returning the whole pattern data source is associated with a pattern of type *AssociationRule*; whenever the user specifies an extensional formula code, this overrides the default behavior.

- Concerning the intensional formula, the user has to specify the name of an existing Prolog predicate, intensionally checking whether a source data item is represented by the pattern (*ARFormulaINT* in this example, see line 19).
- The structure is associated with a function EQUALS, checking the equality between two structure values for the pattern type under definition (lines 4-8).
- The measure is associated with a function THETA, checking whether a measure value is "better than or equal to" another (lines 9-15).

Concerning the mining function for association rules, within PSYCHO, a Java implementation of the Apriori algorithm (Agrawal & Srikant, 1994) exists. Additional mining functions can however be made available. In the current version of PSYCHO, this can be done by defining some Oracle functions. Various measure functions can also be defined. As an example, lines 21-26 of Figure 4 present the statement for creating a

measure function for computing confidence and support over a given data source (identified by variable *varDS*).

Population. In this step, we show how PSYCHO can be used to (1) use various mining functions to extract patterns of a given type; (2) directly insert patterns; and (3) recompute patterns. We wish to outline that only few systems provide support for mining patterns using different mining functions, possibly user-defined. Therefore, this constitutes an important, innovative aspect increasing the extensibility and flexibility of the proposed system. Examples of insertion commands are presented in Figure 5. We first show association rules extraction, using the PSYCHO Java mining function *Apriori* implementing the A-Priori algorithm. We create a class, called *AR30_psycho*, where storing the extracted patterns (line 1). We remark that, if no class is used to store extracted patterns, they are inserted in the system but they cannot be used in queries. Then, we extract association rules from a data source *ItemsDS_30* by using the existing function *Apriori*, and we store

Figure 4. Creation of the AssociationRule pattern type

```
 1: CREATE PATTERN TYPE AssociationRule
 2:   STRUCTURE head CharArray, body CharArray
 3:   DEFINE EQUALS ON p1 USING ret int  CODE
 4:   if Chararray_Equal(self.s.head, p1.s.head)=1 AND Chararray_Equal(self.s.body,p1.s.body)=1
 5:     then ret:= 1;
 6:     else ret:=0;
 7:   end if;
 8:  return ret;
 9:  MEASURE support REAL, confidence REAL
10:   DEFINE THETA ON p2 USING ret int CODE
11:   if (self.m.support >= p2.m.support AND self.m.confidence>=p2.m.confidence)
12:      then ret:= 1;
13:      else ret:=0;
14:   end if;
15:   return ret;
16:  FORMULA EXTENSIONAL ON varDS USING condB varchar2(100), condH varchar2(100)
17:  CODE
18:  ... /* evaluation of the subset of varDS approximated by a pattern of type AssociationRule*/
19:  FORMULA INTENSIONAL ARFormula INT;
20:
21: CREATE MEASURE FUNCTION AR_measure_func FOR AssociationRule ar
22: USING varDS
23: AS  ... /* local parameter declaration*/
24: BEGIN
25:  .../*code for computing confidence and support for association rules over the input dataset*/
26: END;
```

the result in class *AR30_psycho* (lines 3-5). To this purpose, we specify that the support of the extracted rules must be higher than 0.4 and the confidence higher than 0.7 (line 3); the validity period of the extracted rules is set from 01-jul-2005 to 10-aug-2005 (line 4).

Other association rules can be extracted by using the mining algorithms available in Oracle Data Mining ODM (ODM, 2005). Assume a mining function *Apriori_ODM*, calling the ODM one, is available within PSYCHO; new patterns can be extracted from *ItemDS_30* using such a mining function. The resulting patterns can be stored in a new class, named *AR30_ODM*. The PSYCHO code for this operation is presented at lines 7-11, where only rules with support higher than 0.4 and confidence higher than 0.7 are generated.

Single association rules can also be directly inserted in PSYCHO by specifying each component. For example, the direct insertion statement presented at lines 17-21 inserts in class *AR30_psycho* a rule having items "bread" and

"milk" in its *head* and items "jam", "butter", and "wine" in its *body*, representing sale transactions in *ItemsDS_30* data set with support equals to 0.5 and confidence equals to 0.7, valid from 01-aug-2005 till 15-aug-2005.

Finally, within PSYCHO, new patterns can be generated by recomputing measures of existing patterns over a new data source. Line 23 shows an example of a manipulation operation recomputing association rules over the data set *ItemsDS_5* using the *AR_measure_func* measure function. The execution of this operation returns new association rules identical to the existing ones, except for their data source and measure components. In detail, their data source is set to *ItemsDS_5*, and their measure component contains the proper measure values evaluated over *ItemsDS_5* using the input measure function.

Queries. PSY-PQL supports the following querying features: (1) simple queries involving predicates dealing with pattern components; (2) pattern composition; (3) nested queries; and (4)

Figure 5. AssociationRule pattern generation

```
1: CREATE CLASS AR30_psycho OF AssociationRule;
2:
3: EXTRACT PATTERNS OF AssociationRule ar FROM ItemsDS_30 USING Apriori(0.4,0.7)
4: VALID FROM '01-jul-2005' TO '10-aug-2005'
5: INTO CLASS AR30_psycho;
6:
7: CREATE CLASS AR30_ODM OF AssociationRule;
8:
9: EXTRACT PATTERNS OF AssociationRule ar FROM ItemsDS_30 USING AprioriODM(0.4,0.7)
10: VALID FROM '10-jun-2005' TO '10-aug-2005'
11: INTO CLASS AR30_ODM;
12:
13: SELECT *
14: FROM AR30_ODM or INTERSECT JOIN AR30_psycho pr
15: WHERE Chararray_Equal(or.s.head,pr.s.head)=1 AND Chararray_Equal(or.s.body,pr.s.body)=1;
16:
17: DIRECT INSERT PATTERN OF AssociationRule FROM ItemsDS_30
18: STRUCTURE (CharArray('bread','milk'), CharArray('jam','butter','wine') )
19: MEASURE (0.5,0.7)
20: VALID FROM '01-aug-2005' TO '15-aug-2005'
21: INTO CLASS AR30_psycho;
22:
23: RECOMPUTE PATTERNS of AssociationRule ar ON ItemsDS_5 USING AR_measure_func;
```

pattern-data reasoning (cross-over queries). In the following, we present examples for each class of queries.

Simple queries allow the user to select patterns from a given class, according to a variety of predicates. In the WHERE clause of a SELECT statement, selection predicates can be combined using Boolean operators (i.e., NOT, AND, OR). Moreover, PSYCHO supports the analysis of both temporal and semantic pattern validity, through the use of proper querying predicates, according to the notion of pattern validity supported by the

logical model. Queries 1, 2, 3, and 9 in Table 2 are examples of simple queries expressible within PSYCHO over patterns of type *AssociationRule*. In particular, queries 3 and 6 rely on a temporal validity predicate, whereas query 9 applies a semantic validity predicate.

Concerning pattern composition, in the actual release of PSYCHO, two types of join are provided: a general join, called CJOIN, and a specific join, called INTERSECTION JOIN. The CJOIN relies on a user specified composition (or joining) function, defining the structure of the resulting patterns. In particular, it takes two classes and,

Table 2. Simple queries involving AssociationRule patterns

N.	Query	PSY-PQL code
1	Retrieve all association rules from AR30_psycho with support smaller than or equal to 0.75	SELECT * FROM AR30_psycho ar WHERE ar.m.support <= 0.75;
2	Retrieve all association rules from AR30_psycho having at least 1 item in their head and 3 items in their body	SELECT * FROM AR30_psycho ar WHERE ar.s.Head.count>=1 AND ar.s.Body.count>=3;
3	Retrieve all association rules from AR30_psycho having a confidence value greater or equal to 0.75 or which are temporally valid on August, 15 2005	SELECT * FROM AR30_psycho ar WHERE ar.m.confidence >= 0.75 OR isTvalid(ar, '15-aug-2005')=1;
4	Determine all association rules, obtained as the transitive closure (using the Trans_closure_ar composition function) of two existing association rules, and having at least two items in the body	SELECT * FROM AR30_psycho ar1 CJOIN AR30_psycho ar2 WITH Trans_closure_ar WHERE ar2.s.body.count >= 2;
5	Determine all pairs of association rules, generating their intersection	SELECT * FROM AR30_psycho ar1 INTERSECT JOIN AR30_psycho ar2
6	Determine all data represented by association rules in class AR30_psycho	DRILL THROUGH AR30_psycho ar;

7	Determine whether the association rule with PID=10013 and support at least 0.4 is suitable to represent the data set ItemsDS_30, possibly different from the one from which the rule has been generated	DATA COVERING (
		  SELECT *
		  FROM AR30_psycho pr
		  WHERE pr.PID = 10013 AND pr.m.support>=0.4) ar
		FOR ItemsDS_30;

8	Determine among rules in AR30_psycho the ones with confidence at least 0.8 suitable to represent the data set ItemsDS_30 (possibly different from the one from which the rule has been generated)	PATTERN COVERING ItemsDS_30 FOR AR30_psycho ar WHERE ar.m.confidence >= 0.8;
9	Retrieve from AR30_psycho all semantically valid rules (with respect to their data source), with support and confidence greater than or equal to 0.4	SELECT * FROM AR30_psycho ar WHERE isSvalid(ar,ar.d, 'AR_measure_func', AssociationRuleMeasure(null,0.4,0.4))=1;

for each pair of patterns, the first belonging to the first class and the second belonging to the second one, it applies the specified composition function to produce output patterns. On the other hand, the INTERSECTION JOIN takes two classes and returns new patterns, whose structure is a combination of the input structures and whose intensional formula is the conjunction of the input intensional formulas. Queries 4 and 5 in Table 2 are examples of association rule joins. In particular, the CJOIN presented in query 4 relies on the *Trans_closure_ar* composition function, we assume previously defined, which, given a pair of association rules (e.g., A→B and B→C), constructs their transitive closure (i.e., A→C in this case).

PSYCHO also supports pattern-data reasoning; that is, it allows the user to specify PSY-PQL queries involving both data and patterns, the so called cross-over queries. Such kind of queries are quite important in pattern management, since they allow the user to discover interesting (possibly new) correlations between patterns and data. In Table 2, queries 7, 8, and 9 are examples of possible cross-over queries. Moreover, as shown in query 7, PSY-PQL queries can also be nested.

Other Manipulation Operations. PSYCHO supports various types of update operations.

Synchronization operation allows one to synchronize pattern measures with their current data source. For example, statement 1 in Table 3 synchronizes all association rules contained in class *AR30_psycho*, using measure function *AR_measure_func*.

After performing association rules synchronization, it may be useful to validate updated association rules. Validating patterns means possibly recomputing new patterns when the quality of the representation of a data set achieved by the patterns themselves decreases (thus, the recomputed measures are worse than the existing ones) or just synchronizing their measure when the quality increases. For instance, statement 2 in Table 3 validates rules in class *AR30_psycho* and inserts the new created patterns inside the same class.

Clusters of 2D Points

As a further example, we consider clusters of 2D points. Such clusters can be represented in several ways. We consider two distinct representations:

- **Extensional clusters:** In this case, we assume a cluster is represented by the set of points belonging to it.
- **CH-clusters:** In this case, we assume that each cluster is identified by the convex region containing all the points belonging to it. Such region corresponds to the convex hull of such points. We assume to represent the region by listing its vertexes.

Table 3. Update operations involving AssociationRule patterns

N.	Manipulation Operation	PSY-PML code
1	Synchronize association rules in class AR30_psycho, using measure function AR_measure_func.	UPDATE PATTERNS OF AssociationRule ar SYNCHRONIZE USING AR_measure_func WHERE INCLASS(ar,'AR30_psycho')=1;
2	Validate rules in class AR30_psycho and inserts newly created patterns inside the same class.	UPDATE PATTERNS OF AssociationRule ar VALIDATE USING AR_measure_func WHERE inclass(ar, 'AR30_psycho')=1 INTO CLASS AR30_psycho;

The quality of the representation achieved by both types of clusters can be evaluated by the intra distance measure (Han & Kamber, 2001). The definition of such pattern type shows the PSYCHO capabilities in representing and manipulating the pattern formula.

Set-up. We assume that a cluster contains at most 100 points. We also assume two basic Oracle types, named *Point2D* and *Point2DArray*, for modeling 2D points and arrays of 2D points, are available as well as methods for checking equality between pairs of *Point2D* and *Point2DArray* instances. In Figure 6, the PSY-PDL definitions of two distinct pattern types, one for extensional clusters (named *EXTCluster*) and one for CH-clusters (named *CHCluster*), are reported. For both of them, the data source is a relational table with schema (DSID, P), where DSID is a point identifier and P is an instance of *Point2D*.

In defining both pattern types, an extensional formula method is provided (see lines 10-11 and lines 23-24). This method returns, among all points in the pattern data source, the points represented by the cluster. In case of *EXTCluster*, this corresponds to exactly all points belonging to the cluster structure, whereas in case of *CHCluster*, it returns the subset of the data source containing the points which fall inside the convex hull whose vertexes are the ones in the pattern structure. Thus, in this second case the result of the extensional formula constitutes an approximation of the point set represented by the cluster, since it may happen that some points internal to the convex hull describing the cluster structure do not effectively belong to the cluster itself. Additionally, in the case of *CHClusters*, the intensional formula is a Prolog predicate named *convex_hull* (see line 25), defined in file *convex_hull.pl* (Figure 7), which evaluates to true for each point fall-

Figure 6. EXTCluster and CHCluster pattern type definitions

```
 1: CREATE PATTERN TYPE EXTCluster
 2:  STRUCTURE pointset Point2DArray
 3:   DEFINE EQUALS ON p1 USING ret int CODE
 4:    if Pointarray_Equal (self.s.pointset, p1.s.pointset)=1 then ret:= 1; else ret:=0; end if;
 5:    RETURN ret;
 6:  MEASURE IntraDist REAL
 7:   DEFINE THETA ON p2 USING ret int CODE
 8:    if (self.m.IntraDist >= p2.m.IntraDist) then ret:=1; else ret:= 0; end if;
 9:    RETURN ret;
10:  FORMULA EXTENSIONAL ON varDS USING dummy varchar2(100) CODE
11:    ... /* evaluation of the subset of varDS approximated by a pattern of type EXTCluster*/
12: FORMULA INTENSIONAL convex_hull;
13:
14: CREATE PATTERN TYPE CHCluster
15:  STRUCTURE pointset Point2DArray
16:   DEFINE EQUALS ON p1 USING ret int CODE
17:    if Pointarray_Equal (self.s.pointset, p1.s.pointset)=1 then ret:= 1; else ret:=0; end if;
18:    RETURN ret;
19:  MEASURE IntraDist REAL
20:   DEFINE THETA ON p2 USING ret int CODE
21:    if (self.m.IntraDist >= p2.m.IntraDist) then ret:= 1; else ret:= 0; end if;
22:    RETURN ret;
23: FORMULA EXTENSIONAL ON varDS USING dummy varchar2(100) CODE
24:    ... /* evaluation of the subset of varDS approximated by a pattern of type CHCluster*/
25: FORMULA INTENSIONAL convex_hull;
```

Figure 7. convex_hull Prolog predicate

```
convex hull(Points, Xs) :- lin_comb(Points, Lambdas, Zero, Xs), zero(Zero),
polytype(Lambdas).

polytype(Xs) :- positive_sum(Xs, 1).

positive_sum([], Z) :- Z=0.
positive_sum([X|Xs], SumX) :- X >= 0, SumX = X+Sum , positive_sum(Xs, Sum).

zero([]).
zero([Z|Zs]) :- Z=0, zero(Zs).

lin_comb([], [], S1, S1).
lin_comb([Ps|Rest], [K|Ks], S1, S3) :- lin_comb r(Ps, K, S1, S2), lin_comb(Rest, Ks, S2, S3).

lin_comb r([], , [], []).
lin_comb_r([P|Ps], K, [S|Ss], [Kps|Ss1 ]) :- Kps = K*P+S , lin_comb_r(Ps, K, Ss, Ss1 ).
```

Figure 8. Measure function definition for EXTCLuster pattern type

```
1: CREATE MEASURE FUNCTION EC_Measure_func FOR EXTCluster ec
2: USING varDS
3: AS ... /* local variable declaration */
4: BEGIN
5:    ... /* code for computing the average intra-distance value for
6:        patterns of type EXTCluster over the input dataset varDS */
7: END;
```

ing inside the convex hull corresponding to the pattern structure.

We also consider two mining functions, one for each cluster type. The implementation of both mining functions is based on the K-means algorithm (Han & Kamber, 2001) provided by ODM and is parametric with respect to the value of parameter K. We call such functions *KMeansODM* and *KMeansODM_convex*, respectively. In Figure 9 at lines 4-8 and lines 10-14, two examples of extraction operations producing patterns by using these two mining functions are reported.

Similarly to the mining function case, we consider a measure function for each cluster type, named *EC_Measure_func* and *CH_Measure_func*, respectively; the first one computes measures for *EXTcluster* patterns and the second one computes measures for *CHcluster* patterns. Both measure functions compute the intradistance value with respect to the points belonging to the

pattern structure. The PSY-PDL statement used to define *EC_Measure_func* is shown in Figure 8.

Population. In this step, we show how PSYCHO can be used to (1) use various mining functions to generate patterns of type *EXTCluster* and *CHCluster* and (2) directly insert patterns. Suppose the user wants to extract patterns of type EXTCluster from the data set *Points30* by using the *KmeansODM* mining function. First, the user creates two classes for storing the extracted extensional clusters, named *ClassK5_EC* and *ClassK5_CH*, respectively. Then, the user extracts clusters with intradistance greater than 0.3 from data set *Points30* by using the two available mining functions, sets the validity period of the extracted clusters from 10-jun-2005 to 10-jul-2005, and inserts the extracted patterns into the proper class (see Figure 9, lines 4-8). Note that the user may customize the previous extraction operations by

Figure 9. EXTCluster and CHCluster pattern generation

```
1: CREATE CLASS ClassK5_EC OF EXTCluster;
2: CREATE CLASS ClassK5_CH OF CHCluster;
3:
4: EXTRACT PATTERNS OF EXTCluster ec FROM Points30
5. USING KmeansODM(5)
6. WITH (0.3)
7: VALID FROM '10-jun-2005' TO '10-aug-2005'
8: INTO CLASS ClassK5_EC;
9:
10: EXTRACT PATTERNS OF CHCluster cc FROM Points30
11: USING KmeansODM_Convex(5)
12: WITH (0.3)
13: VALID FROM '10-jun-2005' TO '10-jul-2005'
14: INTO CLASS ClassK5_CH;
15:
16: DIRECT INSERT PATTERN OF EXTCluster FROM Points60
17: STRUCTURE(POINT2DARRAY(POINT2D(1,1), POINT2D(2,1), POINT2D(3,1),
18:                        POINT2D(2,2), POINT2D(3,2), POINT2D(2,3)) )
19: VALID FROM CURRENT DATE TO CURRENT DATE+30
20: INTO CLASS ClassK5_EC;
21:
22: DIRECT INSERT PATTERN OF CHCluster FROM Points60
23: STRUCTURE(POINT2DARRAY(POINT2D(1,1), POINT2D(3,1),  POINT2D(3,2), POINT2D(2,3)) )
24: MEASURE (0.3)
25: VALID FROM '01-aug-2005' TO '15-aug-2005'
26:INTO CLASS ClassK5_CH;
```

specifying how many clusters the user wants to obtain as output of the clustering algorithm (the value of parameter K). As already discussed in the case of association rules, PSYCHO supports the direct insertion of patterns. The PSY-PML statement presented at lines 16-20 shows the direct insertion of an *EXT_Cluster* instance in *ClassK5_EC*. Similarly, at lines 22-26, the direct insertion of a *CHCluster* instance in *ClassK5_CH* is reported.

Queries. Table 4 presents several PSYCHO queries involving *EXTCluster* and *CHCluster* patterns. In particular, these queries are primary aimed at pointing out the various pattern representations available in PSYCHO, that is, (1) the pattern data source; (2) items in the data space represented by a pattern; and (3) the subset of the data source which is effectively represented by a certain pattern. In particular, query 1 enumerates the overall set of data from which the cluster has

been extracted, whereas query 2 determines which data are represented by a certain cluster, through its intensional formula. Query 3 determines which data items contained in the source data set *Points30* are effectively represented by a certain cluster of class *ClassK5_EC*. We notice that, for this query, we can use the DATA COVERING operation, relying on the extensional formula and returning the subset of the data source actually represented by the pattern. The obtained data satisfy the intensional formula associated with the selected pattern, since data covering relies on the application of the extensional formula.

Moreover, queries 4 and 5 are primary aimed at showing the usage of the intensional formula.

In particular, query 4 relies on the predicate *icontain*, checking whether a given region of space is contained in the space described by the intensional formula of a given pattern. We outline that this predicate is checked at intensional level, by using the Prolog definition of the intensional

Table 4. Queries involving EXTCluster and CHCluster patterns

N.	Query	PSY-PQL code
1	Determine data from which cluster with PID=1001615 has been extracted.	DRILL THROUGH ClassK5_EC cl WHERE cl.PID = 1001615;
2	Determine data approximated by the cluster with PID=1001615, contained in class ClassK5_EC.	SELECT * FROM ClassK5_EC cl WHERE cl.PID = 1001615;

3	Determine which data items contained in the source data set Points30 are represented by the cluster with PID=1001615, contained in class ClassK5_EC.	DATA COVERING (SELECT *
		        FROM ClassK5_EC cl
		        WHERE cl.PID = 1001615) c
		FOR Points30
		WHERE c.PID = 1001615;

4	Determine clusters in class ClassK5_EC, extracted from data source Points30, containing a certain region of space, characterized by the following formula [X>=2,X=<7,Y>=3,Y=<10].	SELECT * FROM ClassK5_EC cl WHERE cl.d = 'Points30' I_AND icontain(cl.formulaI,[X>=2, X=<7,Y>=3,Y=<10]);
5	Determine clusters in class ClassK5_EC, extracted from data source Points30 intersecting a certain region of space, characterized by the following formula [X>=2,X=<7,Y>=3,Y=<10].	SELECT * FROM ClassK5_EC cl WHERE cl.d = 'Points30' I_AND iintersect(cl.formulaI,[X>=2 ,X=<7,Y>=3,Y=<10]);

formula (therefore, no access to data sources is required). As a consequence, the obtained result is an approximation of the real one since actual points belonging to the cluster are not explicitly taken into account.

SCENARIO 2: PATTERN HIERARCHIES

The aim of the second scenario is to show representation, manipulation, and querying activities for hierarchical patterns. To this purpose, we consider clusters of association rules. In this scenario, we group association rules based on their semantic validity with respect to a certain data source. Even if we apply a very simple clustering criteria, this does not impact the issue we wish to demonstrate. Indeed, it is even possible to extend PSYCHO library with more sophisticated data mining or machine learning algorithms in order to deal with more complex clustering purposes.

Set-up. The considered data source consists in classes of association rules, created in the previous scenario. Starting from those data, clusters of association rules can be modeled by using a pattern type *EXTClusterOfRules*, defined in PSY-PDL as shown in Figure 10. We outline that, as default, an extensional formula returning the whole pattern data source is associated with a pattern of type *EXTClusterOfRule*, but no intensional formula is associated with patterns of this type. Since, for the sake of simplicity, we want to define clusters of association rules based on validity, the used mining function is very simple and just divides a set of association rules into two clusters; such a function is called *EXTClusterOfRulesMF*. Furthermore, we assume the measure function just returns 1 when the pattern is semantically valid with respect to the specified data source.

Otherwise, it returns 0. The measure function *CRules_measure_func* can be easily defined as shown at lines 22-26.

Population. We consider only pattern extraction as shown in Figure 11. We first create a class for storing the extracted clusters, named *ClassCR_1* (see line 1). After that, patterns of type *EXTClusterOfRules* are extracted from the PSYCHO class *AR30_psycho* by using the *EXTClusterOfRuleMF* mining function introduced above, setting the validity period of the extracted clusters starting from August 1, 2005 and ending on September

30, 2005 (see lines 3-7). Note that in this case, the data source is the class *AR30_psycho* and the mining function has a parameter that corresponds to a source data set for association rules, used to check their semantic validity.

Queries. Table 5 presents two queries involving patterns of type *EXTClusterOfRules*. The first one determines clusters of rules containing at least four association rules, whereas the second one is a cross-over query retrieving all association rules contained in a certain cluster of rules.

Figure 10. EXTClusterOfRules pattern type creation

```
1: CREATE TYPE ARset AS varray(100) OF REF AssociationRule;
2: CREATE OR REPLACE FUNCTION ARset_Equal (a ARset, b ARset) RETURN INTEGER
3: AUTHID CURRENT_USER
4: IS ... /* local variable declaration */
5: BEGIN
6:   ... /* code for checking equality between a and b */
7: END ARset_Equal;
8:
9: CREATE PATTERN TYPE EXTClusterOfRules
10: STRUCTURE ruleset ARset
11:   DEFINE EQUALS ON r1 USING ret int CODE
12:   if ARset_Equal(self, p1)=1 then ret:=1; else ret:=0; end if;
13:   return ret;
14: MEASURE Svalidity REAL
15:   DEFINE THETA ON r2 USING ret int CODE
16:   if self.m.Svalidity >= r2.m.Svalidity then ret:=1; else ret:= 0; end if;
17:   return ret;
18: FORMULA EXTENSIONAL ON varDS USING p AssociationRule CODE
19: ... /* evaluation of the subset of varDS approximated by a pattern of type EXTClusterofRules*/
20: FORMULA INTENSIONAL dummy predicate;
21:
22: CREATE MEASURE FUNCTION CRules_measure_func FOR EXTClusterOfRules cr USING varDS AS val real
23: BEGIN
24:   val := isSvalid(cr, 'varDS', 'CRules_own_measure', EXTClusterOfRulesMeasure(null,0));
25:   RETURN MEASURE(val);
26: END;
```

Figure 11. EXTClusterOfRules pattern extraction

```
1: CREATE CLASS ClassCR_1 OF EXTClusterOfRules;
2:
3: EXTRACT PATTERNS OF EXTClusterOfRules ec FROM AR30_psycho
4: USING EXTClusterOfRuleMF('ItemsDS_30')
5: WITH (0)
6: VALID FROM '01-aug-2005' TO '30-sep-2005'
7: INTO CLASS ClassCR_1;
```

Table 5. Queries involving patterns of type EXTClusterOfRules

N.	Query	PSY-PQL code
1	Retrieve all patterns from class ClassCR_1 containing at least four rules	SELECT * FROM ClassCR_1 cr WHERE cr.s.ruleset.count >= 4;
2	Determine the association rule data set from which the cluster with a certain PID, belonging to class ClassCR_1, has been generated	DRILL THROUGH (SELECT * FROM ClassCR_1 c WHERE c.PID = 1001454) a;

CONCLUSION

In this chapter, we have presented PSYCHO, a prototype system for the management of heterogeneous patterns. PSYCHO has been implemented by exploiting object-relational database technologies (provided by the Oracle platform) integrated with logical constraint solving features (provided by the Sicstus Prolog engine) through the usage of object-oriented programming. More precisely, after presenting the main requirements a system for heterogeneous pattern management must support, we have discussed existing solutions and we have then presented PSYCHO features through the illustration of different usage scenarios.

In order to become an effectively usable system for patterns management, PSYCHO functionalities have to be consolidated and extended. Several directions for future work can be identified, including:

- Interoperability aspects allowing the integration of PSYCHO with existing standards for pattern representation, such as PMML, constitute a key functionality in order to make PSYCHO a usable system for pattern management in real applications. To this purpose, an import/export module dedicated to PMML is currently under development. We point out that PMML has been chosen by the authors as the basis for improving interoperability due to the fact that its popularity is rapidly increasing, and it will probably become the de-facto standard for knowledge exchange among distributed sources soon, since it is based on XML.

- The design and development of an open-source version of the system is an interesting challenge. To this end, we need to become independent by a licensed constraint solving engine—like Sicstus Prolog—and by a proprietary DBMS technology—like Oracle. A new PSYCHO version for which we plan to consider an open source DBMS environment is currently under development.

- The development of a graphical user interface to interact with the system and to visualize discovered knowledge in a user-friendly way.

- The experimentation of PSYCHO over real application domains such as retail analysis, clickstream analysis concerning Web navigations, or biomedical applications.

- The enhancement and consolidation of manipulation functionalities provided by PSYCHO for semantic alignment between patterns and the raw data they represent is another interesting topic for future work. Indeed, since in many modern applications, we cannot assume raw data being stable, it would be very helpful for handling concept drift issues to support agile and, possibly, automatic manipulation mechanisms in order to recognize data changes having an impact over patterns and to update them. To this end, we plan to improve the virtual concept drift support already provided by PSYCHO by giving PSYCHO users the ability to promptly recognize data changes and the possibility to deal with them in a real-time fashion. Additionally, in order to fully support real-time alignment between the informative content of the pattern base and the informative content of the data sources, our approach should be revised and enhanced to cope with reactivity, consistency, and maintenance issues. The ability to address these problems becomes very useful in order to deal with stream data, which are very common in many different existing real-world applications.

REFERENCES

Agrawal, R., & Srikant, R. (1994). Fast algorithms for mining association rules in large databases. In *Proceedings of VLDB'94* (pp. 487-499).

Bertino, E., Catania, B., & Maddalena, A. (2004). Toward a language for pattern manipulation and querying. In *Proceedings of the EDBT '04 Workshop on Pattern Representation and Management (PaRMa '04)*.

Catania, B., Maddalena, A., & Mazza, M. (2005). PSYCHO: A prototype system for pattern management. In *Proceedings of VLDB'05* (pp. 1346-1349).

Catania, B., Maddalena, A., Mazza, M., Bertino, E., & Rizzi, S. (2004). A framework for data mining pattern management. In *Proceedings of ECML-PKDD'04* (pp. 87-98). Lecture Notes on Artificial Intelligence 3202.

CINQ. (2001). *The CINQ project*. Retrieved June 15, 2007, from http://www.cinq-project.org

CWM. (2001). *Common warehouse metamodel*. Retrieved June 15, 2007, from http://www.omg.org/cwm

DB2. (2005). DB2 Intelligent Miner. Retrieved June 15, 2007, from http://www-306.ibm.com/software/data/iminer/

De Raedt, L. (2002). A perspective on inductive databases. *ACM SIGKDD Explorations Newsletter, 4*(2), 69-77.

De Raedt, L., Jaeger, M., Lee, S.D., & Mannila, H. (2002). A theory on inductive query answering. In *Proceedings of ICDM'02* (pp. 123-130).

Han, J., Fu, Y., Wang, W., Koperski, K., & Zaiane, O. (1996). DMQL: A data mining query language for relational databases. In *Proceedings of the SIGMOD'96 Workshop on Research Issues in Data Mining and Knowledge Discovery (DMKD'96)*.

Han, J., & Kamber, M. (2001). *Data mining: Concepts and techniques*. Academic Press.

Han, J., Pei, J., & Yin, Y. (2000). Mining frequent patterns without candidate generation. *In Proceedings of ACM SIGMOD '00* (pp. 1-12).

Imielinski, T., & Mannila, H. (1996). A database perspective on knowledge discovery. *Communications of the ACM, 39*(11), 58-64.

Imielinski, T., & Virmani, A. (1999). MSQL: A query language for database mining. *Data Mining and Knowledge Discovery, 2*(4), 373-408.

ISO SQL/MM Part 6. (2001). Retrieved June 15, 2007, from http://www.sql-99.org/SC32/WG4/Progression Documents/FCD/fcd-datamining-2001-05.pdf

Jasper. (2005). *The Jasper Java Interface*. Retrieved June 15, 2007, from http://www.sics.se/sicstus/docs/latest/html/sicstus/Jasper.html

JDM. (2003). *Java Data Mining API*. Retrieved June 15, 2007, from http://www.jcp.org/jsr/detail/73.prt

Johnson, S., Lakshmanan, L.V.S., & Ng, R.T. (2000). The 3W model and algebra for unified data mining. In *Proceedings of VLDB'00* (pp. 21-32).

Meo, R., Lanzi, P.L., & Klemettinen, M. (2003). Database support for data mining applications. *Lecture Notes on Computer Science, 2682.* Springer-Verlag.

Meo, R., Psaila, G., & Ceri, S. (1998). An extension to SQL for mining association rules. *Data Mining and Knowledge Discovery, 2*(2), 195-224.

MS SQL. (2005). Microsoft SQL server analysis server. Retrieved June 15, 2007, from http://www.microsoft.com/sql/evaluation/bi/bianalysis.asp

ODM. (2005). Oracle data mining tools. Retrieved June 15, 2007, from http://www.oracle.com/technology/products/bi/odm

OLEDB. (2005). OLE DB for data mining specification. Retrieved June 15, 2007, from http://www.microsoft.com/data/oledb

PANDA. (2001). The PANDA Project. Retrieved June 15, 2007, from http://dke.cti.gr/panda/

PMML. (2003). Predictive model markup language (version 3.1). Retrieved June 15, 2007, from http://www.dmg.org/pmml-v3-1.html

Rizzi, S., Bertino, E., Catania, B., Golfarelli, M., Halkidi, M., Terrovitis, M., Vassiliadis, P., Vazirgiannis, M., & Vrachnos, E. (2003). Towards a logical model for patterns. In *Proceedings of ER'03* (pp. 77-90).

Sicstus. (2004). *SICStus Prolog (version 3).* Retrieved June 15, 2007, from http://www.sics.se/isl/sicstuswww/site

Tsymbal, A. (2004). *The problem of concept drift: Definitions and related work* (Tech. Rep. No. TCD-CS-2004-15). Trinity College Dublin, Department of Computer Science, Ireland. Retrieved June 15, 2007, from https://www.cs.tcd.ie/publications/tech-reports/reports.04/TCD-CS-2004-15.pdf

Chapter VI
Deterministic Motif Mining in Protein Databases

Pedro Gabriel Ferreira
Universidade do Minho, Portugal

Paulo Jorge Azevedo
Universidade do Minho, Portugal

ABSTRACT

Protein sequence motifs describe, through means of enhanced regular expression syntax, regions of amino acids that have been conserved across several functionally related proteins. These regions may have an implication at the structural and functional level of the proteins. Sequence motif analysis can bring significant improvements towards a better understanding of the protein sequence-structure-function relation. In this chapter, we review the subject of mining deterministic motifs from protein sequence databases. We start by giving a formal definition of the different types of motifs and the respective specificities. Then, we explore the methods available to evaluate the quality and interest of such patterns. Examples of applications and motif repositories are described. We discuss the algorithmic aspects and different methodologies for motif extraction. A brief description on how sequence motifs can be used to extract structural level information patterns is also provided.

INTRODUCTION

Proteins are biological macromolecules involved in all biochemical functions in the life of the cell and therefore in the life of the being. Protein in-formation is encoded in regions of the DNA helix, and these molecules are synthesized through a two step process: *translation* and *transcription* (Cooper, 1994; Hunter, 1993). Proteins are composed of basic unit molecules called *amino acids*.

Twenty different types of amino acids (AAs) exist, all with well differentiated structural and chemical properties.

After being synthesized, proteins acquire a complex 3-dimensional structure in a process called *folding*. The resulting 3D structure, which corresponds to a state of greatest stability (minimal energy), is essential for protein function. This structure is ultimately determined by the linear sequence of amino acids, also called primary structure. Therefore, a closer look at the primary sequence will certainly provide valuable insights about the protein structure and function.

When a set of functionally related sequences is closely analyzed, one can verify that parts of those sequences (subsequences) are common to several or all the analyzed sequences. These subsequences consist of a pattern and are called *sequence patterns* or *motifs*. These motifs occur in protein sequences because they have been preserved through the evolutionary history of the proteins. This suggests that they might play a structural and/or a functional role in the protein's mechanisms. On the other hand, AAs outside these critical regions tend to be less conserved. The discovery of these motifs can be used to support a better understanding of the protein's structure and function. This is due to the fact that the AAs that compose these motifs can be close in the tridimensional arrangement of the protein. Additionally, these motifs can be used to provide evidences and to determine relations with yet uncharacterized proteins.

At the time of this writing,[1] Swiss-Prot (Gasteiger, 2003), which is a comprehensive, annotated, and nonredundant protein knowledge base, contained approximately 208,000 sequences from 9,749 species, with an average length per sequence of 364 AAs. This volume of information demands intelligent and efficient sequence analysis techniques. These methods should look for similarities among the selected proteins and discriminate the regions that have been conserved among a significant number of proteins. These

regions contain well-conserved positions, where the substitutions among different AAs for those positions are less frequent. Motifs can be used to capture the nature of those regions.

In this chapter, we present an overview on the subject of protein motif mining. The chapter has the following outline: First a characterization on the type of extracted patterns is given. Two main classes of motifs are introduced and briefly described (Motif Definition section). Since these two classes have different analysis and algorithmic requirements, we will focus our attention on the class of deterministic patterns. In the Deterministic Motifs section, details of the characteristics of this type of patterns are provided. Next, different ways to evaluate the interest of the motifs (Significance Measures section) are presented, followed by examples of the application of motifs in different contexts (Motif Applications section). In the Motif Databases section, several of the Internet databases that compile and manage protein motifs are surveyed. The motif mining algorithms section describes the algorithmic aspects of the motif extraction process, and some of the most well-known and successful methodologies for motif mining are presented. In the Structural Motifs section, the concept of structural motifs is introduced, and examples of motifs and algorithms are provided. To finish, some conclusions and final remarks are given.

Motif Definition

As previously introduced, a sequence motif describes a region of conserved elements from a set of related sequences. These motifs are eventually related to an important structural and/or functional role of the proteins. Two classes of motifs exist: *probabilistic* and *deterministic*.

Probabilistic motifs consist in a model that simulates the sequences or part of the sequences under consideration. When a given sequence is compared against the motif, the probability of that sequence matching the given motif can be easily calculated. Probabilistic motifs are typically expressed through position weight matrices (PWM) (Gribskov, McLachlan, & Eisenberg, 1987), also called, among other things, Position Specific Scoring Matrices, Templates, or Profiles. A PWM is a matrix of the weighted matches of each of the 20 AAs in each position of the motif. An extra row is added to denote a "do not care" symbol, that is, a symbol that matches any of the AAs. Table 1 shows the scheme of a PWM, which represents a motif of size N. The rows describe a list of amino acids and the columns the motif positions. The value of the cell P_{ij} describes the probability of the amino acid i being found in position j of the motif. In this model, independence is assumed between positions. For a sequence $S = S_1 S_2 ... S_N$ of length N, the likelihood of it being matched by a PWM P is given by formula (1). Since for sequence comparison purposes the logarithms are handled easier than probability values, the log-odds of the P_{ij} cells are usually used. Now, the likelihood of S being matched by P is given by formula (2).

$$\prod_{i=1}^{N} P(S_i, i) \qquad (1)$$

$$\sum_{i=1}^{N} \log P(S_i, i) \qquad (2)$$

Deterministic motifs can be divided into two types: *fixed-length* and *extensible-length*. Fixed-length motifs, also known as (l,d)-*motifs* (Buhler & Tompa, 2001; Pevzner & Sze, 2000), consist of motifs of a fixed size of l symbols, where d possible symbols may have a mismatch with the matched subsequences in the input database. We will discuss more about this type of motifs later in this chapter. Extensible-length motifs have an arbitrary length and are expressed through enhanced regular expressions. Depending on the applications that generate the motifs, different versions of regular expression syntax can be used. A generic format for these motifs is as follows:

$$A_1 - x(p_1, q_1) - A_2 - x(p_2, q_2) - ... - A_n \qquad (3)$$

where A_k is a sequence of consecutive amino acids and $-x(p_i, q_i)-$ a gap greater than p_i and smaller than q_i. A gap corresponds to positions that can be matched by any amino acid. If p_i equals q_i, the gap notation is usually abbreviated to $-x(p_i)-$. If a position is occupied with more than one amino acid, a bracket notation is used. For instance, the notation [ACG] denotes a position that can be occupied by the amino acids A, C, or G.

Table 1. Example of a probabilistic weight matrix

Amino Acid	Position			
	1	2	...	N
A	P_{A1}	P_{A2}	...	P_{AN}
C	P_{C1}	P_{C2}	...	P_{CN}
. . .	...	...	...	...
V	P_{V1}	P_{V2}	...	P_{VN}
*	P_{*1}	P_{*2}	...	P_{*N}

For the sake of simplicity, from now on, we will refer to extensible-length motifs as deterministic motifs, and an explicit reference will be made for fixed-length motifs.

The pattern *[AG]-x(4)-G-K-[ST]* corresponds to the entry PS00017 on the Prosite database (Hulo, 2006). This pattern describes a motif where the first position can be occupied by the amino acid Alanine (A) or Glycine (G), followed by any other four AAs (do not care positions), a Glycine (G), a Lysine (K), and in the last position, it can appear as a Serine (S) or a Threonine (T). A "do not care" position can also be expressed through the symbol ".", so the above pattern can be rewritten as *[AG]. . . .G-K-[ST]*. In a following section, we will describe in more detail some of the motif databases, including Prosite.

Both ways of describing motifs have been pointed out as having advantages and drawbacks (Koonin & Galperin, 2003). Deterministic motifs make use of widely known regular expression syntax, so they are easily understandable by humans. They can be used in any simple application to perform fast searches and matches in large databases. One of the drawbacks of this class of patterns is that they do not capture the complete diversity of the matched sequences. For instance, deterministic patterns do not capture the distribution of the AAs in a given position, for example, the first and last positions of the above example motif. Probabilistic motifs provide more precision for the sequence analysis, at the cost of harder human interpretability. In the next section, we will describe the different types and details concerning deterministic motifs.

Deterministic Motifs

As a result of its representation with regular expressions, deterministic motifs have a great expressive power, as good descriptors for well-conserved regions across several protein sequences.

Furthermore, since they are not confined to a fixed length, they can indicate relations among distant related AAs. Four types of deterministic motifs can be distinguished:

- *Concrete motifs* are patterns admitting only contiguous events; that is, no gaps are allowed. In this case, each position is undoubtedly occupied by the respective AA symbol. Example: *R-G-D* (Prosite entry PS00016).
- *Ambiguous motifs* only contain contiguous events, but some positions may be occupied by more than one symbol. Example: *L-M-A-[EQ]-G-L-Y-N* (Prosite entry PS00033).
- *Rigid gap motifs* only contain gaps with a fixed length; this corresponds to a situation where $p_i = q_i, \forall i$ in formula (3). Example: *Y..Y-Y.C.C* (Prosite entry PS00121).
- *Flexible gap motifs* allow gaps of variable length; this corresponds to a situation where $p_i \leq q_i, \forall i$ in formula (3). Example: *C.C..[GP][FYW]-x(4,8)-C* (Prosite entry PS01186).

For a pattern like *C.[AG].C*, many combinations of subsequences can be matched, more exactly $20 \times 2 \times 20$. Each of these combinations is called *specialization*, for example, *CVAMC*. A more generic combination will be called a *generalization*. *C.[AG].C* is a generalization of *C.A.C* and *C.A.C* a generalization of *CVA.C*.

A motif M' is contained in a motif M and is called *submotif* of M, if it can be obtained by dropping some symbols from M. For example, C.[AG] or [AG].C are submotifs of C.[AG].C. Extending a motif corresponds to appending new symbols to its left or right side. A motif is called *frequent* if it is found in a number of sequences, from the input database, greater or equal than a user specified threshold value. This value is generally called *minimum support*, and it is denoted as σ. The *cover* of the motif represents the list of sequence identifiers where the motif occurs. The cardinality of this list corresponds to the support of the motif.

According to the information that it captures, a motif can be classified as one of three classes: *Maximal, Closed,* or *All.* A motif is said to be *Maximal* (Ester & Zhang, 2004) when it is not contained in any other motif. A motif is called *Closed* (Califano, 2000; Rigoutsos & Floratos, 1998) when all its extensions and specializations result in motifs with smaller support. The *All* class of motifs corresponds to all the possible motif specializations. Maximal motifs are a subset of closed motifs, which are consequently a subset of the *All* class. Table 5 in the motif mining algorithms section presents a list of several motif mining algorithms and the respective features regarding the class and the type of the extracted patterns.

When a user has some predefined idea of the characteristics of the motifs the user is looking for, this previous knowledge can be directly incorporated in the analysis process. This will provide a more focused and efficient motif search. *Constraints* (Ferreira & Azevedo, 2005a; Jonassen, Collins, & Higgins, 1995; Sagot & Viari, 1996) are then used to specify this *a priori* knowledge and can be enumerated as:

- **Symbols constraint:** Restrict the set of symbols that may appear in the motifs.
- **Gap constraint:** Define the minimum distance or the maximum distance that may occur between two adjacent symbols in the motif.
- **Duration or window constraint:** Define the maximum distance between the first and the last symbol of the motifs.
- **Start and end symbol constraint:** Determines that the extracted motifs should start and/or end with the specified symbols.

Each AA has characteristics that make it unique. However, some have similar structural or chemical properties. Table 2 shows an example of AAs grouped according to a common property. These groups of AAs are usually called *substitution sets,* since they express equivalence relations between AAs. Substitution sets are best suited to be used in the deterministic motif extraction (Ester & Zhang, 2004; Sagot & Viari, 1996). For probabilistic motifs, substitution matrices (Durbin, Eddy, Krogh, & Mitchison, 1998) are used. These are AA × AA matrices, where each cell C_{ij} expresses a similarity value between AA i and AA j. The most well known are the PAM and the BLOSUM matrices (Henikoff & Henikoff, 1993).

When substitution sets are used in the motif analysis, AAs within the same group can be exchanged without loss of equivalence. In practice, this feature is equivalent to the concept of ambiguous positions, where positions occupied by more than one AA of the same group are represented by the group label. According to Table 2, the above mentioned motif [*AG*]. . . .*G-K-*[*ST*] is now rewritten as α . . . .*G-K-β.*

SIGNIFICANCE MEASURES

Deterministic motifs are extracted through combinatorial algorithms that perform an exhaustive traversal of the search space, and output motifs are based on the support metric. Protein datasets

Table 2. Example of substitution sets and the respective common property

Label	Group	Property
α	AGP	Small polar
β	ST	Small hydroxyl
γ	FWY	Aromatics
δ	HKR	Basic
ε	ILMV	Medium hydrophobic
ζ	EDNQ	Acid/Amid

are typically characterized by having a relative medium number of sequences (ranging from sets of tens to a few hundreds), a relative long length of the sequences (several hundreds of AAs) and a large density, which is a consequence of a small alphabet size. It results in the fact that if the minimum support is set too high, too few motifs may arise. However, if the support is set too low, too many motifs will be enumerated. Not all these motifs are particularly interesting, and most of them arise by chance. This requires that motifs are evaluated by another measure of significance rather than support. In the literature, many measures of interest and significance have been proposed. Usually, for each proposed motif mining algorithm, a different measure is also proposed. In this section, we will introduce three categories of measures. We will illustrate each category with examples. Some of these measures are not exclusive from the bioinformatics field and can also be found in data mining and machine learning literature. The criterion used for choosing these measures lie in the fact that previous use yielded good results in identifying relevant patterns.

As in Brazma, Jonassen, Eidhammer, and Gilbert (1998a), we assume that a significance measure can be defined as a function in the format $f(m,T) \rightarrow \Re$, where m stands for the motif being evaluated, T a set of possibly related protein sequences. This function returns a number that expresses how relevant or significant m is with respect to T. Although m may be significant with relation to T, it can also occur in many other sequences not related to T. In order to avoid such cases, negative information can be provided to the evaluation function (Barash, Bejerano, & Friedman, 2001; Takusagawa & Gifford, 2004), which is now rewritten as $f(m,T,N) \rightarrow \Re$, where N is a set of sequences considered as negative information. In this case, it will be expected that a motif m will be relevant to set T and not to the set N. If N is omitted, we then consider the negative information as the remaining sequences in the set

of all known sequences—the Swiss-Prot database. Significance measures may have a biological or a statistical meaning. Some measures are calculated exclusively based on the motif information and others on how motifs relate to the sequences where they appear.

Here, we consider that a measure may belong to one of the three following categories:

1. *Class-based* measures are calculated based on the information of the motif with relation to the target and the remaining protein classes/families.
2. *Theoretic-information* measures are calculated based solely on theoretic models like probabilistic or entropy models. In this case, the measure calculation is self-contained; that is, the necessary information is found in the motif itself.
3. *Mixed* measures use both class and theoretic information.

In the next sections, we introduce some measures of interest according to the three categories. It is not our intention to provide an extensive enumeration of all the existing measures, but only to provide the reader a brief introduction to the subject.

Class-Based Measures

The ideal motif is the one that matches all the sequences within the target family and no other sequence outside this family. These patterns are also known as *signatures* (Jonassen et al., 1995) and are the perfect tool to distinguish sequences among different families. Unfortunately, such motifs are not as frequent as desirable. In the bioinformatics context, three measures – *sensitivity* (also known as recall), *specificity*, and *precision* (also known as positive predicted value)—are frequently used to express the quality of the motifs (Brazma et al., 1998a; Hulo, Bairoch, Bulliard, Cerutti, De Castro, Langendijk-Genevaux, et al.,

2006; Jonassen, 2000; Witten & Frank, 2005). Sensitivity (Sn) is used to measure the proportion of sequences of the target family correctly covered by the motif. Specificity (Sp) is used to measure the proportion of sequences outside the target family that are not covered by the motif. Precision measures the proportion of sequences covered by the pattern that belong to the target family. We can therefore distinguish four possible cases:

- **True Positive (T_P):** A sequence that belongs to the target family and matches the motif.
- **True Negative (T_N):** A sequence that does not belong to the target family and does not match the motif.
- **False Negative (F_N):** A sequence that belongs to the target family and does not match the motif.
- **False Positive (F_P):** A sequence that does not belong to the target family and matches the motif.

The three measures are then defined as:

$$Sn = \frac{T_P}{T_P + F_N} \times 100\%; \tag{4}$$

$$Sp = \frac{T_N}{T_N + F_P} \times 100\% \tag{5}$$

$$precision = \frac{T_P}{T_P + F_P} \times 100\%; \tag{6}$$

A motif is considered a signature if both sensitivity and precision are 100%. When a unique value is necessary to score the motifs, measures that combine the information from Table 3 can be used. For instance, the F-measure (formula 7), widely used in the machine learning field (Witten & Frank, 2005), results from a combination of recall and precision and is defined as:

$$F = \frac{2 \times recall \times precision}{recall + precision} = \frac{2 \times T_P}{2 \times T_P + F_N + F_P} \tag{7}$$

Another combined measure is the correlation coefficient (Baldi, Brunak, Chauvin, Andersen, & Nielsen, 2000; Brazma et al., 1998a). This measure uses all the class information, T_P, T_N, F_P, and F_N. Therefore, it can provide a much more balanced evaluation than the F-measure. It is equivalent to the Pearson correlation coefficient and is given by the following formula:

$$Corr = \frac{T_P \times T_N + F_P \times F_N}{\sqrt{(T_P + F_N)(T_P + F_P)(T_N + F_P)(T_N + F_N)}} \tag{8}$$

As a last measure, we introduce the D measure. This measure corresponds to the *discrimination power* (Ben-Hur & Brutlag, 2005) and is particularly useful as a filter. The greater the value of D, the more selective the pattern is:

$$D = \frac{T_P}{|C|} - \frac{F_P}{|\overline{C}|} \tag{9}$$

In this formula, $|C| = T_P + F_N$ and $|\overline{C}| = F_P + T_N$ are, respectively, the number of sequences in the target family and outside that family.

A characteristic of the class-based measures

Table 3. Confusion matrix for the four cases

		Covered Family	
		Positive	Negative
Target Family	Positive	True Positive (T_P)	False Negative (F_N)
	Negative	False Positive (F_P)	True Negative (T_N)

is that they do not rely on the motif itself in order to be calculated. Hence, they can be applied to any type of deterministic motif.

Probability Analysis

When analyzing the probabilistic aspects of the protein sequences, it is generally assumed that sequences can be generated according to one of two models. The Bernoulli model considers that symbols of a sequence are generated according to an independent identically distributed (i.i.d.) process; that is, there is no dependency between the probability distribution of the symbols. The second model is the Markov model. It assumes that the probability distribution of a given symbol depends on the n previous symbols, where n determines the order of the Markov chain (Durbin et al., 1998).

If a Bernoulli model is considered, the occurrence of a motif M in a given sequence is assumed to be an i.i.d. process (Apostolico, Comin, & Parida, 2005). In practice, this means that sequences are considered to be independent and that AAs occur independently of each other. Although this argument is not entirely true, since sequences are believed to be biologically related, it provides a simplification which is a good approximation to the actual verified values (Nevill-Manning, Sethi, Wu, & Brutlag, 1997). Thus, considering a motif M as having the format of formula (3) and, according to Nevill-Manning et al. (1997), the probability of a motif M can be given by the formula:

$$P(M) = P(A_1) \times P(\ -x(p_1,q_1)-)$$

$$\times P(A_2) \times P(-x(p_2,q_2)-) \times \cdots P(A_n) \qquad (10)$$

Since the probability of matching any AA is 1, $P(.) = 1$, then $P(-x(p,q)-) = 1$. Thus, the probability of M can be resumed as:

$$P(M) = \prod_{i=1}^{n} P(A_i) \qquad (11)$$

The probability of a subsequence A_i is given by:

$$P(A_i) = \prod_{a_j \in A_i} \left(\sum_{k=1}^{|A_i|} P(a_{jk}) \right) \qquad (12)$$

The probability of an AA a_j, $P(a_j)$ is given by its frequency[2] at the Swiss-Prot database. Formula (12) is used to calculate the probability of subsequences of AAs. The summation part of the formula handles the ambiguous positions, where a_{jk} stands for the k-th AA in position j of the subsequence. For example, the probability of the subsequence A-[GC].V is $0.0783 \times (0.0693 + 0.0152) \times 1 \times 1 \times 0.0671 = 4.44 \times 10^{-4}$. Multiplying the probability of the motif by the total number of symbols (AAs) in the database provides a good approximation of the number of expected sequences matched by the motif:

Table 4. Example motifs, actual and expected number of matches in the Swiss-Prot database according to the formula 13

Motif	Expected Matches	Actual Matches (release 48.1 Swiss-Prot)
A-C-x(2)-E	5993	4192
A-C-x(2)-E-D-x(1)-L	30	17
Y-x(3)-F-x(3)-F-x(6)-T	201	224
A-[GC]-x(2)-V	33673	33380

$$Exp_{matches} = P(M) \times Num_{symbols} \qquad (13)$$

Table 4 presents the expected and the actual number of matches in the Swiss-Prot database for some example motifs.

In general, only positive information is available, that is, the set of sequences under analysis. Therefore, for the obtained patterns, information, like the number of false positives F_p, is not provided and needs *a posteriori* calculation. In those cases, the computation of the expected matches, according to formula (13), is particularly useful. An alternative would be to get a local copy of the entire database, for instance, the Swiss-Prot, which is available by file transfer protocol (FTP), and run a program that finds matches of the motif in the local database.

Theoretic-Information Measures

Theoretic-information measures quantify the degree of information encoded in a motif. In this section, we provide examples of three of these measures.

In Jonassen et al. (1995), a new measure was introduced to rank the flexible patterns obtained from the Pratt algorithm. This measure expresses the information content of a motif by summing the information of its components (AAs) and decreasing the uncertainty that results from the existence of gaps. It does not take into account the support of the pattern. High information content provides evidences to the significance of the pattern.

In Nevill-Manning et al. (1997) and Ukkonen, Vilo, Brazma, and Jonassen (1996), the minimum description length (MDL principle) is used to score the patterns and to measure the fitness of these patterns with respect to the input sequences. The basic idea of the MDL principle is summarized as: if these sequences hypothetically needed to be transmitted, how much could be saved in the transmission knowing about the presence of the motifs? Thus, according to the MDL principle,

the best motif (or set of motifs) is the one that minimizes the sum of two components: the length of the motif and the length of the sequences when encoded with the motifs.

In Apostolico et al. (2005) and Califano (2000), a Z-Score function is used to evaluate over-represented motifs. For a motif M, this function takes the form:

$$Z(M) = \frac{f(M) - E(M)}{N(M)} \qquad (14)$$

$f(M)$ is the actual number of occurrences (support) of M, $E(M)$ the expected number of occurrences of M, and $N(M)$ represents the expected value of some function of M, for example, the square root of the variance of the support of M in a random database with equal size and composition of the database in analysis. The $E(M)$ can be provided by formula (13), and in the Bernoulli model, the square root of the support variance (Apostolico, 2005) can be calculated according to formula (15).

$$N(M) = \sqrt{N_{symbols} \times P(M) \times (1 - P(M))} \qquad (15)$$

In Apostolico et al. (2005) and Califano (2000), it was generally verified that statistically relevant motifs, discriminated through the Z-Score function, match functionally important regions of the proteins. Another important conclusion obtained from Apostolico et al. (2005) is that for over-represented motifs, the nonmaximal motifs (which are contained on other motifs) have a lower degree of surprise than the maximal motifs. This result yields a clever mechanism to prune motifs just before their significance is computed.

Mixed Measures

A probabilistic or statistically significant pattern may not necessarily occur frequently. The support metric might not always be the most adequate measure of significance. In this case, a significant pattern can be defined as a pattern that occurs more frequently than expected. In this case, significance will represent a measure of expectation.

We will use the definitions from Wu and Brutlag (1995) and Yang and Yu (2001) to define a measure of "*surprise*" of a pattern. The information content *I* of a pattern measure will determine how likely a pattern is to occur, or equivalently, the amount of "surprise" of the pattern when it actually occurs. The information content (Abramson, 1963) of a motif *M* is given by:

$$I(M) = -\log_{|\Sigma|} P(M)$$

$$= I(A_1) + I(A_2) + \cdots + I(A_n) \qquad (16)$$

where

$$I(A_i) = -\log_{|\Sigma|} P(A_i) \text{ and } |\Sigma| = 20 \qquad (17)$$

The information gain (*IG*) measure is introduced to measure the accumulated information of a motif in an amino acid sequence and is given by:

$$IG(M) = I(M) \times [Support(M) - 1] \qquad (18)$$

The fraction *Support*(*M*) − 1 gives the recurrence of the motif *M* in the input database. Since this formula does not account for the motif distribution in the whole universe of sequences, a more balanced measure is the (S)urprise measure. It can be defined as:

$$S(M) = I(M) \times \frac{Support(M \cap C)}{Support(M)}$$

$$= I(M) \times \frac{T_P}{T_P + F_P} \qquad (19)$$

In the formula above, *C* corresponds to the set of sequences under analysis, that is, the target family, and *Support*(*M* ∩ *C*) the number of sequences in *C* covered by *M* (*T_P*).

Finally, we present two widely used information-theoretic measures. The first is called the Mutual-Information measure, derived from the Shannon's entropy theory (Abramson, 1963). The mutual information of two variables *X* and *Y* tells how much the knowledge of *Y* reduces the uncertainty in knowing *X*. This can be used to determine the uncertainty reduction about a set of sequences *C*, when the motif *M* is given. The second measure is the J measure introduced by Smyth and Goodman (1990). This measure combines three important properties: (1) it expresses how well a motif *M* describes a set of sequences C; (2) how *M* reduces the uncertainty in knowing C; and (3) the average content information of *M*. These two measures have many data mining and machine learning applications and are particularly useful for classification purposes.

MOTIF APPLICATIONS

Although motifs are relevant to support a better understanding of the sequences under analysis, they have a wide range of other applications. In this section, we describe some of these applications.

- **Classification:** Classification is the task of finding a set of models or functions that describe and distinguish the different classes of data (Han & Kamber, 2001). These models are built based on a set of previously labeled data. In the bioinformatics context, classes of data may correspond to protein families. In this scenario, classification is used to find for an uncharacterized sequence which family it most resembles. Since motifs may have a tight relation to the proteins function, they can be used as a differentiation factor and therefore provide an important protein function prediction mechanism. In Ben-Hur and Brutlag (2003, 2005), motifs present in a set of sequences are extracted in order to create a feature space, which is then applied to a SVM classifier. In Ferreira and Azevedo

(2005b), rigid gap patterns common to the query sequence and the protein families are extracted. Then, its characteristics are weighted with a Bayes classifier to provide a degree of similarity with relation to the different protein families. Other methods like Blekas, Fotiadis, and Likas (2005) combine probabilistic motifs and neural networks to perform classification. Motifs can also be used in the detection of subfamilies within a larger set of sequence from one family (Ukkonen et al., 1996).

- **Clustering:** Clustering can be defined as the task of grouping similar objects into classes. This is an unsupervised learning technique since it does not make use of the class label information of the objects. Thus, it can be used in those cases where the object information is not known in advance. The goal is to arrange the objects into classes, in a way that the similarity within the class is maximized and the similarity between classes minimized (Han & Kamber, 2001). Once again, the descriptive power of the motifs can be used to perform protein sequence clustering. In Guralnik and Karypis (2001), protein sequences are mapped into motif feature space, after which a *K-means* (Han & Kamber, 2001) based algorithm is used to find clusters in that space.

- **Gene analysis:** One of the most interesting areas of biology is the study of coregulated genes. These are genes regulated by the same protein, and they are expected to have a common motif. Motifs can be used to make inferences about the gene function and their relationship with other genes. In Hill, Hlavacek, Ambrosiano, Wall, Sharp, Cleland, et al. (2001) and Jensen, Shen, and Liu (2005), motif similarity is used to find clusters of coregulated genes. A different approach taken by Rigoutsos, Floratos, Parida, Gao, and Platt (2000) was to apply a motif discovery algorithm (Rigoutsos &

Floratos, 1998) to analyze temporal gene expression data. The algorithm found motifs that express clusters of genes which have a similar or a symmetric behavior during certain time intervals.

MOTIF DATABASES

UniProtKB/Swiss-Prot [http://www.expasy.org/sprot/]

The UniProtKB/Swiss-Prot Protein Knowledgebase (Gasteiger et al., 2003) contains the sequence information of almost all the discovered and sequenced proteins. It has a high level of annotation for each sequence, providing information like the description of the protein function, its domains structure or post-translational modifications. It has a very low level of redundancy. Although it is not a motif repository, we mention it here due to its high level of integration with motif databases. Typically, these databases provide links to the Swiss-Prot sequences where their patterns occur.

Prosite Database [http://www.expasy.org/prosite/]

Prosite (Gasteiger et al., 2003; Hulo et al., 2006) is the oldest and best known sequence motif database. It is a semimanually annotated database. The sequence motifs are characterized by having a high biological significance, typically showing a region in the protein with an important functional or structural role. A family of protein sequences is then described by one or more motifs. Initially, the Prosite entries reported only motifs in the form of regular expressions (with its own adapted syntax). Today, entries are complemented with textual descriptions and PWMs. It also provides references to the literature and to other protein families where the motif occurs. The two key aspects of the Prosite motifs are (1) its capability to identify highly functional regions of the proteins and (2) its ability to be used as a tool to distinguish the members of the families. The quality of these motifs makes this database a reference for comparison of the results from new methods and algorithms. In order to better understand the characteristics of the motifs, we provide some figures and statistics obtained from the analysis of the Prosite database. In release 19.2 (February 2006), Prosite contained 1,929 entries, from which 1,330 were deterministic motifs. From these motifs, 1,030 (77.44%) were rigid gap motifs and 300 (22.56%) from the flexible gap type. The majority of the gaps are of size 1 or 2, with an average gap length of 1.93 and a standard deviation of 1.52. The average precision and sensitivity of the Prosite motifs is respectively 95.9% and 90.16%, which is an indicator of the high quality of the motifs in this database.

As an example of a Prosite entry, we will examine one specific motif from this database. The selected entry is PS00017 which reports the ATP/GTP-binding site motif A, also known as P-loop. This motif appears in a considerable number of proteins that bind ATP or GTP. It is a motif with a high probability of occurrence. A scan to Swiss-Prot (release 49.1) shows that this motif has 17,861 hits in 16,550 different sequences. The pattern has the following format: [AG] - x(4) - G - K - [ST]. We recommend that the reader consult this database and to try out the different tools provided on the Web site.

Blocks [http://blocks.fhcrc.org/]

The Blocks WWW Server (Henikoff & Henikoff, 1994) is a tool that allows a protein or a DNA query sequence to be compared against a database of protein blocks. Each block corresponds to multiple aligned ungapped segments that report highly conserved regions in a family of proteins. The blocks in the database are obtained automatically from groups of proteins from the InterPro (Mulder, Apweiler, Attwood, Bairoch,

Bateman, Binns, et al., 2005). A tool called Block Maker (Henikoff & Henikoff, 1994) can be used to create blocks from a set of related sequences provided by the user.

Prints [http://umber.sbs.man.ac.uk/dbbrowser/PRINTS/]

The Prints database (Attwood, Mitchell, Gaulton, Moulton, & Tabernero, 2006) is a collection of protein motifs fingerprints. A motif corresponds to a local alignment of highly conserved regions of the proteins, and a fingerprint corresponds to a set of motifs that can be used to predict the occurrence of similar motifs in other sequences. Two types of fingerprints exist: (1) simple fingerprints that consist in single motifs and (2) composite fingerprints which combine multiple motifs. The majority of reported fingerprints are of the second type as they have a great expressive and discriminative power.

Pfam [http://www.sanger.ac.uk/Software/Pfam/index.shtml]

Pfam (Finn, Mistry, Schuster-Böckler, Griffiths-Jones, Hollich, Lassmann, et al., 2006) is a database of multiple sequence alignments and Hidden Markov Models that cover many protein families and domains. This database consists in two parts. The first part is the Pfam-A which provides curated and high quality coverage of a large number of protein families. The second part of the database, Pfam-B, contains automatically generated alignments for small protein families and which do not overlap with Pfam-A.

InterPro [http://www.ebi.ac.uk/interpro/]

The InterPro database (Mulder et al., 2005) is an integrated resource of protein families, domains, and sites. This database combines information from multiple databases with different methodologies and different types of biological information. It unifies information for the protein sequences of the Swiss-Prot database with data on functional sites and domains from Prosite, Prints, Pfam, ProDom (Servant, Bru, Carrere, Courcelle, Gouzy, Peyruc, et al., 2002), and the Smart (Schultz, Milpetz, Bork, & Ponting, 1998) databases. By combining all this information, it results in a very powerful integrated diagnostic tool.

eMotif Database [http://motif.stanford.edu/emotif/]

The eMotif database (Huang & Douglas, 2001) provides three different tools for the generation and analysis of protein motifs: Maker, Scan, and Search. The eMotif-Maker program generates rigid gap motifs, using regular expression syntax identical to the one used in Prosite. These motifs are generated from protein sequence multiple alignments. The source of the alignments can be the Prints and the Blocks database or a user input alignment. The motifs are generated according to some degree of specificity, which in this particular case corresponds to the probability of the motif being matched by random sequences. The eMotif-Search is used to search motifs that match subsequences of a given query sequence, and the eMotif-Scan will retrieve protein sequences that match a user input regular-expression (motif).

Different databases report, generate, and provide analysis tools covering different aspects and information about protein families. In practice, this results in each database having its own operational definition of a protein family. In this section, we provided a brief overview to databases somewhat related to sequence motifs. Therefore, many interesting protein databases like SMART, ProDom, DOMO, PIR, ProtoMap, SYSTERS, COG, ProDom-CG, ProClass, and MetaFam, among others, were left out of this analysis. For further details, one should read Henikoff and

Henikoff (2001), which provides a clear and comprehensive overview on the thematics of protein family databases.

MOTIF MINING ALGORITHMS

The problematic of mining motifs and sequence patterns has gathered a great deal of attention from biologists and computer scientists and has been widely investigated for more than 15 years. From the biological point of view, the analysis of sequence motifs provides valuable insights for the comprehension of the sequence-structure-function paradigm. From the computer science point of view, it represents an interesting and challenging problem.

To tackle this problem, many different algorithms and methodologies have been proposed. Some are refinements on previous approaches, while others are completely new ideas. It is difficult to provide a direct comparison on the different algorithmic aspects (like time, space complexity, or the quality of the reported patterns), since the algorithms are usually designed to perform a specific search. For instance, it is difficult to compare two algorithms, when one extracts rigid gap motifs and another is designed for extracting flexible gap motifs or motifs under some specific constraints.

In general, the motif extraction process itself follows a sequence, which has already been identified and described in Brazma et al. (1998a) and Jonassen (2000) as a three-step paradigm:

1. Solution space definition
2. Score and significance definition
3. Algorithm application

In step one, the user defines exactly the type of patterns the user is looking for. According to the Deterministic Motifs section, this implies the definition on the type, class, constraints, substitution sets, minimum support of the motifs, and other relevant information. This step is equivalent to the introduction of background or *a priori* knowledge into the extraction process, since the user is focusing the search on some subset of the solution space.

Depending on the restrictiveness of the conditions applied in step one, a smaller or larger number of motifs can be reported. In both cases, a discrimination function is required in order to score the motifs according to their significance. In the Significance Measures section, we provided some ideas on how to rank a motif and how the different types of measures can be used to evaluate a motif. A critical aspect is the search of over-represented motifs, that is, motifs that appear a number of times greater than expected. If a motif is over-represented and has a low probability of appearance, then there must a biological reason for this. As a result, these motifs should be highlighted to the user. The minimum support, although not the only one, is a measure of over-representation. Hence, the significance of a motif is usually defined as a combination of a scoring function and the support value. Another critical aspect is the length of the motifs. Longer motifs with small support are usually more interesting than smaller motifs with high support. This is due to the fact that the former motifs have probably some biological meaning in contrast to the latter that may arise mainly by chance. Finally, the user should select an algorithm that handles all the input information. Given a set of input sequences and parameter values, the algorithm should return a list of the frequent and best high scoring motifs or a list of all motifs above some predefined level of support and score.

The problem of motif finding is combinatorial in its nature. The performance of the mining algorithms is essentially affected by the size of the output, that is, the number of reported motifs (Califano, 2000; Ester & Zhang, 2004; Ferreira & Azevedo, 2005a; Rigoutsos & Floratos, 1998). This quantity depends on the following variables: number of input database sequences, length of the sequences, similarity between the sequences, and minimum support threshold and constraints. Typical input data are characterized by having a relatively small number of sequences (from tens to a few hundred), with a long length and a small alphabet size (20 symbols in proteins and 4 in DNA sequences). It is generally assumed that these sequences are unaligned. However, algorithms (Huang & Douglas, 2001) have been introduced to extract motifs from an input set of aligned sequences. The difficulty of the motif finding problem demands clever and efficient pruning mechanisms which make the application of such algorithms feasible with responses in useful time. Most of the actual algorithms run on average in almost linear time with respect to the output, and in the worst case, they achieve an exponential time. In particular, it has been proved (Li, Ma, & Wang, 1999) that some of the motif discovery problems are NP-hard. In those cases, in order to find a solution in polynomial time, a relaxation of the original problem is made, where the set of optimal patterns is no longer guaranteed to be found. This is achieved through the introduction of heuristics, randomized and probabilistic strategies, and approximation schemes (Lonardi, 2002).

Next, we provide a brief overview of different methodologies and algorithms that have been designed to tackle this problem. We do not provide a comprehensive survey, since only some of the most representative algorithms of each class are presented. We start distinguishing two motif enumeration approaches: *Bottom-Up* and *Top-Down*. In the Bottom-Up approach, the algorithm starts with an empty motif. Then, it extends the motifs with all the possible symbols, one symbol at a time. If the defined constraints and significance measures are satisfied, the motif continues to be extended; otherwise the extension stops. The process stops when no motifs are left to be extended. In the Top-Down (Ester & Zhang, 2004) approach, the algorithm starts with longer sequences where symbol generalizations and length decrease is successively applied until the sequences fulfill a defined criteria and can be reported as motifs. This latter approach is not as common as the former. For the Bottom-Up approach, the search space can be traversed in a Breadth-first (BFS) or Depth-first manner (DFS). In BFS mode, the motifs are all extended at the same time, level by level. In DFS mode, a motif is successively extended until it does not fulfill the imposed conditions. Then, the algorithm backtracks in the search tree and extends a new motif. Figure 1 shows a lattice structure that represents the search space for an alphabet of two letters and the respective flow of a DFS traversal. Note that not all sequences are traversed. This is due to the minimum support pruning (see the Depth-First Search subsection).

Next, different methodologies and representative algorithms for motif discovery are described. In Lonardi (2002), a detailed description and complexity analysis are provided.

- **Exhaustive search**: This is the simplest approach and consists of a four step method. The user starts by defining the search space and the respective constraints. Next, an exhaustive enumeration of all the motifs in

the search space is made. The third step is to compute the support and the significance of each motif. Finally, the motifs with the highest score or with a score above the defined threshold are outputted. The advantage of this method is that it is a simple approach that is guaranteed to find the best motifs. The greatest drawback lies in the fact that it has a time complexity of $O(|\Sigma|^m)$ for motif length of m and alphabet Σ, which makes this method only suitable to discover small length motifs. This is a very naïve approach, requiring the introduction of pruning techniques. A variation of this methodology, which makes use of an efficient data structure called *suffix tree* (McCreight, 1976; Weiner, 1973), is proposed in an algorithm called *verbumculus* (Apostolico, Gong, & Lonardi, 2003). It provides an exhaustive enumeration in a linear space and time complexity. The biggest drawback is that it only reports concrete patterns, which have a limited expression power. Another algorithm in this class is the *Weeder* (Pavesi, Mauri, & Pesole, 2001) algorithm. It uses an exhaustive enumeration to find rigid motifs allowing a

Figure 1. Tree structure of the search space for an alphabet of two symbols: (a, b); for each sequence the respective support with relation to the example database is presented; dashed lines indicate the flow of the DFS search.

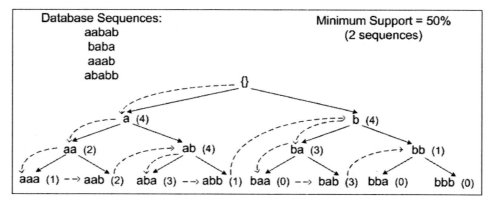

number of mismatches proportional to the length of the pattern.

- **Depth-first search:** This class of algorithms combines Bottom-Up with a DFS approach as described above. Here, the key concept is the minimum support pruning strategy. The concept states that if a sequence is not frequent, all the sequences containing (extensions of it) it will also be not frequent. Thus, a sequence is successively extended until it becomes infrequent. The search is guided by a lattice structure like the one in Figure 1. Note that in this example, sequences *bba* and *bbb* are not visited during the DFS traversal. This is so because sequence *bb* is not frequent for a minimum support of 50% in the example sequence database. Examples of algorithms in this class are the *Pratt* algorithm (Jonassen et al., 1995) which finds high quality frequent flexible gap motifs, and the *gIL* (Ferreira & Azevedo, 2005) that uses a DFS approach to find all the frequent rigid or flexible gap motifs.

- **Shorter pattern combination:** An alternative to the DFS approach is the combination of shorter frequent motifs to form longer motifs. If the suffix of a motif is equal to the prefix of another, they can be combined into a unique and longer motif. This is a suitable strategy to find long motifs. This strategy is divided in two steps. In step one, an enumeration of all motifs with a certain length and user defined characteristics is performed. In step two, an exhaustive combination of the motifs obtained in step one is made. *Teiresias* (Rigoutsos et al., 1998) and *Splash* (Califano, 2000) are two examples of algorithms that find closed rigid gap motifs following this approach. These algorithms run on average with a polynomial time with respect to the output, that is, the number of reported motifs.

- **Exhaustive graph search:** This type of algorithm is based on the idea of searching through all the subsequence combinations of the input sequences that can be possible occurrences of a motif. These algorithms were specially designed to tackle the *(l, d)-motif* problem (Pevzner & Sze, 2000). This problem consists in finding from a set of *n* input sequences a motif M of length *l* which occurs in all the sequences with at most *d* mismatches. Therefore, any two occurrences of M differ at most 2*d* different positions. Since this can be formulated as a graph theory problem, the central idea of the method is based on the notion of expandable clique of a graph. The *Winnower* (Pevzner & Sze, 2000) algorithm was designed to tackle this specific problem. It uses randomized graphs and therefore does not guarantee finding the best solution. It assumes that the motif occurs exactly once per sequence. Depending on the input parameters, it can have a very high time complexity.

- **Random projection search:** The projection algorithm proposed by Buhler and Tompa (2001) was also designed to tackle the (l, d)-motif problem. It uses the projection idea to deduce motif occurrences. Projection can be described as the process of hashing subsequences of the input sequences. For each subsequence, a key is generated, which is based on random subset features of the subsequences like for example some amino acid positions. The keys are then inserted into the hash table cells. A post-processing step uses high scoring cells to cluster instances of motifs. The greatest advantage of this algorithm is the fact that it handles the scalability issues associated with the problem. The biggest drawback is the fact that it is a randomized algorithm. Thus, no guarantees of finding the optimal solution can be given. Typically, the output of this algorithm is used as the input of the Expectation Maximization (Lawrence & Reilly, 1990) refinement algorithm.

Some of these algorithms were originally developed to mine motifs in DNA sequences. Nevertheless, with minor programming changes, they can be used to mine protein sequence databases as well. Typically, two versions of the algorithms are provided for mining the two types of biological sequences. Table 5 summarizes the features of the algorithms described above. The type and class of extracted motifs were already described in deterministic motifs section. The "Best Motif" feature refers to algorithms that optimize their search to find the best scoring motif. The feature "Heuristics" refers to the cases where heuristics are introduced in the mining process to improve the algorithm's efficiency or the quality of the reported motifs. Although the use of such heuristics will eventually lead to the best solution, no absolute guarantee is given in those cases.

STRUCTURAL MOTIFS

In previous sections, we discussed the extraction process of sequence motifs from a set of related sequences. It was also briefly discussed how these motifs can be used to assign function to a newly discovered protein sequence (a task called classification). The central idea behind function classification is that proteins with very similar

sequence encoding will most probably share the same function.

It is well known that during the evolutionary history of a protein, structure is better conserved than sequence (Chothia & Lesk, 1987; Johnson & Lehtonen, 2000). Therefore, it is common to find two proteins with the same function which have significant structural similarity but low resemblance at the primary structure. Extracting patterns in a higher stratum than the sequence level can provide new insights into understanding how proteins acquire their final structure and how structure relates to their function.

Protein information is typically categorized in four different levels (Jones & Hadley, 2000). The first level corresponds to the amino acid sequence information, and it is called *primary structure*. *Secondary structure elements (SSEs)* consist in local regions of the protein with well-defined geometry characteristics. The two basic secondary structures are the *α-helix* and the *β-strand*. A third element that establishes the connection between elements of both types is called *loop* or *coil* (Heringa, 2000). Since 50% of the amino acids will be part of an *α-helix* or a *β-strand*, it is common to describe a protein in terms of its *secondary structure*. The *tertiary structure* corresponds to the coordinate information of atoms in the protein. This information allows a complete visualization of the protein in a 3-dimensional space. If the protein is coupled to other

Table 5. Algorithms and respective features

Algorithm	Concrete	Ambiguous	Rigid	Flexible	Best Motif	All	Closed	Heuristics
Teiresias			X				X	
Splash			X				X	
Pratt				X	X			X
gIL			X	X		X		
Verbumculus	X					X		
Winnower		X				X		X
Weeder			X			X		
Projection		X			X			X

proteins to form a complex macromolecule, the intermolecular interactions are described by the *quaternary structure.*

A *structural motif* is a pattern that provides for a set of functionally related proteins a description of conserved properties at a higher level than the primary structure. Since structure can be described at different levels (e.g., atomic, amino acid, SSEs, etc.) and several features can be reported (e.g., geometry, topology, physic-chemical properties of the amino acids, etc.), different definitions and algorithms for extracting structural motifs have been proposed. Here, we will briefly describe two techniques that use sequence motifs and sequence motif mining algorithms to extract structural motifs.

SPratt: The SPratt (Jonassen, 2000; Jonassen, Eidhammer, Conklin, & Taylor, 2002) method was designed to extract structural motifs from a set of proteins, using the previously proposed method for sequence motif extraction—Pratt (Jonassen, 2000; Jonassen et al., 1995). This is a four step method that can be described as follows: (1) Features describing the structural neighborhood of each amino acid are encoded in a string format; (2) The sequence motif discovery algorithm Pratt is used to extract sequence patterns common to the set of sequences given in the input; (3) Whether the similarity found at the string level is preserved at the structural level is verified. This can be done through a measure of superposition, namely RMSD—root mean square deviation—between the described substructures. (4) Structural patterns are ranked according to a score function that combines the information content of the neighborhood strings and the RMSD values of the substructures.

In a second version of this method—SPratt2 (Jonassen, 2003), the authors follow a similar methodology of SPratt but instead of extracting Prosite-like patterns (see the motif databases section), they devised a new pattern search pro-

cedure where the extracted string patterns consist of sequences of single amino acids separated by gaps of arbitrary size. This improvement allows the mining of a larger number of input structure strings and quicker finding of a more general class of patterns.

SeqFEATURE: The seqFEATURE method (Liang, 2003) relies on the definition of structural motifs from the FEATURE system (Bagley & Altman, 1995; Banatao, Huang, Babbitt, Altman, & Klein, 2001; Liang, 2003; Wei & Altman, 1998). It automatically extracts structural motifs that describe the structural environment around a sequence motif. The FEATURE system extracts structural motifs by describing the physic-chemical environment around functional sites. This description is given by measuring the incidence of the physic-chemical properties at three levels: atomic, residue, and secondary structure for different radial distances. It then compares the set of positive examples of the functional site with a negative control set. This process yields a decision on the significance of the found motifs. The seqFEATURE method makes use of sequence motifs from the eMotif database (Huang & Douglas, 2001) as seed for the automatic creation of structural motifs. The eMotif database is particularly useful in this context since sequence motifs can be obtained at different levels of sensitivity and specificity. After the motifs related to the functional site have been selected, structures from the PDB—Protein Data Bank (Berman, Westbrook, Feng, Gilliland, Bhat, Weissig, et al., 2000), matching the sequence motifs are selected to form the training set. FEATURE is then applied to this set to find structural motifs.

The Calcium binding proteins are involved in a set of vital biological activities. The most common motif found in these proteins is the EF-Hand. This motif (see Table 6) is described at the primary structure level by the sequence motif entry PS00018 at Prosite. At the secondary structure level, this motif typically occurs as a Helix-Loop-Helix pattern (Argos, 1977). The FEATURE model represents a motif in tertiary structure level that describes the 3-dimensional environment around the functional site.

In the same way as several databases have been proposed to manage different types of sequence motifs, structural motif databases also start to emerge. Table 7 summarizes three of these databases and the respective type of structural motifs they provide.

Table 6. Representations of the EF-Hand motif at different structural levels; the primary structure level is described by a sequence motif (Prosite entry PS0018); the secondary structure motif is described by the sequence of its SSEs; the tertiary structure pattern presented is an excerpt of the calcium binding site taken for the webFEATURE database available at http://feature.stanford.edu/webfeature/. The FEA-TURE model describes the 3-dimensional environment around the functional site of the calcium binding proteins; rows describe the different physic-chemical properties and the columns the radial distance. Dark areas represent a high incidence of the respective property.

Structure Level	Pattern
Primary	D - {W} - [DNS] - {ILVFYW} - [DENSTG] - [DNQGHRK] - {GP} - [LIVMC] - [DENQSTAGC] - x(2) - [DE] - [LIVMFYW]
Secondary	Helix-Loop-Helix
Tertiary	

CONCLUSION

In this chapter, we have provided an introduction to the problem of finding patterns in collections of protein sequences. Since this is a broader subject, we have focused on the specific problem of mining deterministic motifs in protein databases. Molecular sequence information is growing at an explosive rate. Such increase in the volume of data demands for the development of automatic and efficient methods for pattern extraction. Human and classical data analysis methods are no longer feasible. Knowledge discovery in databases (KDD), where the data mining and bioinformatics techniques are included, seems to be a promising approach to the problem.

The biological motivation for the development of such techniques was given as an introduction to the problem. Next, we differentiated the two types of patterns that can be extracted from sequence databases, focusing the analysis on deterministic motifs. Details regarding the different features that characterize a motif were provided. Very easily, the motif extraction process may report too many motifs. Thus, significance measures are required to highlight the more biological or statistically significant patterns. Different analysis can be taken to obtain the required effect. Additionally, to the fact that they provide support for a better understanding of the biological processes, deterministic motifs have a wide range of applications in the bioinformatics context. Applications like classification, clustering, or gene analysis are good examples, to name a few. Deterministic motifs are useful to different research communities. This motivates the development of databases with free and worldwide access that gathers and manages sequences and motif information. We dedicated a section to introduce some of these databases. We then described the motif extraction process and introduced several approaches and example algorithms that can be applied in this problem. Since additional protein information is typically available, patterns occurring at the structural level

Table 7. Descriptions of different types of structural motifs, literature references, applications, and the respective databases

Database	References	Structural Motif	Goal
Catalytic Site Atlas	(Bartlett, Porter, Borkakoti, & Thornton, 2002; Porter, Bartlett, & Thornton, 2004; Torrance, Bartlett, Porter, & Thornton, 2005)	Represents and describes several properties of the amino acids residues involved in catalytic reactions.	Identify and documenting enzyme active sites.
Fuzzy Functional Forms (FFF) and Active Site Profiling (ASP) at the Structure-Function Linkage Database (SFLD)	(Cammer, Hoffman, Speir, Canady, Nelson, et al., 2003; Fetrow, Godzik, & Skolnick, 1998; Fetrow & Skolnick, 1998; Pegg, Brown, Ojha, Seffernick, Meng, Morris, et al., 2006)	FFF represents distances and variances between critical residues of the Functional Sites. ASP combines signatures based on sequence and structural information.	Identify Functional Sites in protein structures.
FEATURE	(Bagley & Altman, 1995; Banatao et al., 2001; Liang, 2003; Wei & Altman, 1998)	Represents Physic-Chemical properties at different radial distances around Functional Sites.	Describe the 3D environment around Functional Sites.

can be extracted and combined with sequence information. In the previous section, examples on how sequence motifs and motif mining algorithms can be used to extract structural motifs were presented. Such high level motifs will certainly provide the means for a better understanding of the protein sequence-structure-function paradigm.

ACKNOWLEDGMENT

We are thankful to the two anonymous reviewers for their fruitful comments.

For the author Pedro Gabriel Ferreira, the writing of this chapter was done under the support of a Ph. scholarship, granted by the Fundação para Ciência e Tecnologia from the Ministério da Ciência, Tecnologia e Ensino Superior of the Portuguese Government. Paulo Jorge Azevedo is supported by the Financiamento Pluriannual from the Fundação para Ciência e Tecnologia of the the Ministério da Ciência, Tecnologia e Ensino Superior of the Portuguese Government.

REFERENCES

Abramson, N. M. (1963). *Information theory and coding*. New York: McGraw-Hill.

Apostolico, A., Comin, M., & Parida, L. (2005). Conservative extraction of over-represented extensible motifs. *Bioinformatics, 21*(1), 9-18.

Apostolico, A., Gong, F., & Lonardi, S. (2003). Verbumculus and the discovery of unusual words. *Journal of Computer Science and Technology, 19*(1), 22-41.

Argos, P. (1977). Secondary-structure predictions of calcium-binding proteins. *Biochemistry, 16*(4), 665-672.

Attwood, T., Mitchell, A., Gaulton, A., Moulton, G., & Tabernero, L. (2006). The PRINTS protein fingerprint database: Functional and evolutionary applications. In M. Dunn, L. Jorde, P. Little, & A. Subramaniam (Eds.), *Encyclopaedia of Genetics, Genomics, Proteomics and Bioinformatics*. John Wiley & Sons.

Bagley, S., & Altman, R. (1995). Characterizing the microenvironment surrounding protein sites. *Protein Science, 4*(4), 622-635.

Baldi, P., Brunak, S., Chauvin, Y., Andersen, C., & Nielsen, H. (2000). Assessing the accuracy of prediction algorithms for classification: An overview. *Bionformatics, 16*(5), 412-242.

Banatao, R., Huang, C., Babbitt, P., Altman, R., & Klein, T. (2001). ViewFeature: Integrated feature analysis and visualization. In *Proceedings of the 6th Pacific Symposium on Biocomputing* (pp. 240-250).

Barash, Y., Bejerano, G., & Friedman, N. (2001). A simple hyper-geometric approach for discovering putative transcription factor binding sites. In *Proceedings of the 1st International Workshop on Algorithms in Bioinformatics* (pp. 278-293). Lecture Notes in Computer Science 2149. Springer.

Bartlett, G., Porter, C., Borkakoti, N., & Thornton, J. (2002). Analysis of catalytic residues in enzyme active sites. *Journal of Molecular Biology, 324*(1), 105-121.

Ben-Hur, A., & Brutlag, D. (2003). Remote homology detection: A motif based approach. *Bioinformatics, 19*(1), 26-33.

Ben-Hur, A., & Brutlag, D. (2005). Protein sequence motifs: Highly predictive features of protein function.

Berman, H., Westbrook, J., Feng, Z., Gilliland, G., Bhat, T., Weissig, H., et al. (2000). The protein data bank. *Nucleic Acids Research, 28*(1), 235-242.

Blekas, K., Fotiadis, D., & Likas, A. (2005). Motif-based protein sequence classification using neural networks. *Journal of Computational Biology, 12*(1), 64-82.

Brazma, A., Jonassen, I., Eidhammer, I., & Gilbert, D. (1998a). Approaches to the automatic discovery of patterns in biosequences. *Journal of Computational Biology, 5*(2), 279-305.

Brazma, A., Jonassen, I., Vilo, J., & Ukkonen, E. (1998b). Pattern discovery in biosequences. In *Proceedings of the 4th International Colloquium on Grammatical Inference* (pp. 255--270). Lecture Notes in Artificial Intelligence 1433. Springer.

Buhler, J., & Tompa, M. (2001). Finding motifs using random projections. In *Proceedings of the 5th International Conference on Computational Molecular Biology* (pp. 69-76).

Califano, A. (2000). SPLASH: Structural pattern localization analysis by sequential histograms. *Bioinformatics, 16*(4), 341-357.

Cammer, S., Hoffman, B., Speir, J., Canady, M., Nelson, M., et al.(2003). Structure-based active site profiles for genome analysis and functional family subclassification. *Journal of Molecular Biology, 334*(3), 387-401.

Chothia, C., & Lesk, A. (1986). The relation between the divergence of sequence and structure in proteins. *EMBO Journal, 5*(4), 823-826.

Cooper, N. (1994). *The human genome project: Deciphering the blueprint of heredity.* University Science Books.

Durbin, R., Eddy, S., Krogh, A., & Mitchison, G. (1998). *Biological sequence analysis: Probabilistic models of proteins and nucleic acids.* Cambridge University Press.

Ester, M., & Zhang, Z. (2004). A top-down method for mining most specific frequent patterns in biological sequence data. In *Proceedings of the 4th SIAM International Conference on Data Mining.*

Finn, R., Mistry, J., Schuster-Böckler, B., Griffiths-Jones, S., Hollich, V., Lassmann, T., et al. (2006). Pfam: Clans, Web tools and services [Database issue]. *Nucleic Acids Research, 34,* D247-D251.

Ferreira, P., & Azevedo, P. (2005a). Protein sequence pattern mining with constraints. In *Proceedings of the 9th European Conference on Principles and Practice of Knowledge Discovery in Databases* (pp. 96-107). Lecture Notes in Computer Science 3721. Springer.

Ferreira, P., & Azevedo, P. (2005b). Protein sequence classification through relevant sequence mining and Bayes classifiers. In *Proceedings of the 12th Portuguese Conference on Artificial Intelligence* (pp. 236-247). Lecture Notes in Computer Science 3828. Springer.

Fetrow, J., Godzik, A., & Skolnick, J. (1998). Functional analysis of the *Escherichia coli* genome using the sequence-to-structure-to-function paradigm: Identification of proteins exhibiting the glutaredoxin/thioredoxin disulfide oxidoreductase activity. *Journal of Molecular Biology, 282*(4), 703-711.

Fetrow, J., & Skolnick, J. (1998). Method for prediction of protein function from sequence using the sequence-to-structure-to-function paradigm with application to glutaredoxins/thioredoxins and T1 ribonucleases. *Journal of Molecular Biology, 281*(5), 949-968.

Gasteiger, E., Gattiker, A., Hoogland, C., Ivanyi, I., Appel, R, & Bairoch, A. (2003). *ExPASy: The proteomics server for in-depth protein knowledge and analysis. Nucleic Acids Research, 31*(13), 3784-3788.

Gribskov, M., McLachlan, A., & Eisenberg, D. (1987). Profile analysis: Detection of distantly related proteins. *Proceedings of the National Academy of Sciences, 84*(13), 4355-4358.

Guralnik, V., & Karypis, G. (2001). A scalable algorithm for clustering protein sequences. In *Proceedings of the 1st Workshop on Data Mining in Bioinformatics of the 7th ACM SIGKDD* (pp. 78-80).

Han, J., & Kamber, M. (2001). *Data mining concepts and techniques* (The Morgan Kaufmann Series in Data Management Systems). Morgan Kaufman.

Henikoff, S., & Henikoff, J. (1993). Performance evaluation of amino acid substitution matrices. *Proteins, 17*(1), 49-61.

Henikoff, S., & Henikoff, J. (1994). Protein family classification based on searching a database of blocks. *Genomics, 19*(1), 97-107.

Henikoff, S., & Henikoff, J. (2001). Protein family databases. *Encyclopedia of Life Sciences.*

Heringa, H. (2000). Predicting secondary structure from protein sequences. In D. Higgins & W. Taylor (Eds.), *Bioinformatics: Sequence, structure and databanks: A practical approach.* Oxford University Press.

Hill, D., Hlavacek, W., Ambrosiano, J., Wall, M., Sharp, D., Cleland, T., et al. (2001). Integrated clustering and motif detection for genome-wide expression and sequence data. In *Proceedings of the 2nd International Conference on Systems Biology* (pp. 83-88).

Huang, J., & Douglas, B. (2001). The eMOTIF database. *Nucleic Acids Research, 29*(1), 202-204.

Hulo, N., Bairoch, A., Bulliard, V., Cerutti, L., De Castro, E., Langendijk-Genevaux, P., et al. (2006). *The PROSITE database [Database issue]. Nucleic Acids Research, 34*, D227-D230.

Hunter, L. (1993). Molecular biology for computer scientists. In L. Hunter (Ed.), *Artificial intelligence and molecular biology* (pp. 1-46). AAAI Press.

Jensen, S., Shen, L., & Liu, J. (2005). Combining phylogenetic motif discovery and motif clustering to predict co-regulated genes. *Bioinformatics, 21*(20), 3832-3839.

Johnson, M., & Lehtonen, J. (2000). Comparison of protein three-dimensional structure. In D. Higgins & W. Taylor (Eds.), *Bioinformatics: Sequence, structure and databanks: A practical approach.* Oxford University Press.

Jonassen, I. (2000). Methods for discovering conserved patterns in protein sequences and structures. In D. Higgins & W. Taylor (Eds.), *Bioinformatics: Sequence, structure and databanks: A practical approach.* Oxford University Press.

Jonassen, I., Collins, J., & Higgins, D. (1995). Finding flexible patterns in unaligned protein sequences. *Protein Science, 4*(8), 1587-1595.

Jonassen, I., Eidhammer, I., Conklin, D., & Taylor, W. (2002). Structure motif discovery and mining the PDB. *Bioinformatics, 18*(2), 362-367.

Jones, D., & Hadley, C. (2000). Threading methods for protein structure prediction. In D. Higgins & W. Taylor (Eds.), *Bioinformatics: Sequence, structure and databanks: A practical approach.* Oxford University Press.

Koonin, E., & Galperin, M. (2003). *Sequence-evolution-function: Computational approaches in comparative genomics.* Kluwer Academic Publishers.

Lawrence, C., & Reilly, A. (1990). An expectation maximization (EM) algorithm for the identification and characterization of common sites in unaligned byopolimer sequences. *Proteins, 7*(1), 44-51.

Li, M., Ma, B., & Wang, L. (1999). Finding similar regions in many strings. In *Proceedings of the 31st Annual ACM Symposium on Theory of Computing* (pp. 473-482).

Liang, M., Banatao, D., Klein, T., Brutlag, D., & Altman, R. (2003a). WebFEATURE: An interactive Web tool for identifying and visualizing functional sites on macromolecular structures. *Nucleic Acids Research, 31*(13), 3324-3327.

Liang, M., Brutlag, D., & Altman, R. (2003b). Automated construction of structural motifs for predicting functional sites on protein structures.

In *Proceedings of the 8th Pacific Symposium on Biocomputing* (pp. 204-215).

Lonardi, S. (2002). Pattern discovery in biosequences: Tutorial. In *Proccedings of the 10th International Conference on Intelligent Systems for Molecular Biology.*

McCreight, E. (1976). A space economical space tree construction algorithm. *Journal of ACM, 23*(2), 262-272.

Mulder, N., Apweiler, R., Attwood, T., Bairoch, A., Bateman, A., Binns, D., et al. (2005). InterPro: Progress and status in 2005 [Database issue]. *Nucleic Acids Research, 33*, D201-D205.

Nevill-Manning, C., Sethi, K., Wu, T., & Brutlag, D. (1997). Enumerating and ranking discrete motifs. In *Proceedings of the 5th International Conference on Intelligent Systems for Molecular Biology* (pp. 202-209).

Nevill-Manning, C., Wu, T., & Brutlag, D. (1998). Highly specific protein sequence motifs for genome analysis. *Proceedings of the National Academy of Science, 95*(11), 5865-5871.

Pavesi, G., Mauri, G., & Pesole, G. (2001). An algorithm for finding signals of unknown length in DNA sequences. In *Proceedings of the 9th International Conference on Intelligent Systems for Molecular Biology* (pp. 207-214).

Pegg, S., Brown, S., Ojha, S., Seffernick, J., Meng, E., Morris, J., et al. (2006). Leveraging enzyme structure-function relationships for functional inference and experimental design: the structure-function linkage database. *Biochemistry, 45*(8), 2545-2555.

Pevzner, P., & Sze, S. (2000). Combinatorial approaches to finding subtle signals in DNA sequences. In *Proceedings of the 8th International Conference on Intelligent Systems for Molecular Biology* (pp. 269-278). AAAI Press.

Porter, C., Bartlett, G., & Thornton, J. (2004). The catalytic site atlas: A resource of catalytic sites and residues identified in enzymes using structural data [Database issue]. *Nucleic Acids Research, 32*, D129-D133.

Rigoutsos, I., & Floratos, A. (1998). Combinatorial pattern discovery in biological sequences: The Teiresias algorithm. *Bioinformatics, 14*(1), 55-67.

Rigoutsos, I., Floratos, A., Parida, L., Gao, Y., & Platt, D. (2000). The emergence of pattern discovery techniques in computational biology. *Metabolic Engineering, 2*(3), 159-177.

Sagot, M., & Viari, A. (1996). A double combinatorial approach to discovering patterns in biological sequences. In *Proceedings of the 7th Annual Symposium on Combinatorial Pattern Matching* (pp. 186-208). Springer, 1075.

Schultz, J., Milpetz, F., Bork, P., & Ponting, C. (1998). SMART, a simple modular architecture research tool: Identification of signaling domains. *Proceedings of the National Academy of Science, 95*, 5857-5864.

Servant, F., Bru, C., Carrere, S., Courcelle, E., Gouzy, J., Peyruc, D., et al. (2002). ProDom: Automated clustering of homologous domains. *Briefings in Bioinformatics, 3*(3), 246-251.

Smyth, P., & Goodman, R. (1990). Rule induction using information theory. In G. Piatetsky-Shapiro & W. Frawley (Eds), *Knowledge discovery in databases* (pp. 159-176). MIT Press.

Takusagawa, K., & Gifford, D. (2004). Negative information for motif discovery. In *Proceedings of the 9th Pacific Symposium on Biocomputing* (pp. 360-371).

Torrance, J., Bartlett, G., Porter, C., & Thornton, J. (2005). Using a library of structural templates to recognise catalytic sites and explore their evolution in homologous families. *Journal of Molecular Biology, 347*(3), 565-581.

Ukkonen, E., Vilo, J., Brazma A., & Jonassen, I. (1996). Discovering patterns and subfamilies in biosequences. In *Proceedings of the 4ᵗʰ International Conference on Intelligent Systems for Molecular Biology* (pp. 34-43). AAAI Press.

Wei, L., & Altman, R. (1998). Recognizing protein binding sites using statistical descriptions of their 3D environments. In *Proceedings of the 3ᵗʰ Pacific Symposium on Biocomputing* (pp. 407-508).

Weiner, P. (1973). Linear pattern matching algorithm. In *Proceedings of the 14ᵗʰ IEEE Symposium on Switching and Automata Theory* (pp. 1-11).

Witten, I., & Frank, E. (2005). *Data mining: Practical machine learning tools and techniques.* San Francisco: Morgan Kaufmann.

Wu, T., & Brutlag, D. (1995). Identification of protein motifs using conserved amino acid properties and partitioning techniques. In *Proceedings of the 3ʳᵈ International Conference on Intelligent Systems for Molecular Biology* (pp. 402-410).

Yang, J., & Yu, P. (2001). Mining surprising periodic patterns. In *Proceedings of the 7ᵗʰ ACM SIGKDD International Conference on Knowledge Discovery and Data Mining* (pp. 395-400).

ENDNOTES

[1]   February, 2006—Swiss-Prot Release 49.1.
[2]   Available at the statistics page of the database Web site.

Chapter VII
Data Mining and Knowledge Discovery in Metabolomics

Christian Baumgartner
University for Health Sciences, Medical Informatics and Technology (UMIT), Austria

Armin Graber
BIOCRATES Life Sciences GmbH, Austria

ABSTRACT

This chapter provides an overview of the knowledge discovery process in metabolomics, a young discipline in the life sciences arena. It introduces two emerging bioanalytical concepts for generating biomolecular information, followed by various data mining and information retrieval procedures such as feature selection, classification, clustering, and biochemical interpretation of mined data, illustrated by real examples from preclinical and clinical studies. The authors trust that this chapter will provide an acceptable balance between bioanalytics background information, essential to understanding the complexity of data generation, and information on data mining principals, specific methods and processes, and biomedical applications. Thus, this chapter is anticipated to appeal to those with a metabolomics background as well as to basic researchers within the data mining community who are interested in novel life science applications.

INTRODUCTION

Metabolomics is an evolving discipline that studies unique chemical fingerprints reflecting metabolic changes related to disease onset and progression. Metabolite profiling, an area within metabolomics, measures small molecules, or metabolites, contained in a human cell, tissue, or organ and involved in primary and intermediary metabolism. The biochemical information resulting from metabolite analysis reveals functional endpoints associated with physiological and pathophysiological processes, influenced by both genetic predisposition and environmental factors such as nutrition exercise or medication (Daviss, 2005; Harrigan & Goodacre, 2003; Ryals, 2004; Schmidt, 2004).

Recently, due to significant advances in high-throughput technologies, a wider set of the human metabolome—a thus far largely unexplored source of bioinformation—is now accessible (Beecher, 2003; Dunn, Bailey, & Johnson, 2005). Statistical comparison of metabolite profiles can expose multivariate patterns that have the potential to revolutionize the health care system by specifically capturing latent warning signs of upcoming diseases before any disease symptoms show up. Early disease screening and prevention, as opposed to late disease detection and expensive therapeutic interventions, is probably the primary health care coverage solution for the future.

By definition, these so-called biomarkers are "objectively measured indicators of normal biological processes, pathogenic processes or pharmacological responses to a therapeutic intervention, and ... are intended to substitute for a clinical endpoint (predict benefit or harm) based on epidemiological, therapeutic, pathophysiological or other scientific evidence" (Biomarkers Definitions Working Group, 2001). Interest in the discovery of novel biomarkers originates from their broad range of potential applications and fundamental impact on pharmaceutical industry dynamics and current health care sector principles. Successful implementation of biomarkers in drug discovery can reduce the time and cost of drug development while the application to molecular diagnostics will improve patient compliance in clinical settings and reduce unnecessary costs resulting from false diagnosis in addition to late disease detection (McCandless, 2004; Morris & Watkins, 2005; Stoughton & Friend, 2005).

Qualitative and quantitative metabolite profiling technologies comprise a range of advanced analytical and data processing tools, with the objective of utilizing potential markers as a result of comparison of small molecule components of biological systems. Tandem mass spectrometry (MS/MS), for example, detects hundreds of metabolites simultaneously from microliter quanti-

Figure 1. Mass spectrometry (MS) based technologies used in metabolite profiling. Specific steps for qualitative nontargeted and quantitative targeted profiling are highlighted.

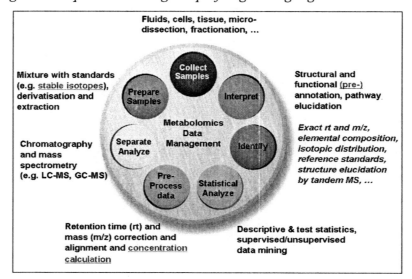

ties of biological samples, such as whole blood, serum, plasma, urine, or other body fluids, from minute amounts, with high precision and sensitivity (Kaltashov & Eyles, 2005; Roschinger, Olgemoller, Fingerhut, Liebl, & Roscher, 2003; Strauss, 2004). Relative quantification is achieved by reference to a wide range of appropriate internal standards. Quality assured data, generated by modern LIMS-controlled technology platforms comprising automated sample preparation, mass spectrometer based analytics and technical validation (Weinberger, Ramsay, & Graber, 2005), are rapidly becoming too voluminous to catalog and interpret by hand. As a result, cutting-edge data mining tools are needed to identify novel and highly relevant information on preprocessed sample data (Baumgartner et al., 2004; Fiehn & Spranger; Huyn, 2001; 2003). However, the identification of biologically meaningful markers is challenged by the deficiency of *a priori* knowledge related to the molecular nature of the disease as well as the biological variability of data.

In recent years, advanced data mining and bioinformatics techniques have been applied to increasingly comprehensive and complex metabolic data sets, with the objective to identify and verify robust and generalizable markers that are biochemically interpretable and biologically relevant in the context of the disease. Ultimately, validated and qualified predictive models can be used for disease screening and therapeutic monitoring (Baumgartner & Baumgartner, 2006; Norton, Huyn, Hastings, & Heller, 2001).

IMPORTANT ASPECTS OF METABOLITE PROFILING

Metabolite Profiling Approaches

As shown in Figure 1, a variety of technologies are exploited for sample preparation, separation, analysis, and data processing in metabolite profiling. Gas (GC) and liquid chromatography

(LC), or capillary electrophoresis (CE) largely use mass spectrometry (MS) to identify and quantify metabolites after separation (Halket, Waterman, Przyborowska, Patel, Fraser, & Bramley, 2005; Jonsson, Gullberg, Nordstrom, Kusano, Kowalczyk, & Sjostrom, 2004; Soga, Ohashi, Ueno, Naraoka, Tomita, & Nishioka, 2003). MS based metabolite profiling technologies typically comprise qualitative nontargeted and quantitative targeted approaches. The selected strategy widely determines the extent of subsequent data preprocessing such as retention time (rt) and mass (m/z) alignment and metabolite identification steps.

The nontargeted approach offers the prospective of covering a broad range of endogenous and drug metabolites. However, the tedious, time-consuming biomolecule identification process based on derived features, that is, primarily retention time and exact mass, limits its throughput performance and hampers a subsequent comprehensive functional interpretation. A targeted profiling scheme is typically used to quantitatively screen for known small molecule compounds, which frequently depict relevant metabolic pathways of the disease being investigated. The targeted molecules are identified by tandem mass spectrometry (MS/MS) utilizing characteristic mass transitions in multiple reaction monitoring (MRM), precursor (PS) and neutral loss (NL) scans. Quantitation is achieved by reference to stable isotopes or other appropriate internal standards added to the preprocessed sample.

A placebo-controlled preclinical trial on diabetes mellitus type II (T2D), exploiting a qualitative and quantitative metabolite profiling approach, was conducted for metabolic characterization of a disease mouse model (db/db) and detailed pharmacodynamic description of a novel candidate drug class. Six groups were studied consisting of healthy and diseased mice, which were either not treated, treated with the novel compound, or placebo-treated (Figure 2). Advantages and limitations of the two complementary profiling methodologies were discussed (Graber, Weinberger, Ramsay, & Wingate, 2005). In particular, differences in performance characteristics, reproducibility of chromatography, complexity of data preprocessing and identification, and derived information content are illustrated. In conclusion, qualitative profiling seems to perform well for exploratory investigations, while the quantitative method has the potential to be employed as a high-content screening technology.

For qualitative LC/MS metabolite profiling, mouse urine and plasma samples were separated by liquid chromatography and analyzed with a quadrupole time of flight (qTOF) MS equipped with an electrospray source. Retention times and masses were aligned utilizing known values of the added internal standards. Raw spectra intensities were filtered with a signal-to-noise threshold, normalized, and scaled, followed by statistical data analysis. As to quantitative targeted MS/MS analysis, mouse urine, plasma, erythrocytes, and liver samples were derivatized (amino acids, acyl-carnitines, sugars) and extracted by solid-phase or in Folch solution (glyco- and phospholipids). These sample preparation procedures were implemented on a liquid handling system. The extracted metabolites were subsequently analyzed by flow injection in combination with multiple reaction monitoring, precursor, and neutral loss scans on a triple quadrupole (QqQ) MS equipped with an electrospray source. Concentrations were calculated from the raw MS spectra exploiting known quantities of the spiked stable isotopes, signal-to-noise filtered and scaled, followed by statistical analysis and biochemical interpretation of the preannotated metabolites (Figure 3).

Data Preprocessing and Metabolite Identification

The nontargeted approach revealed approximately 2,000 peaks per spectrum in full ion scans. As chromatographic column conditions frequently

Figure 2. Placebo-controlled preclinical study on diabetes mellitus type II (T2D). The targeted approach allows quantitative analysis and biochemical interpretation of biofluids and tissue samples in justifiable time. Standard operating procedures (SOPs) target specific compound classes.

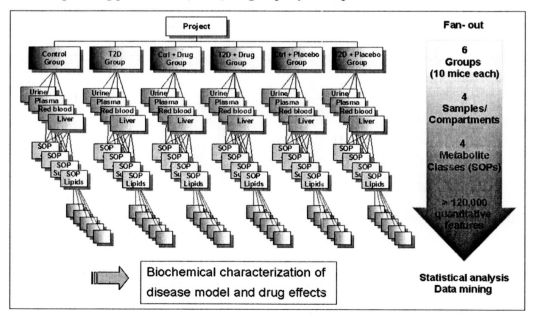

Figure 3. Workflow of two complementary metabolite profiling approaches

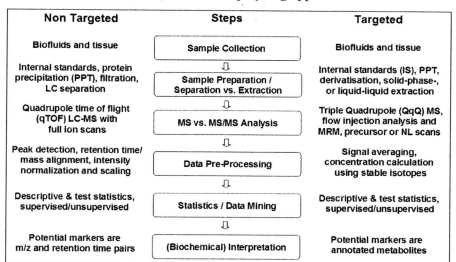

change between LC-MS runs, known retention times of internal standards were used to correct retention time drifts. Furthermore, spectra were mass aligned to match related peaks representing the same underlying chemical component across data sets derived from different samples. Known masses of internal standards were exploited to compensate for such peak drifts and distortions. Additionally, intensities of spectra were normalized utilizing known quantities of internal standards. In this context, merely computational approaches without the need for internal standards are evolving, whereas mass recalibration and intensity normalization are performed exploiting characteristic peaks across runs. Scaling procedures such as z-score can help to enhance the visual comparison between runs. Pareto scaling was used in this study.

Principal component analysis (PCA) discriminated the groups and enabled the selection of putative biomarker candidates. Although the loading plots showed the m/z and retention time pairs that contributed the most to the separation of the groups, interpretation turned out to be cumbersome as significant effort was involved identifying corresponding metabolites (Figure 4). Additionally, concerns about reproducibility of chromatography and standardization of spectra alignment and normalization are all known inherent problems of this approach.

In contrast, quantitative targeted metabolite profiling concentrates on analytes that are known and preannotated and can be detected by MRM, precursor, and neutral loss scans. As flow injection analysis (FIA) supplies a steady stream of ions to the MS over a period of time, intensities can be averaged leading to robust signals. Characteristic mass transitions are used for identification of metabolites and associated internal standards (Figure 5). De-isotoping is a common practice in protein analysis. However, isotope correction is also recommended for certain small molecule compounds and classes (Liebisch, Lieser, Rathenberg, Drobnik, & Schmitz, 2004). These algorithms calculate the theoretical isotope distributions of targeted analytes and compare these isotopic frequencies with measured peak intensities for their isotopic overlap. Compound interferences can be detected,

Figure 4. Example of peak identification in nontargeted metabolite profiling

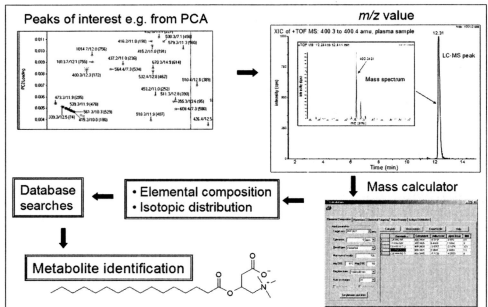

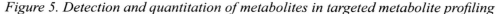

Figure 5. Detection and quantitation of metabolites in targeted metabolite profiling

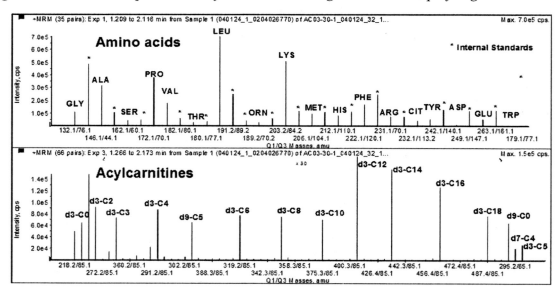

and intensity values for monoisotopic masses can be corrected. Finally, metabolite concentrations are calculated by relating the known concentrations of stable isotopes with the measured ion counts per second (cps).

The applied targeted metabolite profiling methodology utilized a liquid-handling system for fully automated and parallel sample preparation in microtiter format guaranteeing high reproducibility and low coefficients of variation (CVs). Furthermore, analytes and corresponding metabolites were annotated in advance so as to enable fast and direct biochemical and biological interpretation. Up to 825 metabolites were obtained from each compartment, and comparison of the groups enabled identification of the animal disease model and facilitated the immediate biochemical characterization of drug effects.

Role of Data Mining for Biomarker Discovery

Objectives

Targeted metabolite concentration profiling facilitates higher throughput and the versatility for standardized analysis of various biofluids and tissues, which is especially important for comprehensive disease characterizations and efficacy and toxicity assessments in animal model experiments. Direct or surrogate, uni- or multivariate markers are revealed by data mining techniques with the objective to describe diseases at the molecular level, which are subsequently often used to study metabolic and pharmacodynamic changes in various compartments and organs. In general, the identical technology can be applied in various stages of pharmaceutical development, ranging from cell-based systems and animal models to clinical studies. For example, putative biomarkers discovered and verified in the preclinical phase, such as for the characterization of normal biological and pathogenic processes or pharmacological responses to a therapeutic

intervention can be clinically validated with the same analytical technology in human studies. In an intended diagnostic application, clinical studies will have to assess the predictive performance and generalization power of candidate biomarkers in clinical routine, where high specificity is typically required to rule out other diseases.

Data Mining Principles

In addition to descriptive and test statistics, data mining techniques for the analysis of mass spectrometric data primarily include the analysis of mass spectrometric data feature subset selection methods such as PCA, filters, and wrappers (Hall & Holmes, 2003) and classification methods such as logistic regression analysis, support vector machines or neural networks, genetic programming, and cluster analysis (Cristianini & Shawe-Taylor, 2000; Everitt, Landau, & Leese, 2001; Gelman, Carlin, Stern, & Rubin, 2004; Hosmer & Lemeshow, 2000; Mitchell, 1997; Raudys, 2001; Shawe-Taylor & Cristianini, 2004).

Instances of metabolic data derived from biological samples are represented as a numerical vector in a multidimensional space. Here, dimensions or features reflect peaks of aligned mass spectra, that is, corrected m/z and retention time pairs with associated normalized intensity values (nontargeted approach), or a vector of analytes with calculated concentrations that relate to predefined and preannotated metabolites (targeted approach). As principal data mining tasks in biomarker discovery are "supervised", data vectors are defined by a set of tuples $T_{DB} = \{(c_j, m) \mid c_j \in C, m \in M\}$, where c_j is the class label of the collection C of preclassified cohorts (diseased, various stages of disease, treated, normal), and $M = \{m \mid m_l, ..., m_n\}$ is the given feature set, that is, peaks of spectra or metabolite concentrations.

Success of data mining is affected by factors such as noise, redundancy, relevance, or reliability inherent in the experimental data. Thus, feature selection is focused on the process of identifying and removing as much of irrelevant or redundant information as possible and is used as a preprocessing step before classification and biochemical interpretation. One popular categorization of supervised feature selection techniques has coined the terms "filter" and "wrapper" to describe the nature of the metric used to evaluate the worth of features (Hall & Holmes, 2003; Kohavi & John, 1998).

Filters use general characteristics of the data to evaluate attributes and operate independently of any learning algorithm by producing a ranked list of feature candidates. *Wrappers* evaluate feature subsets by using accuracy estimates provided by machine learning algorithms. In general, forward selection search is used to produce a list of features, ranked according to their overall contribution to the accuracy of the attribute subset with respect to the target learning algorithm. Wrappers generally give better results than filters because of the interaction between the search and the learning scheme's inductive bias. However, improved performance comes at the cost of computational expense due to invoking the learning algorithm for every attribute subset considered during the search.

In addition to supervised approaches, PCA is a very popular unsupervised preprocessing step that calculates linear combinations based on the variance of the original data space. Unlike filters or wrappers that identify and assess attributes based on their original variables, PCA is an effective projection method suitable for data compression and dimensionality reduction, where a subset of the new features can be used to describe the instances on a certain percentage of the original information. In general, the first principal component (PC) explains the most variance of data of the original variables; the second PC describes the highest variance in the remaining data after removal of the contribution of the first PC; and so on. In many applications, this sequential reduction leads to a variance concentration in the first few PCs that can be easily visualized for further interpretation.

Filter-Based Feature Selection for Biomarker Discovery

Filter-based feature selection techniques assess features of a given collection (e.g., a list of derived metabolite concentrations, targeted approach) by an appropriate quality measure. Such algorithms finally produce a ranking of the features according to their quality to discriminate predefined classes. Popular methods, for example, are the *information gain* (*IG*) that computes how well a given feature separates data by pursuing reduction of entropy, or *relief/reliefF*, which is an exponent of a correlation-based selection method evaluating the worth of an attribute by repeatedly sampling an instance and considering the value of the given attribute for the nearest instance of the same and different class (Hall & Holmes, 2003).

However, entropy-based or correlation-based approaches are not the single best approaches for all situations, particularly as they do not optimally reflect the characteristics of given MS data structures at normal or disease/treated state. In an effort to improve the performance of feature selection algorithms, data miners should not only have a profound knowledge of different techniques, but should also consider the strengths and weaknesses of the chosen paradigms in the applied domain and derived preprocessed data.

The biomarker identifier (*BMI*), an algorithm recently described by Baumgartner and Baumgartner (2006), makes use of a two-step data processing procedure to discern the discriminatory attributes between two classes of interest (i.e., a set of metabolite profile MS traces from diseased people vs. a set derived from normal samples). Both steps include qualifying and ranking potential marker candidates from a given metabolite collection and discarding irrelevant metabolites (if desired) by thresholding. More specifically, three parameters describing disease related metabolic concentration changes, that is, discriminatory performance, extent of discriminatory space, and variance of concentration values at disease state, were taken into account to develop a quality (score) measure for selecting potential markers candidates.

Figure 6 depicts the BMI scores of measured acylcarnitines on MCADD (n = 63) vs. controls data (n = 1240). Medium chain acyl CoA dehydrogenase deficiency (MCADD), an inborn error of metabolism, is a fatty acid oxidation defect which leads to an accumulation of medium chain acylcarnitines and thus to a decrease in cell energy metabolism (Clayton, Doig, Ghafari, Meaney, Taylor, Leonard, Morris, & Johnson, 1998; Dezateux, 2003; Rinaldo, Matern, & Bennett, 2002). Inborn errors are primarily monogenic diseases due to the change of a single gene, resulting in an enzyme or other protein not being produced or having altered functionality. Such single pathway blockade disorders are characterized by abnormal concentration changes of only a few key metabolites.

Figure 6. Identified key metabolites of the fatty acid metabolism in MCADD using BMI. TS is the discriminatory threshold (μmol/L) between diseased and normal classes, TP* describes the discriminatory power, Δdiff indicates the relative concentration changes, and CV specifies the coefficient of variation at disease state. Parameters TP*, Δdiff, and CV are used to calculate the BMI-score.

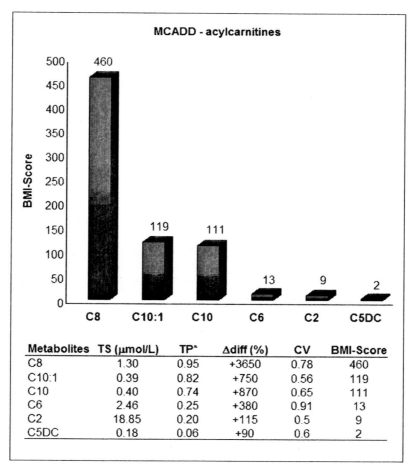

Metabolites	TS (μmol/L)	TP*	Δdiff (%)	CV	BMI-Score
C8	1.30	0.95	+3650	0.78	460
C10:1	0.39	0.82	+750	0.56	119
C10	0.40	0.74	+870	0.65	111
C6	2.46	0.25	+380	0.91	13
C2	18.85	0.20	+115	0.5	9
C5DC	0.18	0.06	+90	0.6	2

Table 1 gives a brief description of seven inborn errors of metabolism regarding their enzyme defects, established diagnostic markers and their natural history to be investigated for identifying disease-specific metabolites. Using BMI, all key metabolites could be identified and prioritized as primary (indicated in bold) and secondary markers according to the current biochemical knowledge on disease metabolism. Here, a score value of $|s| > 100$ enabled a categorization of all established primary markers, and a score value between $20 \leq |s| \leq 100$ enabled a categorization of all secondary markers, which makes BMI an excellent tool for identifying and prioritizing selected metabolites in single pathway blockade disorders (Baumgartner & Baumgartner, 2006).

Arrows $\uparrow$ and $\downarrow$ indicate abnormally enhanced and diminished metabolite concentrations. Bold metabolites denote the established primary diagnostic markers (American College of Medical Genetics/American Society of Human Genetics Test and Technology Transfer Committee Work-

Table 1. Survey of seven inborn errors of metabolism and established diagnostic markers

Amino acid disorders	Enzyme defect/ affected pathway	Diagnostic markers	Symptoms if untreated
Phenylketonuria (PKU)	Phenylalanine hydroxylase or impaired synthesis of biopterin cofactor	**PHE** $\uparrow$ TYR $\downarrow$	Microcephaly, mental retardation, autistic-like behavior, seizures
Organic acid disorders			
Glutaric acidemia, Type I (GA-I)	Glutaryl CoA dehydrogenase	**C5DC** $\uparrow$	Macrocephaly at birth, neurological problems, episodes of acidosis/ ketosis, vomiting
3-Methylcrotonylglycinemia deficiency (3-MCCD)	3-methyl-crotonyl CoA carboxylase	**C5OH** $\uparrow$	Metabolic acidosis and hypoglycemia, some asymptomatic
Methlymalonic acidemia (MMA)	Methlymalonyl CoA mutase or synthesis of cobalamin (B_{12}) cofactor	**C3** $\uparrow$ C4DC $\uparrow$	Life threatening/fatal ketoacidosis, hyperammonemia, later symptoms: failure to thrive, mental retardation
Propionic acidemia (PA)	Propionyl CoA carboxylase α or β subunit or biotin cofactor	**C3** $\uparrow$	Feeding difficulties, lethargy, vomiting and life threatening acidosis
Fatty acid oxidation disorders			
Medium chain acyl CoA dehydrogenase deficiency (MCADD)	Medium chain acyl CoA dehydrogenase	C6 $\uparrow$ **C8** $\uparrow$ **C10** $\uparrow$ **C10:1** $\uparrow$	Fasting intolerance, hypoglycemia, hyperammonemia, acute encephalopathy, cardiomyopathy
3-OH long chain acyl CoA dehydrogenase deficiency (LCHADD)	Long chain acyl CoA dehydrogenase or mitochondrial trifunctional protein	**C16OH** $\uparrow$ C18OH $\uparrow$ C18:1OH $\uparrow$	Hypoglycemia, lethargy, vomiting, coma, seizures, hepatic disease, cardiomyopathy

Figure 7. Feature selection with Information gain and Relief filters. The 12 top ranked metabolites are displayed. The first four bars (Information gain) represent the established diagnostic markers for MCADD (see Table 1).

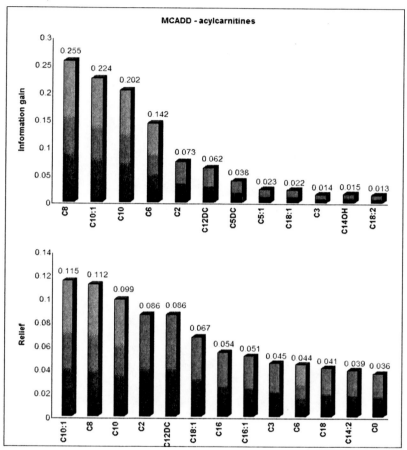

ing Group, 2000; Baumgartner & Baumgartner, 2006).

Comparing BMI results with IG and Relief on MCADD data, IG returned a ranking similar to BMI, but does not allow a convincing prioritization, in particular between the predominant marker C8 (octanyl-carnitine) and the second and third ranked metabolites C10:1 (decenoyl-carnitine) and C10 (decanoyl-carnitine) (Figure 7). Relief turned out inferior, as its heuristics take into account the usefulness of attributes for class prediction along with the level of intercorrelation among them, which seems to be useless on such specific data characteristics. Using PCA, the

groups were discriminated in a meaningful way and enabled the selection of all key metabolites (Figure 8). However, a ranking or even a prioritization of identified subsets with respect to their loadings is not practical by this method.

Metabolite profiles in multigenic diseases such as metabolic syndrome or diabetes mellitus type II reflect more complex metabolic changes typically caused by the interplay of various affected genes and regulatory, signaling, and biochemical pathways. This regularly leads to multiple abnormal enzyme reactions involving several metabolic pathways. In this context, the characterization of the diabetes disease mellitus type II

Figure 8. PCA on MCADD data: Principal component 2 with high loadings of C8-, C10:1-, C10- and C6-acylcarnitines (circle) contributed the most to the separation of the groups. This subset corresponds to the established diagnostic metabolites.

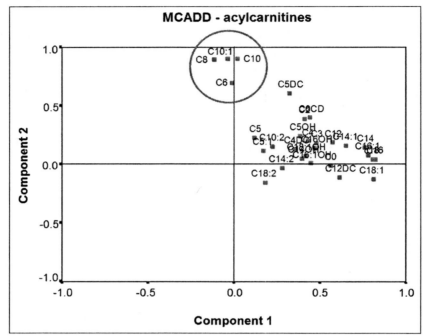

model (Figure 2) revealed several markers that metabolically characterize the mouse model. The study demonstrates that targeted metabolomics is ideally suited to deliver functionally relevant information about the pathophysiology of metabolic disorders including the assessment of ketosis, gluconeogenesis, short term metabolic control, beta-oxidation, oxidative stress, and lipid peroxidation. For instance, the amino acids yielded a wealth of information about the general metabolic condition of the animals, which was consistently confirmed in cellular and extracellular compartments. All the branched-chain amino acids, valine (Val) and leucine/isoleucine (Xle), were elevated in the diabetic animals reflecting a well-known finding in diabetes patients.

This rise most likely results from impaired utilization of these amino acids in peripheral tis-sue, where they usually serve as a major energy source, and is commonly thought to indicate a bad short-term metabolic control (Figures 9A and 9B). Furthermore, phenylalanine (Phe) levels increased while tyrosine (Tyr) concentrations discreased, clearly indicating a reduced activity of the phenylalanine hydroxylase. One of the most plausible explanations for this effect would be a depletion of the enzyme's essential cofactor, tetrahydrobiopterin (BH4), in a situation of marked oxidative stress (Figure 9A). Last of all, the main amino acids, alanine (Ala), glycine (Gly), and serine (Ser), serving as a source for gluconeogenesis, showed consistently lowered concentrations. Elevated gluconeogenesis is a common finding in diabetes models, and the source for this process is very likely to get partly depleted.

These experimental results clearly demonstrate how the incorporation of specific characteristics

Figure 9A. Identified key metabolites of the analyzed amino acid spectrum in diabetes mellitus type II (T2D) data using BMI (mouse model diseased vs. controls); Phe = phenylalanine, Xle = Leucine (Leu) + Isoleucine (Ile), Val = valine, Gly = glycine, Orn = ornathine, and Arg = arginine

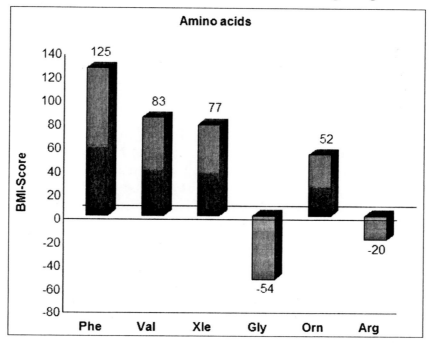

Figure 9B. Impaired metabolic control in diabetes mellitus type II (T2D)

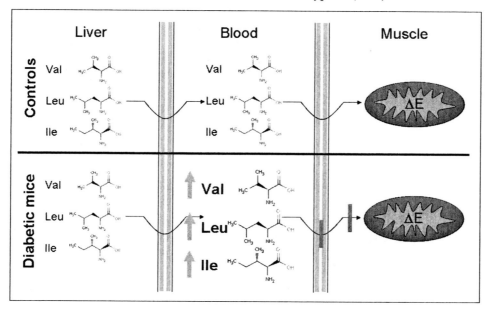

on biological data remarkably improves the performance of feature selection and dimensionality reduction. Ultimately, new developments in this field require target-oriented mining approaches that focus on questions of subset identification combined with straightforward strategies for biochemical interpretation and validation.

Classification on Metabolic Data

The performance of identified marker candidates is determined on their ability to classify instances. Usually, for a supervised classification problem, the training data sets are in the form of a set of tuples $TR = \{(c_j, m) \mid c_j \in C, m \in M\}$, where c_j is the class label and M is the set of attributes (metabolites) for the instances. The task of the learning algorithm is to produce a classifier to classify the instances into the correct class. Validation is now the process of estimating how well a model you have learned from some training data is going to perform on future as-yet-unseen data. Various validation strategies can be applied: The *holdout method (train and test approach)* splits the data set into two groups, where the training set is used to train the classifier and the test set $TS = \{m \mid m \in M\}$ is used to estimate the error rate of the trained classifier. For smaller data sets due to study design, cross-validation (10-fold or leave-one-out cross validation) can be applied. *Ten-fold cross validation*, for instance, generates a 10-fold repetition of the data set. In each of the 10 experiments, nine folds are used for training and the remaining one for testing (Witten & Frank, 2005).

The most common quality measures in a diagnostic setting (diseased vs. normal class) to estimate a classifier's discriminatory performance are accuracy, sensitivity, and specificity. Letting TP stand for true positives, FP for false positives, TN for true negatives, and FN for false negatives, accuracy is calculated by the term (TP+TN)/(TP+FP+TN+FN). Sensitivity is defined as TP/TP+FN, and specificity as TN/TN+FP.

Thus, sensitivity can be seen as a measure of how accurate we are at predicting the positive class, whereas specificity is a measure of how accurately negatives are identified.

Several popular machine learning methods are currently used for classifying metabolomic data: discriminant analysis methods such as linear discriminant analysis or logistic regression analysis constructing a separating linear hyperplane between two data sets (Hosmer & Lemeshow, 2000); classification trees (which are rooted), usually binary trees, with simple classifiers placed at each internal node and a class label at each leaf (Mitchell, 1997); k-NN, an instance-based learning paradigm, where a query object is assigned to the majority class of k-nearest neighbors based on a distance measure (Mitchell, 1997); Bayes classifier, a probabilistic method based on applying Bayes' theorem (Gelman et al., 2004); support vector machines, a method that uses a kernel technique to apply linear classification techniques to nonlinear classification problems (Cristianini & Shawe-Taylor, 2000; Shawe-Taylor & Cristianini, 2004); or artificial neural networks, an information processing paradigm inspired by the biological nervous systems (Raudys, 2001).

Taking a more detailed look at quantified MS data, data distribution in classes can show regions of different densities. If one class contains regions of extremely varying density, many paradigms are not able to globally specify the density of a class. Nevertheless, it is possible to locally examine the density of each class in the region of the sample to be classified, for example, described by a set of k-nearest neighbors. In this context, an important aspect is to separately consider the local cluster structure of each class in order to determine the degree to which a query sample is an outlier. As classes often form clusters, the hypothesis is to introduce a concept combining the "direct density" view with an accurate outlier factor so that a query sample is assigned to the cluster of that class where it fits best. This concept was implemented in a new instance-based algorithm,

LCF, described by Plant, Boehm, Tilg, and Baumgartner (2006), which significantly outperforms traditional classification algorithms, particularly when biological data are characterized by varying local class densities.

Disease Screening

For the clinical routine, the predictive performance and generalization power of candidate biomarkers is utilized to build classification models for disease screening. Typically high sensitivity and specificity are required to rule out other diseases. Additionally, the models have to consider and adjust to the real incidence rate of a disease to calculate false-positive rates, assuming that the prevalence of the disease was artificially controlled in the study.

For the model-building process, feature selection approaches, filters, and wrappers are suitable to define the model inputs. Using the filter approach, the first few top ranked metabolites best distinguish diseased individuals from healthy controls. However, the data miner keeps the task of identifying the relevant subset through continued testing of the classifier's accuracy with the aim of step-by-step optimization. When using wrappers, the interaction between the search and the learning scheme's inductive bias ensures improved classification accuracy, but comes at the cost of computational expense. In this context, it is important to note that identified subsets using wrappers do not ultimately correspond to the top ranked filter results. Consequently, important subsets can be lost, which are ultimately needed when all key metabolites in affected pathways are reviewed for biochemical interpretation and further validation.

More often, *a priori* knowledge on metabolic pathways is considered for defining the classifier's inputs. Demonstrated in a simplified way, an abnormal biochemical reaction can be modeled by an easy ratio describing an irreversible conversion of a reactant into a product (A→B), however affected

by a lower activity up to a blockade of the involved enzyme. For example, due to a blockade of the enzyme phenylalanine hydroxylase, the amino acid phenylalanine (Phe) cannot be metabolized to tyrosine (Tyr). This single pathway defect leads to strongly elevated Phe and slightly decreased Tyr concentration levels in fluid and can be modeled by the term Phe/Tyr. A set of single metabolites combined by constructed features (ratios) as model inputs are helpful tools to further enhance the classification accuracy of a screening model, which in turn reduces unnecessary costs resulting from false diagnosis. In this context, Chace, Sherwin, Hillman, Lorey, and Cunningham (1998) confirmed the improvement of newborn screening for phenylketonuria (PKU) for the first time by the use of the phenylalanine-to-tyrosine ratio. More recent experiments emphasized this hypothesis (Baumgartner Böhm, & Baumgartner, 2005).

Figure 10 illustrates an example of PAHD (phenylalanine hydroxylase deficiency), a disorder embracing both a more severe (classic PKU) and a milder (non-PKU HPA) form, by showing a receiver operating curve (ROC) analysis. A comparison of the screening performance on univariate and multivariate markers including ratios exemplifies a significant increase of sensitivity (primary marker Phe alone: 95.7% vs. Phe + Phe/Tyr: 96.8%) and positive predictive value (44% vs. 50%, the latter value represents 93 false positive cases of 100,000 healthy controls). Preliminary studies (unpublished) on more complex multigenic metabolic diseases tend to express the discriminatory power of multivariate classifiers even more pronounced by modeling apriori knowledge of disease metabolism.

Particularly for screening applications, model-based classifiers such as logistic regression analysis or classification trees are rather used than instance- or kernel-based methods. The use of explicit rules described by the models' target decision function is more practical for the daily screening routine and has shown the highest acceptance rates among clinical personnel. Logistic regression analysis is one of the methods of choice because here class membership is predicted by a probability measure $P(disorder = 1) = \dfrac{1}{1 + e^{-(b_0 + \sum_i b_i x_i)}}$, an additional decision indicator, using a cut-off value of P = 0.5 by default. By employing sharper cut-offs (e.g., $0.25 \leq P \leq 0.75$, that is, between the first and third quartile), this approach can be extended to a prognostic "alarm system" allowing a more effective response to cases of metabolic disorders detected during the screening procedure (Baumgartner et al., 2004; Hosmer & Lemeshow, 2000).

Unsupervised Data Mining for Biomarker Discovery

If class membership is unknown, MS data sets are given as a set of tuples in the form of $T = \{ x_i \mid x_i \in IR^+, i = 1,...,n\}$. Therefore, many unsupervised feature selection methods approach this task as a search problem, where each state in the search space specifies a distinct subset of the possible features. Since the space is exponential in the number of examined attributes, this necessitates the use of a heuristic search procedure. The search procedure is combined with a feature utility estimator to evaluate the relative merit of alternative subsets of attributes.

In general, dimensionality reduction and feature selection techniques map the whole feature space onto a lower dimensional subspace of relevant attributes in which clusters can be found. Unsupervised feature selection is often based on attribute transformations by creating functions of attributes. Examples are PCA, methods based on singular value decomposition (SVD), and other techniques based on wavelets transformation. The major drawbacks are that the transformed attributes often have no intuitive meaning or that data are clustered only in one particular subspace using established dimensionality reduction methods. However, recent approaches to subspace selection methods (RIS) or comparable subspace clustering (CLIQUE, SUBCLU) rely on density-based clustering notations (Agrawal, Gehrke, Gunopulos,

Figure 10. Performance of PAHD screening using ROC-analysis: Improvement of screening by considering apriori knowledge (ratios) in multivariate markers is demonstrated.

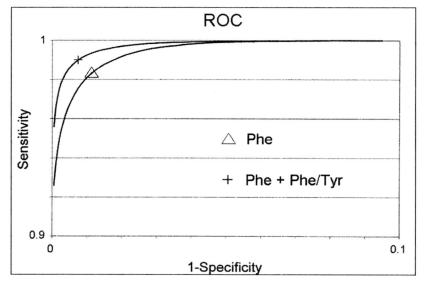

& Raghavan, 1998; Kailing, Kriegel, Kröger, & Wanka, 2003). The most severe problem of these methods is the use of a global density threshold for the definition of clusters due to efficiency reasons. The following difficulties occur when using a global density parameter: The data space dimensionality naturally increases exponentially with each dimension added to the subspace, and the application of one global density parameter to all clusters in one subspace of a fixed dimensionality is not acceptable since the clusters may exceed different density parameters.

SURFING (Baumgartner et al., 2004) tries to overcome this problem by computing all subspaces exhibiting an interesting hierarchical clustering structure ranked according to a quality criterion. This approach facilitates the identification of interesting subspaces of high-dimensional data ranked according to a quality measure and helps to support the complex subspace selection problem of unclassified metabolic data in "unsupervised" biomarker discovery.

For clustering metabolic data into meaningful groups based on the similarity of their aggregate metabolite profiles, established partitioning or hierarchical methods (k-means, single, or average link) are used (Everitt et al., 2001). To better consider local density structures in data, density-based methods, such as DBSCAN (Ester, Kriegel, Sander, & Xu, 1996) or Optics (Ankerst, Breunig, Kriegel, & Sander, 1998), are becoming more popular in this area. Supervised clustering, which, to our knowledge, has not yet been applied to data in the context of metabolite profiling, opens a challenging research field to be employed when class labels of all data are known, with the objective of finding class pure clusters. Data mining innovations in life sciences are definitely needed to better address the issue of given biological data structures.

Biochemical Interpretation, Pathway Visualization, Mapping, and Reconstruction

In a targeted metabolite profiling pilot study on the metabolic syndrome, 375 metabolites were simultaneously quantified in plasma. Unsupervised and supervised data mining techniques were applied to reveal statistically significant, putative markers for disease classification. For instance, the high and low concentration levels of arginine (Arg) and ornithine (Orn), respectively, in patients afflicted with severe metabolic syndrome and cardiovascular disease (MS+) relative to healthy controls, implied an impacted enzyme arginase in the urea cycle, which could be confirmed elsewhere (Jorda, Cabo, & Grisolia, 1981; Wu & Meininger, 1995). A fundamental step of data mining is to verify putative biomarker candidates in a biochemical context by mining the most likely pathways. Therefore, for querying appropriate knowledge bases, powerful search and retrieval tools are needed that map and link discovered marker candidates against a variety of sources such as online repositories or internal databases.

A suite of metabolic explorer tools was developed and exploited to visualize directly affected biochemical pathways, map experimental metabolite concentrations on these graphs, and reconstruct a spectrum of theoretically possible pathways between relevant metabolites. Metabolic information was primarily extracted from the *Kyoto Encyclopedia of Genes and Genomes* (KEGG) (Ogata, Goto, Sato, Fujibuchi, Bono, & Kanehisa, 1999) and stored in a relational database. Dynamic visualization tools and compound, structure, and route finding algorithms were designed and implemented for interactive mining of biochemical pathways and related entities such as reactions, enzymes, and metabolites, facilitating a direct functional annotation of experimental results (path finder retrieval and reconstruction tool, Biocrates life sciences, Innsbruck, Austria).

The main functionality is grouped into three modules:

First, the SEARCHER module allows querying about 4,500 endogenous metabolites and links, each of them to annotated biochemical pathways, where specific entities, for example, reactions and enzymes, are identified that might directly influence the concentration of selected metabolites. Direct hyperlinks to databases, such as GenBank, SWISS-PROT, Prosite, PDB, and OMIM reveal supplementary information about entities. Furthermore, structure based search helps to discover chemically related endogenous compounds that share (Figure 11), for example, substructures, and thus perhaps fragment similarly in a tandem mass spectrometer, which can be very relevant both for method development and compound identification. In this context, metabolites such as arginine and ornithine were searched and investigated, emphasizing their common biochemical pathway, reaction, and involved enzyme, that is, the urea

cycle, arginine amidinohydrolase, and arginase, respectively (Figure 11).

Second, the BROWSER module displays biochemical pathways with their involved enzymes and metabolites, also showing their structures. A variety of graphical layout options support user-friendly navigation in complex pathways. A species filter removes non-existing reactions and enzymes. Metabolite concentrations can be mapped onto biochemical pathways. In this respect, experimentally derived metabolite concentrations, such as arginine and ornithine, were loaded and displayed, revealing that impaired arginase enzyme activity might cause significantly elevated arginine and low ornithine values, respectively (Figure 12).

Third, the ROUTER module reconstructs and displays alternative reaction sequence pathways between two metabolites. Various options are available to reduce the number of possible pathways. For instance, only routes can be considered

Figure 11. SEARCHER module for entity mining and annotated pathway association

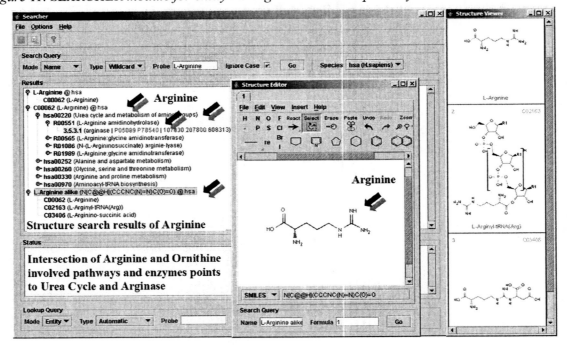

Figure 12. BROWSER module for mapping experimental metabolite concentrations

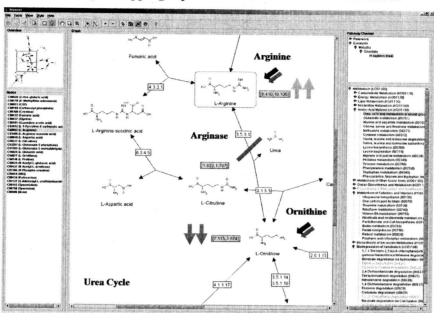

Figure 13. ROUTER module for pathway reconstruction

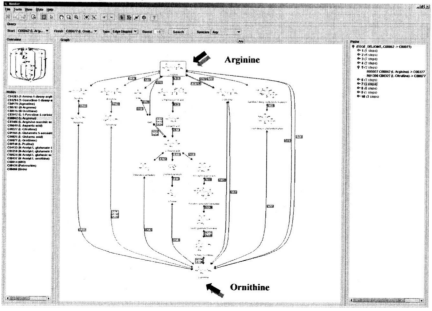

that either have no enzyme or metabolite in common. All enzyme disjoint pathways connecting the two metabolites arginine and ornithine were visualized. Individual reaction steps are depicted in the right panel, whereas the current path is the second one from the left (Figure 13).

Verification, Validation, and Qualification of Marker Candidates

The discovery, biochemical and biological interpretation, statistical verification, and independent validation of biomarker candidates typically require the interdisciplinary expertise and teamwork of biostatisticians, clinicians, biologists, analytical chemists, biochemists, and bioinformaticians, and involve the professional planning, implementation, and control of all steps in a study, ranging from experimental or clinical trial design to the

discovery and validation of putative markers, respectively (Figure 14).

Independently validated biomarkers might be subsequently commercially evaluated for potential clinical use. Biomarkers applied in a molecular diagnostic test have to go through clinical validation, qualification, and regulatory approval prior to commercialization and any use of the molecular diagnostic or theranostic product in clinical routine. Development of an *in vitro* molecular diagnostic device (IVD) and test, typically including an apparatus, software, standard operating procedures (SOPs), and consumables, can take up to 10 years from the discovery of a novel biomarker (Frontline, 2003). However, there is considerable variation depending on several factors, including the resources available to the originating inventors and to what extent diagnostic tests are already in place for the disease in question.

Figure 14. Biomarker discovery, verification, and validation process

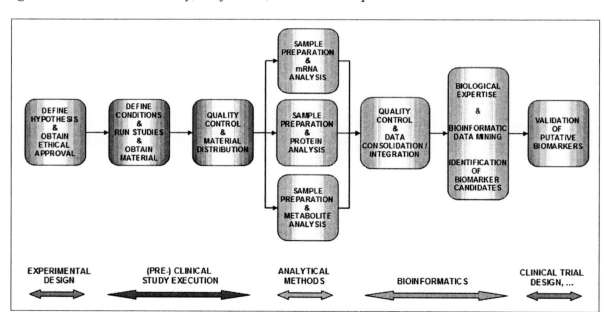

CLINICAL APPLICATIONS IN THE DRUG DEVELOPMENT ARENAS

Interest in the discovery of novel biomarkers originates from their broad range of potential applications and fundamental impact on pharmaceutical industry dynamics and current health care sector principles. Successful implementation of biomarkers in drug discovery can reduce the time and cost of drug development while application to molecular diagnostics will improve patient compliance in clinical settings and reduce unnecessary costs resulting from false diagnosis in addition to late disease detection.

In particular, biochemical and clinical markers are critical for efficient drug development. Biological markers of drug effect, sometimes referred to as surrogate markers, are used when clinical outcome measures such as survival are substantially delayed relative to predictive biochemical changes or clinical effects of the investigational compound. Biomarkers have generally been used for early-phase decision-making studies and accelerated regulatory approvals for much-needed drugs to treat cancer, neurological diseases, and acquired immune deficiency syndrome (Floyd & McShane, 2004).

Preclinical and clinical evaluation of a potential biomarker is often the longest stage of biomarker development, and the required standards and efforts for evaluation or validation depend on the intended use of clinical development. Biomarkers verified for use in preclinical studies can be used to help select appropriate animal models and lead compounds. Biomarkers qualified for use in clinical trials can confirm a drug's pharmacological or biological mechanism of action, guide protocol design, aid patient and dose selection, and help to minimize safety risks.

Theranostics is another emerging field utilizing molecular biomarkers to select patients for treatments that are mostly expected to benefit them and are unlikely to produce side effects. Additionally, theranostics provide an early and objective indica-

tion of treatment efficacy in individual patients, which allows for immediate therapeutic changes if necessary. Therefore, theranostic tests are increasingly used in the areas of cardiovascular disease, cancer, infectious diseases, and prediction of drug toxicity. These tests lead to rapid and accurate diagnosis, contributing to better initial patient management and more efficient use of drugs (Jain, 2005; Picard & Bergeron, 2002; Ross & Ginsburg, 2002)

CONCLUSION

A successful metabolite profiling biomarker discovery study relies on a carefully planned experimental design with clearly defined objectives, a detailed plan and quality control procedures in advance, as is a common practice in controlled clinical trials. Well thought-through experimental designs maximize the information obtained from a given experimental effort, yielding valid and objective conclusions (Ransohoff, 2004).

Experimental flaws and bias jeopardize the predictive performance and generalization power of statistically determined biomarkers. In this context, metabolite profiling has to learn from the past, where insufficient experimental design and deficient reproducibility in early clinical validation studies have acted to restrained the widespread use of serum protein profiling technologies (Baggerly, Morris, Edmonson, & Coombes, 2005; Ransohoff, 2005).

Of course, beyond statistical significance lies the problem of biological significance. Just because a change in expression or concentration is statistically significant, this does not always imply that the change affects the underlying biology. Some genes, proteins, and metabolites are tightly regulated so that small changes in abundance are biologically relevant, while others are loosely regulated and can vary considerably with no biological effect.

Since metabolomics is a very young discipline, open standards for conducting and reporting metabolomic studies are still in development (Metabolomics Standards Initiative Group, 2006). The current focus is on establishing standards for metabolite data annotation and exchange, facilitating the creation of repository databases and related software implementing these standards and promoting the sharing of high-quality, well annotated data within the life science community. Another goal for the future is to extend and consolidate this notion with other functional high-throughput technologies in genomics and proteomics. The data processing standardization group works on reporting requirements associated with statistical analysis and data mining of metabolite data. The ontology group seeks to facilitate the consistent annotation of metabolomics experiments by developing ontology to enable the broader scientific community to understand, interpret, and integrate data. Both guidelines will have a huge impact on the metabolomics-user community, allowing consistent semantic understanding and exchange of data across diverse technologies and laboratories worldwide.

In summary, targeted metabolite concentration profiling in combination with appropriate data mining approaches have the potential to revolutionize clinical diagnosis and drug development. In particular, big pharma is under continuous pressure to discover new targets, novel, more effective, and safer compounds, to speed up biomarker and drug discovery and to generally reduce the cost of pharmaceutical development. Big pharma increasingly relies on biotech companies to fill this innovative gap and future pipelines. In this context, innovative bioanalytical and data mining techniques will play a fundamental role in saving costs by reducing time to market and drug attrition rates (Di Masi, Hansen, & Grabowski, 2003).

ACKNOWLEDGMENT

The authors thank all colleagues at Biocrates life sciences, particularly Klaus Weinberger for his valuable contributions to the biochemical interpretation of the preclinical study on diabetes mellitus type II, and Claudia Plant, Bernhard Pfeifer, and Bernhard Tilg at the University for Health Sciences, Medical Informatics and Technology (UMIT) for their helpful suggestions on biomedical data management and data mining. Financial support was provided in part by KMT (www.kmt.at) and HITT (www.hitt.at).

REFERENCES

Agrawal, R., Gehrke, J., Gunopulos, D., & Raghavan, P. (1998). *Automatic subspace clustering of high dimensional data for data mining applications.* In *Proceedings of the ACM SIGMOD International Conference on Management of Data (SIGMOD' 98)*, Seattle, Washington (pp. 94-105).

American College of Medical Genetics/American Society of Human Genetics Test and Technology Transfer Committee Working Group. (2000). Tandem mass spectrometry in newborn screening. *Genetics in Medicine, 2,* 267-269.

Ankerst, M., Breunig, M.M., Kriegel, H.P., & Sander, J. (1999). *OPTICS: Ordering points to identify the clustering structure.* In *Proceedings of the ACM SIGMOD International Conference on Management of Data (SIGMOD'99)*, Philadelphia, Pennsylvania (pp. 49-60).

Baggerly, K.A., Morris, J.S., Edmonson, S.R., & Coombes, K.R. (2005). Signal in noise: Evaluating reported reproducibility of serum proteomic tests for ovarian cancer. *Journal of the National Cancer Institute, 97,* 307-309.

Baumgartner, C., & Baumgartner, D. (2006). Biomarker discovery, disease classification, and similarity query processing on high-throughput MS/MS data of inborn errors of metabolism. *Journal of Biomolecular Screening, 11*, 90-99.

Baumgartner, C., Böhm, C., & Baumgartner, D. (2005). Modelling of classification rules on metabolic patterns including machine learning and expert knowledge. *Journal of Biomedical Informatics, 38*, 89-98.

Baumgartner, C., Böhm, C., Baumgartner, D., Marini, G., Weinberger, K., Olgemöller, B., Liebl, B., & Roscher, A.A. (2004). Supervised machine learning techniques for the classification of metabolic disorders in newborns. *Bioinformatics, 20*, 2985-2996.

Baumgartner, C., Kailing, K., Kriegel, H.-P., Kröger, P., & Plant, C. (2004). *Subspace selection for clustering high-dimensional data.* In *Proceedings of the 4th IEEE International Conference on Data Mining (ICDM'04)*, Brighton, United Kingdom (pp. 11-18).

Beecher, C. (2003). The human metabolome. In G.G. Harrigan & R. Goodacre (Eds.), *Metabolic profiling: Its role in biomarker discovery and gene function analysis* (pp. 311-319). Boston/Dordrecht/London: Kluwer Academic Publishers.

Biomarkers Definitions Working Group. (2001). Biomarkers and surrogate endpoints: Preferred definitions and conceptual framework. *Clinical Pharmacology and Therapeutics, 69*, 89-95.

Blau, N., Thony, B., Cotton, R.G.H., & Hyland, K. (2001). *Disorders of tetrahydrobiopterin and related biogenic amines.* In C.R. Scriver, S. Kaufman, E. Eisensmith, S.L.C. Woo, B. Vogelstein, & B.

Chace, D.H., Sherwin, J.E., Hillman, S.L., Lorey, F., & Cunningham, G.C. (1998). Use of phenylalanine-to-tyrosine ratio determined by tandem mass spectrometry to improve newborn screening for phenylketonuria of early discharge specimens collected in the first 24 hours. *Clinical Chemistry, 44*, 2405-2409.

Clayton, P.T., Doig, M., Ghafari, S., Meaney, C., Taylor, C., Leonard, J.V., Morris, M., & Johnson, A.W. (1998). Screening for medium chain acyl-CoA dehydrogenase deficiency using electrospray ionisation tandem mass spectrometry. *Archives of Disease in Childhood, 79*, 109-115.

Cristianini, N., & Shawe-Taylor, J. (2000). *An introduction to support vector machines and other kernel-based learning methods.* Cambridge, UK: Cambridge University Press.

Daviss, B. (2005). Growing pains for metabolomics. *The Scientist, 19*, 25-28.

Dezateux, C. (2003). Newborn screening for medium chain acyl-CoA dehydrogenase deficiency: Evaluating the effects on outcome. *European Journal of Pediatrics, 162*(Suppl. 1), S25-S28.

Di Masi, J.A., Hansen, R.W., & Grabowski, H.G. (2003). The price of innovation: New estimates of drug development costs. *Journal of Health Economics, 22*, 151-185.

Donlon, J., Levy, H., & Scriver, C.R. (2004). Hyperphenylalaninemia: Phenylalanine hydroxylase deficiency. In C.R. Scriver, A.L. Beaudet, S.W. Sly, & D. Valle (Eds.); B. Childs, K.W. Kinzler, & B. Vogelstein (Assoc Eds.), *The metabolic and molecular bases of inherited disease.* New York: McGraw-Hill.

Dunn, W.B., Bailey, N.J., & Johnson, H.E. (2005). Measuring the metabolome: Current analytical technologies. *Analyst, 130*, 606-625.

Ester, M., Kriegel, H.P., Sander, J., & Xu, X. (1996). *A density-based algorithm for discovering clusters in large spatial databases with noise.* In *Proceedings of the 2nd International Conference on Knowledge Discovery and Data Mining (KDD'96)*, Menlo Park, California (pp. 226-231). AAAI Press.

Everitt, B.S., Landau, S., & Leese, M. (2001). *Cluster analysis* (4th ed.). New York: Oxford University Press.

Fiehn, O., & Spranger, J. (2003). Use of metabolomics to discover metabolic patterns associated with human diseases. In G.G. Harrigan & R. Goodacre, R. (Eds.), *Metabolic profiling: Its role in biomarker discovery and gene function analysis* (pp. 199-215). Boston/Dordrecht/London: Kluwer Academic Publishers.

Floyd, E., & McShane, T.M. (2004). Development and use of biomarkers in oncology drug development. *Toxicologic Pathology, 32*(Suppl. 1), 106-115.

Frontline Strategic Consulting, Inc. (2003). *Biomarkers: In Vitro diagnostics candidate screening and strategic analysis* (Report # 1420, III-20).

Gelman, A., Carlin, J.B., Stern, H.S., & Rubin, D.B. (2004). *Bayesian data analysis* (2nd ed.). Boca Raton, FL: Chapman & Hall/CRC Press.

Graber, A., Weinberger, K., Ramsay, S., & Wingate, J. (2005). Differences in technology and performance of qualitative and quantitative metabolite profiling approaches. In *Proceedings of the 53rd ASMS Conference on Mass Spectrometry*, San Antonio, Texas.

Halket, J.M., Waterman, D., Przyborowska, A.M., Patel, R.K., Fraser, P.D., & Bramley, P.M. (2005). Chemical derivatization and mass spectral libraries in metabolic profiling by GC/MS and LC/MS/MS. *Journal of Experimental Botany, 56*, 219-243.

Hall, M.A., & Holmes, G. (2003). Benchmarking attribute selection techniques for discrete class data mining. *IEEE Transactions on Knowledge and Data Engineering, 15*, 1437-1447.

Harrigan, G.G., & Goodacre, R. (2003). *Metabolic profiling: Its role in biomarker discovery and gene function analysis*. Boston/Dordrecht/London: Kluwer Academic Publishers.

Hoffmann, G.F., & Zschocke, J. (1999). Glutaric aciduria type I: From clinical, biochemical and molecular diversity to successful therapy. *Journal of Inherited Metabolic Disease, 22*, 381-391.

Hosmer, D.W., & Lemeshow, S. (2000). *Applied logistic regression* (2nd ed.). New York: Wiley.

Huyn, N. (2001). Data analysis and mining in the life sciences. *ACM SIGMOD Record, 30*, 76-85.

Jain, K.K. (2005). Personalised medicine for cancer: From drug development into clinical practice. *Expert Opinion on Oharmacotherapy, 6*, 1463-1476.

Jonsson, P., Gullberg, J., Nordstrom A., Kusano, M., Kowalczyk, M., & Sjostrom, M. (2004). A strategy for identifying differences in large series of metabolomic samples analyzed by GC/MS. *Analytical Chemistry, 76*, 1738-1745.

Jorda, A., Cabo, J., & Grisolia, S. (1981). Changes in the levels of urea cycle enzymes and in metabolites thereof in diabetes. *Enzyme, 26*, 240-244.

Kailing, K., Kriegel, H.P., Kröger, P., & Wanka, S. (2003). Ranking interesting subspaces for clustering high dimensional data. In *Proceedings of the 7th European Conference on Principles and Practice of Knowledge Discovery in Databases (PKDD'03)*, Dubrovnik, Croatia (pp. 241-252).

Kaltashov, I.A., & Eyles, S.J. (2005). *Mass spectrometry in biophysics: Conformation and dynamics of biomolecules*. New York: Wiley.

Kohavi, R., & John, G.H. (1998). The wrapper approach. In H. Liu & H. Motoda (Eds.), *Feature selection for knowledge discovery and data mining* (pp. 33-50). Boston/Dordrecht/London: Kluwer Academic Publishers.

Liebisch, G., Lieser, B., Rathenberg, J., Drobnik, W., & Schmitz, G. (2004). High-throughput quantification of phosphatidylcholine and sphingomyelin by electrospray ionization tandem mass spectrometry coupled with isotope correction algorithm. *Biochimica et Biophysica Acta, 1686,* 108-117.

McCandless, S.E. (2004). A primer on expanded newborn screening by tandem mass spectrometry. *Primary Care, 31,* 583-604.

Metabolomics Standards Initiative Group. (2006). Retrieved June 17, 2007, from http://msi-work-groups.sourceforge.net

Mitchell, T.M. (1997). *Machine learning.* Boston: McGraw-Hill.

Morris, M., & Watkins, S.M. (2005). Focused metabolomic profiling in the drug development process: Advances from lipid profiling. *Current Opinion in Chemical Biology, 9,* 407-412.

Norton, S.M., Huyn, P., Hastings, C.A., & Heller, J.C. (2001). Data mining of spectroscopic data for biomarker discovery. *Current Opinion in Drug Discovery and Development, 4,* 325-331.

Ogata, H., Goto, S., Sato, K., Fujibuchi, W., Bono, H., & Kanehisa, M. (1999). KEGG: Kyoto Encyclopedia of Genes and Genomes. *Nucleic Acids Research, 27,* 29-34.

Picard, F.J., & Bergeron, M.G. (2002). Rapid molecular theranostics in infectious diseases. *Drug Discovery Today, 7,* 1092-1101.

Plant, C., Boehm, C., Tilg, B., & Baumgartner, C. (2006). Enhancing instance-based classification with local density: A new algorithm for classifying unbalanced biomedical data. *Bioinformatics, 22,* 981-988.

Ransohoff, D.F. (2004). Rules of evidence for cancer molecular-marker discovery and validation. *Nature Reviews: Cancer, 4,* 309-314.

Ransohoff, D.F. (2005). Lessons from controversy: Ovarian cancer screening and serum proteomics. *Journal of the National Cancer Institute, 97,* 315-319.

Raudys, S. (2001). *Statistical and neural classifiers.* London: Springer-Verlag.

Rinaldo, P., Matern, D., & Bennett, M.J. (2002). Fatty acid oxidation disorders. *Annual Review of Physiology, 64,* 477-502.

Roschinger, W., Olgemoller, B., Fingerhut, R., Liebl, B., & Roscher, A.A. (2003). Advances in analytical mass spectrometry to improve screening for inherited metabolic diseases. *European Journal of Pediatrics, 162*(Suppl. 1), S67-S76.

Ross, J.S., & Ginsburg, G.S. (2002). Integration of molecular diagnostics with therapeutics: Implications for drug discovery and patient care. *Expert Review of Molecular Diagnostics, 2,* 531-541.

Ryals, J. (2004, June). Metabolomics: An important emerging science. *Business Briefing Pharmatech,* pp. 51-54.

Schmidt, C. (2004). Metabolomics takes its place as latest up-and-coming "omic" science. *Journal of the National Cancer Institute, 96,* 732-734.

Shawe-Taylor, J., & Cristianini, N. (2004). *Kernel methods for pattern analysis.* Cambridge, UK: Cambridge University Press.

Soga, T., Ohashi, Y., Ueno, Y., Naraoka, H., Tomita, M., & Nishioka, T. (2003). Quantitative metabolome analysis using capillary electrophoresis mass spectrometry. *Journal of Proteome Research, 2,* 488-494.

Stoughton, R.B., & Friend, S.H. (2005). How molecular profiling could revolutionize drug discovery. *Nature Reviews: Drug Discovery, 4,* 345-350.

Strauss, A.W. (2004). Tandem mass spectrometry in discovery of disorders of the metabolome. *The Journal of Clinical Investigation, 113,* 354-356.

Weinberger, K.M, Ramsay, S., & Graber, A. (2005). Towards the biochemical fingerprint. *Biosystems Solutions, 12,* 36-37.

Witten, I.H., & Frank, E. (2005). *Data mining: Practical machine learning tools and techniques* (2ⁿᵈ ed.). San Francisco: Morgan Kaufmann Publishers.

Wu, G., & Meininger, C.J. (1995). Impaired arginine metabolism and NO synthesis in coronary endothelial cells of the spontaneously diabetic BB rat. *American Journal of Physiology, 269,* H1312-1318.

Chapter VIII
Handling Local Patterns in Collaborative Structuring

Ingo Mierswa
University of Dortmund, Germany

Katharina Morik
University of Dortmund, Germany

Michael Wurst
University of Dortmund, Germany

ABSTRACT

Media collections on the Internet have become a commercial success, and the structuring of large media collections has thus become an issue. Personal media collections are locally structured in very different ways by different users. The level of detail, the chosen categories, and the extensions can differ completely from user to user. Can machine learning be of help also for structuring personal collections? Since users do not want to have their hand-made structures overwritten, one could deny the benefit of automatic structuring. We argue that what seems to exclude machine learning, actually poses a new learning task. We propose a notation which allows us to describe machine learning tasks in a uniform manner. Keeping the demands of structuring private collections in mind, we define the new learning task of localized alternative cluster ensembles. An algorithm solving the new task is presented together with its application to distributed media management.

INTRODUCTION

Today, large collections of music are available on the Internet. Commercial sites, such as iTunes or Yahoo!, structure their collections based on metadata about the songs like artist, publication date, album, and genre. Individual media collections are organized in very different ways by different persons. A user study reports several organization principles found in physical music collections (Jones, Cunningham, & Jones, 2004), among them the time of day or the situations in which the music is best listened to, the year in which a song has been the favorite, and the room in which to play it (e.g., kitchen, living room, car). In a student project, we found categories of mood, time of day, instruments, occasions (e.g., "when working" or "when chatting"), memories (e.g., "holiday songs from 2005" or "songs heard with Sabine"), and favorites. The same applies for other media collections as, for example, texts or videos. The *level of detail* depends on the interests of the collector. Where some students structure instruments into electronic and unplugged, others carefully distinguish between string quartet, chamber orchestra, symphony orchestra, requiem, and opera. A specialist of jazz designs a hierarchical clustering of several levels, each with several nodes, where a lay person considers jazz just one category.

Where the most detailed structure could become a general taxonomy, from which less finely grained, local structures can easily be computed, categories under headings like "occasions" and "memories" cannot become a general structure for all users. Such categories depend on the personal attitude and life of a user, only. They are truly *local* to the user's collection. Moreover, the classification into a structure is far from being standardized. This is easily seen when thinking of a node "favorite songs". Several users' structures show completely different songs under this label, because different users have different favorites. The same is true for the other categories. We found that even the general genre categories can *extensionally vary* among users, the same song being classified, for example, as "rock'n roll" in one collection and "blues" in another one. Hence, even if (part of) the collections' structure looks the same, their extensions can differ considerably. In summary, structures for personal collections differ in:

- The level of detail.
- The chosen categories.
- The extensions for even the same labels.

This diversity gave rise to new applications under the Web 2.0 paradigm. Systems as *flikr* or *del.icio.us* allow users to annotate objects with arbitrary tags. Such tags complement global properties like artist, album, genre, and so forth, for music collections. In contrast to the global properties, the additional user-assigned tags are *local*; that is, they represent the personal views of a certain user not aiming at a global structure or semantic. These approaches do not include any machine learning support for users. They obey the rule to not destroy hand-made, carefully designed personal structures.

While users like to classify some songs into their own structure, they would appreciate it if a learning system would clean up their collection "accordingly". This means to sort-in songs into the given structure. In addition, users often need to refine their structure since a node in their hierarchy or a class of objects has become too large. Hand-made well-designed structures are often superior to learned ones. Therefore, collaborative approaches are welcome, which allow users to share preferences and knowledge without requiring common semantic or explicit coordination. A structure of another user might serve as a blueprint for refining or enhancing another's structure. The success of collaborative filtering (as in Amazon) shows that users also like to receive personalized recommendations in order to enlarge their collection. Hence, there is some need of support, but it should not force users into a general scheme. An approach which fits the characteristics of users' collections should:

- Not overwrite hand-made structures.
- Not aim at a global model, but enhance a local one.
- Add structure where a category's extension has become too large.

- Take structures of others into account in a collaborative manner.
- Recommend objects which fit nicely into the local structure.
- Deliver several alternatives among which the user can choose.

Due to the last point, such support would not deliver just one result which the user has to accept or otherwise has to stay with the disorderly collection. This of course is also a desirable property of such an approach. Now, the application of structuring music collections has led us to a set of requirements which a machine learning algorithm has to fulfill in order to be of help for users. We do not want to give an ad hoc solution, but try to generalize to *collaborative structuring of personal collections*. Although we will use the setting of the organization of media collections as an example throughout this chapter, the reader should notice that the techniques presented here are not restricted to this domain.

In order to obtain a clear definition of this new learning task, we need to formalize the requirements. The formal notation itself should not be ad hoc, but principled and well based in the general picture of machine learning. Hence, we have developed a uniform description of learning tasks which starts with a most general, generic learning task and is then specialized to the known learning tasks. We derive our new learning task by further specialization and thus embed it into the overall framework (Section 2). While such a uniform framework is of theoretical interest in its own right, we still want to solve the new learning task. We present an approach in the third section. Its use in a distributed setting is exemplified by the application to collaborative media organization in a peer-to-peer network in the fourth section. Experiments on real-world audio data collections in the fifth section show that, in fact, our approach is capable of supporting users to structure their private collections collaboratively.

GENERIC LEARNING TASKS

In the following, we will argue that current learning tasks are not sufficient for the collaborative structuring of personal collections. A learning task is defined by its input and output. In the following, we describe a very general class of learning tasks and show how common learning tasks, as clustering or classification, can be defined by constraining this general class. For each of these learning tasks, we will present at least one example. Also, for each of these classes, we discuss its lack of capabilities for structuring collections according to the given constraints.

Let X denote the set of all possible objects. A function $\varphi: S \rightarrow G$ is a function that maps objects $S \subseteq X$ to a (finite) set G of groups. We denote the domain of a function φ with D_φ. In cases where we have to deal with overlapping and hierarchical groups, we denote the set of groups as 2^G. The input for all learning tasks is a finite set of functions $I \subseteq \Phi = \{ \varphi \mid \varphi: S \rightarrow G \}$. The same holds for the output $O \subseteq \Phi = \{ \varphi \mid \varphi: S \rightarrow G \}$. We can now define a class of generic learning tasks:

Definition 1 (Generic Learning Task)
Given a set $S \subseteq X$, a function set $I \subseteq \Phi$, and a quality function:

$$q: 2^\Phi \times 2^\Phi \times 2^S \rightarrow R$$

with R being partially ordered, a set of output functions O should be found so that $q(I,O,S)$ is maximized.

Constraining the function domains and cardinality of the in- and output functions of this formalization, we can describe many common learning tasks by specifying some details of the functions discussed above. We first describe the abstract formalizations of known learning tasks before we discuss some examples for each task class and also discuss why the known learning tasks are not applicable for collaborative structuring as described above:

$|I| = 1$, $|O| = 1$, $D_\varphi = X$, **Classification:**

The input is $I = \{ \varphi: S \rightarrow G \}$ where S is finite and $S \subseteq X$. In this case, S represents the labeled training examples. G is a set of predefined classes. The task is to find exactly one function $O = \{ \varphi: X \rightarrow G \}$ that is able to assign all possible objects to exactly one class in G. The classification setting can be extended to hierarchical classification with $I = \{ \varphi: S \rightarrow 2^G \}$ and $O = \{ \varphi: X \rightarrow 2^G \}$.

$|I| = 0$, $|O| = 1$, $D_\varphi = S$, **Clustering:**

For traditional clustering, the input set I is empty. The output is $O = \{ \varphi: S \rightarrow G \}$ for a partitioning clustering and $O = \{ \varphi: S \rightarrow 2^G \}$ for a hierarchical and overlapping clustering. S is usually assumed to be finite.

$|I| = 1$, $|O| = 1$, $D_\varphi = S$, **Supervised clustering:**

In contrast to traditional clustering, these clustering schemes use an input set containing one function $I = \{ \varphi: S \rightarrow G \}$. The output is $O = \{ \varphi: S \rightarrow G \}$ for a partitioning clustering and $O = \{ \varphi: S \rightarrow 2^G \}$ for a hierarchical and overlapping clustering. S is usually assumed to be finite.

$|I| > 1$, $|O| = 1$, $D_\varphi = X$, **Classifier ensembles:**

For classifier ensembles, a set of classifiers is given, which is then combined into a global classification function. Thus, $I \subseteq \{ \varphi \mid \varphi: X \rightarrow G \}$, where I is usually assumed to be finite. The output is a single function $O = \{ \varphi: X \rightarrow G \}$ that represents the global classifier model. Please note that the only difference to cluster ensembles is the domain of the input and output functions. Again, hierarchical classifier ensembles could be defined similarly with $I \subseteq \{ \varphi \mid \varphi: X \rightarrow 2^G \}$ and $O = \{ \varphi: X \rightarrow 2^G \}$.

$|I| > 1$, $|O| = 1$, $D_\varphi = S$, **Cluster ensembles:**

For cluster ensembles, a set $I \subseteq \{ \varphi_i \mid \varphi_i: S \rightarrow G_i \}$ of partitions of the objects in S is given. The output is a single partition $O = \{ \varphi: S \rightarrow G \}$. Hierarchical cluster ensembles could be defined similarly with $I \subseteq \{ \varphi_i \mid \varphi_i: S \rightarrow 2^{G_i} \}$ and $O = \{ \varphi: S \rightarrow 2^G \}$.

$|I| = 1$, $|O| > 1$, $D_\varphi = X$, **Alternative classification:**

As for traditional classification, the input set I contains a given function indicating the supervised training points. As output, however, a finite set of functions $O \subseteq \{ \varphi \mid \varphi: X \rightarrow G \}$ should be found that is able to assign all possible objects to exactly one class in G. The classification setting can be extended to hierarchical classification with $I = \{ \varphi: S \rightarrow 2^G \}$ and $O \subseteq \{ \varphi \mid \varphi: X \rightarrow 2^G \}$.

$|I| = 0$, $|O| > 1$, $D_\varphi = S$, **Alternative clustering:**

As for traditional clustering, the input set I is empty. As output, however, a finite set of clusterings on the objects in S is delivered, thus $O \subseteq \{ \varphi_i \mid \varphi_i: S \rightarrow G_i \}$. Again it is easy to define hierarchical alternative clustering with $O \subseteq \{ \varphi_i \mid \varphi_i: S \rightarrow 2^{G_i} \}$.

Known Learning Tasks and Collaborative Structuring

After the formal definition of known learning tasks in the previous section, we will now discuss known instances of these classes of learning tasks and their lack of ability to directly handle the problem of collaborative structuring.

Classification: If there are enough annotated objects, *classification* learning can deliver a decision function φ which maps objects x of the domain X to a class g in a set of classes G. New objects will be classified as soon as they come in, and the user has no burden of annotation anymore. However, classification does not refine the structure.

Clustering: If there is no structure given yet, clustering is the method to choose. The aim of traditional *cluster analysis* is to group a set of previously non-annotated objects into clusters of similar objects. There are several variants of this basic clustering task. Each of them creates a structure of groups G for the not yet annotated objects $S \subseteq X$. Traditional clustering schemes neither take into account the structure which users already have built up nor deliver several alternatives.

Supervised clustering: *Semisupervised or constraint clustering* algorithms allow users to pose constraints on the resulting cluster structure. Constraints state, for example, that two objects must be assigned to the same cluster (Cohn, Caruana, & McCallum, 2003). A variant of semisupervised clustering is *supervised clustering* (Finley & Joachims, 2005). The user provides a cluster structure on a small subset of objects which is then used to cluster the resulting objects. This case can be written as $I = \{ \varphi\colon S' \rightarrow G \}$ where $S' \subseteq X$, we wish to obtain an output function $O = \{ \varphi\colon S \rightarrow G' \}$. Although supervised clustering obeys given groupings, it is not able to incorporate more than one input clustering, it does not preserve label structure, and it does not take locality into account.

Nonredundant data clustering creates alternative structures to a set of given ones (Gondek & Hofmann, 2004). Given a structure G for all objects in the collection, it creates an alternative structure G' for all objects. However, it does not focus on the not yet annotated objects S but restructures also the objects which were already carefully structured. Nonredundant clustering is connected to another area that has recently found increasing attention: *clustering with background knowledge.* In general, the idea of exploiting (user supplied) background knowledge has shown advantages, for example, in text clustering (Hotho, Staab, & Stumme, 2003) or lane finding in global positioning system (GPS) data (Wagstaff, Cardie, Rogers, & Schroedl, 2001). However, these approaches use a feature-based clustering instead of given input clusterings and are hence not applicable to our problem.

Incremental clustering refers to the task of clustering streams of objects, thus to adapt the cluster structure to new objects automatically. Given one input function $I = \{ \varphi\colon S' \rightarrow G \}$, we wish to obtain an output function $O = \{\varphi\colon S' \cup S \rightarrow G'\}$ that additionally clusters the objects S. The cluster quality should be optimized. Often, it is additionally required to alter existing clusters G on S' as little as possible. A very simple method is to check whether a new object is sufficiently similar to one of the current clusters. If this is the case, it is assigned to this cluster; otherwise a new cluster is created that contains only this object (Jain, Murty, & Flynn, 1999). A more sophisticated approach and a theoretical analysis of the problem can be found in Charikar, Chekuri, Feder, and Motwani (2004). Hennig and Wurst (2006) proposed an approach that takes the cost for a user to adapt to a new cluster structure explicitly into account. Again, incremental clustering does not exploit several input clusterings and is hence not applicable for collaborative structuring.

Classifier ensembles: *Classifier ensembles* are one of the most important techniques in supervised learning (Hastie, Tibshirani, and Friedman, 2001). As for traditional classification, classifier ensembles do not refine the structure of the objects.

Cluster ensembles: We may consider the structuring achieved so far as a set of partitions φ_i, each mapping S to a set of groups G_i. *Ensemble clustering* then produces a consensus φ which combines these input partitions (Strehl & Ghosh, 2002). To date, almost all research is concerned with flat cluster ensembles and especially with partition ensembles. Another common assumption of all approaches is that all partitions cover the same set of objects. Several approaches were proposed to merge partitions. The most simple one uses the co-association of objects in the given partitions to derive a binary similarity measure which is then used together with a traditional similarity-based clustering algorithm. The major advantage of this algorithm is its simplicity and the ability to plug it into any state of the art clustering algorithm. Empirical results suggest that it works very well on different problems (Topchy, Jain, & Punch, 2003). A major drawback is the consumption of storage space, because a $|S|^2$ matrix has to be created as input to the clustering procedure.

Another general approach is to search for a median partition among the input partitions, thus a partition that has a maximum average similarity to all other partitions. Several similarity measures are possible. Strehl and Ghosh (2002) proposed mutual information. This measure has however the disadvantage that it cannot be directly optimized. Topchy et al. (2003) proposed other measures like generalized mutual information as it is used in COBWEB. For both, it can be shown that by transforming the input partitions to a set of features (each cluster results in one feature), the problem of finding a median partition is reduced to the k-means clustering problem applied in this feature space.

A third family of algorithms is based on *hyper graph separation* (Strehl & Ghosh, 2002). First, a hyper graph is generated from the input partitions. This hyper graph contains an edge between two objects for each concept they are assigned to.

In addition, in many current applications it is important to consider structures of several users who interact in a network, each offering a clustering $\varphi_i: S_i \rightarrow G_i$. A user with the problem of structuring her leftover objects S might now exploit the cluster models of other users in order to enhance his/her own structure. *Distributed clustering* learns a global model integrating the various local ones (Datta, Bhaduri, Giannella, Wolff, & Kargupta, 2005). However, this global consensus model, again, destroys the structure al-

ready created by the user and does not focus on the set S of not appropriately structured objects.

Cluster ensembles are almost what we need. However, there are three major drawbacks: first, all input clusterings must be defined at least on S. Second, the consensus model does not take the locality of S into account. Finally, merging several heterogeneous user clusterings by a global consensus does not preserve valuable label information.

Alternative classification: To our best knowledge, no classification scheme exists which directly delivers several alternatives for a given classification problem. Although it would be possible to restart nondeterministic classification learners several times, this simple approach would not lead to a diverse set of solutions and is hence not of interest to the user.

There are, however, first approaches for alternative classifier learning if the important problem of automatic feature selection is also taken into account. For supervised learning, there is usually an objective function (as accuracy) that can be optimized by selecting subsets of features (John, Kohavi, & Pfleger, 1994). The total number of features should be minimized during selection since smaller feature sets ease understanding. This leads to a natural competition between the used performance criterion and the number of features, since omitting important features will decrease the performance. Using *multi-objective optimization for feature selection* leads to several output functions using different feature subsets (Emmanouilidis, Hunter, & MacIntyre, 2000). Such an approach is oriented towards the task of structuring personal collections, but it lacks the opportunity to refine the structure of the given objects.

Alternative clustering: For alternative clustering, only *subspace clustering* delivers more than one solution to the user (Agrawal, Gehrke, Gunopulos,

& Raghavan, 1998}. The authors make use of the fact that the density of cells can only decrease with increasing dimensionality. The algorithm therefore searches for dense clusters of maximal dimensionality.

Multi-objective feature selection, as depicted above, can also be applied to clustering. It turns out that, in contrast to the supervised case, the number of features must be maximized in order to find proper solutions (Mierswa & Wurst, 2006). This algorithm naturally yields a diverse set of cluster alternatives respecting different feature subsets. However, both subspace clustering and unsupervised feature selection do not exploit given input functions.

However, still the characteristics of collaborative structuring are not yet met. Whether the user's partial clusterings or those of other peers in a network are given, the situation is the same: current clustering methods deliver a consensus model overwriting the given ones and do not take into account the query set S. In addition, users might want to select among proposed models which the learner delivers. In the media collection setting described before, this would mean that the user might want to select from several different solutions, for example, a structure based on the genre vs. a structure based on musical moods. The practical need of the user in organizing a media collection is not yet covered by existing methods. The situation we are facing is actually a new learning task which will be discussed in the next section.

New Learning Tasks

Following the structure depicted above, we can define several new learning tasks which are in principle better suited for the structuring problem discussed in the introduction:

$|I| > 1, |O| > 1, D_\varphi = S$, **Alternative cluster ensembles:**

Both the input and the output are a finite set of functions $I \subseteq \{ \varphi_i \mid \varphi_i: S \to G_i \}$ and $O \subseteq \{ \varphi_i \mid \varphi_i: S \to G_i \}$. Again, it is easily possible to embed hierarchical clusterings with $I \subseteq \{ \varphi_i \mid \varphi_i: S \to 2^{G_i} \}$ and $O \subseteq \{ \varphi_i \mid \varphi_i: S \to 2^{G_i} \}$.

$|I| > 1, |O| > 1, D_\varphi = X$, **Alternative classifier ensembles:**

For alternative classifier ensembles, both the input and the output are a finite set of functions $I \subseteq \{ \varphi \mid \varphi: X \to G \}$ and $O \subseteq \{ \varphi \mid \varphi: X \to G \}$. Again, it is easily possible to embed hierarchical classifiers with functions $I \subseteq \{ \varphi \mid \varphi: X \to 2^G \}$ and functions $O \subseteq \{ \varphi \mid \varphi: X \to 2^G \}$. Please note that the only difference to alternative cluster ensembles is the domain of the input and output functions.

In this chapter, we will focus on alternative cluster ensembles and embed the problem of locality into this learning task. Locality can be defined twofold. First, locality can be defined regarding the domains S_i of objects on which the input and the output functions are defined. For all ensembles discussed above, these sets are identical. All input functions are defined for the same objects, which is also the set on which the output functions are defined. In general, this must not be the case. Some input functions could be defined only on a local subset of objects, describing a concept that is only locally valid. This is automatically the case if one takes several users into account with, for example, different collections or media data. Second, locality is found in the set of solution functions. While traditional methods deliver exactly one global result, there could be several local results that are valid, as well. To capture this kind of locality, the algorithm must deliver more than one global solution. In the following, we extend the learning task of alternative cluster ensembles in a way that it takes both aspects of locality explicitly into account.

173

Definition 2 (Localized Alternative Cluster Ensembles)

Given a set $S \subseteq X$, a set of input functions $I \subseteq \{ \varphi_i \mid \varphi_i : S_i \rightarrow G_i \}$, and a quality function:

$$q: 2^\Phi \times 2^\Phi \times 2^S \rightarrow R$$

with R being partially ordered, *localized alternative clustering ensembles* deliver output functions $O \subseteq \{ \varphi_i \mid \varphi_i : S_i \rightarrow G_i \}$ so that $q(I,O,S)$ is maximized, and for each $\varphi_i \in O$, it holds that $S \subseteq D_{\varphi_i}$.

Note that in contrast to cluster ensembles, the input clusterings can be defined on any subset S_i of X. Since for all $\varphi_i \in O$, it must hold that $S \subseteq D_{\varphi}$, all output clusterings must at least cover the objects in S. This will ensure that at least the query items which should be structured will be covered by the returned solutions.

AN APPROACH TO LOCALIZED ALTERNATIVE CLUSTER ENSEMBLES

In the following, we describe a clustering method that is based on the idea of bags of clusterings: deriving a new clustering from existing ones by extending the existing clusterings and combining them such, that each of them covers a subset of objects in S. In order to preserve existing label information but allowing the group mapping for new objects, we define the extension of functions φ_i:

Definition 3 (Extended function)

Given a function $\varphi_i : S_i \rightarrow G_i$, the function $\varphi'_i : S'_i \rightarrow G_i$ is the *extended function* for φ_i, if $S_i \subset S'_i$ and $\forall x \in S_i : \varphi_i(x) = \varphi'_i(x)$.

Extended functions allow us to define a bag of extensions of non-overlapping originally labeled subsets that covers the entire collection:

Definition 4 (Bag of clusterings)

Given a set I of functions. A *bag of clusterings* is a function:

$$\varphi_i(x) = \begin{cases} \varphi'_{i1}(x), & \text{if } x \in S'_{i1} \\ \vdots & \vdots \\ \varphi'_{ij}(x), & \text{if } x \in S'_{ij} \\ \vdots & \vdots \\ \varphi'_{im}(x), & \text{if } x \in S'_{im} \end{cases}$$

where each φ'_{ij} is an extension of a $\varphi_{ij} \in I$ and $\{S'_{i1}, \ldots, S'_{im}\}$ is a partitioning of S.

Since each φ'_{ij} is an extension of an input clustering φ_{ij} on a subset S_{ij}, the label information is preserved. Now, we can define the quality for the output, that is, the objective function for our bag of clusterings approach to local alternative clustering ensembles.

Definition 5 (Quality of an Output Function)

The *quality of an individual output function* is measured as:

$$q^*(I, \varphi_i, S) = \sum_{x \in S} \max_{x' \in S_{ij}} sim(x, x') \text{ with } j = h_i(x)$$

where sim is a similarity function sim: $X \times X \rightarrow [0,1]$ and h_i assigns each example to the corresponding function in the bag of clusters, that is, h_i: $S \rightarrow \{1, \ldots, m\}$ with $h_i(x) = j \Leftrightarrow x \in S'_{ij}$. The *quality of a set of output* functions now becomes:

$$q(I, O, S) = \sum_{\varphi_i \in O} q^*(I, \varphi_i, S).$$

Besides this quality function, we want to cover the set S with a bag of clusterings that contains as few clusterings as possible.

The Algorithm

In the following, we present a greedy approach to optimizing the bags of clusterings problem. The main task is to cover S by a bag of clusterings

φ_i. The basic idea of this approach is to employ a sequential covering strategy. In a first step, we search for a function $\varphi_i \in I$ that best fits the set of query objects S. For all objects not sufficiently covered by φ_i, we search for another function in I that fits the remaining objects. This process continues until either all objects are sufficiently covered, a maximal number of steps is reached, or there are no input functions left that could cover the remaining objects. All objects that could not be covered are assigned to the input function φ_j containing the object which is closest to the one to be covered. Alternative clusterings are produced by performing this procedure several times, such that each input function is used at most once.

Before we describe this algorithm in a more formal way, we discuss its function for our media collection example. A user might have a set S of songs which should be structured. Given that a set I of possible structures already exist, the algorithm now tries to find an optimal structure from those which fits a subset of S. The songs of S which are covered by the selected structure are removed from the query set and the process is started anew. Songs which cannot be covered by any of the existing structures are just classified into the already selected structures. The whole process is restarted for the complete set S of songs with the remaining input structures which will lead to alternative solutions for your media collections. The user can then select the final solution which best suits her needs.

We now have to formalize the notion of a function sufficiently covering an object and a function fitting a set of objects such that the quality function is optimized. When is an object sufficiently covered by an input function so that it can be removed from the query set S? We define a threshold based criterion for this purpose:

Definition 6

A function φ *sufficiently covers* an object $x \in S$ (written as $x \sqsubseteq_\alpha \varphi$), if,

$$x \sqsubseteq_\alpha \varphi : \Leftrightarrow \max_{x' \in Z_\varphi} sim(x,x') > \alpha.$$

The set Z_φ of items is delivered by φ. The threshold α allows the balancing of the quality of the resulting clustering and the number of input clusters. A small value of α allows a single input function to cover many objects in S. This, on average, reduces the number of input functions needed to cover the whole query set. However, it may also reduce the quality of the result, as the algorithm covers many objects in a greedy manner, which could be covered better using an additional input function.

Turning it the other way around, when do we consider an input function to fit the objects in S well? First, it must contain at least one similar object for each object in S. This is essentially what is stated in the quality function q*. Second, it should cover as few additional objects as possible. This condition follows from the locality demand. Using only the first condition, the algorithm would not distinguish between input functions which span a large part of the data space and those which only span a small local part. This distinction, however, is essential for treating local patterns in the data appropriately. The situation we are facing is similar to that in information retrieval. The target concept S—the ideal response—is approximated by φ delivering a set of objects—the retrieval result. If all members of the target concept are covered, the retrieval result has the highest recall. If all objects in the retrieval result are members of S, it has the highest precision. We want to apply precision and recall to characterize how well φ covers S. Let $Z\varphi_i$ be the set of objects delivered by φ_i. We can define

$$prec(Z_{\varphi_i}, S) = \frac{1}{|Z_{\varphi_i}|} \sum_{z \in Z_{\varphi_i}} max \{sim(x, z) | x \in S\}$$

and

$$rec(Z_{\varphi_i}, S) = \frac{1}{|S|} \sum_{x \in S} max \{sim(x, z) | z \in Z_{\varphi_i}\}.$$

Please note that using a similarity function which maps identical objects to 1 (and 0 otherwise) leads to the usual definition of precision and recall. The fit between an input function and a set of objects now becomes:

$$q_f^*(Z_{\varphi_i}, S) = \frac{(\beta^2 + 1)rec(Z_{\varphi_i}, S)prec(Z_{\varphi_i}, S)}{\beta^2 rec(Z_{\varphi_i}, S) + prec(Z_{\varphi_i}, S)}.$$

Recall directly optimizes the quality function q*, and precision ensures that the result captures local structures adequately. The fitness $q_f^*(Z_\varphi, S)$ balances the two criteria as it is well known from the f-measure.

Deciding whether φ_i fits S or whether an object $x \in S$ is sufficiently covered requires computing the similarity between an object and a cluster. If the cluster is represented by all of its objects ($Z_{\varphi_i} = S_i$ as used in single-link agglomerative clustering), this important step becomes inefficient. If the cluster is represented by exactly one point ($|Z_{\varphi_i}| = 1$, for example, a centroid in k-means clustering, the similarity calculation is very efficient, but

sets of objects with irregular shape, for instance, cannot be captured adequately. Hence, we adopt the representation by "well scattered points" Z_{φ_i} as representation of φ_i (Guha, Rastogi, & Shim, 1998), where $1 < |Z_{\varphi_i}| < |S_i|$. These points are selected by stratified sampling according to G. Please note that this approach will not ensure that the selected points are prototypical in any sense. In our media collection setting, just a random sample from the clusters are drawn—a set of songs describing the clusters.

We can now dare to compute the fitness q_f^* of all $Z_{\varphi_i} \in I$ with respect to a query set S in order to select the best φ_i for our bag of clusterings. The whole algorithm works as depicted in Figure 1. We start with the initial set of input functions I and the set S of objects to be clustered. In a first step, we select an input function that maximizes $q_f^*(Z_{\varphi_i}, S)$. φ_i is then removed from the set of input functions leading to a set I'. For all objects S' that are not sufficiently covered by φ_i, we again select a function from I' with maximal fit to S'. This process is iterated until all objects are

Figure 1. The sequential covering algorithm finds bags of clusterings in a greedy manner. max_{alt} denotes the maximum number of alternatives in the output, and max_{steps} denotes the maximum number of steps that are performed during sequential covering. The function bag constructs a bag of clusterings by assigning each object $x \in S$ to the function $\varphi_i \in B$ that contains the object most similar to x.

```
O = ∅
I' = I
while (|O| < max_alt) do
    S' = S
    B = ∅
    step = 0
    while ((S' ≠ ∅) ∧ (I' ≠ ∅) ∧ (step < max_steps)) do
        φ_i = arg max_{φ∈J} q_f^*(Z_φ, S')
        I' = I' \ {φ_i}
        B = B ∪ {φ_i}
        S' = S' \ {x ∈ S'|x ⊏_α φ_i}
        step = step + 1
    end while
    O = O ∪ {bag(B, S)}
end while
```

sufficiently covered, a maximal number of steps is reached, or no input functions left that could cover the remaining objects. All input functions selected in this process are combined to a bag of clusters, as described above. Each object $x \in S$ is assigned to the input function containing the object most similar to x. Then, all input functions are extended accordingly (cf. Definition 3). We start this process anew with the complete set S and the reduced set I' of input functions until the maximal number of alternatives is reached.

Regarding computation complexity, the approach works linear in the number of input structures I and query items (e.g., songs) S. As each function is represented by a fixed number of representative points, the number of similarity calculations performed by the algorithm is linear in the number of query objects and in the number of input functions, thus $O(|I| \, |S| \, |Z\varphi_i|)$. The same holds for the memory requirements. If the number of representation objects grows, the runtime is quadratic in the query set S for the worst case.

Incremental Clustering

The aim of incremental clustering is to enrich an existing cluster structure with new objects. The cluster quality should be optimized without altering the given clustering more than necessary. This can easily be achieved in our approach. In the first step of the inner loop of the algorithm described above, we always select the original clustering created by the user. The algorithm then proceeds as usual, exploiting all available clusterings as input functions in order to cover the objects which are not covered by the original structure.

Hierarchical Matching

A severe limitation of the algorithm described so far is that it can only combine complete input clusterings. In many situations, a combination of partial clusterings or even individual clusters

would yield a much better result. This is especially true if local patterns are to be preserved, being captured by maximally specific concepts. Moreover, the algorithm does not yet handle hierarchies. Our motivation for this research was the structuring of media collections. Flat structures are not sufficient with respect to this goal. For example, music collections might be divided into genres and subgenres. We cannot use a standard hierarchical clustering algorithm, since we still want to solve the new task of local alternative cluster ensembles. In the following, we extend our approach to the combination of partial hierarchical functions. A hierarchical function maps objects to a hierarchy of groups.

Definition 7 (Group Hierarchy)
The set G_i of groups associated with a function φ_i builds a *group hierarchy* if there is a relation < such that $(g<g') : \Leftrightarrow (\forall x \in S_i: g' \in \varphi_i(x) \Rightarrow g \in \varphi_i(x))$ and $(G_i, <)$ is a tree. The function φ_i is then called a *hierarchical function*.

It should be possible to match functions that correspond to only a partial group hierarchy. We formalize this notion by defining a hierarchy on functions, which extends the set of input functions such that it contains all partial functions, as well.

Definition 8 (Function Hierarchy)
Two hierarchical functions φ_i and φ_j are in *direct subfunction relation* $\varphi_i \prec \varphi_j$, iff $G_i \subset G_j$, $\forall x \in S_i: \varphi_i(x) = \varphi_j(x) \cap G_i$, and $\neg \exists \varphi': G_i \subset G'_i \subset G_j$. Figure 2 depicts both notions.

Let the set I* be the set of all functions which can be achieved following the direct subfunction relation starting from I, thus:

$$I^* = \{\varphi_i | \exists \varphi_j \in I : \varphi_i \prec^* \varphi_j\}$$

where $\prec^*$ is the transitive hull of $\prec$. While it would be possible to apply the same algorithm as above to the extended set of input functions

Figure 2. The function φ_i is a subfunction of function φ_j, i.e. $\varphi_i \prec \varphi_j$. The groups g_4 and g_5 are subgroups of g_2, and the groups g_2, g_3, g_4 and g_5 are sub groups of g_1.

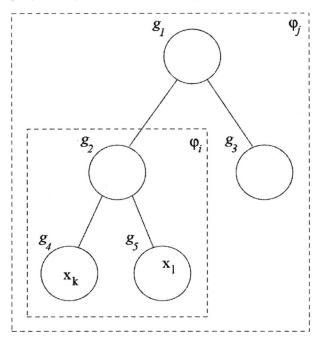

I*, this would be rather inefficient, because the size of I* can be considerably larger than the one of the original set of input functions I. We therefore propose an algorithm which exploits the function hierarchy and avoids multiple similarity computations. Each function $\varphi_i \in$ I* is again associated with a set of representative objects $Z\varphi_i$. We additionally assume the standard taxonomy semantics:

$$\varphi_i \prec \varphi_j \Rightarrow Z_{\varphi_i} \subseteq Z_{\varphi_j}.$$

Now, the precision can be calculated recursively in the following way:

$$prec(Z_{\varphi_i}, S) = \frac{|Z^*_{\varphi_i}|}{|Z_{\varphi_i}|} prec(Z^*_{\varphi_i}, S) +$$
$$\sum_{\varphi_j \prec \varphi_i} \frac{|Z_{\varphi_j}|}{|Z_{\varphi_i}|} prec(Z_{\varphi_j}, S).$$

where $Z\varphi_i{}^* = Z\varphi_i \backslash \bigcup_{\varphi_j \prec \varphi_i} Z\varphi_j$. For recall, a similar function can be derived. Note that neither the number of similarity calculations is greater than in the base version of the algorithm nor are the memory requirements increased.

Moreover, the bottom-up procedure also allows for pruning. We can optimistically estimate the best precision and recall that can be achieved in function hierarchy using all representative objects Z_e for which the precision is already known. The following holds:

$$prec(Z_{\varphi_i}, S) \leq \frac{|Z_e| prec(Z_e, S) + |Z_{\varphi_i} \backslash Z_e|}{|Z_{\varphi_i}|}$$

with $Z_e \subset Z\varphi_j$. An optimistic estimate for the recall is one. If the optimistic f-measure estimate of the hierarchy's root node is worse than the current best score, this hierarchy does not need to be processed further. This is due to the optimistic score increasing with $|Z\varphi_j|$ and $|Z\varphi_j| > |Z\varphi_i|$ for all subfunctions $\varphi_j \prec \varphi_i$. No subfunction of the root can be better than the current best score, if the score of the root is equal or worse than the current best score.

This conversion to hierarchical cluster models concludes our algorithm for Local Alternative Cluster Ensembles (LACE).

A DISTRIBUTED ALGORITHM

The LACE algorithm is well suited for distributed scenarios. We assume a set of nodes connected over an arbitrary communication network. Each node has one or several functions φ_i together with the sets S_i. If a node A has a set of objects S to be clustered, it queries the other nodes and these respond with a set of functions. The answers of the other nodes form the input functions I. The node A computes the output O for S. The node B being queried uses its own functions φ_i as input and determines the best fitting φ_i for S and sends this output back to node A. The algorithm is the same for each node and each node executes the algorithm independently of the other nodes.

We introduce three optimizations to this distributed approach. First, given a function hierarchy, each node returns exactly one optimal function in the hierarchy. This reduces the communication cost, without affecting the result, because all but the optimal function would not be chosen anyway (see pruning in the last section).

Second, input functions returned by other nodes can be represented more efficiently by only containing the objects in the query set, that are sufficiently covered by the corresponding function. Together with the f-measure value q_f^* for the function, this information is sufficient for the querying node in order to perform the algorithm.

In many application areas, we can apply a third optimization. If objects are uniquely identified, such as audio files, films, Web resources, and so forth, they can be represented by these IDs only. In this case, the similarity between two objects is 1, if they have the same ID and 0 otherwise. A distributed version of our algorithm only needs to query other nodes using a set of IDs. This reduces the communication cost and makes matching even more efficient. Furthermore, such queries are already very well supported by current technology, such as p2p search engines.

In a distributed scenario, network latency and communication cost must be taken into account. If objects are represented by IDs, both are restricted to an additional effort of $O(|S| + |I^*|)$. Thus, the algorithm is still linear in the number of query objects.

Distributed Media Management

Together with a group of students, we have developed Nemoz as a framework for studying collaborative music organization. Nemoz is made for experimenting with intelligent functionality of media organization systems. Of course, the basic functions of media systems are implemented: download and import of songs, playing music, retrieving music from a collection based on given metadata, and creating play lists. The data model covers not only the standard metadata (performer, composer, album, year, duration of the song, genre, and comment) and a reference to the location of the song, but also features extracted from the raw data.

Communication among (W)LAN nodes via TCP and UDP is supported by a network service.

Intelligent functions are based on taxonomy data structures. A collection can be organized using several taxonomies in parallel. At each taxonomy node, an extended function can be stored, which decides whether a new song belongs to this node or not. This classifier is the learned model, where the learning task has been performed by one of the methods supplied by the machine learning environment YALE (Mierswa, Wurst, Klinkenberg, Scholz, & Euler, 2006; available at http://yale.sf.net). Based on this data structure, Nemoz already implements several intelligent functions:

- Taxonomies can be defined extensionally by the user.
- Taxonomy nodes can be intensionally defined by a (learned) model.
- New music can be classified into the taxonomy.
- Users can search for similar taxonomies in the network.
- Users can search to music similar to a selected song.
- A taxonomy can be enhanced through the taxonomies of other users automatically (LACE).

Confronted with music data, machine learning encounters a new challenge of scalability. Music databases store millions of records, and each item contains up to several million values. In addition, the shape of the curve defined by these values does not express the crucial aspect of similarity measures for musical objects. The solution to overcome these issues is to extract features from the audio signal which leads to a strong compression of the data set at hand. Feature extraction from audio data has become a hot topic recently. Many manually designed audio features extracted from polyphonic music have been proposed for different applications in music information retrieval (e.g., Moerchen, Ultsch, Thies, & Loehken, 2005; Pampalk, Dixon, & Widmer, 2003; Tzanetakis & Cook, 2002).

Regarding local patterns is also crucial for the process of feature extraction, since a feature set which is valid for the overall collection is hard to find (Pohle, Pampalk, & Widmer 2005). It is not very likely that a feature set delivering excellent performance on the separation of classical and popular music works well also for the separation of music structured according to occasions. This problem already arises for high-level structures like musical genres and is even aggregated due to the locality induced by personal structures.

If there would exist one complete set of features, from which each learning task selects its proper part, the feature problem could be reduced to feature selection. However, there is no tractable feature set to select from. The number of possible feature extractions is so large—virtually infinite—that it would be intractable to enumerate it. Mierswa and Morik (2005) proposed a unified framework for extraction methods which allows for automatically learning the optimal feature extractors for a given learning task. The result is a (nested) sequence of data transformations which calculates the optimal feature set. Learning feature extraction delivers good results, but training the feature extraction is time-consuming and demands a sufficient set of examples.

Beside these problems, emotional or sociocultural aspects of music can hardly be expressed by feature values at all. Clustering schemes merely using audio features as a basis of a similarity measure will fail for this reason. Since Nemoz exploits the hand-made structures provided by other users, these aspects can also be covered. Furthermore, the similarity measures can be improved by transferring successful features together with the structuring (Mierswa & Wurst, 2005).

In Nemoz, each user may create arbitrary, personal classification schemes to organize music. For instance, some users structure their collection according to mood and situations, others according to genres, and so forth. Some of these structures may overlap; for example, the blues genre may cover songs which are also covered by a personal concept "melancholic" of a structure describing moods. Nemoz supports the users in structuring their media objects while not forcing them to use the same set of concepts or annotations. If an ad hoc network has been established, peers support each other in structuring. A user who needs to structure a set of media objects S (e.g., refining an over-full node in a taxonomy) invokes the distributed algorithm described above. Then, the system offers a set of alternative clusterings, each combined from peers' response and covering S (cf. Figure 3).

By recommending tags and structures to other users, we establish emerging views on the underlying space of objects. An important point here is that the LACE approach naturally leads to a social filtering of such views. If someone creates a (partial) taxonomy found useful by many other users, it is often copied. If several taxonomies equally fit a query, a well-distributed taxonomy is recommended with higher probability. This pushes high quality taxonomies and allows to filter random or non-sense taxonomies. While the collaborative approach offers many opportunities, audio features can still be very helpful. The most important is that they allow replacing of exact matches by similar matches. This is essential when dealing with sparse data: that is, the number of objects in the taxonomies is rather small.

Figure 3. Other users have sent taxonomies φ_1 and φ_2 which best fit the query S. LACE sorts objects of S into the selected structure φ_2. The remaining objects S' form a second query set leading to a new response set. The second structure φ'_1 is added together with φ_1 under a new merge node.

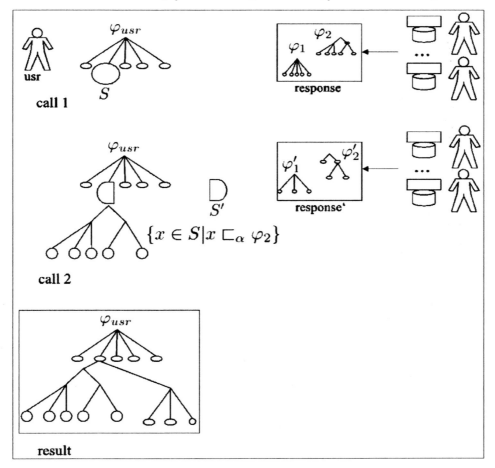

EXPERIMENTS

The evaluation of LACE is performed on a real-world benchmark data set gathered in a student project on distributed audio classification based on peer-to-peer networks (Nemoz). The data set contains 39 taxonomies (functions $\varphi_1, \ldots, \varphi_{39}$) and overall 1,886 songs (Homburg, Mierswa, Moeoller, Morik, & Wurst, 2005). All experiments described in this chapter were performed with the machine learning environment YALE. The evaluation of LACE is performed by subsequently leaving out one function φ_i of the data set. Then we apply clustering to reconstruct this taxonomy. Hence, we can evaluate cluster models in a way similar to classification learning. We have a "ground truth" available. A user taxonomy φ_i is compared with a taxonomy φ, created automatically by clustering as follows. We construct the usual tree distance matrices M and M' for the two taxonomies (cf. Definition 7) and compare these matrices on all pairs (x_i, x_j) of objects in the set S. Each entry M_{ij} of the matrix M is computed as:

$$|\varphi(x_i)| + |\varphi(x_j)| - 2 \cdot |\varphi(x_i) \cap \varphi(x_j)|,$$

for M' the function φ, is used. For instance, the objects x_k and x_l from Figure 2 are both members of g_1 and g_2 and have a tree distance of 2. For the *absolute distance* criterion, the differences between the entries of M and M' are summed-up and divided by the total number of entries. As a second criterion, we use the *correlation* between these tree distances.

Finally, for each cluster in the left-out taxonomy, we search for the best corresponding cluster in the learned taxonomy according to f-measure. The average performance over all user-given clusters is then used as the *FScore* evaluation measure (Steinbach, Karypis, & Kumar, 2000). Note that although we report the FScore, it is not normalized with respect to the number of created clusters. Finer grained structures therefore

always lead to equal or better performance than their coarse grained variants. This, however, does often not reflect the similarity to the user-given taxonomy.

We compare our approach with single-link agglomerative clustering using cosine measure, top-down divisive clustering based on recursively applying kernel k-means (Dhillon Guan & Kulis, 2004) (TD), with random clustering. Localized Alternative Cluster Ensembles were applied using cosine similarity as inner similarity measure. The parameters for all algorithms were chosen globally optimal. This is possible as our evaluation procedure is basically a variant of leave-one-out cross validation. Thus, we can start the evaluation several times on different parameter sets. It turns out that small values for α perform best. In our experiments, we used $\alpha = 0.1$. For β, the optimal value was 1.

TD and random clustering were started five times with different random initializations. We use a set of 20 features which were shown to work well in a wide range of applications (Moerchen, Ultsch, Thies, Loehken, Noecker, & Stamm, 2004) as underlying audio features. Since, here, we want to test the new clustering method, we do not investigate different feature sets. Please refer to Wurst, Morik, and Mierswa (2006) for further details on the experiments.

Table 1 shows the results. As can be seen, the local alternative cluster ensembles approach LACE performs best. Note however, that absolute distance does not lead to results that are representative for agglomerative clustering as such, because it usually builds-up quite deep hierarchies, while the user constructed hierarchies were rather shallow.

A second experiment inspects the influence of the representation on the accuracy. The results of LACE with different numbers of instances at a node are shown in Table 2. Representing functions by all points performs best. Using a single centroid for representing a subtree leads to inferior results, as we already expected. Well-scattered points perform well. We obtain good results even for a very small number of representative objects at each node of the cluster model.

We also evaluated how the number of output functions influences the quality of the result. The result should be clearly inferior with a decreasing number. Table 3 shows the results. On one hand, we observe that even with just one model, that is $|O| = 1$, LACE still outperforms the other methods with respect to tree distance. On the other hand, the results are, indeed, getting worse with fewer alternatives. Providing alternative solutions seems to be essential for improving the quality

of results at least in heterogeneous settings as the one discussed here.

CONCLUSION

Services for media collections are demanded, both for the client side and the server side. In addition to basic services (e.g., player, viewer, etc.) structuring tools are requested. Clustering is a basic technique for this problem. A correct or optimal clustering of objects depends strongly on intentions and preferences of the user. An important

Table 1. The results for different evaluation measures. It can clearly be seen that LACE performs best (Correlation and FScore should be maximized; the distance should be minimized).

Method	Correlation	Absolute distance	FScore
LACE	0.44	0.68	0.63
TD audio	0.19	2.2	0.51
TD ensemble	0.23	2.5	0.55
single-link audio	0.11	9.7	0.52
single-link ensemble	0.17	9.9	0.60
random	0.09	1.8	0.5

Table 2. The influence of the concept representation (i.e., the cardinality of $|Z|$)

Representation	Correlation	Absolute distance	FScore
all points	0.44	0.68	0.63
$|Z| = 10$	0.44	0.68	0.63
$|Z| = 5$	0.41	0.69	0.63
$|Z| = 3$	0.40	0.69	0.62
centroid	0.19	1.1	0.42

Table 3. The influence of the response set cardinality $|O|$

Alternatives	Correlation	Absolute distance	FScore
5	0.44	0.68	0.63
3	0.38	0.73	0.60
1	0.34	0.85	0.56

challenge for new clustering techniques is the question of how to integrate clusterings provided by other users in a way that allows for a certain personalization which reflects the locality of the data and preserves user created clusterings.

We introduced a generic notion of machine learning which can be constrained in order to define well-known learning tasks. We argued that none of these tasks can be used to fulfill the conditions of collaborative structuring. Following this generic notion, we were able to derive several learning tasks like alternative cluster ensembles which are the departing point for solving the collaborative structuring problem. In contrast to other cluster ensemble methods or distributed clustering, a global model (consensus) is not the aim.

Investigating the practical needs carefully has led to the definition of a new learning task, namely learning localized alternative cluster ensembles, where a set of given clustering is taken into account and a set of proposed clusterings is delivered. We have formalized the learning task and developed a greedy approach to solve it. Enhancements for hierarchical structures accomplish the LACE algorithm. It is well suited for distributed settings.

The performance of algorithms solving the localized alternative cluster ensembles task can be measured by a leave-one-structuring-out approach. The proposed algorithm outperforms standard clustering schemes on a real-world data set in the domain of music collections. We also investigated the influence of the number of representative points and the influence of response set cardinality which are important in distributed scenarios.

In our opinion, applications in the Web 2.0 context offer many interesting opportunities for machine learning. Corresponding methods must be user-centric and inherently robust and scalable. LACE is the first and very promising approach to overcome some of the problems associated with this new kind of machine learning application.

REFERENCES

Agrawal, R., Gehrke, J., Gunopulos, D., & Raghavan, P. (1998). Automatic subspace clustering of high dimensional data for data mining applications. *SIGMOD Record, 27*(2), 94-105. ACM Special Interest Group on Management of Data.

Charikar, M., Chekuri, C., Feder, T., & Motwani, R. (2004). Incremental clustering and dynamic information retrieval. *SIAM Journal on Computing, 33*(6).

Cohn, D., Caruana, R., & McCallum, A. (2000). *Semi-supervised clustering with user feedback* (Tech. Rep. No. TR2003-1892). Cornell University.

Datta, S., Bhaduri, K., Giannella, C., Wolff, R., & Kargupta, H. (2005). Distributed data mining in peer-to-peer networks [Special issue]. *IEEE Internet Computing.*

Dhillon, I.-S., Guan, Y., & Kulis, B. (2004). Kernel k-means: Spectral clustering and normalized cuts. In *Proceedings of the Conference on Knowledge Discovery and Data Mining (KDD).*

Emmanouilidis, C., Hunter, A., & MacIntyre, J. (2000). A multiobjective evolutionary setting for feature selection and a commonality-based crossover operator. *In Proceedings of the Congress on Evolutionary Computation (CEC)* (pp. 309-316).

Finley, T., & Joachims, T. (2005). Supervised clustering with support vector machines. In *Proceedings of the International Conference on Machine Learning (ICML).*

Gondek, D., & Hofmann, T. (2004). Non-redundant data clustering. In *Proceedings of the 4th IEEE International Conference on Data Mining (ICDM).*

Guha, S., Rastogi, R., & Shim, K. (1998). CURE: An efficient clustering algorithm for large databases. In *Proceedings of the ACM SIGMOD International Conference on Management of Data* (pp. 73-84).

Hastie, T., Tibshirani, R., & Friedman, J. (2001). *The elements of statistical learning: Data mining, inference, and prediction* (Springer Series in Statistics). Springer.

Hennig, S., & Wurst, M. (2006). Incremental clustering of newsgroup articles. In *Proceedings of the International Conference on Industrial, Engineering and Other Applications of Applied Intelligent Systems (IEA/AIE 06)*.

Homburg, H., Mierswa, I., Moeller, B., Morik, K., & Wurst, M. (2005). A benchmark dataset for audio classification and clustering. In *Proceedings of the International Conference on Music Information Retrieval*.

Hotho, A., Staab, S., & Stumme, G. (2003). Ontologies improve text document clustering. In *Proceedings of the International Conference on Data Mining* (pp. 541-544).

Jain, A.-K., Murty, M.-N., & Flynn, P.-J. (1999). Data clustering: A review. *ACM Computing Surveys, 31*, 264-323.

John, G.-H., Kohavi, R., & Pfleger, K. (1994). Irrelevant features and the subset selection problem. In *Proceedings of the International Conference on Machine Learning (ICML)* (pp. 121-129).

Jones, S., Cunningham, S.-J., & Jones, M. (2004). Organizing digital music for use: An examination of personal music collections. In *Proceedings of the International Conference on Music Information Retrieval*.

Mierswa, I., & Morik, K. (2005). Automatic feature extraction for classifying audio data. *Machine Learning Journal, 58*, 127-149.

Mierswa, I., & Wurst, M. (2005). Efficient case based feature construction for heterogeneous learning tasks. In *Proceedings of the European Conference on Machine Learning (ECML)* (pp. 641-648).

Mierswa, I., & Wurst, M. (2006). Information preserving multi-objective feature selection for unsupervised learning. In *Proceedings of the Genetic and Evolutionary Computation Conference (GECCO)*.

Mierswa, I., Wurst, M., Klinkenberg, R., Scholz, M., & Euler, T. (2006). YALE: Rapid prototyping for complex data mining tasks. In *Proceedings of the 12th ACM SIGKDD International Conference on Knowledge Discovery and Data Mining (KDD 2006)*. ACM Press.

Moerchen, F., Ultsch, A., Thies, M., & Loehken, I. (2006). Modelling timbre distance with temporal statistics from polyphonic music. *IEEE Transactions on Speech and Audio Processing*.

Moerchen, F., Ultsch, A., Thies, M., Loehken, I., Noecker, C., Stamm, M., et al. (2004). *Musicminer: Visualizing perceptual distances of music as topographical maps* (Tech. Rep.). Department of Mathematics and Computer Science, University of Marburg, Germany.

Pampalk, E., Dixon, S., & Widmer, G. (2003). On the evaluation of perceptual similarity measures for music. In *Proceedings of the International Conference on Digital Audio Effects* (pp. 6-12).

Pohle, T., Pampalk, E., & Widmer, G. (2005). Evaluation of frequently used audio features for classification of music into perceptual categories. In *Proceedings of the International Workshop on Content-Based Multimedia Indexing*.

Steinbach, M., Karypis, G., & Kumar, V. (2000). A comparison of document clustering techniques. In *Proceedings of the KDD Workshop on Text Mining*.

Strehl, A., & Ghosh, J. (2002). Cluster ensembles: A knowledge reuse framework for combining partitionings. In *Proceedings of the AAAI*.

Topchy, A.P., Jain, A.K., & Punch, W.F. (2003). Combining multiple weak clusterings. In *Proceedings of the International Conference on Data Mining (ICDM)* (pp. 331-338).

Tzanetakis, G., & Cook, P. (2002). Musical genre classification of audio signals. *IEEE Transactions on Speech and Audio Processing, 10*(5), 293-302.

Wagstaff, K., Cardie, C., Rogers, S., & Schroedl, S. (2001). Constrained k-means clustering with background knowledge. In *Proceedings of the International Conference on Machine Learning (ICML)*.

Wurst, M., Morik, K., & Mierswa, I. (2006). Localized alternative cluster ensembles for collaborative structuring. In *Proceedings of the European Conference on Machine Learning (ECML)*.

Chapter IX
Pattern Mining and Clustering on Image Databases

Marinette Bouet
LIMOS, Blaise Pascal University-Clermont-Ferrand, France

Pierre Gançarski
LSIIT-AFD-Louis Pasteur University, France

Marie-Aude Aufaure
Supélec—INRIA, France

Omar Boussaïd
University LUMIERE Lyon, France

ABSTRACT

Analysing and mining image data to derive potentially useful information is a very challenging task. Image mining concerns the extraction of implicit knowledge, image data relationships, associations between image data and other data or patterns not explicitly stored in the images. Another crucial task is to organise the large image volumes to extract relevant information. In fact, decision support systems are evolving to store and analyse these complex data. This chapter presents a survey of the relevant research related to image data processing. We present data warehouse advances that organise large volumes of data linked with images, and then we focus on two techniques largely used in image mining. We present clustering methods applied to image analysis, and we introduce the new research direction concerning pattern mining from large collections of images. While considerable advances have been made in image clustering, there is little research dealing with image frequent pattern mining. We will try to understand why.

INTRODUCTION

In recent years, most organisations have been dealing with multimedia data integrating differ-ent formats such as images, audio formats, video formats, texts, graphics, or XML documents. For example, a lot of image data have been produced for various professional or domestic domains such as weather forecasting, surveillance flights, satellites, bio-informatics, biomedical imaging, marketing, tourism, press, Web, and so forth. Such data have been at the disposal of all audiences. Faced with the amount of information produced in numerous domains, there has been a growing demand for tools allowing people to efficiently manage, organise, and retrieve multimedia data.

In this chapter, we focus our attention on the media image. Images may be characterised in terms of three aspects—the volume of the data, the pixel matrix, and the high dimensionality of the data. The first aspect is linked to the huge volume of these data (from a few hundred bytes to several gigabytes for the remote sensing images); the second one reflects the intrinsic nature of the pixel matrix. A pixel or a pixel sequence itself does not mean anything: images do not directly contain any information. Yet the presence of one or more pixel sequences often points to the presence of relevant information. In fact, image interpretation and exploitation need extra relevant information including semantic concepts such as annotations or ontologies, cluster characterisation, and so forth. Today, image and, more generally, multimedia retrieval systems have reached their limits owing to this semantic information absence.

Moreover, in the image retrieval context, a logical indexation process is performed to associate a set of metadata (textual and visual features) with images. These image features are stored in numeric vectors. Their high dimensionality, the third image aspect, constitutes a well known problem. All these different points are, in fact, related to image complexity.

Classical data mining techniques are largely used to analyse alphanumerical data. However, in an image context, databases are very large since they contain strongly heterogeneous data, often not structured and possibly coming from different sources within different theoretical or applicative domains (pixel values, image descriptors, annotations, trainings, expert or interpreted knowledge,

etc.). Besides, when objects are described by a large set of features, many of them are correlated, while others are noisy or irrelevant. Furthermore, analysing and mining these multimedia data to derive potentially useful information is not easy. For example, image mining involves the extraction of implicit knowledge, image data relationships, associations between image data, and other data or patterns not explicitly stored in the images.

To circumvent this complexity, we can multiply the number of descriptors. The problem is now to define multidimensional indexes so that searching the nearest neighbours becomes more efficient using the index rather than a sequential search. In the image case, the high dimensionality due to complex descriptors is still an unsolved research problem.

Moreover, another problem is to use external knowledge that could be represented using ontologies or metadata. Taking account of *a priori* knowledge, such as annotation and metadata to build an ontology dedicated to an application, is also a challenge and implies the definition of new descriptors that integrate semantics. As an example, the Web contains many images that are not exploited using the textual part of the Web pages. In this case, the combination of visual and textual information is particularly relevant.

Finally, a crucial task is to organise these large volumes of "raw" data (image, text, etc.) in order to extract relevant information. In fact, decision support systems (DSS) such as data warehousing, data mining, or online analytical processing (OLAP) are evolving to store and analyse these complex data. OLAP and data mining can be seen as two complementary fields. OLAP can easily deal with structuring data before their analysis and with organising structured views. However, this technique is restricted to a simple data navigation and exploration. Data warehouse techniques can help data preprocessing and offer a good structure for an efficient data mining process.

Consequently, new tools must be developed to efficiently retrieve relevant information in specialised and generalised image databases. Different data mining techniques contributions have been or may be developed: reducing the retrieval space in the multidimensional indexation domain, learning by relevance feedback and without relevance feedback, and using the synergy between textual and visual features to better explore and exploit the image database. For instance, a usual way to address the problem of retrieval of relevant information is to perform an automatic classification of images, that is, to classify images into different categories so that each one is composed of images that have a similar content. A more recent approach consists in pattern mining such as rule mining: associations between image content features and non-image content features, associations of different image contents with no spatial relationships, and associations among image contents with spatial relationships.

In this chapter, we present a survey of the relevant research related to image processing. We present data warehouse solutions to organise large volumes of data linked with images, and we focus on two techniques used in image mining. On one hand, we present clustering methods applied to image analysis, and on the other hand, we introduce the new research direction concerning pattern mining from large collections of images.

Because there is a lack of hybrid data mining methods and methodologies which use the complementarity of these image or video data in a collaborative way, and which considers them from different points of view, we shall sketch a multistrategic data mining approach able to handle complex data.

The rest of this chapter is organised as follows. The second section presents data warehouses, classification, and pattern mining techniques related to classical data. The third section presents some relevant work related to these three aspects applied to image mining. The fourth section describes some issues and applications linked with these approaches. The fifth section concludes our study.

DATA WAREHOUSE, PATTERN MINING, AND CLASSIFICATION IN CLASSICAL DATA PROCESSING

This section presents data warehouses, classification, and pattern mining techniques related to classical data. Data warehouses techniques can be seen as a preprocessing stage used to strengthen data structuring. Data mining techniques, such as pattern mining (association rules or frequent pattern search), have been intensively used for many applications. This technique consists in generating rules from facts according to a threshold. Data clustering can be divided into partition, hierarchical, density-based, and conceptual clustering. Some methods are also based on neuronal methods such as self-organised maps. In most cases, the choice of a similarity measure is a crucial point.

Data Warehouses

Data warehousing and OLAP technologies (Inmon, 2005; Kimball & Ross, 2002) are now considered well established. They aim, for instance, to analyse the behaviour of a customer, a product, or a company, and may help monitoring one or several activities (commercial or medical pursuits, patent deposits, etc.). In particular, they help analyse such activities in the form of numerical data. A data warehouse is a subject oriented, integrated, time-variant, and nonvolatile collection of data that supports managerial decision making (Inmon, 2005). Data warehousing has been cited as the highest-priority postmillennium project of more than half of information technology (IT) executives. A large number of data warehousing methodologies and tools are available to support the growing market. However, with so many methodologies to choose from, a major concern for many firms is which one to employ in a given data warehousing project.

Online transactional processing (OLTP) systems are useful for addressing the operational data needs of a firm. However, they are not well suited for supporting decision-support queries or business questions that managers typically need to answer. Such queries are analytical and can be answered using roll up aggregation, drill down, and slicing/dicing of data, which are best supported by OLAP systems. Data warehouses support OLAP applications by storing and maintaining data in multidimensional format (Chaudhuri & Dayal, 1997; Kimball & Ross, 2002). Data in an OLAP warehouse are extracted and loaded from multiple OLTP data sources (including DB2, Oracle, IMS databases, and flat files) using Extract, Transform, and Load (ETL) tools. The warehouse is located in a presentation server. It can span enterprise-wide data needs or can be a collection of "conforming" data marts. Data marts (subsets of data warehouses) are conformed by following a standard set of attribute declarations called a data warehouse bus (Kimball & Ross, 2002). The data warehouse uses a metadata repository to integrate all of its components. The metadata store the definitions of the source data, the data models for target databases, and the transformation rules that convert source data into target data. The concepts of time variance and nonvolatility are essential for a data warehouse (Inmon, 2005). Inmon emphasised the importance of cross-functional slices of data drawn from multiple sources to support a diversity of needs (Inmon, 2005); the foundation of his subject-oriented design was an enterprise data model. Kimball and Ross (2002) introduced the notion of dimensional modeling, which addresses the gap between relational databases and data warehouses.

In classical data warehouses, data volumetry now constitutes the main problem. To tackle the performance problem, several solutions, such as materialised views and index selection or fragmentation, are proposed in the literature. Star schemas are probably the simplest and most used data warehouse models. A star schema is characterised by one or more very large fact tables that contain the primary information in the data ware-

house, and a number of much smaller dimension tables (or lookup tables), each of which contains information about the entries for a particular attribute in the fact table (Chaudhuri & Dayal, 1997; Kimball & Ross, 2002). In a warehousing process, multidimensional modeling allows the creation of appropriated analysis contexts.

The data warehousing and OLAP technologies are now well-suited to be applied in management applications, especially when data are numerical. However, in many domain applications, such as medical or geographical ones, data coming from heterogeneous sources may be represented in different formats (text, images, video, etc.) and/or diversely structured. They may also be differently expressed and periodically changed. These data are called complex data. This complexity may concern the syntactic or the semantic aspect of data and, sometimes, it also concerns data processing. In this chapter, we have chosen to address the particular problem of image data, which represent a typical example of complex data. In the literature, there are a lot of image database applications which are OLTP-oriented databases; that is, their vocation is image data management and not image data analysis. However, a few image data warehouses exist. They are all closely linked to specific applications, such as medical applications (e.g., Wong, Hoo, Knowlton, Laxer, Cao, Hawkins, et al., 2002). The proposed architectures of image data warehouses may be applied only to a given field. They cannot be generalised to other fields. No general methodological approach suitable for image data warehouses has been defined. To do so, we extend the images with the complex data. Henceforth, we will consider the complex data in a general way.

Frequent Pattern Mining

Frequent patterns resulting from mining are represented in a specific form called *association rule*. A typical example of association rule mining is market basket analysis. To analyse customer behaviour (i.e., to obtain information about customers and why they make purchases), Agrawal, Imielinski, and Swami (1993) introduced the association rule concept. Faced with the very huge amount of sales data, the authors developed an algorithm generating all significant rules between items in the database (i.e., an itemset is the set of items in transactions or rules). Such computed rules may be useful for taking decisions and are very easy to interpret. For example, placing products often purchased together at opposite ends of the store may entice customers buying such products to pick up other products along the way. Thus, the discovered association rules may allow stores to lay out products on the shelves more efficiently. An association rule example is "if a customer buys plants, then he also buys compost". Since 1993, a lot of studies concerning extensions (the method may be applied in any domain where object clustering is judicious) and improvements (more efficient algorithms) of association rule mining problems have been proposed; more details may be found in surveys (Goethals, 2005). The association rule search in a database is probably the problem which most strongly contributed to the emergence of data mining.

Today, association rule mining is one of the most popular problems when we look for interesting associations or correlations from a large data items set. More precisely, association rule mining is based on the following concepts. A transaction corresponds to a transaction identifier associated with a finite set of items called itemset. While a transaction database D is a finite multiset of transactions, an association rule is an implication of the form $X \Rightarrow Y$ where the body or antecedent X and the head or consequent Y are itemsets having no item in common. Two measures of rules interestingness are defined: rule support and rule confidence. The support of an association rule $X \Rightarrow Y$ in D is the support of $X \cup Y$ in D where the support of an itemset X in D is the number of transactions in the cover of X in D and the cover of an itemset X in D corresponds

to the transaction identifier set in D that supports X. The confidence of an association rule $X \Rightarrow Y$ in D corresponds to the conditional probability of having Y contained in a transaction, given that X is already contained in this transaction. More intuitively, the rule support represents the usefulness of mined rules while the rule confidence corresponds to their certainty. In fact, an association rule is considered interesting if and only if it is both a frequent association rule (i.e., a rule whose support exceeds a given minimal support threshold) and a confident association rule (i.e., a rule whose confidence exceeds a given minimal confidence threshold). In the same way, a frequent itemset is an itemset whose support exceeds a given minimal support threshold. Thus given a transaction set, the general frequent pattern mining problem consists in generating all association rules whose support and confidence exceed the user or expert-specified minimum threshold values (rf. Agrawal et al., 1993, for further details on the problem description).

In Han and Kamber (2001), association rules are classified into several categories according to different criteria. The authors distinguish association rules according to either the type of values they handle (such as Boolean values and quantitative values), the dimension of data implied in the rules (single/dimensional rules), the level of abstraction of the rules (single/multilevel association rules), or the various extensions to association mining (maximal frequent pattern, frequent closed itemsets). Methods for mining each one of these types of association rules is studied in Han and Kamber (2001, ch. 6).

The problem of association rule mining from large databases is generally decomposed into two steps: the frequent itemset discovering process and the frequent and confident association rule generating process from the previous discovered frequent itemsets. The frequent itemset discovering process is time-consuming as the search space has an exponential size in terms of the number of items occurring in the transaction database.

The first algorithm called *AIS* (Agrawal et al., 1993) proposed to solve the frequent set mining problem was improved and gave rise to the well-known *Apriori* algorithm published independently by Agrawal and Srikant (1994) and Mannila, Toivonen, and Verlamo (1994). The improvement is based on the set support monotonicity property that states "every subset of a frequent itemset is itself a frequent itemset". The Apriori algorithm is based on an iterative approach known as *level-wise* search, where *k-itemsets* (i.e., an itemset containing *k* items) are used to explore (*k*+1)-itemsets. A lot of studies on association rule mining techniques in large databases have been proposed. These studies cover a broad active spectrum of topics concerning fast algorithms based on the level-wise Apriori search (Agrawal & Srikant, 1994; Klemettinen, Mannila, Ronkainen, Toivonen, & Verkamo, 1994) and its variations such as table hashing (Park, Chen, & Yu, 1995), transaction reduction (Agrawal & Srikant, 1994; Han & Fu, 1995; Park et al., 1995), partitioning (Savasere, Omiecinski, & Navathe, 1995), sampling (Toivonen, 1996) with incremental updating and parallel algorithms (Cheung, Han, Ng, & Wong, 1996; Han, Karypis, & Kumar, 1997; Park, Chen, & Yu, 1995a) while passing by mining of generalised and multilevel rules (Han & Fu, 1995; Srikant & Agrawal, 1995). We can also mention mining long patterns and dense data sets (Bayardo, 1998; Bayardo, Agrawal, & Gunopulos, 1999), mining correlations and causal structures (Brin, Motwani, & Silverstein, 1997; Silverstein, Brin, Motwani, & Ullman, 1998), mining ratio rules (Korn, Labrinidis, Kotidis, & Faloutsos, 1998), query-based constraint mining of associations (Ng, Lakshmanan, Han, & Pang, 1998; Srikant, Vu, & Agrawal, 1997), mining cyclic and calendric association rules (Ozden, Ramaswamy, & Silberschatz, 1998; Ramaswamy, Mahajan, & Silberschatz, 1998), mining partial periodicities (Han, Dong, & Yin, 1999), rule mining query languages (Meo, Psaila, & Ceri, 1996), mining of quantitative and multidimensional rules (Fu-

kuda, Morimoto, Morishita, & Tokuyama, 1996; Kamber, Han, & Chiang, 1997; Lent, Swami, & Widom, 1997; Miller & Yang, 1997; Srikant & Agrawal, 1996), and mining of frequently occurring patterns related to time or other sequences (Agrawal & Srikant, 1995).

Data Clustering

The goal of clustering is to identify subsets of data called clusters (or groups) where a cluster usually corresponds to objects that are more similar to each other than they are to objects from other clusters.

There are different ways to group objects. In hard clustering, each object belongs to one and only cluster: the clusters are disjoints. In a soft approach, clusters can be overlapped: an object can belong to zero, one, or several clusters. The probabilistic approach assumes that each object belongs to clusters depending on a probability. Finally, in a fuzzy clustering approach, each object belongs to all the clusters with an assigned membership for each cluster.

Although a lot of clustering algorithms have been developed with a lot of application fields, no one can be used to solve all the problems (Kleinberg, 2002). Comprehensive surveys of clustering principles and techniques can be found in Berkhin (2002), Jain, Murty, and Flynn (1999), and Xu and Wunsch (2005). Traditionally, clustering methods are divided into hierarchical and partitioning techniques. Whereas partitioning algorithms produce a flat structure, hierarchical clustering algorithms organise data into a hierarchical structure such as a tree of clusters or a dendrogram: a cluster node contains child-clusters which are a partitioning of this cluster.

Hierarchical clustering methods, such as CURE (Guha, Rastogi, & Shim, 1998), ROCK (Guha, Rastogi, & Shim, 2000), Chameleon (Karypis, Han, & Kumar, 1999), and BIRCH (Zhang, 1997), are categorised into agglomerative and divisive approaches. Starting with the one object cluster, agglomerative methods iteratively merge clusters, depending on their similarity. Divisive methods start with one cluster containing all objects to be clarified and recursively split clusters until a criterion (number of clusters, size of clusters, etc.) is achieved. To merge or split subsets of objects, the distance between clusters (linkage metric) has to be defined. In fact, most hierarchical clustering algorithms are variant of a single link (minimum distance between objects), a complete link (minimum distance between objects), or an average link. The type of the link metric used significantly affects results: a complete-link algorithm produces tightly bound or compact clusters (Baeza-Yates, 1992) whereas a simple-link algorithm suffers from the chaining effect (Nagy, 1968).

While hierarchical algorithms build clusters iteratively, partitioning algorithms learn clusters directly. The most popular partitioning algorithms are partitioning relocation methods. Such a method tries to discover clusters by iteratively relocating data between subsets. These methods can be categorised into probabilistic clustering, for example, the EM framework (Mitchell, 1998), k-medoid methods, such as CLARA (Kaufman & Rousseew, 1990), and squared-error based methods like K-means (MacQueen, 1967). A density-based partitioning algorithm such as DBSCAN (Ester, Kriegel, Dansder, & Xu, 1996) tries to discover dense connected components which are flexible in terms of their shape.

Partitioning methods take advantage in applications involving large data sets for which the construction of a dendrogram is computationally prohibitive. In most cases, however, the difficult problem is the choice of the number of output clusters. Some methods are proposed to resolve this problem such as ISODATA (Ball & Hall, 1967). In practice, the algorithm is typically run multiple times with different starting states (initial centers of clusters, numbers of clusters), and the "best" output clustering is kept. More complex

search methods, such as evolutionary algorithms (Fogel, 1994), can also be used to explore the solution space better and faster.

Competitive neural networks are often used to cluster data. Based on data correlation, similar data are grouped by the network and represented by a neurone. Data are presented at the input and are associated with the output neuron; the weights between the input neurons and the output neurons are iteratively changed. Among this type of algorithm, the most popular algorithm is the self-organising map (SOM) (Kohonen, 1990).

IMAGE PROCESSING USING DATA WAREHOUSES, PATTERN MINING, AND CLASSIFICATION

Different types of information are related to images: those related to a low-level description (pixels, resolution, texture, and size), content information, and lastly, information linked to the context (domain, etc.). The use of this information must take into account data processing: relevant data should be extracted and structured as a pre-processing stage. Complex data warehousing is a solution allowing us to describe analysis contexts. Among all the existing analysis techniques, patterns discovery can outline associations between images, evolution of geographical areas, and so forth. Image clustering is used to summarise and structure data, and can be useful in the case of image content-based retrieval to reduce the search space.

Complex Data Warehouses: How Image Data Can Be Managed in Such Data Warehouses

In complex data warehouses, new difficulties appear because of data nature and specificity. Structuring, modeling, and analysing image data is a difficult task that requires the use of efficient techniques and powerful tools, such as data mining. complex data produce different kinds of information that are represented as metadata. These metadata are essential when warehousing complex data. Furthermore, domain-specific knowledge becomes necessary to warehouse complex data properly, for example, under the form of ontologies.

Analysing complex data raises, among others, the issue of selecting analysis axes. Data mining may help reach this goal. Furthermore, OLAP operators are not well suited for non-additives complex data measures. In this context, data mining techniques such as clustering can be used to develop appropriate OLAP operators for complex data (Ben Messaoud, Boussaïd, & Loudcher Rabaseda, 2006). Such data mining techniques allow us to perform exploratory analyses while exploiting causality relationships in complex data.

The growing interest concerning the storage and knowledge discovery in complex data has lead research communities to look for new architectures and more suitable processing tools. Indeed, organisations need to deploy data warehouses in order to integrate access and analyse their complex data. For example, a medical file usually consists of data drawn from various forms. A patient's medical history might be recorded as plain text; numerous biological exam results might be differently represented. The medical file could also include radiographies (images) or echographies (video sequences). Successive diagnosis and therapies might be recorded as text or audio documents, and so on. If one needs to explore this kind of data, then the warehousing approach should be adapted to take into account the specificity of such data.

In opposition to classical solutions, complex data warehouse architectures may be numerous and very different from one another. However, two approaches emerge. The first family of architectures is *data-driven* and based on a classical, centralised data warehouse where data are the main focus. XML document warehouses are an example of such solutions (Boussaid, Ben Messaoud, Choquet, & Anthoard, 2006a; Nassis, Rajagopalapillai, Dillon, & Rahayu, 2005; Pokorny, 2001; Rusu, Rahayu, & Taniar, 2005). They often exploit XML views, which are XML documents generated from whole XML documents and/or parts of XML documents (Baril & Bellahsene, 2000). A data cube is then a set of XML views. The second family of architectures includes solutions based on virtual warehousing, which are *process-driven* and where metadata play a major role. These solutions are based on mediator-wrapper approaches (Maiz, Boussaïd, & Bentayeb, 2006; Wiederhold, 1995) and exploit distributed data sources. The schemas of such sources provide the most important information that mediators exploit to answer user queries. Data are collected and modeled in a multidimensional way (as data cubes, to constitute an OLAP analysis context) on the fly to answer a given decision support need.

Note that complex data are generally represented by descriptors that may either be low-level information (an image size, an audio file duration, the speed of a video sequence, etc.) or related to semantics (relationships between objects in a picture, topic of an audio recording, identification of a character in a video sequence, and so on). Processing the data thus turns out to process their descriptors. Original data are stored, for example, as binary large objects (BLOBs), and can also be exploited to extract information that could enrich their own characteristics (descriptors and metadata) (Boussaid, Tanasescu, Bentayeb, & Darmont, 2006b).

In today's competitively managed environment, decision makers must be able to interpret trends, identify factors, and utilise information based on clear, timely data presented in a meaningful format. Warehousing complex data, and particularly image data, is well suited to structuring, storing, accessing, and querying these data. The capacity to organise the image data in the data warehouse structure allows us to carry out online analytical processing of the warehoused data. To increase this ability, it is necessary to enhance the classical OLAP operators with data mining techniques, such as clustering or pattern mining, and to elaborate exploratory and predictive analyses (Ben Messaoud et al., 2006).

Pattern Mining

Image mining (Simoff, Djeraba, & Zaïane, 2002; Zhang, Hsu, & Lee, 2001) is still a recent research field and is not very well developed yet because extracting relevant knowledge from image data still remains a difficult task. Mining association rules relating to images cannot be considered as simply taking each image as a transaction and computing frequent patterns that occur among different images. Image mining raises some new issues (Han & Kamber, 2001) such as rule mining which considers various resolutions, measures, and rules adjustment to the nature of images as well as a detailed attention to the spatial relationships within the images.

In Han and Kamber (2001), three association rule categories are distinguished: associations between image content features and non-image content features, associations among image contents with no spatial relationships, and associations among image contents with spatial relationships. In recent years, there has been some research dealing with rule association mining in image data.

In Zaïne, Han, and Zhu (2000), authors have proposed methods for mining content-based associations with recurrent items and with spatial relationships from large visual data repositories. A progressive resolution refinement approach has been proposed in which frequent itemsets at rough resolutions levels are mined, and progressively, finer resolutions are mined only on candidate frequent itemsets derived from mining through rough resolution levels. The proposed algorithm is an extension of the well-known Apriori algorithm taking account of the number of object occurrences in the images.

Ordonez and Omiecinski (1999) state that the image mining problem relates not only to the data mining field, but also to the fields of the databases, image understanding, and content-based image retrieval. He has proposed a first attempt to combine association rules and images: an algorithm which would discover object association rules in image databases and which would be based on image content. The algorithm relies on four majors steps: feature extraction, object identification, auxiliary image creation, and object mining. The main advantage of this approach is that it does not use any domain knowledge and does not produce meaningless rules or false rules. However, it suffers from several drawbacks, most importantly, the relative slowness of the feature extraction step. It does not work well with complex images either.

Djeraba (2002) proposes an architecture which integrates knowledge extraction from image databases with the image retrieval process. Association rules are extracted to characterise images, and they are also used to classify new images during insertion. In Tollari, Glotin, and Le Maitre (2005), a recent experiment has been carried out to show the dependencies between textual and visual indexation. This experiment was performed on different corpuses containing photographs which were manually indexed by keywords. The authors then compared text-only classification, visual-only classification, and the fusion of textual and visual classification. They have shown that the fusion significantly improves text-only classification.

In Ardizzone, Daurel, Maniscalco, and Rigotti (2001), association rules between low-level descriptors (i.e., colour descriptors) and semantic descriptors (i.e., names of painters) are extracted. The authors recommend using discovered association rules as complementary information to improve indexing, query optimisation in image databases.

Finally, in Morin, Kouomou Chopo, and Chauchat (2005) data mining techniques are used in order to improve time and quality of the content-based retrieval in an image database, namely clustering and association rules. The suggested strategy is based on both an automatic selection of the content-based retrieval features and on the association rules in order to reduce the number of descriptors. Thus the users may carry out their image research without being concerned with nature or quality of the subjacent descriptors. The results so obtained remain relatively satisfactory compared to an exhaustive sequential search. Moreover, during search processing, intermediate results are progressively merged and proposed to the user.

The brevity of this section dedicated to images and pattern mining shows how tiny the intersection of these two fields is. What pattern mining can contribute to image retrieval and image understanding thus remains an open question.

Image Classification

Two domains are concerned with image clustering. On one hand, a key step for structuring the database is image content clustering employed in order to improve "search-by-query" in large image databases. Each image is viewed as a collection of local features (a colour histogram, a textural index, etc.). The goal is to find a mapping between the archive images and the classes (clusters) so that the set of classes provides essentially the same prediction, or information, about the image archive as the entire image-set collection. The generated classes provide a concise summarisation and visualisation of the image content: this process is considered as image-set clustering. Note that the definition of a clustering scheme requires the determination of two major components in the process: the input representation space (used feature space, global vs. local information) and the distance measure defined in the selected feature space.

On the other hand, partitioning pixels from an image into groups of coherent properties by clustering is a popular method of image segmentation: pixels that are similar in low level features (e.g., color or radiometric features) and are connected in the image (4 or 8 connectivity) are grouped into one region. However, the problem lies in the difficulty to define the similarity measurements, for example, to define them in terms of intensity, colour, texture, or other parameters. Each element can be used alone, but they can also be compounded together to represent an image pixel. Thus, each pixel can be associated to become a feature vector.

This section presents three approaches to per-pixel image clustering: the K-means algorithm, the EM one, and the multistrategical approach.

The K-means Algorithm

The K-means algorithm (MacQueen, 1967) attempts to minimise the cost function, $F = \sum_{k \in [1,K]} \sum_{x_i \in C_k} d(x_i, c_k)$, where K is the number of clusters and c_k is the center of the k-th cluster.

First, the initial set of centers is randomly chosen. Then to minimise F, the K-means algorithm iterates two steps:

- **Labeling:** Each object in the data set is assigned to the nearest cluster.
- **Recentering:** A new center for all the clusters is recalculated.

The K-means algorithm is very simple and easy to implement. Its time complexity is O(NKd) where d is the dimension of the objects: such an algorithm can be used to cluster large data sets such as image data.

Figure 1 shows an example of a remotely sensed image. The area (approximately 10 km²) is the eastern part of the agglomeration of Strasbourg (France) with a resolution of 20m in a multispectral mode (three radiometric bands). Its size is 250 x 200 pixels.

Figure 2 shows an instance of a K-means running (with 5 classes and 10 iterations) on the

SPOT remote sensing image. The circle on the first image (on the left) highlights the sub-area which evolves during the 10 iterations. The area is the downtown of Strasbourg and is composed of building areas. At the beginning, some pixels are blue, a colour which corresponds to the "water" class. One can see that almost all these pixels emigrate towards the "gray" class which corresponds to the class of "building" (in agreement with expert evaluation).

Model-Based Clustering

In model-based clustering, individual clusters are described by a probability distribution. Each pixel is assumed to be produced by a probability density associated with one of the K clusters. The maximum likelihood (ML) approach then consid-

Figure 1. Spot image (Strasbourg)

ers that the best estimate for $\theta = \{\theta_k\}_{k \in [1,K]}$ (θ_k is the unknown parameter for the density associated with the k-th cluster) is the one that maximises the log-likelihood given by:

$$\ln(X,\theta) = \sum_{i \in [1,N]} \log \left(\sum_{k \in [1,K]} \pi_k \cdot p(x_i | \theta_k) \right)$$

where π_k is the prior probability for cluster C_k.

In most circumstances, the solution of the likelihood equation cannot be analytically computed. Efficient iterative Expectation-Maximisation (EM) schemes exist to perform the log-likelihood optimisation (Dempster, 1977; McLachlan, 1997). In such schemes, each object x_i carries not only its observable attributes but also a hidden cluster label vector $z_i = (z_{i,k})_{k \in [1,K]}$ with $z_{i,k} = 1$ if $x_i \in C_k$.

Thus the log-likelihood for the data set is given by:

$$E(X,\theta) = \sum_{i \in [1,N]} \sum_{k \in [1,K]} z_{i,k} \cdot \log p(x_i | \theta_k)$$

The summation terms inside *Pog* have been eliminated. One can observe that:

- If the density parameters are known, the cluster label vector can be easily set.
- If cluster label vectors are known, estimating the density parameters is easy.

Figure 2. Example of K-means evolution

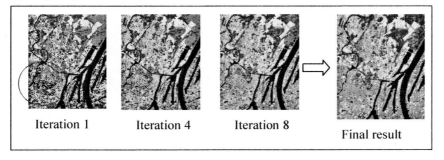

In fact, the EM algorithm iterates two steps:

- E-step (Expectation) to compute the expectation of the complete data.
- M-step (Maximisation) to maximise the log-likelihood of the complete data and then estimate θ.

In the case of multivariate normal (Gaussian) density, the most used for image segmentation, the unknown parameters (μ_k, σ_k) and π_k for each cluster are estimated by the Expectation-Maximisation.

Although the K-means and EM algorithms have been quite successful in both theory and practice, they present some problems. First, these algorithms are very sensitive to the selection of the initial partition: they may converge towards a local minimum if the initial partition is not properly chosen. Second, the number of clusters must be known. Unfortunately, there is no efficient and universal method to identify the number of clusters and the initial partitions. Certain strategies could be used to circumvent these problems. The most frequently used strategy consists in carrying out the algorithms several times with random initial partitions, with or without the same number of clusters, on either the whole data or on subsets from the original data only: the « best » result is then kept. Some techniques deal with the estimation of the number of clusters: ISODATA dynamically adjusts the number of clusters by merging and splitting clusters according to several criteria.

Another relatively recent approach can also be also used. It is based on the idea that the information concerning objects offered by different classifiers is complementary (Kittler, 1998). Thus, the combination of different classification methods may increase their efficiency and accuracy. A single classification is produced from results of methods which have different points of view: all individual classifier opinions are used to derive a consensual decision.

These combining of methods circumvent some

of the limitations of the methods used alone by taking advantage of the complementarities of the different classification methods used. For example, some classifiers only propose a partitioning of the data, whereas others give a hierarchy of classes or concepts as result. Combining the results allows us to automatically adjust the number of clusters of the partitioning methods according to the results presented by the hierarchical methods. Experiments show that this approach decreases the importance of the initial choices.

A collaborative multistrategical clustering process is proposed in (Gançarski & Wemmert, 2005). This process is composed of three main steps: First, a phase of initial classifications is performed: classifications are computed by each method with its parameters. Then, an iterative phase of convergence of the results is performed. The three phases are repeated as long as the results improve in terms of their quality and as long as they converge to become more and more similar:

1. A step of evaluation of the similarity between the results with mapping of the classes.
2. A step of refinement of the results: (1) Conflict detection by evaluating the dissimilarities between results; (2) Local resolution of such conflicts; and (3) Management of these local modifications in the global result.
3. A step of combination of the refined results.

For example, we present a test with six expected classes. The unsupervised classification methods used are:

- The K-means algorithm with four initial random nodes.
- The K-means algorithm with eight initial random nodes.
- The EM algorithm with 15 classes.
- The conceptual classifier Cobweb with an acuity of 18.

Figure 3. Initial clusterings

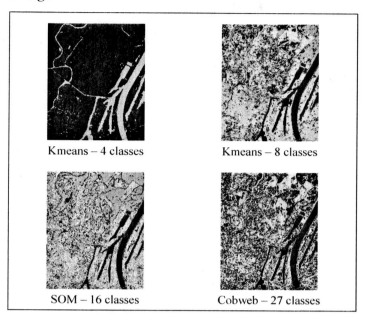

Kmeans – 4 classes   Kmeans – 8 classes

SOM – 16 classes   Cobweb – 27 classes

Figure 4. Final clusterings

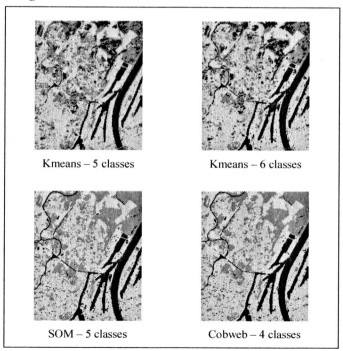

Kmeans – 5 classes   Kmeans – 6 classes

SOM – 5 classes   Cobweb – 4 classes

We have obtained the results[1] (Figure 3). These results have been refined according to multistrategical algorithm. We have obtained the following results (Figure 4).

We applied the multiview voting algorithm described in (Wemmert & Gançarski, 2002) on these results. The unifying result (Figure 5a) is composed of five different classes. We present also in Figure 5b the voting result for all the objects:

- **In white:** All the methods agreed on the classification.
- **In gray:** One method disagreed with the other ones.
- **In black:** The nonconsensual objects (two or more results classified these objects differently).

IMAGE MINING ISSUES

In this section, we present applications using the concepts described above. The first section tries to give some perspectives for image pattern mining. The second section deals with the extraction of information from images and briefly describes its application for the semantic Web. The last section describes an application in the field of remote sensing image databases.

Image Pattern Mining

Image pattern mining can be used for images represented by low-level features such as earth exploration applications or images built from sonar or radar signals. These applications have a common point: the notion of evolution is very important. For example, in the case of images extracted from a sonar signal, the characterisation of seabed sediments and its evolution should be performed using pattern mining techniques. Consider, for example, that the records are grouped according to their localisation (i.e., the geographical areas in which the sonar has been used). Suppose that for one localisation, we have the sediment evolution. Then, it will be easy, using pattern mining techniques, to find common evolutions for a set of localisations.

In the case of earth observation, a potential application is to study the evolution of a particular object or geographic area, such as a dense urban area for example. Pattern mining for content-based image retrieval seems to be less relevant, but should be useful to reduce the search space. Association rules can be defined to determine an image cluster for a particular description. For example, you can state that if the dominant colours are yellow and brown, the images related to this description should be contained in cluster 2.

Figure 5. Unification

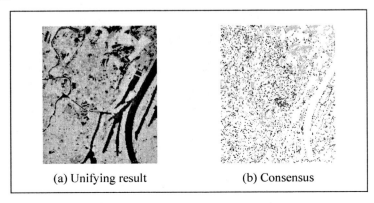

| (a) Unifying result | (b) Consensus |

Few experiments have been realised to use such a technique to reduce the search space. We think that research work could be done in the case of images represented by a set of pixel in order to describe data evolution.

Clustering and Characterisation Rules with the Service of Image Retrieval by Similarity

The content-based image retrieval in large databases is based on two modules: *the logical indexation* and *the retrieval*. While the first one extracts the metadata (textual descriptors: keywords, annotations, and so forth; visual features like colour, shape, texture; spatial localisation, spatial constraints, etc.) associated to images and stores the extracted metadata in the database; the second one assists final users to efficiently retrieve images based on their visual and/or textual descriptions. The retrieval process, by means of a suited distance for each feature, computes the similarity between the user's query and the image database. The best similar images in terms of their similarity value are then displayed by decreasing similarity. In this context, the scope of queries addressed to multimedia databases is very large and may include both objective and subjective content. Three levels of abstraction are distinguished (Eakins, 2002): (1) syntactic level: visual features, spatial localisation, and spatial constraints are used to retrieve images. This level is purely algorithmic. For instance, a query may be "Give me all the images containing red circles"; (2) semantic level including only objective content. In this level, objects appearing in images have to be identified. A query example may be "Give me all the images in which my children appear"; (3) semantic level with subjective content. This level involves complex reasoning about objects or scenes using human perception. Such a query may be "Give me all the images representing the notion of liberty" or "Give me all the images in which my friends are happy".

This level is also related to scene recognition as, for example, a child's birthday: this scene can be characterised by balloons, young faces, candles, cakes, and so forth.

However, content-based image retrieval has reached some limitations, in particular a lack of semantics integration. Textual and visual feature combinations are sometimes not sufficient, particularly when semantic querying is predominant, that is, when the image and its context are necessary (as, for instance, the retrieval of audiovisual sequences about unemployment, the retrieval of images in which there is a strong feeling of sadness). This limit is known as the semantic gap between the visual appearance of an image and the idea the user has in mind of what images, including semantics, the user wants to retrieve. Thus, the content-based retrieval suffers from a lack of expressive power because it does not integrate enough semantics. Semantics is today a crucial point which it is impossible to circumvent as soon as one wishes to integrate, unify, or bring closer the metadata resulting from different sources. A lot of research is going in this direction. For example, we can mention the fusion of ontologies to search resources regardless of their nature (Hunter, 2001). We can also mention the definition of Web page semantics to improve the Web information retrieval since the semantics of a Web page is expressed through both its contexts (static context: author's contribution and dynamic context: user's contribution) and through its content (Grosky, Sreenath, & Fotouhi, 2002). Worth mentioning is also the proposed architecture in Troncy (2003) to reason on descriptions of video documents thanks to an audiovisual ontology.

In the context of content-based retrieval, the problem of lack of semantics prevents final users from making good explorations and exploitations of the image database. In Bouet and Aufaure (2006), image mining is proposed to allow for a better image database exploration by exploiting the visual and textual image characterisation complementarily. The proposed approach is situated in an exploratory context (descriptive data mining). The desired objective may not be achieved without a strong synergy between image mining and visual ontology. On the hand, image mining concerns making associations between images from a large database. To produce a summarised view of an annotated image database and to reduce the research space, clustering and characterisation rules are combined. These data mining techniques are performed separately on visual descriptors and textual information (annotations, keywords, Web pages). On the other hand, a visual ontology is derived from the textual part and enriched with representative images associated to each concept of the ontology. Ontology-based navigation can also be seen as a user-friendly and powerful tool to retrieve relevant information. These two approaches should make the exploitation and the exploration of a large image database easier.

The process called "multimedia mining" is detailed more precisely in the Figure 6. Multimedia mining consists of several methods such as clustering and extraction of characteristic rules from clusters. These clusters and rules extracted from visual and textual descriptors may be seen as metadata associated to the considered image database. While clustering is performed to reduce the research space, the characterisation rules are used to describe each cluster and to classify automatically a new image in the appropriate clusters. Because of their intrinsic nature difference (numeric vs. symbolic), textual descriptions (keywords, annotations, etc.), and visual descriptions (colour, shape, texture, spatial constraints) are dealt with separately, using well-suited techniques. Starting from feature sets (such as colour set, keyword set, texture set, colour and shape set, etc.), the system automatically clusters together similar images using a well-suited method. Then, in order to qualify the previous clusters, a more powerful representation than the cluster centroid may be chosen. These characterisation rules may be obtained either from all the points of a cluster (in order to have the most frequent patterns) or

from a data aggregation (for example, a median histogram in the case of colour clusters, which is representative of the cluster content). In the image context, these rules are in the form of *antecedent* $\Rightarrow$ *consequent* with certain accuracy, where antecedent and consequent correspond respectively to a visual feature value and a cluster. The accuracy is fundamental to estimate the quality of the induced rules. Statistical measures are used to estimate the rule accuracy. As far as the textual description processing is concerned, it requires a preprocessing phase in order to reduce the number of keywords and to keep only relevant keywords. This task is difficult and time-consuming, and needs an expert to validate the results obtained. Textual descriptions need to find a relevant similarity measure. Clustering can be performed by conceptual clustering such as the Cobweb, or by other techniques such as the K-means after the transformation of the initial keywords into numerical vectors. The extracted concepts are then hierarchically organised, using *a priori* knowledge, hierarchical classification techniques, or the expert's knowledge of the application domain.

Once the search space reduction and the cluster characterisation by means of rules has been performed, descriptive metadata are stored in the database. These metadata represent the characteristics discovered and shared by images appearing in the same cluster, and they play an important role because they allow the user to navigate from the textual world towards the visual world, and conversely. The architecture presented in Figure 6 is well-suited to specific databases like fingerprint databases, face databases, and so forth. Indeed, image mining results depend on both the chosen clustering method and the estimated similarity quality. Without a real synergy between application fields, considered visual features, their modeling and the estimation of their similarity degree, the obtained descriptive metadata are not relevant to allow for a more interesting image database exploration. This architecture may also be adapted to general databases, and more particularly to the Web. As Web databases contain images of any domain, visual features are not very representative of particular concepts. This is the reason only the concept extraction phase is made. Visual clusters are deduced from textual clusters since they contain semantics by nature. The visual clusters which we obtain are then characterised by means of rules. This proposed architecture adaptation may be a new way to navigate Web image databases. Web search engines are able to index only Web images having a particular tag related to the image legend. For example, if you search images of "Champs Elysées" using Google Image, the result contains only images whose legend corresponds to the specified keyword. Results are then ranked and presented to the user according to their relevance. Some metadata concerning these images are also added, for example, the format (gif, pdf, etc.), the colour, and so forth. But, if

Figure 6. The multimedia mining process

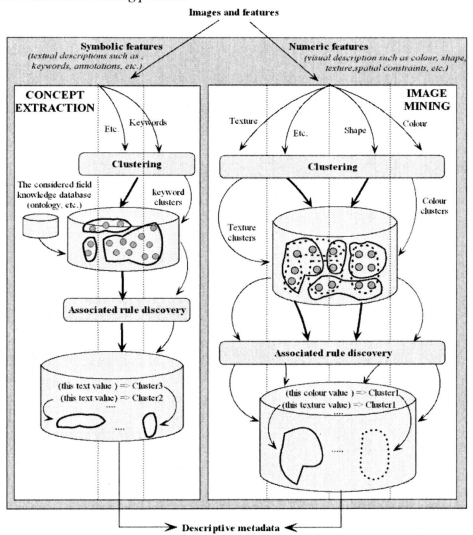

the user wants to retrieve images of the "Champs Elysées" by night and only in black and white, no results are given by the search engine.

Thus, in order to improve the Web images search, we should take into account both textual information in the Web pages and visual information. Textual information can be the legend represented by a special tag, a text under the image, and a free text in the Web page. In this last case, we can extract a word from paragraphs appearing before and after the image, and search frequent words to try to label the images. Some research has been done in this field. Integrating a visual and textual descriptor to improve the Web image search is still an unsolved problem.

Multistrategical Mining of Remote Sensing Images Databases

In the last two decades, the Earth observation offer in optical and radar fields has been multiplied. With the new types of remote sensing images that have appeared since 1999 and the multiplication of the hyperspectral sensors that have several hundreds of bands, the users are faced with a huge stream of images. Since 1999, new types of images (HSR sensors like Quickbird, Orbviewor, hyperspectral sensors like AVIRIS, DAIS, CASI) have been providing a huge amount of data the user has to cope with in terms of spatial, spectral, and temporal resolution, depending on the objectives. In a context of city planning, it is necessary to support the identification, the localisation, and the formalisation of the urban elements (impervious surfaces, vegetation, water).

Very often, the identification step requires some complementary aspects of a set of images and also ancillary data: seasonal to discriminate mineral surfaces (these may or may not be agricultural zones), spectral to supplement the range of the effective spectral answers, and finally, spatial to take into account (1) the relationships between the studied area and (2) the adequacy of the resolution of the pixel in relation to the objects of interest (for example, irrigated natural zones).

However, the lack of methods facilitating the selection of useful data, the improvement of extraction of knowledge and the interpretation assistance adapted to the needs is still compelling. Moreover, these methods do not allow for simultaneous and complementary approaches.

Currently, the tendency is the development of object oriented methods where each object represents a set of homogeneous pixels and is built around some elementary characteristics (spectral, geometrical) and the spatial relationships between objects (contextual texture and topological relations). Monoformalism does not allow for an unequivocal way to identify heterogeneous objects in an urban area. The formalism must be adapted to each scale of analysis. The Fodomust project[2] proposes a multiformalist approach, taking into account the level of creation of the object and its use. This solution provides a complete data mining process allowing for information extraction without data fusion (if not needed).

Due to the heterogeneity and the complexity of remote sensing images, the current methods of extraction and assistance to interpretation are not effective enough to take into account the complementarity of the data. In this project, it is argued that the problem lies in the need to use multiformalisation on several levels of abstraction according to images resolutions. Thus, the main aim of our project is to study and define methods and tools able to simultaneously use different knowledge databases to localise, identify, and characterise objects as being urban elements. These databases are associated with different sources (radiometric sensors, aerial and areal photographs, etc.), data representing the same object information but at different times or in various formats, scales, and file types (free texts, Web documents, taxonomy, etc.)

This is the reason why a complete process of mining complex data sets, using expert knowledge for selecting, extracting, and interpreting remote sensing images, is proposed (Figure 7):

- **Data structuring and organising:** The authors propose an architecture to structure and organise the set of data and metadata that are collected from the various physical data sources. They then design query mechanisms for image databases that exploit both low-level descriptors (date, location, etc.) and high-level semantic descriptors depicting the actual content of the images. This can allow us, on one hand, to select and cluster data sources (by fusion, for instance) and, on the other hand, to eliminate in these sources the noise, redundancies, and nonrelevant information that are massively present in remote sensing images. When exploiting several sources of knowledge and images, data mining may also be performed directly on the raw data.

- **Object construction step:** Image processing techniques (such as image segmentation which change the observed scale from pixels to regions) may greatly help to improve the quality of identification and classification of objects contained in the considered images. Numerous segmentation techniques exist, and we propose to focus on the mathematical morphology principles. Indeed, mathematical morphology is not so often used in remote sensing, whereas it clearly presents several advantages in this application field, in particular, the possibility to characterise the different objects considering some of their properties such as shape, texture, size, topology, spatial relations, and so forth. The objectives are to elaborate multi-images morphological tools, to integrate knowledge into morphological analysis processes and to validate the methods over a large set of images.

- **Multistrategical classification and interpretation:** The authors extend their multistrategy classification methods in order to be able to deal with data from different sources, and to take into account the multi-

formalism paradigm to which the different strategies can contribute some different but complementary skills. Considering a unified representation, it will be possible to perform a multistage learning corresponding to different abstraction levels. Moreover, this extension will result in classification of heterogeneous objects and semisupervised feature selection based on a coevolution of extractors. The results will make the understanding and the use of remote sensing information for general end users easier. User knowledge has to be integrated for operational guidance. It is worthwhile to use given expert knowledge to simplify extraction and classification procedures.

These three distinct phases respectively make it possible to make extractions from the geographical objects initiated from several images, to characterise them by a whole set of descriptors, to treat them using techniques of classification according to multiple strategies, and to identify them while being based on ontology. The process functions in an iterative way, until a satisfactory identification of the objects has been reached. If such objects are neither in ontology, nor in the database, they will be enriched.

The proposed process is under development. The first stage is the most advanced in its development. Architecture has been developed to store the mass of data image as well as the geographical objects which will be built progressively. It is based on PostgreSQL and the associated API PostGIS to manage spatial data. A conceptual diagram of data, which reflects the structure of geographical objects, as well as the bonds which connect them, was defined as a preliminary. This made it possible to implement the database of geographical objects. These geographical objects thus stored will be useful both as a reference and for the process of identification.

In addition, the ontology of the geographical domain was defined to represent knowledge useful for the identification of the objects. This knowledge was acquired in two different ways: (1) by methods of elicitation, in collaboration with geography photo interpreters, to extract and formalise the discriminating attributes and (2) by supervised machine learning (Sheeren, Quirin, Puissant, & Gançarski, 2006). The ontology was developed in OWL under Protégé 2000.

The mechanism making it possible to associate the objects stored in the base with the concepts of ontology is currently being studied. The principle is to extract an object from an image (by using a classifier) and to perform a matching between this object and the concepts of the ontology. According to the degree of similarity of the attributes with the properties of the concepts of ontology, the object will be labeled by the best-matching concept.

CONCLUSION

Detection and recognition of semantic concepts from image databases is a major research challenge. A promising way could be the unsupervised mining of patterns. Patterns are recurrent, predictable occurrences of one or more entities that satisfy statistical, associative, or relational conditions. Together with the statistical aspect, we have presented some research related to the clustering methods applied to knowledge discovery from images in order to summarise image databases. But, we did not find many uses of the pattern mining method when employed to discover associative rules among images or between pixels from one or several images. This raises two questions. The first is trying to discover such relations from im-

Figure 7. Interpretation of remotely sensed image

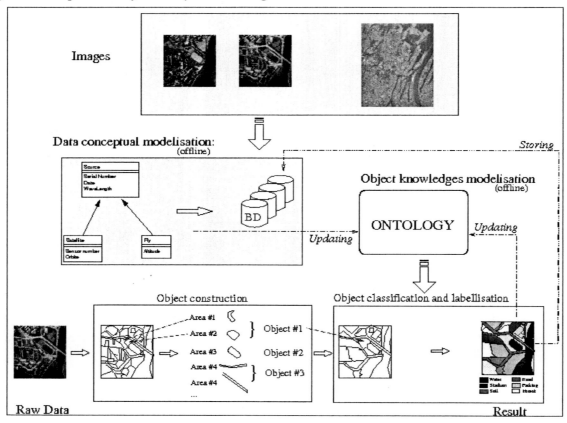

ages relevant. Second, if the answer is yes, how can we make this research effective? Nevertheless, we believe that such an approach can be very useful to highlight relations at the feature level (high level) as well. Patterns at the feature level may represent the occurrence of primitive concepts such as pixel clusters or relations between pixels. At the higher level, patterns may outline relations between semantic concepts and extracted clusters, or relations between semantic concepts themselves.

Even if the clustering approach seems more mature than the approach related to the association rules discovery, we are still faced with many challenges in both domains. The most important in our opinion is to find adequate representations of data: experiments which show that using an image or a pixel directly as a transaction or as an item in a transaction is not efficient.

More specific questions have to be answered, for example: How do we detect patterns starting from images with heterogeneous representation? How do we deal with patterns that may have relatively sparse occurring frequencies? How do we take into account temporality?

And, last but not the least, how do we evaluate the quality of mining results given its unsupervised nature?

REFERENCES

Agrawal, R., Imielinski, T., & Swami, A. (1993). Mining association rules between sets of items in large databases. In *Proceedings of the ACM SIGMOD International Conference on Management of Data (SIGMOD 1993)*, Washington, DC (pp. 207-216). ACM Press.

Agrawal, R., & Srikant, R. (1994). Fast algorithms for mining association rules. In J. Bocca, M. Jarke, & C. Zoniolo (Eds.), *Proceedings of the 20th International Conference on Very Large Data Bases (VLDB 1994)*, Santiago, Chile (pp. 487-499). Morgan Kaufmann.

Agrawal, R., & Srikant, R. (1995). Mining sequential patterns. In *Proceedings of the 11th International Conference on Data Engineering (ICDE 1995)*, Taipei, Taiwan (pp. 3-14). IEEE Computer Society Press.

Ardizzone, E., Daurel, T., Maniscalco, U., & Rigotti, C. (2001). Extraction of association rules between low-level descriptors and semantic descriptors in an image database. In *Proceedings of the 1st International Workshop on Multimedia Data and Document Engineering (MDDE 2001)*, Lyon, France.

Baeza-Yates, R. A. (1992). Introduction to data structure and algorithms related to information retrieval. In *Information retrieval: Data structure and algorithms* (pp. 13-27). Prentice Hall.

Ball, G., & Hall, D. (1967). A clustering technique for summarizing multi-variate data. *Behavioral Sciences, 12*, 153-155.

Baril, X., & Bellahsene, Z. (2000). A view model for XML documents. In D. Patel, I. Choudhury, S. Patel, & S. de Cesare (Eds.), *International Conference on Object Oriented Information Systems*, London, United Kingdom (pp. 429–441).

Bayardo, R. J. (1998). Efficiently mining long patterns from databases. In *Proceedings of the ACM SIGMOD International Conference on Management of Data (SIGMOD 1998)*, Seattle, Washington (pp. 85-93). ACM Press.

Bayardo, R. J., Agrawal, R., & Gunopulos, D. (1999). Constraint-based rule mining in large, dense databases. In *Proceedings of the 15th International Conference on Data Engineering (ICDE 1999)*. Sydney, Australia (pp. 188-197). IEEE Computer Society.

Ben Messaoud, R., Boussaïd, O., & Loudcher Rabaseda, S. (2006). A data mining-based OLAP aggregation of complex data: Application on

XML documents. *International Journal of Data Warehousing and Mining, 2*(4), 1-26.

Berkhin, P. (2002). *Survey of clustering data mining techniques.* San Jose, CA: Accrue Software.

Berners-Lee, T., Hendler, J., & Lassila, O. (2001). The Semantic Web. *Scientific American, 284*(5), 34-43.

Bouet, M., & Aufaure, M. A. (2006). New image retrieval principle: Image mining and visual ontology. In V. A. Petrushin & L. Khan (Eds.), *Multimedia data mining and knowledge discovery.* Springer.

Boussaid, O., Ben Messaoud, R., Choquet, R., & Anthoard, S. (2006a). XWarehousing: An XML-based approach for warehousing complex data. In *Proceedings of the 10th East-European Conference on Advances in Databases and Information Systems (ADBIS06)*, Thessaloniki, Greece (pp. 39-54). Lecture Notes in Computer Science 4152.

Boussaid, O., Tanasescu, A., Bentayeb, F., & Darmont, J. (2006b). Integration and dimensional modelling approaches for complex data warehousing. *Journal of Global Optimization, 37*(4), 571-591.

Brin, S., Motwani, R., & Silverstein, C. (1997). Beyond market baskets: Generalizing association rules to correlations. In *Proceedings of the ACM SIGMOD International Conference on Management of Data (SIGMOD 1997)*, Tucson, Arizona (pp. 265-276). ACM Press.

Chaudhuri, S., & Dayal, U. (1997). An overview of data warehousing and OLAP technology. *SIGMOD Record, 26*(1), 65-74.

Cheung, D. W. L., Han, J., Ng, V., & Wong, C. Y. (1996). Maintenance of discovered association rules in large databases: An incremental updating technique. In *Proceedings of the 12th International Conference on Data Engineering (ICDE 1996)*, New Orleans, Louisiana (pp. 106-114). IEEE Computer Society Press.

Djeraba, C. (2003). Association and content-based retrieval. *IEEE Transactions on Knowledge and Data Engineering, 15*(1).

Eakins, J. P. (2002). Towards intelligent image retrieval. *Pattern Recognition, 35*, 3-14.

Ester, M., Kriegel, H. P., Dansder, J., & Xu, X. (1996). A density-based algorithm for discovering clusters in large spatial databases with noise. In *Proceedings of the Second ACM SIGKDD*, Portland, Oregon (pp. 226-231).

Fogel, D. (1994). An introduction to simulated evolutionary optimization. *IEEE Transactions on Neural Networks, 5*(1), 3-14.

Fukuda, T., Morimoto, Y., Morishita, S., & Tokuyama, T. (1996). Data mining using two-dimensional optimized association rules: Scheme, algorithms, and visualization. In *Proceedings of the ACM SIGMOD International Conference on Management of Data (SIGMOD 1996)*, Montreal, Quebec, Canada (pp. 13-23). ACM Press.

Gançarski, P., & Wemmert, C. (2005). Collaborative multi-strategy classification: Application to per-pixel analysis of images. In *Proceedings of the Sixth International Workshop on Multimedia Data Mining (ACM SIGKDD)*, Chicago, Illinois.

Goethals, B. (2005). Frequent set mining. In *The data mining and knowledge discovery handbook* (pp. 377-397). Springer.

Gomez-Perez, A., & Rojas, M. D. (1999). Ontological reengineering and reuse. In D. Fensel & R. Studer (Eds.), *Proceedings of the 11th European Workshop on Knowledge Acquisition, Modeling and Management (EKAW'99)*, Germany (pp. 139-156). Lecture Notes in Artificial Intelligence 1621. Springer-Verlag.

Grosky, W. I., Sreenath, D. V., & Fotouhi, F. (2002). Emergent semantics and the multimedia semantic Web. *SIGMOD Record, 4*.

Gruber, T. (1993). Toward principles for the design of ontologies used for knowledge sharing [Special issue]. *International Journal of Human-Computer Studies*.

Guha, S., Rastogi, R., & Shim, K. (1998). CURE: An efficient clustering algorithm for large databases. In *Proceedings of the ACM SIGMOD International Conference on Management of Data* (pp. 73-84).

Guha, S., Rastogi, R., & Shim, K. (2000). ROCK: A robust clustering algorithm for categorical attributes. *Information Systems, 25*(5), 345-366.

Han, J., Dong, G., & Yin, Y. (1999). Efficient mining of partial periodic patterns in time series database. In *Proceedings of the 15th International Conference on Data Engineering (ICDE 1999)*, Sydney, Australia (pp. 106-115). IEEE Computer Society.

Han, J., & Fu, J. (1995). Discovery of multiple-level association rules from large databases. In *Proceedings of the 21st International Conference on Very Large Data Bases (VLDB 1995)*, Zurich, Switzerland (pp. 420-431). Morgan Kaufmann.

Han, J., & Kamber, M. (2001). *Data mining: Concepts and techniques* (pp. 225-278, 395-449). San Francisco, CA: Morgan Kaufmann.

Han, E. H., Karypis, G., & Kumar, V. (1997). Scalable parallel data mining for association rules. In *Proceedings of the ACM SIGMOD International Conference on Management of Data (SIGMOD 1997)*, Tucson, Arizona (pp. 277-288). ACM Press.

Hunter, J. (2001). Adding multimedia to the semantic Web: Building an MPEG-7 ontology. In *Proceedings of the First International Semantic Web Working Symposium (SWWS'01)*, Stanford, California (pp. 261-283).

Inmon, W. (2005). *Building the data warehouse* (4th ed.). John Wiley & Sons.

Jain, A. K., Murty, M. N., & Flynn, P. J. (1999). Data clustering: A review. *ACM Computing Surveys, 31*(3).

Kamber, M., Han, J., & Chiang, J. (1997). Meta-rule-guided mining of multi-dimensional association rules using data cubes. In *Proceedings of the 3rd International Conference on Knowledge Discovery and Data Mining (KDD 1997)*, Newport Beach, California (pp. 207-210). The AAAI Press.

Karypis, G., Han, E., & Kumar, V. (1999). Chameleon: Hierarchical clustering using dynamic model. *IEEE Computer, 32*(8), 68-75.

Kaufman, L., & Rousseew, P. (1990). *Finding groups in data: An introduction to cluster analysis*. New York: John Wiley & Sons.

Kimball, R., & Ross, M. (2002). *The data warehouse toolkit*. John Wiley & Sons.

Kleinberg, J. (2002). An impossibility theorem for clustering. *Proceedings of the Conference on Advances in Neural Information Processing Systems, 15*, 463-470.

Klemettinen, M., Mannila, H., Ronkainen, P., Toivonen, H., & Verkamo, A. I. (1994). Finding interesting rules from large sets of discovered association rules. In *Proceedings of the 3rd ACM International Conference on Information and Knowledge Management (CIKM 1994)*, Gaithersburg, Maryland (pp. 401-407). ACM Press.

Kohonen, T. (1990). Self-organizing map. *Proceeding of IEEE, 78*(9), 1464-1480.

Korn, F., Labrinidis, A., Kotidis, Y., & Faloutsos, C. (1998). Ratio rules: A new paradigm for fast, quantifiable data mining. In *Proceedings of the 24th International Conference on Very Large Data Bases (VLDB 1998)*, New York, New York (pp. 582-593). Morgan Kaufmann.

Lent, B., Swami, A. N., & Widom, J. (1997). Clustering association rules. In *Proceedings of the 13th International Conference on Data Engineering (ICDE 1997)*, Birmingham, United Kingdom (pp. 220-231). IEEE Computer Society.

MacQueen, J. (1967). Some methods for classification and analysis of multivariate observations. *In* L. M. Le Cam & J. Neyman (Eds.), *Proceedings of the Fifth Berkeley Symposium on Mathematical Statistics and Probability* (vol. 1, pp. 281-297). Berkeley: University of California Press.

Maiz, N., Boussaïd, O., & Bentayeb, F. (2006). Ontology-based mediation system. In *Proceedings of the 13th ISPE International Conference on Concurrent Engineering: Research and Applications (CE 2006)*, Antibes, France (pp. 181-189).

Mannila, H., Toivonen, H., & Verkamo, A. I. (1994). Efficient algorithms for discovering association rules. In U. Fayyad & R. Uthurusamy (Eds.), *Proceedings of the AAAI Workshop Knowledge Discovery in Databases (KDD'94)* (pp. 181-192). AAAI Press.

Meo, R., Psaila, G., & Ceri, S. (1996). A new SQL-like operator for mining association rules. In *Proceedings of the 22nd International Conference on Very Large Data Bases (VLDB 1996)*, Bombay, India (pp. 122-133). Morgan Kaufmann.

Miller, R. J., & Yang, Y. (1997). Association rules over interval data. In *Proceedings of the ACM SIGMOD International Conference on Management of Data (SIGMOD 1997)*, Tucson, Arizona (pp. 452-461). ACM Press.

Mitchell, T. (1998). *Machine learning.* New York: McGraw-Hill.

Morin, A., Kouomou Chopo, A., & Chauchat, J. H. (2005). Dimension reduction and clustering for query-by-example in huge image databases. In *Proceedings of the 3rd World Conference on Computational Statistics and Data Analysis*, Chypre.

Nagy, G. (1968). State of the art in pattern recognition. *Proceedings of the IEEE, 56*, 836-862.

Nassis, V., Rajagopalapillai, R., Dillon, T. S., & Rahayu, W. (2005). Conceptual and systematic design approach for XML document warehouses. *International Journal of Data Warehousing and Mining, 1*(3), 63-87. Idea Group Inc.

Ng, R. T., Lakshmanan, L. V. S., Han, J., & Pang, A. (1998). Exploratory mining and pruning optimizations of constrained associations rules. In *Proceedings of the ACM SIGMOD International Conference on Management of Data (SIGMOD 1998)*, Seattle, Washington (pp. 13-24). ACM Press.

Noy, N. F., Fergerson, R. W., & Musen, M. A. (2000). The knowledge model of Protege-2000: Combining interoperability and flexibility. In *Proceedings of the Second International Conference on Knowledge Engineering and Knowledge Management.*

Ordonez, C., & Omiecinski, E. (1999). Discovering association rules based on image content. In *Proceedings of the IEEE Advances in Digital Libraries Conference (ADL'99)*, Baltimore, Maryland (pp. 38-49).

Ozden, B., Ramaswamy, S., & Silberschatz, A. (1998). Cyclic association rules. In *Proceedings of the 14th International Conference on Data Engineering (ICDE 1998)*, Orlando, Florida (pp. 412-421). IEEE Computer Society.

Park, J. S., Chen, M. S., & Yu, P. S. (1995). An effective hash-based algorithm for mining association rules. In Proceedings of the 1995 ACM SIGMOD International Conference on Management of Data Volume, San Jose, California. *SIGMOD Record, 24*(2), 175-186. ACM Press.

Park, J. S., Chen, M. S., & Yu, P. S. (1995a). Efficient parallel data mining for association rules. In *Proceedings of the 4th International Conference on Information and Knowledge Management*

(CIKM 1995), Baltimore, Maryland (pp. 31-36). ACM Press.

Pokorny, J. (2001). Modelling stars using XML. In *DOLAP'01: Proceedings of the 4ᵗʰ ACM International Workshop on Data Warehousing and OLAP* (pp. 24-31).

Ramaswamy, S., Mahajan, S., & Silberschatz, A. (1998). On the discovery of interesting patterns in association rules. In *Proceedings of the 24ᵗʰ International Conference on Very Large Data Bases (VLDB 1998)*, New York City, New York (pp. 368-379). Morgan Kaufmann.

Rusu, L. I., Rahayu, J. W., & Taniar, D. (2005). A methodology for building XML data warehouses. *International Journal of Data Warehousing and Mining, 1*(2), 23-48. Idea Group Inc.

Savasere, A., Omiecinski, E., & Navathe, S. B. (1995). An efficient algorithm for mining association rules in large databases. In *Proceedings of the 21ˢᵗ International Conference on Very Large Data Bases (VLDB 1995)*, Zurich, Switzerland (pp. 432-444). Morgan Kaufmann.

Sheeren, D., Quirin, A., Puissant, A., & Gançarski, P. (2006). Discovering rules with genetic algorithms to classify urban remotely sensed data. In *Proceedings of the IEEE International Geoscience and Remote Sensing Symposium (IGARSS'06)*.

Silverstein, C., Brin, S., Motwani, R., & Ullman, J. (1998). Scalable techniques for mining causal structures. *Data Mining Knowledge Discovery, 4*(2-3), 163-192.

Simoff, S. J., Djeraba, C., & Zaïane, O. R. (2002). MDM/KDD2002: Multimedia data mining between promises and problems. *ACM SIGKDD Explorations, 4*(2).

Srikant, R., & Agrawal, R. (1995). Mining generalized association rules. In *Proceedings of the 21ˢᵗ International Conference on Very Large Data*

Bases (VLDB 1995), Zurich, Switzerland (pp. 407-419). Morgan Kaufmann.

Srikant, R., & Agrawal, R. (1996). Mining quantitative association rules in large relational tables. In *Proceedings of the ACM SIGMOD International Conference on Management of Data (SIGMOD 1996)*, Montreal, Quebec, Canada (pp. 1-12). ACM Press.

Srikant, R., Vu, Q., & Agrawal, R. (1997). Mining association rules with item constraints. In *Proceedings of the 3ʳᵈ International Conference on Knowledge Discovery and Data Mining (KDD 1997)*, Newport Beach, California (pp. 67-73). The AAAI Press.

Toivonen, H. (1996). Sampling large databases for association rules. In *Proceedings of the 22ⁿᵈ International Conference on Very Large Data Bases (VLDB 1996)*, Bombay, India (pp. 134-145). Morgan Kaufmann.

Tollari, S., Glotin, H., & Le Maitre, J. (2005). Enhancement of textual images classification using segmented visual contents for image search engine. *Multimedia Tools and Applications, 25*, 405-417).

Troncy, R. (2003). Integration structure and semantics into audio-visual documents. In D. Fensel et al. (Eds.), *Proceedings of ISWC2003* (pp. 566-581). Lecture Notes in Computer Science 2870.

Wemmert, C. & Gançarski, P. (2002). A multiview voting method to combine unsupervised clarifications. In *Proceedings of the IASTED Artificial Intelligence and Applications Conference*.

Wiederhold, G. (1995). Mediation in information systems. *ACM Computing Surveys, 27*(2), 265-267.

Wong, S. T. C., Hoo, K. S., Knowlton, R. C., Laxer, K. D., Cao, X., Hawkins, R. A., Dillon, W. P., & Arenson, R. L. (2002). Design and applications of a multimodality image data warehouse framework. *The Journal of the American Medical Informatics Association, 9*(3), 239-254.

Xu, R., & Wunsch, D. (2005). Survey of clustering algorithms. *IEEE Transactions on Neural Networks, 16*(13), 645-678.

Zaïne, O. R., Han J., & Zhu, H. (2000). Mining recurrent items in multimedia with progressive resolution refinement. In *Proceedings of the International Conference on Data Engineering (ICDE'00)*, San Diego, California.

Zhang, J., Hsu, W., & Lee, M. L. (2001). Image mining: Issues, frameworks and techniques. In *Proceedings of the Second International Workshop on Multimedia Data Mining (MDM/KDD)*, San Francisco, California.

Zhang, T., Ramakrishman, R., & Livny, M. (1996). BIRCH: An efficient data clustering algorithm for very large databases. In *Proceedings of the International Conference on Management of Data* (pp. 103-114).

ENDNOTES

[1]   In all the results, the colours have been randomly chosen by the authors.

[2]   http://lsiit.u-strasbg.fr/afd/fodomust.

Chapter X
Semantic Integration and Knowledge Discovery for Environmental Research

Zhiyuan Chen
University of Maryland, Baltimore County (UMBC), USA

Aryya Gangopadhyay
University of Maryland, Baltimore County (UMBC), USA

George Karabatis
University of Maryland, Baltimore County (UMBC), USA

Michael McGuire
University of Maryland, Baltimore County (UMBC), USA

Claire Welty
University of Maryland, Baltimore County (UMBC), USA

ABSTRACT

Environmental research and knowledge discovery both require extensive use of data stored in various sources and created in different ways for diverse purposes. We describe a new metadata approach to elicit semantic information from environmental data and implement semantics-based techniques to assist users in integrating, navigating, and mining multiple environmental data sources. Our system contains specifications of various environmental data sources and the relationships that are formed among them. User requests are augmented with semantically related data sources and automatically presented as a visual semantic network. In addition, we present a methodology for data navigation and pattern discovery using multi-resolution browsing and data mining. The data semantics are captured and utilized in terms of their patterns and trends at multiple levels of resolution. We present the efficacy of our methodology through experimental results.

INTRODUCTION

The urban environment is formed by complex interactions between natural and human systems. Studying the urban environment requires the collection and analysis of very large datasets that span many disciplines, have semantic (including spatial and temporal) differences and interdependencies, are collected and managed by multiple organizations, and are stored in varying formats. Scientific knowledge discovery is often hindered because of challenges in the integration and navigation of these disparate data. Furthermore, as the number of dimensions in the data increases, novel approaches for pattern discovery are needed.

Environmental data are collected in a variety of units (metric or SI), time increments (minutes, hours, or even days), map projections (e.g., UTM or State Plane) and spatial densities. The data are stored in numerous formats, multiple locations, and are not centralized into a single repository for easy access. To help users (mostly environmental researchers) identify data sets of interest, we use a metadata approach to extract semantically related data sources and present them to the researchers as a semantic network. Starting with an initial search (query) submitted by a researcher, we exploit stored relationships (metadata) among actual data sources to enhance the search result with additional semantically related information. Although domain experts need to manually construct the initial semantic network, which may only include a small number of sources, we introduce an algorithm to let the network expand and evolve automatically based on usage patterns. Then, we present the semantic network to the user as a visual display of a hyperbolic tree; we claim that semantic networks provide an elegant and compact technique to visualize considerable amounts of semantically relevant data sources in a simple yet powerful manner.

Once users have finalized a set of environmental data sources, based on semantic networks, they can access the actual sources to extract data and perform techniques for knowledge discovery. We introduce a new approach to integrate urban environmental data and provide scientists with semantic techniques to navigate and discover patterns in very large environmental datasets.

Our system provides access to a multitude of heterogeneous and autonomous data repositories and assists the user to navigate through the abundance of diverse data sources as if they were a single homogeneous source. More specifically, our contributions are:

1. **Recommendation of additional and relevant data sources:** We present our approach to recommend data sources that are potentially relevant to the user's search interests. Currently, it is tedious and impractical for users to locate relevant information sources by themselves. We provide a methodology that addresses this problem and automatically supplies users with additional and potentially relevant data sources that they might not be aware of. In order to discover these additional recommendations, we exploit semantic relationships between data sources. We define *semantic networks* for interrelated data sources and present an algorithm to automatically refine, augment, and expand an initial and relatively small semantic network with additional and relevant data sources; we also exploit *user profiles* to tailor resulting data sources to specific user preferences.

2. **Visualization and navigation of relevant data sources:** The semantic network with the additional sources is shown to the user as a visual hyperbolic tree improving usability by showing the semantic relationships among relevant data sources in a visual way. After the user has decided on the choice of relevant data sources of interest (based on our metadata approach) and has accessed the actual data, we also assist the user in navigating through the plethora of environmental data

using visualization and navigation techniques that describe data at multiple levels of resolution, enabling pattern and knowledge discovery at different semantic levels. We achieve that, using wavelet transformation techniques, and we demonstrate resilience of wavelet transformation to noisy data.

3. **Implementation of a prototype system:** Finally, we have designed and implemented a prototype system as a proof of concept for our techniques. Using this system we have demonstrated the feasibility of our contributions and have conducted a set of experiments verifying and validating our approach.

This article is organized as follows. First, we present related work on data integration using semantics, and on exploration of multi-dimensional data. Next, we present our research methodology on semantic networks and pattern discovery with wavelet transformations. Then, we describe our prototype implementation and the experiments we conducted. Our conclusions are presented in the final section.

RELATED WORK

Data Integration

There is a rich body of existing work on data integration problems. The fundamental problem is to enable interoperation across different heterogeneous sources of information. In general, this problem manifests itself either as schema mismatches (schema integration) or data incompatibilities (data integration) while accessing disparate data sources. Several surveys identifying problems and proposed approaches on schema and data integration have been written over the years (Batini, Lenzerini, & Navathe, 1986; Ouksel & Sheth, 1999; Rahm & Bernstein, 2001). There has been a significant amount of work on data inte-

gration, especially on resolving discrepancies of different data schemas using a global (mediated) schema (Friedman, Levy, & Millstein, 1999; Levy, Rajaraman, & Ordille, 1996; Miller et al., 2001; Papakonstantinou, Garcia-Molina, & Ullman, 1996; Rahm & Bernstein, 2001; Ram, Park, & Hwang, 2002). More recently, there exists work on decentralized data sharing (Bowers, Lin, & Ludascher, 2004; Doan, Domingos, & Halevy, 2003; Halevy, Ives, Suciu, & Tatarinov, 2003; Rodriguez-Gianolli, Garzetti, Jiang, Kementsietsidis, Kiringa, Masud, Miller, and Mylopoulos, 2005; Tatarinov, & Halevy, 2004) and on integrating data in web-based databases (Bowers et al., 2004; Chang, He, & Zhang, 2005; Dispensa & Brulle, 2003). Clustering, classification and ontologies have also been extensively used as a tool to solve semantic heterogeneity problems (Jain & Zhao, 2004; Kalfoglou & Schorlemmer, 2003; Ram & Park, 2004; Sheth et al., 2004; Sheth, Arpinar, & Kashyap, 2003; Sheth et al., 2002; Zhao & Ram, 2002, 2004).

All the previously mentioned work takes a deep integration approach, where the data schemas (or query interface for integrating web databases) of all sources are integrated. However, this approach is often too restrictive for environmental research because: (1) there are so many different types of data collected by so many different groups that it is impractical for all of them to agree on a universal mediated schema; (2) unlike companies, environmental researchers often share data in an ad hoc way, e.g., a company may purchase products from several fixed suppliers while environmental researchers may use any dataset collected by other researchers but related to their current research task.

There has been much effort by the ecology research community to integrate its data (EML, ORS, SEEK). These systems take a *shallow integration* approach where only metadata is integrated; they allow researchers to store metadata in a centralized database and to select datasets by searching the metadata using keyword or SQL-based search. Such systems avoid the problem of defining a global-mediated data schema and allow researchers to share data in an ad hoc way. A semantics-based integration approach for geospatial data is presented in (Ram, Khatri, Zhang, & Zeng, 2001).

The main problem of existing systems for integrating environmental data is that they provide limited support to assist users in finding data sources semantically related to their research. Most existing systems assume researchers have full knowledge of what keywords to search and provide no assistance in selecting data sources based on relationships between them. However, unlike business applications, environmental research is more explorative and researchers are interested in searching semantically related datasets. Although experienced researchers may find all related keywords, inexperienced researchers such as graduate students may have trouble doing this. The only exception is the SEEK project (Bowers et al., 2004; Bowers & Ludascher, 2004), which uses an ontology for ecology concepts to find related datasets. However, SEEK assumes the ontology will be completely given by domain experts, while our approach augments such knowledge by incremental and automatic refinement of the semantic network.

There has also been work on discovering semantic similarity in (Fankhauser, Kracker, & Neuhold, 1991) based on generalization/specialization, and positive/negative association between classes; in our article, we do not restrict our work to these types of classes only, instead, we let the users identify the degree of relevance between data sources as their own semantic interpretation. Although our approach gives more emphasis on the user's semantics, it may require more manual work to calculate the semantic relationships in the semantic network, since it is user-based. To reduce the amount of manual work, we start with a small manually created semantic network, and then we apply an algorithm that we designed and implemented, to automatically expand, refine,

and augment the semantic network by taking advantage of observed usage patterns. Another difference with (Fankhauser et al., 1991) is the way that the degree of relevance is calculated. They use triangular norms (T-norms) from fuzzy logic, while we use conditional probabilities. Relevant to our work is the topic of discovering and ranking semantic relationships for the Semantic Web (Aleman-Meza, Halaschek-Wiener, Arpinar, Ramakrishnan, & Sheth, 2005; Sheth et al., 2004). However, relationship ranking is not in the scope of this article.

Using Wavelets for Exploration of Multidimensional Data

In order to study long-term environmental factors, we need to evaluate measures across multiple dimensions such as time and geographic space at different dimensional hierarchies. An example of the type of queries that have to be answered is, "How do stream temperature and precipitation change over time and space?" In order to answer such queries, the system must integrate diverse sets of information, which is typically facilitated by dimensional modeling techniques (Kimball, 2002) and online analytical processing (OLAP). The challenge stems from the fact that such dimensional models grow exponentially in size with the number of dimensions and dimensional hierarchies. Current OLAP techniques, however, rely on the intuition of the decision maker in navigating through this lattice of cuboids and only provide navigation tools such as drill down and roll up. There have been very few attempts made to address this issue, most notably the work done by (Sarawagi, Agrawal, & Megiddo, 1998) and (Kumar, Gangopadhyay, & Karabatis, in press). However, the major deficiency of the existing work in this area is that the volume of data after a few drill-downs becomes prohibitively large, which hinders the effectiveness of the method. In order to help end users (scientists or engineers) discover and analyze patterns from large datasets, we have developed a methodology for visualization of data at multiple levels of dimensional hierarchy and pattern discovery through data mining techniques (Han & Kamber, 2000; Mitchell, 1997) at multiple levels of resolution.

The last decade has seen an explosion of interest in wavelets (Daubechies, 1992; Goswami & Chan, 1999), a subject area that has coalesced from roots in mathematics, physics, electrical engineering and other disciplines. Wavelets have been developed as a means to provide low-resolution views of data with the ability to reconstruct high-resolution views if necessary. Wavelet transformation has been applied in numerous disciplines such as compression and de-noising of audio signals and images, finger print compression, edge detection, object detection in two-dimensional images, and image retrieval (Stollnitz, Derose, & Salesin, 1996). There have been few studies on approximate query answering through lossy compression of multi-dimensional data cubes (Matias, Vitter, & Wang, 1998; Smith, Li, & Jhingran, 2004; Vitter & Wang, 1999; Vitter, Wang, & Iyer, 1998), data cleaning, and time-series data analysis (Percival & Walden, 2000). However, no study has been done on utilizing wavelet transformation to provide decision support. We use wavelets to provide coarse, low-resolution views to researchers with

the capability of retrieving high-resolution data by zooming into selected areas.

Generally speaking, wavelet transformation is a tool that divides up data, functions, or operators into different frequency components and then studies each component with a resolution matched to its scale (Daubechies, 1992). A wavelet has many desirable properties such as compact support, vanishing moments and dilating relation and other preferred properties such as smoothness (Chui & Lian, 1996). The core idea behind a discrete wavelet transformation (DWT) is to progressively smooth the data using an iterative procedure and keep the detail along the way. The DWT is performed using the pyramid algorithm (Mallat, 1989) in $O(N)$ time.

RESEARCH DESIGN AND METHODS

Overview of the Architecture

The overall architecture of our system is shown in Figure 1. It consists of a data integration component, a data warehouse, and visualization, navigation, and pattern discovery component, all for the semantic utilization of heterogeneous data

Figure 1. System architecture with data integration and knowledge discovery components

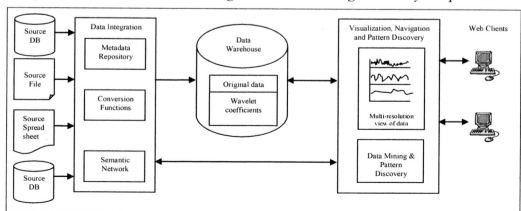

sources. The data integration component consists of a metadata repository, a semantic network, and a set of conversion functions. The metadata repository stores information about the source data including descriptions of each particular source along with information on its syntax and semantics. In our approach the metadata layer is not a global schema. Instead we collect various information artifacts about the sources to assist in finding relationships and correspondences among data in different sources. We also store information on how to access the data (including location identifier, access method, access rights, username, etc.) and how to transform the data to the canonical form if needed through conversion functions (on measurement units, formats, etc.), as explained in the following section.

The semantic network contains relationships between sources. Users request data sources by searching the metadata repository and our system will automatically use the semantic network to return not only the requested ones but also to recommend additional and related data sources that users might not know about. Once the users decide on the final selection of the sources they may download data directly to their local machines. Data being downloaded can be converted to canonical form for possible analysis. This is achieved by a set of conversion functions that are part of the integration component. Data that are integrated are stored in the data warehouse. The data warehouse is a multidimensional model of commonly used source data, which also stores wavelet coefficients. Once users have obtained data, they can visualize, navigate, and discover patterns at different dimensions and resolutions to aid knowledge discovery.

Data Integration

In this section, we address issues related to (1) data sources and relationships that form among them, (2) semantic networks, for recommendation of additional and relevant data sources visualized

as hyperbolic trees, and (3) automatic expansion and augmentation of the semantic network by observing user patterns.

Describing Data Sources and Their Relationships

The plethora of diverse data in environmental research poses significant integration problems. Some data sources may be structured or semi-structured databases with varying data models (relational, object-oriented, object-relational, etc.); some may be available as spreadsheets, while others may be flat files. Data may also contain spatial information in raster or vector formats.

We take a metadata approach, in which we store information about the data, which is collected and stored in the metadata layer with details from both scientific and storage perspectives. For example, many ecosystem study projects collect data related to climate (e.g., precipitation depth, wind speed, wind velocity, air temperature, humidity), soils (e.g., temperature, water content, trace gases), and streams (e.g., depth, flow rate, temperature, nutrients, pathogens, toxics, biota). For each such category, we store its definition, measurement unit, collection frequency, and measurement location, to create an accurate description of what is being collected, how it is measured, where it is stored, and how it is accessed. Usually, this type of information is available from the data sources themselves. It is part of a routine process to specify specific metadata information when users submit data at the data sources. Additional information may also be stored from external sources (e.g., the Open Research System (ORS)). In general, information about data sources is not significantly large, especially when compared with the amount of actual data at the sources; metadata information can be collected from the sources either automatically (through an application programming interface (API) if available) or manually. All such information is kept in the metadata repository and it serves the purpose of a universal registry; similar but not identical to universal description, discovery and integration (UDDI) for Web services. The metadata repository, stored in an object-relational database, is augmented with information on additional data sources as needed.

This work expands on the specification of relationships among database objects stored in heterogeneous database systems (Georgakopoulos, Karabatis, & Gantimahapatruni, 1997; Karabatis, Rusinkiewicz, & Sheth, 1999; Rusinkiewicz, Sheth, & Karabatis, 1991; Sheth & Karabatis, 1993). We have created a methodology allowing researchers to derive semantic relationships among data sources based on source descriptions in the metadata layer. These semantic relationships form a semantic network of related information, which assists users to discover additional information, relevant to their search but possibly unknown to them. We realize that some relationships may not be captured initially in the metadata repository, especially when semantic incompatibilities prevent direct identification of data (such as problems related to synonyms, homonyms, etc.). Nevertheless, missing relationships are captured and added to the metadata repository by observing researchers' usage patterns when they interact with the semantic network, as will be explained further in the current section. The notion of relationships between concepts is also related to the topic maps or concept maps (TopicMap), and Semantic Web (W3C) for XML and web documents containing metadata about concepts. However, our work does not limit itself only to XML or web data, but can be used to describe data in general.

Converting Data to a Canonical Form

Environmental data sources may have differences in formats, data units, spatial and temporal granularities, and may be collected at different time intervals. We have implemented methods and/or applications to convert between different units and formats. In addition, spatial and temporal disparities are resolved using spatial and temporal join/aggregation operations and integrating data at the appropriate level. As an example, suppose that we need to integrate stream chemical and biological data collected at each site with land use and land cover data. In our data warehouse model, each site belongs to a stream reach, and each stream reach belongs to a sub-watershed (the land area that drains to a particular point along a stream segment and is represented by a polygon feature). Land use/land cover data is also collected on areas represented by polygons (although these polygons are different and smaller than polygons for sub-watersheds). Thus, we aggregate stream data to sub-watershed level, and then aggregate land use/land cover data to areas represented by the same set of polygons for sub-watersheds using re-projection, spatial joins, or overlay functions provided by ArcObjects, the API included in the ESRI's ArcGIS software suite (www.esri.com/software/arcgis).

Using Semantic Networks to Expand User Queries

In this section, we provide details on the creation and utilization of semantic networks. We formally define semantic networks and we present techniques to extract information from semantic networks and recommend additional and relevant data sources to users in their search of related data sources. We also present an algorithm to automatically refine, and dynamically augment semantic networks; Semantic networks have long been used to represent relationships (Masterman, 1961). We take advantage of their structure to elicit additional semantic information for environmental data.

Definition 1. *We formally define a semantic network G(V,E,W) as a graph G where:*

- V is the set of nodes in the network. Each node represents a data source or data set.

For convenience, we use data source and data set interchangeably in this article.

- *E* is the set of directed edges in the network. An edge (v_i, v_j) indicates that node v_i is semantically related to node v_j.
- *W* is a $|V| * |V|$ relevance score matrix, where $W(i,j)$ is a number in range of [0,1] and represents the degree of relevance (or relevance score) between nodes v_j and v_i.

Figure 2 depicts an example semantic network related to fish population. The number on each edge represents the relevance score associated with the two adjacent nodes. Based on these scores, we can infer the relevance between any two nodes in the network. We consider each relevance score as a conditional probability and assume they are independent of each other (Rice, 1994). For example, the relevance score between fish population and stream temperature can be considered as the conditional probability of a researcher interested in stream temperature given that he or she is interested in fish population.

Using the standard notation for conditional probability, we have:

P(surfaces | fish) = P(surfaces, stream temperature | fish) because the user will be interested in impervious surfaces, assuming the user is also interested in stream temperature.

Using chain rules and assuming all conditional probabilities are independent (Rice, 1994), we have:

Figure 2. An example semantic network

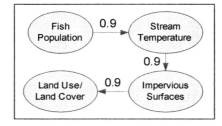

P(surfaces, temperature | fish) = P(temperature | fish) * P(surfaces | temperature) = 0.9 * 0.9 = 0.81.

In general, if v_i and v_j are two nodes, there are k paths $p_1, ..., p_k$ between v_i and v_j, where path p_l $(1 <= l <= k)$ consists of nodes $v_{l1}, ..., v_{l|pl|+1}$ $(|p_l|$ is the length of path p_l).

The relevance score *rs* between v_i and v_j is,

$$rs = \min(1, \sum_{pl} \prod_{1 \le i \le |pl|} w(l_i, l_{i+1})) \qquad (1)$$

The above formula computes the relevance score between v_i and v_j as the sum of relevance scores for all paths connecting v_i and v_j. For each such path, the relevance score between the two endpoints is computed as the product of relevance scores for all edges along the path. There can be more detailed types of semantic relationships (cause-effect, is-a, and is-part-of), or to use more advanced inference rules without the independent assumption on the conditional probabilities, but these extensions are beyond the scope of this article.

Construction of Semantic Network

We assume that domain experts have provided an initial semantic network, i.e., a set of edges and nodes with their relevance scores. Based on this initial semantic network, we compute the relevance scores between any pair of nodes in the network, and create the matrix *W*.

Let us consider the example in Figure 2. Suppose matrix *R* stores the relevance scores of all edges in the initial semantic network. The first, second, third, and fourth row (column) in the matrix corresponds to edges from (to) fish, temperature, surface data, and land data. R_{ij} stores the relevance score from node *i* to node *j*.

$$R = \begin{pmatrix} 0 & 0.9 & 0 & 0 \\ 0 & 0 & 0.9 & 0 \\ 0 & 0 & 0 & 0.9 \\ 0 & 0 & 0 & 0 \end{pmatrix}$$

Based on formula (1), the relevance score between any pair of nodes equals the sum of relevance scores of all paths between them. Using matrix multiplication rules, and for any given pair (i, j) with $i \neq j$, we calculate the sum of relevance scores of all paths between i and j with length k. It is equal to R^k_{ij} where R^k is the multiplication of k matrices R. For example, the relevance scores of all paths with length 2 is:

$$R^2 = R * R = \begin{pmatrix} 0 & 0 & 0.81 & 0 \\ 0 & 0 & 0 & 0.81 \\ 0 & 0 & 0 & 0 \\ 0 & 0 & 0 & 0 \end{pmatrix}$$

There are two non-zero entries: $R^2_{13} = 0.81$, identifying the relevance score between fish data to surface data, and $R^2_{24} = 0.81$ identifying the score between temperature and land data. Hence, the relevance score rs between any pair of nodes in the network can be computed using the following formula:

$$rs = \sum_{1 \leq i \leq N} R^i \tag{2}$$

Using Semantic Networks to Elicit Additional Semantics

A user in search of ecosystem data sources may perform a keyword search or submit a regular SQL query to our system, which in turn will find data sources that directly satisfy the user's conditions. We call these data sources exact answers. In addition to the exact answers, we describe a novel approach to enhance and augment the result set with additional sources, semantically relevant to the exact answers, which the user might not be aware of. We achieve this goal by exploiting the semantic network, and returning all data sources whose relevance score with the exact answers is higher than a threshold. For simplicity, we have set the threshold in our system to 0.5 but a user can adjust it according to how closely additional data sources should be related to the exact answers.

For example, suppose a user wants to find all data sources related to 'fish population.' The exact answer contains only the fish population data set because only that data set contains the keyword 'fish population.' However, using the semantic network in Figure 2, our system will return all other three data sources in the figure because they are also related to the fish population according to the semantic network. Therefore, we can automatically recommend to the users additional semantic information (data sources) relevant to the exact answers.

Visualizing Semantic Networks

Most existing systems for ecological research (EML) return data sources as a list, and it is difficult for users to go through them when the list is long. Our system utilizes a hyperbolic tree technique (Lamping, Rao, & Pirolli, 1995) to visualize data sources and the semantic relationships they form. Figure 3 shows an example of such a tree. The main benefit of this technique is to show users the entire set of exact answers and additional related data sources at a glance, as a visualization of all relevant nodes and edges forming a semantic network. In addition, users can dynamically adjust the display size of a data source of their choice and automatically bring it to the foreground concentrating on a specific data source and all its edges connecting it to the relevant sources.

Dealing with Different User Preferences

We also consider the issue that different domain experts may not have the same interests; instead they may need to utilize different semantic networks (if available) pertaining to their own specialties. For example, a stream chemist may not be interested in land use/land cover, contrary to an urban developer who would certainly focus on it. We address this problem by creating different user profiles, each corresponding to a separate semantic network with its own bias towards a certain specialty. Initially, domain experts will define a set of profiles. A new user will select a profile before using our system, and can change this selection at any time. For each profile, we also track the usage patterns by users and collect information that is used to dynamically refine and augment the network based on these patterns. Therefore, although an initial profile may not completely satisfy every user, it will adapt to user preferences after some period of time.

Refining and Augmenting the Semantic Network

The key idea to automatically refine, evolve, and augment the semantic network is to monitor usage patterns. Once the initial semantic network (or a given profile) has been created by a domain expert, users can query the metadata repository for data sources. The system provides exact answers and recommends additional data sources (displayed visually as in Figure 3). Then, the users select (click on) those data sources potentially relevant to their research. They submit their queries to the data sources, while the metadata repository keeps copies of queries to identify query patterns. Based on the usage of these patterns by users, we can infer additional relationships that form between data sources. These relationships are used to automatically expand, enhance and refine the semantic network.

As an example, suppose two users have asked for data sources related to 'fish population.' *User1* selects all four data sources in Figure 2, while *User2* selects only fish, temperature, and land data. Let F, T, S, L represent fish, temperature, surfaces, and land, respectively. We assume that users agree to incorporate every edge connecting two sources that they selected in the network, but disagree with all other edges of sources they did not select. For example, *User1* agrees with the edges F-T, T- S, and S-L. However, *User2* agrees with the edge F-T, but not the other two. The issue is how *User2* selects the land data, which is only related to fish via surface data in the current network, and *User2* does not select surface. We

Figure 3. Visualiing a semantic network as a hyperbolic tree

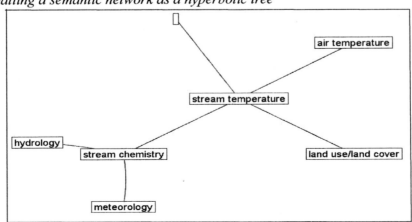

assume the user agrees with relationship between fish and land, where fish is an exact answer and land is a selected source that is not covered by any existing edges that the user agrees with. Thus, we propose the Algorithm 1 to automatically augment and refine the network.

This algorithm first creates a copy of the current network at step 1. At step (2a) it identifies the edges that users agree on based on usage patterns. At step (2b), the algorithm identifies new edges not in the current network, but necessary for users to select those sources connected by these edges. For instance, in the above example, if the usage patterns consists of $Q_1 = \{F, T, S, L\}$, and $Q_2 = \{F, T, L\}$. At step 2a), the algorithm will add to S_1 edges F-T, T-S, S-L for Q_1, and F-T for Q_2. Thus, $S_1 = \{F-T, T-S, S-L, F-T\}$. At step 2b), the algorithm will add to S_2 edge F-L. Thus,

$S_2 = \{F-L\}$. At step 3, the algorithm re-computes the relevance scores for the existing edges. The new score consists of two components, the first component is the current score, and the second component is the score based on usage patterns. These two components are combined using a weight d, which is also called an *aging factor* because it determines how quickly the new score converges to the usage patterns. We set the aging factor $d = 0.5$ in this article. In the above example, the new scores are:

R(fish-temperature) = 0.9 * 0.5 + 1 * 0.5 = 0.95
R(temperature-surfaces) = 0.9 * 0.5 + 0.5 * 0.5 = 0.7
R(surfaces-land) = 0.9 * 0.5 + 0.5 * 0.5 = 0.7
*R(fish-land) = 0.5 * 0.5 = 0.25.*

Algorithm 1. Automatic refinement of semantic network

Input: current network N, a set of usage patterns {Q1, ..., Qm}, where each Qi consists of a set of exact answers and a set of related answers selected by users.

Output: a refined network N'

  1. Create N' as exact copy of N

  2. For each user query Qi,

   a. Identify all edges in the current network N that link two selected sources and add them to a multi-set S1.

   b. For any source selected by users but is not covered by an edge in N, generate an edge from the exact answer to that source and add it to a multi-set S2.

  3. For each edge AB in existing network N

   There are three possible cases:

   a. AB appears in S1. The new relevance score r(AB) equals

   r(AB) * d + Occ(AB) / Occ(A) * (1-d)

   where d is an aging factor ranging from 0 to 1, Occ(AB) is the number of times edge AB appears in S1, and Occ(A) is the number of times node A is selected in usage patterns.

   b. AB does not appear in S1, and A is never selected. The score of AB remains unchanged.

   c. AB does not appear in S1, but A is selected. The new score equals r(AB) * d

  4. For each edge AB in S2, add it to the new network N' with relevance score Occ(AB)/ Occ(A), where Occ(AB) is the number of times edge AB appears in S2, and Occ(A) is the number of times node A is selected in usage patterns.

Data Navigation: A Visual Approach

Visualization of data can be proven to be a significant decision support tool. It can provide deep insights into data that are very difficult to capture by automatic means. Since environmental data often have different spatial and temporal granularities, environmental researchers are interested in viewing data at multiple resolutions. For example, a spike in stream flow, precipitation, and nitrogen content will tell a scientist that there is an influx of nitrogen in the stream due to a precipitation event. However, a steady increase or decrease in stream flow, precipitation, and nitrogen content for several years will indicate a possible change in the longer term. Furthermore, the recent development of wireless sensors and sensor networks has allowed for the collection of environmental data at high temporal resolution. In consequence, researchers often need to visualize this data for long time scales, that is, at lower resolutions.

Therefore, we present an effective multiresolution visualization method using wavelets to help researchers discover patterns, trends, and surprises. The main benefit of using wavelets compared to using fixed levels of resolutions is that wavelets allow finer and more flexible levels of resolutions. For example, fixed levels allow users to view stream temperature at minutes, hours, and days, while wavelets allow users to view the temperature at one minute, two minute, or four minute spans, and so on.

In this article, we apply wavelet transformations—we used Haar wavelets (Goswami & Chan, 1999), and we are currently experimenting with other wavelet transforms—for numerical attributes. If the data contains spatial or temporal attributes (e.g., indicating the location or time the measurements were collected), we always sort the data records in the spatial or temporal order and apply wavelet transformations to the sequence of the measurement attributes in this order. Otherwise, we view the measurement attributes as a sequence in the order that records are stored in

the database, and apply wavelet transformations. Of course, in the latter case, the different levels of resolutions do not have spatial or temporal meanings, and only provide a lower-resolution view of the data.

The generated wavelet coefficients are then stored in an object-relational database (Oracle 10g). We have developed an algorithm (see Goswami & Chan, 1999) to reconstruct not only the complete set of the original data but also a certain subset of it, at appropriate levels of resolutions. The utility of reconstructing a subset of the original dataset stems from the fact that a decision maker may want to find out only that part of the original dataset that was used to generate a particular coefficient.

We developed a visualization tool to help environmental scientists visually inspect temporal and spatial datasets for noticeable trends and relationships. Figure 4 depicts a prototype interface developed in Visual Basic which allows users to spatially locate and select data collection sites and visualize time-series data for the selected sites. The top pane connects to the ESRI's ArcSDE® Geodatabase system where the user can navigate spatially using zooming and panning tools. The bottom pane connects to a DBMS which stores raw data along with wavelet-transformed data at various levels of temporal resolution. The left side of the interface allows the user to (1) select the site or sites of interest spatially or from a list, (2) select the time period of the visualization, (3) select the dataset (4) select the type of visualization, and (5) interactively control the temporal resolution of the visualization. The user can select a site, or sites, either spatially by using the GIS interface, or by selecting specific sites based on the site name. Once a site is chosen, the user can select the time period of the visualization by providing the date and time. Then the user can select whether he or she may want to visualize the data using a line graph, bar graph, or scatter plot. The visualization is then displayed in the bottom pane of the interface. The slider below

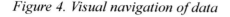

Figure 4. Visual navigation of data

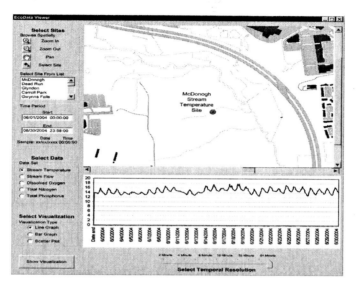

the displayed data allows the user to control the temporal resolution of the visualization. The slider goes from the resolution of the raw data on the left to the level *n* wavelet transformation on the right. The scale on the slider can change, based on a combination of the time period of the raw dataset and the level of wavelet transformations available. Data at the selected resolution will be reconstructed from the stored wavelet coefficients and shown to users. Figure 4 shows the McDonogh stream temperature site along with time series data at the 64 minute resolution for the month of June, 2004.

Pattern Discovery Through Multi-Resolution Data Mining

Multi-resolution data mining is similar in concept to online analytical mining (OLAM) (Han, 1998; Han, Chee, & Chiang, 1998). Conceptually, it allows a user to mine the data at different levels of the dimension hierarchy. We propose to augment the dimensional hierarchies with wavelet coef-

ficients at different levels of decomposition and provide mining capabilities including association rule mining, classification, and clustering. This approach provides the benefits of OLAM, but in addition, it enables users to select the appropriate levels of resolution that would be ideally suited for mining the data. If the data is noisy, wavelet decomposition could reduce noise in the data and would result in a better classifier. We illustrate the efficacy of using wavelet decomposition in classification and its resilience on noise in the following section.

IMPLEMENTATION AND EXPERIMENTAL RESULTS

We have conducted preliminary experiments to validate our approaches of using semantic networks to help environmental researchers find related data sources and using wavelets to identify patterns in different data resolutions. Our major findings are:

- Users of our system concluded that our query expansion and visualization interface surpasses the traditional exact query interface. In all cases we tested, our query expansion interface returned more data sources than the exact query interface. They also found value in the automatic adaptation and augmentation of the semantic network based on profiles and refinement techniques.

- Wavelet transformation is a promising tool to discover patterns at different resolutions of data. Our experiments demonstrated that for a real data set and a benchmark data set, wavelet transformation preserved most patterns in the data while it was used to convert data to a lower resolution. More interestingly, our results also showed that wavelet transformation is very robust to noise in data and in some cases even improved the quality of discovered patterns.

We first describe the implementation details, and then proceed to experimental results.

Implementation

We used Oracle 10g to store metadata of data sources and semantic networks using the database schema in Figure 5. We use three relational tables (sources, edges, network) to store information about data sources, keywords, and relevance scores. The Edges table stores the edges and their relevance scores in the semantic network. The Network table stores the relevance scores between any pair of nodes in the semantic network, which is computed from the Edge table. We implemented the algorithms described in the previous section as PL/SQL stored procedures for the construction, query expansion, and dynamic augmentation of the semantic network.

We implemented a semantic network query interface (written in Visual Basic) for researchers to search data sources with semantic terms related to their research; this interface is based on the semantic network and metadata repository and is shown in Figure 6. The user first needs to select a profile then provide keywords and finally submit the search to database. Our query expansion procedure will augment the query and return all sources related to the given keywords in the results window. The user can then visualize the relationships (as edges) between returned sources by clicking the 'view network' button. Figure 7 shows the hyperbolic visualization of the results obtained in Figure 6. We use a publicly available Hyperbolic Tree Java Library (http://sourceforge. net/projects/hypertree/) to display hyperbolic trees. Users can also record their selections by first checking the sources of interest and then clicking 'record.' Recorded selections are used as usage patterns to dynamically augment the network as described in the previous section. We have also implemented a Haar wavelet transformation as a stored procedure in an Oracle server and inserted the results into a table, which will be later used for pattern discovery.

Experiments with Semantic Networks

Setup: *We evaluated our semantic network approach using data sets collected by the Baltimore Ecosystem Study (http://www.beslter.org/). Table 1 summarizes the details of these data sets.*

Figure 5. Database schema for the semantic network

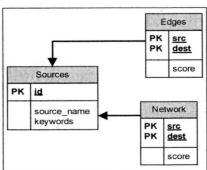

Figure 6. Query interface using semantic networks

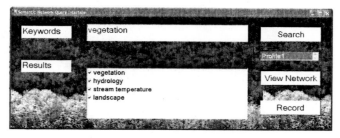

Figure 7. Visualization of results of Figure 6

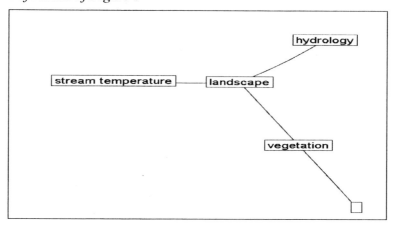

We asked an environmental researcher to define the edges in the initial semantic network between these data sets. The researcher created three different semantic networks corresponding to three different profiles of users interested in vegetation, stream temperature, and stream chemistry respectively. Figure 8 shows the networks where *Pi* identifies the score in the ith profile. In this experiment, the researcher considered the relationships bidirectional.

We ran two experiments to test our search interface and the semantic network refinement algorithm. In the first experiment, we asked another researcher to use our search interface to find related data sources and asked him to give us feedback on the appropriateness of the results. Due to limited resources, we asked that researcher to take on alternate roles of three different types of users and then we selected one of the three profiles. The researcher posted three example queries as follows:

- **Query 1:** What data sets are related to riparian vegetation? The researcher selected profile 1 and searched the data sources with keyword 'vegetation.'
- **Query 2:** What factors contribute to the fluctuations in stream temperature? The researcher selected profile 2 and used 'stream temperature' as the keyword.
- **Query 3:** What factors may affect the stream chemistry? The researcher selected profile 3 and used 'stream chemistry' as the keyword.

Table 1. Data sources used in semantic network experiments

Data Source Name	Description	Location
Vegetation	Riparian vegetation of the Gwynns Falls Watershed in Baltimore area	http://www.ecostudies.org/pub/besveg/riparian.zip
Hydrology	Streamflow data collected along the Gwynns Falls in Baltimore area	http://waterdata.usgs.gov/md/nwis/nwisman?site_no=01589352
Stream Temperature	Stream temperature of the Gwynns Falls Watershed	As an Excel file on local file server
Meteorology	Baltimore meteorological station data	http://www.ecostudies.org/pub/bes_206.zip
Stream Chemistry	Stream chemistry data of the Gwynns Falls Watershed	As a text file on local file server
Landscape	Satellite image data of Baltimore area landscape (forests, grass, crops, etc.)	As a text file on local file server

Table 2. Adapted from A Primer on Landsat 7 (http://imaging,geocomm,com/features/sensor/landsat7)

Spectral Bandwidth Ranges for Landsat 7 ETM+ Sensor (μ)		
Band Number	Wavelength Range	Recommended Application
Band 1	0.45 - 0.52 (blue-green)	soil and vegetation discrimination and forest type mapping
Band 2	0.53 - 0.61 (green)	vegetation discrimination, plant vigor
Band 3	0.63 - 0.69 (red)	detection of roads, bare soil, and vegetation type
Band 4	0.78 - 0.90 (near-infrared)	biomass estimation, separation of water from vegetation, soil moisture discrimination
Band 5	1.55 - 1.75 (mid-infrared)	discrimination of roads, bare soils, and water
Band 6	10.4 - 12.5 (thermal infrared)	measuring plant heat stress and thermal mapping
Band 7	2.09 - 2.35 (mid-infrared)	discrimination of mineral and rock types, interpreting vegetation cover and soil moisture
Band 8	.52 - .90 (panchromatic)	for enhanced resolution and increased detection ability

In the second experiment, we asked the researcher to select a set of data sources in the results of Query 4 that he thought was most related to the question he asked. We then ran our algorithm to refine the semantic network based on his selection and compared the results for Query 4 with the results using the original network. Our search interface returned the following results:

- **Query 1:** Vegetation, hydrology, stream temperature, and landscape.

- **Query 2:** Stream temperature, meteorology, and landscape.
- **Query 3:** Hydrology, meteorology, stream chemistry, and landscape.

In all cases, the exact search interface only returned one data source with the search keyword, while our search interface returned multiple sources (4 for Query 1 and 3, and 3 for Query 2). We also asked the researcher to look at the results returned by our interface, and he found the answers returned by our search interface actually related to these research questions.

In the second experiment, the user selected only the first three data sources for Query 3. When the researcher ran Query 3 on the refined network, the 'landscape' data source is no longer in the search results due to the refinement. This reflected the user selection.

In summary, our experiments verified that our system exploits data source relationships that are maintained in semantic networks and supplies users with additional data sources that are relevant to their original search, but they might not be aware of.

Experiments for Knowledge Discovery using Wavelet Transformations

We conducted several experiments to test our hypothesis that wavelet transformation results in preserving patterns in data. In the first experiment, we used remote sensing data from the Landsat 7 ETM+ sensor. Data from the Landsat 7 ETM+ sensor is typically used by environmental scientists to characterize the landscape in terms of land cover. The Landsat 7 ETM+ sensor captures wavelength values for 8 spectral bands based on the reflectance of the earth's surface. Table 2 shows the range of wavelengths captured in each band and its recommended application.

We downloaded a Landsat 7 ETM+ scene from October 5, 2001, covering central Maryland (path 15/row 33), from the Global Land Cover Facility (http://glcf.umiacs.umd.edu/data/). We extracted spectral information from the Landsat image and a subset was evaluated for a 1.2 km² area in northern Baltimore County, Maryland. We then manually classified land cover values of crop, grass, forest, or water based on high resolution aerial photography. The resulting dataset consisted of eight attributes representing the spectral bands and one class attribute representing the four distinct land cover values. The spectral bands were used to identify whether the land cover is 'grass,' 'forest,' 'water,' or 'crops'. This yielded 1193 instances that were divided into two groups. Group 1 had 616 instances that were used for training and group 2 had 577 instances that were used for testing. We performed the following steps. We (1) divided the data into two disjoint sets—a test set and a training set; (2) performed first level of

Figure 9. Performance comparison

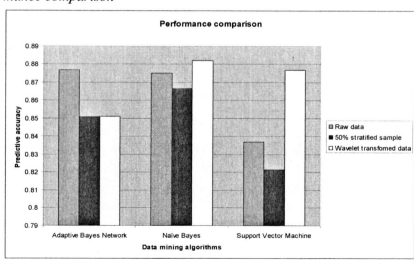

Figure 10. Performance comparison on noisy data

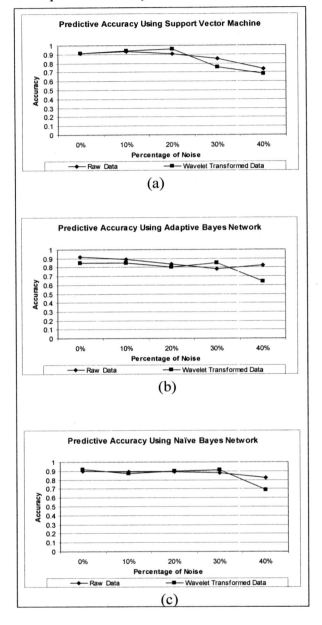

Haar wavelet transformation on the raw data; (3) created a 50% stratified sample of the training set of the raw data; (4) created three classifiers based on raw data, 50% stratified sample, and wavelet transformed data; and (5) compared the predictive accuracy on test data for the three classifiers.

Two sets of three different classifiers were built using an adaptive Bayes network, a naïve Bayes method, and support vector machines (with linear kernel function) for the raw data and approximate coefficients from a Haar wavelet transformation of the raw data. We used Oracle 10g as the database and Oracle Data Miner for the mining functions. The reason for testing with a stratified sample is that the Haar wavelet transform reduces the data size by half. Hence the size of the training set for raw data is twice as large as that of the wavelet transformed data. As shown in Figure 9, in two out of three methods (naïve Bayes and support vector machine), the use of a Haar wavelet transform resulted in a better classifier than both (1) the raw data with twice the size of the training set and (2) a 50% stratified sample that had the same size of the training set. For the adaptive Bayes network, a wavelet transform resulted in 2% loss of predictive accuracy as compared with the raw data, but had a slightly higher predictive accuracy when tested with a training set of the same size.

In addition, we decided to test the sensitivity of classifier accuracy on a noisy dataset. For these experiments, we used the Iris plant dataset from the UCI machine learning repository (http://www. ics.uci.edu/~mlearn/MLSummary.html). The dataset contained 150 instances with four attributes and three class labels. The attributes represent sepal length, sepal height, petal length, and petal width and the class variable refers to one of three types of iris plant. Again, the same environment was used to test the predictive accuracy of three classifiers: an adaptive Bayes network, a naïve Bayes method, and support vector machine. In each case, we introduced random noise following standard normal distribution to 10%-40% of the instances. As shown in Figures 10a-c, use of the Haar wavelet transform resulted in a classifier with a comparable predictive accuracy to the raw data. It is evident that the raw data outperforms the wavelet transformed data with 40% noise with the disparity in performance being more pronounced in the adaptive Bayes and naïve Bayes methods. This indicates a threshold in the noise-to-signal ratio below which the benefit of wavelet transformation is lost. Wavelets can be applied to any numerical attributes assuming that the data is sorted in the order that they are stored in the database. This approach has also

been used by many existing studies (Matias et al., 1998; Smith et al., 2004; Vitter & Wang, 1999; Vitter et al., 1998). The only difference is that the levels of resolutions do not have temporal or spatial meanings. While more research is needed to establish the efficacy of wavelet transformation, these preliminary experiments do indicate that wavelet transformation holds promise as a robust tool for pattern discovery at multiple levels of data and as a method for data reduction in very large datasets with little degradation in predictive accuracy.

CONCLUSION

In this article, we have described a methodology for data integration and pattern discovery for environmental research using data semantics. We used semantics to integrate multiple data sources to answer user queries for environmental research. Our methodology to describe the data sources is based on a metadata approach and takes advantage of data interrelationships represented as a semantic network. User queries are automatically expanded using a relevance score matrix and a semantic network, which can be visualized as a hyperbolic tree. We have utilized user profiles to capture diverse user preferences to precisely answer user queries, and have presented an algorithm to automatically expand, augment and refine the semantic network by observing usage patterns. We have demonstrated that our semantic integration techniques offer a powerful, straightforward and user-friendly approach for the visualization of significant amounts of environmental data sources.

In addition to enabling search for data in the integrated system described above, we also allow users to navigate through multi-dimensional data through visualization, implemented using wavelet transformation. We have used Haar wavelets that decompose data by averaging and differencing consecutive, non-overlapping pairs of data at each level of decomposition. Thus, users can visualize multiple levels of data and roll-up or drill down at different levels of hierarchy. They can also apply data mining techniques such as classification at different levels of resolution. We have illustrated that patterns in the data are well preserved at first level decomposition with 50% reduction in data size. We have also demonstrated the resilience of wavelet transformation to noisy data.

The research presented in this article is being enhanced by further development of the described methodologies and further experimentation with pattern discovery at multiple levels of resolution. We plan to incorporate data mining and machine learning techniques to aid in the enhancement and refinement of the semantic network. The methodology presented in this article can also be applied to other application areas where search, visualization, and pattern discovery of data from multiple sources are needed.

ACKNOWLEDGMENT

This material is based upon work partly supported by the National Science Foundation under Grant Nos. DEB-0423476 and BES-0414206 and by U.S. Environmental Protection Agency under grants R-82818201-0 and CR83105801. Although the research described in this article has been funded in part by the U.S. Environmental Protection Agency, it has not been subjected to the agency's required peer and policy review and therefore does not necessarily reflect the views of the agency and no official endorsement should be inferred.

REFERENCES

Aleman-Meza, B., Halaschek-Wiener, C., Arpinar, I. B., Ramakrishnan, C., & Sheth, A. P. (2005). Ranking complex relationships on the Semantic Web. *IEEE Internet Computing*, 37-44.

Batini, C., Lenzerini, M., & Navathe, S. (1986). A comparative analysis of methodologies for database schema integration. *ACM Computing Surveys, 18*(4), 323-364.

Bowers, S., Lin, K., & Ludascher, B. (2004). *On integrating scientific resources through semantic registration*. Paper presented at the Scientific and Statistical Database Management.

Bowers, S., & Ludascher, B. (2004). *An ontology-driven framework for data transformation in scientific workflows*. Paper presented at the International Workshop on Data Integration in the Life Sciences.

Chang, K. C.-C., He, B., & Zhang, Z. (2005). *Toward large scale integration: Building a MetaQuerier over databases on the Web*. Paper presented at the CIDR.

Chui, C. K., & Lian, J. (1996). A study of orthonormal multiwavelets. *Applied Numerical Mathematics: Transactions of IMACS, 20*(3), 273-298.

Daubechies, I. (1992). *Ten lectures on wavelets*. Capital City Press.

Dispensa, J. M., & Brulle, R. J. (2003). The Sprawling Frontier: Politics of Watershed Management. *Submitted to Rural Sociology*.

Doan, A., Domingos, P., & Halevy, A. Y. (2003). Learning to match the schemas of data sources: A multistrategy approach. *Machine Learning, 50*(3), 279-301.

EML. *Ecological Metadata Language. http://knb. ecoinformatics.org/software/eml/*

Fankhauser, P., Kracker, M., & Neuhold, E. J. (1991). Semantic vs. structural resemblance of classes. *SIGMOD Record, 20*(4), 59-63.

Friedman, M., Levy, A., & Millstein, T. (1999). *Navigational plans for data integration*. Paper presented at the AAAI/IAAI.

Georgakopoulos, D., Karabatis, G., & Ganti-mahapatruni, S. (1997). Specification and management of interdependent data in operational systems and data warehouses. *Distributed and Parallel Databases, An International Journal, 5*(2), 121-166.

Goswami, J. C., & Chan, A. K. (1999). *Fundamentals of wavelets: Theory, algorithms and applications*: John Wiley.

Halevy, A. Y., Ives, Z. G., Suciu, D., & Tatarinov, I. (2003). *Schema mediation in peer data management systems.* Paper presented at the ICDE.

Han, J. (1998). *Towards on-line analytical mining in large databases.* Paper presented at the ACM SIGMOD.

Han, J., Chee, S., & Chiang, J. (1998). *Issues for on-line analytical mining of data warehouses.* Paper presented at the Proceedings of 1998 SIGMOD'96 Workshop on Research Issues on Data Mining and Knowledge Discovery DMKD, Seattle, Washington.

Han, J., & Kamber, M. (2000). *Data Mining: Concepts and Techniques*: Morgan Kaufmann.

Hyperion. The Hyperion Project. http://www.cs.toronto.edu/db/hyperion/.

Jain, H., & Zhao, H. (2004). *Federating heterogeneous information systems using Web services and ontologies.* Paper presented at the Tenth Americas Conference on Information Systems, New York.

Kalfoglou, Y., & Schorlemmer, M. (2003). Ontology mapping: The state of the art. *Knowledge Engineering Review, 18*(1), 1-31.

Karabatis, G., Rusinkiewicz, M., & Sheth, A. (1999). Interdependent database systems. In *Management of Heterogeneous and Autonomous Database Systems* (pp. 217-252). San Francisco, CA: Morgan-Kaufmann.

Kimball, R. (2002). *The data warehouse toolkit* (2nd ed.).

Kumar, N., Gangopadhyay, A., & Karabatis, G. (in press). Supporting mobile decision making with association rules and multi-layered caching. *Decision Support Systems.*

Lamping, J., Rao, R., & Pirolli, P. (1995). *A Focus+Context Technique Based on Hyperbolic Geometry for Visualizing Large Hierarchies.* Paper presented at the Proceedings ACM Conference Human Factors in Computing Systems.

Levy, A. Y., Rajaraman, A., & Ordille, J. J. (1996). *Querying heterogeneous information sources using source descriptions.* Paper presented at the VLDB.

Mallat, S. G. (1989). A theory for multiresolution signal decomposition: The wavelet representation. *IEEE Transactions on Pattern Analysis and Machine Intelligence, 11*, 674-693.

Masterman, M. (1961). Semantic message detection for machine translation, using an interlingua. *NPL*, pp. 438-475.

Matias, Y., Vitter, J. S., & Wang, M. (1998). *Wavelet-based histograms for selectivity estimation.* Paper presented at the ACM SIGMOD.

Miller, R. J., Hernandez, M. A., Haas, L. M., Yan, L., Ho, C. T. H., Fagin, R., et al. (2001). The clio project: managing heterogeneity. *SIGMOD Record, 30*(1).

Mitchell, T. M. (1997). *Machine learning*: McGraw-Hill.

ORS. *Open Research System. http://www.orspublic.org*

Ouksel, A., & Sheth, A. P. (1999). Special issue on semantic interoperability in global information systems. *SIGMOD Record, 28*(1).

Papakonstantinou, Y., Garcia-Molina, H., & Ullman, J. (1996). *Medmaker: A mediation system based on declarative specifications.* Paper presented at the ICDE.

Percival, D. B., & Walden, A. T. (2000). *Wavelet methods for time series analysis.* Cambridge University Press.

Rahm, E., & Bernstein, P. A. (2001). A survey of approaches to automatic schema matching. *VLDB Journal, 10*(4).

Ram, S., Khatri, V., Zhang, L., & Zeng, D. (2001). *GeoCosm: A semantics-based approach for information integration of geospatial data.* Paper presented at the Proceedings of the Workshop on Data Semantics in Web Information Systems (DASWIS2001), Yokohama, Japan.

Ram, S., & Park, J. (2004). Semantic conflict resolution ontology (SCROL): An ontology for detecting and resolving data and schema-level semantic conflicts. *IEEE Transactions on Knowledge and Data Engineering, 16*(2), 189-202.

Ram, S., Park, J., & Hwang, Y. (2002). *CREAM: A mediator based environment for modeling and accessing distributed information on the Web.* Paper presented at the British National Conference on Databases (BNCOD).

Rice, J. A. (1994). *Mathematical statistics and data analysis.* Duxbury Press.

Rodriguez-Gianolli, P., Garzetti, M., Jiang, L., Kementsietsidis, A., Kiringa, I., Masud, M., Miller, R., & Mylopoulos, J. (2005). Data Sharing in the Hyperion Peer Database System. In *Proceedings of the International Conference on Very Large Databases (VLDB).*

Rusinkiewicz, M., Sheth, A., & Karabatis, G. (1991). Specifying interdatabase dependencies in a multidatabase environment. *IEEE Computer, 24*(12), 46-53.

Sarawagi, S., Agrawal, R., & Megiddo, N. (1998). *Discovery-driven exploration of OLAP data cubes.* Paper presented at the International Conference on Extending Database Technology.

SEEK. *The Science Environment for Ecological Knowledge.* http://seek.ecoinformatics.org

Sheth, A., Aleman-Meza, B., Arpinar, I. B., Bertram, C., Warke, Y., Ramakrishanan, C., et al. (2004). Semantic association identification and knowledge discovery for national security applications. *Journal of Database Management, 16*(1).

Sheth, A., Arpinar, I. B., & Kashyap, V. (2003). Relationships at the heart of Semantic Web: Modeling, discovering, and exploiting complex semantic relationships. In M. Nikravesh, B. Azvin, R. Yager & L. A. Zadeh (Eds.), *Enhancing the power of the Internet studies in fuzziness and soft computing.* Springer-Verlag.

Sheth, A., Bertram, C., Avant, D., Hammond, B., Kochut, K., & Warke, Y. (2002). Managing semantic content for the web. *IEEE Internet Computing, 6*(4), 80-87.

Sheth, A., & Karabatis, G. (1993, May). *Multi-database Interdependencies in Industry.* Paper presented at the ACM SIGMOD, Washington DC.

Smith, J. R., Li, C.-S., & Jhingran, A. (2004). A wavelet framework for adapting data cube views for OLAP. *IEEE Transactions on Knowledge and Data Engineering, 16*(5), 552-565.

Stollnitz, E. J., Derose, T. D., & Salesin, D. H. (1996). *Wavelets for Computer Graphics Theory and Applications*: Morgan Kaufmann Publishers.

Tatarinov, I., & Halevy, A. Y. (2004). *Efficient Query Reformulation in Peer-Data Management Systems.* Paper presented at the SIGMOD.

TopicMap. *XML Topic Maps (XTM)* 1.0 http://www.topicmaps.org/xtm/

UDDI. *Universal description, discovery and integration.* http://www.uddi.org

Vitter, J. S., & Wang, M. (1999). *Approximate computation of multidimensional aggregates of sparse data using wavelets.* Paper presented at the ACM SIGMOD.

Vitter, J. S., Wang, M., & Iyer, B. (1998). *Data Cube Approximation and Histograms via Wavelets.* Paper presented at the 7th CIKM.

W3C. Semantic Web. http://www.w3.org/2001/sw/.

Zhao, H., & Ram, S. (2002). *Applying classification techniques in semantic integration of heterogeneous data sources.* Paper presented at the Eighth Americas Conference on Information Systems, Dallas, TX.

Zhao, H., & Ram, S. (2004). Clustering schema elements for semantic integration of heterogeneous data sources. *Journal of Database Management, 15*(4), 88-106.

This work was previously published in Journal of Database Management, Vol. 18, Issue 1, edited by K. Siau, pp. 43-68, copyright 2007 by IGI Publishing, formerly known as Idea Group Publishing (an imprint of IGI Global).

Chapter XI
Visualizing Multi Dimensional Data

César García-Osorio
University of Burgos, Spain

Colin Fyfe
The University of Paisley, UK

ABSTRACT

This chapter gives a survey of some existing methods for visualizing multi dimensional data, that is, data with more than three dimensions. To keep the size of the chapter reasonably small, we have limited the methods presented by restricting ourselves to numerical data. We start with a brief history of the field and a study of several taxonomies; then we propose our own taxonomy and use it to structure the rest of the chapter. Throughout the chapter, the iris data set is used to illustrate most of the methods since this is a data set with which many readers will be familiar. We end with a list of freely available software and a table that gives a quick reference for the bibliography of the methods presented.

INTRODUCTION

The advent of the personal computer has provided mankind with enormous benefits: we have access to more information than ever before and have such access virtually 24 hours per day, 7 days per week thanks to the Internet. However, it is in the nature of humankind that we always wish for more: in this case, we have all this data but actually finding information within the data is often an extremely complex task. This chapter will devote itself to this problem. We will restrict ourselves to numeric data: this is the simplest and perhaps most frequent form of data in which we seek information. The numeric data will often be multi dimensional: we might envisage information about an individual consisting of height, weight, bank balance, and so on, so that each of these fields constitutes one dimension of a long description of the individual. Thus, if we have 10 fields, we have a 10-dimensional vector describing each individual. The task then might be to identify groups of individuals, all of whom share some common characteristic. For example, it is known that tall people tend to earn more than their shorter brethren (a fact which causes some of us some disquiet). In order to ascertain this fact, we must have a way of identifying structure across dimension boundaries. This chapter will investigate methods for performing such identifications in a semi-automated manner.

We state semi-automated since we believe that the computer and the human both have roles to play in identifying structure: the computer is very good at handling large volumes of data and manipulating such data in an automatic manner; but humans are very good at pattern identification much better than computers (consider how face recognition systems have failed to live up to our expectations, even now). Therefore, we envisage a partnership between the human and the computer software with each performing the role to which they are best suited. The computer software will manipulate the multi dimensional data and present it to the human in a way which facilitates the human's pattern matching. An example of this is Exploratory Projection Pursuit (see later) in which the high-dimensional data is projected onto a two dimensional subspace in such a way that the structure of the data (for example, clusters) is most easily identified by the human eye. Another example is the use of Andrews' Curves in which each data point is represented by a curve. A human can run an eye along a set of curves (representing the members of the data set) and identify particular regions of the curve which are optimal for identifying clusters in the data set.

However, interestingly, several of the methods which we use to find structure (i.e., the computer software part of the partnership) are based on neural networks, the network of neurons which we have in our brains. Does this suggest that humans might be able to dispense with the computer soft-

ware and perform the whole task themselves? It is a nice thought but common experience suggests that it is not so; we require intelligent software to help us find structure in multi dimensional data sets.

HISTORY

Let us see first a quick review of the history of visualization techniques. The roots of information visualization as a practical field can be established in the works of Tukey (1977), Bertin (1981, 1983), and Tufte (1983) who focused on 2D and 3D visualization and produced general rules for the plane, colour composition, and attribute mapping, among others. The use of the attributes of a database as dimensions was the rationale behind the study of the multi dimensional techniques. The contents of this chapter can be classified into this last category. However, the study of multivariate visualization began some centuries before; following Wong and Bergeron (1997), the evolution of the field can be divided into four periods:

1. **The searching stage (from 1782 to 1976):** Characterized by relatively small sized data and tools for data visualization that usually consisted of colour pencils and graph paper.
2. **The awakening stage (from 1977 to 1985):** Two and three dimensional spatial data were the most common data types being studied, although multivariate data started gaining more attention.
3. **The discovery stage (from 1986 to 1991):** The limited availability of high speed graphics hardware during the previous stage was gradually conquered. Most of the visualization methods presented in this chapter were developed in this period.
4. **The elaboration and assessment stage (from 1992 to present):** This period has been a retrenchment in the development of

new visualization techniques. Some of the most recently developed tools are elaborations of work done in previous stages.

In this chapter, we will focus on visualization techniques for numerical data, when the number of attributes to represent is higher than three. The data visualization field includes also visualization of non-numerical data, hierarchical and graph relations, and time series and temporal data. A full review of the entire field is beyond the scope of this chapter. A general overview can be found in Wong and Bergeron (1997); Ferreira de Oliveira and Levkowitz (2003); and Keim (1997, 2002). Nevertheless, we start with a short description of some taxonomies of visualization methods, and then we present our own vision of the field that we have used to structure the remainder of the chapter. After that, we explain in detail each class in our classification emphasizing some of the more significant visualization methods belonging to that class. We will finish by giving a list of some of the software tools for data visualization freely available on the Internet.

TAXONOMIES OF VISUALIZATION METHODS

There is no universal consensus on the best taxonomy. In the following subsections, we present two of the more elaborate ones. As well, we give our own vision of the field, a taxonomy use to organize this chapter.

Taxonomy of Techniques by Shneiderman

In addition to the visual information seeking mantra—"Overview first, zoom and filter, then details-on-demand—Shneiderman (1996) propounded a task by data type taxonomy of information visualizations. The seven tasks are:

- **Overview:** Gain an overview of the entire collection.
- **Zoom:** Zoom in on items of interest allowing a more detailed view.
- **Filter:** Filter out uninteresting items reducing the size of search.
- **Details-on-demand:** Select an item or group and get details when needed.
- **Relate:** View relationships among items
- **History:** Keep a history of actions to support undo, replay, and progressive refinement allowing a mistake to be undone, or a series of steps to be replayed.
- **Extract:** Allow extraction of subcollections and saving, printing, or dragging to another application.

The seven data types considered are:

- **1-dimensional:** Linear data types include textual documents, program source code, and lists of names in alphabetical order.
- **2-dimensional:** Planar or map data include geographic maps, floor plans, or newspaper layouts.
- **3-dimensional:** Real-world objects such as molecules, the human body, and buildings. The user must cope with understanding their position and orientation when viewing the objects.
- **Multi dimensional:** Items with n attributes become points in a n-dimensional space.
- **Temporal:** This data type is different from the 1-dimensional data type because now the items have a start and finish time and items may overlap.
- **Tree:** Collections of items, where each item has a link to one parent item (except the root). Items and the links between parent and children can have multiple attributes.
- **Network:** The items are linked to an arbitrary number of other items and the relationships among items cannot be captured with a tree structure.

Taxonomies of Techniques by Keim

Keim and Kriegel (1996) categorize the visualization techniques into the following:

- **Geometric techniques.** The aim of those techniques is to find "interesting" transformations of multi dimensional data sets. This class includes Scatterplot Matrix (Becker & Cleveland, 1987; Chambers, Cleveland, Keliner & Tukey, 1983), Principal Component Analysis (Jolliffe, 1986), Factor Analysis (Lewis-Beck, 1994), Multi dimensional Scaling (Kruskal & Wish, 1978; Shepard, Romney, & Nerlove, 1972; Torgerson, 1952), Projection Pursuit (Huber, 1985), Parallel Coordinates (Inselberg, 1985; Inselberg, Chen, Shieh, & Lee, 1990), and so forth.

- **Icon-based techniques.** Every multi dimensional item is mapped onto an icon or glyph. The data values determine the geometric and/or colour characteristics of the glyph. The amount of observations that it is possible to visualize at the same time is quite limited, and depends on the characteristics of the icon. Examples are Chernoff Faces (Chernoff, 1973), Star Icons (Ward, 1994), Colour Icons (Levkowitz, 1991), and Stick Figure Icons (Grinstein, Pickett, & Williams,

1989). Later, we will give more details about the first of these methods.

- **Pixel-oriented techniques.** In these techniques, the data attributes are mapped onto pixels; the colour of each pixel depends on the values of the attributes. An important aspect is the spatial distribution of the pixels (Keim & Kriegel, 1994); some examples are the recursive pattern technique, the circle segments technique, and the spiral technique.

- **Hierarchical techniques.** The multi dimensional space is divided hierarchically in subspaces. Examples are Dimensional Stacking (LeBlanc, Ward, & Wittels, 1990) and Worlds-within-Worlds (Behsers & Feiner, 1990).

- **Graph-based techniques.** These are specialized techniques for presenting large graphs using specific layout algorithms, query languages, and abstraction techniques. For example, the Treemap (Shneiderman, 1992), a method that recursively subdivides a 2-D rectangular space to visualize large hierarchies.

The previous classification is extended by Keim (2000) with another two orthogonal criteria: the distortion technique and the interaction

Figure 1. The classification of information visualization techniques (Adapted from Keim, 2000)

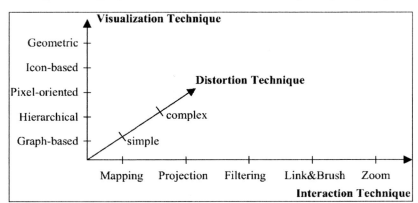

Figure 2. The classification of information visualization techniques (Adapted from Keim, 2002)

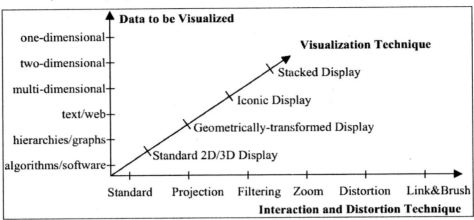

technique. The first is to show portions of the data with different levels of detail. The second allows the user to directly interact with the visualization. The three criteria are shown as orthogonal axes of a classification system as we can see in Figure 1. It is worth noting that the distortion techniques alone deserve their own taxonomy that has been analyzed by Leung and Apperley (1994).

In Keim (2002), the interaction and distortion criteria are combined in one axis, the data to be visualized is added as a new criteria, and the visualization techniques are presented slightly changed as we can see in Figure 2. The methods proposed in this chapter fall into the geometric techniques category of Keim (2000), or similarly in the geometrically transformed display category used in Keim (2002).

Our Own Taxonomy

We have grouped the visualization methods presented in this chapter, all of them to deal with numerical data,[1] according to the following classification:

- **Linear projection methods.** A lower dimensional representation of the data is obtained using a linear projection of the multi dimensional space. Some examples

are Principal Component Analysis (PCA) (Hotelling, 1933; Jolliffe, 1986), Exploratory Projection Pursuit (EPP) (Friedman, 1987; Friedman & Tukey, 1974; Jones & Sibson, 1987), and Scatterplot Matrix (Becker & Cleveland, 1987; Chambers et al., 1983).

- **Topology preservation methods.** A nonlinear mapping between the multi dimensional space and the lower-dimensional representation is used trying to maintain the topology of the multi dimensional space: Sammon mapping (Sammon, 1969), Curvilinear Component Analysis (CCA) (Demartines & Hérault, 1997), Self Organizing Maps (SOM) (Kohonen, 1992, 2001), and Spring Models (Chalmers, 1996; Morrison & Chalmers, 2003).

- **Multi dimensional representations.** This time there is no dimension reduction; instead of that, all the values of the coordinates are used to obtain the graphical representation; examples are Chernoff Faces (Chernoff, 1973), Parallel Coordinates (Inselberg & Dimsdale, 1990; Wegman, 1991), Andrews' Curves (Andrews, 1972), and Multi dimensional Stacking (LeBlanc et al., 1990).

- **Grand tour methods.** Instead of one static representation of the data, a sequence of projections is used to study the structure of

Figure 3. The Gaussian distribution and its higher order moments

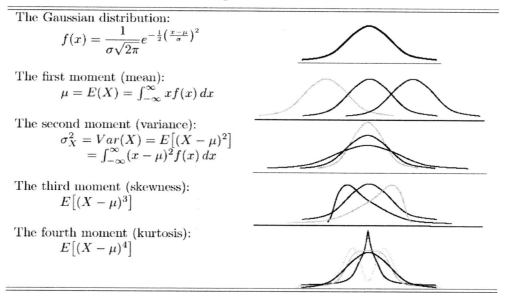

The Gaussian distribution:
$$f(x) = \frac{1}{\sigma\sqrt{2\pi}}e^{-\frac{1}{2}\left(\frac{x-\mu}{\sigma}\right)^2}$$

The first moment (mean):
$$\mu = E(X) = \int_{-\infty}^{\infty} xf(x)\,dx$$

The second moment (variance):
$$\sigma_X^2 = Var(X) = E\left[(X-\mu)^2\right]$$
$$= \int_{-\infty}^{\infty}(x-\mu)^2 f(x)\,dx$$

The third moment (skewness):
$$E\left[(X-\mu)^3\right]$$

The fourth moment (kurtosis):
$$E\left[(X-\mu)^4\right]$$

the data. Some of the algorithms (Asimov, 1985; Wegman, 1990; Wegman & Solka, 2002) used to obtain such a sequence are the Asimov-Buja winding algorithm, the random curve algorithm, the fractal curve algorithm, and the pseudo grand tour.

LINEAR PROJECTION METHODS

Sometimes, it is possible to see the structure of a multi dimensional data set just by changing the basis of the considered space. However, the decision as to what basis to use would require a fore-knowledge of the pattern one wants to identify. One possible solution to this problem is the use of the directions which explain most of the variance in the data set; such directions are called the *principal component directions* of the data set. The rationale for this is that without any information about the distribution of the data set, the standard assumption is to suppose that the data set follows a Gaussian distribution

(see Figure 3), and in Gaussian distributions the amount of information is directly proportional to the variance. Even if the distribution is not Gaussian, there is liable to be more information in high variance projections than in a low variance projection. The use of the principal component projections to analyze a data set is known as Principal Component Analysis (Hotelling, 1933; Jolliffe, 1986). When the distribution is not a Gaussian, instead of maximizing the variance, we can try to maximize other moments of the distribution[2] (Table 3). This last approach gives rise to a set of techniques known as Exploratory Projection Pursuit (Friedman, 1987; Friedman & Tukey, 1974; Jones & Sibson, 1987). In the following sections, we give more details about these two techniques.

Principal Component Analysis

For some data sets, the projection onto the principal components (or PCs) lets us visualize clearly their structure. In this way, we can try to discover

Figure 4. An example in which the projection onto the PC directions reveals for us structure in the dataset (in this case, the existence of two clusters)

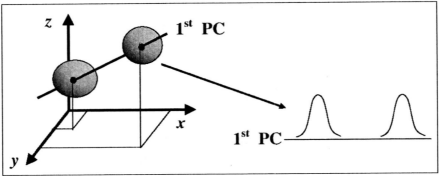

the structure of a multi dimensional data set by projecting it onto the subspace defined by the first principal components (usually the first two or three). The projection onto the first principal component explains most of the variance of the data; then the projection onto the second principal component, which is orthogonal to the first one, explains the next most, and so on. In Figure 4, we can see an example of this. We have a data set with three variables (in this case the dimensionality of the data set makes a graphical representation possible, but with greater than three dimensions, this is not the case), and we can discover the existence of the clusters when we project it onto the one dimensional space of the first principal component (actually, in this case, we can see the histogram of the projection).

The principal components represent the most important linear characteristics of the data. The aim of PCA is the identification of the dependency

Figure 5. The first two principal components of the iris data set

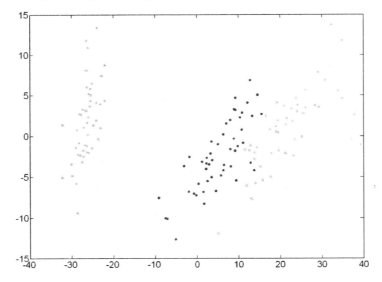

existing between the variables; see Jolliffe (1986) for an extensive treatment of this technique. The higher the correlation between the variables and the fewer the number of the independent variables, the more the dimensionality can be reduced.

Using PCA a multi dimensional data set can be represented by a few principal components (from the point of view of graphical representation, the ideal number is two or three), so PCA can be considered as much a feature extraction technique as a data compression technique. Figure 5 shows the first two principal components of a four dimensional data set, the well known iris data set (Ripley, 1996).

How to Calculate the Principal Components

There exist several algebraic methods to calculate the principal components of a data set: the power method, Householder transformation and Lanczos method, and also neural networks algorithms; a good review of these is presented by Diamantaras and Kung (1996). The most famous of the neural network methods is Oja's algorithm (Oja, 1982, 1989; Oja, Ogawa, & Wangviwattana, 1992a, 1992b); here we are interested in a negative feed-

back implementation of PCA defined by (1)-(3) (Fyfe, 1993, 1995a). Let us have an N-dimensional input vector, $\mathbf{x}$, and an M-dimensional output vector, $\mathbf{y}$, with w_{ij} as the weight linking the jth input to the ith output. The learning rate η is a small value which will be annealed to zero over the course of training the network. The activation passing from input to output through the weights is described by (1). The activation is then fed back though the weights from the outputs and the error, $\mathbf{e}$, calculated for each input dimension. Finally the weights are updated using simple Hebbian learning (see later).

$$y_i = \sum_{j=1}^{N} w_{ij} x_j, \forall i \qquad (1)$$

$$e_j = x_j - \sum_{i=1}^{M} w_{ij} y_i \qquad (2)$$

$$\Delta w_{ij} = \eta e_j y_i \qquad (3)$$

Several variations of this network have been used to perform clustering with topology preservation (Fyfe, 1995b), to perform Factor Analysis (Charles & Fyfe, 1998; Fyfe & Charles, 1999), and

Figure 6. An example in which the projection onto the first PC does not give information about the structure of the data set

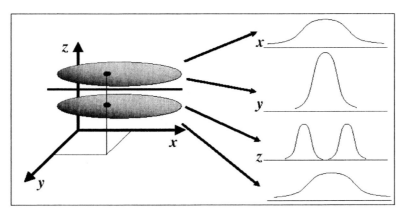

to perform Exploratory Projection Pursuit (Fyfe, 1997; Fyfe & Baddeley, 1995).

Exploratory Projection Pursuit

Sometimes the projection onto the principal components does not give any clue about the structure of the data set; in Figure 6, we can see that this time the projection onto the first principal component direction (that is approximately the x-axis direction) does not give any information about the structure in the data set. Something similar happens with the projection onto the y axis. On the contrary, the projection onto the z-axis reveals the existence of two clusters to us. In circumstances like this, we can use Exploratory Projection Pursuit.

Exploratory Projection Pursuit (Friedman, 1987) is a generic name for the set of techniques designed to identify structure in multidimension data sets. In such data sets, structure often exists across data field boundaries, and one way to reveal such structure is to project the data onto a lower dimension space and then look for structure in this lower dimension projection by eye. However, we need to determine what constitutes the best subspace onto which the data should be projected.

Exploratory Projection Pursuit is a technique for exploring multi dimensional spaces. As we have seen, PCA searches for filters in a data set which maximize the variance of the projections of the data onto these filters. EPP can be thought of as an extension of PCA since it is a technique for finding projections which maximise some statistic over the data set. For example, when we wish to identify clusters in a data set, their presence might be revealed by a negative fourth moment (kurtosis) in the projections. EPP has also been implemented using artificial neural networks (Fyfe, 1997; Fyfe & Baddeley, 1995).

As noted by Diaconis and Freedman (1984), the typical projection of multi dimensional data will have a Gaussian distribution, and so little

structure will be evident. This has led researchers to suggest that what they should be looking for is a projection which gives a distribution as different from a Gaussian as possible. Thus we typically define an index of "interestingness" in terms of how far the resultant projection is from a Gaussian distribution. Since the Gaussian distribution is totally determined by its first two moments, we usually sphere the data (make it zero mean and with covariance matrix the identity matrix) so that we have a level playing field to determine departures from Gaussianity. In this section, we will review two methods of performing Exploratory Projection Pursuit with neural algorithms based on the network introduced in the previous section. In García-Osorio and Fyfe (2003), we propose a new method which is a combination of these two and compare the three methods.

The Output Functions EPP Algorithm

Two common measures of deviation from a Gaussian distribution are based on the higher order moments of the distribution (see Figure 3). Skewness is based on the normalized third moment of the distribution and basically measures if the distribution is symmetrical. Kurtosis is based on the normalized fourth moment of the distribution and measures the heaviness of the tails of a distribution. A bimodal distribution will often also have a negative kurtosis, and therefore, kurtosis can signal that a particular distribution shows evidence of clustering. Whilst these measures have their drawbacks as measures of deviation from normality (particularly their sensitivity to outliers), their simplicity makes them ideal for explanatory purposes.

The only difference between the PCA network and the EPP network is that a function of the output activations is calculated and used in the simple Hebbian learning procedure. We have for N dimensional input data and M output neurons,

$$y_i = \sum_{j=1}^{N} w_{ij} x_j \qquad (4)$$

$$e_j = x_j - \sum_{i=1}^{M} w_{ij} y_i \qquad (5)$$

$$r_i = f\left(\sum_{j=1}^{N} w_{ij} x_j\right) = f(y_i) \qquad (6)$$

$$\Delta w_{ij} = \eta_t r_i e_j \qquad (7)$$

$$= \eta_t f\left(\sum_{k=1}^{N} w_{ik} x_k\right) \left\{ x_j - \sum_{l=1}^{M} w_{lj} \sum_{p=1}^{N} w_{lp} x_p \right\} \qquad (8)$$

where r_i is the value of the function $f(.)$ on the ith output neuron. Thus (8) may be written in matrix form as:

$$\Delta \mathbf{W}(t) = \eta(t)[\mathbf{I} - \mathbf{W}(t)\mathbf{W}^T(t)]\mathbf{x}(t) f(\mathbf{x}^T(t)\mathbf{W}(t)) \qquad (9)$$

where t is an index of time and $\mathbf{I}$ is the identity matrix.

Following Karkunen and Joutsensalo (1994), we can derive (9) as an approximation to the maximization of a function of the weights $J(\mathbf{W}) = \sum_{i=1}^{M} E(g[\mathbf{x}^T \mathbf{w}_i]|\mathbf{w}_i)$ with $E(.)$ the expectation operator and $\mathbf{w}_i$ the weight vector into the ith output neuron.

We must ensure that the optimal solution is kept bounded; otherwise there is nothing to stop the weights from growing without bound. Formally,

$$\text{let } J(\mathbf{W}) = \sum_{i=1}^{M} E(g[\mathbf{x}^T \mathbf{w}_i]|\mathbf{w}_i)$$
$$+ \frac{1}{2}\sum_{i=1}^{M}\sum_{j=1}^{M} \lambda_{ij}[\mathbf{w}_i^T \mathbf{w}_j - a_{ij}] \qquad (10)$$

where the last term enforces the constraints $\mathbf{w}_i^T \mathbf{w}_j - a_{ij}$ using the Lagrange multipliers λ_{ij}. As usual, we differentiate this equation with respect to the weights and with respect to the Lagrange multipliers. This yields respectively, at a stationary point,

$$\frac{\partial J(\mathbf{W})}{\partial \mathbf{W}} = E(\mathbf{x}g'(\mathbf{x}^T\mathbf{W})|\mathbf{W}) + \mathbf{W}\boldsymbol{\Lambda} = 0 \text{ and} \qquad (11)$$

$$\mathbf{W}^T\mathbf{W} = \mathbf{A} \qquad (12)$$

where $g'(\mathbf{x}^T\mathbf{W})$ is the elementwise derivative of $g'(\mathbf{x}^T\mathbf{W})$ with respect to $\mathbf{W}$, $\mathbf{A}$ is the matrix of parameters a_{ij} (often the identity matrix) and $\boldsymbol{\Lambda}$ is the matrix of Lagrange multipliers. Equations (11) and (12) define the optimal points of the process. Premultiplying (11) by $\mathbf{W}^T$ and inserting (12), we get,

$$\boldsymbol{\Lambda} = -\mathbf{A}^{-1}\mathbf{W}^T E(\mathbf{x}g'(\mathbf{x}^T\mathbf{W})|\mathbf{W})$$

and using this value and reinserting this optimal value of $\boldsymbol{\Lambda}$ into (11) yields the equation,

$$\frac{\partial J(\mathbf{W})}{\partial \mathbf{W}} = [\mathbf{I} - \mathbf{W}\mathbf{A}^{-1}\mathbf{W}^T]E(\mathbf{x}g'(\mathbf{x}^T\mathbf{W})|\mathbf{W}) \qquad (13)$$

We wish to use an instantaneous version of this in a gradient ascent algorithm,

$$\Delta \mathbf{W} \propto \frac{\partial J(\mathbf{W})}{\partial \mathbf{W}}$$

to yield

$$\Delta \mathbf{W} = \mu[\mathbf{I} - \mathbf{W}\mathbf{A}^{-1}\mathbf{W}^T]\mathbf{x}g'(\mathbf{x}^T\mathbf{W}) \qquad (14)$$

We will be interested in the special case where the $\mathbf{W}$ values form an orthonormal basis of the data space and so $\mathbf{A} = \mathbf{I}$, the identity matrix. Therefore, we can equate (14) with (9).

Summing up, the network operation is

Feedforward:

$$y_i = \sum_{j=1}^{N} w_{ij} x_j, \forall i$$

Feedback:

$$e_j = x_j - \sum_{i=1}^{M} w_{ij} y_i$$

Weight change:

$$\Delta w_{ij} = \eta f(y_i) e_j$$

where the function $f(.)$ is determined by the function $g(.)$ which we wish to maximize.

The Maximum Likelihood EPP Algorithm

Various researchers (Karhunen & Joutsensalo, 1994; Xu, 1993) have shown that the learning rules (1)-(3) can be derived as an approximation to the best linear compression of the data. Thus we may start with the cost function,

$$J = 1^T E\{(\mathbf{x} - \mathbf{W}\mathbf{y})^2\} \tag{15}$$

which we minimize to get (3).

We may show that the minimization of J is equivalent to minimizing the negative log probabilities of the residual, **e**, if **e** is Gaussian and thus is equal to maximizing the probabilities of the residual (Bishop, 1995). Let the probability of the residuals $p(\mathbf{e}) = (1/Z)\exp(-\mathbf{e}^2)$ where Z is a normalization term. Then we can denote a general cost function associated with the network as,

$$J = -\log p(\mathbf{e}) = (\mathbf{e})^2 + K \tag{16}$$

Intuitively, J gives a measure as to how probable the residual is under the current model parameters. Since the only parameters which can be

changed are the weights which both feed forward and backward, these are the parameters which we must adapt in order to make the residuals more likely under the model. Therefore, performing gradient descent on J we have,

$$\Delta \mathbf{W} \propto -\frac{\partial J}{\partial \mathbf{W}} = -\frac{\partial J}{\partial \mathbf{e}}\frac{\partial \mathbf{e}}{\partial \mathbf{W}} \approx \mathbf{y}(2\mathbf{e})^T \tag{17}$$

where we have discarded a relatively unimportant term (Karhunen & Joutsensalo, 1994).

An extension of the above was considered by Corchado and Fyfe (2002) and Fyfe and McDonald (2002) with a more general cost function:

$$J = f_1(e) = f_1(\mathbf{x} - \mathbf{W}\mathbf{y}) \tag{18}$$

Let us now consider the residual after the feedback to have probability density function:

$$p(\mathbf{e}) = \frac{1}{Z}\exp(-|\mathbf{e}|^p) \tag{19}$$

Then we can denote a general cost function associated with this network as,

$$J = -\log p(\mathbf{e}) = (\mathbf{e})^p + K \tag{20}$$

where K is a constant. Therefore performing gradient descent on J we have,

$$\Delta \mathbf{W} \propto -\frac{\partial J}{\partial \mathbf{W}} = -\frac{\partial J}{\partial \mathbf{e}}\frac{\partial \mathbf{e}}{\partial \mathbf{W}} \approx p\mathbf{y}\big(|\mathbf{e}|^{p-1}\,\text{sign}(\mathbf{e})\big)^T \tag{21}$$

We would expect that for leptokurtotic residuals (more kurtotic than a Gaussian distribution), values of $p < 2$ would be appropriate, while platykurtotic residuals (less kurtotic than a Gaussian), values of $p > 2$ would be appropriate. It has been shown (Hyvarinen, Karhunen, & Oja, 2001) that it is less important to get exactly the correct distribution when searching for a specific source than it is to get an approximately correct distribution; that is, all super-Gaussian signals can be retrieved using a generic leptokurtotic distribution and all sub-Gaussian signals can be retrieved using a generic platykurtotic distribution.

Therefore, the network operation is:

Feedforward:

$$y_i = \sum_{j=1}^{N} w_{ij} x_j, \forall i$$

Feedback:

$$e_j = x_j - \sum_{i=1}^{M} w_{ij} y_i$$

Weight change:

$$\Delta w_{ij} = \eta y_i \operatorname{sign}(e_j) |e_j|^{p-1}$$

where the value of p is determined by the type of structure we seek.

Now the nature and quantization of the interestingness is in terms of how likely the residuals are under a particular model of the probability density function of the residual. As with standard EPP, we also sphere the data before applying the learning method to the sphered data.

Scatter Plot Matrix

This technique is one of the oldest and most popular methods for projecting multi dimensional data (Becker, Cleveland, & Wilks, 1987; Cleveland & McGill, 1988). With this technique, instead of having only one representation of the data, we can view the data from different perspectives. In the scatterplot matrix, which is also named the Draftman's display of axes, if we have an N-dimensional data set, the scatter plot matrix will have N rows and N columns, and the ith row and jth column of this matrix is a plot of the data projected onto the i and j axes, showing the relations between each pair of variables and the nature of these relationships (direct or indirect, linear or nonlinear, degree of relationship, etc.).

The presence of outliers and clusters in the data can be identified as well. Figure 7 shows the scatterplot matrix for the iris data set.

The basic idea of the scatter plot matrix can be presented with a few variations:

1. The diagonal plot is simply a 45 degree line, so an alternative to that is to plot the univariate histogram (as in Figure 7) or to print the variable label.
2. Since the scatter plot matrix is symmetrical, it is possible to omit the plots below the diagonal, or use the upper portion to print the correlation coefficients.
3. It can be helpful to overlay some type of fitted curve on the scatter plots.
4. As proposed by Becker and Cleveland (1987), we can use the scatter plot matrix with interaction techniques such as brushing and linking. Below we go a bit more deeply into these techniques.

The main drawback of the scatter plot matrix is that as we increase the dimensionality, we leave less screen space for each projection. Ware and Beatty (1988) present a technique to lighten this problem by means of the use of colour. Each point is a coloured patch rather than a black point on a white background. We can use three of the dimensions to determine the amount of red, green, and blue that gives the final colour.

Other visualization tools that use some of the ideas in the scatter plot matrix representation are the Hyperbox of Alpern and Carter (1991) and the HyperSlice of Wijk and Leire (1993). The former presents the different orthogonal projections of the data set onto the faces of an N-dimensional box, that is depicted in a 2-dimensional way, instead of onto the cells of a matrix grid. The latter uses the same matrix arrangement but presents slices of scalar functions of many variables instead of orthogonal data projections.

Figure 7. Scatterplot for the iris dataset

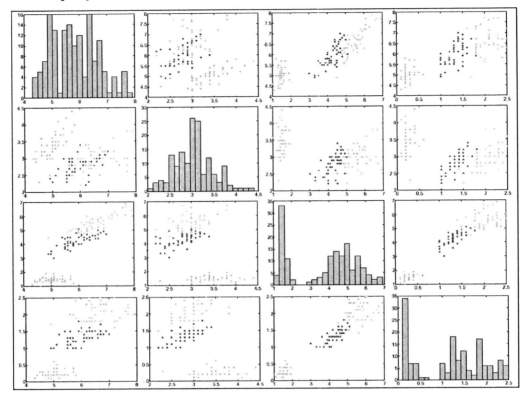

Brushing and Linking

The brushing technique has its origin as an interaction technique used in combination with scatterplot matrices. Becker and Cleveland (1987, p. 128) state:

The central object in brushing is the *brush*, a rectangle that is superimposed on the screen .... The data analyst moves the brush to different positions on the scatterplot matrix by moving a mouse. There are four basic *brushing operations*—highlight, shadow highlight, delete, and label. Each operation is carried out in one of three *paint modes*—transient, lasting, and undo. At any time, the data analyst can stop the brushing and change one or more of the features—the shape of the brush, the operation, or the paint mode—and then resume the brushing. The brushing meth-

odology provides a medium within which a data analyst can invent data analytic methods, which we call *brush techniques*.

Basically, with brushing operations, we change some of the attributes (e.g., colour, glyph, visibility, labeling) of the points or lines we use to represent the data. The idea is to isolate clusters or other interesting subsets of a data set by, for example, painting that subset with a colour. Then the linking lets us identify the selected points in all the other projection panels in the scatterplot matrix, since the changed attribute changes at the same time in all views of the data. In this way, the highlight operation changes the colour or glyph of the points within the current panel in all the other panels, the shadow highlight changes the visibility in the other panels, the delete operation simply eliminates the points within the brush, and the label shows the associated label, if any, for the brushed points. In transient mode, only the points under the brush are affected by the corresponding operation. In lasting mode, points inside the brush remain affected even after the brush no longer covers them. Finally, the undo mode is used to restore the attribute value changed by a previous brushing operation.

Although brushing and linking were proposed originally in the context of scatterplot matrices, these techniques can be used with any kind of graphical representation. With the use of the same attribute value for the data points in all representations, we can track coherent clusters or subsets of the data through different representations. With an animation, we can follow the cluster of subsets of the data through the time evolution of the animation.

TOPOLOGY PRESERVATION METHODS

The techniques shown in the previous section are not adequate to reveal nonlinear structures, such as structures consisting of arbitrarily shaped clusters or curved manifolds, since they describe the data in terms of a linear subspace.

So, we need techniques that project the data in higher dimensions to lower dimensions (2 or 3 dimensions) without losing the characteristics of the local topology of the data. One way to achieve topology preservation is to preserve the distances between the points in the original data set, which means that:

1. The projections of two close points should remain close (conversely, the projection of distant points should be distant).
2. If the projections of two points are close, it is because, in the original multi dimensional space, the two points were close (if the projections are distant, the original points were distant).

Techniques such as multi dimensional scaling (Kruskal & Wish, 1978; Shepard et al., 1972; Torgerson, 1952) achieve both of the previous properties. Techniques such as the self organizing map (Kohonen, 1992, 2001) only achieve the second property. In the following we give details of some of the topology preservation techniques.

Multi dimensional Scaling

Every time we view a world map, we are seeing the result of applying a process of multi dimensional scaling (Kruskal & Wish, 1978; Shepard et al., 1972; Torgerson, 1952). Basically, in the world map, we have a 2-dimensional representation of the distance between cities that are on the surface of a sphere, and hence in a 3-dimensional space.

The key idea of MDS is to give a visual representation of the distances between a set of points in a multi dimensional space. We want to maintain as much as possible the distances between the points in the multi dimensional space.[3] To measure how closely we have reproduced the distances, a stress function is used, whose general form is:

$$S = \sum_{ij} a_{ij} (\delta_{ij} - d_{ij})^2 \qquad (22)$$

where δ_{ij} is the distance between two data points $\mathbf{x}_i$ and $\mathbf{x}_j$, d_{ij} is the distance between the corresponding projected points $\mathbf{y}_i$ and $\mathbf{y}_j$, and a_{ij} is a scale or weighting factor. Taking:

$$a_{ij} = \left(\sum_{ij} d_{ij}^2 \right)^{-1}$$

gives a classical stress function, known as Kruskal's stress (Kruskal & Wish, 1978). We want to minimize the stress function. There exists multiple variants of MDS that use slightly different cost functions and optimization algorithms. In the following subsection, we give details of one of these.

Sammon Mapping

Sammon mapping (Sammon, 1969) performs MDS by using as a weighting factor:

$$a_{ij} = \left(\delta_{ij} \sum_{ij} \delta_{ij} \right)^{-1}$$

that gives the stress function,

$$S = \frac{1}{\sum_{ij} \delta_{ij}} \sum_{ij} \frac{(\delta_{ij} - d_{ij})^2}{\delta_{ij}} \qquad (23)$$

which emphasizes the preservation of the local distances. One possible way to obtain a configuration of projected points that minimizes this stress function is to employ a gradient descent algorithm:

3. Initialize the Sammon mapping with random coordinates (2D).

4. Calculate the relative pair wise error of each data point between spaces.
5. Calculate a gradient which shows the direction to minimize the error.
6. Move the data points in the Sammon mapping according to the gradient.
7. Repeat steps 2-4 until the error is below a given limit, or no improvement is seen.

This algorithm has some disadvantages. First, it lacks generalization, which means that if we want to add new points, we need to recalculate the projection. Second, a local minimum in the error surface could be reached, therefore we may need to try a significant number of experiments with different random initializations. Finally, it is very computationally intensive: with N points, in each iteration $N(N-1)/2$, distances must be calculated, resulting in $O(N^2)$ complexity per iteration. However the problem of generalization can be alleviated using neural network implementations of the Sammon mapping; de Ridder and Duin (1997) present a comparison. In Figure 8, we can see the result of apply this algorithm to the iris data set.

Figure 8. Sammon projection of the iris data set

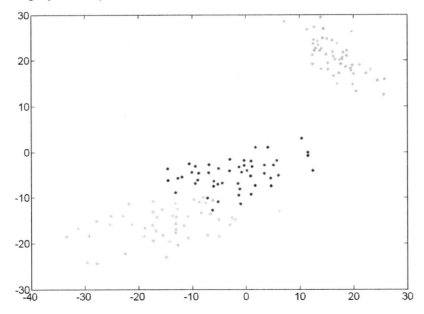

Spring Models

Within the class of MDS algorithms, one of the simpler are the spring model algorithms. These are based on the work of Fruchterman and Reingold (1991) who simulate the forces within a set of springs that interconnect a set of rings, until equilibrium is obtained. In their original work, the rings were associated with nodes of a graph and the springs with the arcs. The equilibrium of the system gives a configuration with certain aesthetic characteristics (for example, the same length for all the arcs). In the context of MDS, it is considered that the springs are connecting every pair of points of a data set; the repulsion or attraction spring forces are proportional to the difference between the multi dimensional distances and the bidimensional distances of the layout we want to obtain. The combination of forces applied over a point is used to calculate its velocity, and the velocity is used to obtain its position. At the equilibrium of the system, the projection maintains the similarities and dissimilarities of the multi dimensional data set. Since it is necessary to calculate the forces for every pair of points and the number of iterations is proportional to N, the number of data points, the simulation gives an algorithm of complexity $O(N^3)$.

Chalmers (1996) presents a way to obtain a good approximation to the final configuration with less complexity. The key idea of the algorithm is the reduction of the amount of forces that it is necessary to calculate for each point. Every point has two associated sets. One is ordered and maintains the closest neighbours found so far. The second is recalculated at every iteration by randomly sampling the full data set; if one of the points in the second set is closer than one of the points in the first; the former is substituted by the latter. In this way, with each iteration, the neighbour set will be more representative of the most similar points. For each point, only the forces applied by the springs associated with points in these two sets are considered. Since the sizes of these sets are constant, the complexity of the algorithm is reduced to $O(N^2)$ and the quality of the obtained layout is still good.

Morrison, Ross, and Chalmers (2002, 2003) introduce an additional improvement. In a first phase, only a set S of sqrt(N) points randomly sampled from the original data set is considered, and the full simulation is performed. The complexity of this step is O(sqrt(N)·sqrt(N)), that is, $O(N)$. Now, for every of the N−sqrt(N) remaining elements, the closest point within the sqrt(N) point used in the first step is found; that closest point is called the "parent" point. The point is located around the parent point taking also into account the forces of a sample of points over S. As a final stage of fine-tuning, a constant number of iterations of the simulation over the full data set are executed. The final complexity of the process is $O(N$·sqrt(N)).

A last improvement is proposed by Morrison and Chalmers (2003). This time the search for the parent elements is performed using distance discretization and a subset of selected points (pivots). The idea is to precalculate the distances to the pivots, and use those distances and the triangle inequality to reduce the distance calculations. With this strategy, it is possible to reduce the complexity down to $O(N^{5/4})$.

Self Organizing Map

Contrary to the MDS methods, self organizing maps do not preserve distances, but these artificial neural networks are also used for dimensionality reduction, clustering, and visualization. They were first described by Teuvo Kohonen (1995), and so are also known as Kohonen maps.

The SOM has usually a rectangular or hexagonal two dimensional structure of interconnected artificial neurons (see Figure 9). The weights of these neurons can be seen as the coordinates of a vector that lies in the multi dimensional space we want to explore (they are called model vectors, prototype vectors, or centres). The process that organizes the positions of these vectors is an unsupervised competitive learning mechanism that works as follows:

12. Randomly select a training pattern, **x**, from the input data set.
13. Find the neuron, *c*, whose centre is closest to the input pattern[4]; that neuron will be the *winning neuron* or the so called *Best Matching Unit* (BMU) for the pattern.
14. Adjust the centres toward the data vector for the winning neuron and all its neighbours using the following equation:

$$\Delta \mathbf{w}_i = \eta(\mathbf{x} - \mathbf{w}_i)\Lambda(i, c)$$

where η is the learning rate, and Λ is often a monotonically decreasing function of the distance between *i* and *c*, known as the *neighbourhood function*. Normally this function is a Gaussian of a difference of Gaussians (though this is not monotonically decreasing).
15. Repeat steps 1-3 for new inputs until some convergence criterion is reached.

This results in the network learning positions for the centres of its neurons which cover the input space and are determined by the density of the data in the input space.

The computational complexity of the SOM is $O(K^2)$, where *K* is the number of neurons in the grid: each learning step requires $O(K)$ computations, and to achieve a sufficient statistical accuracy, the number of iterations should be at least some multiple of *K*. In some uses of the SOM, the number of neurons is of the order of the number of input samples; in these situations, the computational complexity of the SOM is of the same order of magnitude as in the MDS algorithms.

Once trained, it is possible to use different methods to visualize the SOM structure (Vesanto, 1999). In Figure 10, we can see four different ways to represent a SOM trained using the iris data set (as it is usual with this three clusters data set, one of the clusters is easily identifiable). The U-matrix (unified distance matrix), is perhaps the most popular method of displaying SOMs. The distance between adjacent neurons is calculated and presented with different colourings, darker colours representing larger distances. Light areas represent clusters and dark areas indicate cluster boundaries. The D-matrix can be constructed as an averaged version of the U-matrix, in which the size of each map unit is inversely proportional to the average distance to its neighbours. The similarity colouring is obtained by spreading a colour map on top of the principal component projection of the prototype vectors. Areas with similar colours are close to each other in the input space.

A New Family of Algorithms

Most topology preserving algorithms have concentrated on modifying adaptive clustering rules so the final mapping has an element of topology

Figure 9. Examples of SOM architectures

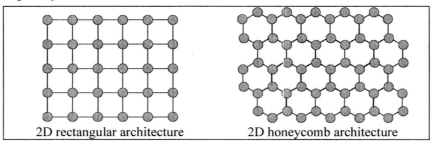

| 2D rectangular architecture | 2D honeycomb architecture |

Figure 10. Examples of SOM visualisations methods

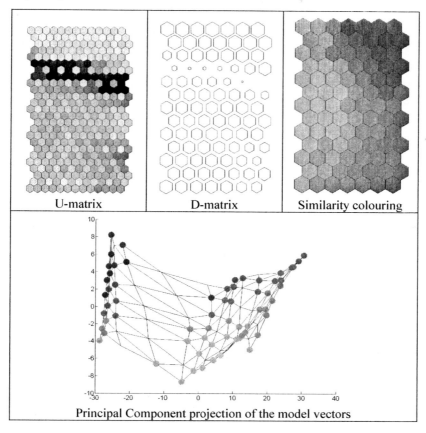

| U-matrix | D-matrix | Similarity colouring |

Principal Component projection of the model vectors

preservation. However, an alternative was suggested by Bishop, Svensén, and Williams (1998) who created a probabilistic model of data analysis based on a mixture of experts. Each expert is represented by a point in latent space, $\mathbf{t}_1, \mathbf{t}_2, \ldots, \mathbf{t}_K$. Each latent point is mapped through a series of basis functions, $\varphi_1(\mathbf{t}_i), \varphi_2(\mathbf{t}_i), \ldots, \varphi_M(\mathbf{t}_i)$, to an intermediate feature space before being mapped linearly to the data space so that each $\mathbf{t}_i \to \mathbf{m}_i$ through $m_i = \sum_{j=1}^{M} w_j \varphi_j(t_i)$ a prototype in data space. The parameters of the model are adjusted to make the data as likely as possible under this model.

We (Fyfe, 2000, 2006) have used this model with a product of experts underlying model and shown that by updating the parameters according to,

$$\Delta_n w_{md} = \eta \sum_{k=1}^{K} \varphi_m(t_k)(x_d^{(n)} - m_d^{(k)}) r_{kn} \qquad (27)$$

where we have used Δ_n to signify the change when the nth data point is presented, η is a learning rate, and $x_d^{(n)}$ denotes the dth dimension of the nth data point. A similar convention is used with the prototypes. r_{kn} is the responsibility that the kth latent point takes for the nth data point and is calculated from,

$$r_{kn} = \frac{\exp(-\gamma d(x_n, m_k))}{\sum_{j=1}^{K} \exp(-\gamma d(x_n, m_j))}. \qquad (28)$$

This was shown to perform a topology preserving mapping of data sets.

Now, while the basic method has a probabilistic underpinning, it may also be seen to be a minimization of the mean square error between the prototypes and the data while allocating responsibilities to the prototypes for the data. It has recently been shown (Zhang, 2000; Zhang, Hsu, & Dayal, 1999) that replacing the mean squared error with an error function based on harmonic averages gives an algorithm for clustering K-means in a manner which solves the problem of local minima for K-means (it is well known that the final converged prototypes for K-means is dependent on the initial conditions of the prototypes). We have applied this algorithm with the above underlying latent space and shown that it too can provide a topology preserving mapping (Fyfe, 2006; Pena & Fyfe, 2005). An example of this mapping on a data set of 118 samples of 18 dimensional data representing the quantity of pigments at various frequencies is shown in Figure 11. To create this diagram, we trained a map and then allocated

the data points to the underlying 2-dimensional latent space using the responsibilities of each latent point for the data point as a measure of how strong it should be in the allocation of the point to latent space. Thus each data point x_n is mapped to $\sum_n r_{kn} \mathbf{t}_n$. We see that the mapping (which was not given the class information) has allocated the points to clusters which in general identify a single type. In Figure 12, we show the results of zooming into the central part of Figure 11: two classes which appeared confounded are actually easy to disambiguate using the responsibilities. This is something which is not possible if we simply quantize to a single latent point.

Other Methods

All the visualization methods presented in this section can also be categorized within the field of manifold learning. That field is rich in techniques; the ones presented above are only some of them. Let us now briefly present some others.

Figure 11. The nine species of algae as represented on a two dimensional latent space

Figure 12. Zooming into the central portion of Figure 11

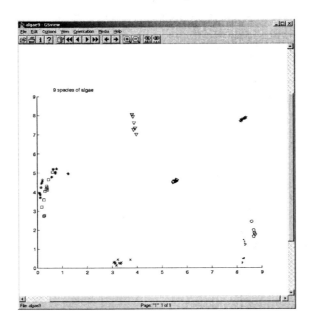

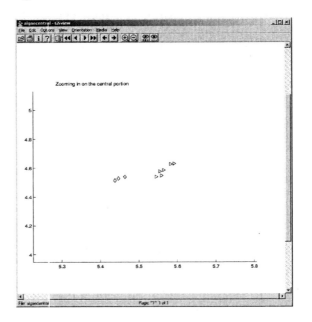

Principal Curves

Principal curves are one of the nonlinear generalizations of principal components. They were first defined by Hastie and Stuetzle (1989) as *self-consistent*, smooth, 1-dimensional curves that pass through the *middle* of a *p*-dimensional data set, providing a nonlinear summary of the data (see Figure 13). An introduction and very good review of the field can be found at http://www.iro.umontreal.ca/~kegl/research/pcurves/.

The Elastic Net

Also known as the elastic map, it was first suggested by Durbin and Willshaw (1987) as a solution to the traveling salesman problem, although Gorban and Zinevyev (2001) have also applied it to visualization and manifold learning. It can be thought of as a variant of the SOM with a different learning rule. Recently, a model has been proposed that unifies both paradigms (Tereshko & Allinson, 2000, 2002a, 2002b).

Curvilinear Component Analysis

Previously known as vector quantization and projection (VQP), but renamed CCA in order to evoke other *CA; it is a neural implementation of Sammon mapping preceded by a vector quantization to reduce the computational load (Demartines & Heráult, 1993, 1997). As with Sammon maps, it favours the local topology but the weighting does not use distance values in the multi dimensional space; instead CCA uses a decreasing function, *F*, of the low-dimensional distances. The function *F* is also parameterized by a neighbourhood width, λ, in the style of the neighbourhood parameter of the SOM. The error function is:

$$E_{CCA} = \sum_{ij} (\delta_{ij} - d_{ij}) F_\lambda(d_{ij}) \qquad (29)$$

The result of applying this projection method to the iris data set is shown in Figure 14.

Isomap and Curvilinear Distance Analysis

The key idea in both algorithms is the use of an approximation to the geodesic distances instead of Euclidean distances. Every point is linked to the *k* closest points or, alternatively, to the set of points closer than a radius ε. This gives a graph that is used to approximate the geodesic distances, first determining the shortest path between two

Figure 13. Example of principal curve through the middle of a bidimensional data set

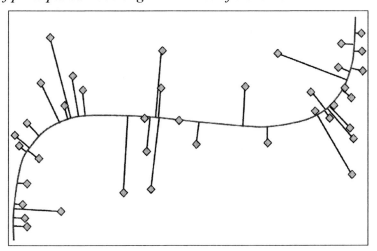

Figure 14. The CCA projection of the iris data set

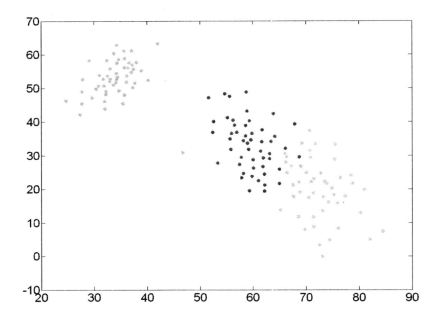

points in the graph, then summing the Euclidean distances between the sequence of points in the path. Figure 15 clarifies the difference between the Euclidean distance and the geodesic distance.

In both algorithms, instead of using the full data set, a reduced set of points is selected. The differences between the two algorithms are in the way they select the subset of points and in the way they use the obtained geodesic distances. In the modern version of Isomap proposed by Tenenbaum, de Silva, and Langford (2000),[5] a subset of points is obtained by random selection from the original data set. After computing the geodesic distances, the obtained matrix of distances is used to perform traditional metric MDS and to obtain the projection of the subset of points. In Curvilinear Distance Analysis (Lee, Lendasse, Donckers, & Verleysen, 2000), the points in the graph are obtained through vector quantization of the original data set. Then CCA is applied over the subset using the geodesic distances. Fi-

nally, the projection of the original data points is computed using a piecewise linear interpolator. Lee, Lendasse, and Verleysen (2002) have made a comparison between the two methods.

Locally Linear Embedding

Contrary to the metric MDS, the method of Locally Linear Embedding, proposed by Roweis and Saul (2000), does not try to preserve distance but the local structure of the data. It assumes that the data manifold is locally linear, and hence each data point can be obtained as a linear combination of its nearest neighbours. First, it calculates the weights, $\mathbf{W}_{ij}$, that best describe each point $\mathbf{x}_i$ as a function of its neighbourhood, that is, the weights that minimize the error function:

$$\varepsilon(\mathbf{W}) = \sum_i \left\| \mathbf{x}_i - \sum_j \mathbf{W}_{ij}\mathbf{x}_j \right\|^2 \qquad (30)$$

Figure 15. (a) Two points in a spiral, (b) the Euclidian distance between the two same points, and (c) the geodesic distance

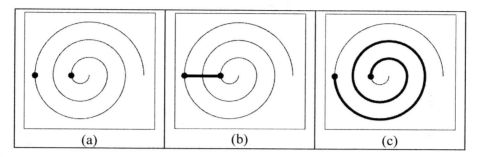

subject to $\Sigma_j \mathbf{W}_{ij} = 1$ and $\mathbf{W}_{ij} = 0$ if $\mathbf{x}_j$ does not belong to the set of neighbours of $\mathbf{x}_i$. Second, it finds the projections $\mathbf{y}_i$ associated with each $\mathbf{x}_i$ that best reproduce the same reconstruction weights, that is, that minimize the following error function:

$$\phi(\mathbf{Y}) = \sum_i \left\| \mathbf{y}_i - \sum_j \mathbf{W}_{ij}\mathbf{y}_j \right\|^2 \qquad (31)$$

Both problems can be solved using algebraic techniques.

Isotop

Designed by Lee and Verleysen (2002) to overcoming some of the limitation of the SOM, Isotop shares with CDA the initial vector quantization to obtain prototypes (or model vectors) of the original data set, the construction of a graph to approximate geodesic distances between these prototypes and the use of a piecewise linear interpolator in the last stage of the algorithm to obtain the projection of the original points by means of the projection of the prototypes. The main difference is how they obtain the projections of the prototypes. Now, instead of using CCA, an update rule similar to the SOM is used. However, the neighbourhood of the model vector is determined by the graph obtained in the first stages.

A comparison with LLE is presented in Lee, Archambeau, and Verleysen (2003a).

REPRESENTATION OF MULTI DIMENSIONAL DATA

In the previous sections, we have outlined some of the existing methods to project the multi dimensional data onto a lower dimension that makes the graphical representation possible. In this section, we present methods that, instead of searching for projections of the data, try to represent graphically all the dimensions of the data.

Chernoff Faces

The original idea was presented by Chernoff (1973). It consists of representing each multi dimensional observation with a face cartoon. The multiple values of the observations are used in the drawing process as parameters used, which control features such as:

- The shape of the upper and lower part of the face (5 variables).
- The length of nose (1 variable).
- The vertical position, curvature, and width of mouth (3 variables).
- The vertical position, separation, slant, eccentricity, and size of eyes (5 variables).
- The position of pupils (1 variable).
- The vertical position, size, and slant of eyebrows (3 variables).

Figure 16. Three examples of Chernoff's faces

Hence, different values give different face cartoons (see Figure 16). The use of Chernoff's faces makes the visually identification of clusters easy and also facilitates the detection of outliers in multi dimensional data. The explanation of this is that people have built-in face recognizers, or as Chernoff (1973, p. 363) says: "People grow up studying and reacting to faces all of the time. Small and barely measurable differences are easily detected and evoke emotional reactions from long catalogue buried in the memory."

This method has been used in a broad range of disciplines: economics (Moriarity, 1979; Smith & Taffler, 1996), marketing (Nel, Pitt & Wcbb, 1994), medicine (Lott & Durbridge, 1990), sociology (Apaiwongse, 1995; Sawasdichai & Poggenpohl, 2002), and so on. One problem with this method is the subjective assignment of variables to features. Different assignments will give different face shapes. The effect of these assignments has been investigated by Chernoff and Rizvi (1975). As pointed out by Saxena and Navanneetham (1991), the comparison with other methods, discussed in Hamner, Turner, and Young (1987); Saxena and Navaneetham (1986); and Tidmore and Turner (1983), shows that Chernoff faces perform quite well in the identification of clusters. Saxena and Navanneetham themselves analyze the effect of the size, dimensionality, and number of clusters when using Chernoff's faces. In Lee, Reilly, and Butavicius (2003b), this visualization tool is evaluated in the context of binary data visualization.

Subsequent researchers have wanted to increase the dimensionality of the data set with which Chernoff faces can be used, by means of using asymmetric faces (Flury & Riedwyl, 1981). Another variant uses, as graphical objects, schematic pictures of castles and trees (Kleiner & Hartigan, 1981) or, more recently, pictures that resemble bugs (Chuah & Eick, 1998). Taking advantage of the powerful graphical capabilities of the modern computer, more recently, the construction of more realistic faces (not just caricatures) has been proposed (Loizides & Slater, 2002; Müller & Alexa, 1998), and instead of doing a mapping from the data to face features, the data is used to change the emotional features of the faces; in this way, even an isolated face can transmit information to the viewer (for example, a happy face could mean a good financial situation).

Andrews' Curves

Andrews (1972) described his curves early on in the computing era; it is an interesting observation that he thought it necessary to counsel: "an output device with relatively high precision ... is required". Current standard PC software is quite sufficient for the purpose. The method is another way to attempt to visualize and hence to find structure in multi dimensional data. Each data point $\mathbf{x} = \{ x_1, x_2, ..., x_d \}$ defines a finite Fourier series:

$$f_{\mathbf{x}}(t) = x_1 / \sqrt{2} + x_2 \cos(t)$$
$$+ x_3 \sin(t) + x_4 \cos(2t) + x_5 \sin(2t) + ...$$

$$(32)$$

and this function is then plotted for $-\pi < t < \pi$. Thus each data point may be viewed as a line between $-\pi$ and π. This formula can be thought of as the projection of the data point onto the vector:

$$\left(\frac{1}{\sqrt{2}}, \sin(t), \cos(t), \sin(2t), \cos(2t), \dots \right)$$

If there is structure in the data, it may be visible in the Andrews' Curves of the data. An example of Andrews' Curves on the iris data set is shown in Figure 17. The data set is four dimensional (only the first four terms of (32) are used). We see that one type of iris is easily identifiable from the other two, but there is some difficulty in differentiating between these two. Thus $t = 3$ gives us a value for a linear projection of the data which differentiates one type of data from the rest. But the fact that we cannot see any clear distinction between the other two types of iris in the figure does not necessarily mean that it is not possible to find a projection which will do so: the Andrews parameters are limited by the proper-

ties of the trigonometric functions (e.g., $\sin^2() + \cos^2() = 1$), which means that we have a very constrained relationship between the parameters of the projection for x_2 and x_3.

These curves have been utilized in fields as different as neurology (Kokiol & Hacke, 1991), sociology (Spencer, 2003), biology (Murphy, 2003), and semiconductor manufacturing (Rietman, Lee, & Layadi, 1998; Rietman & Layadi, 2000). Some of their uses include the quality control of products (Kulkarmi & Paranjape, 1984), the detection of period and outliers in time series (Embrechts, Herzberg, & Ng, 1986), or the visualization of learning in artificial neural networks (Gallagher, 2000). Khattree and Naik (2002) have suggested their utilization in robust design and in correspondence analysis.

Properties

These curves have several useful properties, some of which are:

Figure 17. An Andrews' Plot of the iris data set. It is clear that one type of iris is distinct from the other two but differentiating between the other two is less easy

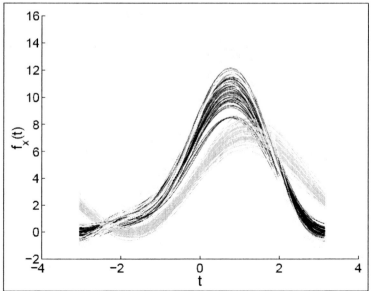

16. Mean preservation. The function corresponding to the mean of a set of N multivariate observations is the pointwise mean of the functions corresponding to these

$$f_{\bar{\mathbf{x}}}(t) = \frac{1}{N} \sum_{i=1}^{N} f_{\mathbf{x}_i}(t)$$

17. Distance preservation. The distance between two function is,

$$\|f_{\mathbf{x}}(t) - f_{\mathbf{y}}(t)\|_{L_2}$$

$$= \int_{\pi}^{\pi} \left[f_{\mathbf{x}}(t) - f_{\mathbf{y}}(t) \right]^2 dt$$

which is proportional to the Euclidean distance between the corresponding points

$$\|f_{\mathbf{x}}(t) - f_{\mathbf{y}}(t)\|_{L_2}$$

$$= \pi \|\mathbf{x} - \mathbf{y}\|^2 = \pi \sum_{i=1}^{d} (x_i - y_i)^2$$

18. One-dimensional projections. For a particular value of $t = t_0$, the function value $f_x(t_0)$ is proportional to the length of the projection of the vector $(x_1, x_2, ..., x_d)$ on the vector,

$$\mathbf{f_1}(t_0) = (1/\sqrt{2}, \sin(t_0),$$

$$\sin(2t_0), \cos(2t_0), \cdots)$$

19. Linear relationships. If a point $\mathbf{y}$ lies on a line joining $\mathbf{x}$ and $\mathbf{z}$, then for all values of t, $f_y(t)$ is between $f_x(t)$ and $f_z(t)$.

Also, if the components of the data are uncorrelated with common variance σ^2, the Andrews' Curves representations preserve that variance. This variance preservation property lets us perform a test of significance using the curves, although this "*is less useful since most multivariate data are either correlated and/or have unequal variances across the variables*" (Khattree & Naik, 2002, p. 413).

All these properties were noted by Andrews (1972). The last one was generalized by Goodchild and Vijayan (1974) to the case of unequal and not necessarily orthogonal variances. Tests of significance at particular values of t are still possible, but not so the overall tests mentioned by Andrews (1972).

However, the Andrews' Curves also have a drawback, in that they suffer from strong dependence on the order of the variables; that is, if we change the order of variables, the shape of the curves is completely different. That is why Embrechts and Herzberg (1991) propose to try different arrangements of the variables to find more suitable Andrews' Curves. In García-Osorio and Fyfe (2005b), we propose a way of combining in the display two different arrangements. Besides, as pointed out by Andrews (1972), in the plots, low frequencies are more readily seen than high frequencies. For this reason, it is useful to associate the most important variables with low frequencies.

Variations

Some variations of the Andrews' Curves have been proposed throughout the years. Andrews (1972) proposed the use of different integers to give the general formulation:

$$f_{\mathbf{x}}(t) = x_1 \sin(n_1 t) +$$

$$+ x_2 \cos(n_1 t) + x_3 \sin(n_2 t) + x_4 \cos(n_2 t) + \dots \quad (33)$$

The restriction to using integers is because of the distance preserving property; without integers, this property is lost. Andrews compared the curve with values $n_1 = 2$, $n_2 = 4$, $n_3 = 8$, ... with the original formulation and concluded that the former is more space filling but more difficult to interpret when it is used for visual inspection.

Embrechts and Herzberg (1991) investigate the effect of rescaling and reordering the coefficients and the interpretation of the plots when one or more coordinates are made equal to zero. They propose the use of other kinds of orthogonal functions such as Legendre and Chebychev polynomials. They give many examples of these variations using the iris data set. Embrechts, Herzberg, Kalbfleisch, Traves, and Whitla (1995) completes this study with a new variation consisting of the use of wavelet functions. All these variations have been used later by Rietman and Layadi (2000) as a help to monitor the manufacture of silicon wafers; they also point to a previous work (Rietman et al., 1998) in which they used another variation consisting of drawing the Andrews' Curves using polar coordinates.

A bivariate version of Andrews' Plots has been proposed by Koziol and Werner (1991):

Given two vectors of observations $x^T = (x_1, ..., x_p)$ and $y^T = (y_1, ..., y_p)$ where the (x_i, y_i), $i = 1, 2, ..., p$ are naturally paired, from the functions,

$$f_x(t) = x_1/\sqrt{2} + x_2 \sin(t)$$
$$+ x_3 \cos(t) + x_4 \sin(2t) + x_5 \cos(2t) + \cdots$$

$$f_y(t) = y_1/\sqrt{2}$$
$$+ y_2 \sin(t) + y_3 \cos(t) + y_4 \sin(2t) + y_5 \cos(2t) + \cdots$$

and plot $(t, f_x(t), f_y(t))$ for a set of t-values in the range $-\pi \leq t \leq \pi$.

A similar idea to the previous one, but this time to obtain a three dimensional Andrews' Plot, has been proposed by Wegman and Shen (1993). They were concerned with the connection between Andrews' Curves and the grand tour[6] noted by Crawford and Fall (1990). They show that Andrews' Curves are not a real 1-dimensional grand tour. The problem is that Andrews' Curves do not exhaust all possible orientations of a 1-dimensional vector. They propose a generalization of Andrews' Curves which is more space filling and which can be used to obtain a bidimensional pseudo grand tour. Now, two orthogonal vectors are used:

$$\mathbf{w}_1 = \sqrt{\frac{2}{d}}$$
$$\left(\sin(\lambda_1 t), \cos(\lambda_1 t), ..., \sin(\lambda_{\frac{d}{2}} t), \cos(\lambda_{\frac{d}{2}} t) \right)$$

$$\mathbf{w}_2 = \sqrt{\frac{2}{d}}$$
$$\left(\cos(\lambda_1 t), -\sin(\lambda_1 t), ..., \cos(\lambda_{\frac{d}{2}} t), -\sin(\lambda_{\frac{d}{2}} t) \right)$$

with the λ_j linearly independent over the rationals to increase the space filling property of the curves, but losing the distance preservation property.[7]

If we use surfaces instead of curves, we can obtain three orthogonal vector we can use to obtain a 3-dimensional pseudo grand tour (García-Osorio & Fyfe, 2005b):

$$\mathbf{w}_1 \propto$$
$$\left(\cos(\lambda_1 t) \cos(\mu_1 s), \cos(\lambda_1 t) \sin(\mu_1 s), \sin(\lambda_1 t), ... \right)$$

$$\mathbf{w}_2 \propto$$
$$\left(\sin(\lambda_1 t) \cos(\mu_1 s), \sin(\lambda_1 t) \sin(\mu_1 s), \cos(\lambda_1 t), ... \right)$$

$$\mathbf{w}_3 \propto \left(\sin(\mu_1 s), \cos(\mu_1 s), 0, ... \right)$$

Khattree and Naik (2002) have suggested the function,

$$g_y(t) = \frac{1}{\sqrt{2}} \Big\{ y_1 + y_2 \big(\sin(t)$$
$$+ \cos(t) \big) + y_3 \big(\sin(t) - \cos(t) \big)$$
$$+ y_4 \big(\sin(2t) + \cos(2t) \big)$$
$$+ y_5 \big(\sin(2t) - \cos(2t) \big) + \cdots \Big\}, -\pi \leq t \leq \pi$$

$$(34)$$

So, every y_i is exposed to a sine function as well as a cosine function. As they note, one of the advantages of this formulation is that the trigonometric terms in (34) do not simultaneously vanish at any given t. They also establish an interesting relation between the Andrews' Curves and the eigenvectors of a symmetric positive definite circular covariance matrix.

Parallel Coordinates

Parallel coordinates are an invention of Alfred Inselberg originally developed as a device for visualizing multi dimensional geometry (Inselberg, 1985); it was their utility as air traffic collision detectors (Inselberg, Chen, Shieh, & Lee, 1990) which initially brought serious and broader interest to this new tool (Inselberg, n.d.). Later, Wegman (1991) proposed their use as a data analysis tool and enhanced them by combining them with the grand tour (Wegman & Luo, 1991).

The parallel coordinate plots can be thought of as a generalization of the 2-dimensional Cartesian plot. Instead of using orthogonal axes, the axes are drawn parallel to each other. Instead of using a "dot" to represent the location of a "point" and the values of its coordinates, a "line" is used which connects the coordinates of the point on the axes. So the points became lines. If we draw the lines associated with points lying on the same line, we discover that they intersect at a point, which is the dual of the line where the points lie. So, in parallel coordinates plots, the dual of points are lines and the dual of lines are points. Also, now we can draw as many axes as we want, so we can represent points of dimensionality greater than three. In Figure 18, the iris data set is represented using parallel coordinates. The set of dualities are:

- A point in Cartesian coordinates becomes a line in parallel coordinates (a poly line if we consider more than two dimensions, and hence we draw more than two parallel axes) and vice versa.

- An ellipse in Cartesian coordinates maps into a "line hyperbola" in parallel coordinates. Maybe Figure 19 can clarify the strange notion of line hyperbola. In general, a point conic in Cartesian coordinates becomes a line conic in parallel coordinates.

- Rotations in Cartesian coordinates become translations in parallel coordinates and vice versa.

- Points of inflection in Cartesian space become cusps in parallel coordinate space and vice versa.

Because of these duality properties, parallel coordinate displays allow interpretations of statistical data in an analogous way to the 2-dimensional Cartesian scatter plots. In the statistical setting, as pointed out by Wegman and Luo (1991), the following interpretations can be made:

- For highly negatively correlated pairs, the dual line segments in parallel coordinates tend to cross near a single point between the two parallel coordinates axes. So an X-shape between axes signals negative correlation between the respective variables.

- For highly positively correlated data, lines tend not to intersect between the parallel coordinates axes. Parallel or almost parallel lines between axes indicates positive correlation between variables.

Two of the most common objections to parallel coordinate plots are the dependency on the order of the axes in order to identify the relations between variables (the pairwise comparison between consecutive axes is easy, but this comparison is not so easy when the axes are not adjacent) and the bad *data-ink* ratio[8] or heavy overplotting (as lines are used to represent points, when the size of the data set is too large, the parallel coordinate plot becomes a messy clutter of ink). To minimize the first, Wegman (1991) presents in Appendix A an algorithm for constructing a minimal set of permutations to insure adjacency of every pair of axes. If the number of axes is *d*, only (*d*+1)/2 permutations are needed. To address the second, in the same paper, Wegman proposes the utilization of parallel coordinate density plots, that is, the use of colours to represent the density of observations. More details were given in a subsequent paper (Wegman & Luo, 1997).

The use of parallel coordinates as a data analysis tool has been perfected later by means of using the grand tour and the saturation brushing mechanism (Wegman & Luo, 1991; Wegman, Poston, & Solka, 1998). This last technique allows a very fast calculation of the densities of the lines. Quoting Wegman and Solka (Wegman & Solka, 2002, p. 449):

The idea of saturation brushing is to desaturate a brushing colour until it contains only a very small component of colour and hence is very nearly black. Most modern computers have a so-called α-channel which allows for compositing of overplots. The α-channel is used in computer graphics as a device for incorporating transparency. However, by using such a device to build up colour intensity, we can obtain a visual indication of how much overplotting there is at a pixel. In effect, the brighter, more saturated a pixel is, the more overplotting.

An alternative to saturation brushing for processing high volume data sets is the hierarchical parallel coordinates proposed by Fua, Ward, and Rundensteiner (1999). They *"use data aggregation techniques to collapse data into clusters, and show the population and extents of clusters with bands of varying translucency"* (Fua et al., 1999, p. 44). Other improvements have to do with interaction techniques (Graham & Kennedy, 2003; Hauser, Ledermann, & Doleisch, 2002; Siirtola, 2000, 2003).

Figure 18. The parallel coordinates resentation of the iris data set

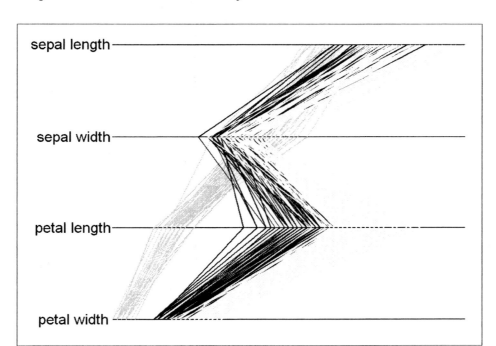

Figure 19. Parallel coordinate plot of ellipse points

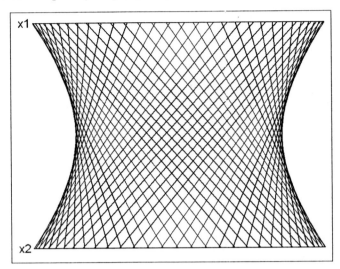

The idea of saturation brushing is to desaturate a brushing colour until it contains only a very small component of colour and hence is very nearly black. Most modern computers have a so-called α-channel which allows for compositing of overplots. The α-channel is used in computer graphics as a device for incorporating transparency. However, by using such a device to build up colour intensity, we can obtain a visual indication of how much overplotting there is at a pixel. In effect, the brighter, more saturated a pixel is, the more overplotting.

GRAND TOUR

The idea of the grand tour method, introduced by Asimov (1985) and Buja and Asimov (1986), is to generate a continuous sequence of low dimensional projections of a multi dimensional data set. The animation obtained can be thought of as a generalization of rotations in multi dimensional space. From that point of view, the grand tour shares a common objective with exploratory projection pursuit techniques. In both cases, the human ability for visual pattern recognition is exploited.

To create a two dimensional grand tour, we need to generate a sequence of planes in the multi dimensional space of the data. Two conditions are required: (1) the sequence should be dense in the set of all planes in the multi dimensional space, and (2) the sequence should be smooth to give a visual impression of the data points moving in a continuous way. Several algorithms have been proposed to achieve these two conditions (Asimov, 1985; Asimov & Buja, 1994; Wegman & Solka, 2002). They are based on obtaining a general rotation in the multi dimensional space, the dimension of which is d. To obtain a frame of the grand tour, we multiply the data set by a generalized rotation matrix $\mathbf{Q}$ of dimension $d{\times}d$. The matrix $\mathbf{Q}$ is obtained by multiplying $p = d(d-1)/2$ matrices, $R_{ij}(\theta_{ij})$, each of which rotates the $e_i e_j$ plane through an angle of θ_{ij} (an outline of this matrix is shown below). Now the algorithms differ in the way they obtain the angles θ_{ij}. In *The Asimov-Buja winding algorithm*, the p angles θ_{ij} are taken from the coordinates of the vector $\alpha(t) = (\lambda_1 t, \lambda_2 t, \dots \lambda_p t)$ that defines a mapping from $\mathbb{R}$ onto $[0,2\pi]^p$, where t is the time parameter, the $\lambda_j t$ are taken modulo 2π and $\lambda_1 t, \dots \lambda_p t$, and are real numbers linearly independent over the rational numbers. With these conditions, this vector defines a curve over a p-torus that does not intersect itself. *The random curve algorithm* just randomly takes two points $\mathbf{s}_i, \mathbf{s}_j \in [0,2\pi]^p$ and creates a linear interpolant between them going from $\mathbf{s}_i$ to $\mathbf{s}_j$, then takes a third point s_k and joins it with $\mathbf{s}_j$ and so on. In *The fractal curve algorithm*, a p-dimensional Hilbert or Peano curve is constructed that tours through the p-dimensional hypercube $[0,2\pi]^p$. (See Box 1).

As we have commented in the section about Andrews' Curves, although it does not strictly obtain a grand tour, the more simpler of the algorithms is based on the use of the variant of Andrews' Curves proposed by Wegman (1990).

Originally, the grand tour was designed with the aim of obtaining two dimensional projections; with the arrival of parallel coordinates is possible to use higher dimensional projections, which was noted first by Edward J. Wegman (1990). Wegman and Luo (1997) give an interesting example about the combined use of parallel coordinates and grand tours.

An enhancement of the grand tour, called the tracking grand tour (TGT), is presented by Huh and Kim (2002). In the TGT during the grand tour, the old frames instead of being substituted by the new ones, are maintained for a while *"that shows the trace of the touring process as small 'comet trails' of the projected points"* (Huh & Kim, 2002, p. 721).

In Wegman, Poston, and Solka (1998), the image grand tour, another variation of the grand tour, is proposed. This time the idea of the grand tour is used to combine in a single gray scale image several multispectral images of the same scene. The grand tour is, through the different combinations of the multispectral images, a continuously changing gray scale image with variable contributions from the collected images. The image grand tour has been successfully applied to the detection of mines in a minefield. Symanzik, Wegman, Braverman, and Luo (2002) show more applications of the image grand tour.

SOFTWARE TOOLS AND REFERENCE TABLE

Since most of the methods presented in this chapter are dynamic or have a component of interaction, the best way to understand them is to use them. For most of them, there exist tools that automate the process of obtaining the graphical representation. Here we give a list with the Web addresses from which they can be downloaded and a short comment about their visualization capabilities (for some of them it is possible to find a more complete review in ATKOSoft S.A., 1997).

Box 1.

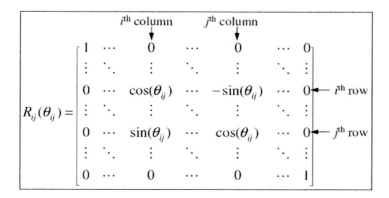

- **XmdvTool (http://davis.wpi.edu/~xmdv/):** Scatter plots, star glyphs, hierarchical parallel coordinates, dimensional stacking, proximity colouring, pixel-oriented techniques.
- **GGobi (http://www.ggobi.org/):** Parallel coordinates, grand tour, brushing and linking, scatter plots.
- **VisDB (http://www.dbs.informatik.uni-muenchen.de/dbs/projekt/visdb/visdb.html):** Pixel-oriented techniques, stick figure icons, parallel coordinates.
- **Parallel Coordinate Explorer (http://www.cs.uta.fi/~hs/pce/):** Parallel coordinates and brushing.
- **CrystalVision (ftp://www.galaxy.gmu.edu/pub/software/CrystalVision.exe):** Parallel coordinates, grand tour, saturation brushing.
- **parvis (http://home.subnet.at/flo/mv/parvis/):** Parallel coordinates, axis histograms, brush fuzziness.
- **ViDaExpert (http://www.ihes.fr/~zinovyev/vida/vidaexpert.htm):** Linear discriminant analysis, PCA, elastic maps.
- **HiSee (https://sourceforge.net/projects/hisee/):** PCA, Sammon mapping.
- **Visual Attribute Explorer (http://www.alphaworks.ibm.com/tech/visualexplorer):** Parallel coordinate plots, attribute bar chart.
- **Martin's Parallel Coordinate Curves Applet (http://www.dcs.napier.ac.uk/~marting/parCoord/):** Parallel coordinates curves.
- **SOM Toolbox for Matlab (http://www.cis.hut.fi/projects/somtoolbox/):** Self organizing maps, Sammon mapping, CCA, PCA.
- **Datatool (http://www.datatool.com/):** Scatter plots, colour scatter plots.
- **Parallax (http://www.kdnuggets.com/software/parallax/):** Parallel coordinates (from the inventor of parallel coordinates, nonfree).
- **Data Loom (http://s92417348.onlinehome.us/software/dataloom/):** Parallel coordinates (for Macintosh).
- **The Visualization Toolkit (http://www.visualizationtoolkit.org/):** C++ library to make the creation of useful graphics and visualization applications much easier.
- **Mondrian (http://rosuda.org/Mondrian/):** Parallel coordinates, saturation brushing, mosaic plot, scatter plots, maps, bar charts, histograms, box plots.
- **Manet (http://rosuda.org/Manet/):** Scatter plots, box plots, mosaic plots, histograms, polygon plots.
- **Matlab package for Isomap (http://isomap.stanford.edu/IsomapR1.tar):** Isomap projections.
- **Matlab code for LLE (http://www.cs.toronto.edu/~roweis/lle/code.html):** LLE projections.
- **John Aldo Lee code for Nonlinear Projections (http://www.dice.ucl.ac.be/~lee/):** Self organizing maps, Sammon mapping, CDA, Isotop.
- TreeMap (http://www.cs.umd.edu/hcil/treemap/index.shtml#download), TreeMap java Library (http://sourceforge.net/projects/treemap/), and Microsoft Treemapper with Excel Add-In (http://research.microsoft.com/community/treemapper/).
- MANI fold learning Matlab demo (http://www.math.umn.edu/~wittman/mani/): Principal Component Analysis, Multi dimensional Scaling, Isomap, Local Linear Embedding.
- Interactive Java tools for exploring high dimensional data (http://www.jstatsoft.org/v06/i01/bradley/): parallel coordinates, scatter plot matrix.

This chapter was designed to be mainly an entry point to the field of multi dimensional representation and visualization; it has provided many references to the methods and variations of the

Box 2.

Technique	References
Andrews' Curves	(Andrews, 1972; García-Osorio & Fyfe, 2005b; Khattree & Naik, 2002; Wegman & Shen, 1993)
Chernoff Faces	(Chernoff, 1973)
Colour Icons	(Levkowitz, 1991)
Curvilinear Component Analysis	(Demartines & Hérault, 1997)
Curvilinear Distance Analysis	(Lee, 2000)
Dimensional Stacking	(LeBlanc et al., 1990)
Elastic Net or Elastic Map	(Durbin & Willshaw, 1987; Gorban & Zinevyev, 2001)
Exploratory Projection Pursuit	(Friedman, 1987; Friedman & Tukey, 1974; Jones & Sibson, 1987)
Factor Analysis	(Lewis-Beck, 1994)
Grand Tour Methods	(Asimov, 1985; Wegman, 1990; Wegman et al., 1998; Wegman & Solka, 2002)
Harmonic Topographic Map Products of Experts	(Peña & Fyfe, 2005)
Hyperbox	(Alpern & Carter, 1991)
HyperSlice	(Wijk & Leire, 1993)
Isomap	(Tenenbaum et al., 2000)
Isotop	(Lee & Verleysen, 2002)
Locally Linear Embedding	(Roweis & Saul, 2000)
Multi dimensional Scaling	(Kruskal & Wish, 1978; Shepard, Romney & Nerlove, 1972; Torgerson, 1952)
Multi dimensional Stacking	(LeBlanc et al., 1990)
Parallel Coordinates	(Inselberg, 1985; Inselberg et al., 1990; Wegman, 1991; Wegman & Luo, 1991; Wegman & Solka, 2002)
Parallel Coordinates	(Inselberg & Dimsdale, 1990; Wegman, 1991)
Pixel-oriented Techniques	(Keim & Kriegel, 1994)
Principal Component Analysis	(Hotelling, 1933; Jolliffe, 1986)
Principal Curves	(Hastie & Stuetzle, 1989)
Projection Pursuit	(Huber, 1985)
Sammon Mapping	(Sammon, 1969)
Scatterplot Matrices	(Chambers et al., 1983; Becker & Cleveland, 1987)
Self Organizing Maps	(Kohonen, 1992, 2001; Vesanto, 1999)
Spring Models	(Chalmers, 1996; Fruchterman & Reingold, 1991; Morrison & Chalmers, 2003)
Star Icons	(Ward, 1994)
Stick Figure Icons	(Grinstein et al., 1989)
Treemap	(Shneiderman, 1992)
Worlds-within-Worlds	(Behsers & Feiner, 1990)

basic methods and applications have been given throughout the chapter. As a convenient way to summarize the background here, we give a table with the main references for each of the methods and its main variations. (See Box 2).

CONCLUSION

In this chapter, we have shown how wide and diverse the data mining and visualization fields are. This fact is even more clear if we consider the lack of a commonly accepted taxonomy for the field. The variety of tools, far from being a drawback, is an advantage, or actually a need. Some of them are more suitable for identifying clusters, others can handle more data records. For each data set there exists an appropriate tool. The main conclusion we can state here is that there is not a tool better than the others over all data sets. The important thing is to provide data analysts with a set of tools, in which they can choose the tool most suitable for the data set they are investigating.

REFERENCES

Alpern, B., & Carter, L. (1991). The hyperbox. In G.M. Nielson & L. Rosenblum (Eds.), *Proceedings of IEEE Visualization '91*, San Diego, California (pp. 133-139).

Andrews, D. F. (1972). Plots of high dimensional data. *Biometrics, 28*, 125-136.

Apaiwongse, T. S. (1995). Facial display of environmental policy uncertainty. *Journal of Business Psychology, 10*, 65-74.

Asimov, D. (1985). The grand tour: A tool for viewing multi dimensional data. *SIAM Journal on Scientific and Statistical Computing, 6*(1), 128-143.

Asimov, D. A., & Buja, A. (1994). Grand tour via geodesic interpolation of 2-frames. In R. J. Moorhead II, D. E. Silver, & S. Uselton (Eds.), *Proceedings of the SPIE Visual Data Exploration and Analysis—Volume Conference, 2178,* 145-153.

ATKOSoft S.A. (1997). Survey on visualisation methods and software tools. Retrieved June 23, 2007, from http://europa.eu.int/en/comm/eurostat/research/supcom.96/30/result/a/visualisation_methods.pdf

Becker, R. A., & Cleveland, W. S. (1987). Brushing scatterplots. *Technometrics, 29*, 127-142.

Becker, R. A., Cleveland, W. S., & Wilks, A. R. (1987). Dynamic graphics for data analysis. *Statistical Science, 2*(4), 355-383.

Behsers, C. G., & Feiner, S. K. (1990). Visualizing *n*-dimensional virtual worlds with *n*-Vision. *Computer Graphics, 24*(2), 37-38.

Bertin, J. (1981). *Graphics and graphic information processing.* Berlin, Germany: Walter De Gruyter.

Bertin, J. (1983). *Semiology of graphics.* Madison, WI: University of Wiscosin Press.

Bishop, C. (1995). *Neural networks for pattern recognition.* Oxford: Clarendon Press.

Bishop, C. M., Svensén, M., & Williams, C. K. I. (1998). GTM: The generative topographic mapping. *Neural Computation, 10*(1), 215-235.

Buja, A., & Asimov, D. (1986). Grand tour methods: An outline. In D. Allen (Ed.), *Computer science and statistics: Proceedings of the Seventeenth Symposium on the Interface* (pp. 63-67). Amsterdam: North Holland. Elsevier Science Publisher B.V.

Chalmers, M. (1996). A linear iteration time layout algorithm for visualising high-dimensional data. In *Proceedings of IEEE Visualization 96*, San Francisco, California (pp. 127-132).

Chambers, J. M., Cleveland, W. S., Keliner, B., & Tukey, P. A. (1983). *Graphical methods for data analysis*. New York: Chapman and Hall.

Charles, D., & Fyfe, C. (1998). Modelling multiple cause structure using rectification constraints. *Network: Computation in Neural Systems, 9*, 167-182.

Chernoff, H. (1973). The use of faces to represent points in *k*-dimensional space graphically. *Journal of American Statistical Association, 68*, 361-368.

Chernoff, H., & Rizvi, M. H. (1975). Effect on classification error of random permutations of features in representing multivariate data by faces. *Journal of American Statistical Association, 70*, 548-554.

Chuah, M. C., & Eick, S. G. (1998). Information rich glyphs for software management data. *IEEE Computer Graphics and Applications, 18*(4), 24-29.

Cleveland, W. S., & McGill, M. E. (Eds.). (1988). *Dynamic graphics for statistics*. Belmont, CA: Wadsworth & Brooks.

Corchado, E., & Fyfe, C. (2002). Maximum likelihood Hebbian learning. In *Proceedings of the Tenth European Symposium on Artificial Neural Networks, ESANN2002* (pp. 143-148). d-side publications.

Crawford, S. L., & Fall, T. C. (1990). Projection pursuit techniques for visualizing high-dimensional data sets. In G. M. Nielson, B. Shrivers, & L. J. Rosenblum (Eds.), *Visualization in scientific computing* (pp. 94-108). Los Alamitos, CA: IEEE Computer Society Press.

Demartines, P., & Hérault, J. (1993). Vector quantization and projection neural network. In J. Mira, J. Cabestany, A. Prieto (Eds.), *International Workshop on Artificial Neural Networks* (pp. 328-333). Springer-Verlag. Lecture Notes in Computer Science 686.

Demartines, P., & Hérault, J. (1997). Curvilinear component analysis: A self-organizing neural network for nonlinear mapping of data sets. *IEEE Transactions on Neural Networks, 8*(1), 148-154.

de Ridder, D., & Duin, R. P. W. (1997). Sammon's mapping using neural networks: A comparison. *Pattern Recognition Letters, 18*(11-13), 1307-1316.

Diaconis, P., & Freedman, D. (1984). Asymptotics of graphical projections. *The Annals of Statistics, 12*(3), 793-815.

Diamantaras, K. I., & Kung, S. Y. (1996). *Principal component neural networks: Theory and applications*. John Wiley & Sons.

Durbin, R., & Willshaw, D. (1987). An analogue approach to the traveling salesman problem using an elastic net method. *Nature, 326*(6114), 689-691.

Embrechts, P., & Herzberg, A. M. (1991). Variations of Andrews' plots. *International Statistical Review, 59*(2), 175-194.

Embrechts, P., Herzberg, A. M., Kalbfleisch, H. K., Traves, W. N., & Whitla, J. R. (1995). An introduction to wavelets with applications to Andrews' plots. *Journal of Computational and Applied Mathematics, 64*, 41-56.

Embrechts, P., Herzberg, A. M., & Ng, A. C. (1986). An investigation of Andrews' plots to detect period and outliers in time series data. *Communications in Statistics: Simulation and Computation, 15*(4), 1027-1051.

Ferreira de Oliveira, M. C., & Levkowitz, H. (2003). From visual data exploration to visual data mining: A Survey. *IEEE Transactions on Visualization and Computer Graphics, 9*(3), 378-394.

Flury, B., & Riedwyl, H. (1981). Graphical representation of multivariate data by means of asymmetrical faces. *Journal of American Statistical Association, 76*, 757-765.

Friedman, J. H. (1987). Exploratory projection pursuit. *Journal of the American Statistical Association, 82*(397), 249-266.

Friedman, J. H., & Tukey, J. W. (1974). A projection pursuit algorithm for exploratory data analysis. *IEEE Transactions on Computers, c-23*(9), 881-889.

Fruchterman, T., & Reingold, E. (1991). Graph drawing by force-directed placement. *Software—Practice and Experience, 21*(11), 1129-1164.

Fua, Y.-H., Ward, M. O., & Rundensteiner, E. A. (1999). Hierarchical parallel coordinates for exploration of large datasets. In *Proceedings of the 10th IEEE Visualization 1999 Conference (VIS '99): Celebrating Ten Years*, San Francisco, California (pp. 43-50). SIGGRAPH: ACM Special Interest Group on Computer Graphics and Interactive Techniques. IEEE Computer Society Press.

Fyfe, C. (1993). PCA properties of interneurons. In *From Neurobiology to Real World Computing, ICANN 93* (pp. 183-188).

Fyfe, C. (1995a). Introducing asymmetry into interneuron learning. *Neural Computation, 7*(6), 1167-1181.

Fyfe, C. (1995b). Radial feature mapping. In *International Conference on Artificial Neural Networks, ICANN95, Neuronimes '95 Scientific Conference, 2*, 27-32, Paris, France.

Fyfe, C. (1997). A comparative study of two neural methods of exploratory projection pursuit. *Neural Networks, 10*(2), 257-262.

Fyfe, C. (2005). Topographic product of experts. In *International Conference on Artificial Neural Networks, ICANN2005*.

Fyfe, C. (2006). Two topographic maps for data visualization. *Data Mining and Knowledge Discovery*.

Fyfe, C., & Baddeley, R. (1995). Non-linear data structure extraction using simple hebbian networks. *Biological Cybernetics, 72*(6), 533-541.

Fyfe, C., & Charles, D. (1999). Using noise to form a minimal overcomplete basis. In *Proceedings of the Seventh International Conference on Artificial Neural Networks, ICANN99* (pp. 708-713).

Fyfe, C., & MacDonald, D. (2002). Epsilon-insensitive Hebbian learning. *Neurocomputing, 47*, 35-57.

Gallagher, M. (2000). *Multi-layer perceptron error surfaces: Visualization, structure and modelling*. Doctoral thesis, Department of Computer Science and Electrical Engineering, University of Queensland.

García-Osorio, C., & Fyfe, C. (2003). Three neural exploratory projection pursuit algorithms. In *Proceedings of the European Symposium on Intelligent Technologies, Hybrid Systems and their implementation on Smart Adaptive Systems (EUNITE 2003)* (pp. 409-420).

García-Osorio, C., & Fyfe, C. (2005a). The combined use of self-organizing maps and Andrews' curves. *International Journal of Neural Systems, 15*(3), 1-10.

García-Osorio, C., & Fyfe, C. (2005b). Visualization of high-dimensional data via orthogonal curves. *Journal of Universal Computer Science, 11*(11), 1806-1819.

Gnanadesikan, R. (1977). *Methods for statistical data analysis of multivariate observations*. New York: John Wiley & Sons.

Goodchild, N. A., & Vijayan, K. (1974). Significance tests in plots of multi-dimensional data in two dimensions. *Biometrics, 30*, 209-210.

Gorban, A. N., & Zinovyev, A. Y. (2001). *Visualization of data by method of elastic maps and its applications in genomics, economics and sociology* (Tech. Rep. No. IHES M/01/36). Institut des Hautes Etudes Scientifiques.

Graham, M., & Kennedy, J. (2003). Using curves to enhance parallel coordinate visualisations. In *Proceedings of the Seventh International Conference on Information Visualization (IV'2003)* (pp. 10-16). London, UK: IEEE Computer Society.

Grinstein, G., Pickett, R., & Williams, M. G. (1989). EXVIS: An exploratory visualization environment. In *Proceedings of Graphics Interface '89* (pp. 254-259).

Hamner, C. G., Turner, D. W., & Young, D. M. (1987). Comparison of several graphical methods for representing multivariate data. *Computer and Mathematics with Applications, 13*, 647-655.

Hastie, T. J., & Stuetzle, W. (1989). Principal curves. *Journal of the American Statistical Association, 84*(406), 502-516.

Hastie, T., Tibshirani, R., & Friedman, J. (2001). *The elements of statistical learning.* Springer.

Hauser, H., Ledermann, F., & Doleisch, H. (2002). Angular brushing of extended parallel coordinates. In *IEEE Symposium on Information Visualization 2002 (InfoVis 2002)* (pp. 127-130). Boston: IEEE Computer Society Press.

Hotelling, H. (1933). Analysis of a complex of statistical variables into principal components. *Journal of Educational Psychology, 24*, 417-441, 498-520.

Huber, P. J. (1985). Projection pursuit. *Annals of Statistics, 13*, 435-475.

Huh, M. Y., & Kim, K. (2002). Visualization of multi dimensional data using modifications of the grand tour. *Journal of Applied Statistics, 29*(5), 721-728.

Hyvarinen, A., Karhunen, J., & Oja, E. (2001). *Independent component analysis.* Wiley.

Inselberg, A. (n.d.). *Parallel coordinates: How it happened.* Retrieved June 23, 2007, from http://www.math.tau.ac.il/~aiisreal/

Inselberg, A. (1985). The plane with parallel coordinates. *The Visual Computer, 1,* 69-91.

Inselberg, A., Chen, Y., Shieh, M., & Lee, H. (1990). Planar conflict resolution algorithms for air traffic control. In *Proceedings of the 2nd Canadian Conference on Computational Geometry* (pp. 160-164).

Inselberg, A., & Dimsdale, B. (1990). Parallel coordinates: A tool for visualizing multi dimensional geometry. In *Proceedings of Visualization '90*, Los Alamitos, California (pp. 361-378). SIGGRAPH: ACM Special Interest Group on Computer Graphics and Interactive Techniques, IEEE Computer Society Press.

Jolliffe, I. (1986). *Principal component analysis.* Springer-Verlag.

Jones, M. C., & Sibson, R. (1987). What is projection pursuit. *Journal of The Royal Statistical Society,* 1-37.

Karhunen, J. & Joutsensalo, J. (1994). Representation and separation of signals using nonlinear PCA type learning. *Neural Networks, 7*(1), 113-127.

Keim, D. A. (1997). Visual techniques for exploring databases (Invited tutorial). In *Proceedings of the International Conference on Knowledge Discovery in Databases (KDD'97)*, Newport Beach, California. Retrieved June 23, 2007, from http://www.dbs.informatik.uni-muenchen.de/~daniel/KDD97.pdf

Keim, D. A. (2000). Designing pixel-oriented visualization techniques: Theory and applications. *IEEE Transactions on Visualization and Computer Graphics, 6*(1), 59-72.

Keim, D. A. (2002). Information visualization and visual data mining. *IEEE Transactions on Visualization and Computer Graphics, 8*(1), 1-8.

Keim, D. A., & Kriegel, H.-P. (1994). VisDB: Database exploration using multi dimensional visualization. *IEEE Computer Graphics and Applications, 14*(5), 44-49.

Keim, D. A., & Kriegel, H.-P. (1996). Visualization techniques for mining large databases: A comparison. *IEEE Transactions on Knowledge and Data Engineering, 8*(6), 923-938.

Khattree, R., & Naik, D. N. (2002). Andrews plots for multivariate data: Some new suggestions and applications. *Journal of Statistical Planning and Inference, 100,* 411-425.

Kleiner, B., & Hartigan, J. (1981). Representing points in many dimensions by trees and castles. *Journal of American Statistical Association, 76,* 260-269.

Kohonen, T. (1992). Self-organized formation of topologically correct feature maps. *Biological Cybernetics, 43,* 59-69.

Kohonen, T. (2001). *Self-organizing maps* (3rd ed.). Springer.

Kokiol, J. A., & Hacke, W. (1991). A bivariate version of Andrews plots. *IEEE Transactions on Biomedical Engineering, 38*(12), 1271-1274.

Kruskal, J. B., & Wish, M. (1978). *Multi dimensional scaling.* Beverly Hills: Sage Publications.

Kulkarmi, S. R., & Paranjape, S. R. (1984). Use of Andrews' function plot technique to construct control curves for multivariate process. *Communications in Statistics - Theory Methods, 13*(20), 2511-2533.

LeBlanc, J., Ward, M. O., & Wittels, N. (1990). Exploring n-dimensional databases. In A. Kaufman (Ed.), *Proceedings of the 1st Conference on Visualization '90,* San Francisco, California (pp. 230-237). IEEE Computer Society Technical Committee on Computer Graphics, IEEE Computer Society Press.

Lee, J. A., Archambeau, C., & Verleysen, M. (2003a). Locally linear embedding versus Isotop. In *ESANN'2003 Proceedings of the European Symposium on Artificial Neural Networks* (pp. 527-534). d-side publications.

Lee, J. A., Lendasse, A., Donckers, N., & Verleysen, M. (2000). A robust nonlinear projection method. In M. Verleysen (Ed.), *ESANN'2000 Proceedings of the European Symposium on Artificial Neural Networks* (pp. 13-20). D-Facto Publications.

Lee, J. A., Lendasse, A., & Verleysen, M. (2002). Curvilinear distance analysis versus Isomap. In M. Verleysen (Ed.), *ESANN'2002 Proceedings of the European Symposium on Artificial Neural Networks* (pp. 185-192). d-side publications.

Lee, J. A., & Verleysen, M. (2002). Nonlinear projection with the Isotop method. In J. R. Dorronsoro (Ed.), *ICANN 2002 Proceedings of the International Conference on Artificial Networks,* Madrid, Spain (pp. 933-938). Lecture Notes in Computer Science 2415. Springer.

Lee, M. D., Reilly, R. E., & Butavicius, M. E. (2003b). An empirical evaluation of Chernoff Faces, star glyphs, and spatial visualizations for binary data. In *Proceedings of the Australian Symposium on Information Visualisation* (pp. 1-10). Australian Computer Society.

Leung, Y. K., & Apperley, M. D. (1994). A review and taxonomy of distortion-oriented presentation Techniques. *ACM Transactions on Computer-Human Interaction, 1*(2), 126-160.

Levkowitz, H. (1991). Color icons: Merging color and texture perception for integrated visualization of multiple parameters. In G. M. Nielson & L. Rosenblum (Eds.), *Proceedings of IEEE Visualization '91,* San Diego, California (pp. 164-170). SIGGRAPH: ACM Special Interest Group on Computer Graphics and Interactive Techniques, IEEE Computer Society Press.

Lewis-Beck, M. S. (Ed.). (1994). *Factor analysis and related techniques.* London: Sage Publications.

Loizides, A., & Slater, M. (2002). The empathic visualisation algorithm (EVA): An automatic mapping from abstract data to naturalistic visual structure. In *Sixth International Conference on Information Visualization (IV'02)* (pp. 705-712).

Lott, J. A., & Durbridge, T. C. (1990). Use of Chernoff Faces to follow trends in laboratory data. *Journal of Clinical Laboratory Analysis, 4*(1), 59-63.

Moriarity, S. (1979). Communicating financial information through multi dimensional graphics. *Journal of Accounting Research, 17*(1), 205-224.

Morrison, A., & Chalmers, M. (2003). Improving hybrid MDS with pivot-based searching. In *Proceedings of IEEE Information Visualization 2003*, Seattle, Washington (pp. 85-90).

Morrison, A., Ross, G., & Chalmers, M. (2002). A hybrid layout algorithm for sub-quadratic multi dimensional scaling. In *Proceedings of IEEE Information Visualisation 2002*, Boston, Massachusetts (pp. 152-160).

Morrison, A., Ross, G., & Chalmers, M. (2003). Fast multi dimensional scaling through sampling, springs and interpolation. *Information Visualization, 2*(1), 68-77.

Müller, W., & Alexa, M. (1998). Using morphing for information visualization. In *Proceedings of the 1998 Workshop on New Paradigms in Information Visualization and Manipulation* (pp. 49-52). ACM Press.

Murphy, J. F. (2003). *Methods for collection and processing of gene expression data.* Doctoral thesis, California Institute of Technology, Pasadena, California.

Nel, D., Pitt, L., & Webb, T. (1994). Using Chernoff Faces to portray service quality data. *Journal of Marketing Management, 10*, 247-255.

Oja, E. (1982). A simplified neuron model as a principal component analyser. *Journal of Mathematical Biology, 16*, 267-273.

Oja, E. (1989). Neural networks, principal components and subspaces. *International Journal of Neural Systems, 1*, 61-68.

Oja, E., Ogawa, H., & Wangviwattana, J. (1992a). Principal component analysis by homogeneous neural networks (Part 1: The weighted subspace criterion). *IEICE Transactions on Information & Systems, E75-D*, 366-375.

Oja, E., Ogawa, H., & Wangviwattana, J. (1992b). Principal component analysis by homogeneous neural networks (Part 2: Analysis and extensions of the learning algorithms). *IEICE Transactions on Information & Systems, E75-D*(3), 375-381.

Peña, M., & Fyfe, C. (2005). The harmonic topographic map. In *The Irish Conference on Artificial Intelligence and Cognitive Science, AICS05*.

Rietman, E. A., Lee, J. T. C., & Layadi, N. (1998). Dynamic images of plasma processes: Use of fourier blobs for endpoint detection during plasma etching of patterned wafers. *Journal of Vacuum Science and Technology, 16*(3), 1449-1453.

Rietman, E. A., & Layadi, N. (2000). A study on $R^m \rightarrow R^1$ maps: Application to a 0.16-m via etch process endpoint. *IEEE Transactions on Semiconductor Manufacturing, 13*(4), 457-468.

Ripley, B. D. (1996). *Pattern recognition and neural networks.* Cambridge University Press.

Roweis, S. T., & Saul, L. K. (2000). Nonlinear dimensionality reduction by locally linear embedding. *Science, 290*(5500), 2323-2326.

Sammon, J. (1969). A nonlinear mapping for data structure analysis. *IEEE Transactions on Computation, C-18*(5), 401-409.

Sawasdichai, N., & Poggenpohl, S. (2002). User purposes and information-seeking behaviors in Web-based media: A user-centered approach to information design on Websites. In *Proceedings of the Conference on Designing Interactive Systems* (pp. 201-212). ACM Press.

Saxena, P. C., & Navaneetham, K. (1986). The validation of Chernoff Faces as clustering algorithm. In *Proceedings of the VIII Annual Conference of the Indian Society for Probability and Statistics*, Kolhapur, Shivaji University (pp. 179-193).

Saxena, P. C., & Navaneetham, K. (1991). The effect of cluster size, dimensionality, and number of clusters on recovery of true cluster structure through Chernoff-type Faces. *The Statistician, 40*, 415-425.

Shepard, R. N., Romney, A. K., & Nerlove, S. B. (Eds.). (1972). *Multi dimensional scaling: Theory and applications in the behavioral sciences* (vol. 1). Seminar Press, Inc.

Shneiderman, B. (1992). Tree visualization with treemaps: A 2D space-filling approach. *ACM Transactions on Graphics, 11*(1), 92-99.

Shneiderman, B. (1996). The eyes have it: A task by data type taxonomy for information visualization. In *Proceedings of the IEEE Workshop on Visual Languages '96* (pp. 336-343). IEEE Computer Society Press.

Siirtola, H. (2000). Direct manipulation of parallel coordinates. In J. Roberts (Ed.), *Proceedings of the International Conference on Information Visualization (IV'2000)* (pp. 373-378). IEEE Computer Society.

Siirtola, H. (2003). Combining parallel coordinates with the reorderable matrix. In J. Roberts (Ed.), *Proceedings of the International Conference on Coordinated and Multiple Views in Exploratory Visualization (CMV 2003)* (pp. 63-74). London, UK: IEEE Computer Society.

Smith, M., & Taffler, R. (1996). Improving the communication of accounting information through cartoon graphics. *Journal of Accounting, Auditing and Accountability, 9*(2), 68-85.

Spencer, N. H. (2003). Investigating data with Andrews plots. *Social Science Computer Review, 21*(2), 244-249.

Symanzik, J., Wegman, E. J., Braverman, A. J., & Luo, Q. (2002). New applications of the image grand tour. *Computing Science and Statistics, 34*, 500-512.

Tenenbaum, J. B. (1998). Mapping a manifold of perceptual observations. In M. I. Jordan, M. J. Kearns, & S. A. Solla (Eds.), *Advances in neural information processing systems* (vol. 10, pp. 682-688). Cambridge, MA: MIT Press.

Tenenbaum, J. B., de Silva, V., & Langford, J. C. (2000). A global geometric framework for nonlinear dimensionality reduction. *Science, 290*(5500), 2319-2323.

Tereshko, V., & Allinson, N. M. (2000). Common framework for "topographic" and "elastic" computations. In D. S. Broomhead, E. A. Luchinskaya, P. V. E. McClintock, & T. Mullin (Eds.), *Stochaos: Stochastic and chaotic dynamics in the lakes: AIP Conference Proceedings, 502*, 124-129.

Tereshko, V., & Allinson, N. M. (2002a). Combining lateral and elastic interactions: Topology-preserving elastic nets. *Neural Processing Letters, 15*, 213-223.

Tereshko, V., & Allinson, N. M. (2002b). Theory of topology-preserving elastic nets. In W. Klonowski (Ed.), *Attractors, Signals and Synergetics, EUROATTRACTOR 2000* (pp. 215-221). PABS Science Publications.

Tidmore, F. E., & Turner, D. W. (1983). On clustering with Chernoff-type Faces. *Communications in Statistics, A12*(14), 381-396.

Torgerson, W. S. (1952). Multi dimensional scaling: I. Theory and methods. *Psychometrika, 17*(4), 401-419.

Tufte, E. R. (1983). *The visual display of quantitative information*. Cheshire, CT: Graphics Press.

Tukey, J. (1977). *Exploratoy data analysis*. Reading, MA: Addison-Wesley.

Vesanto, J. (1999). SOM-based data visualization methods. *Intelligent-Data-Analysis, 3*, 111-126.

Ward, M. O. (1994). XmdvTool: Integrating multiple methods for visualizing multivariate data. In G. M. Nielson & L. Rosenblum (Eds.), *Proceedings of the Conference on Visualization '94*, Washinton, DC (pp. 326-333). Session: Visualization systems table of contents.

Ware, C., & Beatty, J. C. (1988). Using color dimensions to display data dimensions. *Human Factors, 30*(2), 127-142.

Wegman, E. J. (1990). Hyperdimensional data analysis using parallel coordinates. *Journal of the American Statistical Association, 411*(85), 664-675.

Wegman, E. J. (1991). The Grand Tour in *k*-dimensions. In C. Page & R. LePage (Eds.), *Computing Science and Statistics: Proceedings of the 22ⁿᵈ Symposium on the Interface* (pp. 127-136). Springer-Verlag.

Wegman, E. J., & Luo, Q. (1991). Construction of line densities for parallel coordinate plots. In A. Buja & P. Tukey (Eds.), *Computing and graphics in statistics* (pp. 107-124). New York: Springer-Verlag.

Wegman, E. J., & Luo, Q. (1997). High dimensional clustering using parallel coordinates and the Grand Tour. *Computing Science and Statistics, 28*, 352-360.

Wegman, E. J., Poston, W. L., & Solka, J. L. (1998). Image grand tour (Tech. Rep. TR 150). The Center for Computational Statistics. Retrieved June 24, 2007, from ftp://www.galaxy.gmu.edu/pub/papers/Image_Tour.pdf

Wegman, E. J., & Shen, J. (1993). Three-dimensional Andrews plots and the Grand Tour. *Computing Science and Statistics, 25*, 284-288.

Wegman, E. J., & Solka, J. L. (2002). On some mathematics for visualising high dimensional data. *Indian Journal of Statistics, 64*(Series A, 2), 429-452.

Wijk, J. J. v., & Liere, R. v. (1993). Hyperslice visualization of scalar functions of many variables. In G. M. Nielson & R. D. Bergeron (Eds.), *Proceedings of IEEE Visualization '93*, San Jose, California (pp. 119-125).

Wong, P. C., & Bergeron, R. D. (1997). 30 years of multi dimensional multivariate visualization. In G. M. Nielson, H. Hagan, & H. Muller (Eds.), *Scientific visualization: Overviews, methodologies and Techniques* (pp. 3-33). Los Alamitos, CA: IEEE Computer Society Press.

Xu, L. (1993). Least mean square error reconstruction principle for self-organizing neural-nets. *Neural Networks, 6*(5), 627-648.

Zhang, B. (2000). *Generalized k-harmonic means: Boosting in unsupervised learning* (Technical report). Palo Alto, CA: HP Laboratories.

Zhang, B., Hsu, M., & Dayal, U. (1999). *K-harmonic means: A data clustering algorithm* (Technical report). Palo Alto, CA: HP Laboratories.

ENDNOTES

[1] Although the Andrews' Curves have been used by Embrechts, Herzberg, and Ng (1986) to represent time series, as well.

[2] Depending on the values of these moments, we can speak about *skewed* distributions when distributions are not symmetric; *leptokurtotic* or *super-Gaussian* distributions when distributions are more kurtotic than a Gaussian distribution, and conversely *platykurtotic* or *sub-Gaussian* distributions when distributions are less kurtotic than a Gaussian distribution.

[3] Actually, MDS is not limited to the use of a distance matrix; it is possible to use any other kind of dissimilarity or similarity matrix (for

example, the matrix of correlations among variables).

4. The closeness criterion is usually the Euclidean distance between the model vectors and the input pattern.

5. There exists a previous version of the algorithm (Tenenbaum, 1998) that used a different method to approximate the geodesic distances.

6. Multivariate visualization method that consists of looking at the data from all points of view by presenting a continuous sequence of low dimensional projections; we will discuss this in more detail in Section 7.

7. Khattree and Naik (2002) point to Gnanadesikan (1977) who attribute a special case of this formulation to Tukey. Tukey used as lambdas the square roots of 1, 2, 3, 5, … (the prime numbers).

8. This concept is discussed by Tufte (1983).

Chapter XII
Privacy Preserving Data Mining, Concepts, Techniques, and Evaluation Methodologies

Igor Nai Fovino
Joint Research Centre, Italy

ABSTRACT

Intense work in the area of data mining technology and in its applications to several domains has resulted into the development of a large variety of techniques and tools able to automatically and intelligently transform large amounts of data in knowledge relevant to users. However, as with other kinds of useful technologies, the knowledge discovery process can be misused. It can be used, for example, by malicious subjects in order to reconstruct sensitive information for which they do not have an explicit access authorization. This type of "attack" cannot easily be detected, because, usually, the data used to guess the protected information, is freely accessible. For this reason, many research efforts have been recently devoted to addressing the problem of privacy preserving in data mining. The mission of this chapter is therefore to introduce the reader to this new research field and to provide the proper instruments (in term of concepts, techniques, and examples) in order to allow a critical comprehension of the advantages, the limitations, and the open issues of the privacy preserving data mining techniques.

INTRODUCTION

We live today in the information society. Every second, millions of information are stored in some "Information Repository" located everywhere in the world. Every second, millions of information are retrieved, shared, and analyzed by someone. On the basis of the information stored in a database, people develop economical strategies and make decisions having an important effect on the lives of other people. Moreover, this information is used in critical applications, in order to manage and to maintain, for example, nuclear plants, defense sites, energy and water grids, and so on. Information is a precious asset for the life of our society.

In such a scenario, information protection assumes a prominent role. A relevant amount of information stored in a database is related to personal data or, more in general, to information accessible only by a restricted number of users (we call this information "Sensitive Information"). Let us consider as an example the case of a Hospital Health Database. In such a database, records are collected related to the patients of the hospital. The data stored in such database are extremely useful; in fact they allow keeping track of the medical history of the patients, to make an automatic profile analysis, to extract statistical data related to a certain disease, and so on. However, such data can even be considered extremely sensitive. For example, the information *"Patient A has been, in the past, affected by the psychological problem Y"* is an information which, if freely accessible, could have a strong impact on the social life of Mr. A.

It is evident that the concept of *Information Privacy* is a not negligible issue in this context. In the scientific literature, several definitions exist for privacy. At this moment, in order to introduce the context, we briefly define privacy as *limited access to a person and to all the features related to the person.* In the database context, the privacy property is usually satisfied by the use of access control techniques. This approach guarantees a high level of privacy protection against attacks, having as the final goal the direct access to the information stored in a database. Access control methods, however, result nowadays prone to a more sophisticated family of privacy attacks based on the use of data mining techniques. Data mining (DM) techniques has been defined as "The nontrivial extraction of implicit, previously unknown, and potentially useful information from data" (Frawley, Piatetsky-Shapiro, & Matheus, 2002). In other words, by using DM techniques,

it is possible to extract new and implicit information from known information. This characteristic constitutes, per se, an enormous advantage in the analysis of immense datasets. However, the malicious use of such techniques is a serious threat against privacy protection.

In a typical database, a large number of relationships (both explicit and implicit) exist between the different information. These relationships constitute a potential privacy breach. In fact, by applying some access control methods, one can avoid the direct access to sensitive information. However, sensitive information, by the presence of these relationships, influences in some way or other information. It is then possible, by applying DM techniques to the accessible information to reconstruct indirectly the sensitive information, violating in such a way the privacy property.

Let us consider the previous Health Database example. In such a case, we can make the hypothesis that only authorized personnel have full access to all the data stored in the database. However, considering that such data can be useful even for some analysis based on statistics, we can imagine a control access policy which allows different levels of access; that is, there exist different user profiles which can access different portions of data. Such a scenario is very common in the real world and guaranteed to avoid the *direct* access to a target data by non-authorized people. However, as claimed previously, due to the relationships among the different data contained in a database, one, by the use of data mining techniques, someone may be able to indirectly infer sensible data starting from the analysis of the public data.

Recently, a new class of data mining methods, known as privacy preserving data mining (PPDM) algorithms, has been developed by the research community working on security and knowledge discovery. The aim of these algorithms is the extraction of relevant knowledge from large amounts of data, while protecting at the same time sensitive information. The main scope of this chapter is then to give a high level overview of the existing privacy preserving data mining techniques giving to the reader the proper instruments to understand how such techniques can be evaluated in order to identify the most suitable for a target real case.

The chapter is organized as follows: after a brief overview of the data mining techniques, allowing the creation of a "common starting base", in the third section, the privacy preserving problem is presented within the data mining perspective. Then, taxonomy criteria are defined, allowing us to give a constructive high level presentation of the main PPDM approaches. In the fourth section, after a preliminary description of the state of the art in the field of evaluation methodologies for PPDM, an unified evaluation framework is presented. Finally, in the fifth section, a discussion on the future directions of PPDM is presented.

A DATA MINING OVERVIEW

Data mining can be assumed to be a particular type of knowledge discovery process. More precisely, it can be defined as the analysis of observational data sets to find unsuspected relationships and to summarize the data in novel ways, understandable and useful to the owner. From a historical point of view, we can see the data mining techniques as the natural result of the database technology evolution started with the introduction of data collection techniques, continued with the development of data management techniques, and followed by the introduction of the data analysis techniques of which DM is a part.

Data mining can be assumed to be a combination of techniques and theories from other research fields (machine learning, statistics, database systems). For this reason, different classification schemas can be used to characterize the data mining methods. As explained by Chen, Han, and Yu (1996), it is possible to classify data mining techniques by adopting different metrics:

- **Kinds of target databases:** Relational, transaction, object-oriented, deductive, spatial, temporal, multimedia, heterogeneous, active, and legacy databases.
- **Kind of knowledge to be mined:** As we have mentioned, different kinds of knowledge (or patterns) exist that are possible to extract from a database: association rules, classification rules, and clusters.
- **Kinds of techniques to be utilized:** Data mining algorithms can also be categorized according to the driven method into autonomous knowledge, data-driven, query-driven, and interactive data miners.

In the following, very brief, overview of data mining techniques (we remember here that the topic of this chapter is related to privacy preserving data mining and not to data mining), we will follow the "Kinds of Knowledge" classification.

Association Rule Mining

The main goal of association rule mining is to discover frequent patterns, associations, correlations, or causal structures among sets of items or objects in transaction databases, relational databases, and other information repositories. An association rule is an expression $X \rightarrow Y$, where X and Y are sets of items. A good example allowing for the understanding of the concept of rule association is the classic market-basket database, where rules like "A customer that buys products x1 and x2 will also buy product y with probability c%" can be mined.

More formally:

Definition 1. *Let* $J = \{i_1, i_2, i_3, in\}$ *be a set of items. Let D a set of database transactions where each transaction T is a set of items such that* $T \subseteq J$. *Let A be a set of items. A transaction T contains an itemset A if and only if* $A \subset T$. *An association rule is an implication of the form* $A \rightarrow B$ *where* $A \subset J, B \subset J,$ *and* $A \cap B = \varphi$.

Definition 2. *The rule* A → B *holds in the transaction set* D *with a support* s *where* s *is the percentage of transactions in D that contains* A ∪ B.

Definition 3. *The rule* A → B *has a* **confidence** c *in the transaction set* D *if* c *is the percentage of transaction in* D *containing* A *that also contain* B.

Roughly speaking, *confidence* denotes the strength of implication, and *support* indicates the frequencies of the occurring patterns in the rule. Usually, especially in sparse databases, it is possible to extract a wide number of rules. Intuitively, not all these rules can be identified as "Of Interest". Piatetsky-Shapiro (1991) and Agrawal, Imielinski, and Swami (1993) therefore introduced the concept of strong rule, that is, a rule with a reasonable (under such criteria) level of support and confidence. Traditionally, the association rule mining task consists in identifying a set of strong association rules.

Clustering Techniques

The main goal of a clustering operator is to find a reasonable framing of the records (data) according to some criteria (Han & Kamber, 2000). If we consider a machine learning point of view, we can think of the frames as non-evident (hidden) patterns; the individuation of such patterns can be seen as unsupervised learning and the results as a data concept. It is possible to give here a very brief classification of the clustering techniques:

- **Hierarchical methods:** Hierarchical clustering builds a cluster hierarchy or, in other words, a tree of clusters, also known as a dendrogram. Some interesting algorithms based on such an approach are the SLINK algorithm (Sibson, 1973), the CLINK algorithm (Defays, 1977), and the AGlomerative NESting (AGNES) algorithm (Kaufman & Rousseeuw, 1990).

- **Partitioning relocation methods:** They divide data into several subsets. Because checking all possible subsets is computationally infeasible, some greedy heuristics are used in order to obtain an iterative optimization. This introduces the concept of Relocation Schema that reassigns the points in the different clusters during this process. Some of these methods can be classified as probabilistic models (MClachlan & Basford, 1988). In such a context, the SNOB algorithm (Wallace & Dowe, 1994) and the AUTOCLASS algorithm (Cheeseman & Stutz, 1996) have a significant position in the scientific literature.

- **Density-based partitioning:** Such a class of algorithms represents the implementation of the idea that an open set in a Euclidean space can be divided into a set of its connected components. The discriminator is then the density; in this way, a cluster grows in any direction allowing clusters with not well-defined or pre-fixed shape. The algorithm density based spatial clustering of applications with noise (DBSCAN) (Ester, Kriegel, Sander, & Xu, 1996) represents a reference point in this context.

- **Methods Based on co-occurrence of categorical data:** These methods are developed in order to identify clusters in the context of categorical database. We recall here that a categorical database is one in which the values of the items can assume a limited range of fixed values. A typical example is the Market Basket database, in which each record contains sequences of 0 and 1 representing what the customer has in the shopping basket. In this context, cluster must be created searching for the co-occurrence between the different records. The shared nearest neighbors (SNN) algorithm (Ertoz, Steinbach, & Kumar, 2003) is representative of this class of methods.

Classification Techniques

Data classification is the process which finds the common properties among a set of objects in a database and classifies them into different classes, according to a classification model. The basic idea of Classification Techniques is to use some limited set of records, named Sample or Training set, in which every object has the same number of items of the real database, and in which every object has already associated a label identifying its classification. The objective of the classification methodologies can be summarized as:

- **Sample set analysis:** The sample set is analyzed in order to produce a description or a model for each class using the features available in the data.
- **Accuracy evaluation:** The accuracy of the model is evaluated. Only if the accuracy is over a certain threshold, the model will be used in the following step.
- **Test data analysis**: Using the model previously obtained, a classification of new test data is executed. Moreover, the model can be used to improve an already existing data description.

The possible approaches to classification are traditionally divided into four main classes:

- **Decision tree induction:** This is a supervised learning method that constructs decision trees from a set of examples (Quinlan, 1993).
- **Bayesian classification:** It uses the principle of *Bayesian Classification Error* in order to build classification models (Domingos & Pazzani, 1996).
- **Backpropagation:** It is a neural network based process which performs learning on a multilayer feedforward network layer (Rumelhart, Hinton, & Williams, 1986).

- **Classification based on association rule mining:** it is based on the possibility to transform every implication X$\rightarrow$Y (association rule) into a classification.

PRIVACY PRESERVING DATA MINING

As already claimed in the introduction, the rapid evolution of data mining has given a lot of benefits in data analysis and knowledge discovery. Such technology has been applied to a wide range of fields from financial data analysis (Dhar, 1998) to intrusion detection systems (Lee & Stolfo, 1998) and so on. However, as any technology, it is not good or malicious by definition. That is obvious even for data mining. The example of the Health Database made in the previous section easily explains which is the main threat represented by the malicious use of data mining techniques. This type of "attack" cannot easily be detected, because, usually, the data used to guess the protected information are freely accessible. To address this problem is the main goal of a relatively new field of research named privacy preserving data mining.

The "Privacy Preserving" Problem

Before going through a classification of the existing PPDM techniques, it is necessary to give at least a description of the problem for which such techniques have been developed.

As described by Lindel and Pinkas (2002), to define correctly the privacy preserving problem, it is necessary first to define a data representation. One of the most popular data representations is by data tables (Pawlak, 1991). Adopting such a representation, it is easy to think about a relational database as a collection of data tables linked by some "relations". Starting from the data representation suggested by Pawlak (1991), a data table can be defined as a pair T = (U,A) such that:

1. U is a non-empty finite set, called the universe.
2. A is a non-empty finite set of primitive attributes.
3. Every primitive attribute $a \in A$ is a total function $a : U \rightarrow V_a$, where V_a is the set of values of a, called the domain of a.

The attributes associated with a data table can be generally divided into three sets (Hsu et al., 2001):

- **Key attributes:** They are used to identify a data record. They directly identify individuals (which are, of course, directly associated to elements in the universe U).
- **Public attributes:** Their values are normally accessible to the authorized people. These attributes, as we will see in the rest of the chapter, if not adequately protected, may be used to break the privacy of an individual record.
- **Confidential attributes:** The values that are considered sensible and that we want to absolutely protect.

Hsu, Liau, and Wang (2001), in order to identify the privacy problem well, reorganize a data table as a data matrix, mapping the universe U to the rows of a matrix T, in a way that allow us to have in the first part of the matrix (positions $1..m_1$) all the public attributes (pub(T)) and, in the second part (position $m_1+1..m_2$), the private (or sensible) attributes (conf(T)). Ideally, as introduced by Hsu et al. (2001) database managers or people with full access rights are in possession of a triple (U,T,J) where U is the universe of individuals, T is the data matrix, and J is a function $J:U \rightarrow t_1...t_n$ that assigns to each individual a data record. On the other hand, a user who accesses the database also has another triple $(U,pub(T),J_1)$, where J_1 is a function defined as $J_1: U \rightarrow pub(t_1), pub(t_2)...,$

$pub(t_n)$ and where pub(t_1) is the portion of a given record t_1 of the matrix containing the public data. Given this formal definition, it is possible now to characterize the Privacy Preserving Problem as follow:

How can T be modified in such a way the user would not know any individual's confidential attribute values and the modified matrix is kept as informative as possible?

Mapping this problem on the specific case of data mining, it can be rewritten as follows:

How can T be modified in such a way the use of data mining techniques do not give as result any individual's confidential attribute or confidential "information", while preserving at the same time the utility of such data for authorized uses?

More formally, a Privacy Breach in such a context can be defined as:

Definition 4. Let *Tk be a tabular DB (as in the previous description), a privacy breach under the data mining perspective exist if exists a function* $B:T \rightarrow T$ *such that* $B(J_1(T_k))= T_b$ *where* $T_b \subseteq T_k$ *and* $\exists t_i \in T_b \mid t_i \in conf(T_k)$.

In other words, the breach exists if it is possible to identify a function which, taking as input a set of public data (we remember here that $J_1(T_k)$=pub(T_k)); it is able to construct a new database T_b containing some item t_i which was originally in the subset of the confidential items. Intuitively, function *B* might exist because a relationship exists between confidential data and public data which can be used in order to reconstruct or guess the sensible information. The PPDM techniques then, usually, have as one of their topics the suppression or the "falsification" of such relationships.

Methods Taxonomy

In this section, a first complete taxonomy and classification of the PPDM algorithms is given, based on the analysis by Verykios, Bertino, Nai Fovino, Parasiliti, Saygin, and Theodoridis (2004). In this analysis, various PPDM techniques are mainly classified on the basis of the privacy preservation technique used for the data modification (PPDM techniques are always based on data modification):

1 **Heuristic-based:** Make use of some heuristics in order to modify selected values of the database.
2 **Cryptography-based:** Make use of cryptographic schemas in order to protect the sensible data (i.e., secure multiparty computation).
3 **Reconstruction-based:** Where the original distribution of the data is reconstructed from the randomized data.

Figure 1 shows a taxonomy of the existing PPDM algorithms according to those dimensions.

Heuristic Based Techniques

Atallah, Bertino, Elmagarmid, Ibrahim, and Verykios (1999) have shown how the selective data sanitization is a NP-Hard problem. However, the use of specific heuristics can be used to approximate and, in some way, circumvent the optimal sanitization problem. In the same work, Atallah et al., in order to protect some large itemsets, propose a heuristic for the modification of the data contained in a categorical database based on data perturbation. More specifically, the procedure was to change a selected set of 1-values to 0-values, so that the support of sensible rules is lowered in such a way that the utility of the released database is kept to some maximum value.

A derived approach presented by Dasseni, Verykios, Elmagarmid, and Bertino (2001) ex-

Figure 1. A taxonomy of the developed PPDM algorithms

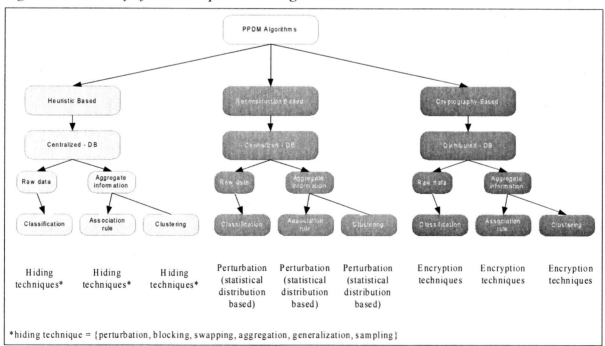

tends the sanitization of sensitive large itemsets to the sanitization of sensitive rules.

The technique adopted in this approach tries to avoid the generation of sensitive rules by adopting two alternative solutions:

- Hiding the frequent itemsets from which they are derived.
- Decreasing the confidence of the sensitive rules under a target threshold.

The goal of these strategies is obtained by modifying the 1-value in the binary database into a 0-value or the 0-value turned into a 1-value, in such a way to modify the support or the confidence of the rule one wants to protect. However, such strategies have some side effects. In fact, the modification of the database can be equated to the injection of new false information. Such a phenomenon is known in the literature as "Ghost Rule Injection". Moreover, by modifying the items in the database, there is even the risk to hide nonsensitive rules, downgrading in such a way the information content of the database. We name these rules "Lost Rules".

A complete approach based on this idea has been presented by Verykios, Elmagarmid, Bertino, Saygin, and Dasseni (2003). In the same context, Oliveira and Zaiane (2002) propose a heuristic-based framework for preserving privacy in mining frequent itemsets. They focus on hiding a set of frequent patterns, containing highly sensitive knowledge.

The algorithms they propose only remove information from a transactional database and can be easily classified as *nonperturbative* algorithms. Such algorithms are based on a item-restriction approach, allowing the avoidance of additional noise to the data and limit the removal of real data. What is interesting is that proposing such algorithms, Oliveira and Zaiane introduce some

measures quantifying the effectiveness and the efficiency of their algorithms.

A completely different approach was introduced by Sweeney (2002). Sweeney proposes a heuristic-based approach for protecting raw data through generalization and suppression techniques. The methods she proposes provide what is known in the literature as *K-Anonymity*. More in detail, we can say that a database is K-anonymous with respect to some attributes if at least k transactions exist in the database for each combination of the attribute values. Therefore, we can convert a database A into a new database A_1 that guarantees the K-anonymity with respect to a target, sensible attribute, by performing some generalizations on the values of such attributes. As a side-effect, however, the generalized attributes are susceptible to a *cell distortion* due to the different level of generalization applied in order to achieve K-anonymity.

The problem of privacy preservation in data mining has also been addressed in the context of clustering techniques. Oliveira and Zaiane (2003) have introduced a family of geometric data transformation methods for performing a clustering analysis while ensuring at the same time privacy preservation.

Conventional perturbation methods proposed in the context of statistical databases do not apply well to data clustering, leading to very different results in clustering analysis. Therefore, they adopt some techniques proposed for image processing in order to distort data before the mining process. More in detail, they consider the case in which confidential numerical attributes are distorted in order to meet privacy protection in clustering analysis, notably on partition-based and hierarchical methods. In this specific situation, they introduce a particular transformation (GDTM), in which the inputs are a vector V composed of confidential numerical attributes and a vector N representing the uniform noise, while the output is the transformed vector subspace VO.

Reconstruction Based Techniques

The reconstruction based techniques address the data mining privacy problem by perturbing the data and reconstructing the distributions at an aggregate level. An example of a reconstruction based technique is the one proposed by Agrawal and Srikant (2000) for estimating the probability distribution of original numeric data values, in order to build a decision tree classifier from perturbed training data. More in detail, the question they addressed was whether, given a large number of users who want to make this perturbation, it is still possible to construct a sufficiently accurate predictive model. They suggest two algorithms for the case of classification. The algorithms were based on a Bayesian procedure for correcting perturbed distribution. This approach obviously preserves the individual privacy; in fact, reconstructing the distribution does not release any type of information related to a target individual.

Another reconstruction based approach was proposed by Agrawal and Aggarwal (2001). It is based on an Expectation Maximization (EM) algorithm for distribution reconstruction, which converges to the maximum likelihood estimate of the original distribution on the perturbed data. The basic idea of this class of algorithms is the following: by perturbing the data and reconstructing distributions at an aggregate level in order to perform the mining, it is possible to retain privacy while accessing the information implicit in the original attributes. However, the problem of this technique is related with the reconstruction of the data. In fact, depending on the approach adopted, the data reconstruction may cause an information loss. Even if in some situation this information loss can be ignored, it is important to pay attention to the reconstruction process. Agrawal and Aggarwal propose the use of the EM algorithm to make the reconstruction in order to mitigate this problem.

In the context of categorical databases, Evfimievski, Srikant, Agrawal, and Gehrke (2002) propose a framework for mining association rules from transactions, guaranteeing at the same time that only true associations are mined. However, the most relevant contribution from the work of Evfimievski et al. (2002) is the first formal definition of *privacy breach*. In fact, they show that an itemset A results in a privacy breach of level ρ if the probability that an item in A belongs to a nonrandomized transaction, given that A is included in a randomized transaction and is greater or equal to ρ.

Finally, to conclude the overview of the reconstruction based techniques, another reconstruction based technique is proposed by Rivzi and Haritsa (2003). Their approach is based on a two-step mining process. In the first step, they suggest applying a distortion method to preprocess the data, and in the second step, a mining process is applied on the data.

Cryptography Based Techniques

The cryptography techniques have been introduced in PPDM in order to solve the secure multiparty computation (SMC) problem. In detail, in order to understand what the SMC problem is, let us consider the following example: two or more partners want to make a computation that needs as input some private data which any partner wants to maintain reserved. The problem is then how to allow the different partners to be able to compute the results without disclosing the private data.

An example of cryptography based technique is the one proposed by Kantarcioglu and Clifton (2002). In their work, the authors address the problem of privacy-preserving association rule mining over a horizontally partitioned database by applying cryptographic techniques in order to keep the amount of shared information low. The proposed solution can be divided into three phases:

1. Each party first encrypts its own itemsets using commutative encryption.

2. Each party encrypts the already encrypted itemsets of the other parties.
3. A party transmits a token containing its frequency count and a random value to its neighbor.
4. The neighbor adds its frequency count and sends the token to the other parties.
5. A comparison is realized between the final and initiating parties in order to identify if the final result is greater than the threshold plus the random value.

Another cryptography based approach is described by Vaidya and Clifton (2002). This approach addresses the problem of association rule mining in vertically partitioned data. In other words, its aim is to determine the item frequency when transactions are split across different sites, without revealing the contents of individual transactions.

PPDM EVALUATION METHODOLOGIES

Considering the large amount of different privacy preserving data mining techniques that have been developed over the last years, it could be difficult to understand which method is the most suitable in a target context. Moreover, there is an effective difficulty in the results comparison between different approaches. It is then necessary to provide a complete suite of parameters allowing to the clear evaluation and comparison of the different approaches (Oliveira & Zaiane, 2004).

In this section, we present the results on this topic (Bertino & Nai Fovino, 2005; Bertino, Nai Fovino, & Parasiliti, 2005) and, more in detail, a framework which allows one to compare the various privacy preserving techniques on a common platform.

State of the Art in the Evaluation Methodologies for PPDM

By recalling the approaches analyzed in the previous sections, we focus in this section on the parameters used by the different authors of PPDM algorithms in order to prove the properties of their algorithms. Moreover, on the basis of the presented parameters, we make some considerations on the goals that PPDM must (or should) satisfy. This short presentation will act as the basis on which we will build the remaining part of this chapter.

In the evaluation of their heuristic-based framework for preserving privacy in mining frequent itemsets, Oliveira and Zaiane (2002) introduce some measures quantifying the effectiveness and the efficiency of their algorithms. The first parameter is evaluated in terms of:

- **Hiding failure:** The percentage of restrictive patterns that are discovered from the sanitized database.
- **Misses cost:** The percentage of nonrestrictive patterns that are hidden after the sanitization process.
- **Artifactual pattern:** The percentage of discovered patterns that are artifacts.

Moreover, the specification of a *disclosure threshold* φ, representing the percentage of sensitive transactions that are not sanitized, allows us to obtain a trade-off between the hiding failure and the number of misses.

Oliveira and Zaiane, in the same work, measure the efficiency of their algorithms in terms of:

- **CPU time:** Used by keeping constant both the size of the database and the set of restrictive patterns, and then increasing the size of the input data, to measure the scalability.

- **Frequency histograms dissimilarity:** Allows the measurement of the dissimilarity between the sanitized and the original database.
- **Size differences:** Used in order to obtain another dissimilarity parameter.
- **Content differences:** Used as third dissimilarity parameter.

As explained in section 3.2.1, Sweeney (2002) proposes a heuristic based approach for protecting raw data through generalization and suppression techniques. We can consider the cell distortion that normally affects a database sanitized by K-anonymity a first measure of DQ impact of the sanitization process on the target database. Sweeney measures the cell distortion as the ratio of the domain of the attribute to the height of the attribute generalization which is a hierarchy. In the same article, the concept of *precision* is also introduced. Given a table *T*, the *precision* represents the information loss incurred by the conversion process from a table *T* to a K-anonymous table *Tk*. More in detail, as reported by Sweeney, the *precision* of a table Tk is measured as follows:

Given a database DB *with* NA *attributes and* N *transactions, if we identify as generalization scheme a domain generalization hierarchy* GT *with a depth* h, *it is possible to measure the quality of a sanitized database* SDB *as:*

$$Quality(SDB) = 1 - \frac{\sum_{i=1}^{i=N_t} \sum_{j=1}^{j=N} \frac{h}{|GT_{Ai}|}}{|DB| * |N_A|} \qquad (1)$$

where $\frac{h}{|GT_{Ai}|}$ *represent the detail loss for each cell sanitized.*

Agrawal and Srikant (2002) introduce a quantitative measure to evaluate the amount of privacy offered by a method and evaluate the proposed method against this measure. More in detail, if we assume to know that, with a certain confidence *conf(v)*, a value *v* falls in a certain interval, then we can use the dimension of such interval as the measure of the amount of privacy guaranteed. In the same work, Agrawal and Srikant assess the accuracy of the proposed algorithms for Uniform and Gaussian perturbation and for fixed privacy level.

Moreover, Agrawal and Aggarwal (2001) propose some metrics in order to evaluate privacy and information loss. These authors in their considerations start from a point of view completely different from the one specified in Agrawal and Srikant (2002). In fact, in this work, the authors take into account the possibility that both the perturbed individual records and the reconstructed distribution are available to the user as well as the perturbing distribution, as it is specified by Evfimievski (2002). The metric resulting by this hypothesis is based then on the concept of mutual information between the original and the perturbed records.

In other words, in order to evaluate the privacy introduced by the use of a PPDM algorithm, Agrawal and Aggarwal suggest modeling even the hypothetical knowledge owned by an adversary who wants to maliciously guess sensitive data. Therefore, the average conditional privacy of an attribute A, given some other information, modeled with a random variable B, is defined as 2h(A|B), where h(A|B) is the conditional differential entropy of A given B representing a measure of uncertainty inherent in the value of A, given the value of B.

In order to assess the information loss, that is, the lack of precision in estimating the original distribution from the perturbed data, Agrawal and Aggarwal suggest calculating half of the expected value of the L1-norm between the original distribution and the reconstructed one. Such a metric measures the difference between the original distribution and its estimated reconstruction in terms of area. All these metrics have non-negligible property as universal since they can be applied to any reconstruction algorithm.

Evfimievski (2002), in order to evaluate the privacy breaches, counts the occurrences of an itemset in a randomized transaction and in its sub-items in the corresponding nonrandomized transaction. Out of all sub-items of an itemset, the item causing the worst privacy breach is chosen. Therefore, considering each combination of transaction size and itemset size, the worst and the average value of this breach level are computed over all frequent itemsets. The itemset size giving the worst value for each of these two values is selected.

Rivzi and Haritsa (2003) propose a privacy measure dealing with the probability with which the user's distorted entries can be reconstructed. Roughly speaking, the probability that a given 1 or 0 in a transactional database can be reconstructed is estimated as a privacy measure.

Kantarcioglu and Clifton (2002) evaluate the methods they propose in terms of communication and computation costs:

- **Communication cost:** The number of messages exchanged among the sites, required by the protocol in order to reach its scope.
- **Computation cost:** The number of encryption and decryption operations required by the specific algorithm.

Oliveira and Zaiane (2003), in their work on Clustering PPDM, define a performance measure that quantify the fraction of data points that are preserved in the corresponding clusters mined from the distorted database. More in detail, a specific parameter, called *misclassification error*, is also introduced for measuring the amount of legitimate data points that are not well-classified in the distorted database. Finally, the privacy ensured by such techniques is measured as the variance difference between the actual and the perturbed values.

A Unified Evaluation Methodology

In order to define which set of parameters is the most suitable to evaluate PPDM algorithms, it is previously necessary to define which are the main goals a PPDM algorithm should satisfy and then, starting from these considerations, reflect on the dimensions to be taken into account in the evaluation phase. On the basis of the content of the previous section, it is evident that a PPDM algorithm must satisfy the following requirements:

1. It should prevent the discovery of sensible information.
2. The sanitized database should be resistant to the various data mining techniques.
3. It should not compromise the access and use of nonsensitive data.
4. It should be usable on large amounts of data.
5. It should not have an exponential computational complexity.
6. It should not consume a high amount of resources.

The actual generation of PPDM algorithms does not satisfy completely all these goals at the same time. Let us take as an example the point (2): its satisfaction implies that an algorithm has to make its sanitization process taking into consideration the different data models under which the same information may be represented and then guessed by the use of different DM techniques. Such characteristic is, to our knowledge at the moment, not fully satisfied by any of the existing PPDM algorithms.

Bertino et al. (2005) proposed a first framework intended to be used for the evaluation of different kinds of PPDM techniques. Such a framework is based on the following evaluation dimensions:

- **Efficiency:** It measures how good the performances of a privacy preserving algorithm are in terms of resources consumption. It can be used to measure goal (6).

- **Scalability:** It evaluates the efficiency trend of a PPDM algorithm for increasing sizes of the data. It can be used to measure the goal number (4).
- **Data quality:** It measures the impact of the sanitization on the quality of the information contained in the sanitized database. It is related with goal number (3).
- **Hiding failure:** It measures the ability of a target PPDM algorithm to fulfill completely its mission (hide all the requested information). It is related to the goal (1).
- **Privacy level:** It estimates how well the information have been hidden. It can be used to give an alternative measure to the goal (1) and partially to the goal (2).

In the following, we will each evaluation criteria in-depth.

Operational Parameters

The *Operational parameters* are mainly related to the computational properties of the algorithms. In this class of parameters, we consider the efficiency, scalability, hiding failure, and complexity. In what follows, a detailed definition of these parameters is given.

Efficiency

As introduced previously, the amount of resources used by a privacy preserving data mining algorithm gives in some way a measure of its *Efficiency*. This kind of performance is assessed considering three main dimensions: time and space, and, for distributed algorithms, communication costs caused by the traffic generated for information exchange among the distributed entities involved in the sanitization process. More in detail:

- *Time requirements* are evaluated measuring the consumed CPU time, the theoretical computational cost, or the average of the number of operations required by the PPDM technique.
- *Space requirements* are measured by evaluating the average amount of memory that must be allocated in order to implement and run the given algorithm.
- *Communication requirements*, as already defined before, are evaluated in terms of the number of communications among all the sites involved in the distributed data mining task.

Scalability

Eager, Zahorjan, and Lazowska (1989) claim that, intuitively, scalability implies a favorable comparison between a larger version of some parallel system with either a sequential version of that same system or a theoretical parallel machine. He relates scalability to the concept of *speedup*. More in detail, let *time*(*n,x*) be the time required by an n–processor system to execute a program to solve a of problem of size *x*; the speedup on a problem of size *x* with *n* processors is the execution time on one processor divided by the time on *n* processors:

$$speedup(n, x) = \frac{time(1, x)}{time(n, x)} \qquad (2)$$

Moreover, Eager relates Efficiency with speedup as follows:

$$efficiency(n, x) = \frac{speedup(n, x)}{n} = \frac{time(1, x)}{n * time(n, x)} \qquad (3)$$

Intuitively, a system with a linear speedup (speedup(n, x) = n) can be assumed to be scalable. We can thus propose a first definition:

Definition 5. *A system is scalable if efficiency (n, x) = 1 for all algorithms, number of processors n, and problem sizes x.*

This is not a useful definition, however. As Amdhal (1967) notes, *many parallel algorithms have a sequential (or at least not completely parallel) component, yielding poor efficiency for a sufficiently large number of processors.* Moreover, there exists the size problem: is it constant or not?

Some approaches to scalability are based on the concept of *theoretical parallel machines* (Fortune & Wyllie, 1978) and on the comparison between the efficiency of the real machine with the theoretical one. A PPDM algorithm has to be designed and implemented so that it is scalable with larger and larger data sets. The less rapid the decrease in the efficiency of a PPDM algorithm for increasing data dimensions, the better its scalability. We can then define the scalability as:

Definition 6. *Letting* A *be an algorithm for PPDM and* D *a database to be sanitized, we define the scalability of the algorithm* A *as the efficiency trend for increasing values in data sizes of* D.

Therefore, the parameter concerns the increase of both performance and storage requirements together with the costs of the communications required by a distributed technique when data sizes increase.

Formally, we define the scalability as the speedup of a monoprocessor computation in a function of the size increase of the database:

$$\text{Scalab} = (\text{speedup}(1, \text{size}(t))) \qquad (4)$$

Obviously, given this definition, it is easy to extend it in the case in which we want to evaluate the PPDM algorithm in a multiprocessor context. However, we are not actually interested in this type of application.

Hiding Failure

As defined before, such a metric is quantified by calculating the percentage of sensitive informa-

tion that is still discovered, after the data has been sanitized. It is interesting to note here that actually, most of the existing Privacy Preserving data mining techniques guarantee by construction a level of hiding failure equal to zero.

Complexity

If an algorithm halts, we define its running time to be the sum of the costs of each instruction carried out. Within the RAM model of computation, arithmetic operations involve a single instruction and could be assumed to have a unit cost. By computing then the computational cost of an algorithm, we have in some way an alternative measure of the efficiency and scalability of an algorithm. It represents the theoretical measure of the algorithm behavior.

Privacy Level

In our society the, term *"Privacy"* is overloaded, and can, in general, assume a wide range of different meanings. From a philosophical point of view, Schoeman (1984) and Walters (2001) identify three possible definitions of privacy:

1. Privacy as the right of a person to determine which personal information about himself/herself may be communicated to others.
2. Privacy as the control over access to information about oneself.
3. Privacy as limited access to a person and to all the features related to the person.

What is interesting from our point of view is the concept of "Controlled Information Release" emerging from the previous definitions. From this idea, as in Bertino et al. (2005), we consider privacy:

Definition 7. *"The right of an entity to be secure from unauthorized disclosure of sensitive information that are contained in an electronic repository or that can be derived as aggregate* *and complex information from data stored in an electronic repository".*

As we already noted, PPDM algorithms act in very different ways in order to hide the sensitive information. For this reason, we believe that when evaluating a set of PPDM algorithms, it is necessary to take into account such considerations.

The Privacy Evaluation in PPDM

The question we want to answer in this section is: Are there some observable phenomena linked with the privacy variation? By analyzing the privacy definition, it is evident that it is strongly related to the information contained in the sanitized database. The sanitization acts as a "Confusion Agent" that avoids the Malicious User be able to see clearly the reality. In physics, the confusion of a system is strongly related to the Entropy of a system. The *Oxford English Dictionary* gives the first definition of entropy: "For a closed system, the quantitative measure of the amount of thermal energy not available to do work". If we substitute "Thermal Energy" with "Information", we obtain that the entropy in some way is the amount of information not available to do work (to be used). Moreover, if we assume the original database to be an ordered universe, the sanitization introduces some disorder. The biggest is the disorder, the biggest is the number of possibilities in which it is possible to rearrange the universe, and then more difficult is to recover the sensitive information.

To summarize, the intuition is that in some way the entropy of the database is related to the privacy introduced by the sanitization. In 1949, Shannon and Weaver wrote a famous paper: "A Mathematical Theory of Communication". What is interesting to underline is that, when talking about the information and communication channel, they defined the concept of *Information Content*, claiming that the information contained in a data sent along a communication channel is inversely related to the probability of occurrence.

Thus, our hypothesis is that it is possible to measure the privacy introduced by a PPDM algorithm measuring the variation of Information Content associated to the database.

The Privacy Level Measure

A metric for evaluating the privacy level offered by a PPDM method is proposed from Agrawal and Srikant (2000). In their work, the authors argue that if the perturbed value of an attribute can be estimated, with a confidence c, to belong to an interval [a,b], then the privacy is estimated by (b − a) with confidence c. Even if the intuition behind this privacy evaluation technique is interesting, such a metric has a non-negligible lack; in fact, it does not take into account the distribution of the original data along with the perturbed data. Agrawal and Aggarwal (2001), in order to solve such a problem, propose a new metric based on the concept of information entropy.

Shannon (1949) defines the concept of *Information Entropy* as:

Let X *be a random variable which takes on a finite set of values according to a probability distribution* p(x). *Then, the entropy of this probability distribution is defined as:*

$$h(x) = -\sum p(x) * \log_2(p(x)) \qquad (5)$$

or, in the continuous case:

$$h(x) = -\int f(x) * \log_2(f(x)) \qquad (6)$$

where f(x) *denotes the density function of the continuous random variable* x.

By projecting the Shannon definition of information in the Privacy Preserving data mining context, Agrawal and Aggarwal argue that because the entropy represents the information content of a datum, the entropy after data sanitization should be higher than the entropy before the sanitization.

For this reason, Agrawal and Aggarwal (2001) measure the level of privacy inherent in an attribute X, given some information modeled by Y, by the following quantity:

$$\prod(X \mid Y) = 2^{-\int f_{X,Y}(x,y)*\log_2 f_{X,Y=y}(x))dxdy} \qquad (7)$$

in which the exponent is the conditional entropy of a random variable X (modeling the original data) given a random variable Y, modeling the sanitized (perturbed) data. The measure of the privacy level by measuring the entropy level, has the non-negligible property to be very general and applicable with some refinement, to a wide range of different PPDM contexts.

In order to give an example of its use, Bertino et al. (2005) show how to apply the Entropy concept to the Association Rule context. The approach adopted is based on the work of Smyth and Goodman (1992). In their work, they use the concept of Information Entropy to measure the amount of information contained in the association rules extracted from a database, with the aim of ranking and thus characterizing the most important rules in terms of information they contain.

Roughly speaking, they represent a rule y ⇒ x as a condition *if Y = y then X = x* with a certain probability *p*. Making a step in the direction of the Entropy Theory, the two random variables can be assumed as two communicating entities connected by a discrete memoryless channel. The channel transition probabilities are the conditional probabilities between the two variables. A rule corresponds to a particular input event **Y** = y, rather than the average overall input events as is defined for communication channels, and p, the rule probability, is the transition probability p(X=x|Y = y).

With such considerations, it is easy to calculate the hypothetical *Instantaneous Information* (i.e., the information we have about X knowing that **Y** = y occurs), which can be represented as a function f(**X:Y** = y). Shannon (1949) defines one of the requirement for f as:

$$Ey[f(\mathbf{X:Y} = y)] = I(\mathbf{X:Y}) \qquad (8)$$

where Ey is the expectation with respect to the random variable **Y**.

Blachman (1968) showed that f(**X:Y**=y) is not unique, and it has two possible solutions, the *i-measure* and the *j-measure*:

$$i(X : Y = y)$$
$$= \sum_x p(x)*\log(\frac{1}{p(x)}) - \sum_x p(x \mid y)*\log(\frac{1}{p(x \mid y)}) \qquad (9)$$

$$j(X : Y = y) = \sum_x p(x \mid y)*\log(\frac{p(x \mid y)}{p(x)}) \qquad (10)$$

Moreover, Blachman showed that only the j measure is not negative. Adapting this measure to the case of a rule (a rule gives information about the event X = x and its complement $\bar{x}$), it is possible to obtain the following function:

$$j_r(x, Y = y) = p(x \mid y)*\log\frac{p(x \mid y)}{p(x)}$$
$$+ (1 - p(x \mid y))*\log\frac{1 - p(x \mid y)}{1 - p(x)} \qquad (11)$$

representing the cross-entropy of a rule.

Finally, it is possible to define a J-measure representing the entropy of a rule as:

$$J(X,Y = y) = p(y)jr(X, Y = y) \qquad (12)$$

where the term *p(y)* is the probability of the rule antecedent.

If we consider the association rules model and a specific rule y ⇒ x, the value p(y), that is, the probability of antecedent, is equal to frequency of y and the value p(x|y) is the probability that the variable X assumes the value x, given that y is the value of variable Y. It represents the strength of the rule *if Y = y then X = x* and it is referred to as *confidence* of the rule. Bertino et al. (2005) define a parameter *entropy privacy* (EP) as:

$$EP = J(X, Y = y) - J1(X, Y = y) \qquad (13)$$

where J1 is the J-measure after the operation of data hiding.

Some preliminary tests we executed show that the simple J-measure does not provide an intuitive evaluation parameter. In fact, as the Information Theory suggests, we would expect as a result that when the confidence decreases, the level of entropy increases. Indeed, in some particular cases, trend is not what we expected to obtain. This is due to the fact that the J-measure represents the average conditional mutual information or, in other words, the difference between the *a priori* and *a posteriori* probabilistic distributions of the two random variables X and Y.

On the base of this observation, we note that if:

- $P(X \wedge Y) < P(X) \times P(Y)$ the two variables X and Y are negatively correlated.
- $P(X \wedge Y) > P(X) \times P(Y)$ the two variables X and Y are positively correlated.
- $P(X \wedge Y) = P(X) \times P(Y)$ the two variables X and Y are independent.

By remembering that:

$$\frac{P(X \wedge Y)}{P(Y)} = P(X \mid Y) \qquad (14)$$

we observe that the J-measure does not take into account the type of correlation between the involved random variables. In fact that can happen only in the case where during the sanitization process, the confidence of the rule remains under the value of the support. In this case, when the confidence value decreases, the J-measure value increases. Studying the J-measure function, it is possible to see that it always has a minimum. The derived function is negative when $p(x|y) < p(x)$ and positive when $p(x|y) > p(x)$. For this reason, we finally adopt as measure the derivative of the J-measure (for making the steps easy to understand, s is equal to p(x), b is equal to p(y), and x is equal to (p(x|y))):

$$J'(X : Y = y) = p(y) * (\log_2(\frac{p(x \mid y)}{p(x)}) - \log_2(\frac{1 - p(x \mid y)}{1 - p(x)})) \qquad (15)$$

Finally, we measure the amount of privacy introduced by the following expression:

$$Level\ of\ privacy = (J'1 - J') \qquad (16)$$

where J'1 is the calculated after the sanitization and J' is measured before sanitization.

Data Quality

As noted before, the main part of the PPDM techniques has an impact on the data quality of the information contained in the sanitized database. If such aspect could be not relevant in certain contexts, it assumes a prominent position in those contexts in which, on the basis of the information stored in a database, relevant, critical decisions are made. Let us consider, for example, the case already described of a medical database. What might happen if during the sanitization critical items of the patient records have been changed? It is then extremely important to be able to identify the PPDM techniques which, in a given context, minimize the impact of the information data quality.

We are then interested in assessing whether, given a target database, the sanitization phase will compromise the quality of the mining results that can be obtained from the sanitized database. In order to understand better how to measure DQ we introduce a formalization of the sanitization phase. In a PPDM process, a given database DB is modified in order to obtain a new database DB'.

Definition 8. *Let* DB *be the database to be sanitized. Let* P_{DB} *be the set of all the aggregate information contained in* DB. *Let* $H\_{DB} \subseteq P_{DB}$

be the set of the sensitive information to hide. A transformation $\xi : D \rightarrow D$, *where D is the set of possible instances of a* DB *schema, is a perfect sanitization if* $P_{\xi(DB)} = P_{DB} - H_{DB}$.

In other words, the ideal sanitization is the one that completely removes the sensitive high level information, while preserving at the same time the other information. This would be possible in the case in which constraints and relationship between the data and between the information contained in the database do not exist or, roughly speaking, assuming the information to be a simple aggregation of data, if the intersection between the different information is always equal to $\varnothing$. However, this hypothetical scenario, due to the complexity of modern databases, is not possible. In fact, we must take into account not only the high level information contained in the database, but we must also consider the relationships between different information or different data. In order to identify the possible parameters that can be used to assess the DQ in the context of PPDM algorithms, we performed a set of sanitization tests over different databases.

Observing the results, we identified the following four categories of damages (or loss of quality) to the informative asset of the database:

- **Ambiguous transformation:** This is the case in which the transformation introduces some uncertainty in the nonsensitive information, that can then be misinterpreted. It is, for example, the case of aggregation algorithms and Perturbation algorithms. It can be viewed even as a precision lack when for example some numerical data are standardized in order to hide some information.

- **Incomplete transformation:** The sanitized database results are incomplete. More specifically, some values of the attributes contained in the database are marked as "Blank". For this reason, information may

result incompletely and cannot be used. This is typically the effect of the Blocking PPDM algorithm class.

- **Meaningless transformation:** In this case the sanitized database contains information without meaning. That happens in many cases when perturbation or heuristic based algorithms are applied without taking into account the meaning of the information stored in the database.

- **Implicit constraints violation:** Every database is characterized by some implicit constraints derived from the external world that are not directly represented in the database in terms of structure and relation (the example of medicines A and B presented in the previous section could be an example). Transformations that do not consider these constraints risk compromising the database, introducing inconsistencies in the database.

Therefore, we identify as most appropriate DQ parameters for PPDM algorithms:

- **Accuracy:** It measures the proximity of a sanitized value *a'* to the original value *a*
- **Completeness:** It evaluates the percentage of data from the original database that are missing from the sanitized database
- **Consistency:** It measures the amount of semantic constraints holding on the data that are still satisfied after the sanitization

In the following, we present the formal definitions of these parameters as introduced by Bertino and Nai (2005). Let *OD* be the original database and *SD* be the sanitized database resulting from the application of the PPDM algorithm. Without losing generality and in order to make simpler the following definitions, we assume that *OD* (and consequently *SD*) be composed by a single relation. We also adopt the positional notation to denote attributes in relations. Thus, let od_i (sd_i) be the *i*-th tuple in *OD* (*SD*), then od_{ik} (sd_{ik}) denotes the kth attribute of od_i (sd_i). Moreover, let *n* be the total number of the attributes of interest, we assume that attributes of positions *1,...,m* (*m≤n*) are the primary key attributes of the relation.

Definition 9. Let sd_j be a tuple of *SD*. We say that sd_j is **Accurate** if $\neg\exists\ od_i \in OD$ such that $((od_{ik} = sd_{jk})\ \forall\ k=1..m\ ^\wedge\exists(od_{if} \neq sd_{jf}),(sd_{jf} \neq NULL), f=m+1,..,n)$

Definition 10. A sd_j is **Complete** if $(\exists od_i \in OD$ such that $(od_{ik} = sd_{jk})\ \forall\ k=1..m)\ ^\wedge(\neg\exists\ (sd_{jf}=NULL), f=m+1,..,n)$

Let *C* be the set of the constraints defined on database *OD*. In what follows, we denote with c_{ij} the jth constraint on attribute *i*. We assume here constraints on a single attribute, but, as we show in Section 4, it is easily possible to extend the measure to complex constraints.

Definition 11. An instance sd_k is **Consistent** if $\neg\exists\ c_{ij} \in C$ such that $c_{ij}(sd_{kl})=false, i=1..n$

Starting from these definitions, it is possible to introduce three metrics (Table 1) that allow us to measure the lack of accuracy, completeness, and consistency. More specifically, we define the lack of accuracy as the proportion of non-accurate items (i.e., the amount of items modified during the sanitization), with respect to the number of items contained in the sanitized database. Similarly, the lack of completeness is defined as the proportion

of noncomplete items (i.e., the items substituted with a NULL value during the sanitization) with respect to the total number of items contained in the sanitized database. The consistency lack is simply defined as the number of constraints violation in *SD* due to the sanitization phase.

The Information Quality Model

In the previous section, we have presented a way to measure DQ in the sanitized database.

These parameters are, however, not sufficient. In fact, a high number of *aggregated information* are usually stored in a database. Moreover, different information stored in a real database may have a different relevance and then when measuring the impact of a PPDM algorithm on the data quality, it is necessary even to take into account if it has been modified relevant or not relevant information.

Bertino and Nai (2005) provide a formal description that allows the magnification of the aggregate information of interest for a target database and the relevance of DQ properties for each aggregate information (AI) and for each attribute involved in the AI. They call such schema *Information Quality Schema (IQS)*.

Data Quality Evaluation of IQS

By adopting the IQS scheme, it is possible then to associate to every relevant information contained in the analyzed database, a minimum level of quality required (represented by Definitions 9, 10,

Table 1. Data quality parameters

Name	Short Explanation	Expression
Accuracy Lack	*The proportion of non-accurate items in SD*	$\lambda_{SD} = \dfrac{\mid SD_{nacc}\mid}{\mid SD\mid}$
Completeness Lack	*The proportion of noncomplete items in SD*	$\vartheta_{SD} = \dfrac{\mid SD_{nc}\mid}{\mid SD\mid}$
Consistency Lack	*The number of constraints violations in SD*	$\varpi_{SD} = N_c$

Figure 2. An information quality schema associated with a target aggregate information

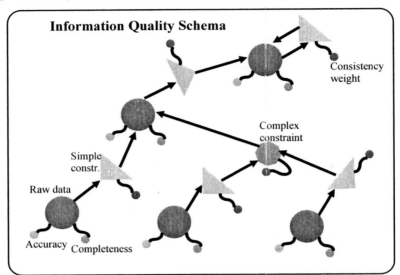

and 11). Starting from this schema, Bertino and Nai (2005) propose a methodology allowing us to measure the quality impact of a target PPDM algorithm over a defined database. This methodology is organized in two main phases:

- **Search:** In this phase, all the tuples modified in the sanitized database are identified. The primary keys of all these transactions (we assume that the sanitization process does not change the primary key) are stored in a set named *evalset*. This set is the input of the Evaluation phase.
- **Evaluation:** In this phase, the accuracy, consistency, and completeness associated with the information quality model are evaluated using information on the accuracy and completeness weight associated with the DMG and related to the transactions in Evalset.

Once the evaluation process is complete, a set of values is associated the database that gives the balanced level of accuracy, completeness, and consistency.

A Three-Steps Framework for the Evaluation of PPDM Algorithms

In many real world applications, it is necessary to take into account also other parameters that are not directly related to DQ. On the other hand, DQ should represent the invariant of a PPDM evaluation and should be used to identify the best algorithm within a set of previously selected "Best Algorithms". To preselect this "best set", we suggest using the *Operational Parameters* presented before plus a *coarse data quality measure* (depending on the specific class of PPDM algorithms) as a discriminator to select the algorithms that have an acceptable behavior. Once we have identified the *Best Set*, we are able to apply our DQ-driven evaluation. We now present a three-step evaluation framework based on the previous concepts.

1. A set of "Interesting" PPDMs is selected. These algorithms are tested on a generic database and evaluated according the general parameters (efficiency, scalability, hiding failure, coarse data quality, level of privacy).

The result of this step is a restricted set of *Candidate algorithms*

2. A test database with the same characteristics of the target database is generated. An IQM schema with the AIS and the related DMG is the result of this step.

3. The information driven DQ evaluation algorithm is applied in order to identify the algorithm that finally will be applied.

This top down analysis is useful not only for the specific case of PPDM evaluation, but, if well developed, is a powerful tool to understand the real information contents, its value, and the relation between the information stored in a given database.

CONCLUSION

This chapter presents an overview of the most relevant contributions in the context of Privacy Preserving Data Mining. Starting from a survey of the existing PPDM algorithms, we have presented a classification of these algorithms using as criteria several parameters related to the type of data mining techniques for which they are developed and the type of technique adopted to hide the data (distortion, blocking, etc.). Moreover, techniques allowing the evaluation and choosing of the most suitable PPDM algorithm for a target scenario have been presented.

However, the PPDM world is far from being completely explored; there exist a large number

Figure 3. The evaluation framework

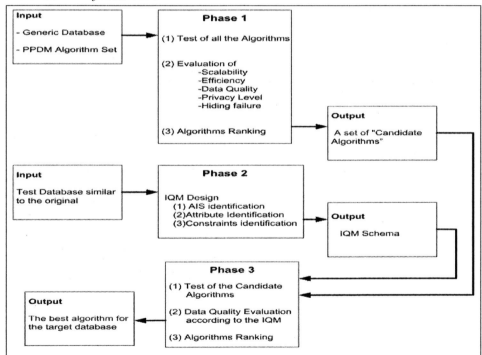

of aspects that are not yet analyzed. The PPDM algorithms of the present generation have a non-negligible impact on the data quality of the sanitized database, as showed by Bertino et al. (2005). For this reason, there is today the need to develop a new generation of PPDM algorithms which take into consideration the data quality and then the usability of the data to be protected. In this context, a second interesting direction is the exploration of the presented DQ concepts in the context of distributed database (Vertically and Horizontally partitioned), focusing the attention on the trade-off between DQ, privacy, and trust.

The PPDM approach is based on prevention: we modify a database in order to prevent the information disclosure. In some particular and critical context, the data modification is unacceptable. The third direction to be explored in the future is then related to the study of a malicious data mining intrusion detection system that should be useful in the context of critical online database.

REFERENCES

Adam, N., & Worthmann, J. (1989). Security-control methods for statistical databases: A comparative study. *ACM Comput. Surv., 21*(4), 515-556. ACM Press.

Agrawal, D., & Aggarwal, C. C. (2001). On the design and quantification of privacy preserving data mining algorithms. In *Proceedings of the 20th ACM Symposium on Principle of Database System* (pp. 247-255). ACM Press.

Agrawal, R., Imielinski, T., & Swami, A. (1993, May). Mining association rules between sets of items in large databases. In *Proceedings of ACM SIGMOD* (pp. 207-216). ACM Press.

Agrawal, R., & Srikant, R. (2000). Privacy preserving data mining. In *Proceedings of the ACM SIGMOD Conference of Management of Data* (pp. 439-450). ACM Press.

Amdahl, G. M. (1967). Validity of the single-processor approach to achieving large scale computing capabilities. In *AFIPS Conference Proceedings* (pp. 483-485). Morgan Kaufmann Publishers Inc.

Atallah, M. J., Bertino, E., Elmagarmid, A. K., Ibrahim, M., & Verykios, V. S. (1999). Disclosure limitation of sensitive rules. In *Proceedings of the IEEE Knolwedge and Data Engineering Workshop* (pp. 45-52). IEEE Computer Society.

Bertino, E., & Nai Fovino, I. (2005). Information driven evaluation of data hiding algorithms. In *Proceedings of the 7th International Conference on Data Warehousing and Knowledge Discovery*, Copenaghen, Denmark. Springer-Verlag.

Bertino, E., Nai Fovino, I., & Parasiliti Provenza, L. (2005). A framework for evaluating privacy preserving data mining algorithms. *Data Mining and Knowledge Discovery Journal*. Kluwert.

Blachman, N. M. (1968). The amount of information that y gives about X. *IEEE Trans. Inform. Theon., IT-14*, 27-31. IEEE Press.

Cheeseman, P., & Stutz, J. (1996). Bayesian classification (AutoClass): Theory and results. *Advances in Knowledge Discovery and Data Mining*. AAAI Press/MIT Press.

Chen, M. S., Han, J., & Yu, P. S. (1996). Data mining: An overview from a database perspective. *IEEE Transactions on Knowledge and Data Engineering, 8*(6), 866-883.

Chin, F. Y., & Ozsoyoglu, G. (1981, March). Statistical database design. *ACM Trans. Database Syst., 6*(1), 113-139. ACM Press.

Chin, F. Y., & Ozsoyoglu, G. (1982, April). Auditing and inference control in statistical databases. *IEEE Trans. Softw. Eng., SE-8*(6), 574-582. IEEE Press.

Cox, L. H. (1980, June). Suppression methodology and statistical disclosure control. *J. Am. Stat. Assoc., 75*(370), 377-385.

Dasseni, E., Verykios, V. S., Elmagarmid, A. K., & Bertino, E. (2001). Hiding association rules by using confidence and support. In *Proceedings of the 4th Information Hiding Workshop* (pp. 369-383). Springer-Verlag.

Defays, D. (1977). An efficient algorithm for a complete link method. *The Computer Journal, 20*, 364-366.

Denning, D. (1980). Secure statistical databases with random sample queries. *ACM TODS, 5*(3), 291-315.

Denning, D. E. (1982). *Cryptography and data security*. Reading, MA: Addison-Wesley.

Denning, D. E., & Schlorer, J. (1983). Inference control for statistical databases. *Computer, 16*(7), 69-82. IEEE Press.

Dhar, V. (1998). Data mining in finance: Using counterfactuals to generate knowledge from organizational information systems. *Information Systems, 23*(7), 423-437.

Domingo-Ferrer, J., & Torra, V. (2002). A quantitative comparison of disclosure control methods for microdata. In P. Doyle, J. Lane, J. Theeuwes, & L. Zayatz (Eds.), *Confidentiality, disclosure and data access: Theory and practical applications for statistical agencies* (pp. 113-134). North-Holland.

Domingos, P., & Pazzani, M. (1996). Beyond independence: Conditions for the optimality of the simple Bayesian classifier. In *Proceedings of the Thirteenth International Conference on MachineLearning* , San Francisco, California (pp. 105-112). Morgan Kaufmann.

Duncan, G. T., Keller-McNulty, S. A., & Stokes, S. L. (2001). *Disclosure risks vs. data utility: The R-U confidentiality map* (Tech. Rep. No. 121). National Institute of Statistical Sciences.

Dwork, C., & Nissim, K. (2004). Privacy preserving data mining in vertically partitioned database. *Proceedings of Crypto 2004, 3152*, 528-544.

Eager, D. L., Zahorjan, J., & Lazowska, E. D. (1989). Speedup versus efficiency in parallel systems. *IEEE Trans. on Computers, C-38*(3), 408-423. IEEE Press.

Ertoz, L., Steinbach, M., & Kumar, V. (2003). Finding clusters of different sizes, shapes, and densities in noisy, high dimensional data. In *Proceedings of the SIAM International Conference on Data Mining*.

Ester, M., Kriegel, H. P., Sander, J., & Xu, X. (1996). A density-based algorithm for discovering clusters in large spatial databases with noise. In *Proceedings of the 2nd ACM SIGKDD*, Portland, Oregon (pp. 226-231). AAAI Press.

Evfimievski, A. (2002). Randomization in privacy preserving data mining. *SIGKDD Explor. Newsl., 4*(2), 43-48. ACM Press.

Evfimievski, A., Srikant, R., Agrawal, R., & Gehrke, J. (2002). Privacy preserving mining of association rules. In *Proceedings of the 8th ACM SIGKDDD International Conference on Knowledge Discovery and Data Mining*. Elsevier Ltd.

Fortune, S., & Wyllie, J. (1978). Parallelism in random access machines. In *Proceedings of the Tenth ACM Symposium on Theory of Computing* (pp. 114-118). ACM Press.

Frawley, W., Piatetsky-Shapiro, G., & Matheus, C. (1992). Knowledge discovery in databases: An overview. *AI Magazine*, pp. 213-228.

Ghosh, S. P. (1984). An application of statistical databases in manufacturing testing. In *Proceedings of IEEE COMPDEC Conference* (pp. 96-103). IEEE Press.

Ghosh, S. P. (1985). An application of statistical databases in manufacturing testing. *IEEE Trans. Software Eng., SE-11*(7), 591-596. IEEE Press.

Han, J., & Kamber, M. (2000, August). *Data mining: Concepts and techniques* (The Morgan Kaufmann Series in Data Management Systems). Morgan Kaufmann Publishers.

Hsu, T., Liau, C., & Wang, D. (2001). A logical model for privacy protection. *Lecture Notes in Computer Science, 2200*, 110-124. Springer-Verlag.

Kantarcioglu, M., & Clifton, C. (2002). Privacy preserving distributed mining of association rules on horizontally partitioned data. In *Proceedings of the ACM SIGMOD Workshop on Research issues in Data Mining and Knowledge Discovery* (pp. 24-31). IEEE Educational Activities Department.

Kaufman, L., & Rousseeuw, P. (1990). *Finding groups in data: An introduction to cluster analysis.* New York: John Wiley & Sons.

Lee, W., & Stolfo, S. (1998, January). Data mining approaches for intrusion detection. In *Proceedings of the Seventh USENIX Security Symposium (SECURITY '98)*, San Antonio, Texas.

Lindell, Y., & Pinkas, B. (2002). Privacy preserving data mining. *Journal of Cryptology, 15*, 177-206. Springer-Verlag.

MClachlan, G., & Basford, K. (1988). *Mixture models: Inference and applications to clustering.* New York: Marcel Dekker.

Oliveira, S. R. M., & Zaiane, O. R. (2002). Privacy preserving frequent itemset mining. In *Proceedings of the IEEE International Conference on Privacy, Security and Data Mining* (pp. 43-54). Australian Computer Society, Inc.

Oliveira, S. R. M., & Zaiane, O. R. (2003). Privacy preserving clustering by data transformation. In *Proceedings of the 18th Brazilian Symposium on Databases*, Manaus, Amazonas, Brazil (pp. 304-318).

Oliveira, S. R. M., & Zaiane, O. R. (2004). Toward standardization in privacy preserving data mining. In *Proceedings of the ACM SIGKDD 3rd Workshop on Data Mining Standard* (pp. 7-17). ACM Press.

Palley, M. A., & Simonoff, J. S. (1987, December). The use of regression methodology for compromise of confidential information in statistical databases. *ACM Trans. Database Syst., 12*(4), 593-608.

Pawlak, Z. (1991). *Rough sets theoretical aspects of reasoning about data.* Kluwer Academic Publishers.

Piatetsky-Shapiro, G. (1991). Discovery, analysis, and presentation of strong rules. *Knowledge Discovery in Databases, 229-238.* AAAI/MIT Press.

Quinlan, J. R. (1993). *C4.5: Programs for machine learning.* Morgan Kaufmann.

Rizvi, S. J., & Haritsa, J. R. (2003). Maintaining data privacy in association rule mining. In *Proceedings of the 28th International Conference on Very Large Databases.* Morgan Kaufmann.

Rumelhart, D. E., Hinton, G. E., & Williams, R. J. (1986). Learning internal representations by error propagation. In *Parallel distributed processing: Explorations in the microstructure of cognition* (vol. 1, pp. 318–362). Cambridge, MA: MIT Press.

Sande, G. (1984). Automated cell suppression to reserve confidentiality of business statistics. In *Proceedings of the 2nd International Workshop on Statistical Database Management* (pp. 346-353).

Schlorer, J. (1983). Information loss in partitioned statistical databases. *Comput. J., 26*(3), 218-223. British Computer Society.

Schoeman, F. D. (1984). *Philosophical dimensions of privacy: An anthology.* Cambridge University Press.

Shannon, C. E., & Weaver, W. (1949). *The mathematical theory of communication.* Urbana, IL: University of Illinois Press.

Shoshani, A. (1982). Statistical databases: Characteristics, problems, and some solutions. In *Proceedings of the Conference on Very Large Databases (VLDB)* (pp. 208-222). Morgan Kaufmann Publishers Inc.

Sibson, R. (1973). SLINK: An optimally efficient algorithm for the single link cluster method. *Computer Journal, 16,* 30-34.

Smyth, P., & Goodman, R. M. (1992). An information theoretic approach to rule induction from databases. *IEEE Transactions on Knowledge and Data Engineering, 3*(4), 301-316. IEEE Press.

Sweeney, L. (2002). Achieving k-anonymity privacy protection using generalization and suppression. *International Journal on Uncertainty, Fuzzyness and Knowledge-based System,* 571-588. World Scientific Publishing Co., Inc.

Wallace, C., & Dowe, D. (1994). Intrinsic classification by MML: The snob program. In *Proceedings of the 7th Australian Joint Conference on Artificial Intelligence*, Armidale, Australia (pp. 37- 44). World Scientific Publishing Co.

Walters, G. J. (2001). *Human rights in an information age: A philosophical analysis* (ch. 5). University of Toronto Press.

Willenborg, L., & De Waal, T. (2001). Elements of statistical disclosure control. *Lecture Notes in Statistics, 155.* New York: Springer-Verlag.

Vaidya, J., & Clifton, C. (2002). Privacy preserving association rule mining in vertically partitioned data. In *Proceedings of the 8th ACM SIGKDD International Conference on Knowledge Discovery and Data Mining* (pp. 639-644). ACM Press.

Verykios, V. S., Bertino, E., Nai Fovino, I., Parasiliti, L., Saygin, Y., & Theodoridis, Y. (2004). State-of-the-art in privacy preserving data mining. *SIGMOD Record, 33*(1), 50-57. ACM Press.

Verykios, V. S., Elmagarmid, A. K., Bertino, E., Saygin, Y., & Dasseni, E. (2003). Association rule hiding. *IEEE Transactions on Knowledge and Data Engineering.* IEEE Educational Activities Department.

Chapter XIII
Mining Data–Streams

Hanady Abdulsalam
Queen's University, Canada

David B. Skillicorn
Queen's University, Canada

Pat Martin
Queen's University, Canada

ABSTRACT

Data analysis or data mining have been applied to data produced by many kinds of systems. Some systems produce data continuously and often at high rates, for example, road traffic monitoring. Analyzing such data creates new issues, because it is neither appropriate, nor perhaps possible, to accumulate it and process it using standard data-mining techniques. The information implicit in each data record must be extracted in a limited amount of time and, usually, without the possibility of going back to consider it again. Existing algorithms must be modified to apply in this new setting. This chapter outlines and analyzes the most recent research work in the area of data-stream mining. It gives some sample research ideas or algorithms in this field and concludes with a comparison that shows the main advantages and disadvantages of the algorithms. It also includes a discussion and possible future work in the area.

INTRODUCTION

Since many recent applications such as Internet traffic monitoring, telecommunications billing, near-earth asteroid tracking, closed-circuit television, and sales tracking produce a huge amount of data to be monitored, it is not practical to store the data physically. The data is instead presented as continuous streams. We define a data-stream to be an endless, real-time, and ordered sequence of records. Systems that analyze such streams have been called data-stream management systems

(DSMSs). Because streams are endless, results and models that depend on observing the entire data cannot be computed exactly, and some kind of approximation is required. Because streams are real-time, analysis should be fast enough to accommodate high input rates. Otherwise, the underfitting problem might occur; that is, although there is enough data to produce complex models, only simple and inaccurate models are produced since the system is unable to take full advantage of the data (Domingos & Hulten, 2001). Analysis, moreover, cannot require more than amortized constant time for each record, and analysis that depends on multiple passes over the data cannot be carried out, at least not without new algorithms.

A number of example DSMSs appear in the literature. Some are general DSMSs, for example, STREAM (Arasu, et al., 2003; Babcock, Babu, Datar, Motwani, & Widow, 2002), the Stanford data-stream management system, and Aurora (Abadi, et al., 2003). Others were developed for special applications; for example, COUGAR (Bonnet, Gehrke, & Seshadri, 2001) is a sensor system developed at Cornell University, used in sensor networks for monitoring and managing data, and the Tribeca network monitoring system (Sullivan & Heybey, 1998) is a DSMS designed to support network traffic analysis.

We now consider the main subject of this chapter: data-stream mining. Data-stream mining poses new challenges, such as understanding the trade-offs between accuracy and limited access to the data records; developing new algorithms that avoid multiple passes over the data while still producing similar results; and understanding the relationship between the amount of data seen and accuracy. Performance issues are of critical importance since they determine how much processing can be applied per data object.

Three kinds of data-stream mining can be distinguished:

1. **Occurrence mining:** The stream is continuously scanned for occurrences of a particular pattern or set of patterns. For example, the stream may be scanned for records with particular attribute values that trigger an alarm, or for certain combinations of records occurring in close proximity. Occurrence mining is similar to the use of continuous queries (Terry, Goldberg, Nichols, & Oki, 1992) in database systems, which are queries issued once and executed continuously over a data-stream upon receiving new data points. We will not discuss occurrence mining further.

2. **Multipass mining:** Extracting information requires more than one pass over the data. Clearly such a model cannot be built from the stream directly but requires some sample to be collected and used as if it were a standard dataset.

    Windows of adjacent records are often used to extract a sample that can be made available for off-line analysis. Windows may be defined as:

    *   **Time based:** An interval of timestamps on the data records, for example, all records from the last hour.
    *   **Order based:** An interval of record identifiers, for example, the last 100 records or the recent set of records that can fit into the memory buffer.

    Standard data-mining techniques can be applied in multipass mining with little, if any, change so we will not discuss them further.

3. **Online mining:** A model of the data is built continuously and incrementally from the records as they flow into the system. Such models can be simple, for example, accumulating the sum of some attribute of each of the records, or can be complicated, for example, building a decision tree based on the stream as training data.

    There are three important classes of online mining techniques:

- Constructing summaries of the data so far in a compact format. Many types of summaries have been suggested: synopses (Acharya, Gibbons, & Poosala, 1999b; Babcock, Babu, Datar, Motwani, Widom, 2002), sketches (Ganguly, Garofalakis, & Rastogi, 2004; Krishnamurthy, Sen, Zhang, & Chen, 2003), random sampling (Acharya et al., 1999a; Babcock et al., 2002; Chaudhuri & Motwani, 1999; Chaudhuri, Motwani, & Narasayya, 1999), histograms (Ioannidis & Poosala, 1999; Zhou, Qin, & Qian, 2005), wavelets (Chakrabarti, Garofalakis, Rastogi, & Shim, 2000; Vitter & Wang, 1999; Zhu & Shasha, 2003), or batch processing (Babcock et al., 2002), which all record a selected history of what has been seen in the stream so far.
- Building predictors from the data. Such models predict some property, either a class label or a numerical value for new records. Prediction techniques from mainstream data mining must usually be modified substantially to work in an online way.
- Clustering the data. Such models group records in ways that reflect their underlying similarities and dissimilarities. Again, clustering techniques from mainstream data mining must be adapted to be used on stream data.

Stream-based data-mining algorithms can also be categorized by their requirements for the data, and the quality of their results:

- Is the result of the stream-based algorithm equivalent to one of the results produced by a standard algorithm, or is it an approximation to such a result?

- Is the model built incrementally and smoothly from records in the stream, or must there be some batching of the data?
- Must the model builder see every record of the stream, or can it use a sample?
- Does the algorithm discount older data, either by reducing or removing its effects?

We focus in this chapter on the three online mining techniques of data-streams, namely summarization, techniques, and clustering techniques, and show the research work in the area. The chapter is structured as follows: The next section introduces stream-based summarization techniques. The section after describes techniques for stream-based prediction. The later section describes techniques for stream-based clustering. Each section concludes with a comparative analysis of the major work in the area. The last section states some conclusions and outlines possible future research in this area.

DATA-STREAM SUMMARIZATION

In this section, we consider three major forms of data-stream summarization, namely maintaining statistics of data-streams, identifying frequent records in data-streams, and detecting changes in data-streams.

Maintaining Statistics of Data-Streams

One of the important problems in the field of data-stream mining is maintaining statistics of data records. Examples of such statistics are mean, median, standard deviation, sum, max, and min. Approximation techniques are required to estimate these statistics of data-streams, in the sense that they always capture properties of the stream "so far". Such statistics are useful for understanding a stream's overall behavior, as well as detecting deviations from stationarity.

To solve the problem of maintaining statistics of data-streams, two approaches have been considered. The first is to use incremental calculations that reflect only a recent window of data (Zhu & Shasha, 2002). This approach does not really use approximation techniques, nor does it reflect properties of the whole stream. It is useful for applications that need to know recent statistics, such as the number of current users using a network router.

The second solution is to store summaries of the properties of the data records. The calculated statistics capture all the history of the stream, but with some approximation (Babcock, Datar, & Motwani, 2003; Bulut & Singh, 2005; Datar, Gionis, Indyk, & Motwani, 2002). Algorithms differ in the precise way they capture and record summaries but, almost always, they give more weight to recent data. A simple example of an application using this approach is recording the maximum temperature reached so far in a city to be kept in forecasting records. We now give some example algorithms.

Algorithms

STATSTREAM is a data-stream monitoring system proposed by Zhu and Shasha (2002). Its main idea is to divide windows into subwindows, called basic windows, that fit into main memory. Summaries are stored for each basic window and the sum over the entire window is updated by adding the summary for the new basic window and removing the summary of the oldest basic window. Using basic windows enables the algorithm to find statistics for large windows that cannot fit into memory.

Bulut and Singh (2005) propose a framework for monitoring streams. The main contribution of the framework is its feature extraction technique. They maintain the function to be monitored at multiple resolutions so that the higher-level aggregates depend on the lower levels to compute their values. They use multiple levels to be able to work with variable-length queries. More space is required, however, to store the aggregates of all the levels. The authors therefore propose either batch processing, or what they called the minimum bounding rectangle (MBR). The MBR only stores the minimum and maximum values over a number of windows, c, in the same level, and uses them to approximate the required aggregate. The required space is therefore reduced by a factor of c.

Datar et al. (2002) use a different approach to maintaining stream statistics. They assume that streams contain binary data, and they count the number of 1s appearing in the stream. They call their algorithm BASIC COUNTING. It maintains an exponential histogram (EH), which stores the timestamps of all the 1s' bits that are within the current sliding window. The total count is then approximated by having two counters; one is for the last bucket ($LAST$) and the other for the total count including the last bucket ($TOTAL$), so the approximate count is $TOTAL - \frac{1}{2} LAST$, since the last bucket may have expired records.

Babcock et al. (2003) propose an algorithm for maintaining the variance over a data-stream. The algorithm defines a set of buckets, within an exponential histogram, called the suffix buckets $\{B_{1*}, B_{2*}..., B_{m*}\}$, where m is the total number of buckets in the window, and B_m is the oldest bucket that may contain expired records. A suffix bucket B_{i*} is defined to be the set of elements that arrived after the bucket B_i, that is $B_{i*} = \bigcup_{l=1}^{i-1} B_l$. To approximate the average at time t, B_{m*} statistics and the active portion of the oldest bucket B_m are used.

Analysis

We give our analysis of the above mentioned algorithms in the area of maintaining statistics of data-streams. See Tables 1 and 2 for performance and design choices, respectively. Note that, in all the stream-summarization techniques, we do not consider the time complexity in our analysis since all the algorithms maintain simple and inexpensive statistics, so we assume constant per-record time complexity for all of them.

Identifying Frequent Records (Hot Lists)

Identifying frequent records (hot lists) is a problem that can be thought of in two ways: either finding *those records whose frequency is above some threshold*, or finding the *k most frequent* records in a stream. Both problems are important problems with practical applications. Approximation techniques are required to estimate the counts or frequencies of the records. Hot list algorithms can be divided into *counter-based* algorithms and *sketch-based* algorithms (Metwally, Agrawal, & El Abbadi, 2005).

Counter-Based Algorithms

Counter-based algorithms (Arasu & Manku, 2004; Gaber, Krishnaswamy, & Zaslavsky, 2004; Karp, Papadimitriou, & Shenker, 2003; Manku & Motwani, 2002; Metwally et al., 2005) are probabilistic algorithms based on sampling. They select

Table 1. Performance for algorithms that maintain statistics of data-streams

Space Complexity

• STATSTREAM (Zhu & Shasha, 2002):
    ◦ $O(k)$ where k is the number of the basic windows of the current sliding window.
    ◦   Best space complexity.
• Bulut and Singh:
    ◦   Requires space to store the aggregates at multiple levels. However, when using the MBRs, the space complexity reduces by a factor of c.
    ◦   Worst space complexity.
• Algorithms using histograms (Babcock et al., 2003; Datar et al., 2002):
    ◦ $O(\log n)$,where n is the size of the stream seen so far.
    ◦   Moderate algorithms; they require reasonable space and give reasonable approximations.

Table 2. Design choices for algorithms that maintain statistics of data-streams

Technique	Flexibility

• STATSTREAM (Zhu & Shasha, 2002) does not use approximate answers
• Others (Babcock et al., 2003; Bulut & Singh, 2005; Datar et al., 2002), each approximate the required aggregates in a different way:
    ◦ .   Both Datar et al. and Babcock et al. use histograms.
    ◦   Bulut and Singh use the MBR.
    ◦   Histograms give better approximation than MBRs since histogram approximation is only done on the oldest bucket, which might have some expired records.
    ◦   MBR is poor for non-normally distributed data-streams.
	• STATSTREAM (Zhu & Shasha, 2002) and BASICCOUNTING (Datar et al., 2002):
	    ◦ Not flexible enough to be applied to different durations of a stream.
	    ◦ Only computes the required aggregates for the most recent window.
	• The other two algorithms (Babcock et al., 2003; Bulut & Singh, 2005):
	    ◦ Have the ability to approximate the aggregates over earlier durations of the stream given that they are within a reasonable period of time from the current time (not very old).

a sample of the stream using some probabilistic criterion and keep a counter for each record in the set that reflects its approximated frequency at any time. The set of sampled records changes with time according to some algorithmic constraints.

One of the major results in this area is due to Manku and Motwani (2002). The authors consider only the problem of finding the most frequent records. They propose an algorithm called STICKYSAMPLING that requires the user to specify three parameters: a threshold percentage s, an error ε ($\varepsilon \ll s$), and a failure probability δ. Suppose that the length of the stream seen so far is n. The algorithm guarantees that all the output records have frequency counts greater than sn with error ε and probability $(1-\delta)$. That is, there are no false negatives, but there might be false positives that have true frequencies not less than $(s - \varepsilon)n$. The input elements are sampled using a sampling rate that is exponentially decremented every $2t$ time steps, where $t = \log(s^{-1}\delta^{-1})/\varepsilon$.

Another counter-based algorithm, called the SPACE SAVING algorithm, is proposed by Metwally et al. (2005). It is an integrated approach for solving both the most frequent records and the top k element problems. The authors argue that a solution for both problems can be found by estimating the frequencies of the elements of the sampled set, and always storing them in a sorted order (sampled list) using a summary data structure. They monitor only the sampled records and replace the less promising records with new records.

Sketch-Based Algorithms

Sketch-based algorithms (Arasu & Manku, 2004; Charikar, Chen, & Farach-Colton, 2002; Golab, DeHaan, Demaine, López-Ortiz, & Munro, 2003; Manku & Motwani, 2002) are deterministic algorithms that monitor the entire stream of data by keeping summaries of the past data. For this purpose, they use histograms, bit-maps, or application-specific data structures.

LOSSYCOUNTING is a sketch-based algorithm proposed by Manku and Motwani (2002). It takes a percentage threshold s and an error ε as inputs. The input stream is divided into buckets of width $w = \lceil 1/\varepsilon \rceil$. Each bucket has an ID associated with it and the current bucket ID is $b_{current} = n/w$, where n is the number of elements seen so far. Each bucket keeps track of the counts of the records included in it. Nonpromising records having small counts are deleted to save memory.

COUNTSKETCH is a sketch-based algorithm proposed by Charikar et al. (2002) to find the top k records of a stream. It uses a number of hash functions applied to input records to update a set of counters associated with each hash function. In other words, each record arrival updates a different set of counters, giving better overall estimation. The total count of a record is then retrieved by taking the median of the expected values of the counters it has updated. The authors use the median since it is less sensitive to outliers and more robust than the mean.

Table 3. Performance of algorithms that identify frequent records in data-streams

Accuracy of results	Space Complexity

• Sketch-based give better accuracy in general.
   o Good for bursty data-streams
• Counter-based are better for normally distributed data since they represent the whole stream with a small sample.
   o They need less per-record time to compute their results.
	• Sketch-based algorithms need more space to store the summaries → their space is dependent on stream size.
	• Counter-based algorithms need less space since they only store a sample of the data points → their space is independent of the stream size.

Analysis

We summarize hot-list algorithm accuracies and space complexities in Table 3.

Detecting Changes in Data-Streams

Detecting changes in data-streams has applications in areas such as network monitoring, traffic management, intrusion detection, and system analysis. In addition, change detection can be considered as a precursor of some stream applications that build models from the data. Data-stream change-detection algorithms can be divided into two types, namely those that detect a change in the distribution of the underlying process that is generating the data (Dasu, Krishnan, Venkata-subramanian, & Yi, 2005; Kifer, Ben-David, & Gehrke, 2004; Krishnamurthy et al., 2003) and those that detect stream bursts, that is, sudden large and unusual changes in a data-stream (Zhou et al., 2005; Zhu & Shasha, 2003), which can be of interest for applications such as stock markets.

Detecting Distribution Changes

We consider two approaches to detecting distribution changes. The first approach is based on what is called the two-window paradigm. The system keeps track of two windows of data: the current window of data, and a reference window that captures the underlying distribution of the stream. The system compares the data distributions of both windows using some distance measure.

The second approach is to use the old data distribution to predict the new incoming data distribution, and then compare the predicted distribution with the actual one. If the prediction error is significant, then the distribution of the stream has changed.

Kifer et al. (2004) and Dasu et al. (2005) propose algorithms for detecting distribution changes in a stream that are based on using multiple pairs of the two-window paradigm. Kifer et al. use a distance measure based on the *total variation* measure (Ihara, 1993), replacing the probability distributions with the empirical weights of records, since there is no prior knowledge of the distributions of the two samples. Dasu et al. use the well known *KL* distance (relative entropy) (Ihara, 1993) to measure the difference between two windows' distributions. The *KL* distance is a distance measure that depends on the probability mass function of two known distributions. The algorithm of Dasu et al., however, assumes no prior knowledge of the two windows' distributions, and therefore, measures the empirical probability mass function for each window's records. It also tests the change significance, using bootstrap methods (Davison & Hinkley, 1997) and hypothesis testing that depend on a user-defined threshold.

Krishnamurthy et al. (2003) use a prediction model to detect stream distribution changes. They use sketches to summarize the data based on some probability measures. The proposed algorithm has only been tested for off-line data. However, the authors claim that it is suitable for stream applications. The main idea of the algorithm is to depend on the sketches to compute an observed value for the current time interval, compute a forecast value for the same interval depending on the past observed values, and then find the difference between the two computed values. If the difference is greater than some threshold, then a change has been detected.

Detecting Stream Bursts

Detecting stream bursts is easier than detecting distribution changes since a stream burst can be deduced directly from the summaries of the data. Zhou et al. (2005) propose an algorithm for detecting stream bursts. They rely on having a ratio threshold and adaptive window sizes. The algorithm depends on a linear scan of a data structure, which they call an inverted histogram (IH), for summarizing an incoming stream by storing suffix sums. They check the most recent two consecutive windows for bursts using the summaries in the IH when each record arrives.

Zhu and Shasha (2003) propose an algorithm for detecting bursts in data-streams using wavelets. They use what they call the elastic sliding window model, which is a model that has a range of windows to be checked to detect different types of stream bursts, either small sudden bursts or long-lasting stream bursts. They propose a modified version of Haar wavelets which they call the Shifted Wavelet Tree (*SWT*). This gives overlaps between windows in the same level such that any window of size $w \leq 2^i$ is covered by intervals at level $i+1$ and all the higher levels. They use either an online approach or a batch approach to compute their required statistics and update the SWT.

Analysis

We summarize the accuracies and complexities for algorithms to detect changes in stream in Table 4.

DATA-STREAM PREDICTION

The goal of prediction is to build a model that relates the attributes of data records to some property of interest. If the property is a label for each record, then prediction is called classification. If the property is a numerical value, then prediction is called regression. For example, we may want to predict whether each frame captured by a closed-circuit television camera contains a human face or not (classification), or we may want to predict the wind velocity in each frame based on the position of objects such as flags (regression).

Standard prediction is usually considered in three phases. In the first phase, a model is built using data, called the training data, for which the property of interest is already known. In the second phase, the model is used to predict the property of interest for data, called test data, for which the property of interest is known, but which the model has not previously seen. In the third phase, the model is used to predict the property of interest for new data (deployment). The model's performance on test data provides a good estimate of how well it will perform on new data, and so provides a way of assessing the adequacy of the model before deployment.

The three phases are carried out in sequence in conventional prediction. In a stream setting, there is no natural way to separate the phases, so we must formulate the problem in a different way. In what follows, we assume that some subset of the stream records are already labeled with the property of interest and so can be used for training

Table 4. Performance for algorithms that detect changes of data-streams

Accuracy of results	Space Complexity
• Algorithms that store the actual data (Dasu et al., 2005; Kifer et al., 2004) are more accurate than algorithms that use summaries (Krishnamurthy et al., 2003; Zhou et al., 2005; Zhu & Shasha, 2003). • Checking the change-significance affects accuracy as well. ° Dasu et al. use a bootstrap method to check the significance, while others (Kifer et al., 2004; Krishnamurthy et al., 2003; Zhou et al., 2005; Zhu & Shasha, 2003) check for change significance using a threshold value. The bootstrap method is a well-known and efficient statistical measure that gives more accurate results.	• Detecting distribution changes: ° Algorithms that need space to store multiple data samples to represent the previous distribution of the data-stream and the most recent data (Dasu et al., 2005; Kifer et al., 2004) need more space. ° Algorithms that Store only summaries of old data (Krishnamurthy et al., 2003) need less space. • Detecting a stream burst needs less space than detecting distribution changes. ° Zhou et al. require linear space to store the IH they use in their computations, while Zhu and Shasha need to store more data since SWT requires storing summaries for overlapping windows.

or testing. Other records are not labeled, and we wish to generate appropriate labels for them as they arrive. In some settings, it is appropriate to insist that predictions must be made for all unlabeled records, perhaps after some initial time. Alternatively, predictions may only need to be made for some records defined by an external analyst, perhaps for a particular window of data.

Conventional prediction handles concept drift, that is a change in the criteria for prediction, by rebuilding the predictive model from scratch whenever necessary (Hulten, Spencer, & Domingos, 2001). In a stream setting, it is possible to incorporate incremental rebuilding in a natural way so that the current model always reflects recent labeled data.

In fact, in the area of data-stream prediction, research is only concerned about the stream classification algorithms. No real work has been done on the data-stream regression. We will, therefore, not discuss any regression algorithms further.

Standard Classification

A popular technique for standard classification is the decision tree (DT). A decision tree is a tree data structure in which internal nodes contain rules, usually (in)equalities on attribute values, and leaves have assigned class labels (that is, one of a set of predicted values for the property of interest). Decision trees are built from training data by determining the attribute whose value is most informative, based on one of a number of criteria such as information gain, and using a rule based on that attribute as the root of the tree. Rules at the next level of the tree are determined in a similar way using the records that satisfy the initial inequality or not and the remaining attributes. When the set of training records that remain at the end of a branch is entirely or almost entirely from a single class, the branch is not extended further, and the leaf is labeled with the class label. An example of a simple decision tree is shown in Figure 1.

A decision tree is used for prediction by testing a new record against the rule at the root of the tree, passing it down to one of the branches depending on the outcome of the rule application, and repeating until the record reaches a leaf. The class label of that leaf is used as the predicted class. Two popular decision tree predictor building algorithms are the ID3 and C4.5 algorithms (Dunham, 2003).

Figure 1. Example of a decision tree

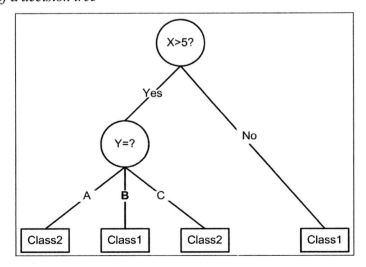

Data-Stream Classification Techniques

Many data-stream classification techniques are based on decision trees with some variations because of the requirements of streams (Chu, Wang, & Zaniolo, 2004; Domingos & Hulten, 2000; Fan, 2004; Fan, Huang, & Yu, 2004; Gama, Medas, & Rocha, 2003, 2004; Hulten et al., 2001; Wang, Fan, Yu, & Han, 2003; Zhu, Wu, & Yang, 2004). The biggest problem is that measures of attribute importance used to determine the best choice of attribute and the inequality usually require counts or probabilities computed over all of the training data. Clearly, this is not possible when the data is a stream.

One solution is to use the Hoeffding bound to estimate when a variable such as information gain is sufficiently well approximated from a sample of the attribute values (Domingos & Hulten, 2000). In other words, the Hoeffding bound tells us when a sample of the data records is large enough that the information we learn from it is good enough to make a decision about the next rule to apply.

The Hoeffding bound states that: "Given a random variable r in the range R, and n independent observations of r, having mean value $\bar{r}$, the true mean of r is at least $\bar{r} - \varepsilon$, where:

$$\varepsilon = \sqrt{\frac{R^2 \ln(1/\delta)}{2n}},$$

with probability $1-\delta$, where δ is a user-defined threshold probability" (Domingos & Hulten, 2000). In other words, using Hoeffding bounds assures that no split is made unless there is a confidence of $1-\delta$ that this attribute is the best attribute for splitting at that point of the execution.

The Hoeffding bounds are achieved by the following. Assume that we have a general function G that checks an attribute's goodness for splitting at a specific internal node of the decision tree. At each point in tree construction, G is calculated for all attributes, and the best and second best attributes are chosen to calculate $\Delta \bar{G} = G_{highest} - G_{second\ highest}$. The algorithm then recalculates G for all attributes as each new record arrives and updates $\Delta \bar{G}$ continuously until it satisfies the stopping condition, that is, $\Delta \bar{G} > \varepsilon$. That means the true value of the largest G is within a range of the value ε of the approximated G with probability $1-\delta$. Therefore, the attribute with the highest G is the best choice for splitting at the current node with confidence $1-\delta$. The tree grows with time, since the input stream is infinite. Whenever a new record must be classified, the current tree is used.

We now discuss the key ideas of some example stream-classification algorithms that are based on the decision tree family of algorithms. Domingos and Hulten (2000) propose the very fast decision tree (VFDT) algorithm for classifying high-speed streaming data. VFDT is the base for many algorithms that use decision trees. It is capable of building decision trees that require constant memory and constant per-record construction time.

VFDT follows the basic steps of building a Hoeffding tree described above, but with some modifications. When there are two close best G values while building the decision tree (i.e., $\Delta \bar{G} > \varepsilon$ is false for a long time), VFDT considers the situation to be a tie. Therefore, it allows a user to define a threshold value, τ, and split on the best attribute found so far whenever $\Delta \bar{G} < \varepsilon < \tau$ holds, in order to break the tie. Also, VFDT computes G for tree nodes periodically instead of after each single record arrival to save processing time, and it drops unpromising attributes with small values of G to save memory. To achieve better efficiency, VFDT uses a standard decision-tree algorithm to create an initial tree off-line, using a small number of records. This provides a reasonable initial approximation to the online classification tree.

VFDT is efficient; however, it does not consider concept drift. Therefore, an improvement for VFDT was proposed by Hulten et al. (2001), called the concept-adapting very fast decision tree (CVFDT) algorithm, which addresses concept drift while maintaining similar efficiency and speed to VFDT. It is an incremental algorithm based on windows.

The main idea behind CVFDT is to grow alternative subtrees for intermediate nodes. Whenever there is an internal subtree that poorly reflects the current concept, CVFDT replaces this node with the alternative subtree that has better performance. Depending on the available memory, CVFDT defines a maximum limit on the total number of alternative subtrees that can exist at the same time. If there are alternative subtrees that are not making any progress, CVFDT prunes them to save memory.

Another improvement on the VFDT approach is to use ensembles (Chu et al., 2004; Fan, 2004; Gama et al., 2004; Wang et al., 2003; Zhu et al., 2004), which are trees built using different parts of the data-stream. These trees are deployed as an ensemble by using each of them to classify new records and then using voting to combine the predictions of each individual tree. For example, five trees could be grown independently using five different windows of data from the stream. These five trees would produce five predictions of the class label for new records, and the class with a plurality of votes would be the prediction of the whole ensemble. It is also possible to extend this simple voting scheme so that each individual tree's prediction is given a weight, perhaps based on its test accuracy, or its size. The overall prediction becomes the plurality of the weighted votes. Another possible extension is to use only the prediction of the most-accurate tree out of a number of current trees in the ensemble, based on some test criterion. We present some example algorithms in the following paragraphs.

Wang et al. (2003) propose a weighted-classifier ensemble algorithm. Classifier weights depend on the data distribution of the windows used to train them, so that the classifiers built from data having a distribution similar to the current distribution are assigned higher weights. Clearly, this addresses the concept-drift problem, as the classifiers representing the current and recent distributions are more heavily favored.

Each classifier is given a weight that is inversely proportional to its expected classification error using the mean-square error measure. The expected error is approximated by comparing the new classifier results to the results of the latest classifier. After assigning the weights, only the best k classifiers are considered, if necessary, for the testing phase, and their results are combined using weighted averaging.

Zhu et al. (2004) propose an algorithm called attribute-oriented dynamic classifier selection (AO-DSC). It is based on the dynamic classifier selection technique (DCS) that trains multiple classifiers on the data-stream as it flows in, and chooses the most accurate classifier. Only the most recent k classifiers are considered and an evaluation set to measure the accuracy of the base classifiers is used.

All of the above stream classification algorithms are based on decision trees. There are other stream-classification algorithms that are based on the K-Nearest Neighbors (KNN) algorithm (Aggarwal, Han, Wang, & Yu, 2004; Gaber et al., 2004). The KNN considers the entire training data as the prediction model, and predicts new records to have the class label of the majority of the nearest k records in the training set. As for decision-tree-based algorithms, the problem in applying the KNN idea to streaming data is that the training set is infinite. The data used for classification must therefore be a subset of the available data, so there are issues about which data should be chosen and how it should be summarized.

Gaber et al. (2004) propose a light weight classification (LWClass) algorithm based on the KNN algorithm and the concept of output granularity. They define the algorithm's output granularity to be the number of results that can fit into the main memory before performing an incremental step (i.e., going to next window). To build a classifier from a stream, LWClass stores a number of training records, according to the output granularity.

Then, for each new arrival of a training record, LWClass finds the nearest training record already stored, using some distance measure, and checks if the new record has the same class as the nearest stored record. If so, the weight of the stored record is increased; otherwise, it is decreased. Whenever the weight of any stored record reaches zero, it is deleted from memory to create space for new records.

Aggarwal et al. (2004) propose an algorithm that uses an off-line model for training the system, and an online model for the classification phase on user request. They rely on the off-line microclustering concept (Aggarwal, Han, Wang, & Yu, 2003). The microclusters store training data statistics in snapshots and consider them as the prediction model. The user specifies the duration at which the classification process is to be applied,

Table 5. Data-stream classification algorithm performance

Time Complexity	Space Complexity

• Testing phase time is of more concern.
• For DT:
  ◦ Worst case: $O(\log t)$ where t is the number of nodes in the tree.
  ◦ Expected: $O(t)$.
  ◦ Light calculations per testing sample.
  ◦ Using ensemble classifiers: $O(m \log t)$ where m is the number of ensembles.
  ◦ However, m can be neglected since the number of classifiers is always limited, except for the AO-DSC (Zhu et al., 2004), since it takes time to evaluate the classifiers and choose the most accurate one.
• For KNN:
  ◦ Worst case: $O(nd)$, where n is the number of stored data and d is the number of attributes.
  ◦ Need expensive calculation per testing sample.
• Obviously, DT-based algorithms have a better time complexity than KNN-based algorithms.
	• DT: $O(ldvc)$, where:
	  ◦ l: number of leaves
	  ◦ d: number of attributes
	  ◦ v: maximum number of values per attribute
	  ◦ c: number of classes
	  ◦ Independent of data size → scalable
	  ◦ CVFDT (Hulten et al., 2001) need space to store alternative trees → $O(wdvc)$, w: number of nodes in the tree and alternative subtrees.
	  ◦ Ensemble classifiers (Chu et al., 2004; Fan, 2004; Gama et al., 2004; Wang et al., 2003; Zhu et al., 2004) need more space to build multiple DTs, however, they all fit into memory.
	• KNN: depends on the size of training data → not scalable.

Table 6. Data-stream classification algorithms design choices

Underlying Classification Techniques	Classification Accuracy

• DT based algorithms:
  ◦ Most popular for streaming applications.
  ◦ Simple and efficient.
  ◦ Time and space complexities are independent on data size → scalable.
• KNN based algorithms:
  ◦ Simple.
  ◦ Not scalable → not practical.
	• Both DT and KNN give good accuracy.
	• However, KNN builds the predictor on part of the data → accuracy reduced.
	• DT is preferred because it is based on the Hoeffding bounds.
	• DT may lead to overfitting.
	• KNN is better for outlier handling because it only depends on the k nearest neighbors.
	• KNN is better for data that change in nature, such that it builds the predictor on the recent window of data.
	• DT algorithms that do not consider the concept drift problem (Domingos & Hulten, 2000; Gama et al., 2003, 2004) have the least accuracy.

and the system chooses the appropriate snapshots of training data. The system considers an evaluation data set (1% of training records) to be used in measuring the most accurate k microclusters. Then the KNN algorithm is applied. At any time, the number of the stored microclusters is $C \log n$, where C is the maximum capacity of a snapshot and n is the size of the input stream seen so far. Each microcluster requires $O(d)$ memory, where d is the number of attributes.

Analysis

We now analyze the above stream-classification algorithms. Tables 5 and 6 compare the algorithms' performance and design, respectively. Table 5 gives a comparison of the algorithms' time and space complexities. Table 6 considers the main design choices, their underlying classification techniques and classification accuracies.

DATA-STREAM CLUSTERING

Data clustering is the process of gathering input data into a number of groups or clusters. Each cluster contains data records that are similar to each other, while being dissimilar to records in other clusters. The difficulty in applying such techniques to data-streams is that it is impossible to see all of the data records before deciding the best way to cluster them. Therefore, clustering algorithms over data-streams use approximation techniques that store important statistics needed by the clustering algorithms, and tentative clusters that reflect the data seen so far. In this section, we describe how standard data-clustering algorithms can be modified to apply to streaming data, and examine and compare the different data-stream clustering techniques.

Standard Data Clustering

Standard clustering algorithms can be divided into two main types, namely hierarchical clustering algorithms and partitional clustering algorithms (Dunham, 2003; Kantardzic, 2003). Hierarchical clustering algorithms produce a tree in which each leaf represents a data record, and each internal node represents a cluster. The parent of a set of nodes represents a cluster that is the union of the clusters below it, so that the clustering structure can be understood at different granularities by considering different levels of the tree. The tree structure is called a dendrogram. An example is shown in Figure 2. The main advantage of hierarchical clustering is that it does not require the number of clusters to be known in advance.

Two kinds of algorithms are used to build hierarchical clustering. Agglomerative algorithms start by assuming each data record is a cluster on its own, and then repeatedly join the two most similar clusters until all of the records are in a single cluster (at the root of the tree). They build the dendrogram upwards from the leaves to the root. Divisive algorithms start by assuming that the data records form a single cluster, and then repeatedly divide one of the existing clusters into two subclusters. They build the dendrogram downwards from the root to the leaves.

Partitional clustering algorithms divide the data records into a fixed number of disjoint clusters

Figure 2. Example of a dendogram

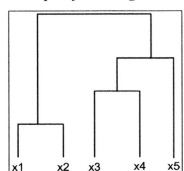

(sometimes records may be members of more than one cluster probabilistically). These algorithms need to know the number of clusters in advance, which can be problematic in practice. Partitional algorithms are preferred for large datasets because their results are easier to interpret than those of hierarchical algorithms.

Both kinds of clustering algorithms (hierarchical and partitional) use some measure of similarity between records and/or clusters to decide where boundaries between clusters should be. Some common measures of similarity are distance (for example, Euclidean distance) or likelihood (for example, based on a set of distributions).

K-means is a common partitional clustering algorithm (Dunham, 2003; Kantardzic, 2003). It is widely used, perhaps because of its simplicity, although it assumes that the best model for cluster shape is spherical, and that most clusters are about the same size. When these assumptions are violated, *k*-means can produce quite poor results.

The goal of *k*-means is to find a clustering that minimizes the total squared-error, E^2, of the distance of each record from its cluster center. This can be accomplished by first finding the centroid for each cluster. Suppose we have *k* clusters and each cluster C_j, $1 \leq j \leq k$ has n_j data records. The centroid of a cluster C_j is the mean vector M_j of that cluster:

$$M_j = \left(1/n_j\right)\sum_{i=1}^{n_j} x_{ij},$$

where x_{ij} is the ith data sample included in cluster C_j. The squared-error, e^2, for C_j is then calculated using:

$$e_j^2 = \sum_{j=1}^{n_j} \left(x_{ij} - M_j\right)^2.$$

Finally, the total squared-error E^2 for the clustering is calculated as:

$$E^2 = \sum_{j=1}^{k} e_j^2.$$

The simplest implementation of *k*-means starts by assigning data records to *k* clusters randomly, and then finds the centroid for each of the initial clusters. Each record is then assigned to the closest cluster centroid. The centroids of these new clusters are calculated, records are reassigned, and the process repeats. The algorithm terminates when no change in allocations of records to clusters takes place. *K*-means has a well-known variant that is used, for example, in discrete input data problems. It is called the *k*-medians algorithm. In this variant, the centroid must be one of the input data records, usually the one closest to the calculated centroid.

Data-Stream Clustering Techniques

We now consider how clustering algorithms can be applied to data-streams. As mentioned before, clustering algorithms over data-streams must use approximation techniques. Most existing data-stream clustering algorithms are based on the *k*-means algorithm in one way or another. This is because the *k*-means algorithm is incremental in nature since it accesses the inputs one by one and updates the clustering structure incrementally, unlike other clustering algorithms that consider the whole dataset and have multiple generations, as in genetic algorithms and self organizing maps. Also, the *k*-means algorithm calculations are light calculations compared to other algorithms as it only calculates the Euclidean distance between any incoming item and the existing cluster centers. The per-item time is therefore minimized. Because the *k*-means algorithm inherently requires multiple passes over the data, applying the algorithm requires collecting windows of data.

Many solutions have been proposed to the problem of applying *k*-means on streaming data. We consider three common solutions. The first solution is to have the clustering done in multiple layers (Babcock et al., 2003; Guha et al., 2000). Each window of data is clustered into a number of clusters, and only the cluster centers and some summary data (for example, diameters) are kept in memory. Then, whenever the number of cluster centers becomes large, these centers are reclustered to form another layer of clustering, and the summaries are updated to represent the new layer of clustering as well.

The second solution is to use an incremental clustering method with generations (Gaber et al., 2004; Gupta & Grossman, 2004; Ordonez, 2003). A generation is actually a window of recent data. In this solution, important calculations for each data record are done upon each new record's arrival; however, the clustering operation that produces the final clustering structure of the current stage is performed whenever all the window's records accumulate. Incremental algorithms have a constant space complexity and a time complexity of $O(n)$, where n is the number of data points seen so far.

The third solution is not to create an approximate clustering at all times. Algorithms instead find clusters for a defined set of records, perhaps defined by an analyst. The advantage of this solution is that it only needs to maintain simple online summaries, and the actual clustering is done off-line on request.

Guha et al. (2000) use the multiple layers idea for clustering. They use constant-factor approximation algorithms (Hochbaum, 1997) to compute k-medians in one pass and store a summary of past data to be used in clustering computations. Similar work is done by Babcock et al. (2003). They rely on the multiple layer clustering idea as well, but they use an exponential histogram (EH) to store summary information about the data. Both algorithms require a space of $O(n^\varepsilon)$, for windows of size n^ε, where $\varepsilon < \frac{1}{2}$ and n is the number of data records seen so far, and a time complexity of $O(n^{\varepsilon+1})$ using an approximation factor of $2^{O(1/\varepsilon)}$.

The GenIc algorithm proposed by Gupta and Grossman (2004) is an example of an incremental algorithm. GenIc, which stands for single-pass generalized incremental algorithm

for clustering, combines ideas from incremental algorithms and windowed algorithms. It updates the existing clusters with each new data record's arrival (incremental step) by finding the nearest cluster center to it. At the end of each window of data (a generation), it merges clusters to get k final clusters (window step). Cluster centers are assigned a weight value depending on the number of points assigned to each of them. The centers are considered in the next-generation clustering results only if the ratio between the number of points assigned to this center and the total number of data points is above some selected threshold. The first incoming points of the data-stream are chosen to be initial cluster centers. Some variations include keeping the discarded clusters in case they can be used later, or combining the lightweight clusters that are assigned to be discarded with heavy-weight clusters if they exist within their neighbors' boundaries.

Aggarwal et al. (2003) propose two algorithms that produce clustering based on a defined period of time: CluStream, a framework for clustering streams that are of changing nature, and HPStream (Aggarwal et al., 2004), a framework for projected clustering of high-dimensional data-streams. Projected clustering means that the clustering process does not take all the attributes into consideration when finding similarities; instead, it clusters the data using the similarities of a subset of attributes.

The underlying idea of both of these algorithms is to use two components: an online component and an off-line component. The online component, called the online microclustering component, maintains summary statistics of the data seen so far. The off-line component, called the off-line macroclustering component, uses these stored summaries to cluster the data. HPStream is an extension of CluStream to handle projected clustering.

Although all of the above mentioned algorithms use the k-means clustering algorithm in one way or another, there are algorithms for stream clustering that are based on other ideas. The STREAM system (Arasu et al., 2003) uses a clustering algorithm that relies on a concept called the facility cost, which involves finding clusters such that the total cost is minimized (O'Callaghan, Mishra, Meyerson, Guha, & Motwani, 2002). The number of clusters k is not fixed; instead the best k is found such that the total cost is minimized. This is usually more desirable than having to specify a fixed k in advance, since in practice the appropriate number of clusters to represent a given data-stream may not be known in advance.

STREAM clusters data windows using a local search method, and only the cluster centers are stored, each with the number of data points assigned to it. The cluster center cost is calculated using the center weight and the distance from each point to this center. Whenever the number of stored cluster centers becomes large, the centers themselves are reclustered. It is important to note that no single step that affects the overall change in cluster structure is performed if the new structure has greater cost than the current one. The number of centers to test for a change is a randomly chosen $\log k$ points. Therefore, this algorithm has a time complexity of $O(nm + k \log k)$, where n is the number of data points seen so far and m is the number of the initial facilities (cluster centers). The space complexity is constant.

Rodrigues, Gama, and Pedroso (n.d.) propose the online divisive agglomerative clustering system (ODAC) as a hierarchical stream-clustering approach. For each window of data, ODAC starts with the divisive step that searches the clusters from the largest diameter to the smallest, trying to find a cluster that has a good splitting point according to a predefined splitting threshold. If it finds a cluster worth splitting, then it does so. If no candidates are found, the system proceeds to an agglomerative step, where it searches for a possible aggregation of two clusters.

ODAC uses the correlation between two records as its distance measure. A change of cluster structure (split or aggregate) is not actually per-

formed unless it produces a better cluster quality. Since ODAC uses a hierarchical structure to store the cluster structures, its space complexity is $O(\log n)$, and its time complexity is $O(n \log n)$, where n is the number of data records seen so far.

Finally, a novel approach to data-stream clustering was proposed by Motoyoshi, Miura, and Shioya (2004). They cluster data-streams incrementally using regression analysis (Dunham, 2003). They assume that there are linear correlations among the records in the data-stream, so that the clusters should form linear subspaces in the attribute space. With this assumption, local regression can be used to detect clusters.

The algorithm proposed by Motoyoshi et al. (2004) accesses the data as windows. For each window, it creates a number of initial clusters by finding sets of approximately collinear records using inner products (which correspond to the cosine of the angle between records regarded as vectors). Clusters are combined using two measures: the Mahalanobis distance between them, and a similarity measure, the F-value test method for multiple regression analysis. Both tests have to be successful in order to be able to combine two clusters. The time and space complexities are $O(nm^2)$ and $O(m)$, respectively, where n is the number of data records seen so far and m is the number of values kept in memory. The value of m is large since the algorithm does not summarize the input data values; instead, it keeps the actual values.

Analysis

We give our analysis of stream-clustering techniques. Tables 7 and 8 compare the stream-clustering algorithms with respect to performance and design choices, respectively. Table 7 considers performance in terms of the time and space complexities. The design choices listed in Table 8 are the approximation technique used, the clustering technique used, and the output format.

Table 7. Data-stream clustering algorithm performance

Time Complexity	Space Complexity

• Optimal: $O(n)$
• Algorithms that have $O(n)$ complexity:
  ○ Incremental (Gaber *et al.*, 2004; Gupta & Grossman, 2004; Ordonez, 2003).
  ○ Online component of the online-off-line algorithms (Aggarwal *et al.*, 2003; Aggarwal *et al.*, 2004).
	• Optimal: $O(1)$
	• Algorithms that have $O(1)$ complexity:
	  ○ Incremental (Gaber *et al.*, 2004; Gupta & Grossman, 2004; Ordonez, 2003).
	  ○ STREAM (O'Callaghan et al., 2002).
	• Online-off-line algorithms have $O(log\ n)$ complexity → Reasonable

Table 8. Data-stream clustering algorithms design choices

Approximation technique: Sliding Window	Underlying clustering technique	Output format

• Consider new data with some percentage of old structure (Gaber et al., 2004; Motoyoshi et al., 2004; O'Callaghan et al., 2002; Ordonez, 2003).
  ○ Good for applications with data changing in nature.
• Consider old data summaries (Guha et al., 2000; Rodrigues et al., n.d.)
  ○ Good for stable data-stream applications.
• Consider only heavy-weighted old clusters (Gupta & Grossman, 2004).
  ○ Modest and fair solution.
	• Partitional: *k*-means/*k*-medians
	  ○ Defined number of clusters.
	  ○ Light calculations → Less time/record.
	• Hierarchical (Rodrigues et al., n.d.)
	  ○ Expensive computations for splitting/aggregating. → More time
	  ○ Not suitable for streams
	• Regression analysis (Motoyoshi et al., 2004)
	  ○ Only good for line-shaped clusters → Not general.
	• We consider *k*-means based stream clustering algorithms the most suitable for streaming data among other used algorithms.
		• Continuous (Babcock et al., 2003; Guha et al., 2000).
		  ○ Use approximations → least efficient.
		• Upon user request (Aggarwal et al., 2003; Aggarwal et al., 2004; Babcock et al., 2003).
		  ○ Flexible and general.
		  ○ Most efficient.
		  ○ More time.
		• Periodic (Gaber et al., 2004; Gupta & Grossman, 2004; Motoyoshi et al., 2004; O'Callaghan et al., 2002; Ordonez, 2003; Rodrigues et al., n.d.).
		  ○ Modest and fair solution.

RESEARCH ISSUES

Although researchers in the data-stream mining field have successfully addressed many of the issues that are of major concern of data-streams, the area is still new and it has many open problems. Actually, what has been addressed so far is related to having stream-mining systems that can handle the endless flow data of data by being incremental, fast, and clever enough to approximate answers with a certain level of accuracy, based on the stream samples that have been seen so far. The concept drift problem has also been a major concern of the existing stream-mining systems. It is still, however, an open problem for lots of stream-mining algorithms.

Despite all the addressed problems in the field of data-stream mining, there are other interesting open research issues to consider. We list some of the most important ones here:

- The trade-offs between model performance and computational capability needs to be understood.
- The accuracy of the data-stream mining systems does not reflect real-life applica-

tion needs. A system should be able to give accuracy according to the requirements of the application.

- The area of data-stream regression algorithms should be further improved.

- Although the field of distributed data-stream mining systems is one of the research directions that are recently considered, the interaction between different data-stream mining systems or data-stream mining systems and standard data-mining systems is an issue that is not yet addressed.

- The privacy of data coming from different sources for data-stream mining systems is one of the important problems that have not been considered by data-stream mining techniques.

- The practical upper limits of data rates should be studied in order for the current data-stream mining algorithms to remain effective.

- The opportunities to go beyond adaptations of standard data-mining algorithms to discover entirely new algorithms appropriate for stream data is an interesting open problem.

CONCLUSION

Data-streams represent the continuous data generated by reactive systems, which produce a conceptually endless stream of data, often at high speed. Data-stream analysis and mining requires novel algorithms that are able to produce models of the data in an online way, looking at each data record only once, and within a limited amount of time. Although standard data-analysis and data-mining algorithms are a useful starting point, they must typically be adapted to operate in the stream setting. We have described some of the ideas that have been suggested and tried, analyzed them, and provided an assessment of their effectiveness.

For data summarization, most stream-based algorithms provide approximations with bounded errors to properties or statistics of the stream as a whole. Some of these techniques are unexpectedly effective, suggesting that they have a role to play in standard data mining as well.

For prediction, techniques for only a limited number of models are known. The use of Hoeffding bounds has been important, since it allows attribute selection methods used in decision trees to be generalized to stream data. The idea of bounding the error of an approximate value based on how much raw data has been seen once again plays an important role.

For clustering, the challenge is that standard partitional clustering algorithms are almost all based on iterations of two-phase algorithms; the first phase determines the fit of model parameters based on the data, and the second phase determines the fit of the data based on the model parameters. Simulating the effect of such iterations is difficult with only one pass over the data. Most algorithms replace each iteration by a new window of data, assuming an underlying stationarity in the distribution of the attribute values.

REFERENCES

General

Davison, A. C., & Hinkley, D. V. (1997). *Bootstrap methods and their applications.* Cambridge University Press.

Dellaert, F. (2002). *The expectation maximization algorithm* (Tech. Rep. No. GIT-GVU-02-20). College of Computing, Georgia Institute of Technology.

Dunham, M. H. (2003). *Data mining: Introductory and advanced topics.* Prentice Hall.

Hochbaum, D. S. (1997). *Approximation algorithms for NP-Hard problems*. PWS Publishing Company.

Ihara, S. (1993). *Information theory for continuous systems*. World Scientific Publiching Co.

Kantardzic, M. (2003). *Data mining: Concepts, models, methods, and algorithms*. IEEE Press.

Montgomery, D. C., & Runger, G. C. (1994). *Applied statistics and probability for engineers*. John Wiley & Sons, Inc.

Stone, M. (1974). Cross-validatory choice and assessment of statistical predictions (with discussion). *Journal of the Royal Statistical Society Series B, 36*, 111-147.

Data-Stream Management Systems

Abadi, D., Carney, D., Cetintemel, U., Cherniack, M., Convey, C., Lee, S., Stonebraker, M., Tatbul, N., & Zdonik, S. (2003). Aurora: A new model and architecture for data stream management. *Journal of Very Large Data Bases (VLDB), 12*(2), 120-139.

Acharya, S., Gibbons, P. B., & Poosala, V. (1999). *Congressional samples for approximate answering of group-by queries* (Technical report). Bell Laboratories, Murray Hill.

Acharya, S., Gibbons, P. B., Poosala, V., & Ramaswamy, S. (1999). Join synopses for approximate query answering. In *Proceedings of the ACM International Conference on Management of Data (SIGMOD)*, Philadelphia, Pennsylvania.

Arasu, A., Babcock, B., Babu, S., Datar, M., Ito, K., Nishizawa, I., Rosenstein, J., & Widom, J. (2003). STREAM: The Stanford data stream management system. *IEEE Data Engineering Bulletin, 26*(1).

Babcock, B., Babu, S., Datar, M., Motwani, R., & Widom, J. (2002). Models and issues in data stream systems. In *Proceedings of the 21st ACM SIGACT-SIGMOD-SIGART Symposium on Principles of Database Systems (PODS)*, Madison, Wisconsin (pp. 1-16).

Babcock, B., Datar, M., & Motwani, R. (2002). Sampling from a moving window over streaming data. In *Proceedings of the 13th Annual ACM-SIAM Symposium on Discrete Algorithms (SODA)*, San Francisco, California (pp. 633-634).

Babcock, B., Datar, M., & Motwani, R. (2003). Load shedding techniques for data stream systems. In *Proceedings of the 2003 Workshop on Management and Processing of Data Streams (MPDS)*, San Diego, California.

Babcock, B., Datar, M., & Motwani, R. (2004). Load shedding for aggregation queries over data streams. In *Proceedings of the 20th International Conference on Data Engineering (ICDE)*, Boston, Massachusetts (pp. 350-361).

Bonnet, P., Gehrke, J. E., & Seshadri, P. (2001). Towards sensor database systems. In *Proceedings of the 2nd International Conference on Mobile Data Management (MDM)*, Hong Kong, China (pp. 3-14).

Chakrabarti, K., Garofalakis, M. N., Rastogi, R., & Shim, K. (2000). Approximate query processing using wavelets. In *Proceedings of the 26th International Conference on Very Large Data Bases (VLDB)*, Cairo, Egypt (pp. 111-122).

Chaudhuri, S., & Motwani, R. (1999). On sampling and relational operators. *IEEE Data Engineering Bulletin, 22*(4), 41-46.

Chaudhuri, S., Motwani, R., & Narasayya, V. R. (1999). On random sampling over joins. In *Proceedings ACM SIGMOD International Conference on Management of Data (SIGMOD)*, Philadelphia, Pennsylvania (pp. 263-274).

Ganguly, S., Garofalakis, M., & Rastogi, R. (2004). Processing data-stream join aggregates using skimmed sketches. In *Proceedings of the 9th International Conference on Extending Database Technology (EDBT)*, Heraklion, Crete, Greece (pp. 569-586).

Golab, L., & Ozsu, M. T. (2003). Issues in data stream management. *ACM SIGMOD Record, 32*(2), 5-14.

Ioannidis, Y. E., & Poosala, V. (1999). Histogram-based approximation of set-valued query-answers. In *Proceedings of the 25th International Conference on Very Large Data Bases (VLDB)*, Edinburgh, Scotland, United Kingdom (pp. 174-185).

Sullivan, M., & Heybey, A. (1998). Tribeca: A system for managing large databases of network traffic. In *Proceedings of the USENIX Annual Technical Conference*, New Orleans, Louisiana.

Tatbul, N., Cetintemel, U., Zdonik, S., Cherniack, M., & Stonebraker, M. (2003). Load shedding in a data stream manager. In *Proceedings of the 29th International Conference on Very Large Data Bases(VLDB)*, Berlin, Germany (*pp*. 309-320).

Terry, D. B., Goldberg, D., Nichols, D., & Oki, B. M. (1992). Continuous queries over append-only databases. In *Proceedings of the 1992 ACM SIGMOD International Conference on Management of Data* (pp. 321-330).

Vitter, J. S., & Wang, M. (1999). Approximate computation of multidimensional aggregates of sparse data using wavelets. In *Proceedings of the ACM SIGMOD International Conference on Management of Data (SIGMOD)*, Philadelphia, Pennsylvania (pp. 193-204).

Data-Stream Mining—General

Domingos, P., & Hulten. G. (2001). Catching up with the data: Research issues in mining data streams. In *Proceedings of the 2001 ACM SIGMOD Workshop on Research Issues in Data Mining and Knowledge Discovery (DMKD)*, Santa Barbara, California.

Data-Stream Summarization—Maintaining Statistics

Bulut, A., & Singh, A. K. (2005). A unified framework for monitoring data streams in real time. In *Proceedings of the 21st International Conference on Data Engineering (ICDE)*, Tokyo, Japan (pp. 44-55).

Datar, M., Gionis, A., Indyk, P., & Motwani, R. (2002). Maintaining stream statistics over sliding windows. In *Proceedings of the 13th Annual ACM-SIAM Symposium on Discrete Algorithms (SODA)*, San Francisco, California (pp. 635-644).

Zhu, Y., & Shasha, D. (2002). StatStream: Statistical monitoring of thousands of data streams in real time. In *Proceedings of the 28th International Conference on Very Large Data Bases (VLDB)*, Hong Kong, China (pp. 358-369).

Data-Stream Summarization—Frequent Records

Arasu, A., & Manku, G. S. (2004). Approximate counts and quantiles over sliding windows. In *Proceedings of the 23rd ACM SIGMOD-SIGACT-SIGART Symposium on Principles of Database Systems (PODS)*, Paris, France (pp. 286-296).

Charikar, M., Chen, K., & Farach-Colton, M. (2002). Finding frequent items in data streams. In *Proceedings of the 29th International Colloquium on Automata, Languages and Programming (ICALP)*, Malaga, Spain (pp. 693-703).

Golab, L., DeHaan, D., Demaine, E. D., López-Ortiz, A., & Munro, J. I. (2003). Identifying frequent items in sliding windows over on-line packet streams. In *Proceedings of the 2003 ACM SIGCOMM Internet Measurement Conference (IMC)*, Miami, Florida (pp. 173-178).

Karp, R. M., Papadimitriou, C. H., & Shenker, S. (2003). A simple algorithm for finding frequent elements in streams and bags. *ACM Transactions on Database Systems (TODS), 28*(1), 51-55.

Manku, G. S., & Motwani, R. (2002). Approximate frequency counts over data streams. In *Proceedings of the 28th International Conference on Very Large Data Bases (VLDB)*, Hong Kong, China (pp. 346-357).

Metwally, A., Agrawal, D., & El Abbadi, A. (2005). Efficient computation of frequent and top-k elements in data streams. In *Proceedings of the 10th International Conference on Database Theory (ICDT)*, Edinburgh, United Kingdom (pp. 398-412).

Data-Stream Summarization— Detecting Changes

Dasu, T., Krishnan, S., Venkatasubramanian, S., & Yi, K. (2005). *An information-theoretic approach to detecting changes in multi-dimensional data streams* (Tech. Rep. No. CS-2005-06).

Kifer, D., Ben-David, S., & Gehrke, J. (2004). Detecting change in data streams. In *Proceedings of the 30th International Conference on Very Large Data Bases (VLDB)*, Toronto, Canada (pp. 180-191).

Krishnamurthy, B., Sen, S., Zhang, Y., & Chen, Y. (2003). Sketch-based change detection: Methods, evaluation, and applications. In *Proceedings of the 3rd ACM SIGCOMM Internet Measurement Conference (IMC)*, Miami Beach, Florida (pp. 234-247).

Zhou, A., Qin, S., & Qian, W. (2005). Adaptively detecting aggregation bursts in data streams. In *Proceedings of the 10th International Conference of Database Systems for Advanced Applications (DASFAA)*, Beijing, China (pp. 435-446).

Zhu, Y., & Shasha, D. (2003). Efficient elastic burst detection in data streams. In *Proceedings of the 9th ACM SIGKDD International Conference on Knowledge Discovery and Data Mining (KDD)*, Washington, DC (pp. 336-345).

Data-Stream Prediction

Aggarwal, C. C., Han, J., Wang, J., & Yu, P. S. (2004). On demand classification of data streams. In *Proceedings of the 10th ACM SIGKDD International Conference on Knowledge Discovery and Data Mining (KDD)*, Seattle, Washington (pp. 503-508).

Chu, F., & Wang, Y., & Zaniolo, C. (2004). An adaptive learning approach for noisy data streams. In *Proceedings of the 4th IEEE International Conference on Data Mining (ICDM)*, Brighton, United Kingdom (pp. 351-354).

Domingos, P., & Hulten, G. (2000). Mining high-speed data streams. In *Proceedings of the 6th ACM SIGKDD International Conference on Knowledge Discovery and Data Mining (KDD)*, Boston, Massachusetts (pp. 71-80).

Fan, W. (2004). Systematic data selection to mine concept-drifting data streams. In *Proceedings of the 10th ACM SIGKDD International Conference on Knowledge Discovery and Data Mining (KDD)*, Seattle, Washington (pp. 128-137).

Fan, W., Huang, Y., & Yu, P. S. (2004). Decision tree evolution using limited number of labeled data items from drifting data streams. In *Proceedings of the 4th IEEE International Conference on Data Mining (ICDM)*, Brighton, United Kingdom (pp. 379-382).

Gama, J., Medas, P., & Rocha, R. (2004). Forest trees for on-line data. In *Proceedings of the 2004 ACM Symposium on Applied Computing (SAC)*, Nicosia, Cyprus (pp. 632-636).

Gama, J., Rocha, R., & Medas, P. (2003). Accurate decision trees for mining high-speed data streams. In *Proceedings of the 9th ACM SIGKDD International Conference on Knowledge Discovery and Data Mining (KDD)*, Washington, DC (pp. 523-528).

Hulten, G., Spencer, L., & Domingos, P. (2001). Mining time-changing data streams. In *Proceedings of the 7th ACM SIGKDD International Conference on Knowledge Discovery and Data mining (KDD)*, San Francisco, California (pp. 97-106).

Wang, H., Fan, W., Yu, P., & Han, J. (2003). Mining concept-drifting data streams using ensemble classifiers. In *Proceedings of the 9th ACM SIGKDD International Conference on Knowledge Discovery and Data Mining (KDD)*, Washington, DC (pp. 226-235).

Zhu, X., Wu, X., & Yang, Y. (2004). Dynamic classifier selection for effective mining from noisy data streams. In *Proceedings of the 4th IEEE International Conference on Data Mining (ICDM)*, Brighton, UK (pp. 305-312).

Data-Stream Clustering

Aggarwal, C. C., Han, J., Wang, J., & Yu, P. (2003). A framework for clustering evolving data streams. In *Proceedings of 29th International Conference on Very Large Data Bases (VLDB)*, Berlin, Germany (pp. 81-92).

Aggarwal, C. C., Han, J., Wang, J., & Yu, P. (2004). A framework for high dimensional projected clustering of data streams. In *Proceedings of the 30th International Conference on Very Large Data Bases (VLDB)*, Toronto, Canada (pp. 852-863).

Babcock, B., Datar, M., Motwani, R., & O'Callaghan, L. (2003). Maintaining variance and k-medians over data stream windows. In *Proceedings of the 22nd ACM SIGACT-SIGMOD-SIGART Symposium on Principles of Database Systems(PODS)*, San Diego, California (pp. 234-243).

Barbara, D. (2002), "Requirements for clustering data streams", in *ACM SIGKDD Knowledge Discovery in Data and Data Mining Explorations Newsletter*, Vol.3, No.2, pp. 23-27.

Gaber, M. M., Krishnaswamy, S., & Zaslavsky, A. (2004). Cost-efficient mining techniques for data streams. In *Proceedings of the 1st Australasian Workshop on Data Mining and Web Intelligence (DMWI)*, Dunedin, New Zealand.

Guha, S., Mishra, N., Motwani, R., & O'Callaghan, L. (2000). Clustering data streams. In *Proceedings of the 41st Annual Symposium on Foundations of Computer Science, (FOCS)*, Redondo Beach, California (pp. 359-366).

Gupta, C., & Grossman, R. L. (2004). GenIc: A single pass generalized incremental algorithm for clustering. In *Proceedings of the 1st Workshop on Secure Data Management (SDM)*, Toronto, Canada.

Motoyoshi, M., Miura, T., & Shioya, I. (2004). Clustering stream data by regression analysis. In *Proceedings of the 1st Australasian Workshop on Data Mining and Web Intelligence (DMWI)*, Dunedin, New Zealand.

O'Callaghan, L., Mishra, N., Meyerson, A., Guha, S., & Motwani, R. (2002). Streaming-data algorithms for high quality clustering. In *Proceedings of the 18th International Conference on*

Data Engineering (ICDE), San Jose, California (pp. 685-696).

Ordonez, C. (2003). Clustering binary data streams with K-means. In *Proceedings of the 8th ACM*

SIGMOD Workshop on Research Issues in Data Mining and Knowledge Discovery (DMKD), San Diego, California (pp. 12-19).

Rodrigues, P., Gama, J., & Pedroso, J. P. *Hierarchical time-series clustering for data streams*. Master's thesis, University of Porto.

Compilation of References

Abadi, D., Carney, D., Cetintemel, U., Cherniack, M., Convey, C., Lee, S., Stonebraker, M., Tatbul, N., & Zdonik, S. (2003). Aurora: A new model and architecture for data stream management. *Journal of Very Large Data Bases (VLDB), 12*(2), 120-139.

Abiteboul, S., Quass, D., McHugh, J., Widom, J., & Wiener, J. (1997). The Lorel query language for semistructured data. *International Journal on Digital Libraries, 1*(1).

Abramson, N. M. (1963). *Information theory and coding.* New York: McGraw-Hill.

Acharya, S., Gibbons, P. B., & Poosala, V. (1999). *Congressional samples for approximate answering of group-by queries* (Technical report). Bell Laboratories, Murray Hill.

Acharya, S., Gibbons, P. B., Poosala, V., & Ramaswamy, S. (1999). Join synopses for approximate query answering. In *Proceedings of the ACM International Conference on Management of Data (SIGMOD)*, Philadelphia, Pennsylvania.

Adam, N., & Worthmann, J. (1989). Security-control methods for statistical databases: A comparative study. *ACM Comput. Surv., 21*(4), 515-556. ACM Press.

Agarwal, R., & Srikant, R. (1994). Fast algorithms for mining association rules. In *Proceedings of the 20th International Conference on Very Large Data Bases* (pp. 487-499), Morgan Kaufmann.

Agarwal, R., & Srikant, R. (1995). Mining sequential patterns. In *Proceedings of the International Conference on Data Engineering* (pp. 3-14), IEEE Computer Society Press, Taipei, Taiwan.

Agarwal, R., Aggarwal, C., & Prasad, V. (1999). A tree projection algorithm for generation of frequent itemsets. *Journal of Parallel and Distributed Computing, 61*(3), 350-371.

Aggarwal, C. C., Han, J., Wang, J., & Yu, P. (2003). A framework for clustering evolving data streams. In *Proceedings of 29th International Conference on Very Large Data Bases (VLDB)*, Berlin, Germany (pp. 81-92).

Aggarwal, C. C., Han, J., Wang, J., & Yu, P. (2004). A framework for high dimensional projected clustering of data streams. In *Proceedings of the 30th International Conference on Very Large Data Bases (VLDB)*, Toronto, Canada (pp. 852-863).

Aggarwal, C. C., Han, J., Wang, J., & Yu, P. S. (2004). On demand classification of data streams. In *Proceedings of the 10th ACM SIGKDD International Conference on Knowledge Discovery and Data Mining (KDD)*, Seattle, Washington (pp. 503-508).

Agrafiotis, D. K. (1997). A new method for analyzing protein sequence relationships based on Sammon maps. *Protein Science, 6*(2), 287-293.

Agrawal, D., & Aggarwal, C. C. (2001). On the design and quantification of privacy preserving data mining algorithms. In *Proceedings of the 20th ACM Symposium on Principle of Database System* (pp. 247-255). ACM Press.

Agrawal, R., & Srikant, R. (1994). Fast algorithms for mining association rules. In *Proceedings of the 20th Conference on VLDB*, Santiago, Chile (pp. 487-499).

Agrawal, R., & Srikant, R. (1995). Mining sequential patterns. In *Proceedings of the 11ᵗʰ International Conference on Data Engineering (ICDE 1995)*, Taipei, Taiwan (pp. 3-14). IEEE Computer Society Press.

Agrawal, R., & Srikant, R. (2000). Privacy preserving data mining. In *Proceedings of the ACM SIGMOD Conference of Management of Data* (pp. 439-450). ACM Press.

Agrawal, R., Gehrke, J., Gunopulos, D., & Raghavan, P. (1998). *Automatic subspace clustering of high dimensional data for data mining applications*. In *Proceedings of the ACM SIGMOD International Conference on Management of Data (SIGMOD' 98)*, Seattle, Washington (pp. 94-105).

Agrawal, R., Imielinski, T., & Swami, A. (1993). Mining association rules between sets of items in large databases. In *Proceedings of the ACM SIGMOD International Conference on Management of Data (SIGMOD 1993)*, Washington, DC (pp. 207-216). ACM Press.

Agrawal, R., Imielinski, T., & Swami, A. (1993, May). Mining association rules between sets of items in large databases. In *Proceedings of ACM SIGMOD* (pp. 207-216). ACM Press.

Aleman-Meza, B., Halaschek-Wiener, C., Arpinar, I. B., Ramakrishnan, C., & Sheth, A. P. (2005). Ranking complex relationships on the Semantic Web. *IEEE Internet Computing*, 37-44.

Alpern, B., & Carter, L. (1991). The hyperbox. In G.M. Nielson & L. Rosenblum (Eds.), *Proceedings of IEEE Visualization '91*, San Diego, California (pp. 133-139).

Amdahl, G. M. (1967). Validity of the single-processor approach to achieving large scale computing capabilities. In *AFIPS Conference Proceedings* (pp. 483-485). Morgan Kaufmann Publishers Inc.

American College of Medical Genetics/American Society of Human Genetics Test and Technology Transfer Committee Working Group. (2000). Tandem mass spectrometry in newborn screening. *Genetics in Medicine, 2*, 267-269.

Andrews, D. F. (1972). Plots of high dimensional data. *Biometrics, 28*, 125-136.

Ankerst, M., Breunig, M.M., Kriegel, H.P., & Sander, J. (1999). *OPTICS: Ordering points to identify the clustering structure*. In *Proceedings of the ACM SIGMOD International Conference on Management of Data (SIGMOD'99)*, Philadelphia, Pennsylvania (pp. 49-60).

Apaiwongse, T. S. (1995). Facial display of environmental policy uncertainty. *Journal of Business Psychology, 10*, 65-74.

Apostolico, A., Comin, M., & Parida, L. (2005). Conservative extraction of over-represented extensible motifs. *Bioinformatics, 21*(1), 9-18.

Apostolico, A., Gong, F., & Lonardi, S. (2003). Verbumculus and the discovery of unusual words. *Journal of Computer Science and Technology, 19*(1), 22-41.

Arasu, A., & Manku, G. S. (2004). Approximate counts and quantiles over sliding windows. In *Proceedings of the 23ʳᵈ ACM SIGMOD-SIGACT-SIGART Symposium on Principles of Database Systems (PODS)*, Paris, France (pp. 286-296).

Arasu, A., Babcock, B., Babu, S., Datar, M., Ito, K., Nishizawa, I., Rosenstein, J., & Widom, J. (2003). STREAM: The Stanford data stream management system. *IEEE Data Engineering Bulletin, 26*(1).

Ardizzone, E., Daurel, T., Maniscalco, U., & Rigotti, C. (2001). Extraction of association rules between low-level descriptors and semantic descriptors in an image database. In *Proceedings of the 1ˢᵗ International Workshop on Multimedia Data and Document Engineering (MDDE 2001)*, Lyon, France.

Arenas, M., & Libkin, L. (2004). A normal form for XML documents. *ACM Transactions on Database Systems, 29*(1), 195-232.

Argos, P. (1977). Secondary-structure predictions of calcium-binding proteins. *Biochemistry, 16*(4), 665-672.

Asimov, D. (1985). The grand tour: A tool for viewing multidimensional data. *SIAM Journal on Scientific and Statistical Computing, 6*(1), 128-143.

Asimov, D. A., & Buja, A. (1994). Grand tour via geodesic interpolation of 2-frames. In R. J. Moorhead II, D. E. Silver,

& S. Uselton (Eds.), *Proceedings of the SPIE Visual Data Exploration and Analysis—Volume Conference, 2178*, 145-153.

Atallah, M. J., Bertino, E., Elmagarmid, A. K., Ibrahim, M., & Verykios, V. S. (1999). Disclosure limitation of sensitive rules. In *Proceedings of the IEEE Knolwedge and Data Engineering Workshop* (pp. 45-52). IEEE Computer Society.

ATKOSoft S.A. (1997). Survey on visualisation methods and software tools. Retrieved June 23, 2007, from http://europa.eu.int/en/comm/eurostat/research/supcom.96/30/result/a/visualisation_methods.pdf

Attwood, T., Mitchell, A., Gaulton, A., Moulton, G., & Tabernero, L. (2006). The PRINTS protein fingerprint database: Functional and evolutionary applications. In M. Dunn, L. Jorde, P. Little, & A. Subramaniam (Eds.), *Encyclopaedia of Genetics, Genomics, Proteomics and Bioinformatics*. John Wiley & Sons.

Augurusa, E., Braga, D., Campi, A., & Ceri, S. (2003). Design and implementation of a graphical interface to XQuery. In *Proceedings of the ACM Symposium on Applied Computing* (pp. 1163-1167). ACM Press.

Babcock, B., Babu, S., Datar, M., Motwani, R., & Widom, J. (2002). Models and issues in data stream systems. In *Proceedings of the 21st ACM SIGACT-SIGMOD-SIGART Symposium on Principles of Database Systems (PODS)*, Madison, Wisconsin (pp. 1-16).

Babcock, B., Datar, M., & Motwani, R. (2002). Sampling from a moving window over streaming data. In *Proceedings of the 13th Annual ACM-SIAM Symposium on Discrete Algorithms (SODA)*, San Francisco, California (pp. 633-634).

Babcock, B., Datar, M., & Motwani, R. (2003). Load shedding techniques for data stream systems. In *Proceedings of the 2003 Workshop on Management and Processing of Data Streams (MPDS)*, San Diego, California.

Babcock, B., Datar, M., & Motwani, R. (2004). Load shedding for aggregation queries over data streams. In *Proceedings of the 20th International Conference on Data Engineering (ICDE)*, Boston, Massachusetts (pp. 350-361).

Babcock, B., Datar, M., Motwani, R., & O'Callaghan, L. (2003). Maintaining variance and k-medians over data stream windows. In *Proceedings of the 22nd ACM SIGACT-SIGMOD-SIGART Symposium on Principles of Database Systems(PODS)*, San Diego, California (pp. 234-243).

Baeza-Yates, R. A. (1992). Introduction to data structure and algorithms related to information retrieval. In *Information retrieval: Data structure and algorithms* (pp. 13-27). Prentice Hall.

Baggerly, K.A., Morris, J.S., Edmonson, S.R., & Coombes, K.R. (2005). Signal in noise: Evaluating reported reproducibility of serum proteomic tests for ovarian cancer. *Journal of the National Cancer Institute, 97*, 307-309.

Bagley, S., & Altman, R. (1995). Characterizing the microenvironment surrounding protein sites. *Protein Science, 4*(4), 622-635.

Baldi, P., Brunak, S., Chauvin, Y., Andersen, C., & Nielsen, H. (2000). Assessing the accuracy of prediction algorithms for classification: An overview. *Bionformatics, 16*(5), 412-242.

Ball, G., & Hall, D. (1967). A clustering technique for summarizing multi-variate data. *Behavioral Sciences, 12*, 153-155.

Ball, P. (2002). Algorithm makes tongue tree. *Nature, 22*, January.

Banatao, R., Huang, C., Babbitt, P., Altman, R., & Klein, T. (2001). ViewFeature: Integrated feature analysis and visualization. In *Proceedings of the 6th Pacific Symposium on Biocomputing* (pp. 240-250).

Banerjee, A., & Ghosh, J. (2001). Clickstream clustering using weighted longest common subsequences. In *Proceedings of Workshop on Web Mining in the 1st International SIAM Conference on Data Mining* (pp. 33-40).

Bao, J., Shen, J., Liu, X., & Liu, H. (2005). The heavy frequency vector-based text clustering. *International Journal of Business Intelligence and Data Mining, 1*(1), 42-53, Inderscience Publishers.

Baralis, E., Garza, P., Quintarelli, E., & Tanca, L. (2006). *Answering XML queries by means of data summaries* (Tech.

Rep. No. 2006.43). Milano, Italy: Politecnico di Milano, Dipartimento di Elettronica e Informazione.

Barash, Y., Bejerano, G., & Friedman, N. (2001). A simple hyper-geometric approach for discovering putative transcription factor binding sites. In *Proceedings of the 1ˢᵗ International Workshop on Algorithms in Bioinformatics* (pp. 278-293). Lecture Notes in Computer Science 2149. Springer.

Barbara, D. (2002), "Requirements for clustering data streams", in *ACM SIGKDD Knowledge Discovery in Data and Data Mining Explorations Newsletter*, Vol.3, No.2, pp. 23-27.

Baril, X., & Bellahsene, Z. (2000). A view model for XML documents. In D. Patel, I. Choudhury, S. Patel, & S. de Cesare (Eds.), *International Conference on Object Oriented Information Systems*, London, United Kingdom (pp. 429–441).

Bartlett, G., Porter, C., Borkakoti, N., & Thornton, J. (2002). Analysis of catalytic residues in enzyme active sites. *Journal of Molecular Biology, 324*(1), 105-121.

Basu, S., Banerjee, A., & Mooney, R. J. (2002). Semisupervised clustering by seeding. In *Proceedings of the 19ᵗʰ International Conference on Machine Learning (ICML-2002)*, Sydney, Australia (pp. 19-26).

Basu, S., Banerjee, A., & Mooney, R. J. (2004). Active semisupervision for pairwise constrained clustering. In *Proceedings of the SIAM International Conference on Data Mining (SDM-2004)*, Lake Buena Vista, Florida (pp. 333-344).

Basu, S., Bilenko, M., & Mooney, R. J. (2004). A probabilistic framework for semisupervised clustering. In *Proceedings of KDD-2004*, Seattle, Washington (pp. 59-68).

Batini, C., Lenzerini, M., & Navathe, S. (1986). A comparative analysis of methodologies for database schema integration. *ACM Computing Surveys, 18*(4), 323-364.

Baumgartner, C., & Baumgartner, D. (2006). Biomarker discovery, disease classification, and similarity query processing on high-throughput MS/MS data of inborn errors of metabolism. *Journal of Biomolecular Screening, 11*, 90-99.

Baumgartner, C., Böhm, C., & Baumgartner, D. (2005). Modelling of classification rules on metabolic patterns including machine learning and expert knowledge. *Journal of Biomedical Informatics, 38*, 89-98.

Baumgartner, C., Böhm, C., Baumgartner, D., Marini, G., Weinberger, K., Olgemöller, B., Liebl, B., & Roscher, A.A. (2004). Supervised machine learning techniques for the classification of metabolic disorders in newborns. *Bioinformatics, 20*, 2985-2996.

Baumgartner, C., Kailing, K., Kriegel, H.-P., Kröger, P., & Plant, C. (2004). *Subspace selection for clustering high-dimensional data.* In *Proceedings of the 4ᵗʰ IEEE International Conference on Data Mining (ICDM'04)*, Brighton, United Kingdom (pp. 11-18).

Bayardo, R. J. (1998). Efficiently mining long patterns from databases. In *Proceedings of the ACM SIGMOD International Conference on Management of Data (SIGMOD 1998)*, Seattle, Washington (pp. 85-93). ACM Press.

Bayardo, R. J., Agrawal, R., & Gunopulos, D. (1999). Constraint-based rule mining in large, dense databases. In *Proceedings of the 15ᵗʰ International Conference on Data Engineering (ICDE 1999)*. Sydney, Australia (pp. 188-197). IEEE Computer Society.

Becker, R. A., & Cleveland, W. S. (1987). Brushing scatterplots. *Technometrics, 29*, 127-142.

Becker, R. A., Cleveland, W. S., & Wilks, A. R. (1987). Dynamic graphics for data analysis. *Statistical Science, 2*(4), 355-383.

Beecher, C. (2003). The human metabolome. In G.G. Harrigan & R. Goodacre (Eds.), *Metabolic profiling: Its role in biomarker discovery and gene function analysis* (pp. 311-319). Boston/Dordrecht/London: Kluwer Academic Publishers.

Behsers, C. G., & Feiner, S. K. (1990). Visualizing *n*-dimensional virtual worlds with *n*-Vision. *Computer Graphics, 24*(2), 37-38.

Ben Messaoud, R., Boussaïd, O., & Loudcher Rabas'eda, S. (2006). A data mining-based OLAP aggregation of complex data: Application on XML documents. *International Journal of Data Warehousing and Mining, 2*(4), 1-26.

Benedetto, D., Caglioti, E., & Loreto, V. (2002). Language trees and zipping. *Physics Review Letters, 88*(4) 1-4.

Ben-Hur, A., & Brutlag, D. (2003). Remote homology detection: A motif based approach. *Bioinformatics, 19*(1), 26-33.

Ben-Hur, A., & Brutlag, D. (2005). Protein sequence motifs: Highly predictive features of protein function.

Bennett, C. H., Gacs, P., Li, M., Vitanyi, P. M. B., & Zurek, W. (1998). Information distance. *IEEE Transactions on Information Theory, 44*(4), 1407-1423.

Bergroth, L., Hakonen, H., & Raita, T. (2000). A survey of longest common subsequence algorithm. The *7th International Symposium on String Processing and Information Retrieval* (pp. 39-48).

Berkhin, P. (2002). *Survey of clustering data mining techniques.* San Jose, CA: Accrue Software.

Berman, H., Westbrook, J., Feng, Z., Gilliland, G., Bhat, T., Weissig, H., et al. (2000). The protein data bank. *Nucleic Acids Research, 28*(1), 235-242.

Berners-Lee, T., Hendler, J., & Lassila, O. (2001). The Semantic Web. *Scientific American, 284*(5), 34-43.

Bertin, J. (1981). *Graphics and graphic information processing.* Berlin, Germany: Walter De Gruyter.

Bertin, J. (1983). *Semiology of graphics.* Madison, WI: University of Wiscosin Press.

Bertino, E., & Nai Fovino, I. (2005). Information driven evaluation of data hiding algorithms. In *Proceedings of the 7th International Conference on Data Warehousing and Knowledge Discovery*, Copenaghen, Denmark. Springer-Verlag.

Bertino, E., Catania, B., & Maddalena, A. (2004). Toward a language for pattern manipulation and querying. In *Proceed-*

ings of the EDBT '04 Workshop on Pattern Representation and Management (PaRMa '04).

Bertino, E., Nai Fovino, I., & Parasiliti Provenza, L. (2005). A framework for evaluating privacy preserving data mining algorithms. *Data Mining and Knowledge Discovery Journal.* Kluwert.

Bezerra, E., Xexéo, G. B., & Mattoso, M. L. Q. (2006, April). *Semisupervised clustering of XML documents: Getting the most from structural information.* Paper presented at the 3rd International Workshop on XML Schema and Data Management (XSDM'06), Atlanta, Georgia.

Bilenko, M., Basu, S., & Mooney, R. J. (2004). Integrating constraints and metric learning in semisupervised clustering. In *Proceedings of the 21st International Conference on Machine Learning (ICML-2004)*, Ban□, Canada (pp. 81-88).

Biomarkers Definitions Working Group. (2001). Biomarkers and surrogate endpoints: Preferred definitions and conceptual framework. *Clinical Pharmacology and Therapeutics, 69*, 89-95.

Bishop, C. (1995). *Neural networks for pattern recognition.* Oxford: Clarendon Press.

Bishop, C. M., Svensén, M., & Williams, C. K. I. (1998). GTM: The generative topographic mapping. *Neural Computation, 10*(1), 215-235.

Blachman, N. M. (1968). The amount of information that y gives about X. *IEEE Trans. Inform. Theon., IT-14*, 27-31. IEEE Press.

Blau, N., Thony, B., Cotton, R.G.H., & Hyland, K. (2001). *Disorders of tetrahydrobiopterin and related biogenic amines.* In C.R. Scriver, S. Kaufman, E. Eisensmith, S.L.C. Woo, B. Vogelstein, & B.

Blekas, K., Fotiadis, D., & Likas, A. (2005). Motif-based protein sequence classification using neural networks. *Journal of Computational Biology, 12*(1), 64-82.

Boncz, P. A., Grust, T., Manegold, S., Rittinger, J., & Teubner, J. (2005). *Pathfinder: Relational XQuery over multi-gigabyte XML inputs in interactive time* (Tech. Rep. No. INS-E0503). Amsterdam: CWI.

Boncz, P., Flokstra, J., Grust, T., van Keulen, M., Manegold, S., Mullender, S., Nes, N., Rittinger, J., Teubner, J., & Zhang, Y. (2006). *MonetDB/XQuery*. Retrieved June 13, 2007, from http://monetdb.cwi.nl/XQuery/

Bonnet, P., Gehrke, J. E., & Seshadri, P. (2001). Towards sensor database systems. In *Proceedings of the 2nd International Conference on Mobile Data Management (MDM)*, Hong Kong, China (pp. 3-14).

Bouet, M., & Aufaure, M. A. (2006). New image retrieval principle: Image mining and visual ontology. In V. A. Petrushin & L. Khan (Eds.), *Multimedia data mining and knowledge discovery*. Springer.

Boussaid, O., Ben Messaoud, R., Choquet, R., & Anthoard, S. (2006a). XWarehousing: An XML-based approach for warehousing complex data. In *Proceedings of the 10th East-European Conference on Advances in Databases and Information Systems (ADBIS06)*, Thessaloniki, Greece (pp. 39-54). Lecture Notes in Computer Science 4152.

Boussaid, O., Tanasescu, A., Bentayeb, F., & Darmont, J. (2006b). Integrationand dimensional modelling approaches for complex data warehousing. *Journal of Global Optimization*.

Bowers, S., & Ludascher, B. (2004). *An ontology-driven framework for data transformation in scientific workflows*. Paper presented at the International Workshop on Data Integration in the Life Sciences.

Bowers, S., Lin, K., & Ludascher, B. (2004). *On integrating scientific resources through semantic registration*. Paper presented at the Scientific and Statistical Database Management.

Braga, D., Campi, A., & Ceri, S. (2005). XQBE (XQuery by example): A visual interface to the standard XML query language. *ACM Transaction on Database Systems, 30*(2), 398-443.

Bray, T., Paoli, J., & Sperberg-McQueen, C. M. (2000). Extensible markup language (XML) 1.0 (2nd ed., W3C Recommendation).

Brazma, A., Jonassen, I., Eidhammer, I., & Gilbert, D. (1998a). Approaches to the automatic discovery of patterns in biosequences. *Journal of Computational Biology, 5*(2), 279-305.

Brazma, A., Jonassen, I., Vilo, J., & Ukkonen, E. (1998b). Pattern discovery in biosequences. In *Proceedings of the 4th International Colloquium on Grammatical Inference* (pp. 255--270). Lecture Notes in Artificial Intelligence 1433. Springer.

Brin, S., Motwani, R., & Silverstein, C. (1997). Beyond market baskets: Generalizing association rules to correlations. In *Proceedings of the ACM SIGMOD International Conference on Management of Data (SIGMOD 1997)*, Tucson, Arizona (pp. 265-276). ACM Press.

Buchner, A., & Mulvenna, M. D. (1998). Discovering internet marketing intelligence through online analytical Web usage mining. *SIGMOD Record, 27*(4), 54-61.

Buhler, J., & Tompa, M. (2001). Finding motifs using random projections. In *Proceedings of the 5th International Conference on Computational Molecular Biology* (pp. 69-76).

Buja, A., & Asimov, D. (1986). Grand tour methods: An outline. In D. Allen (Ed.), *Computer science and statistics: Proceedings of the Seventeenth Symposium on the Interface* (pp. 63-67). Amsterdam: North Holland. Elsevier Science Publisher B.V.

Bulut, A., & Singh, A. K. (2005). A unified framework for monitoring data streams in real time. In *Proceedings of the 21st International Conference on Data Engineering (ICDE)*, Tokyo, Japan (pp. 44-55).

Buneman, P., Davidson, S. B., Hillebrand, G. G., & Suciu, D. (1996). A query language and optimization techniques for unstructured data. In H. V. Jagadish & I. S. Mumick (Eds.), *ACM SIGMOD International Conference on Management of Data* (pp. 505-516). ACM Press.

Buneman, P., Davidson, S., Fan, W., Hara, C., & Tan, W. (2001a). Reasoning about keys for XML. In G. Ghelli & G. Grahne (Eds.), *8th International Workshop on Database Programming Languages* (pp. 133-148). Springer-Verlag. Lecture Notes in Computer Science 2397.

Buneman, P., Fan, W., Siméon, J., & Weinstein, S. (2001b). Constraints for semistructured data and XML. *ACM SIGMOD Record, 30*(1), 47-54.

Cadez, I. V., Heckerman, D., Meek, C., Smyth, P., & White, S. (2000). Visualization of navigation patterns on a Web site using model-based clustering. In *Proceedings of the Sixth International Conference on Knowledge Discovery and Data Mining*, ACM Press, Boston, pp. 280-284.

Califano, A. (2000). SPLASH: Structural pattern localization analysis by sequential histograms. *Bioinformatics, 16*(4), 341-357.

Cammer, S., Hoffman, B., Speir, J., Canady, M., Nelson, M., et al.(2003). Structure-based active site profiles for genome analysis and functional family subclassification. *Journal of Molecular Biology, 334*(3), 387-401.

Catania, B., Maddalena, A., & Mazza, M. (2005). PSYCHO: A prototype system for pattern management. In *Proceedings of VLDB'05* (pp. 1346-1349).

Catania, B., Maddalena, A., Mazza, M., Bertino, E., & Rizzi, S. (2004). A framework for data mining pattern management. In *Proceedings of ECML-PKDD'04* (pp. 87-98). Lecture Notes on Artificial Intelligence 3202.

Ceccarelli, M., & Maratea, A. (2005). Semisupervised fuzzy c-means clustering of biological data. Paper presented at WILF 2005 (pp. 259-266).

Ceri, S., Comai, S., Damiani, E., Fraternali, P., Paraboschi, S., & Tanca, L. (1999). XML-GL: A graphical languaguage for querying and restructuring XML documents. *Computer Networks, 31*(1-2), 1171-1188.

Chace, D.H., Sherwin, J.E., Hillman, S.L., Lorey, F., & Cunningham, G.C. (1998). Use of phenylalanine-to-tyrosine ratio determined by tandem mass spectrometry to improve newborn screening for phenylketonuria of early discharge specimens collected in the first 24 hours. *Clinical Chemistry, 44*, 2405-2409.

Chakrabarti, K., Garofalakis, M. N., Rastogi, R., & Shim, K. (2000). Approximate query processing using wavelets. In *Proceedings of the 26th International Conference on Very Large Data Bases (VLDB)*, Cairo, Egypt (pp. 111-122).

Chalmers, M. (1996). A linear iteration time layout algorithm for visualising high-dimensional data. In *Proceed-*

ings of IEEE Visualization 96, San Francisco, California (pp. 127-132).

Chambers, J. M., Cleveland, W. S., Keliner, B., & Tukey, P. A. (1983). *Graphical methods for data analysis.* New York: Chapman and Hall.

Chang, H., & Yeung, D.-Y. (2004). Locally linear metric adaptation for semisupervised clustering. In *Proceedings of the Twenty-first International Conference on Machine Learning*, New York, New York (p. 20). ACM Press.

Chang, K. C.-C., He, B., & Zhang, Z. (2005). *Toward large scale integration: Building a MetaQuerier over databases on the Web.* Paper presented at the CIDR.

Charikar, M., Chekuri, C., Feder, T., & Motwani, R. (2004). Incremental clustering and dynamic information retrieval. *SIAM Journal on Computing, 33*(6).

Charikar, M., Chen, K., & Farach-Colton, M. (2002). Finding frequent items in data streams. In *Proceedings of the 29th International Colloquium on Automata, Languages and Programming (ICALP)*, Malaga, Spain (pp. 693-703).

Charles, D., & Fyfe, C. (1998). Modelling multiple cause structure using rectification constraints. *Network: Computation in Neural Systems, 9*, 167-182.

Chaudhuri, S., & Dayal, U. (1997). An overview of data warehousing and OLAP technology. *SIGMOD Record, 26*(1), 65-74.

Chaudhuri, S., & Motwani, R. (1999). On sampling and relational operators. *IEEE Data Engineering Bulletin, 22*(4), 41-46.

Chaudhuri, S., Motwani, R., & Narasayya, V. R. (1999). On random sampling over joins. In *Proceedings ACM SIGMOD International Conference on Management of Data (SIGMOD)*, Philadelphia, Pennsylvania (pp. 263-274).

Cheeseman, P., & Stutz, J. (1996). Bayesian classification (AutoClass): Theory and results. *Advances in Knowledge Discovery and Data Mining.* AAAI Press/MIT Press.

Chen, G., Wei, Q., Kerre, E., & Wets, G. (2003, September). Overview of fuzzy associations mining. In *Proceedings of* the 4th *International Symposium on Advanced Intelligent Systems*, Jeju, Korea.

Chen, M. S., Han, J., & Yu, P. S. (1996). Data mining: An overview from a database perspective. *IEEE Transactions on Knowledge and Data Engineering, 8*(6), 866-883.

Chen, X., Kwong, S., & Li, M. (1999). A compression algorithm for DNA sequences and its applications in genome comparison. In K. Asai, S. Myano, & T. Takagi (Eds.), *Genome informatics* (pp. 51-61). *Proceedings of the 10th Workshop on Genome Informatics, Universal Academy Press, Tokyo,* (Also in RECOMB 2000).

Chernoff, H. (1973). The use of faces to represent points in *k*-dimensional space graphically. *Journal of American Statistical Association, 68,* 361-368.

Chernoff, H., & Rizvi, M. H. (1975). Effect on classification error of random permutations of features in representing multivariate data by faces. *Journal of American Statistical Association, 70,* 548-554.

Cheung, D. W. L., Han, J., Ng, V., & Wong, C. Y. (1996). Maintenance of discovered association rules in large databases: An incremental updating technique. In *Proceedings of the 12th International Conference on Data Engineering (ICDE 1996),* New Orleans, Louisiana (pp. 106-114). IEEE Computer Society Press.

Chin, F. Y., & Ozsoyoglu, G. (1981, March). Statistical database design. *ACM Trans. Database Syst., 6*(1), 113-139. ACM Press.

Chin, F. Y., & Ozsoyoglu, G. (1982, April). Auditing and inference control in statistical databases. *IEEE Trans. Softw. Eng., SE-8*(6), 574-582. IEEE Press.

Chothia, C., & Lesk, A. (1986). The relation between the divergence of sequence and structure in proteins. *EMBO Journal, 5*(4), 823-826.

Chu, F., & Wang, Y., & Zaniolo, C. (2004). An adaptive learning approach for noisy data streams. In *Proceedings of the 4th IEEE International Conference on Data Mining (ICDM),* Brighton, United Kingdom (pp. 351-354).

Chu, W. W. (2000). Medical digital library to support scenario specific information retrieval. In *Proceedings of the Kyoto International Conference on Digital Libraries* (p. 388).

Chuah, M. C., & Eick, S. G. (1998). Information rich glyphs for software management data. *IEEE Computer Graphics and Applications, 18*(4), 24-29.

Chui, C. K., & Lian, J. (1996). A study of orthonormal multiwavelets. *Applied Numerical Mathematics: Transactions of IMACS, 20*(3), 273-298.

Chung, C.-W., Min, J.-K., & Shim, K. (2002). Apex: An adaptive path index for xml data. In M. J. Franklin, B. Moon, & A. Ailamaki (Eds.), *ACM SIGMOD International Conference on Management of Data* (pp. 121-132). ACM Press.

CINQ. (2001). *The CINQ project.* Retrieved June 15, 2007, from http://www.cinq-project.org

Clayton, P.T., Doig, M., Ghafari, S., Meaney, C., Taylor, C., Leonard, J.V., Morris, M., & Johnson, A.W. (1998). Screening for medium chain acyl-CoA dehydrogenase deficiency using electrospray ionisation tandem mass spectrometry. *Archives of Disease in Childhood, 79,* 109-115.

Cleveland, W. S., & McGill, M. E. (Eds.). (1988). *Dynamic graphics for statistics.* Belmont, CA: Wadsworth & Brooks.

Cohen, E., Krishnamurthy, B., & Rexford, J. (1998). Improving end-to-end performance of the Web using server volumes and proxy liters. *Proceedings of the ACM SIGCOMM,* Vancouver, British Columbia, Canada: ACM Press.

Cohn, D., Caruana, R., & McCallum, A. (2000). *Semi-supervised clustering with user feedback* (Tech. Rep. No. TR2003-1892). Cornell University.

Consens, M. P., & Mendelzon, A. O. (1990). Graphlog: A visual formalism for real life recursion. In *Proceedings of the ACM SIGACT-SIGMOD-SIGART Symposium on Principles of Database Systems* (pp. 404-416). ACM Press.

Cooley, R., Mobasher, B., & Srivastava, J. (1999). Data preparation for mining world wide Web browsing patterns. *Knowledge and Information Systems, 1*(1), 5-32.

Cooper, N. (1994). *The human genome project: Deciphering the blueprint of heredity.* University Science Books.

Corchado, E., & Fyfe, C. (2002). Maximum likelihood Hebbian learning. In *Proceedings of the Tenth European Symposium on Artificial Neural Networks, ESANN2002* (pp. 143-148). d-side publications.

Cox, L. H. (1980, June). Suppression methodology and statistical disclosure control. *J. Am. Stat. Assoc., 75*(370), 377-385.

Crawford, S. L., & Fall, T. C. (1990). Projection pursuit techniques for visualizing high-dimensional data sets. In G. M. Nielson, B. Shrivers, & L. J. Rosenblum (Eds.), *Visualization in scientific computing* (pp. 94-108). Los Alamitos, CA: IEEE Computer Society Press.

Cristianini, N., & Shawe-Taylor, J. (2000). *An introduction to support vector machines and other kernel-based learning methods.* Cambridge, UK: Cambridge University Press.

Cross, V., & Sudkamp, T. (2002). *Similarity and computability in fuzzy set theory: Assessments and applications* (Vol. 93 of Studies in Fuzziness and Soft Computing). Physica-Verlag.

CWM. (2001). *Common warehouse metamodel.* Retrieved June 15, 2007, from http://www.omg.org/cwm

Damiani, E., Oliboni, B., Quintarelli, E., & Tanca, L. (2003). *Modeling semistructured data by using graph-based constraints* (Tech. Rep. No. 27/03). Milano, Italy: Politecnico di Milano, Dipartimento di Elettronica e Informazione.

Dasseni, E., Verykios, V. S., Elmagarmid, A. K., & Bertino, E. (2001). Hiding association rules by using confidence and support. In *Proceedings of the 4th Information Hiding Workshop* (pp. 369-383). Springer-Verlag.

Dasu, T., Krishnan, S., Venkatasubramanian, S., & Yi, K. (2005). *An information-theoretic approach to detecting changes in multi-dimensional data streams* (Tech. Rep. No. CS-2005-06).

Datar, M., Gionis, A., Indyk, P., & Motwani, R. (2002). Maintaining stream statistics over sliding windows. In *Proceedings of the 13th Annual ACM-SIAM Symposium on Discrete Algorithms (SODA)*, San Francisco, California (pp. 635-644).

Datta, S., Bhaduri, K., Giannella, C., Wolff, R., & Kargupta, H. (2005). Distributed data mining in peer-to-peer networks [Special issue]. *IEEE Internet Computing.*

Daubechies, I. (1992). *Ten lectures on wavelets.* Capital City Press.

Davidson, I., & Ravi, S. (2005a). Clustering under constraints: Feasibility issues and the k-means algorithm. In *Proceedings of the 5th SIAM Data Mining Conference.*

Davidson, I., & Ravi, S. (2005b). *Hierarchical clustering with constraints: Theory and practice.* Paper presented at the Ninth European Conference on Principles and Practice of Knowledge Discovery in Databases (PAKDD-2005), Porto, Portugal.

Davison, A. C., & Hinkley, D. V. (1997). *Bootstrap methods and their applications.* Cambridge University Press.

Daviss, B. (2005). Growing pains for metabolomics. *The Scientist, 19*, 25-28.

DB2. (2005). DB2 Intelligent Miner. Retrieved June 15, 2007, from http://www-306.ibm.com/software/data/iminer/

De Raedt, L. (2002). A perspective on inductive databases. *ACM SIGKDD Explorations Newsletter, 4*(2), 69-77.

De Raedt, L., Jaeger, M., Lee, S.D., & Mannila, H. (2002). A theory on inductive query answering. In *Proceedings of ICDM'02* (pp. 123-130).

de Ridder, D., & Duin, R. P. W. (1997). Sammon's mapping using neural networks: A comparison. *Pattern Recognition Letters, 18*(11-13), 1307-1316.

Defays, D. (1977). An efficient algorithm for a complete link method. *The Computer Journal, 20*, 364-366.

Delgado, M., Marin, D., Sanchez, D., & Vila, M.A. (2003). Fuzzy association rules: General model and applications. *IEEE Transactions on Fuzzy Systems, 11*(2), 214-225.

Dellaert, F. (2002). *The expectation maximization algorithm* (Tech. Rep. No. GIT-GVU-02-20). College of Computing, Georgia Institute of Technology.

Demartines, P., & Hérault, J. (1993). Vector quantization and projection neural network. In J. Mira, J. Cabestany, A. Prieto (Eds.), *International Workshop on Artificial Neural Networks* (pp. 328-333). Springer-Verlag. Lecture Notes in Computer Science 686.

Demartines, P., & Hérault, J. (1997). Curvilinear component analysis: A self-organizing neural network for nonlinear mapping of data sets. *IEEE Transactions on Neural Networks, 8*(1), 148-154.

Denning, D. (1980). Secure statistical databases with random sample queries. *ACM TODS, 5*(3), 291-315.

Denning, D. E. (1982). *Cryptography and data security.* Reading, MA: Addison-Wesley.

Denning, D. E., & Schlorer, J. (1983). Inference control for statistical databases. *Computer, 16*(7), 69-82. IEEE Press.

Deutch, A., Fernandez, M., Florescu, D., Levy, A., & Suciu, D. (1998). *XML-QL: A query language for XML.* Paper presented at QL'98–W3C Workshop on Query Languages.

Dezateux, C. (2003). Newborn screening for medium chain acyl-CoA dehydrogenase deficiency: Evaluating the effects on outcome. *European Journal of Pediatrics, 162*(Suppl. 1), S25-S28.

Dhar, V. (1998). Data mining in finance: Using counterfactuals to generate knowledge from organizational information systems. *Information Systems, 23*(7), 423-437.

Dhillon, I.-S., Guan, Y., & Kulis, B. (2004). Kernel k-means: Spectral clustering and normalized cuts. In *Proceedings of the Conference on Knowledge Discovery and Data Mining (KDD).*

Di Masi, J.A., Hansen, R.W., & Grabowski, H.G. (2003). The price of innovation: New estimates of drug development costs. *Journal of Health Economics, 22*, 151-185.

Diaconis, P., & Freedman, D. (1984). Asymptotics of graphical projections. *The Annals of Statistics, 12*(3), 793-815.

Diamantaras, K. I., & Kung, S. Y. (1996). *Principal component neural networks: Theory and applications.* John Wiley & Sons.

Dispensa, J. M., & Brulle, R. J. (2003). The Sprawling Frontier: Politics of Watershed Management. *Submitted to Rural Sociology.*

Djeraba, C. (2003). Association and content-based retrieval. *IEEE Transactions on Knowledge and Data Engineering, 15*(1).

Doan, A., Domingos, P., & Halevy, A. Y. (2003). Learning to match the schemas of data sources: A multistrategy approach. *Machine Learning, 50*(3), 279-301.

Domingo-Ferrer, J., & Torra, V. (2002). A quantitative comparison of disclosure control methods for microdata. In P. Doyle, J. Lane, J. Theeuwes, & L. Zayatz (Eds.), *Confidentiality, disclosure and data access: Theory and practical applications for statistical agencies* (pp. 113-134). North-Holland.

Domingos, P., & Hulten, G. (2000). Mining high-speed data streams. In *Proceedings of the 6th ACM SIGKDD International Conference on Knowledge Discovery and Data Mining (KDD)*, Boston, Massachusetts (**pp. 71-80).**

Domingos, P., & Hulten. G. (2001). Catching up with the data: Research issues in mining data streams. In *Proceedings of the 2001 ACM SIGMOD Workshop on Research Issues in Data Mining and Knowledge Discovery (DMKD)*, Santa Barbara, California.

Domingos, P., & Pazzani, M. (1996). Beyond independence: Conditions for the optimality of the simple Bayesian classifier. In *Proceedings of the Thirteenth International Conference on Machine Learning*, San Francisco, California (pp. 105-112). Morgan Kaufmann.

Donlon, J., Levy, H., & Scriver, C.R. (2004). Hyperphenylalaninemia: Phenylalanine hydroxylase deficiency. In C.R. Scriver, A.L. Beaudet, S.W. Sly, & D. Valle (Eds.); B. Childs, K.W. Kinzler, & B. Vogelstein (Assoc Eds.), *The metabolic and molecular bases of inherited disease.* New York: McGraw-Hill.

Dougherty, J., Kohavi, R., & Sahami, M. (1995). Supervised and unsupervised discretization of continuous features. In A. Prieditis & S. Russell (Ed.), *Machine learning: Proceedings of the 12th International Conference* (pp. 194-202). Morgan Kaufmann.

Dubois, D., & Prade, H. (1988). *Possibility theory*. Plenum Press.

Dubois, D., & Prade, H. (1992). Gradual inference rules in approximate reasoning. *Information Sciences, 61*(1-2), 103-122.

Dubois, D., & Prade, H. (1996). What are fuzzy rules and how to use them. *84*, 169-185.

Dubois, D., & Prade, H. (1997). The three semantics of fuzzy sets. *90*(2), 141-150.

Dubois, D., Fargier, H., & Prade, H. (1996a). Possibility theory in constraint satisfaction problems: Handling priority, preference and uncertainty. *Applied Intelligence, 6*, 287-309.

Dubois, D., Fargier, H., & Prade, H. (1996b). Refinements of the maximin approach to decision making in fuzzy environment. *Fuzzy Sets and Systems, 81*, 103-122.

Dubois, D., Hüllermeier, E., & Prade, H. (2006). A systematic approach to the assessment of fuzzy association rules. *Data Mining and Knowledge Discovery, 13*(2), 167.

Dubois, D., Prade, H., & Sudkamp, T. (2005). On the representation, measurement, and discovery of fuzzy associations. *IEEE Transactions on Fuzzy Systems, 13*(2), 250-262.

Duda, R. O., Hart, P. E., & Stork, D. G. (2001). *Pattern classification* (2nd ed.). New York: John Wiley & Sons.

Duncan, G. T., Keller-McNulty, S. A., & Stokes, S. L. (2001). *Disclosure risks vs. data utility: The R-U confidentiality map* (Tech. Rep. No. 121). National Institute of Statistical Sciences.

Dunham, M. H. (2003). *Data mining: Introductory and advanced topics*. NJ: Prentice Hall.

Dunham, M. H. (2003). *Data mining: Introductory and advanced topics*. Prentice Hall.

Dunn, W.B., Bailey, N.J., & Johnson, H.E. (2005). Measuring the metabolome: Current analytical technologies. *Analyst, 130*, 606-625.

Durbin, R., & Willshaw, D. (1987). An analogue approach to the traveling salesman problem using an elastic net method. *Nature, 326*(6114), 689-691.

Durbin, R., Eddy, S., Krogh, A., & Mitchison, G. (1998). *Biological sequence analysis: Probabilistic models of proteins and nucleic acids*. Cambridge University Press.

Dwork, C., & Nissim, K. (2004). Privacy preserving data mining in vertically partitioned database. *Proceedings of Crypto 2004, 3152*, 528-544.

Eager, D. L., Zahorjan, J., & Lazowska, E. D. (1989). Speedup versus efficiency in parallel systems. *IEEE Trans. on Computers, C-38*(3), 408-423. IEEE Press.

Eakins, J. P. (2002). Towards intelligent image retrieval. *Pattern Recognition, 35*, 3-14.

Elmasari, R., & Navathe, S. B. (1994). *Fundamentals of database systems* (2nd ed.). Benjamin/Cummings.

Embrechts, P., & Herzberg, A. M. (1991). Variations of Andrews' plots. *International Statistical Review, 59*(2), 175-194.

Embrechts, P., Herzberg, A. M., & Ng, A. C. (1986). An investigation of Andrews' plots to detect period and outliers in time series data. *Communications in Statistics: Simulation and Computation, 15*(4), 1027-1051.

Embrechts, P., Herzberg, A. M., Kalbfleisch, H. K., Traves, W. N., & Whitla, J. R. (1995). An introduction to wavelets with applications to Andrews' plots. *Journal of Computational and Applied Mathematics, 64*, 41-56.

EML. *Ecological Metadata Language*. http://knb.ecoinformatics.org/software/eml/

Emmanouilidis, C., Hunter, A., & MacIntyre, J. (2000). A multiobjective evolutionary setting for feature selection and a commonality-based crossover operator. *In Proceedings of the Congress on Evolutionary Computation (CEC)* (pp. 309-316).

Ertoz, L., Steinbach, M., & Kumar, V. (2003). Finding clusters of different sizes, shapes, and densities in noisy, high dimensional data. In *Proceedings of the SIAM International Conference on Data Mining*.

Ester, M., & Zhang, Z. (2004). A top-down method for mining most specific frequent patterns in biological sequence data. In *Proceedings of the 4th SIAM International Conference on Data Mining*.

Ester, M., Kriegel, H. P., Dansder, J., & Xu, X. (1996). A density-based algorithm for discovering clusters in large spatial databases with noise. In *Proceedings of the Second ACM SIGKDD*, Portland, Oregon (pp. 226-231).

Ester, M., Kriegel, H. P., Sander, J., & Xu, X. (1996). A density-based algorithm for discovering clusters in large spatial databases with noise. In *Proceedings of the 2nd ACM SIGKDD*, Portland, Oregon (pp. 226-231). AAAI Press.

Ester, M., Kriegel, H.P., Sander, J., & Xu, X. (1996). *A density-based algorithm for discovering clusters in large spatial databases with noise*. In *Proceedings of the 2nd International Conference on Knowledge Discovery and Data Mining (KDD'96)*, Menlo Park, California (pp. 226-231). AAAI Press.

Everitt, B.S., Landau, S., & Leese, M. (2001). *Cluster analysis* (4th ed.). New York: Oxford University Press.

Evfimievski, A. (2002). Randomization in privacy preserving data mining. *SIGKDD Explor. Newsl., 4*(2), 43-48. ACM Press.

Evfimievski, A., Srikant, R., Agrawal, R., & Gehrke, J. (2002). Privacy preserving mining of association rules. In *Proceedings of the 8th ACM SIGKDDD International Conference on Knowledge Discovery and Data Mining*. Elsevier Ltd.

Fan, W. (2004). Systematic data selection to mine concept-drifting data streams. In *Proceedings of the 10th ACM SIGKDD International Conference on Knowledge Discovery and Data Mining (KDD)*, Seattle, Washington (pp. 128-137).

Fan, W., Huang, Y., & Yu, P. S. (2004). Decision tree evolution using limited number of labeled data items from drifting data streams. In *Proceedings of the 4th IEEE International Conference on Data Mining (ICDM)*, Brighton, United Kingdom (pp. 379-382).

Fankhauser, P., Kracker, M., & Neuhold, E. J. (1991). Semantic vs. structural resemblance of classes. *SIGMOD Record, 20*(4), 59-63.

Fayyad, U.M., Piatetsky-Shapiro, G., & Smyth, P. (1996). From data mining to knowledge discovery: An overview. In *Advances in Knowledge Discovery and Data Mining*. MIT Press.

Ferreira de Oliveira, M. C., & Levkowitz, H. (2003). From visual data exploration to visual data mining: A Survey. *IEEE Transactions on Visualization and Computer Graphics, 9*(3), 378-394.

Ferreira, P., & Azevedo, P. (2005a). Protein sequence pattern mining with constraints. In *Proceedings of the 9th European Conference on Principles and Practice of Knowledge Discovery in Databases* (pp. 96-107). Lecture Notes in Computer Science 3721. Springer.

Fetrow, J., & Skolnick, J. (1998). Method for prediction of protein function from sequence using the sequence-to-structure-to-function paradigm with application to glutaredoxins/thioredoxins and T1 ribonucleases. *Journal of Molecular Biology, 281*(5), 949-968.

Fetrow, J., Godzik, A., & Skolnick, J. (1998). Functional analysis of the *Escherichia coli* genome using the sequence-to-structure-to-function paradigm: Identification of proteins exhibiting the glutaredoxin/thioredoxin disulfide oxidoreductase activity. *Journal of Molecular Biology, 282*(4), 703-711.

Fiehn, O., & Spranger, J. (2003). Use of metabolomics to discover metabolic patterns associated with human diseases. In G.G. Harrigan & R. Goodacre, R. (Eds.), *Metabolic profiling: Its role in biomarker discovery and gene function analysis* (pp. 199-215). Boston/Dordrecht/London: Kluwer Academic Publishers.

Finley, T., & Joachims, T. (2005). Supervised clustering with support vector machines. In *Proceedings of the International Conference on Machine Learning (ICML)*.

Finn, R., Mistry, J., Schuster-Böckler, B., Griffiths-Jones, S., Hollich, V., Lassmann, T., et al. (2006). Pfam: Clans, Web tools and services [Database issue]. *Nucleic Acids Research, 34*, D247-D251.

Floyd, E., & McShane, T.M. (2004). Development and use of biomarkers in oncology drug development. *Toxicologic Pathology, 32*(Suppl. 1), 106-115.

Flury, B., & Riedwyl, H. (1981). Graphical representation of multivariate data by means of asymmetrical faces. *Journal of American Statistical Association, 76*, 757-765.

Fogel, D. (1994). An introduction to simulated evolutionary optimization. *IEEE Transactions on Neural Networks, 5*(1), 3-14.

Forgey, E. W. (1965). Cluster analysis of multivariate data efficiency vs. interpretability of classifications. *Biometrics, 21*(3), 768-769.

Fortune, S., & Wyllie, J. (1978). Parallelism in random access machines. In *Proceedings of the Tenth ACM Symposium on Theory of Computing* (pp. 114-118). ACM Press.

Frawley, W., Piatetsky-Shapiro, G., & Matheus, C. (1992). Knowledge discovery in databases: An overview. *AI Magazine*, pp. 213-228.

Friedman, J. H. (1987). Exploratory projection pursuit. *Journal of the American Statistical Association, 82*(397), 249-266.

Friedman, J. H., & Tukey, J. W. (1974). A projection pursuit algorithm for exploratory data analysis. *IEEE Transactions on Computers, c-23*(9), 881-889.

Friedman, M., Levy, A., & Millstein, T. (1999). *Navigational plans for data integration.* Paper presented at the AAAI/IAAI.

Frontline Strategic Consulting, Inc. (2003). *Biomarkers: In Vitro diagnostics candidate screening and strategic analysis* (Report # 1420, III-20).

Fruchterman, T., & Reingold, E. (1991). Graph drawing by force-directed placement. *Software—Practice and Experience, 21*(11), 1129-1164.

Fu, L. (2005). Novel efficient classifiers based on data cube. *International Journal of Data Warehousing and Mining, 1*(3), 15-27.

Fu, Y., Sandhu, K., & Shih, M. (1999). Clustering of Web users based on access patterns. *Workshop on Web Usage Analysis and User Profiling.*

Fua, Y.-H., Ward, M. O., & Rundensteiner, E. A. (1999). Hierarchical parallel coordinates for exploration of large datasets. In *Proceedings of the 10th IEEE Visualization 1999 Conference (VIS '99): Celebrating Ten Years*, San Francisco, California (pp. 43-50). SIGGRAPH: ACM Special Interest Group on Computer Graphics and Interactive Techniques. IEEE Computer Society Press.

Fukuda, T., Morimoto, Y., Morishita, S., & Tokuyama, T. (1996). Data mining using two-dimensional optimized association rules: Scheme, algorithms, and visualization. In *Proceedings of the ACM SIGMOD International Conference on Management of Data (SIGMOD 1996)*, Montreal, Quebec, Canada (pp. 13-23). ACM Press.

Fyfe, C. (1993). PCA properties of interneurons. In *From Neurobiology to Real World Computing, ICANN 93* (pp. 183-188).

Fyfe, C. (1995a). Introducing asymmetry into interneuron learning. *Neural Computation, 7*(6), 1167-1181.

Fyfe, C. (1995b). Radial feature mapping. In *International Conference on Artificial Neural Networks, ICANN95, Neuronimes '95 Scientific Conference, 2*, 27-32, Paris, France.

Fyfe, C. (1997). A comparative study of two neural methods of exploratory projection pursuit. *Neural Networks, 10*(2), 257-262.

Fyfe, C. (2005). Topographic product of experts. In *International Conference on Artificial Neural Networks, ICANN2005.*

Fyfe, C. (2006). Two topographic maps for data visualization. *Data Mining and Knowledge Discovery.*

Fyfe, C., & Baddeley, R. (1995). Non-linear data structure extraction using simple hebbian networks. *Biological Cybernetics, 72*(6), 533-541.

Fyfe, C., & Charles, D. (1999). Using noise to form a minimal overcomplete basis. In *Proceedings of the Seventh*

International Conference on Artificial Neural Networks, ICANN99 (pp. 708-713).

Fyfe, C., & MacDonald, D. (2002). Epsilon-insensitive Hebbian learning. *Neurocomputing, 47,* 35-57.

Gaber, M. M., Krishnaswamy, S., & Zaslavsky, A. (2004). Cost-efficient mining techniques for data streams. In *Proceedings of the 1st Australasian Workshop on Data Mining and Web Intelligence (DMWI)*, Dunedin, New Zealand.

Gallagher, M. (2000). *Multi-layer perceptron error surfaces: Visualization, structure and modelling.* Doctoral thesis, Department of Computer Science and Electrical Engineering, University of Queensland.

Gama, J., Medas, P., & Rocha, R. (2004). Forest trees for on-line data. In *Proceedings of the 2004 ACM Symposium on Applied Computing (SAC)*, Nicosia, Cyprus (pp. 632-636).

Gama, J., Rocha, R., & Medas, P. (2003). Accurate decision trees for mining high-speed data streams. In *Proceedings of the 9th ACM SIGKDD International Conference on Knowledge Discovery and Data Mining (KDD)*, Washington, DC (pp. 523-528).

Gançarski, P., & Wemmert, C. (2005). Collaborative multi-strategy classification: Application to per-pixel analysis of images. In *Proceedings of the Sixth International Workshop on Multimedia Data Mining (ACM SIGKDD)*, Chicago, Illinois.

Ganguly, S., Garofalakis, M., & Rastogi, R. (2004). Processing data-stream join aggregates using skimmed sketches. In *Proceedings of the 9th International Conference on Extending Database Technology (EDBT)*, Heraklion, Crete, Greece (pp. 569-586).

García-Osorio, C., & Fyfe, C. (2003). Three neural exploratory projection pursuit algorithms. In *Proceedings of the European Symposium on Intelligent Technologies, Hybrid Systems and their implementation on Smart Adaptive Systems (EUNITE 2003)* (pp. 409-420).

García-Osorio, C., & Fyfe, C. (2005a). The combined use of self-organizing maps and Andrews' curves. *International Journal of Neural Systems, 15*(3), 1-10.

García-Osorio, C., & Fyfe, C. (2005b). Visualization of high-dimensional data via orthogonal curves. *Journal of Universal Computer Science, 11*(11), 1806-1819.

Gasteiger, E., Gattiker, A., Hoogland, C., Ivanyi, I., Appel, R, & Bairoch, A. (2003). *ExPASy: The proteomics server for in-depth protein knowledge and analysis. Nucleic Acids Research, 31*(13), 3784-3788.

Gelman, A., Carlin, J.B., Stern, H.S., & Rubin, D.B. (2004). *Bayesian data analysis* (2nd ed.). Boca Raton, FL: Chapman & Hall/CRC Press.

Georgakopoulos, D., Karabatis, G., & Gantimahapatruni, S. (1997). Specification and management of interdependent data in operational systems and data warehouses. *Distributed and Parallel Databases, An International Journal, 5*(2), 121-166.

Ghosh, S. P. (1984). An application of statistical databases in manufacturing testing. In *Proceedings of IEEE COMPDEC Conference* (pp. 96-103). IEEE Press.

Ghosh, S. P. (1985). An application of statistical databases in manufacturing testing. *IEEE Trans. Software Eng., SE-11*(7), 591-596. IEEE Press.

Gnanadesikan, R. (1977). *Methods for statistical data analysis of multivariate observations.* New York: John Wiley & Sons.

Goethals, B. (2005). Frequent set mining. In *The data mining and knowledge discovery handbook* (pp. 377-397). Springer.

Goethals, B., & Zaki, M. J. (2004). *Advances in frequent itemset mining implementation: Report on FIMI'03.* SIGKDD Explorations Newsletter, 6(1), 109-117.

Golab, L., & Ozsu, M. T. (2003). Issues in data stream management. *ACM SIGMOD Record, 32*(2), 5-14.

Golab, L., DeHaan, D., Demaine, E. D., López-Ortiz, A., & Munro, J. I. (2003). Identifying frequent items in sliding windows over on-line packet streams. In *Proceedings of the 2003 ACM SIGCOMM Internet Measurement Conference (IMC)*, Miami, Florida (pp. 173-178).

Gomez-Perez, A., & Rojas, M. D. (1999). Ontological reengineering and reuse. In D. Fensel & R. Studer (Eds.), *Proceedings of the 11ᵗʰ European Workshop on Knowledge Acquisition, Modeling and Management (EKAW'99)*, Germany (pp. 139-156). Lecture Notes in Artificial Intelligence 1621. Springer-Verlag.

Gondek, D., & Hofmann, T. (2004). Non-redundant data clustering. In *Proceedings of the 4ᵗʰ IEEE International Conference on Data Mining (ICDM)*.

Goodchild, N. A., & Vijayan, K. (1974). Significance tests in plots of multi-dimensional data in two dimensions. *Biometrics, 30*, 209-210.

Gorban, A. N., & Zinovyev, A. Y. (2001). *Visualization of data by method of elastic maps and its applications in genomics, economics and sociology* (Tech. Rep. No. IHES M/01/36). Institut des Hautes Etudes Scientifiques.

Goswami, J. C., & Chan, A. K. (1999). *Fundamentals of wavelets: Theory, algorithms and applications*: John Wiley.

Graber, A., Weinberger, K., Ramsay, S., & Wingate, J. (2005). Differences in technology and performance of qualitative and quantitative metabolite profiling approaches. In *Proceedings of the 53ʳᵈ ASMS Conference on Mass Spectrometry*, San Antonio, Texas.

Graham, M., & Kennedy, J. (2003). Using curves to enhance parallel coordinate visualisations. In *Proceedings of the Seventh International Conference on Information Visualization (IV'2003)* (pp. 10-16). London, UK: IEEE Computer Society.

Grahne, G., & Zhu, J. (2002). Discovering approximate keys in XML data. In *Proceedings of the 11ᵗʰ International Conference on Information and Knowledge Management* (pp. 453-460). ACM Press.

Gribskov, M., McLachlan, A., & Eisenberg, D. (1987). Profile analysis: Detection of distantly related proteins. *Proceedings of the National Academy of Sciences, 84*(13), 4355-4358.

Grinstein, G., Pickett, R., & Williams, M. G. (1989). EXVIS: An exploratory visualization environment. In *Proceedings of Graphics Interface '89* (pp. 254-259).

Grira, N., Crucianu, M., & Boujemaa, N. (2004). Unsupervised and semisupervised clustering: A brief survey. In *A review of machine learning techniques for processing multimedia content: Report of the MUSCLE European Network of Excellence (FP6)* (p. 11).

Grira, N., Crucianu, M., & Boujemaa, N. (2005, November 6-12). Active semisupervised fuzzy clustering for image database categorization. In *Proceedings of the 6ᵗʰ ACM SIGMM International Workshop on Multimedia Information Retrieval*, Singapore.

Grosky, W. I., Sreenath, D. V., & Fotouhi, F. (2002). Emergent semantics and the multimedia semantic Web. *SIGMOD Record, 4*.

Gruber, T. (1993). Toward principles for the design of ontologies used for knowledge sharing [Special issue]. *International Journal of Human-Computer Studies*.

Guha, S., Mishra, N., Motwani, R., & O'Callaghan, L. (2000). Clustering data streams. In *Proceedings of the 41ˢᵗ Annual Symposium on Foundations of Computer Science, (FOCS)*, Redondo Beach, California (pp. 359-366).

Guha, S., Rastogi, R., & Shim, K. (1998). CURE: An efficient clustering algorithm for large databases. In *Proceedings of the ACM SIGMOD International Conference on Management of Data* (pp. 73-84).

Guha, S., Rastogi, R., & Shim, K. (2000). ROCK: A robust clustering algorithm for categorical attributes. *Information Systems, 25*(5), 345-366.

Gupta, C., & Grossman, R. L. (2004). GenIc: A single pass generalized incremental algorithm for clustering. In *Proceedings of the 1ˢᵗ Workshop on Secure Data Management (SDM)*, Toronto, Canada.

Guralnik, V., & Karypis, G. (2001). A scalable algorithm for clustering protein sequences. In *Proceedings of the 1ˢᵗ Workshop on Data Mining in Bioinformatics of the 7ᵗʰ ACM SIGKDD* (pp. 78-80).

Halevy, A. Y., Ives, Z. G., Suciu, D., & Tatarinov, I. (2003). *Schema mediation in peer data management systems.* Paper presented at the ICDE.

Halket, J.M., Waterman, D., Przyborowska, A.M., Patel, R.K., Fraser, P.D., & Bramley, P.M. (2005). Chemical derivatization and mass spectral libraries in metabolic profiling by GC/MS and LC/MS/MS. *Journal of Experimental Botany, 56,* 219-243.

Hall, M.A., & Holmes, G. (2003). Benchmarking attribute selection techniques for discrete class data mining. *IEEE Transactions on Knowledge and Data Engineering, 15,* 1437-1447.

Hamner, C. G., Turner, D. W., & Young, D. M. (1987). Comparison of several graphical methods for representing multivariate data. *Computer and Mathematics with Applications, 13,* 647-655.

Han, E. H., Karypis, G., & Kumar, V. (1997). Scalable parallel data mining for association rules. In *Proceedings of the ACM SIGMOD International Conference on Management of Data (SIGMOD 1997),* Tucson, Arizona (pp. 277-288). ACM Press.

Han, E. H., Karypis, G., Kumar, V., & Mobasher, B. (1998). Hypergraph based clustering in high-dimensional data sets: A summary of results. *Bulletin of the Technical Committee on Data Engineering, 21*(1), 15-22.

Han, J. (1998). *Towards on-line analytical mining in large databases.* Paper presented at the ACM SIGMOD.

Han, J., & Fu, J. (1995). Discovery of multiple-level association rules from large databases. In *Proceedings of the 21st International Conference on Very Large Data Bases (VLDB 1995),* Zurich, Switzerland (pp. 420-431). Morgan Kaufmann.

Han, J., & Kamber, M. (2000). *Data Mining: Concepts and Techniques*: Morgan Kaufmann.

Han, J., & Kamber, M. (2000, August). *Data mining: Concepts and techniques* (The Morgan Kaufmann Series in Data Management Systems). Morgan Kaufmann Publishers.

Han, J., & Kamber, M. (2001). *Data mining concepts and techniques* (The Morgan Kaufmann Series in Data Management Systems). Morgan Kaufman.

Han, J., & Kamber, M. (2001). *Data mining: Concepts and techniques* (pp. 225-278, 395-449). San Francisco, CA: Morgan Kaufmann.

Han, J., Chee, S., & Chiang, J. (1998). *Issues for on-line analytical mining of data warehouses.* Paper presented at the Proceedings of 1998 SIGMOD'96 Workshop on Research Issues on Data Mining and Knowledge Discovery DMKD, Seattle, Washington.

Han, J., Dong, G., & Yin, Y. (1999). Efficient mining of partial periodic patterns in time series database. In *Proceedings of the 15th International Conference on Data Engineering (ICDE 1999),* Sydney, Australia (pp. 106-115). IEEE Computer Society.

Han, J., Fu, Y., Wang, W., Koperski, K., & Zaiane, O. (1996). DMQL: A data mining query language for relational databases. In *Proceedings of the SIGMOD'96 Workshop on Research Issues in Data Mining and Knowledge Discovery (DMKD'96).*

Han, J., Pei, J., & Yin, Y. (2000). Mining frequent patterns without candidate generation. *In Proceedings of ACM SIGMOD '00* (pp. 1-12).

Harinarayan, V., Rajaraman, A., & Ullman, J. D. (1996). Implementing data cubes efficiently. In H. V. Jagadish & I. S. Mumick (Eds.), *1996 ACM SIGMOD International Conference on Management of Data* (pp. 205-216). ACM Press.

Harrigan, G.G., & Goodacre, R. (2003). *Metabolic profiling: Its role in biomarker discovery and gene function analysis.* Boston/Dordrecht/London: Kluwer Academic Publishers.

Hartigan, J. A. (1975). *Clustering algorithms.* New York: John Wiley & Sons.

Hastie, T. J., & Stuetzle, W. (1989). Principal curves. *Journal of the American Statistical Association, 84*(406), 502-516.

Hastie, T., Tibshirani, R., & Friedman, J. (2001). *The elements of statistical learning: Data mining, inference, and prediction* (Springer Series in Statistics). Springer.

Hastie, T., Tibshirani, R., & Friedman, J. (2001). *The elements of statistical learning.* Springer.

Hauser, H., Ledermann, F., & Doleisch, H. (2002). Angular brushing of extended parallel coordinates. In *IEEE Symposium on Information Visualization 2002 (InfoVis 2002)* (pp. 127-130). Boston: IEEE Computer Society Press.

He, H., & Yang, J. (2004). Multiresolution indexing of XML for frequent queries. In *Proceedings of the 20th International Conference on Data Engineering* (pp. 683-694). IEEE Computer Society.

Henikoff, S., & Henikoff, J. (1993). Performance evaluation of amino acid substitution matrices. *Proteins, 17*(1), 49-61.

Henikoff, S., & Henikoff, J. (1994). Protein family classification based on searching a database of blocks. *Genomics, 19*(1), 97-107.

Henikoff, S., & Henikoff, J. (2001). Protein family databases. *Encyclopedia of Life Sciences.*

Hennig, S., & Wurst, M. (2006). Incremental clustering of newsgroup articles. In *Proceedings of the International Conference on Industrial, Engineering and Other Applications of Applied Intelligent Systems (IEA/AIE 06).*

Heringa, H. (2000). Predicting secondary structure from protein sequences. In D. Higgins & W. Taylor (Eds.), *Bioinformatics: Sequence, structure and databanks: A practical approach.* Oxford University Press.

Hill, D., Hlavacek, W., Ambrosiano, J., Wall, M., Sharp, D., Cleland, T., et al. (2001). Integrated clustering and motif detection for genome-wide expression and sequence data. In *Proceedings of the 2nd International Conference on Systems Biology* (pp. 83-88).

Hochbaum, D. S. (1997). *Approximation algorithms for NP-Hard problems.* PWS Publishing Company.

Hoffmann, G.F., & Zschocke, J. (1999). Glutaric aciduria type I: From clinical, biochemical and molecular diversity to successful therapy. *Journal of Inherited Metabolic Disease, 22*, 381-391.

Homburg, H., Mierswa, I., Moeller, B., Morik, K., & Wurst, M. (2005). A benchmark dataset for audio classification and clustering. In *Proceedings of the International Conference on Music Information Retrieval.*

Hosmer, D.W., & Lemeshow, S. (2000). *Applied logistic regression* (2nd ed.). New York: Wiley.

Hotelling, H. (1933). Analysis of a complex of statistical variables into principal components. *Journal of Educational Psychology, 24*, 417-441, 498-520.

Hotho, A., Staab, S., & Stumme, G. (2003). Ontologies improve text document clustering. In *Proceedings of the International Conference on Data Mining* (pp. 541-544).

Hsu, T., Liau, C., & Wang, D. (2001). A logical model for privacy protection. *Lecture Notes in Computer Science, 2200*, 110-124. Springer-Verlag.

Huang, J., & Douglas, B. (2001). The eMOTIF database. *Nucleic Acids Research, 29*(1), 202-204.

Huber, P. J. (1985). Projection pursuit. *Annals of Statistics, 13*, 435-475.

Huber, P.J. (1981). *Robust statistics.* Wiley.

Huh, M. Y., & Kim, K. (2002). Visualization of multidimensional data using modifications of the grand tour. *Journal of Applied Statistics, 29*(5), 721-728.

Huhtala, Y., Karkkainen, J., Porkka, P., & Toivonen, H. (1999). TANE: An efficient algorithm for discovering functional and approximate dependencies. *The Computer Journal, 42*(2), 100-111.

Hüllermeier, E. (2001). Implication-based fuzzy association rules. In *Proceedings of the 5th European Conference on Principles and Practice of Knowledge Discovery in Databases*, Freiburg, Germany (pp. 241-252).

Hüllermeier, E. (2002). Association rules for expressing gradual dependencies. In *Proceedings of the 6th European Conference on Principles and Practice of Knowledge Discovery in Databases*, Helsinki, Finland (pp. 200-211).

Hüllermeier, E. (2005b). Fuzzy sets in machine learning and data mining: Status and prospects. *Fuzzy Sets and Systems, 156*(3), 387-406.

Hüllermeier, E. (Ed.). (2005a). Fuzzy sets in knowledge discovery [Special Issue]. *Fuzzy Sets and Systems, 149*(1).

Hulo, N., Bairoch, A., Bulliard, V., Cerutti, L., De Castro, E., Langendijk-Genevaux, P., et al. (2006). *The PROSITE database [Database issue]. Nucleic Acids Research, 34,* D227-D230.

Hulten, G., Spencer, L., & Domingos, P. (2001). Mining time-changing data streams. In *Proceedings of the 7ᵗʰ ACM SIGKDD International Conference on Knowledge Discovery and Data mining (KDD)*, San Francisco, California (pp. 97-106).

Hunter, J. (2001). Adding multimedia to the semantic Web: Building an MPEG-7 ontology. In *Proceedings of the First International Semantic Web Working Symposium (SWWS'01)*, Stanford, California (pp. 261-283).

Hunter, L. (1993). Molecular biology for computer scientists. In L. Hunter (Ed.), *Artificial intelligence and molecular biology* (pp. 1-46). AAAI Press.

Huyn, N. (2001). Data analysis and mining in the life sciences. *ACM SIGMOD Record, 30,* 76-85.

Hyperion. The Hyperion Project. http://www.cs.toronto.edu/db/hyperion/.

Hyvarinen, A., Karhunen, J., & Oja, E. (2001). *Independent component analysis*. Wiley.

Ihara, S. (1993). *Information theory for continuous systems.* World Scientific Publiching Co.

Imielinski, T., & Mannila, H. (1996). A database perspective on knowledge discovery. *Communications of the ACM, 39*(11), 58-64.

Imielinski, T., & Virmani, A. (1999). MSQL: A query language for database mining. *Data Mining and Knowledge Discovery, 2*(4), 373-408.

Inmon, W. (2005). *Building the data warehouse* (4ᵗʰ ed.). John Wiley & Sons.

Inselberg, A. (1985). The plane with parallel coordinates. *The Visual Computer, 1,* 69-91.

Inselberg, A. (n.d.). *Parallel coordinates: How it happened.* Retrieved June 23, 2007, from http://www.math.tau.ac.il/~aiisreal/

Inselberg, A., & Dimsdale, B. (1990). Parallel coordinates: A tool for visualizing multidimensional geometry. In *Proceedings of Visualization '90*, Los Alamitos, California (pp. 361-378). SIGGRAPH: ACM Special Interest Group on Computer Graphics and Interactive Techniques, IEEE Computer Society Press.

Inselberg, A., Chen, Y., Shieh, M., & Lee, H. (1990). Planar conflict resolution algorithms for air traffic control. In *Proceedings of the 2ⁿᵈ Canadian Conference on Computational Geometry* (pp. 160-164).

Ioannidis, Y. E., & Poosala, V. (1999). Histogram-based approximation of set-valued query-answers. In *Proceedings of the 25ᵗʰ International Conference on Very Large Data Bases (VLDB)*, Edinburgh, Scotland, United Kingdom (pp. 174-185).

ISO SQL/MM Part 6. (2001). Retrieved June 15, 2007, from http://www.sql-99.org/SC32/WG4/Progression Documents/FCD/fcd-datamining-2001-05.pdf

Jain, A. K., & Dubes, R. C. (1988). Algorithms for clustering Data. NJ: Prentice Hall.

Jain, A. K., Murty, M. N., & Flynn, P. J. (1999). Data clustering: A review. *ACM Computing Surveys, 31*(3), 264-323.

Jain, H., & Zhao, H. (2004). *Federating heterogeneous information systems using Web services and ontologies.* Paper presented at the Tenth Americas Conference on Information Systems, New York.

Jain, K.K. (2005). Personalised medicine for cancer: From drug development into clinical practice. *Expert Opinion on Oharmacotherapy, 6,* 1463-1476.

Jancey, R. C. (1966). Multidimensional group analysis. *Australian Journal on Botany, 14*(1), 127-130.

Jasper. (2005). *The Jasper Java Interface.* Retrieved June 15, 2007, from http://www.sics.se/sicstus/docs/latest/html/sicstus/Jasper.html

JDM. (2003). *Java Data Mining API.* Retrieved June 15, 2007, from http://www.jcp.org/jsr/detail/73.prt

Jensen, S., Shen, L., & Liu, J. (2005). Combining phylogenetic motif discovery and motif clustering to predict co-regulated genes. *Bioinformatics, 21*(20), 3832-3839.

Joachims, T., Freitag, D., & Mitchell, T. (1997). Webwatcher: A tour guide for the world wide Web. The 15th *International Joint Conference on Artificial Intelligence* (pp. 770-777), Nagoya, Japan.

John, G.-H., Kohavi, R., & Pfleger, K. (1994). Irrelevant features and the subset selection problem. In *Proceedings of the International Conference on Machine Learning (ICML)* (pp. 121-129).

Johnson, M., & Lehtonen, J. (2000). Comparison of protein three-dimensional structure. In D. Higgins & W. Taylor (Eds.), *Bioinformatics: Sequence, structure and databanks: A practical approach.* Oxford University Press.

Johnson, S., Lakshmanan, L.V.S., & Ng, R.T. (2000). The 3W model and algebra for unified data mining. In *Proceedings of VLDB'00* (pp. 21-32).

Jolliffe, I. (1986). *Principal component analysis.* Springer-Verlag.

Jonassen, I. (2000). Methods for discovering conserved patterns in protein sequences and structures. In D. Higgins & W. Taylor (Eds.), *Bioinformatics: Sequence, structure and databanks: A practical approach.* Oxford University Press.

Jonassen, I., Collins, J., & Higgins, D. (1995). Finding flexible patterns in unaligned protein sequences. *Protein Science, 4*(8), 1587-1595.

Jonassen, I., Eidhammer, I., Conklin, D., & Taylor, W. (2002). Structure motif discovery and mining the PDB. *Bioinformatics, 18*(2), 362-367.

Jones, D., & Hadley, C. (2000). Threading methods for protein structure prediction. In D. Higgins & W. Taylor (Eds.), *Bioinformatics: Sequence, structure and databanks: A practical approach.* Oxford University Press.

Jones, M. C., & Sibson, R. (1987). What is projection pursuit. *Journal of The Royal Statistical Society,* 1-37.

Jones, S., Cunningham, S.-J., & Jones, M. (2004). Organizing digital music for use: An examination of personal music collections. In *Proceedings of the International Conference on Music Information Retrieval.*

Jonsson, P., Gullberg, J., Nordstrom A., Kusano, M., Kowalczyk, M., & Sjostrom, M. (2004). A strategy for identifying differences in large series of metabolomic samples analyzed by GC/MS. *Analytical Chemistry, 76,* 1738-1745.

Jorda, A., Cabo, J., & Grisolia, S. (1981). Changes in the levels of urea cycle enzymes and in metabolites thereof in diabetes. *Enzyme, 26,* 240-244.

Kailing, K., Kriegel, H.P., Kröger, P., & Wanka, S. (2003). Ranking interesting subspaces for clustering high dimensional data. In *Proceedings of the 7th European Conference on Principles and Practice of Knowledge Discovery in Databases (PKDD'03),* Dubrovnik, Croatia (pp. 241-252).

Kalfoglou, Y., & Schorlemmer, M. (2003). Ontology mapping: The state of the art. *Knowledge Engineering Review, 18*(1), 1-31.

Kaltashov, I.A., & Eyles, S.J. (2005). *Mass spectrometry in biophysics: Conformation and dynamics of biomolecules.* New York: Wiley.

Kamber, M., Han, J., & Chiang, J. (1997). Metarule-guided mining of multi-dimensional association rules using data cubes. In *Proceedings of the 3rd International Conference on Knowledge Discovery and Data Mining (KDD 1997),* Newport Beach, California (pp. 207-210). The AAAI Press.

Kantarcioglu, M., & Clifton, C. (2002). Privacy preserving distributed mining of association rules on horizontally partitioned data. In *Proceedings of the ACM SIGMOD Workshop on Research issues in Data Mining and Knowledge Discovery* (pp. 24-31). IEEE Educational Activities Department.

Kantardzic, M. (2003). *Data mining: Concepts, models, methods, and algorithms.* IEEE Press.

Karabatis, G., Rusinkiewicz, M., & Sheth, A. (1999). Interdependent database systems. In *Management of Heterogeneous and Autonomous Database Systems* (pp. 217-252). San Francisco, CA: Morgan-Kaufmann.

Karhunen, J. & Joutsensalo, J. (1994). Representation and separation of signals using nonlinear PCA type learning. *Neural Networks, 7*(1), 113-127.

Karp, R. M., Papadimitriou, C. H., & Shenker, S. (2003). A simple algorithm for finding frequent elements in streams and bags. *ACM Transactions on Database Systems (TODS), 28*(1), 51-55.

Karypis, G., Han, E., & Kumar, V. (1999). Chameleon: Hierarchical clustering using dynamic model. *IEEE Computer, 32*(8), 68-75.

Kaufman, L., & Rousseeuw, P. (1990). *Finding groups in data: An introduction to cluster analysis.* New York: John Wiley & Sons.

Kay, M. (2006). *Saxon: The XSLT and XQuery processor.* Retrieved June 13, 2007, from http://saxon.sourceforge.net/

Keim, D. A. (1997). Visual techniques for exploring databases (Invited tutorial). In *Proceedings of the International Conference on Knowledge Discovery in Databases (KDD'97)*, Newport Beach, California. Retrieved June 23, 2007, from http://www.dbs.informatik.uni-muenchen.de/~daniel/KDD97.pdf

Keim, D. A. (2000). Designing pixel-oriented visualization techniques: Theory and applications. *IEEE Transactions on Visualization and Computer Graphics, 6*(1), 59-72.

Keim, D. A. (2002). Information visualization and visual data mining. *IEEE Transactions on Visualization and Computer Graphics, 8*(1), 1-8.

Keim, D. A., & Kriegel, H.-P. (1994). VisDB: Database exploration using multidimensional visualization. *IEEE Computer Graphics and Applications, 14*(5), 44-49.

Keim, D. A., & Kriegel, H.-P. (1996). Visualization techniques for mining large databases: A comparison. *IEEE Transactions on Knowledge and Data Engineering, 8*(6), 923-938.

Khattree, R., & Naik, D. N. (2002). Andrews plots for multivariate data: Some new suggestions and applications. *Journal of Statistical Planning and Inference, 100*, 411-425.

Kifer, D., Ben-David, S., & Gehrke, J. (2004). Detecting change in data streams. In *Proceedings of the 30th International Conference on Very Large Data Bases (VLDB)*, Toronto, Canada (pp. 180-191).

Kim, H. J., & Lee, S. G. (2002). User-feedback driven document clustering technique for information organization. *IEICE Transactions on Information and Systems, E85-D*(6), 1043-1048.

Kimball, R. (2002). *The data warehouse toolkit* (2nd ed.).

Kimball, R., & Ross, M. (2002). *The data warehouse toolkit.* John Wiley & Sons.

Klein, D., Kamvar, S. D., & Manning, C. D. (2002). From instance level constraints to space-level constraints: Making the most of prior knowledge in data clustering. In *Proceedings of the ICML-2002* (pp. 307-314).

Kleinberg, J. (2002). An impossibility theorem for clustering. *Proceedings of the Conference on Advances in Neural Information Processing Systems, 15*, 463-470.

Kleinberg, J., & Tardos, E. (1999). Approximation algorithms for classification problems with pairwise relationships: Metric labeling and Markov random fields. In *Proceedings of the FOCS '99 40th Annual Symposium on Foundations of Computer Science*, Washington, DC (p. 14). IEEE Computer Society.

Kleiner, B., & Hartigan, J. (1981). Representing points in many dimensions by trees and castles. *Journal of American Statistical Association, 76*, 260-269.

Klement, E.P., Mesiar, R., & Pap, E. (2002). *Triangular norms.* Kluwer Academic Publishers.

Klemettinen, M., Mannila, H., Ronkainen, P., Toivonen, H., & Verkamo, A. I. (1994). Finding interesting rules from large sets of discovered association rules. In *Proceedings of the 3rd ACM International Conference on Information and Knowledge Management (CIKM 1994)*, Gaithersburg, Maryland (pp. 401-407). ACM Press.

Kohavi, R., & John, G.H. (1998). The wrapper approach. In H. Liu & H. Motoda (Eds.), *Feature selection for knowledge discovery and data mining* (pp. 33-50). Boston/Dordrecht/London: Kluwer Academic Publishers.

Kohonen, T. (1985). Median strings. *Pattern Recognition Letters, 3*(1), 309-313.

Kohonen, T. (1990). Self-organizing map. *Proceeding of IEEE, 78*(9), 1464-1480.

Kokiol, J. A., & Hacke, W. (1991). A bivariate version of Andrews plots. *IEEE Transactions on Biomedical Engineering, 38*(12), 1271-1274.

Konstan, J. A., Miller, B. N., Maltz, D., Herlocker, J. L., Gordon, L. R., & Riedl, J. (1997). GroupLens: Applying collaborative filtering to Usenet news. *Communications of the ACM, 40*(3), 77-87.

Koonin, E., & Galperin, M. (2003). *Sequence-evolution-function: Computational approaches in comparative genomics.* Kluwer Academic Publishers.

Korn, F., Labrinidis, A., Kotidis, Y., & Faloutsos, C. (1998). Ratio rules: A new paradigm for fast, quantifiable data mining. In *Proceedings of the 24th International Conference on Very Large Data Bases (VLDB 1998)*, New York, New York (pp. 582-593). Morgan Kaufmann.

Krishnamurthy, B., Sen, S., Zhang, Y., & Chen, Y. (2003). Sketch-based change detection: Methods, evaluation, and applications. In *Proceedings of the 3rd ACM SIGCOMM Internet Measurement Conference (IMC)*, Miami Beach, Florida (pp. 234-247).

Kruskal, J. B., & Wish, M. (1978). *Multidimensional scaling.* Beverly Hills: Sage Publications.

Kulkarmi, S. R., & Paranjape, S. R. (1984). Use of Andrews' function plot technique to construct control curves for multivariate process. *Communications in Statistics - Theory Methods, 13*(20), 2511-2533.

Kumar, N., Gangopadhyay, A., & Karabatis, G. (in press). Supporting mobile decision making with association rules and multi-layered caching. *Decision Support Systems.*

Kumar, P., Rao, M. V., Krishna, P. R., Bapi, R. S., & Laha, A. (2005). Intrusion detection system using sequence and set preserving metric. *Proceedings of IEEE International Conference on Intelligence and Security Informatics* (pp. 498-504), LNCS Springer Verlag, Atlanta.

Lamping, J., Rao, R., & Pirolli, P. (1995). *A Focus+Context Technique Based on Hyperbolic Geometry for Visualizing Large Hierarchies.* Paper presented at the Proceedings ACM Conference Human Factors in Computing Systems.

Lawrence, C., & Reilly, A. (1990). An expectation maximization (EM) algorithm for the identification and characterization of common sites in unaligned byopolimer sequences. *Proteins, 7*(1), 44-51.

LeBlanc, J., Ward, M. O., & Wittels, N. (1990). Exploring n-dimensional databases. In A. Kaufman (Ed.), *Proceedings of the 1st Conference on Visualization '90*, San Francisco, California (pp. 230-237). IEEE Computer Society Technical Committee on Computer Graphics, IEEE Computer Society Press.

Lee, C.H.L., Liu, A., & Chen, W.S. (2006). Pattern discovery of fuzzy time series for financial prediction. *IEEE Transactions on Knowledge and Data Engineering, 18*(5), 613-625.

Lee, J. A., & Verleysen, M. (2002). Nonlinear projection with the Isotop method. In J. R. Dorronsoro (Ed.), *ICANN 2002 Proceedings of the International Conference on Artificial Networks,* Madrid, Spain (pp. 933-938). Lecture Notes in Computer Science 2415. Springer.

Lee, J. A., Archambeau, C., & Verleysen, M. (2003a). Locally linear embedding versus Isotop. In *ESANN'2003 Proceedings of the European Symposium on Artificial Neural Networks* (pp. 527-534). d-side publications.

Lee, J. A., Lendasse, A., & Verleysen, M. (2002). Curvilinear distance analysis versus Isomap. In M. Verleysen (Ed.), *ESANN'2002 Proceedings of the European Symposium on Artificial Neural Networks* (pp. 185-192). d-side publications.

Lee, J. A., Lendasse, A., Donckers, N., & Verleysen, M. (2000). A robust nonlinear projection method. In M. Verleysen (Ed.), *ESANN'2000 Proceedings of the European Symposium on Artificial Neural Networks* (pp. 13-20). D-Facto Publications.

Lee, M. D., Reilly, R. E., & Butavicius, M. E. (2003b). An empirical evaluation of Chernoff Faces, star glyphs, and spatial visualizations for binary data. In *Proceedings of the Australian Symposium on Information Visualisation* (pp. 1-10). Australian Computer Society.

Lee, W., & Stolfo, S. (1998, January). Data mining approaches for intrusion detection. In *Proceedings of the Seventh USENIX Security Symposium (SECURITY '98)*, San Antonio, Texas.

Lent, B., Swami, A. N., & Widom, J. (1997). Clustering association rules. In *Proceedings of the 13th International Conference on Data Engineering (ICDE 1997)*, Birmingham, United Kingdom (pp. 220-231). IEEE Computer Society.

Leung, Y. K., & Apperley, M. D. (1994). A review and taxonomy of distortion-oriented presentation Techniques. *ACM Transactions on Computer-Human Interaction, 1*(2), 126-160.

Levenshtein, L. I. (1966). Binary codes capable of correcting deletions, insertions, and reversals. *Soviet Physics-Doklady, 10*(7), 707-710.

Levkowitz, H. (1991). Color icons: Merging color and texture perception for integrated visualization of multiple parameters. In G. M. Nielson & L. Rosenblum (Eds.), *Proceedings of IEEE Visualization '91*, San Diego, California (pp. 164-170). SIGGRAPH: ACM Special Interest Group on Computer Graphics and Interactive Techniques, IEEE Computer Society Press.

Levy, A. Y., Rajaraman, A., & Ordille, J. J. (1996). *Querying heterogeneous information sources using source descriptions*. Paper presented at the VLDB.

Lewis-Beck, M. S. (Ed.). (1994). *Factor analysis and related techniques*. London: Sage Publications.

Ley, M. (2005). *DBLP bibliography server*. Retrieved June 13, 2007, from http://dblp.uni-trier.de/xml

Li, M., & Vitanyi, P. M. B. (1997). *An introduction to Kolmogorov complexity and its applications* (2nd ed.). New York: Springer-Verlag.

Li, M., & Vitanyi, P. M. B. (2001). Algorithmic complexity. In N. J. Smelser, & P. B. Baltes (Eds.), *International Encyclopedia of the Social & Behavioral Sciences* (pp. 376-382), Oxford: Pergamon.

Li, M., Badger, J. H., Chen, X., Kwong, S., Kearney, P., & Zhang, H. (2001). An information-based sequence distance and its application to whole mitochondrial genome phylogeny. *Bioinformatics, 17*(2), 149-154.

Li, M., Chen, X., Li, X., Ma, B., & P. M. B. Vitányi (2004). The similarity metric. *IEEE Transactions on Information Theory, 50*, 3250-3264.

Li, M., Ma, B., & Wang, L. (1999). Finding similar regions in many strings. In *Proceedings of the 31st Annual ACM Symposium on Theory of Computing* (pp. 473-482).

Liang, M., Banatao, D., Klein, T., Brutlag, D., & Altman, R. (2003a). WebFEATURE: An interactive Web tool for identifying and visualizing functional sites on macromolecular structures. *Nucleic Acids Research, 31*(13), 3324-3327.

Liang, M., Brutlag, D., & Altman, R. (2003b). Automated construction of structural motifs for predicting functional sites on protein structures. In *Proceedings of the 8th Pacific Symposium on Biocomputing* (pp. 204-215).

Lieberman, H. L. (1995). Letizia: An agent that assists Web browsing. *Proceedings of the International Joint Conference on Artificial Intelligence* (pp. 924-929), Montreal, Canada: Morgan Kaufmann.

Liebisch, G., Lieser, B., Rathenberg, J., Drobnik, W., & Schmitz, G. (2004). High-throughput quantification of phosphatidylcholine and sphingomyelin by electrospray ionization tandem mass spectrometry coupled with isotope correction algorithm. *Biochimica et Biophysica Acta, 1686*, 108-117.

Lindell, Y., & Pinkas, B. (2002). Privacy preserving data mining. *Journal of Cryptology, 15*, 177-206. Springer-Verlag.

Loizides, A., & Slater, M. (2002). The empathic visualisation algorithm (EVA): An automatic mapping from abstract data to naturalistic visual structure. In *Sixth International Conference on Information Visualization (IV'02)* (pp. 705-712).

Lonardi, S. (2002). Pattern discovery in biosequences: Tutorial. In *Proccedings of the 10ᵗʰ International Conference on Intelligent Systems for Molecular Biology.*

Lott, J. A., & Durbridge, T. C. (1990). Use of Chernoff Faces to follow trends in laboratory data. *Journal of Clinical Laboratory Analysis, 4*(1), 59-63.

MacQueen, J. (1967). Some methods for classification and analysis of multivariate observations. *In* L. M. Le Cam & J. Neyman (Eds.), *Proceedings of the Fifth Berkeley Symposium on Mathematical Statistics and Probability* (vol. 1, pp. 281-297). Berkeley: University of California Press.

MacQueen, J. B. (1967). Some methods for classification and analysis of multivariate observations. In L. M. LeCam & N. Neyman (Eds.), *Proceedings of the Fifth Berkeley Symposium on Mathematical Statistics and Probability* (vol. 1, pp. 281-297).

Maiz, N., Boussaïd, O., & Bentayeb, F. (2006). Ontology-based mediation system. In *Proceedings of the 13ᵗʰ ISPE International Conference on Concurrent Engineering: Research and Applications (CE 2006)*, Antibes, France (pp. 181-189).

Mallat, S. G. (1989). A theory for multiresolution signal decomposition: The wavelet representation. *IEEE Transactions on Pattern Analysis and Machine Intelligence, 11*, 674-693.

Manku, G. S., & Motwani, R. (2002). Approximate frequency counts over data streams. In *Proceedings of the 28ᵗʰ International Conference on Very Large Data Bases (VLDB)*, Hong Kong, China (pp. 346-357).

Mannila, H., & Meek, C. (2000). Global partial orders from sequential data. *Proceedings of the 6ᵗʰ International Conference on Knowledge Discovery and Data Mining* (pp. 161-168).

Mannila, H., Toivonen, H., & Verkamo, A. I. (1994). Efficient algorithms for discovering association rules. In U. Fayyad & R. Uthurusamy (Eds.), *Proceedings of the AAAI Workshop Knowledge Discovery in Databases (KDD'94)* (pp. 181-192). AAAI Press.

Masterman, M. (1961). Semantic message detection for machine translation, using an interlingua. *NPL*, pp. 438-475.

Matias, Y., Vitter, J. S., & Wang, M. (1998). *Wavelet-based histograms for selectivity estimation.* Paper presented at the ACM SIGMOD.

McCandless, S.E. (2004). A primer on expanded newborn screening by tandem mass spectrometry. *Primary Care, 31*, 583-604.

McCreight, E. (1976). A space economical space tree construction algorithm. *Journal of ACM, 23*(2), 262-272.

MClachlan, G., & Basford, K. (1988). *Mixture models: Inference and applications to clustering.* New York: Marcel Dekker.

McQueen, J. (1967). Some methods for classification and analysis of multivariate observations. *Proceedings Fifth Berkeley Symposium on Math. Statistics and Probability.*

Meo, R., Lanzi, P.L., & Klemettinen, M. (2003). Database support for data mining applications. *Lecture Notes on Computer Science, 2682.* Springer-Verlag.

Meo, R., Psaila, G., & Ceri, S. (1996). A new SQL-like operator for mining association rules. In *Proceedings of the 22ⁿᵈ International Conference on Very Large Data Bases (VLDB 1996)*, Bombay, India (pp. 122-133). Morgan Kaufmann.

Meo, R., Psaila, G., & Ceri, S. (1998). An extension to SQL for mining association rules. *Data Mining and Knowledge Discovery, 2*(2), 195-224.

Merialdo, P. (2003). *SIGMOD RECORD in XML.* Retrieved June 13, 2007, from http://www.acm.org/sigmod/record/xml

Metabolomics Standards Initiative Group. (2006). Retrieved June 17, 2007, from http://msi-workgroups.sourceforge.net

Metwally, A., Agrawal, D., & El Abbadi, A. (2005). Efficient computation of frequent and top-k elements in data streams. In *Proceedings of the 10th International Conference on Database Theory (ICDT)*, Edinburgh, United Kingdom (pp. 398-412).

Mierswa, I., & Morik, K. (2005). Automatic feature extraction for classifying audio data. *Machine Learning Journal, 58*, 127-149.

Mierswa, I., & Wurst, M. (2005). Efficient case based feature construction for heterogeneous learning tasks. In *Proceedings of the European Conference on Machine Learning (ECML)* (pp. 641-648).

Mierswa, I., & Wurst, M. (2006). Information preserving multi-objective feature selection for unsupervised learning. In *Proceedings of the Genetic and Evolutionary Computation Conference (GECCO)*.

Mierswa, I., Wurst, M., Klinkenberg, R., Scholz, M., & Euler, T. (2006). YALE: Rapid prototyping for complex data mining tasks. In *Proceedings of the 12th ACM SIGKDD International Conference on Knowledge Discovery and Data Mining (KDD 2006)*. ACM Press.

Miller, R. J., & Yang, Y. (1997). Association rules over interval data. In *Proceedings of the ACM SIGMOD International Conference on Management of Data (SIGMOD 1997)*, Tucson, Arizona (pp. 452-461). ACM Press.

Miller, R. J., Hernandez, M. A., Haas, L. M., Yan, L., Ho, C. T. H., Fagin, R., et al. (2001). The clio project: managing heterogeneity. *SIGMOD Record, 30*(1).

Milner, R. (1980). A calculus of communicating system. *Lecture Notes in Computer Science, 92*. Berlin: Springer-Verlag.

Mitchell, T. M. (1997). *Machine learning*: McGraw-Hill.

Mobasher, B. (2004). Web usage mining and personalization. In M. P. Singh (Ed.), *Practical handbook of Internet computing*. CRC Press.

Mobasher, B., Colley, R., & Srivastava, J. (2000). Automatic personalization based on Web usage mining. *Communications of the ACM, 43*(8), 142-151.

Mobasher, B., Cooley, R., & Srivastava, J. (1999). Creating adaptive Web sites through usage based clustering of URLs. *Proceedings of the 1999 Workshop on Knowledge and Data Engineering Exchange*.

Mobasher, B., Dai, H., & Luo, M. N. T. (2002). Discovery and evaluation of aggregate usage profiles for Web personalization. *Data Mining and Knowledge Discovery, 6*, 61-82.

Moerchen, F., Ultsch, A., Thies, M., & Loehken, I. (2006). Modelling timbre distance with temporal statistics from polyphonic music. *IEEE Transactions on Speech and Audio Processing*.

Moerchen, F., Ultsch, A., Thies, M., Loehken, I., Noecker, C., Stamm, M., et al. (2004). *Musicminer: Visualizing perceptual distances of music as topographical maps* (Tech. Rep.). Department of Mathematics and Computer Science, University of Marburg, Germany.

Montgomery, D. C., & Runger, G. C. (1994). *Applied statistics and probability for engineers*. John Wiley & Sons, Inc.

Moriarity, S. (1979). Communicating financial information through multidimensional graphics. *Journal of Accounting Research, 17*(1), 205-224.

Morin, A., Kouomou Chopo, A., & Chauchat, J. H. (2005). Dimension reduction and clustering for query-by-example in huge image databases. In *Proceedings of the 3rd World Conference on Computational Statistics and Data Analysis*, Chypre.

Morris, M., & Watkins, S.M. (2005). Focused metabolomic profiling in the drug development process: Advances from lipid profiling. *Current Opinion in Chemical Biology, 9*, 407-412.

Morrison, A., & Chalmers, M. (2003). Improving hybrid MDS with pivot-based searching. In *Proceedings of IEEE Information Visualization 2003*, Seattle, Washington (pp. 85-90).

Morrison, A., Ross, G., & Chalmers, M. (2002). A hybrid layout algorithm for sub-quadratic multidimensional scaling. In *Proceedings of IEEE Information Visualisation 2002*, Boston, Massachusetts (pp. 152-160).

Morrison, A., Ross, G., & Chalmers, M. (2003). Fast multidimensional scaling through sampling, springs and interpolation. *Information Visualization, 2*(1), 68-77.

Motoyoshi, M., Miura, T., & Shioya, I. (2004). Clustering stream data by regression analysis. In *Proceedings of the 1st Australasian Workshop on Data Mining and Web Intelligence (DMWI)*, Dunedin, New Zealand.

Motro, A. (1989). Using integrity constraints to provide intensional answers to relational queries. In P. M. G. Apers & G. Wiederhold (Eds.), *Fifteenth International Conference on Very Large Data Bases* (pp. 237-245). Morgan Kaufmann.

Mount, D. W. (2004). *Bioinformatics: Sequence and genome analysis* (2nd ed.). Cold Spring Harbor, NY: Cold Spring Harbor Laboratory Press.

MS SQL. (2005). Microsoft SQL server analysis server. Retrieved June 15, 2007, from http://www.microsoft.com/sql/evaluation/bi/bianalysis.asp

Mulder, N., Apweiler, R., Attwood, T., Bairoch, A., Bateman, A., Binns, D., et al. (2005). InterPro: Progress and status in 2005 [Database issue]. *Nucleic Acids Research, 33*, D201-D205.

Müller, W., & Alexa, M. (1998). Using morphing for information visualization. In *Proceedings of the 1998 Workshop on New Paradigms in Information Visualization and Manipulation* (pp. 49-52). ACM Press.

Murphy, J. F. (2003). *Methods for collection and processing of gene expression data*. Doctoral thesis, California Institute of Technology, Pasadena, California.

Nagy, G. (1968). State of the art in pattern recognition. *Proceedings of the IEEE, 56*, 836-862.

Nassis, V., Rajagopalapillai, R., Dillon, T. S., & Rahayu, W. (2005). Conceptual and systematic design approach for XML document warehouses. *International Journal of Data Warehousing and Mining, 1*(3), 63-87. Idea Group Inc.

Nel, D., Pitt, L., & Webb, T. (1994). Using Chernoff Faces to portray service quality data. *Journal of Marketing Management, 10*, 247-255.

Nevill-Manning, C., Sethi, K., Wu, T., & Brutlag, D. (1997). Enumerating and ranking discrete motifs. In *Proceedings of the 5th International Conference on Intelligent Systems for Molecular Biology* (pp. 202-209).

Nevill-Manning, C., Wu, T., & Brutlag, D. (1998). Highly specific protein sequence motifs for genome analysis. *Proceedings of the National Academy of Science, 95*(11), 5865-5871.

Ng, R. T., Lakshmanan, L. V. S., Han, J., & Pang, A. (1998). Exploratory mining and pruning optimizations of constrained associations rules. In *Proceedings of the ACM SIGMOD International Conference on Management of Data (SIGMOD 1998)*, Seattle, Washington (pp. 13-24). ACM Press.

Ngu, D. S. W., & Wu, X. (1997). SiteHelper: A localized agent that helps incremental exploration of the world wide Web. *Proceedings of the 6th International World Wide Web Conference* (pp. 691-700), Santa Clara, CA: ACM Press.

Nong, Y. (2003). *The handbook of data mining*. NJ: Lawrence Erlbaum Associates.

Norton, S.M., Huyn, P., Hastings, C.A., & Heller, J.C. (2001). Data mining of spectroscopic data for biomarker discovery. *Current Opinion in Drug Discovery and Development, 4*, 325-331.

Noy, N. F., Fergerson, R. W., & Musen, M. A. (2000). The knowledge model of Protege-2000: Combining interoperability and flexibility. In *Proceedings of the Second International Conference on Knowledge Engineering and Knowledge Management*.

O'Callaghan, L., Mishra, N., Meyerson, A., Guha, S., & Motwani, R. (2002). Streaming-data algorithms for high quality clustering. In *Proceedings of the 18th International Conference on Data Engineering (ICDE)*, San Jose, California (pp. 685-696).

O'Conner, M., & Herlocker, J. (1999). Clustering items for collaborative filtering. *Proceedings of the ACM SIGIR Workshop on Recommender Systems*. Berkeley, CA: ACM Press.

ODM. (2005). Oracle data mining tools. Retrieved June 15, 2007, from http://www.oracle.com/technology/products/bi/odm

Ogata, H., Goto, S., Sato, K., Fujibuchi, W., Bono, H., & Kanehisa, M. (1999). KEGG: Kyoto Encyclopedia of Genes and Genomes. *Nucleic Acids Research, 27,* 29-34.

Oja, E. (1982). A simplified neuron model as a principal component analyser. *Journal of Mathematical Biology, 16,* 267-273.

Oja, E. (1989). Neural networks, principal components and subspaces. *International Journal of Neural Systems, 1,* 61-68.

Oja, E., Ogawa, H., & Wangviwattana, J. (1992a). Principal component analysis by homogeneous neural networks (Part 1: The weighted subspace criterion). *IEICE Transactions on Information & Systems, E75-D,* 366-375.

Oja, E., Ogawa, H., & Wangviwattana, J. (1992b). Principal component analysis by homogeneous neural networks (Part 2: Analysis and extensions of the learning algorithms). *IEICE Transactions on Information & Systems, E75-D*(3), 375-381.

OLEDB. (2005). OLE DB for data mining specification. Retrieved June 15, 2007, from http://www.microsoft.com/data/oledb

Oliveira, S. R. M., & Zaiane, O. R. (2002). Privacy preserving frequent itemset mining. In *Proceedings of the IEEE International Conference on Privacy, Security and Data Mining* (pp. 43-54). Australian Computer Society, Inc.

Oliveira, S. R. M., & Zaiane, O. R. (2003). Privacy preserving clustering by data transformation. In *Proceedings of the 18th Brazilian Symposium on Databases,* Manaus, Amazonas, Brazil (pp. 304-318).

Oliveira, S. R. M., & Zaiane, O. R. (2004). Toward standardization in privacy preserving data mining. In *Proceedings of the ACM SIGKDD 3rd Workshop on Data Mining Standard* (pp. 7-17). ACM Press.

Ordonez, C. (2003). Clustering binary data streams with K-means. In *Proceedings of the 8th ACM SIGMOD Workshop on Research Issues in Data Mining and Knowledge Discovery (DMKD),* San Diego, California (pp. 12-19).

Ordonez, C., & Omiecinski, E. (1999). Discovering association rules based on image content. In *Proceedings of the IEEE Advances in Digital Libraries Conference (ADL'99),* Baltimore, Maryland (pp. 38-49).

ORS. *Open Research System.* http://www.orspublic.org

Ouksel, A., & Sheth, A. P. (1999). Special issue on semantic interoperability in global information systems. *SIGMOD Record, 28*(1).

Ozden, B., Ramaswamy, S., & Silberschatz, A. (1998). Cyclic association rules. In *Proceedings of the 14th International Conference on Data Engineering (ICDE 1998),* Orlando, Florida (pp. 412-421). IEEE Computer Society.

Palley, M. A., & Simonoff, J. S. (1987, December). The use of regression methodology for compromise of confidential information in statistical databases. *ACM Trans. Database Syst., 12*(4), 593-608.

Pampalk, E., Dixon, S., & Widmer, G. (2003). On the evaluation of perceptual similarity measures for music. In *Proceedings of the International Conference on Digital Audio Effects* (pp. 6-12).

PANDA. (2001). The PANDA Project. Retrieved June 15, 2007, from http://dke.cti.gr/panda/

Papakonstantinou, Y., Garcia-Molina, H., & Ullman, J. (1996). *Medmaker: A mediation system based on declarative specifications.* Paper presented at the ICDE.

Papakonstantinou, Y., Garcia-Molina, H., & Widom, J. (1995). Object exchange across heterogeneous information sources. In P. S. Yu & A. L. P. Chen (Eds.), *Eleventh International Conference on Data Engineering* (pp. 251-260). IEEE Computer Society.

Paredaens, J., Peelman, P., & Tanca, L. (1995). G-Log: A declarative graphical query language. *IEEE Transactions on Knowledge and Data Engineering, 7*(3), 436-453.

Park, D. (1980). Concurrency and automata on infinite sequences. *Lecture Notes in Computer Science, 104,* 167-183. Berlin: Springer-Verlag.

Park, J. S., Chen, M. S., & Yu, P. S. (1995). An effective hash-based algorithm for mining association rules. In Proceedings of the 1995 ACM SIGMOD International Conference on Management of Data Volume, San Jose, California. *SIGMOD Record, 24*(2), 175-186. ACM Press.

Park, J. S., Chen, M. S., & Yu, P. S. (1995a). Efficient parallel data mining for association rules. In *Proceedings of the 4th International Conference on Information and Knowledge Management (CIKM 1995)*, Baltimore, Maryland (pp. 31-36). ACM Press.

Paterson, M., & Danc'ik, V. (1994). Longest common subsequences. *Proceedings of the 19th International Symposium Mathematical Foundations of Computer Science* (127-142).

Pavesi, G., Mauri, G., & Pesole, G. (2001). An algorithm for finding signals of unknown length in DNA sequences. In *Proceedings of the 9th International Conference on Intelligent Systems for Molecular Biology* (pp. 207-214).

Pavlov, D., Mannila, H., & Smyth, P. (2001). *Beyond independence: Probabilistic models for query approximation on binary transaction data* (Tech. Rep. No. 09/01). University of California Irvine, Information and Computer Science.

Pawlak, Z. (1991). *Rough sets theoretical aspects of reasoning about data.* Kluwer Academic Publishers.

Pegg, S., Brown, S., Ojha, S., Seffernick, J., Meng, E., Morris, J., et al. (2006). Leveraging enzyme structure-function relationships for functional inference and experimental design: the structure-function linkage database. *Biochemistry, 45*(8), 2545-2555.

Peña, M., & Fyfe, C. (2005). The harmonic topographic map. In *The Irish Conference on Artificial Intelligence and Cognitive Science, AICS05.*

Percival, D. B., & Walden, A. T. (2000). *Wavelet methods for time series analysis.* Cambridge University Press.

Perkowitz, M., & Etzioni, O. (1998). Adaptive Web sites: Automatically synthesizing Web pages. *Proceedings of the 15th National Conference on Artificial Intelligence* (pp. 727-732), Madison, WI: AAAI.

Perkowitz, M., & Etzioni, O. (2000). Adaptive Web sites. *Communications of the ACM, 43*(8), 152-158.

Pevzner, P., & Sze, S. (2000). Combinatorial approaches to finding subtle signals in DNA sequences. In *Proceedings of the 8th International Conference on Intelligent Systems for Molecular Biology* (pp. 269-278). AAAI Press.

Piatetsky-Shapiro, G. (1991). Discovery, analysis, and presentation of strong rules. *Knowledge Discovery in Databases,* 229-238. AAAI/MIT Press.

Picard, F.J., & Bergeron, M.G. (2002). Rapid molecular theranostics in infectious diseases. *Drug Discovery Today, 7*, 1092-1101.

Pitkow, J., & Pirolli, P. (1999). Mining longest repeating subsequences to predict world wide Web surfing. *Proceedings of 2nd USENIX Symposium on Internet Technologies and Systems.*

Plant, C., Boehm, C., Tilg, B., & Baumgartner, C. (2006). Enhancing instance-based classification with local density: A new algorithm for classifying unbalanced biomedical data. *Bioinformatics, 22*, 981-988.

PMML. (2003). Predictive model markup language (version 3.1). Retrieved June 15, 2007, from http://www.dmg.org/pmml-v3-1.html

Pohle, T., Pampalk, E., & Widmer, G. (2005). Evaluation of frequently used audio features for classification of music into perceptual categories. In *Proceedings of the International Workshop on Content-Based Multimedia Indexing.*

Pokorný, J. (2001). Modelling stars using XML. In *DOLAP '01: Proceedings of the 4th ACM International Workshop on Data Warehousing and OLAP* (pp. 24-31).

Porter, C., Bartlett, G., & Thornton, J. (2004). The catalytic site atlas: A resource of catalytic sites and residues identified in enzymes using structural data [Database issue]. *Nucleic Acids Research, 32*, D129-D133.

Porter, M. F. (1980). An algorithm for suffix stripping. *Readings in Information Retrieval, 14*(3), 130-137. Morgan Kaufmann.

Prade, H. (1988). Raisonner avec des règles d'inférence graduelle: Une approche basée sur les ensembles flous. *Revue d'Intelligence Artificielle, 2*(2), 29-44.

Quinlan, J. R. (1993). *C4.5: Programs for machine learning.* Morgan Kaufmann.

Qun, C., Lim, A., & Ong, K. W. (2003). D(k)-index: An adaptive structural summary for graph-structured data. In *Proceedings of the 2003 ACM SIGMOD International Conference on Management of Data* (pp. 134-144). ACM Press.

Rahm, E., & Bernstein, P. A. (2001). A survey of approaches to automatic schema matching. *VLDB Journal, 10*(4).

Ram, S., & Park, J. (2004). Semantic conflict resolution ontology (SCROL): An ontology for detecting and resolving data and schema-level semantic conflicts. *IEEE Transactions on Knowledge and Data Engineering, 16*(2), 189-202.

Ram, S., Khatri, V., Zhang, L., & Zeng, D. (2001). *GeoCosm: A semantics-based approach for information integration of geospatial data.* Paper presented at the Proceedings of the Workshop on Data Semantics in Web Information Systems (DASWIS2001), Yokohama, Japan.

Ram, S., Park, J., & Hwang, Y. (2002). *CREAM: A mediator based environment for modeling and accessing distributed information on the Web.* Paper presented at the British National Conference on Databases (BNCOD).

Ramaswamy, S., Mahajan, S., & Silberschatz, A. (1998). On the discovery of interesting patterns in association rules. In *Proceedings of the 24th International Conference on Very Large Data Bases (VLDB 1998)*, New York City, New York (pp. 368-379). Morgan Kaufmann.

Ransohoff, D.F. (2004). Rules of evidence for cancer molecular-marker discovery and validation. *Nature Reviews: Cancer, 4*, 309-314.

Ransohoff, D.F. (2005). Lessons from controversy: Ovarian cancer screening and serum proteomics. *Journal of the National Cancer Institute, 97*, 315-319.

Raudys, S. (2001). *Statistical and neural classifiers.* London: Springer-Verlag.

Rice, J. A. (1994). *Mathematical statistics and data analysis.* Duxbury Press.

Rietman, E. A., & Layadi, N. (2000). A study on $R^m \rightarrow R^1$ maps: Application to a 0.16-m via etch process endpoint. *IEEE Transactions on Semiconductor Manufacturing, 13*(4), 457-468.

Rietman, E. A., Lee, J. T. C., & Layadi, N. (1998). Dynamic images of plasma processes: Use of fourier blobs for endpoint detection during plasma etching of patterned wafers. *Journal of Vacuum Science and Technology, 16*(3), 1449-1453.

Rigoutsos, I., & Floratos, A. (1998). Combinatorial pattern discovery in biological sequences: The Teiresias algorithm. *Bioinformatics, 14*(1), 55-67.

Rigoutsos, I., Floratos, A., Parida, L., Gao, Y., & Platt, D. (2000). The emergence of pattern discovery techniques in computational biology. *Metabolic Engineering, 2*(3), 159-177.

Rinaldo, P., Matern, D., & Bennett, M.J. (2002). Fatty acid oxidation disorders. *Annual Review of Physiology, 64*, 477-502.

Ripley, B. D. (1996). *Pattern recognition and neural networks.* Cambridge University Press.

Rizvi, S. J., & Haritsa, J. R. (2003). Maintaining data privacy in association rule mining. In *Proceedings of the 28th International Conference on Very Large Databases.* Morgan Kaufmann.

Rizzi, S., Bertino, E., Catania, B., Golfarelli, M., Halkidi, M., Terrovitis, M., Vassiliadis, P., Vazirgiannis, M., & Vrachnos, E. (2003). Towards a logical model for patterns. In *Proceedings of ER'03* (pp. 77-90).

Rodrigues, P., Gama, J., & Pedroso, J. P. *Hierarchical time-series clustering for data streams.* Master's thesis, University of Porto.

Rodriguez-Gianolli, P., Garzetti, M., Jiang, L., Kementsietsidis, A., Kiringa, I., Masud, M., Miller, R., & Mylopoulos, J. (2005). Data Sharing in the Hyperion Peer Database System. In *Proceedings of the International Conference on Very Large Databases (VLDB).*

Roschinger, W., Olgemoller, B., Fingerhut, R., Liebl, B., & Roscher, A.A. (2003). Advances in analytical mass spectrometry to improve screening for inherited metabolic diseases. *European Journal of Pediatrics, 162*(Suppl. 1), S67-S76.

Ross, J.S., & Ginsburg, G.S. (2002). Integration of molecular diagnostics with therapeutics: Implications for drug discovery and patient care. *Expert Review of Molecular Diagnostics, 2*, 531-541.

Roweis, S. T., & Saul, L. K. (2000). Nonlinear dimensionality reduction by locally linear embedding. *Science, 290*(5500), 2323-2326.

Rumelhart, D. E., Hinton, G. E., & Williams, R. J. (1986). Learning internal representations by error propagation. In *Parallel distributed processing: Explorations in the microstructure of cognition* (vol. 1, pp. 318–362). Cambridge, MA: MIT Press.

Rusinkiewicz, M., Sheth, A., & Karabatis, G. (1991). Specifying interdatabase dependencies in a multidatabase environment. *IEEE Computer, 24*(12), 46-53.

Ruspini, E.H. (1969). A new approach to clustering. *Information Control, 15*, 22-32.

Ruspini, E.H. (1991). On the semantics of fuzzy logic. *International Journal of Approximate Reasoning, 5*, 45-88.

Rusu, L. I., Rahayu, J. W., & Taniar, D. (2005). A methodology for building XML data warehouses. *International Journal of Data Warehousing and Mining, 1*(2), 23-48. Idea Group Inc.

Ryals, J. (2004, June). Metabolomics: An important emerging science. *Business Briefing Pharmatech*, pp. 51-54.

Safar, M. (2005). K nearest neighbor search in navigation systems. *Mobile Information Systems, 1*(3), 207–224, IOS Press.

Sagot, M., & Viari, A. (1996). A double combinatorial approach to discovering patterns in biological sequences. In *Proceedings of the 7th Annual Symposium on Combinatorial Pattern Matching* (pp. 186-208). Springer, 1075.

Salton, G., & Buckley, C. (1988). Term-weighting approaches in automatic text retrieval. *Information Processing and Management, 24*(5), 513-523.

Sammon, J. (1969). A nonlinear mapping for data structure analysis. *IEEE Transactions on Computation, C-18*(5), 401-409.

Sande, G. (1984). Automated cell suppression to reserve confidentiality of business statistics. In *Proceedings of the 2nd International Workshop on Statistical Database Management* (pp. 346-353).

Sankoff, D., & Kruskal, J. B. (1983). *Time warps, string edits, and macromolecules: The theory and practice of sequence comparison.* Reading, MA: Addison-Wesley Publishing Company.

Sarawagi, S., Agrawal, R., & Megiddo, N. (1998). *Discovery-driven exploration of OLAP data cubes.* Paper presented at the International Conference on Extending Database Technology.

Savasere, A., Omiecinski, E., & Navathe, S. (1995, September). An efficient algorithm for mining association rules in large databases. In *Proceedings of the 21st International Conference on Very Large Data Bases*, Zurich, Switzerland (pp. 11-15).

Savasere, A., Omiecinski, E., & Navathe, S. B. (1995). An efficient algorithm for mining association rules in large databases. In *Proceedings of the 21st International Conference on Very Large Data Bases (VLDB 1995)*, Zurich, Switzerland (pp. 432-444). Morgan Kaufmann.

Sawasdichai, N., & Poggenpohl, S. (2002). User purposes and information-seeking behaviors in Web-based media: A user-centered approach to information design on Websites. In *Proceedings of the Conference on Designing Interactive Systems* (pp. 201-212). ACM Press.

Saxena, P. C., & Navaneetham, K. (1986). The validation of Chernoff Faces as clustering algorithm. In *Proceedings of the VIII Annual Conference of the Indian Society for Probability and Statistics*, Kolhapur, Shivaji University (pp. 179-193).

Saxena, P. C., & Navaneetham, K. (1991). The effect of cluster size, dimensionality, and number of clusters on recovery of true cluster structure through Chernoff-type Faces. *The Statistician, 40*, 415-425.

Schlorer, J. (1983). Information loss in partitioned statistical databases. *Comput. J., 26*(3), 218-223. British Computer Society.

Schmidt, C. (2004). Metabolomics takes its place as latest up-and-coming "omic" science. *Journal of the National Cancer Institute, 96*, 732-734.

Schoeman, F. D. (1984). *Philosophical dimensions of privacy: An anthology.* Cambridge University Press.

Schultz, J., Milpetz, F., Bork, P., & Ponting, C. (1998). SMART, a simple modular architecture research tool: Identification of signaling domains. *Proceedings of the National Academy of Science, 95*, 5857-5864.

Schweizer, B., & Sklar, A. (1983). *Probabilistic metric spaces.* New York: North-Holland.

SEEK. *The Science Environment for Ecological Knowledge.* http://seek.ecoinformatics.org

Servant, F., Bru, C., Carrere, S., Courcelle, E., Gouzy, J., Peyruc, D., et al. (2002). ProDom: Automated clustering of homologous domains. *Briefings in Bioinformatics, 3*(3), 246-251.

Setubal, J. C., & Meidanis, J. (1987). *Introduction to computational molecular biology.* Boston: PWS Publishing Company.

Shahabi, C., Zarkesh, A. M., Adibi, J. & Shah, V. (1997). Knowledge discovery from users Web-page navigation. *Proceedings of the 7th International Workshop on Research Issues in Data Engineering High Performance Database Management for Large-Scale Applications* (p. 20), IEEE Computer Society, Washington, D.C.

Shannon, C. E., & Weaver, W. (1949). *The mathematical theory of communication.* Urbana, IL: University of Illinois Press.

Shawe-Taylor, J., & Cristianini, N. (2004). *Kernel methods for pattern analysis.* Cambridge, UK: Cambridge University Press.

Sheeren, D., Quirin, A., Puissant, A., & Gançarski, P. (2006). Discovering rules with genetic algorithms to classify urban remotely sensed data. In *Proceedings of the IEEE International Geoscience and Remote Sensing Symposium (IGARSS'06).*

Shepard, R. N., Romney, A. K., & Nerlove, S. B. (Eds.). (1972). *Multidimensional scaling: Theory and applications in the behavioral sciences* (vol. 1). Seminar Press, Inc.

Sheth, A., & Karabatis, G. (1993, May). *Multidatabase Interdependencies in Industry.* Paper presented at the ACM SIGMOD, Washington DC.

Sheth, A., Aleman-Meza, B., Arpinar, I. B., Bertram, C., Warke, Y., Ramakrishanan, C., et al. (2004). Semantic association identification and knowledge discovery for national security applications. *Journal of Database Management, 16*(1).

Sheth, A., Arpinar, I. B., & Kashyap, V. (2003). Relationships at the heart of Semantic Web: Modeling, discovering, and exploiting complex semantic relationships. In M. Nikravesh, B. Azvin, R. Yager & L. A. Zadeh (Eds.), *Enhancing the power of the Internet studies in fuzziness and soft computing.* Springer-Verlag.

Sheth, A., Bertram, C., Avant, D., Hammond, B., Kochut, K., & Warke, Y. (2002). Managing semantic content for the web. *IEEE Internet Computing, 6*(4), 80-87.

Shneiderman, B. (1992). Tree visualization with treemaps: A 2D space-filling approach. *ACM Transactions on Graphics, 11*(1), 92-99.

Shneiderman, B. (1996). The eyes have it: A task by data type taxonomy for information visualization. In *Proceedings of the IEEE Workshop on Visual Languages '96* (pp. 336-343). IEEE Computer Society Press.

Shoshani, A. (1982). Statistical databases: Characteristics, problems, and some solutions. In *Proceedings of the Conference on Very Large Databases (VLDB)* (pp. 208-222). Morgan Kaufmann Publishers Inc.

Sibson, R. (1973). SLINK: An optimally efficient algorithm for the single link cluster method. *Computer Journal, 16*, 30-34.

Sicstus. (2004). *SICStus Prolog (version 3)*. Retrieved June 15, 2007, from http://www.sics.se/isl/sicstuswww/site

Siirtola, H. (2000). Direct manipulation of parallel coordinates. In J. Roberts (Ed.), *Proceedings of the International Conference on Information Visualization (IV'2000)* (pp. 373-378). IEEE Computer Society.

Siirtola, H. (2003). Combining parallel coordinates with the reorderable matrix. In J. Roberts (Ed.), *Proceedings of the International Conference on Coordinated and Multiple Views in Exploratory Visualization (CMV 2003)* (pp. 63-74). London, UK: IEEE Computer Society.

Silverstein, C., Brin, S., Motwani, R., & Ullman, J. (1998). Scalable techniques for mining causal structures. *Data Mining Knowledge Discovery, 4*(2-3), 163-192.

Simoff, S. J., Djeraba, C., & Zaïane, O. R. (2002). MDM/ KDD2002: Multimedia data mining between promises and problems. *ACM SIGKDD Explorations, 4*(2).

Simon, I. (1987). Sequence comparison: Some theory and some practice. In M. Gross, & D. Perrin (Eds.), *Electronic dictionaries and automata in computational linguistics* (pp. 79-92), Berlin: Springer-Verlag, Saint Pierre d'Oeron, France.

Sleepycat Software. (2006). *Berkeley DB XML*. Retrieved June 13, 2007, from http://www.sleepycat.com/products/bdbxml.html/

Smith, J. R., Li, C.-S., & Jhingran, A. (2004). A wavelet framework for adapting data cube views for OLAP. *IEEE Transactions on Knowledge and Data Engineering, 16*(5), 552-565.

Smith, M., & Taffler, R. (1996). Improving the communication of accounting information through cartoon graphics. *Journal of Accounting, Auditing and Accountability, 9*(2), 68-85.

Smyth, P., & Goodman, R. (1990). Rule induction using information theory. In G. Piatetsky-Shapiro & W. Frawley (Eds), *Knowledge discovery in databases* (pp. 159-176). MIT Press.

Smyth, P., & Goodman, R. M. (1992). An information theoretic approach to rule induction from databases. *IEEE Transactions on Knowledge and Data Engineering, 3*(4), 301-316. IEEE Press.

Soga, T., Ohashi, Y., Ueno, Y., Naraoka, H., Tomita, M., & Nishioka, T. (2003). Quantitative metabolome analysis using capillary electrophoresis mass spectrometry. *Journal of Proteome Research, 2*, 488-494.

Spencer, N. H. (2003). Investigating data with Andrews plots. *Social Science Computer Review, 21*(2), 244-249.

Spiliopoulou, M., & Faulstich, L. C. (1999). WUM A tool for Web utilization analysis. In Extended version of *Proceedings of EDBT Workshop* (pp. 184-203), Springer Verlag.

Srikant, R., & Agrawal, R. (1995). Mining generalized association rules. In *Proceedings of the 21st International Conference on Very Large Data Bases (VLDB 1995)*, Zurich, Switzerland (pp. 407-419). Morgan Kaufmann.

Srikant, R., & Agrawal, R. (1996). Mining quantitative association rules in large relational tables. In *Proceedings of the ACM SIGMOD International Conference on Management of Data (SIGMOD 1996)*, Montreal, Quebec, Canada (pp. 1-12). ACM Press.

Srikant, R., Vu, Q., & Agrawal, R. (1997). Mining association rules with item constraints. In *Proceedings of the 3rd International Conference on Knowledge Discovery and Data Mining (KDD 1997)*, Newport Beach, California (pp. 67-73). The AAAI Press.

Staples, J., & Robinson, P. J. (1986). Unification of quantified terms. In R. M. K. J. H. Fasel (Ed.), Graph reduction. *Lecture Notes in Computer Science, 279*, 426-450. Springer-Verlag.

Steinbach, M., Karypis, G., & Kumar, V. (2000). A comparison of document clustering techniques. In *Proceedings of the KDD Workshop on Text Mining*.

Stollnitz, E. J., Derose, T. D., & Salesin, D. H. (1996). *Wavelets for Computer Graphics Theory and Applications*: Morgan Kaufmann Publishers.

Stone, M. (1974). Cross-validatory choice and assessment of statistical predictions (with discussion). *Journal of the Royal Statistical Society Series B, 36*, 111-147.

Stormer, H. (2005). Personalized Web sites for mobile devices using dynamic cascading style sheets. *International Journal of Web Information Systems, 1*(2), Troubador Publishing, UK, 83-88.

Stoughton, R.B., & Friend, S.H. (2005). How molecular profiling could revolutionize drug discovery. *Nature Reviews: Drug Discovery, 4*, 345-350.

Strauss, A.W. (2004). Tandem mass spectrometry in discovery of disorders of the metabolome. *The Journal of Clinical Investigation, 113*, 354-356.

Strehl, A., & Ghosh, J. (2002). Cluster ensembles: A knowledge reuse framework for combining partitionings. In *Proceedings of the AAAI*.

Sudkamp, T. (2005). Examples, counterexamples, and measuring fuzzy associations. *Fuzzy Sets and Systems, 149*(1).

Sullivan, M., & Heybey, A. (1998). Tribeca: A system for managing large databases of network traffic. In *Proceedings of the USENIX Annual Technical Conference*, New Orleans, Louisiana.

Sweeney, L. (2002). Achieving k-anonymity privacy protection using generalization and suppression. *International Journal on Uncertainty, Fuzzyness and Knowledge-based System*, 571-588. World Scientific Publishing Co., Inc.

Symanzik, J., Wegman, E. J., Braverman, A. J., & Luo, Q. (2002). New applications of the image grand tour. *Computing Science and Statistics, 34*, 500-512.

Takusagawa, K., & Gifford, D. (2004). Negative information for motif discovery. In *Proceedings of the 9th Pacific Symposium on Biocomputing* (pp. 360-371).

Tan, L., Taniar, D., & Smith, K. A. (2005). A clustering algorithm based on an estimated distribution model. *International Journal of Business Intelligence and Data Mining, 1*(2), 229-245, Inderscience Publishers.

Tatarinov, I., & Halevy, A. Y. (2004). *Efficient Query Reformulation in Peer-Data Management Systems.* Paper presented at the SIGMOD.

Tatbul, N., Cetintemel, U., Zdonik, S., Cherniack, M., & Stonebraker, M. (2003). Load shedding in a data stream manager. In Proceedings of the 29th International Conference on Very Large Data Bases(VLDB), Berlin, Germany *(pp. 309-320).*

Tenenbaum, J. B. (1998). Mapping a manifold of perceptual observations. In M. I. Jordan, M. J. Kearns, & S. A. Solla (Eds.), *Advances in neural information processing systems* (vol. 10, pp. 682-688). Cambridge, MA: MIT Press.

Tenenbaum, J. B., de Silva, V., & Langford, J. C. (2000). A global geometric framework for nonlinear dimensionality reduction. *Science, 290*(5500), 2319-2323.

Tereshko, V., & Allinson, N. M. (2000). Common framework for "topographic" and "elastic" computations. In D. S. Broomhead, E. A. Luchinskaya, P. V. E. McClintock, & T. Mullin (Eds.), *Stochaos: Stochastic and chaotic dynamics in the lakes: AIP Conference Proceedings, 502*, 124-129.

Tereshko, V., & Allinson, N. M. (2002a). Combining lateral and elastic interactions: Topology-preserving elastic nets. *Neural Processing Letters, 15*, 213-223.

Tereshko, V., & Allinson, N. M. (2002b). Theory of topology-preserving elastic nets. In W. Klonowski (Ed.), *Attractors, Signals and Synergetics, EUROATTRACTOR 2000* (pp. 215-221). PABS Science Publications.

Terry, D. B., Goldberg, D., Nichols, D., & Oki, B. M. (1992). Continuous queries over append-only databases. In *Proceedings of the 1992 ACM SIGMOD International Conference on Management of Data* (pp. 321-330).

Tidmore, F. E., & Turner, D. W. (1983). On clustering with Chernoff-type Faces. *Communications in Statistics, A12*(14), 381-396.

Toivonen, H. (1996). Sampling large databases for association rules. In *Proceedings of the 22nd International Conference on Very Large Data Bases (VLDB 1996)*, Bombay, India (pp. 134-145). Morgan Kaufmann.

Tollari, S., Glotin, H., & Le Maitre, J. (2005). Enhancement of textual images classification using segmented visual contents for image search engine. *Multimedia Tools and Applications, 25*, 405-417).

Topchy, A.P., Jain, A.K., & Punch, W.F. (2003). Combining multiple weak clusterings. In *Proceedings of the International Conference on Data Mining (ICDM)* (pp. 331-338).

TopicMap. *XML Topic Maps (XTM)* 1.0 http://www.topic-maps.org/xtm/

Torgerson, W. S. (1952). Multidimensional scaling: I. Theory and methods. *Psychometrika, 17*(4), 401-419.

Torrance, J., Bartlett, G., Porter, C., & Thornton, J. (2005). Using a library of structural templates to recognise catalytic sites and explore their evolution in homologous families. *Journal of Molecular Biology, 347*(3), 565-581.

TPC-H. (2005). *The TPC benchmark H. Transaction Processing Performance Council.* Retrieved June 13, 2007, from http://www.tpc.org/tpch/default.asp

Troncy, R. (2003). Integration structure and semantics into audio-visual documents. In D. Fensel et al. (Eds.), *Proceedings of ISWC2003* (pp. 566-581). Lecture Notes in Computer Science 2870.

Tsymbal, A. (2004). *The problem of concept drift: Definitions and related work* (Tech. Rep. No. TCD-CS-2004-15). Trinity College Dublin, Department of Computer Science, Ireland. Retrieved June 15, 2007, from https://www.cs.tcd.ie/publications/tech-reports/reports.04/TCD-CS-2004-15.pdf

Tufte, E. R. (1983). *The visual display of quantitative information.* Cheshire, CT: Graphics Press.

Tukey, J. (1977). *Exploratoy data analysis.* Reading, MA: Addison-Wesley.

Tzanetakis, G., & Cook, P. (2002). Musical genre classification of audio signals. *IEEE Transactions on Speech and Audio Processing, 10*(5), 293-302.

UDDI. *Universal description, discovery and integration.* http://www.uddi.org

Ukkonen, E., Vilo, J., Brazma A., & Jonassen, I. (1996). Discovering patterns and subfamilies in biosequences. In *Proceedings of the 4th International Conference on Intelligent Systems for Molecular Biology* (pp. 34-43). AAAI Press.

Vaidya, J., & Clifton, C. (2002). Privacy preserving association rule mining in vertically partitioned data. In *Proceedings of the 8th ACM SIGKDD International Conference on Knowledge Discovery and Data Mining* (pp. 639-644). ACM Press.

Verykios, V. S., Bertino, E., Nai Fovino, I., Parasiliti, L., Saygin, Y., & Theodoridis, Y. (2004). State-of-the-art in privacy preserving data mining. *SIGMOD Record, 33*(1), 50-57. ACM Press.

Verykios, V. S., Elmagarmid, A. K., Bertino, E., Saygin, Y., & Dasseni, E. (2003). Association rule hiding. *IEEE Transactions on Knowledge and Data Engineering.* IEEE Educational Activities Department.

Vesanto, J. (1999). SOM-based data visualization methods. *Intelligent-Data-Analysis, 3*, 111-126.

Vitter, J. S., & Wang, M. (1999). *Approximate computation of multidimensional aggregates of sparse data using wavelets.* Paper presented at the ACM SIGMOD.

Vitter, J. S., Wang, M., & Iyer, B. (1998). *Data Cube Approximation and Histograms via Wavelets.* Paper presented at the 7th CIKM.

W3C. Semantic Web. http://www.w3.org/2001/sw/.

Wagsta, K., & Cardie, C. (2000). Clustering with instance-level constraints. In *Proceedings of the Seventeenth International Conference on Machine Learning*, San Francisco, California (pp. 1103-1110). Morgan Kaufmann Publishers.

Wagsta, K., Cardie, C., Rogers, S., & Schröedl, S. (2001). Constrained k means clustering with background knowledge. In *Proceedings of the Eighteenth International Conference on Machine Learning (ICML-2001)*, San Francisco, California (pp. 577-584). Morgan Kaufmann Publishers.

Wallace, C., & Dowe, D. (1994). Intrinsic classification by MML: The snob program. In *Proceedings of the 7th Australian Joint Conference on Artificial Intelligence*, Armidale, Australia (pp. 37- 44). World Scientific Publishing Co.

Walters, G. J. (2001). *Human rights in an information age: A philosophical analysis* (ch. 5). University of Toronto Press.

Wang, H., Fan, W., Yu, P., & Han, J. (2003). Mining concept-drifting data streams using ensemble classifiers. In *Proceedings of the 9th ACM SIGKDD International Conference on Knowledge Discovery and Data Mining (KDD)*, Washington, DC (pp. 226-235).

Wang, H., Wang, W., Yang, J., & Yu, P. S. (2002). lustering by pattern similarity in large data sets, *SIGMOD Conference* (pp. 394-398).

Wang, J., Xindong Wu, X., & Zhang, C., (2005). Support vector machines based on K-means clustering for real-time business intelligence systems. *International Journal of Business Intelligence and Data Mining, 1*(1), 54-64, Inderscience Publishers.

Ward, M. O. (1994). XmdvTool: Integrating multiple methods for visualizing multivariate data. In G. M. Nielson & L. Rosenblum (Eds.), *Proceedings of the Conference on Visualization '94*, Washinton, DC (pp. 326-333). Session: Visualization systems table of contents.

Ware, C., & Beatty, J. C. (1988). Using color dimensions to display data dimensions. *Human Factors, 30*(2), 127-142.

Wegman, E. J. (1990). Hyperdimensional data analysis using parallel coordinates. *Journal of the American Statistical Association, 411*(85), 664-675.

Wegman, E. J. (1991). The Grand Tour in *k*-dimensions. In C. Page & R. LePage (Eds.), *Computing Science and Statistics: Proceedings of the 22nd Symposium on the Interface* (pp. 127-136). Springer-Verlag.

Wegman, E. J., & Luo, Q. (1991). Construction of line densities for parallel coordinate plots. In A. Buja & P. Tukey (Eds.), *Computing and graphics in statistics* (pp. 107-124). New York: Springer-Verlag.

Wegman, E. J., & Luo, Q. (1997). High dimensional clustering using parallel coordinates and the Grand Tour. *Computing Science and Statistics, 28*, 352-360.

Wegman, E. J., & Shen, J. (1993). Three-dimensional Andrews plots and the Grand Tour. *Computing Science and Statistics, 25*, 284-288.

Wegman, E. J., & Solka, J. L. (2002). On some mathematics for visualising high dimensional data. *Indian Journal of Statistics, 64*(Series A, 2), 429-452.

Wegman, E. J., Poston, W. L., & Solka, J. L. (1998). Image grand tour (Tech. Rep. TR 150). The Center for Computational Statistics. Retrieved June 24, 2007, from ftp://www.galaxy.gmu.edu/pub/papers/Image_Tour.pdf

Wei, L., & Altman, R. (1998). Recognizing protein binding sites using statistical descriptions of their 3D environments. In *Proceedings of the 3th Pacific Symposium on Biocomputing* (pp. 407-508).

Weinberger, K.M, Ramsay, S., & Graber, A. (2005). Towards the biochemical fingerprint. *Biosystems Solutions, 12*, 36-37.

Weiner, P. (1973). Linear pattern matching algorithm. In *Proceedings of the 14th IEEE Symposium on Switching and Automata Theory* (pp. 1-11).

Wiederhold, G. (1995). Mediation in information systems. *ACM Computing Surveys, 27*(2), 265-267.

Wijk, J. J. v., & Liere, R. v. (1993). Hyperslice visualization of scalar functions of many variables. In G. M. Nielson & R. D. Bergeron (Eds.), *Proceedings of IEEE Visualization '93*, San Jose, California (pp. 119-125).

Willenborg, L., & De Waal, T. (2001). Elements of statistical disclosure control. *Lecture Notes in Statistics, 155*. New York: Springer-Verlag.

Witten, I., & Frank, E. (2005). *Data mining: Practical machine learning tools and techniques*. San Francisco: Morgan Kaufmann.

Witten, I.H., & Frank, E. (2005). *Data mining: Practical machine learning tools and techniques* (2nd ed.). San Francisco: Morgan Kaufmann Publishers.

Wong, P. C., & Bergeron, R. D. (1997). 30 years of multi-dimensional multivariate visualization. In G. M. Nielson,

H. Hagan, & H. Muller (Eds.), *Scientific visualization: Overviews, methodologies and Techniques* (pp. 3-33). Los Alamitos, CA: IEEE Computer Society Press.

Wong, S. T. C., Hoo, K. S., Knowlton, R. C., Laxer, K. D., Cao, X., Hawkins, R. A., Dillon, W. P., & Arenson, R. L. (2002). Design and applications of a multimodality image data warehouse framework. *The Journal of the American Medical Informatics Association, 9*(3), 239-254.

World Wide Web Consortium. (1998). *Extensible markup language (XML) 1.0*. Retrieved June 13, 2007, from http://www.w3C.org/TR/REC-xml/

World Wide Web Consortium. (1999). *XML Path Language XPath Version 1.0*. Retrieved June 13, 2007, from http://www.w3C.org/TR/xpath.html

World Wide Web Consortium. (2002). *XQuery: An XML Query Language*. Retrieved June 13, 2007, from http://www.w3C.org/TR/REC-xml/

Wu, G., & Meininger, C.J. (1995). Impaired arginine metabolism and NO synthesis in coronary endothelial cells of the spontaneously diabetic BB rat. *American Journal of Physiology, 269*, H1312-1318.

Wu, T., & Brutlag, D. (1995). Identification of protein motifs using conserved amino acid properties and partitioning techniques. In *Proceedings of the 3rd International Conference on Intelligent Systems for Molecular Biology* (pp. 402-410).

Wurst, M., Morik, K., & Mierswa, I. (2006). Localized alternative cluster ensembles for collaborative structuring. In *Proceedings of the European Conference on Machine Learning (ECML)*.

Xing, E. P., Ng, A. Y., Jordan, M. I., & Russell, S. (2002). Distance metric learning with application to clustering with side-information. In S. T. S. Becker & K. Obermayer (Eds.), *Advances in neural information processing systems* (vol. 15, pp. 505–512). Cambridge, MA: MIT Press.

Xu, L. (1993). Least mean square error reconstruction principle for self-organizing neural-nets. *Neural Networks, 6*(5), 627-648.

Xu, R., & Wunsch, D. (2005). Survey of clustering algorithms. *IEEE Transactions on Neural Networks, 16*(13), 645-678.

Yan, T. W., Jacobsen, M., Garcia-Molina, H., & Dayal, U. (1996). From user access patterns to dynamic hypertext linking. *Proceedings of the 5th International World Wide Web Conference on Computer Networks and ISDN Systems* (pp. 1007-1014), The Netherlands, Elsevier Science Publishers B. V. Amsterdam.

Yang, B., & Hurson, A. R., (2005). Similarity-based clustering strategy for mobile ad hoc multimedia databases. *Mobile Information Systems, 1*(4), 253-273, IOS Press.

Yang, J., & Yu, P. (2001). Mining surprising periodic patterns. In *Proceedings of the 7th ACM SIGKDD International Conference on Knowledge Discovery and Data Mining* (pp. 395-400).

Zadeh, L.A. (1965). Fuzzy sets. *Information and Control, 8*, 338-353.

Zadeh, L.A. (1973). New approach to the analysis of complex systems. *IEEE Transactions on Systems, Man, and Cybernetics, 3*(1).

Zadeh, L.A. (1978). Fuzzy sets as a basis for a theory of possibility. *1*(1).

Zadeh, L.A. (1983). A computational approach to fuzzy quantifiers in natural languages. *Comput. Math. Appl., 9*, 149-184.

Zaïne, O. R., Han J., & Zhu, H. (2000). Mining recurrent items in multimedia with progressive resolution refinement. In *Proceedings of the International Conference on Data Engineering (ICDE'00)*, San Diego, California.

Zhang, B. (2000). *Generalized k-harmonic means: Boosting in unsupervised learning* (Technical report). Palo Alto, CA: HP Laboratories.

Zhang, B., Hsu, M., & Dayal, U. (1999). *K-harmonic means: A data clustering algorithm* (Technical report). Palo Alto, CA: HP Laboratories.

Zhang, J., Hsu, W., & Lee, M. L. (2001). Image mining: Issues, frameworks and techniques. In *Proceedings of the*

Second International Workshop on Multimedia Data Mining (MDM/KDD), San Francisco, California.

Zhang, T., Ramakrishman, R., & Livny, M. (1996). BIRCH: An efficient data clustering algorithm for very large databases. In *Proceedings of the International Conference on Management of Data* (pp. 103-114).

Zhang, T., Ramakrishnan, R., & Livny, M. (1996). BIRCH: An efficient data clustering method for very large databases. In *ACM SIGKDD International Conference on Management of Data* (pp. 103-114).

Zhang, Y., Xu, G., & Zhou, X. (2005). A latent usage approach for clustering Web transaction and building user profile. *ADMA* (pp. 31-42).

Zhao, H., & Ram, S. (2002). *Applying classification techniques in semantic integration of heterogeneous data sources.* Paper presented at the Eighth Americas Conference on Information Systems, Dallas, TX.

Zhao, H., & Ram, S. (2004). Clustering schema elements for semantic integration of heterogeneous data sources. *Journal of Database Management, 15*(4), 88-106.

Zhou, A., Qin, S., & Qian, W. (2005). Adaptively detecting aggregation bursts in data streams. In *Proceedings of the 10th International Conference of Database Systems for Advanced Applications (DASFAA)*, Beijing, China (pp. 435-446).

Zhou, B., Hui, S. C., & Fong, A. C. M. (2005). A Web usage lattice based mining approach for intelligent Web personalization. *International Journal of Web Information Systems, 1*(3) 137-145.

Zhu, X., Wu, X., & Yang, Y. (2004). Dynamic classifier selection for effective mining from noisy data streams. In *Proceedings of the 4th IEEE International Conference on Data Mining (ICDM)*, Brighton, UK (pp. 305-312).

Zhu, Y., & Shasha, D. (2002). StatStream: Statistical monitoring of thousands of data streams in real time. In *Proceedings of the 28th International Conference on Very Large Data Bases (VLDB)*, Hong Kong, China (pp. 358-369).

Zhu, Y., & Shasha, D. (2003). Efficient elastic burst detection in data streams. In *Proceedings of the 9th ACM SIGKDD International Conference on Knowledge Discovery and Data Mining (KDD)*, Washington, DC (pp. 336-345).

About the Contributors

Florent Masseglia is currently a researcher for the INRIA (Sophia Antipolis, France). He did research work in the Data Mining Group at the LIRMM (Montpellier, France) from 1998 to 2002 and received a PhD in computer science from Versailles University, France in 2002. His research interests include data mining (particularly sequential patterns and applications such as Web usage mining) and databases. He is member of the steering committees of the French Working Group on Mining Complex Data and the International Workshop on Multimedia Data Mining. He has co-edited several special issues about mining complex or multimedia data. He also has co-chaired workshops on mining complex data and co-chaired the 6th and 7th editions of the International Workshop on Multimedia Data Mining in conjunction with the KDD conference. He is the author of numerous publications about data mining in journals and conferences, and he is a reviewer for international journals.

Pascal Poncelet is a professor and the head of the data mining research group in the Computer Science Department at the Ecole des Mines d'Alès in France. He is also co-head of the department. Professor Poncelet has previously worked as lecturer (1993-1994) and as associate professor, respectively, in the Medierannée University (1994-1999) and Montpellier University (1999-2001). His research interest can be summarized as advanced data analysis techniques for emerging applications. He is currently interested in various techniques of data mining with application in Web mining and text mining. He has published a large number of research papers in refereed journals, conferences, and workshops, and been reviewer for some leading academic journals. He is also co-head of the French CNRS Group "I3" on Data Mining.

Maguelonne Teisseire received a PhD in computing science from the Méditerrané University, France, in 1994. Her research interests focused on behavioral modeling and design. She is currently an assistant professor of computer science and engineering in Montpellier II University and Polytech'Montpellier, France. She is the head of the Data Mining Group at the LIRMM Laboratory Lab, Montpellier, France, since 2000. Her research interests focus on advanced data mining approaches when considering that data are time ordered. Particularly, she is interested in text mining and sequential patterns. Her research takes part on different projects supported by either National Government (RNTL) or regional projects. She has published numerous papers in refereed journals and conferences either on behavioral modeling or data mining.

* * * * *

Hanady Abdulsalam is currently a PhD candidate in the School of Computing at Queen's University in Kingston, Ontario, Canada. She received her BSc and MSc in computer engineering from Kuwait University, Kuwait in 2000 and 2002, respectively. Her research interests are in the areas of databases and data mining. She is currently a member of the Database Systems laboratory supervised by Professor P. Martin and the Smart Information Management Laboratory supervised by Professor D. Skillicorn in the School of Computing at Queen's University.

Marie-Aude Aufaure obtained her PhD in computer science from the University of Paris 6 in 1992. From 1993 to 2001, she was associated-professor at the University of Lyon; then, she has integrated a French research center in computer science (INRIA) during two years. Now, she is professor at Supélec and scientific partner of the Inria Axis project. Her research interests deal with the combination of data mining techniques and ontologies to improve the retrieval process of complex data. Another research interest concerns the construction of a Web knowledge base in a specific domain to improve the retrieval process. Her work has been published in international journals, books, and conferences.

Paulo Jorge Azevedo received is MSc and PhD in computing from the Imperial College at the University of London in 1991 and 1995. He is an auxiliar professor in the Department of Informatics at the University of Minho. His research interests include bioinformatics, data mining, machine learning, data warehousing, and logic programming.

Elena Baralis is full professor at the Dipartimento di Automatica e Informatica of the Politecnico di Torino since January 2005. She holds a Dr Ing in electrical engineering and a PhD in computer engineering, both from Politecnico di Torino. Her current research interests are in the field of databases, in particular, data mining, sensor databases, and data privacy. She has published over 40 papers in journals and conference proceedings. She has served on the program committees of several international conferences and workshops, among which VLDB, ACM CIKM, DaWak, ACM SAC, PKDD. She has managed several Italian and EU research projects.

Christian Baumgartner is associate professor of biomedical engineering and head of the Research Group for Clinical Bioinformatics at the Institute of Biomedical Engineering, University for Health Sciences, Medical Informatics and Technology (UMIT), Hall in Tirol, Austria. He received his M.Sc. and PhD in biomedical engineering at Graz University of Technology, Austria. Dr. Baumgartner is the author of more than 30 publications in refereed journals and conference proceedings, reviewer of grant applications and biomedical journals, and has also been considered as a member of the program committee in different scientific conferences. His main research interests include knowledge discovery and data mining in biomedicine, clinical bioinformatics, computational biology, and functional imaging.

Eduardo Bezerra is a professor at Federal Center of Technological Education CSF (CEFET/RJ) since 2005. He has received the Doctor of Science degree from COPPE/UFRJ in 2006. His current interests include computational intelligence, intelligent systems, and database systems. He has also worked as a software engineering consultant for more than 10 years, with different companies, and is author of a book on object oriented systems modeling.

Marinette Bouet received her PhD in computer science from the University of Nantes in 2000. She is currently an associate professor in computer science at Polytech'Clermont-Ferrand of the University of Clermont-Ferrand II, France. She works on multimedia data retrieval and, more particularly, on data mining techniques used in the complex data retrieval process. Another topic of interest relates to Web service description.

Omar Boussaid is an associate professor in computer science at the School of Economics and Management of the University of Lyon 2, France. He received his PhD in computer science from the University of Lyon 1, France in 1988. Since 1995, he has been in charge of the master's degree Computer Science in Engineering for Decision and Economic Evaluation at the University of Lyon 2. He is a member of the Decision Support Databases research group within the ERIC laboratory. His main research subjects are data warehousing, multidimensional databases, and OLAP. His current research concerns complex data warehousing, XML warehousing, data mining-based multidimensional modeling, OLAP and data mining coupling, and mining metadata in RDF form.

Barbara Catania is associate professor at the Department of Computer and Information Sciences of the University of Genoa, Italy. In 1993, she graduated from the University of Genoa, Italy, in information sciences. She received her PhD in computer science from the University of Milan, Italy, in 1998. She has been visiting researcher at the European Computer-Industry Research Center of Bull, ICL, and Siemens in Munich, Germany, and at the National University of Singapore. Her main research interests include deductive and constraint databases, spatial databases, XML and Web databases, pattern management, indexing techniques, and database security.

Pedro Gabriel Ferreira graduated in systems and informatics engineering at University of Minho in 2002. He worked as a research assistant in the IT group at Philips Research–Holland in 2002 and did a full year as a software analyst in 2003. He is a PhD student in the Department of Informatics at the University of Minho since 2003, and works in collaboration with the Department of Computer Science and Artificial Intelligence at the University of Granada, Spain. His research interests include data mining, bioinformatics, and computational biology.

Igor Nai Fovino received an MS in computer science with full marks in 2002 and the PhD in computer science in March 2006 with full marks. He worked as research collaborator at University of Milano in the field of privacy preserving data mining. In 2004, he was visiting researcher at CERIAS Research Centre (West-Lafayette, Indiana, USA). He is a scientific officer at the Joint Research Centre of the European Commission and contractual professor at the Insubria University. His main research activities are related to computer security and, more specifically, system survivability, secure protocols, and privacy preserving data mining.

Professor Colin Fyfe is an active researcher in artificial neural networks, genetic algorithms, artificial immune systems, and artificial life, having written over 280 refereed papers, several book chapters, and two books. He is a member of the editorial board of the *International Journal of Knowledge-Based Intelligent Engineering Systems* and an associate editor of the *International Journal of Neural Systems* *and Neurocomputing*. He currently supervises six PhD students and has acted as director of studies for 16 PhDs (all successful) since 1998. Nine former PhD students now hold academic posts, including one other professor and one senior lecturer. He is a member of the academic advisory board of the International Computer Science Conventions group and is a committee member of the EU-funded project, EUNITE: the European Network of Excellence on Intelligent Technologies for Smart Adaptive Systems. He has been visiting researcher at the University of Strathclyde, 1993-1994, at the Riken Institute, Tokyo, in January 1998 and at the Chinese University of Hong Kong in 2000, and visiting professor at the University of Vigo, Spain, the University of Burgos, Spain, the University of Salamanca, Spain, Cheng Shiu University, Taiwan, and the University of South Australia.

Pierre Gançarski received his PhD in computer science from the Strasbourg University (Louis Pasteur). He is currently an associate professor in computer sciences at the Department of Computer Science of the Strasbourg University. His current research interests include collaborative multistrategical clustering with applications to complex data mining and remote sensing analysis. Another topic of interest is about use of genetic approaches for feature weighting in clustering of complex data.

Paolo Garza is a research assistant in the Database and Data Mining Group at the Dipartimento di Automatica e Informatica of the Politecnico di Torino since January 2005. He holds a master's degree and a PhD in computer engineering, both from Politecnico di Torino. His current research interests include data mining and database systems. In particular, he has worked to supervised classification of structured and unstructured data, clustering, and itemsets mining algorithms.

Armin Graber, CEO and director of bioinformatics at Biocrates, manages corporate and business development and is responsible for software products related to metabolomics information extraction and knowledge discovery from bioanalytical data sets to create added value for drug development and medical diagnostics. As head of bioinformatics at Applied Biosystems in Massachusetts, Dr. Graber was responsible for the development and application of innovative solutions and workflows for information discovery in proteomics and metabolomics. He was co-founder of the Research Center and collaborator in the establishment of the proteomics facility at Celera in Maryland. Previously, Dr Graber worked at Novartis Pharmaceuticals in New Jersey, where he led a multisite data warehouse project involving consolidation, analysis, and reporting of quality control and production data. At Sandoz, Dr. Graber had the opportunity to develop high-throughput screening application for selection of superior microorganisms.

Eyke Hüllermeier, born in 1969, obtained his PhD in computer science in 1997 and a habilitation degree in 2002, both from the University of Paderborn, Germany. From 1998 to 2000, he has spent two years as a visiting scientist at the Institut de Recherche en Informatique de Toulouse, France. In 2004, he became an associate professor at the University of Magdeburg, Germany. Currently, he holds a full professorship in the Department of Mathematics and Computer Science at the University of Marburg, Germany. Professor Hüllermeier has published more than 90 papers in books, international journals, and conferences. His current research interests are focused on methodical foundations of knowledge engineering and applications in bioinformatics.

Anna Maddalena is a researcher in computer science at the Department of Computer and Information Sciences of the University of Genoa, Italy, where she received her PhD in computer science in May 2006. In 2001, she graduated from the University of Genoa, Italy, in computer science. Her main research interests include pattern and knowledge management, data mining, data warehousing, and XML query processing.

Pat Martin is a professor and associate director of the School of Computing at Queen's University. He holds a BSc and a PhD from the University of Toronto and a M.Sc. from Queen's University. He is also a faculty fellow with IBM's Centre for Advanced Studies. His research interests include database system performance, Web services, and autonomic computing systems.

Marta Mattoso is a professor of the Department of Computer Science at the COPPE Institute from Federal University of Rio de Janeiro (UFRJ) since 1994, where she co-leads the Database Research Group. She has received the Doctor of Science degree from UFRJ. Dr. Mattoso has been active in the database research community for more than 10 years, and her current research interests include distributed and parallel databases, data management aspects of Web services composition, and genome data management. She is the principal investigator in research projects in those areas, with fundings from several Brazilian government agencies, including CNPq, CAPES, FINEP, and FAPERJ. She has published over 60 refereed international journal articles and conference papers. She has served in program committees of international conferences and is a reviewer of several journals. She is currently the director of publications at the Brazilian Computer Society.

Ingo Mierswa studied computer science at the University of Dortmund from 1998 to 2004. He worked as a student assistant in the collaborative research center 531 where he started to develop the machine learning environment YALE. Since April 2004, he has been a research assistant and PhD student at the Artificial Intelligence Unit of the University of Dortmund. He is mainly working on multi-objective optimization for numerical learning and feature engineering. Today, he is a member of the project A4 of the collaborative research center 475.

Katharina Morik received her PhD at the University of Hamburg 1981 and worked in the well-known natural language project HAM-ANS at Hamburg from 1982 to 1984. Then, she moved to the technical university Berlin and became the project leader of the first German machine learning project. From 1989 to 1991, she was leading a research group for machine learning at the German National Research Center for Computer Science at Bonn. In 1991, she became full professor at the University of Dortmund. She is interested in all kinds of applications of machine learning. This also covers cognitive modeling of theory acquisition and revision.

Cesar Garcia-Osorio received an ME in computer engineering from the University of Valladolid in Spain and obtained his PhD in computer science from the University of Paisley in Scotland, United Kingdom, for a thesis about visual data mining. The major areas of his research interest focus primarily on visualization, visual data mining, neural networks, machine learning, and genetic algorithms. He is a member of the Computational Intelligence and Bioinformatics research group. He is currently a lecturer of artificial intelligence and expert systems, automata and formal languages, and language processors at the University of Burgos, Spain.

Elisa Quintarelli received her master's degree in computer science from the University of Verona, Italy. In January 2002, she completed the PhD program in computer and automation engineering at Politecnico di Milano and is now assistant professor at the Dipartimento di Elettronica e Informazione, Politecnico di Milano. Her main research interests concern the study of efficient and flexible techniques for specifying and querying semistructured and temporal data, the application of data-mining techniques to provide intensional query answering. More recently, her research has been concentrated on context aware data management.

David Skillicorn is a professor in the School of Computing at Queen's University, where he heads the Smart Information Management Laboratory. He is also the coordinator for Research in Information Security in Kingston (RISK). He is an adjunct professor at the Royal Military College of Canada. His research interests are in data mining, particularly for counterterrorism and fraud; he has also worked extensively in parallel and distributed computing.

Letizia Tanca obtained her master's degree in mathematical logic; she then worked as a software engineer and later obtained her PhD in computer science in 1988. She is a full professor at Politecnico di Milano. During her career, she has taught and teaches courses on databases and the foundations of computer science. She is the author of several papers on databases and database theory, published in international journals and conferences. She has taken part in several national and international projects. Her research interests range over all database theory, especially on deductive and graph-based query languages. More recently, her research has been concentrated on context aware data management for mobile computing. She is currently chairperson of the degree and master courses in computer engineering at the Politecnico di Milano, Leonardo campus.

Michael Wurst studied computer science with a minor in philosophy at the University of Stuttgart. He specialized in artificial intelligence and distributed systems. From 2000 until 2001, he had an academic stay in Prague, Czech Republic and worked on the student research project "Application of Machine Learning Methods in a Multi-Agent System" at the Electrotechnical Department of the Czech Technical University. Since 2001, he has been a PhD student at the Artificial Intelligence Unit where he mainly works on distributed knowledge management, clustering, and distributed data mining.

Geraldo Xexéo, DSc 1994 (COPPE/UFRJ), Eng 1988 (IME), is a professor at the Federal University of Rio de Janeiro since 1995. His current interests include P2P systems for cooperative work, data quality, information retrieval and extraction, and fuzzy logic. Professor Xexéo has supervised more than 20 theses in the database and software engineering fields, with more than 60 articles published. He also has a strong interest in information systems, as he was a software engineering consultant for more than 10 years, with different companies.

Index

A

aggregate information (AI) 296
algorithms 68, 69, 70, 71, 72, 73, 78
ambiguous motifs 120
amino acids (AAs) 117, 118
Andrews' Curves 238, 259, 260, 261
application programming interface (API) 219
Apriori algorithm 193
association
  analysis 10, 14
  rule 89, 90, 91, 92, 93, 94, 96
Attribute-Oriented Dynamic Classifier Selection
    (AO-DSC) 313
automated learning 1
average levensthein distance (ALD) 29, 35

B

binary large objects (BLOBs) 195
bioanalytics 142
biomarker identifier (BMI) 149
BLOSUM (BLOck SUbstitution Matrix) 23
Breadth-first (BFS) 131
brush techniques 249

C

capillary electrophoresis (CE) 144
classification rules 164
cluster 89, 90, 95, 97, 109
  validation 18, 35
Communication requirements 290
concept-adapting very fast decision tree
    (CVFDT) 312
concept drift 94, 116
concrete motifs 120

counts per second (cps) 148
Curvilinear Component Analysis (CCA) 241

D

data
  driven 195
  management 86
  mining
    algorithms 280, 299, 320
  mining (DM) 41, 89, 90, 91, 96, 97, 126, 136,
      138, 190, 192, 195, 203, 278, 279, 280,
      282, 285, 305, 320
  model 41, 289
  preprocessing 144, 145
  quality 294, 296
  semantics 214
  warehouse 189, 190, 191
database management system (DBMS) 49
DB2 intelligent miner 98
decision
  support
    systems (DSS) 189
  tree (DT) 311, 312, 313, 324
density based spatial clustering of applications
    with noise (DBSCAN) 281
depth-first manner (DFS) 131
discrete wavelet transformation (DWT) 218
document-level constraints 79
domain patterns 46
dynamic classifier Selection technique (DCS)
    313

E

exact pattern 46
Expectation Maximization (EM) 198, 286